ADAM & ANDY

THE *Complete* ADVENTURES

2005-2013

Written and Illustrated by

James Asal

ADAM & ANDY. The Complete Adventures 2005-2013

ISBN 978-0-359-84123-3

This book is dedicated with love to my partner Timothy
without who none of this would have been necessary.

Introduction

If you're reading this, it's likely you are well acquainted with the world of Adam, Andy, and their extended family of friends and relatives.

"Adam & Andy" began in 1995 as a series of photocopied, stapled comic books shared with friends. The initial story concerned the first meeting and budding romance of a pensive, mercurial Adam and the beefy, carefree Andy. The artwork was primitive; the storylines were dramatic, brimming with complicated characters, troubled pasts, and difficult relationships.

After 8 issues and 150 weekly episodes, "Adam & Andy" went online and became of the earliest webcomics debuting on May 15, 1999.

The original storylines and continuity were discarded in favor of a simplified approach.

Humor had already become more prominent in the strip, and so the revamped comic was amusing instead of emotional. Gone, too, were most of the supporting characters. This allowed for fresh, uncomplicated scenarios without any baggage. Adam and Andy were, in effect, back at square one.

One somewhat unique element to the strip is that the characters age in real time. Adam and Andy were age 30 at the start of the first story and are now in their mid-fifties. The lone exception to this rule is Baxter the dog, a fixture in the comic for 18 years and counting. That's one hardy beagle!

The comics contained in this volume run from January 2005 through December 2013.

Memorable storylines produced during this time include the then-new concept of "civil unions," Andy gaining weight, Mrs. Bittshschlapp's sister coming to visit, Adam and Andy's lakeside retreat and Adam and Andy being thrown in the pokey due to misunderstandings and misidentification.

Andy's sister Diana and her son Tommy were reintroduced after an absence of several years. Current followers of "Adam & Andy" will see hints of the character which the adult Tommy ultimately became.

Another key character from this period is Larry Bolt, "the horny friend." Playful, amorous Larry first appeared during Adam and Andy's adventure at the lake, and he moves to town permanently in

an early 2012 story. Larry fills the role of a more typical, randy gay "bear," just slightly older than Adam and Andy.

The extended storyline involving Mrs. Bittschlapp and her scheming sister Angelica marked an important transition for "Mrs. B" from nutty next-door neighbor to beloved, but abrasive, member of the family.

The strips in this book were created in various sizes and configurations, owing as much to artistic license as to my whim. This creates a few vexing page layout issues; the odd spacing and whitespace between some comics is necessary to preserve their original aspect ratio.

All in all, the work presented here is not always consistent, but it is prolific. And fun.

- James Asal

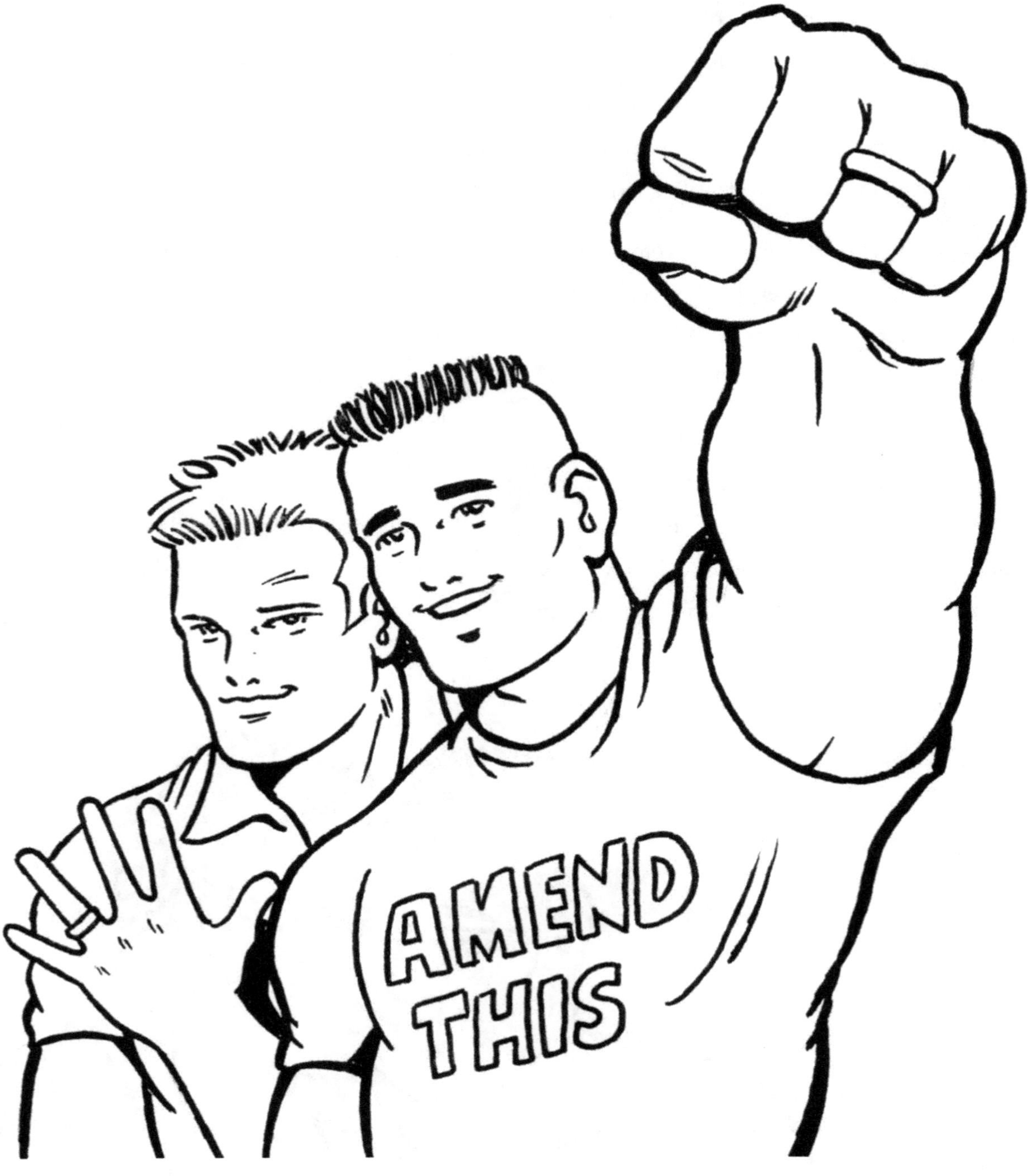
AMEND
THIS

The Players

ADAM: mild neurotic

ANDY: cheerful slob

BAXTER: spoiled beagle

MRS. BITTSCHLAPP: the lady next door

ZUMA & SHEILA: the hash slingers

CHET: the pot stirring coworker

LARRY: the horny friend

DIANA: Andy's sister

TOMMY: Diana's son

A note about the comics

The comics in this book were created over a period of several years in different sizes and configurations. Most of the work is presented "as is," meaning as they were originally written and drawn. Some strips have been retouched with minor edits as needed. All the comics are presented in chronological order.

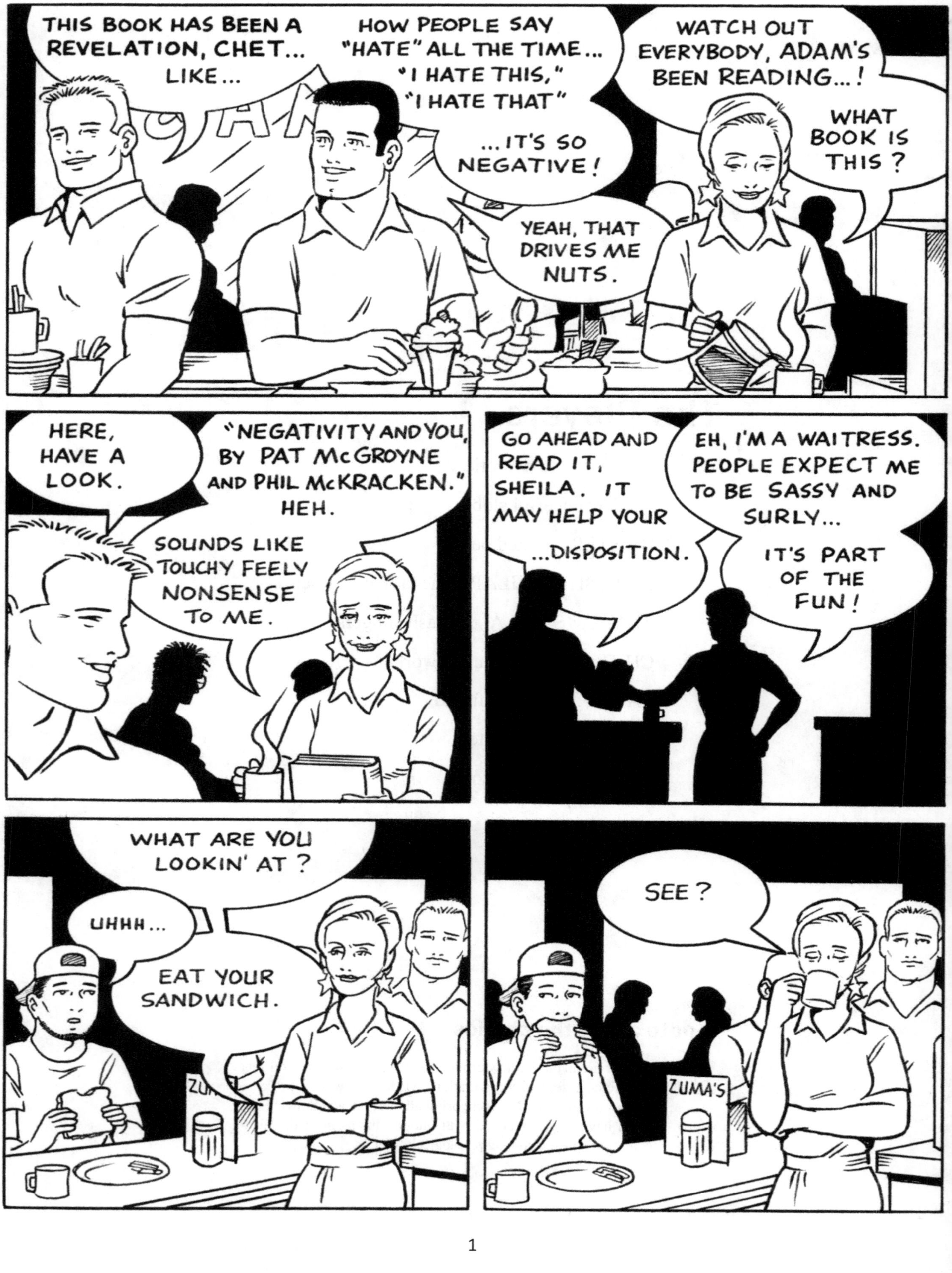

THIS BOOK HAS BEEN A REVELATION, CHET... LIKE...
HOW PEOPLE SAY "HATE" ALL THE TIME... "I HATE THIS," "I HATE THAT"
...IT'S SO NEGATIVE!
YEAH, THAT DRIVES ME NUTS.
WATCH OUT EVERYBODY, ADAM'S BEEN READING...!
WHAT BOOK IS THIS?
HERE, HAVE A LOOK.
"NEGATIVITY AND YOU, BY PAT McGROYNE AND PHIL McKRACKEN." HEH.
SOUNDS LIKE TOUCHY FEELY NONSENSE TO ME.
GO AHEAD AND READ IT, SHEILA. IT MAY HELP YOUR
...DISPOSITION.
EH, I'M A WAITRESS. PEOPLE EXPECT ME TO BE SASSY AND SURLY...
IT'S PART OF THE FUN!
WHAT ARE YOU LOOKIN' AT?
UHHH...
EAT YOUR SANDWICH.
ZUMA'S
SEE?
ZUMA'S

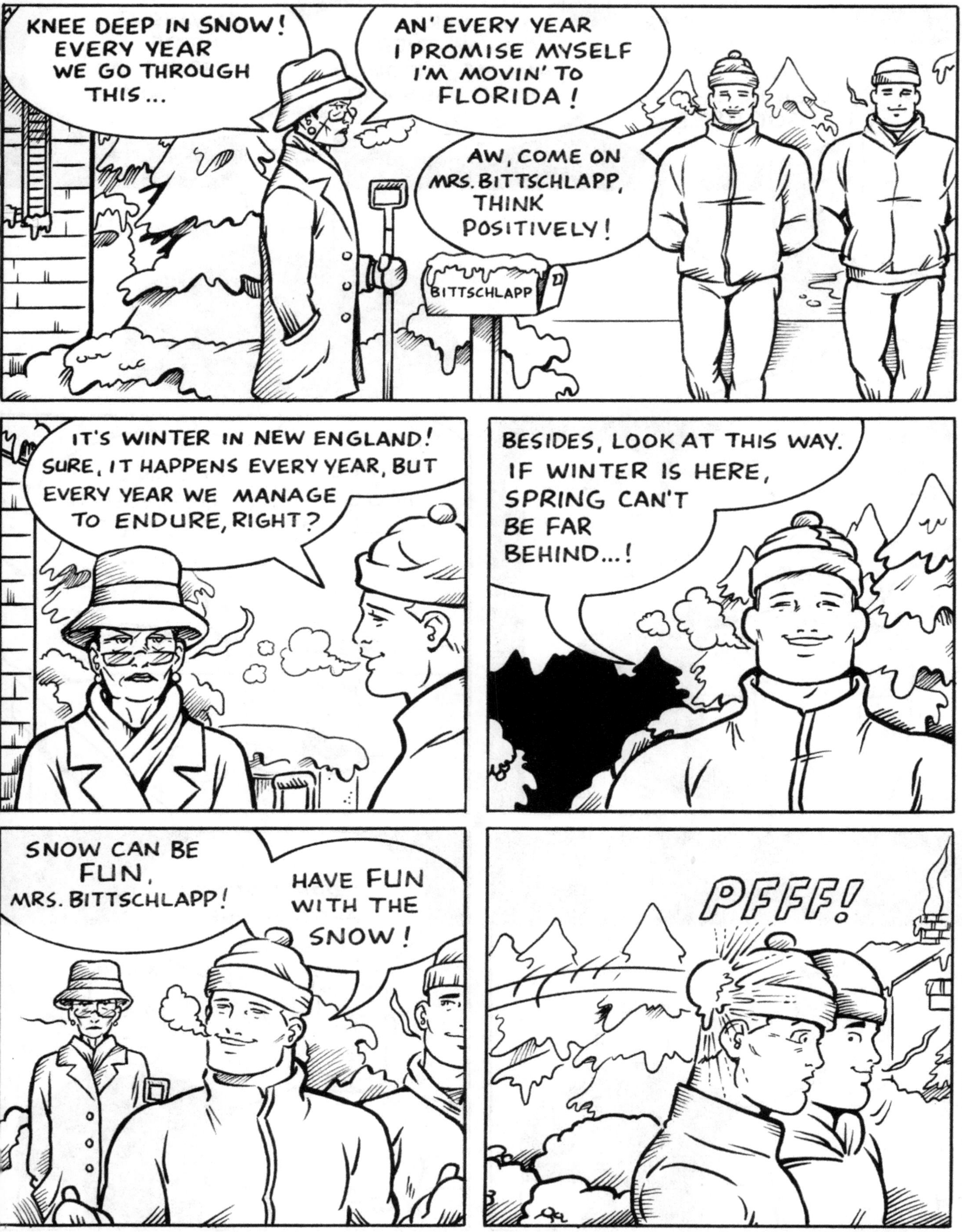
KNEE DEEP IN SNOW! EVERY YEAR WE GO THROUGH THIS...
AN' EVERY YEAR I PROMISE MYSELF I'M MOVIN' TO FLORIDA!
AW, COME ON MRS. BITTSCHLAPP, THINK POSITIVELY!
BITTSCHLAPP
IT'S WINTER IN NEW ENGLAND! SURE, IT HAPPENS EVERY YEAR, BUT EVERY YEAR WE MANAGE TO ENDURE, RIGHT?
BESIDES, LOOK AT THIS WAY. IF WINTER IS HERE, SPRING CAN'T BE FAR BEHIND...!
SNOW CAN BE FUN, MRS. BITTSCHLAPP!
HAVE FUN WITH THE SNOW!
PFFF!

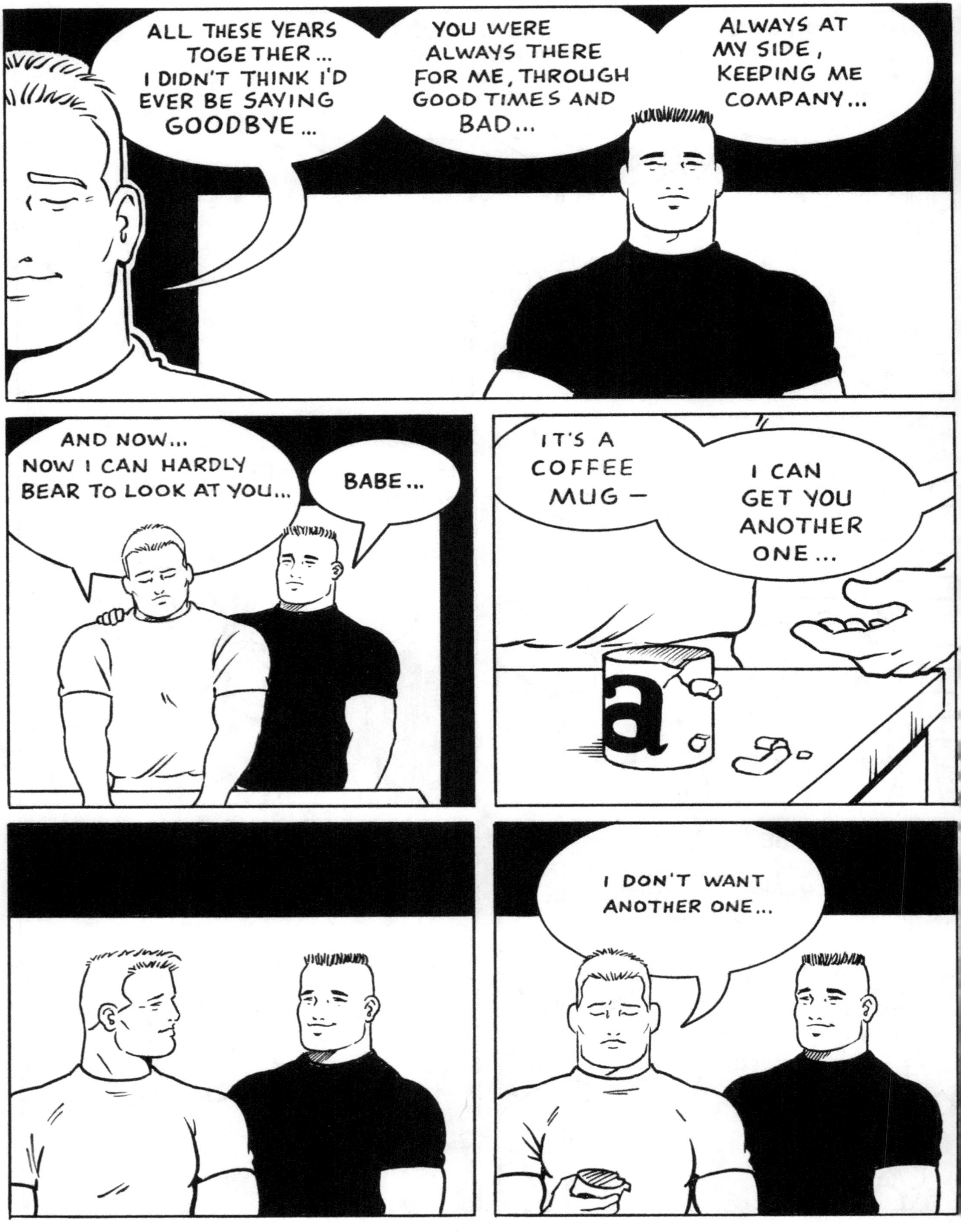
ALL THESE YEARS TOGETHER... I DIDN'T THINK I'D EVER BE SAYING GOODBYE...
YOU WERE ALWAYS THERE FOR ME, THROUGH GOOD TIMES AND BAD...
ALWAYS AT MY SIDE, KEEPING ME COMPANY...
AND NOW... NOW I CAN HARDLY BEAR TO LOOK AT YOU...
BABE...
IT'S A COFFEE MUG –
I CAN GET YOU ANOTHER ONE...
a
I DON'T WANT ANOTHER ONE...

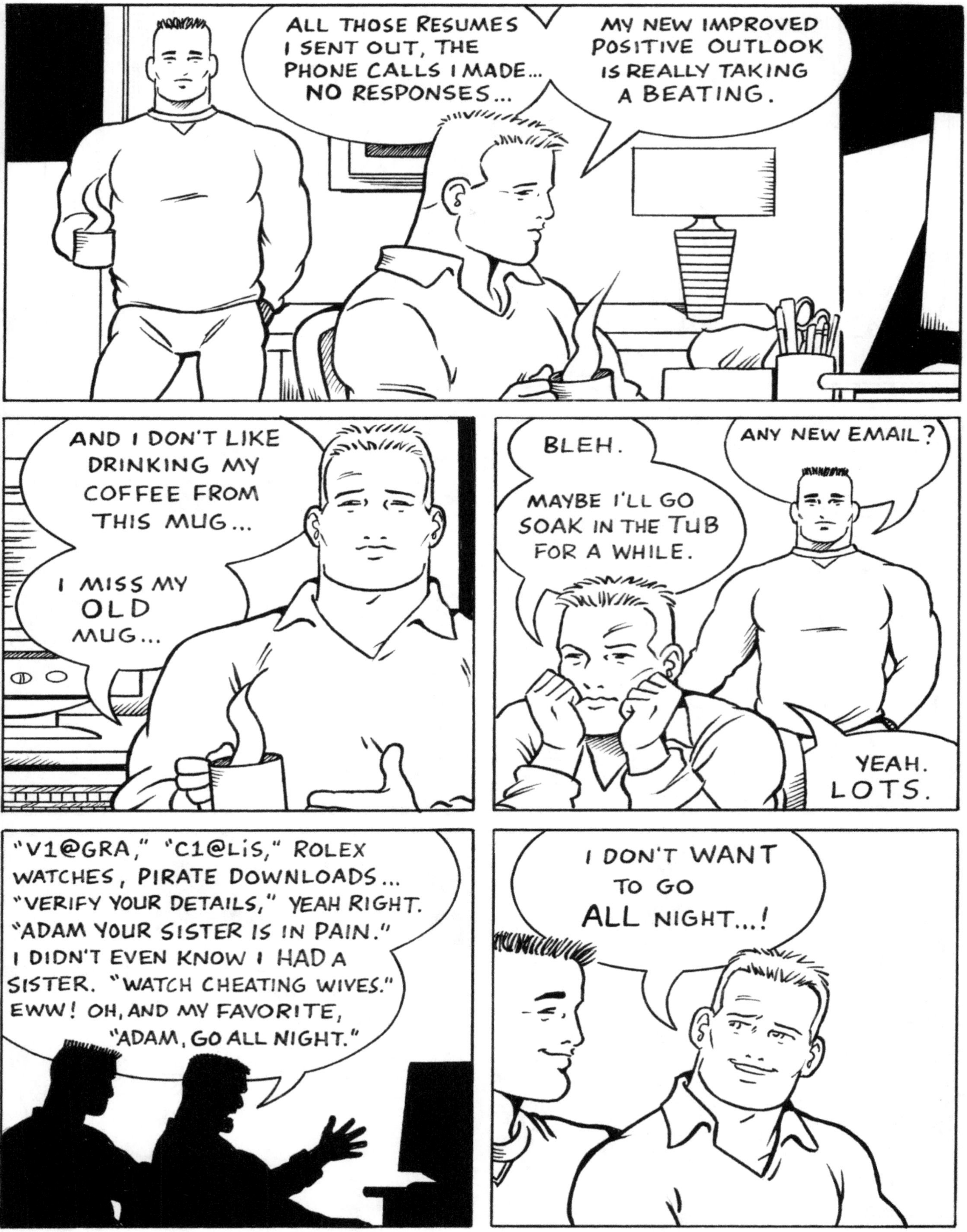
ALL THOSE RESUMES I SENT OUT, THE PHONE CALLS I MADE... NO RESPONSES...
MY NEW IMPROVED POSITIVE OUTLOOK IS REALLY TAKING A BEATING.
AND I DON'T LIKE DRINKING MY COFFEE FROM THIS MUG...
I MISS MY OLD MUG...
BLEH.
MAYBE I'LL GO SOAK IN THE TUB FOR A WHILE.
ANY NEW EMAIL?
YEAH. LOTS.
"V1@GRA," "C1@LIS," ROLEX WATCHES, PIRATE DOWNLOADS... "VERIFY YOUR DETAILS," YEAH RIGHT. "ADAM YOUR SISTER IS IN PAIN." I DIDN'T EVEN KNOW I HAD A SISTER. "WATCH CHEATING WIVES." EWW! OH, AND MY FAVORITE, "ADAM, GO ALL NIGHT."
I DON'T WANT TO GO ALL NIGHT...!

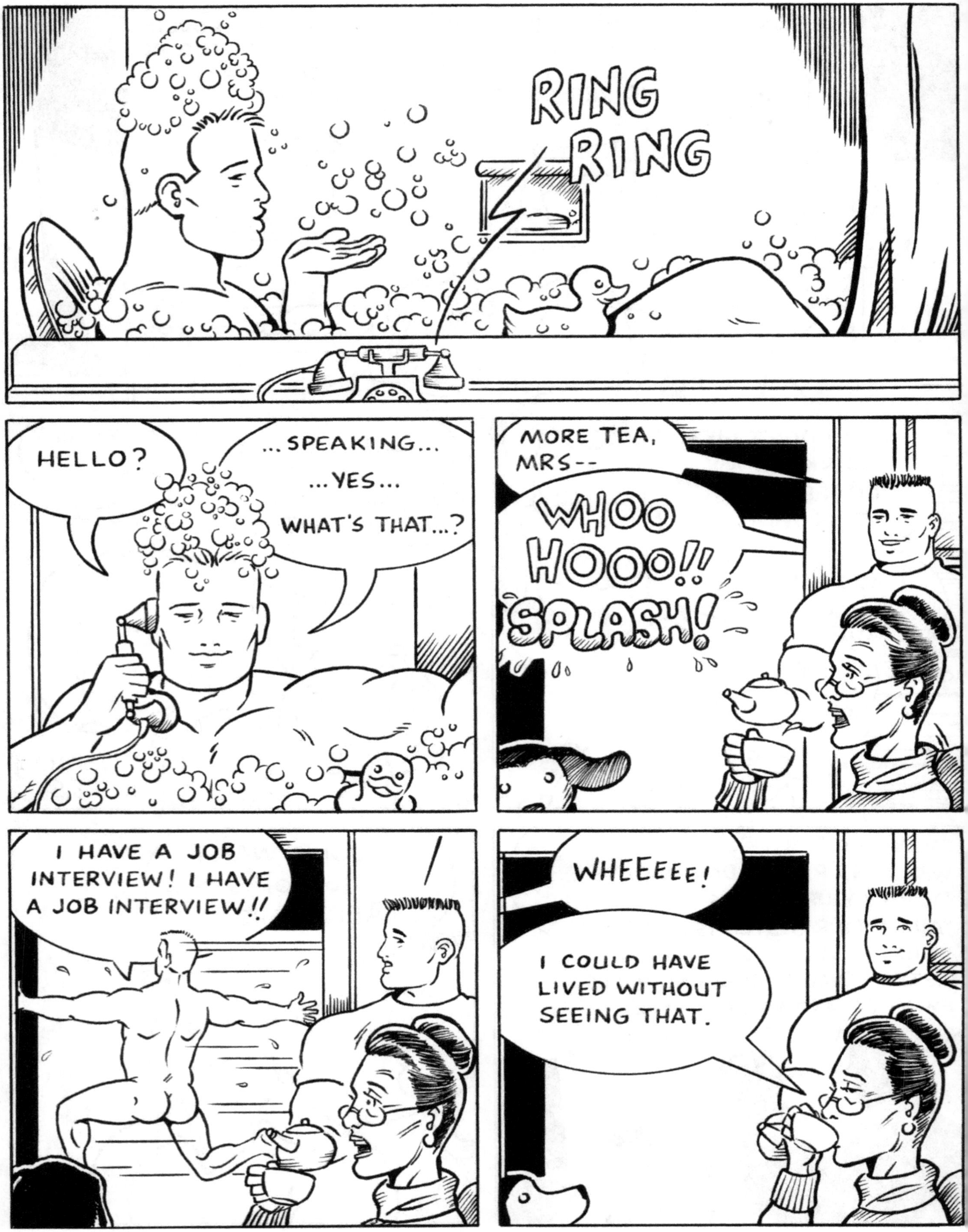
RING
RING
HELLO?
...SPEAKING...
...YES...
WHAT'S THAT...?
MORE TEA, MRS--
WHOO HOOO!!
SPLASH!
I HAVE A JOB INTERVIEW! I HAVE A JOB INTERVIEW!!
WHEEEEEE!
I COULD HAVE LIVED WITHOUT SEEING THAT.

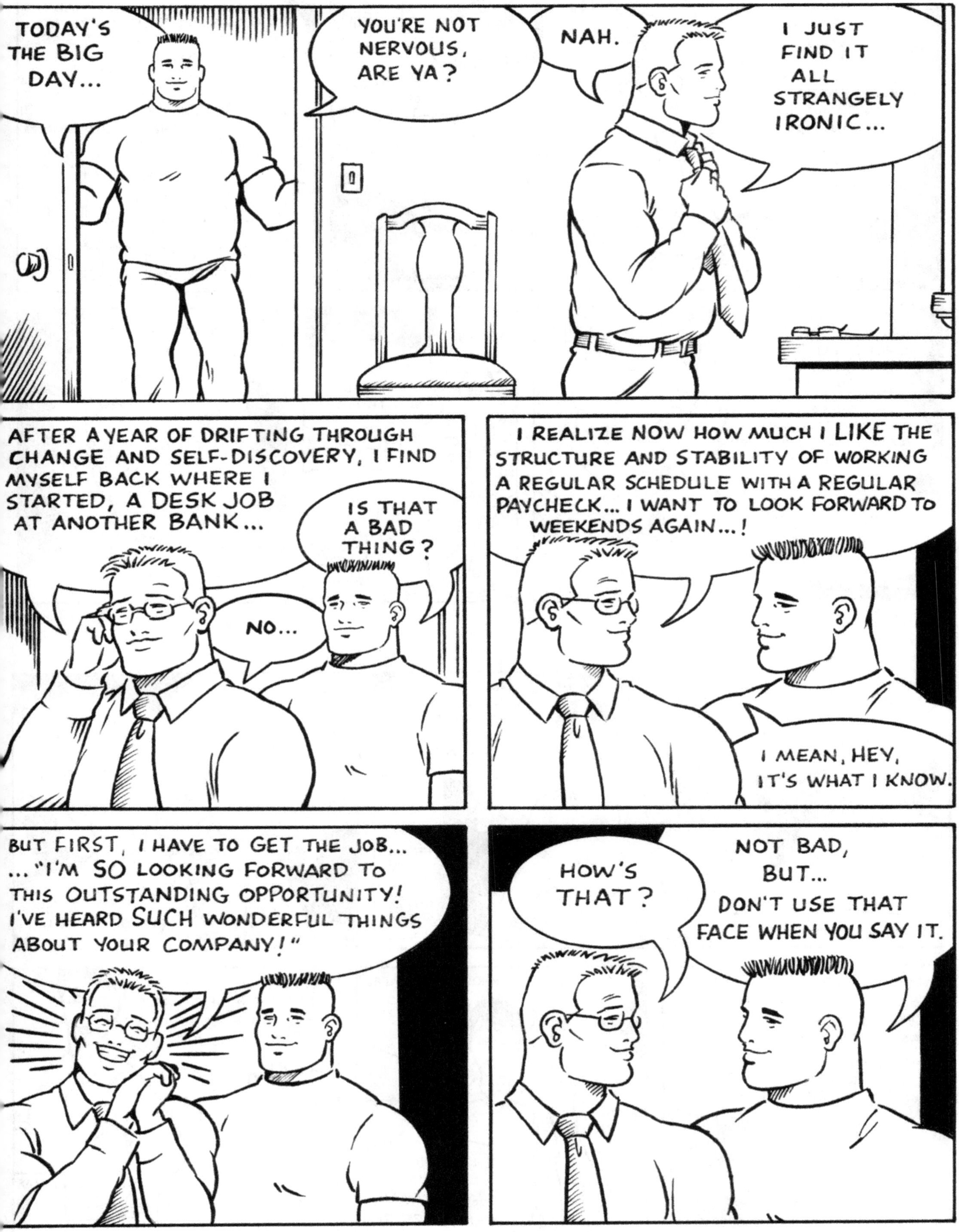
TODAY'S THE BIG DAY...
YOU'RE NOT NERVOUS, ARE YA?
NAH.
I JUST FIND IT ALL STRANGELY IRONIC...
AFTER A YEAR OF DRIFTING THROUGH CHANGE AND SELF-DISCOVERY, I FIND MYSELF BACK WHERE I STARTED, A DESK JOB AT ANOTHER BANK...
IS THAT A BAD THING?
NO...
I REALIZE NOW HOW MUCH I LIKE THE STRUCTURE AND STABILITY OF WORKING A REGULAR SCHEDULE WITH A REGULAR PAYCHECK... I WANT TO LOOK FORWARD TO WEEKENDS AGAIN...!
I MEAN, HEY, IT'S WHAT I KNOW.
BUT FIRST, I HAVE TO GET THE JOB... ..."I'M SO LOOKING FORWARD TO THIS OUTSTANDING OPPORTUNITY! I'VE HEARD SUCH WONDERFUL THINGS ABOUT YOUR COMPANY!"
HOW'S THAT?
NOT BAD, BUT... DON'T USE THAT FACE WHEN YOU SAY IT.

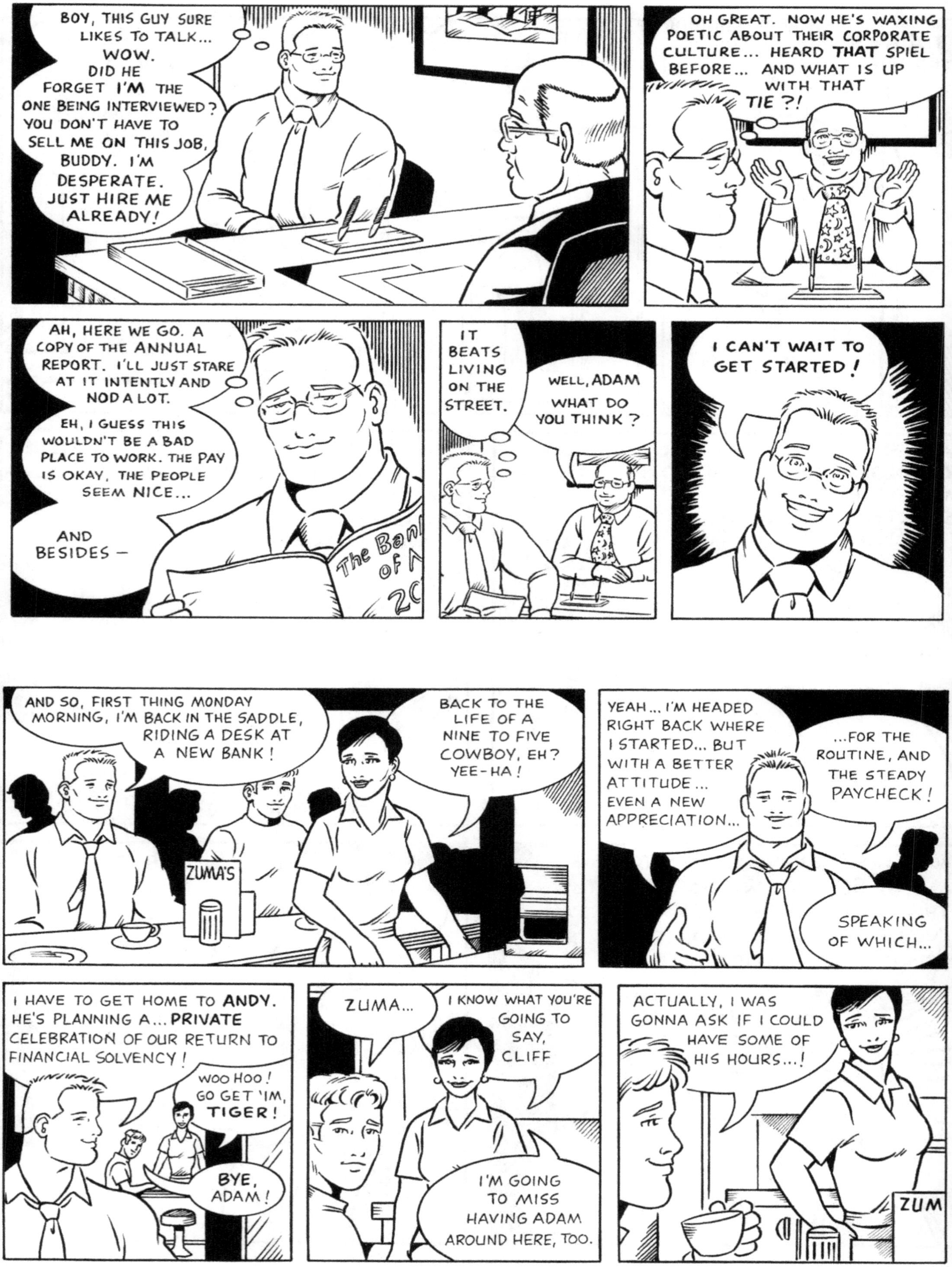
BOY, THIS GUY SURE LIKES TO TALK... WOW. DID HE FORGET I'M THE ONE BEING INTERVIEWED? YOU DON'T HAVE TO SELL ME ON THIS JOB, BUDDY. I'M DESPERATE. JUST HIRE ME ALREADY!
OH GREAT. NOW HE'S WAXING POETIC ABOUT THEIR CORPORATE CULTURE... HEARD THAT SPIEL BEFORE... AND WHAT IS UP WITH THAT TIE?!
AH, HERE WE GO. A COPY OF THE ANNUAL REPORT. I'LL JUST STARE AT IT INTENTLY AND NOD A LOT.
EH, I GUESS THIS WOULDN'T BE A BAD PLACE TO WORK. THE PAY IS OKAY, THE PEOPLE SEEM NICE...
AND BESIDES —
IT BEATS LIVING ON THE STREET.
WELL, ADAM WHAT DO YOU THINK?
I CAN'T WAIT TO GET STARTED!
AND SO, FIRST THING MONDAY MORNING, I'M BACK IN THE SADDLE, RIDING A DESK AT A NEW BANK!
BACK TO THE LIFE OF A NINE TO FIVE COWBOY, EH? YEE-HA!
ZUMA'S
YEAH... I'M HEADED RIGHT BACK WHERE I STARTED... BUT WITH A BETTER ATTITUDE... EVEN A NEW APPRECIATION...
...FOR THE ROUTINE, AND THE STEADY PAYCHECK!
SPEAKING OF WHICH...
I HAVE TO GET HOME TO ANDY. HE'S PLANNING A... PRIVATE CELEBRATION OF OUR RETURN TO FINANCIAL SOLVENCY!
WOO HOO! GO GET 'IM, TIGER!
BYE, ADAM!
ZUMA...
I KNOW WHAT YOU'RE GOING TO SAY, CLIFF
I'M GOING TO MISS HAVING ADAM AROUND HERE, TOO.
ACTUALLY, I WAS GONNA ASK IF I COULD HAVE SOME OF HIS HOURS...!
ZUM

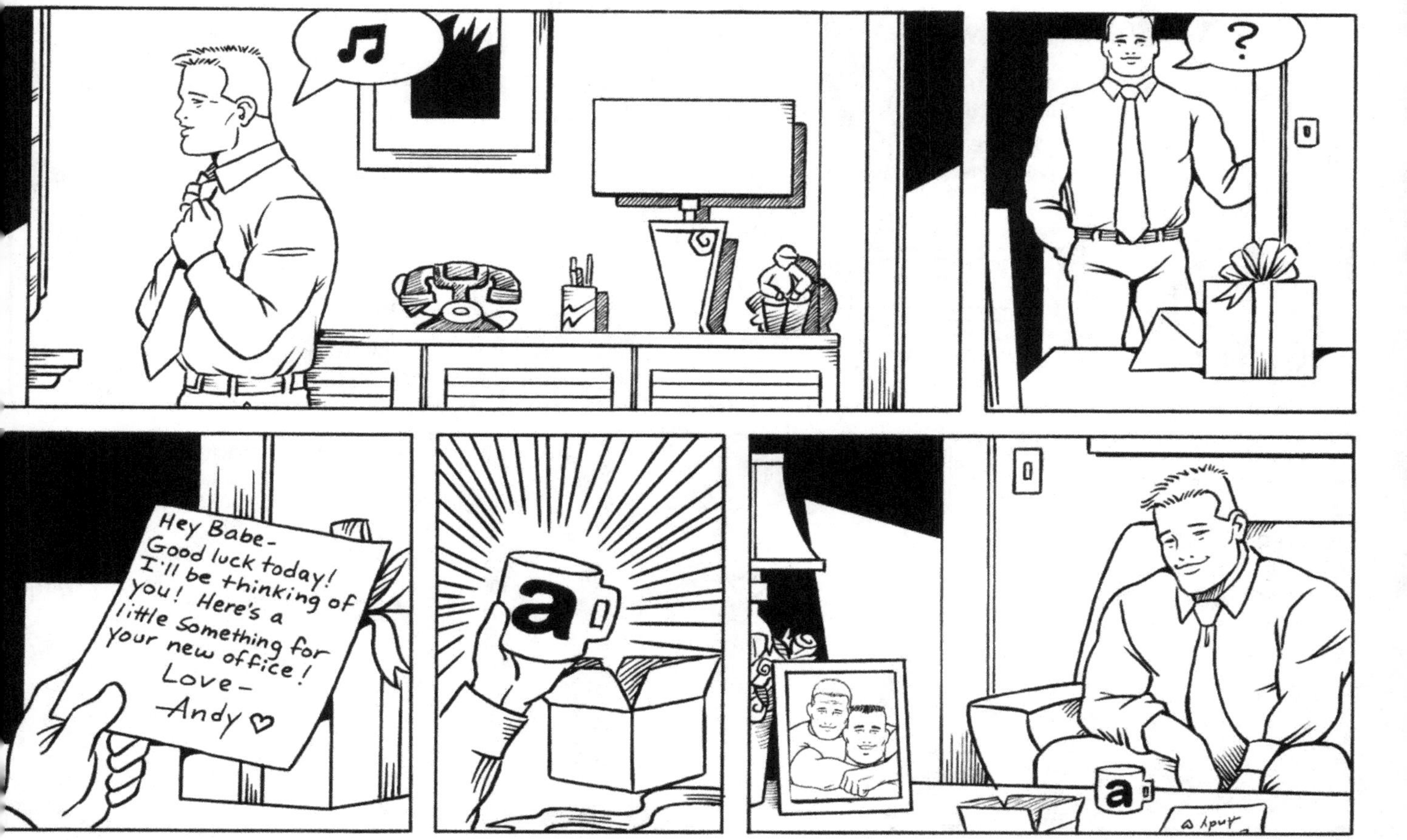
Hey Babe-
Good luck today! I'll be thinking of you! Here's a little Something for your new office!
Love-
-Andy

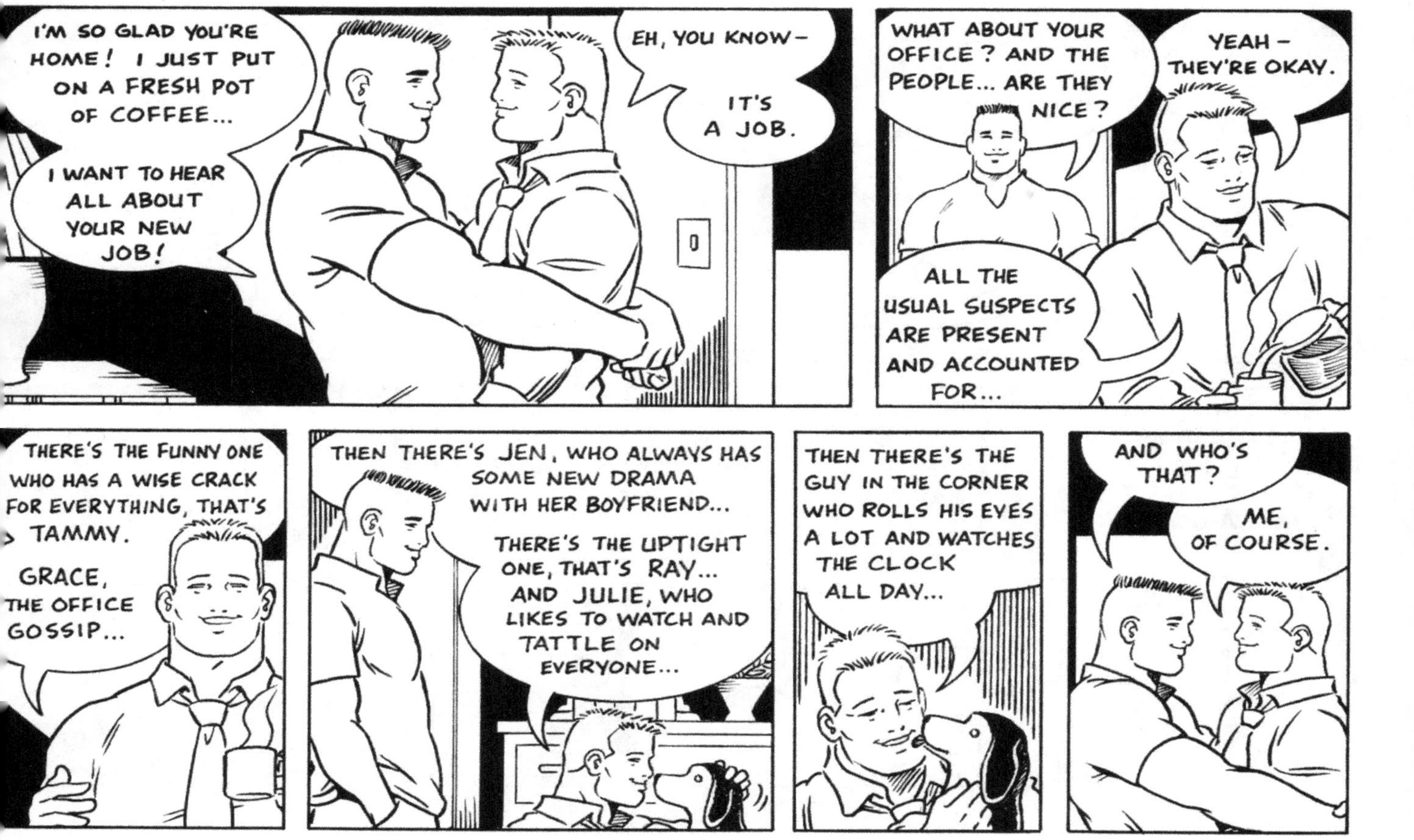
I'M SO GLAD YOU'RE HOME! I JUST PUT ON A FRESH POT OF COFFEE...
I WANT TO HEAR ALL ABOUT YOUR NEW JOB!
EH, YOU KNOW-
IT'S A JOB.
WHAT ABOUT YOUR OFFICE? AND THE PEOPLE... ARE THEY NICE?
YEAH - THEY'RE OKAY.
ALL THE USUAL SUSPECTS ARE PRESENT AND ACCOUNTED FOR...
THERE'S THE FUNNY ONE WHO HAS A WISE CRACK FOR EVERYTHING, THAT'S TAMMY.
GRACE, THE OFFICE GOSSIP...
THEN THERE'S JEN, WHO ALWAYS HAS SOME NEW DRAMA WITH HER BOYFRIEND...
THERE'S THE UPTIGHT ONE, THAT'S RAY... AND JULIE, WHO LIKES TO WATCH AND TATTLE ON EVERYONE...
THEN THERE'S THE GUY IN THE CORNER WHO ROLLS HIS EYES A LOT AND WATCHES THE CLOCK ALL DAY...
AND WHO'S THAT?
ME, OF COURSE.

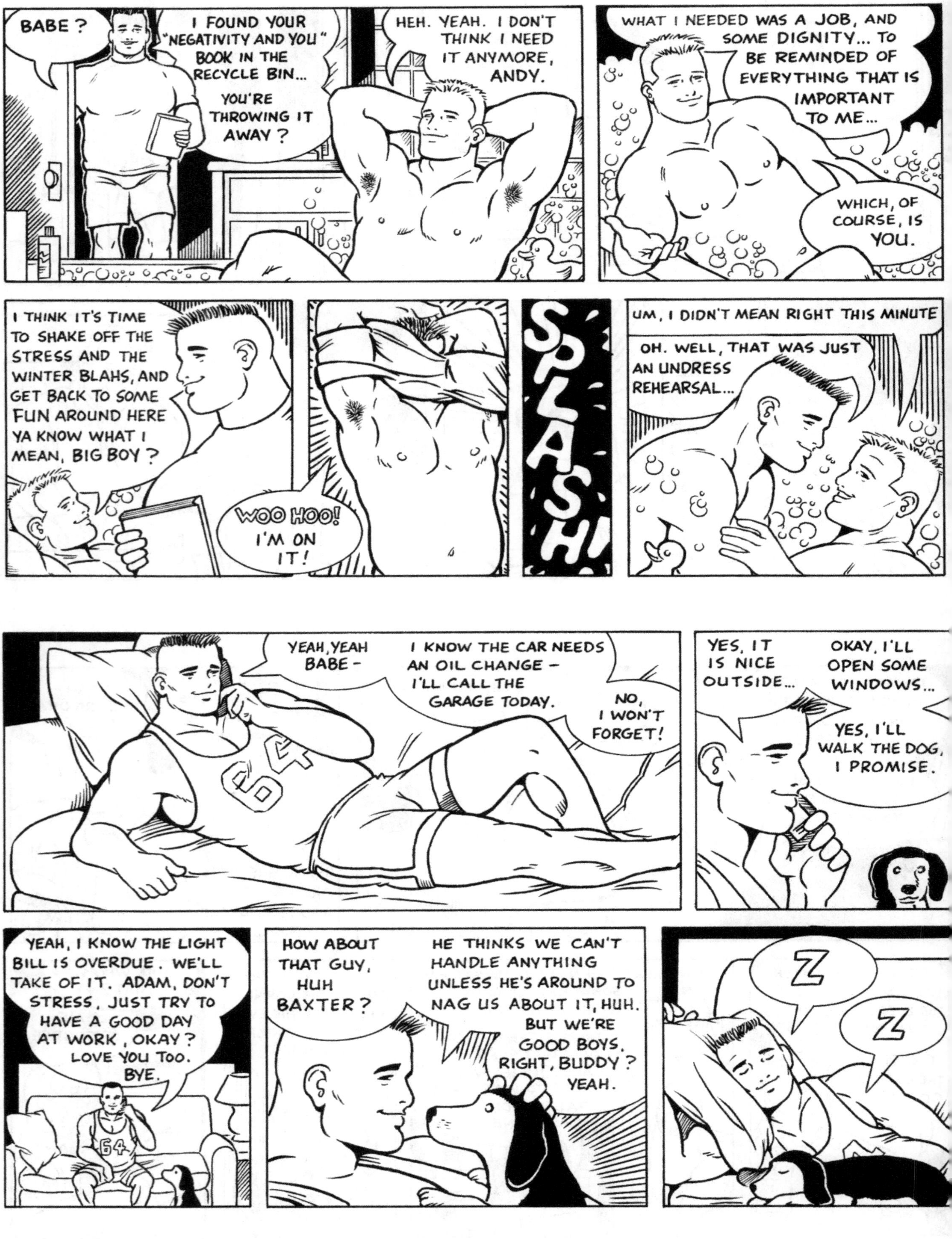
BABE?
I FOUND YOUR "NEGATIVITY AND YOU" BOOK IN THE RECYCLE BIN...
YOU'RE THROWING IT AWAY?
HEH. YEAH. I DON'T THINK I NEED IT ANYMORE, ANDY.
WHAT I NEEDED WAS A JOB, AND SOME DIGNITY... TO BE REMINDED OF EVERYTHING THAT IS IMPORTANT TO ME...
WHICH, OF COURSE, IS YOU.
I THINK IT'S TIME TO SHAKE OFF THE STRESS AND THE WINTER BLAHS, AND GET BACK TO SOME FUN AROUND HERE YA KNOW WHAT I MEAN, BIG BOY?
WOO HOO! I'M ON IT!
SPLASH!
UM, I DIDN'T MEAN RIGHT THIS MINUTE
OH. WELL, THAT WAS JUST AN UNDRESS REHEARSAL...
YEAH, YEAH BABE -
I KNOW THE CAR NEEDS AN OIL CHANGE - I'LL CALL THE GARAGE TODAY.
NO, I WON'T FORGET!
YES, IT IS NICE OUTSIDE...
OKAY, I'LL OPEN SOME WINDOWS...
YES, I'LL WALK THE DOG, I PROMISE.
YEAH, I KNOW THE LIGHT BILL IS OVERDUE. WE'LL TAKE OF IT. ADAM, DON'T STRESS, JUST TRY TO HAVE A GOOD DAY AT WORK, OKAY? LOVE YOU TOO. BYE.
HOW ABOUT THAT GUY, HUH BAXTER?
HE THINKS WE CAN'T HANDLE ANYTHING UNLESS HE'S AROUND TO NAG US ABOUT IT, HUH.
BUT WE'RE GOOD BOYS. RIGHT, BUDDY? YEAH.
Z
Z

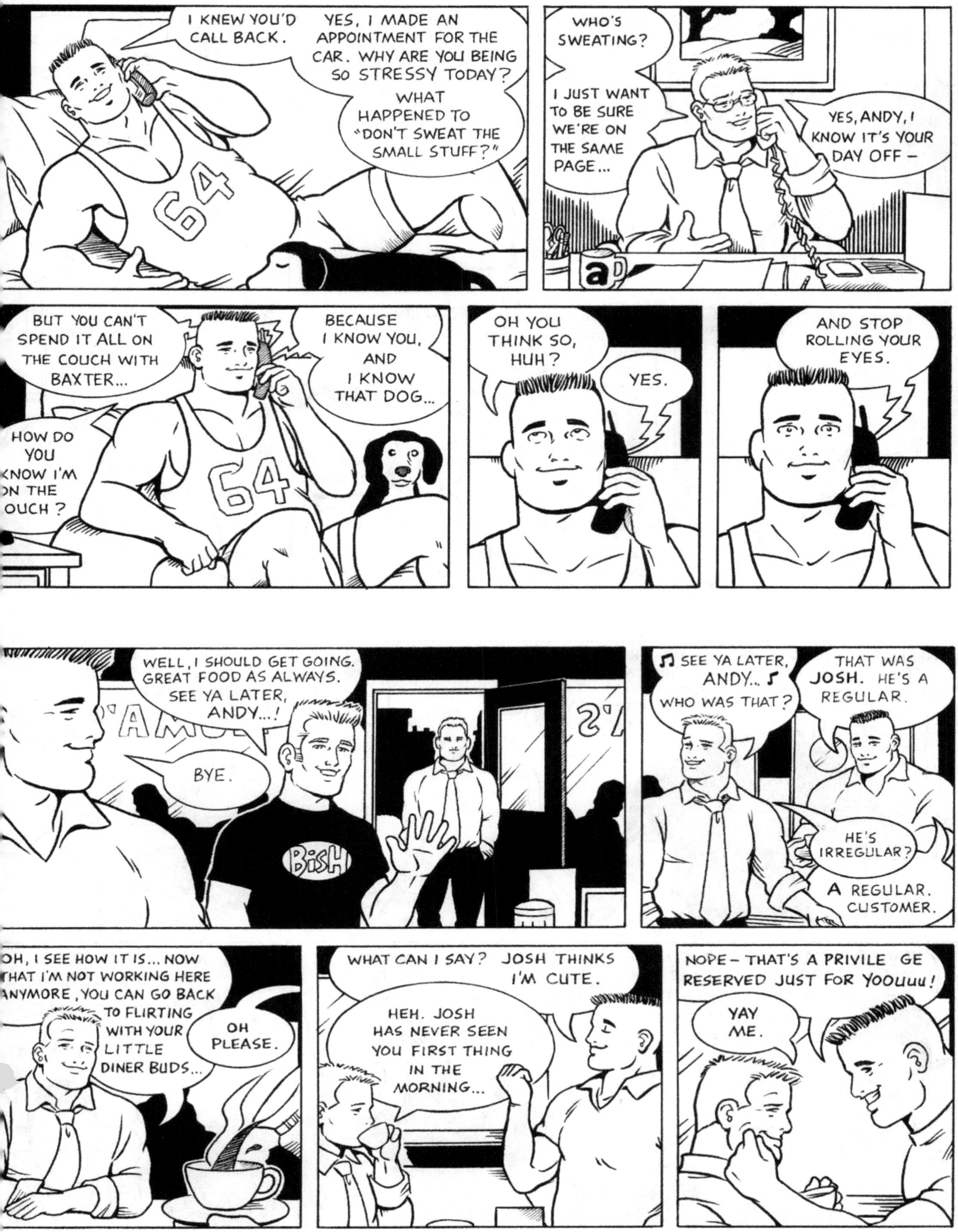
I KNEW YOU'D CALL BACK.
YES, I MADE AN APPOINTMENT FOR THE CAR. WHY ARE YOU BEING SO STRESSY TODAY?
WHAT HAPPENED TO "DON'T SWEAT THE SMALL STUFF?"
WHO'S SWEATING?
I JUST WANT TO BE SURE WE'RE ON THE SAME PAGE...
YES, ANDY, I KNOW IT'S YOUR DAY OFF –
BUT YOU CAN'T SPEND IT ALL ON THE COUCH WITH BAXTER...
HOW DO YOU KNOW I'M ON THE COUCH?
BECAUSE I KNOW YOU, AND I KNOW THAT DOG...
OH YOU THINK SO, HUH?
YES.
AND STOP ROLLING YOUR EYES.
WELL, I SHOULD GET GOING. GREAT FOOD AS ALWAYS. SEE YA LATER, ANDY...!
BYE.
SEE YA LATER, ANDY..
WHO WAS THAT?
THAT WAS JOSH. HE'S A REGULAR.
HE'S IRREGULAR?
A REGULAR. CUSTOMER.
OH, I SEE HOW IT IS... NOW THAT I'M NOT WORKING HERE ANYMORE, YOU CAN GO BACK TO FLIRTING WITH YOUR LITTLE DINER BUDS...
OH PLEASE.
WHAT CAN I SAY? JOSH THINKS I'M CUTE.
HEH. JOSH HAS NEVER SEEN YOU FIRST THING IN THE MORNING...
NOPE – THAT'S A PRIVILE GE RESERVED JUST FOR YOOuuu!
YAY ME.

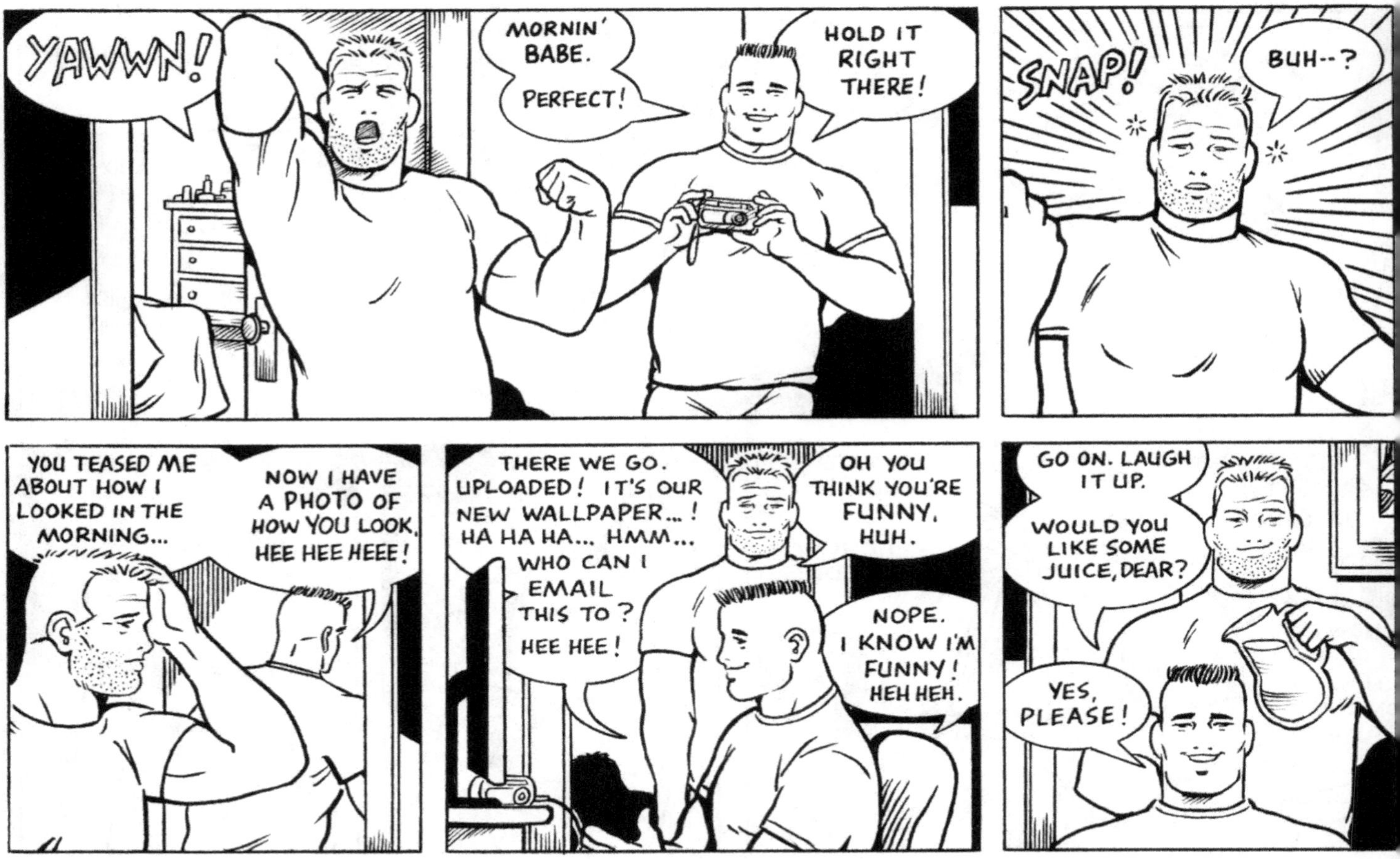
YAWWN!
MORNIN' BABE.
PERFECT!
HOLD IT RIGHT THERE!
SNAP!
BUH--?
YOU TEASED ME ABOUT HOW I LOOKED IN THE MORNING...
NOW I HAVE A PHOTO OF HOW YOU LOOK, HEE HEE HEEE!
THERE WE GO. UPLOADED! IT'S OUR NEW WALLPAPER...! HA HA HA... HMM... WHO CAN I EMAIL THIS TO? HEE HEE!
OH YOU THINK YOU'RE FUNNY, HUH.
NOPE. I KNOW I'M FUNNY! HEH HEH.
GO ON. LAUGH IT UP.
WOULD YOU LIKE SOME JUICE, DEAR?
YES, PLEASE!

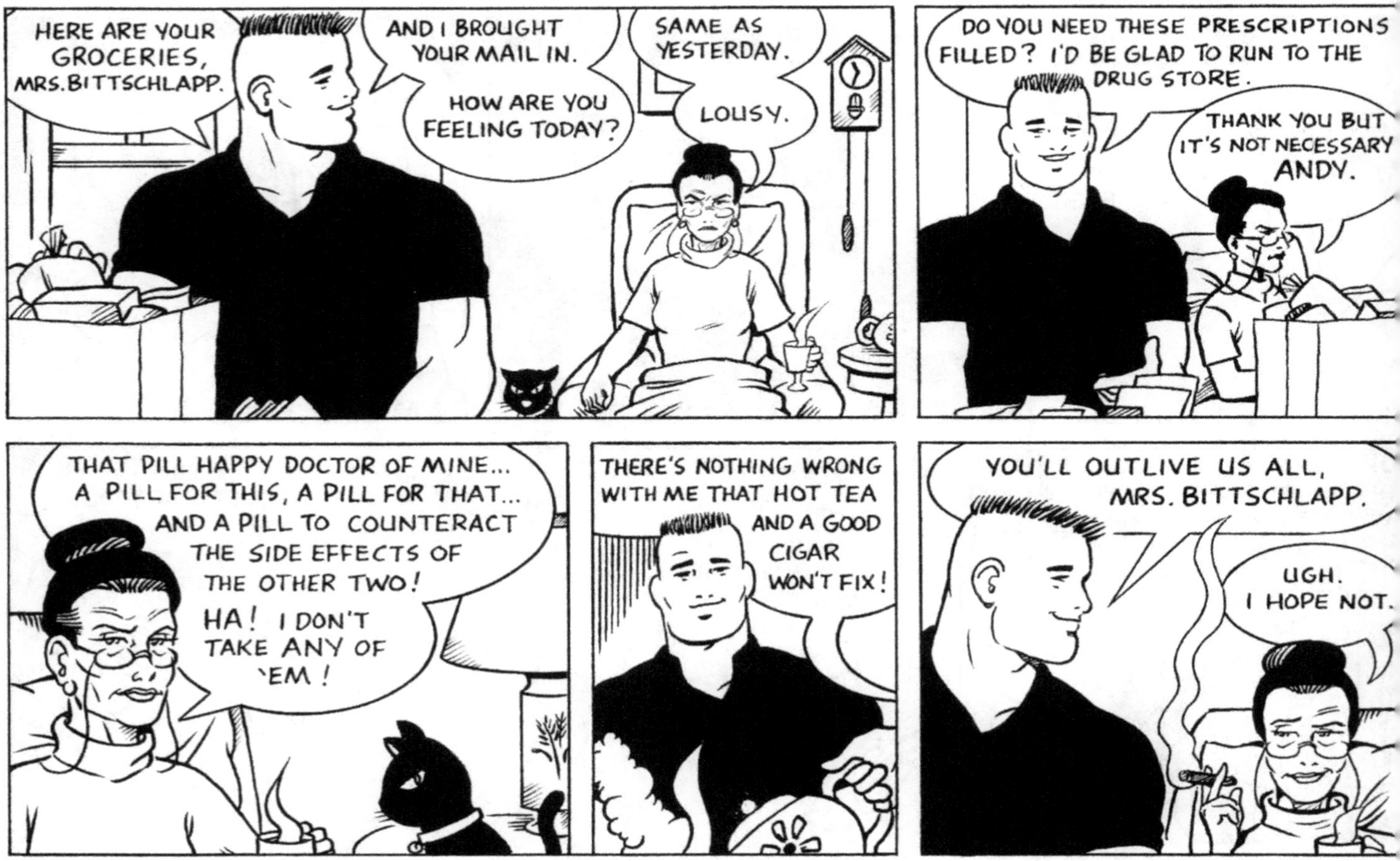
HERE ARE YOUR GROCERIES, MRS. BITTSCHLAPP.
AND I BROUGHT YOUR MAIL IN.
HOW ARE YOU FEELING TODAY?
SAME AS YESTERDAY.
LOUSY.
DO YOU NEED THESE PRESCRIPTIONS FILLED? I'D BE GLAD TO RUN TO THE DRUG STORE.
THANK YOU BUT IT'S NOT NECESSARY ANDY.
THAT PILL HAPPY DOCTOR OF MINE... A PILL FOR THIS, A PILL FOR THAT... AND A PILL TO COUNTERACT THE SIDE EFFECTS OF THE OTHER TWO!
HA! I DON'T TAKE ANY OF 'EM!
THERE'S NOTHING WRONG WITH ME THAT HOT TEA AND A GOOD CIGAR WON'T FIX!
YOU'LL OUTLIVE US ALL, MRS. BITTSCHLAPP.
UGH. I HOPE NOT.

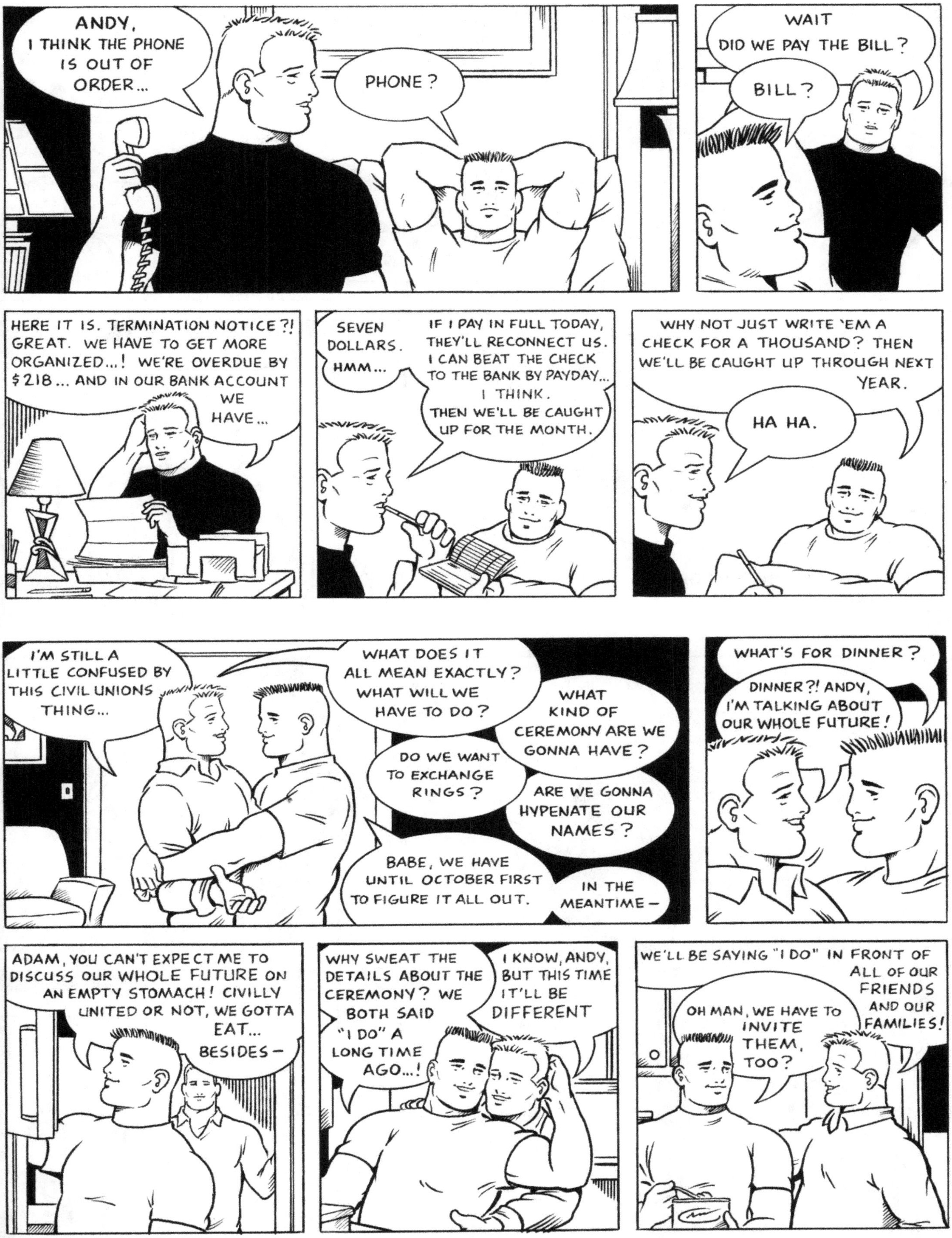
ANDY, I THINK THE PHONE IS OUT OF ORDER...
PHONE?
WAIT DID WE PAY THE BILL?
BILL?
HERE IT IS. TERMINATION NOTICE?! GREAT. WE HAVE TO GET MORE ORGANIZED...! WE'RE OVERDUE BY $218... AND IN OUR BANK ACCOUNT WE HAVE...
SEVEN DOLLARS. HMM...
IF I PAY IN FULL TODAY, THEY'LL RECONNECT US. I CAN BEAT THE CHECK TO THE BANK BY PAYDAY... I THINK. THEN WE'LL BE CAUGHT UP FOR THE MONTH.
WHY NOT JUST WRITE 'EM A CHECK FOR A THOUSAND? THEN WE'LL BE CAUGHT UP THROUGH NEXT YEAR.
HA HA.
I'M STILL A LITTLE CONFUSED BY THIS CIVIL UNIONS THING...
WHAT DOES IT ALL MEAN EXACTLY? WHAT WILL WE HAVE TO DO?
WHAT KIND OF CEREMONY ARE WE GONNA HAVE?
DO WE WANT TO EXCHANGE RINGS?
ARE WE GONNA HYPENATE OUR NAMES?
BABE, WE HAVE UNTIL OCTOBER FIRST TO FIGURE IT ALL OUT.
IN THE MEANTIME—
WHAT'S FOR DINNER?
DINNER?! ANDY, I'M TALKING ABOUT OUR WHOLE FUTURE!
ADAM, YOU CAN'T EXPECT ME TO DISCUSS OUR WHOLE FUTURE ON AN EMPTY STOMACH! CIVILLY UNITED OR NOT, WE GOTTA EAT... BESIDES—
WHY SWEAT THE DETAILS ABOUT THE CEREMONY? WE BOTH SAID "I DO" A LONG TIME AGO...!
I KNOW, ANDY, BUT THIS TIME IT'LL BE DIFFERENT
WE'LL BE SAYING "I DO" IN FRONT OF ALL OF OUR FRIENDS AND OUR FAMILIES!
OH MAN, WE HAVE TO INVITE THEM, TOO?

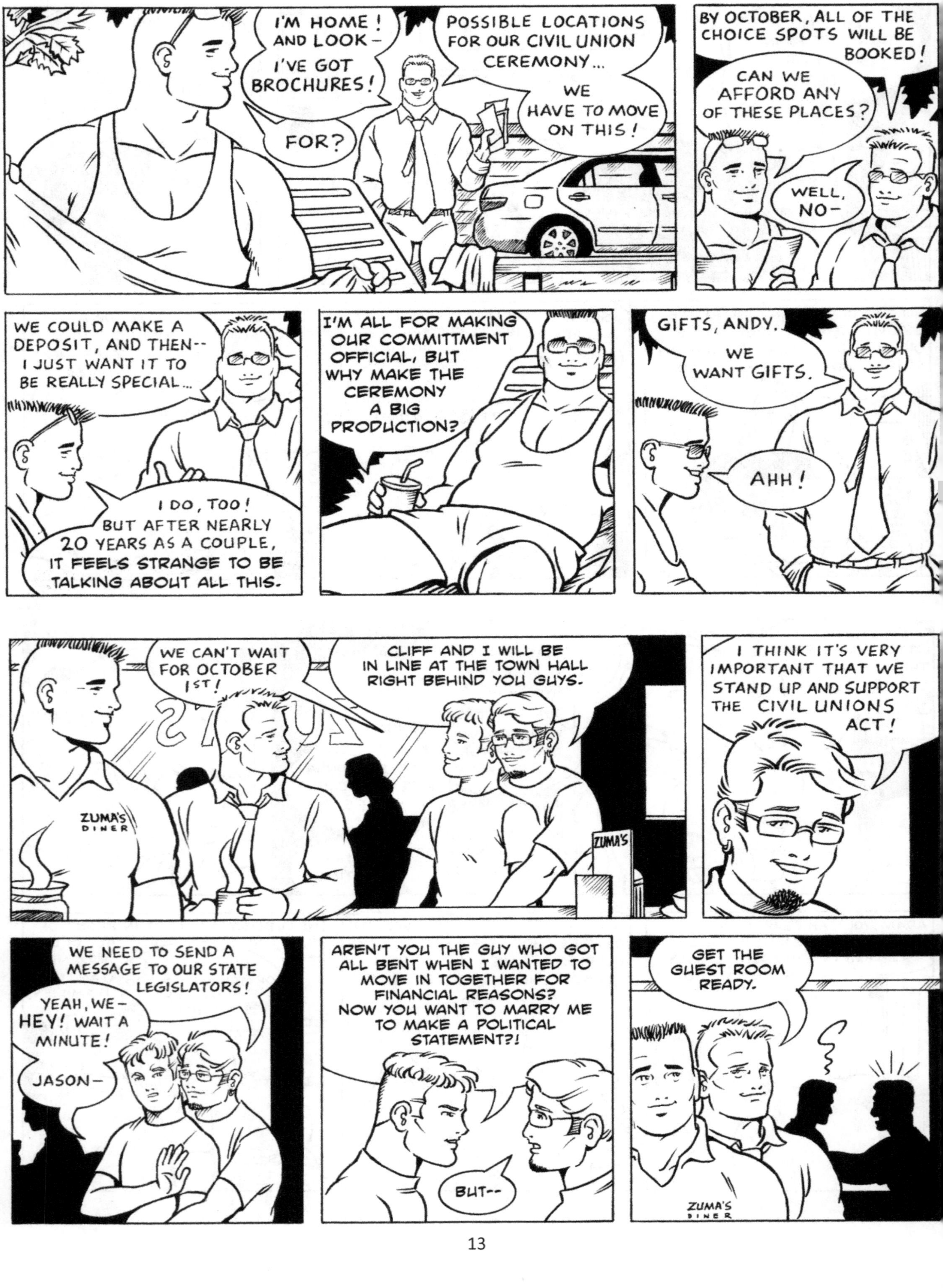

I'M HOME! AND LOOK– I'VE GOT BROCHURES!
FOR?
POSSIBLE LOCATIONS FOR OUR CIVIL UNION CEREMONY...
WE HAVE TO MOVE ON THIS!
BY OCTOBER, ALL OF THE CHOICE SPOTS WILL BE BOOKED!
CAN WE AFFORD ANY OF THESE PLACES?
WELL, NO–
WE COULD MAKE A DEPOSIT, AND THEN-- I JUST WANT IT TO BE REALLY SPECIAL...
I DO, TOO! BUT AFTER NEARLY 20 YEARS AS A COUPLE, IT FEELS STRANGE TO BE TALKING ABOUT ALL THIS.
I'M ALL FOR MAKING OUR COMMITTMENT OFFICIAL, BUT WHY MAKE THE CEREMONY A BIG PRODUCTION?
GIFTS, ANDY.
WE WANT GIFTS.
AHH!
ZUMA'S DINER
WE CAN'T WAIT FOR OCTOBER 1ST!
CLIFF AND I WILL BE IN LINE AT THE TOWN HALL RIGHT BEHIND YOU GUYS.
ZUMA'S
I THINK IT'S VERY IMPORTANT THAT WE STAND UP AND SUPPORT THE CIVIL UNIONS ACT!
WE NEED TO SEND A MESSAGE TO OUR STATE LEGISLATORS!
YEAH, WE– HEY! WAIT A MINUTE!
JASON–
AREN'T YOU THE GUY WHO GOT ALL BENT WHEN I WANTED TO MOVE IN TOGETHER FOR FINANCIAL REASONS? NOW YOU WANT TO MARRY ME TO MAKE A POLITICAL STATEMENT?!
BUT--
GET THE GUEST ROOM READY.
ZUMA'S DINER

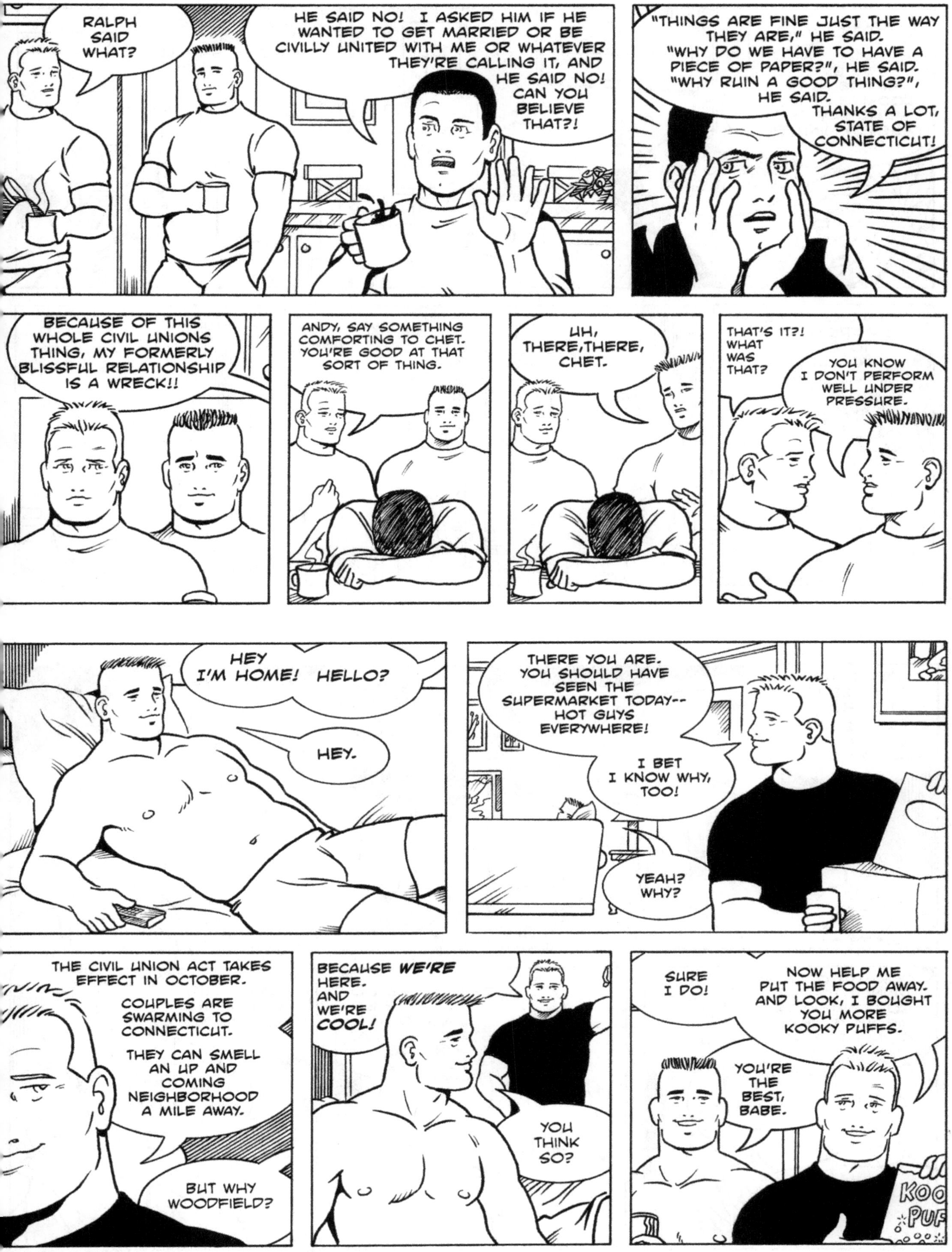
RALPH SAID WHAT?
HE SAID NO! I ASKED HIM IF HE WANTED TO GET MARRIED OR BE CIVILLY UNITED WITH ME OR WHATEVER THEY'RE CALLING IT, AND HE SAID NO! CAN YOU BELIEVE THAT?!
"THINGS ARE FINE JUST THE WAY THEY ARE," HE SAID. "WHY DO WE HAVE TO HAVE A PIECE OF PAPER?", HE SAID. "WHY RUIN A GOOD THING?", HE SAID.
THANKS A LOT, STATE OF CONNECTICUT!
BECAUSE OF THIS WHOLE CIVIL UNIONS THING, MY FORMERLY BLISSFUL RELATIONSHIP IS A WRECK!!
ANDY, SAY SOMETHING COMFORTING TO CHET. YOU'RE GOOD AT THAT SORT OF THING.
UH, THERE, THERE, CHET.
THAT'S IT?! WHAT WAS THAT?
YOU KNOW I DON'T PERFORM WELL UNDER PRESSURE.
HEY I'M HOME! HELLO?
HEY.
THERE YOU ARE. YOU SHOULD HAVE SEEN THE SUPERMARKET TODAY-- HOT GUYS EVERYWHERE!
I BET I KNOW WHY, TOO!
YEAH? WHY?
THE CIVIL UNION ACT TAKES EFFECT IN OCTOBER.
COUPLES ARE SWARMING TO CONNECTICUT.
THEY CAN SMELL AN UP AND COMING NEIGHBORHOOD A MILE AWAY.
BUT WHY WOODFIELD?
BECAUSE *WE'RE* HERE. AND WE'RE *COOL!*
YOU THINK SO?
SURE I DO!
NOW HELP ME PUT THE FOOD AWAY. AND LOOK, I BOUGHT YOU MORE KOOKY PUFFS.
YOU'RE THE BEST, BABE.

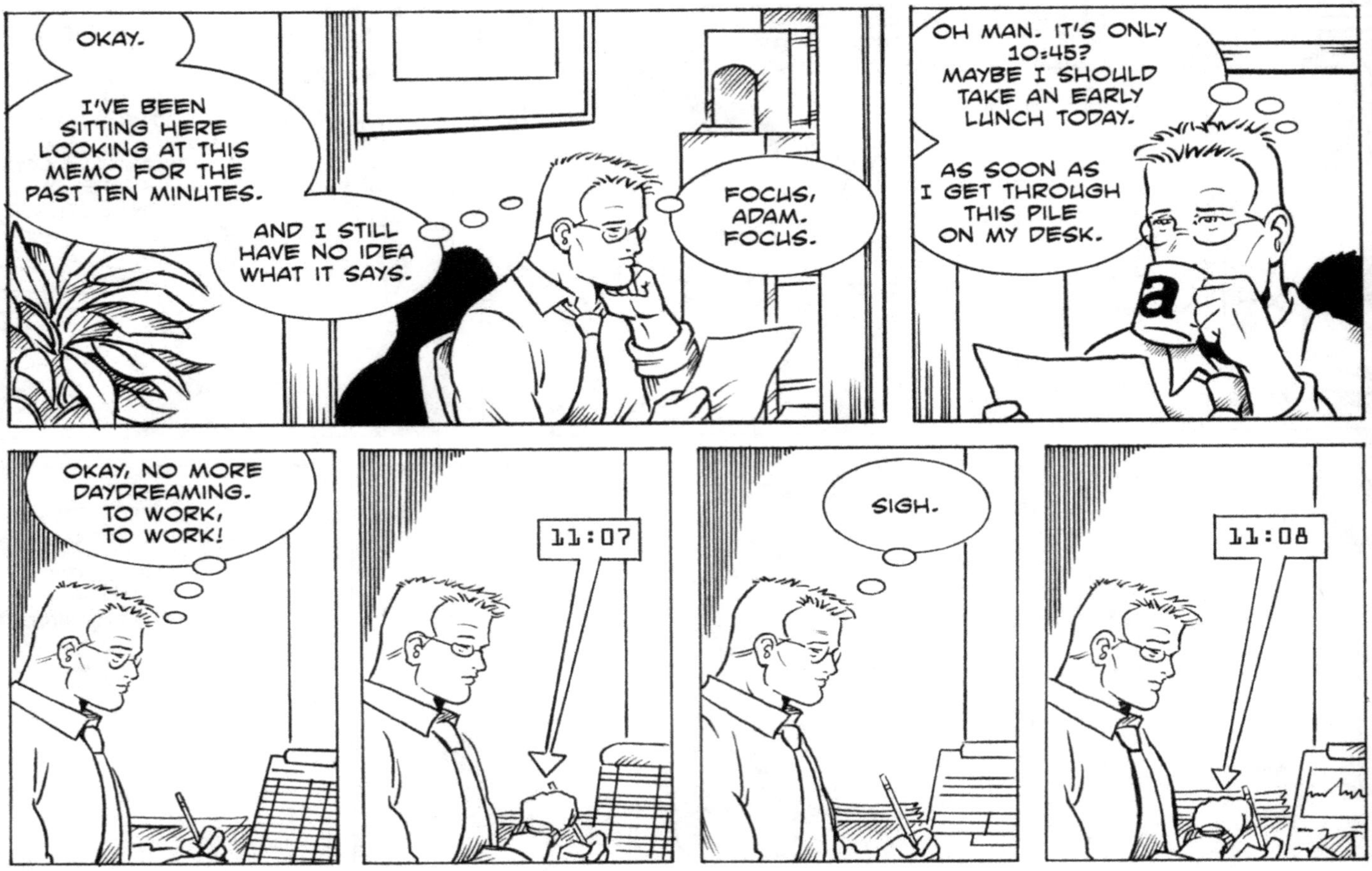
OKAY.
I'VE BEEN SITTING HERE LOOKING AT THIS MEMO FOR THE PAST TEN MINUTES.
AND I STILL HAVE NO IDEA WHAT IT SAYS.
FOCUS, ADAM. FOCUS.
OH MAN. IT'S ONLY 10:45? MAYBE I SHOULD TAKE AN EARLY LUNCH TODAY.
AS SOON AS I GET THROUGH THIS PILE ON MY DESK.
a
OKAY, NO MORE DAYDREAMING. TO WORK, TO WORK!
11:07
SIGH.
11:08

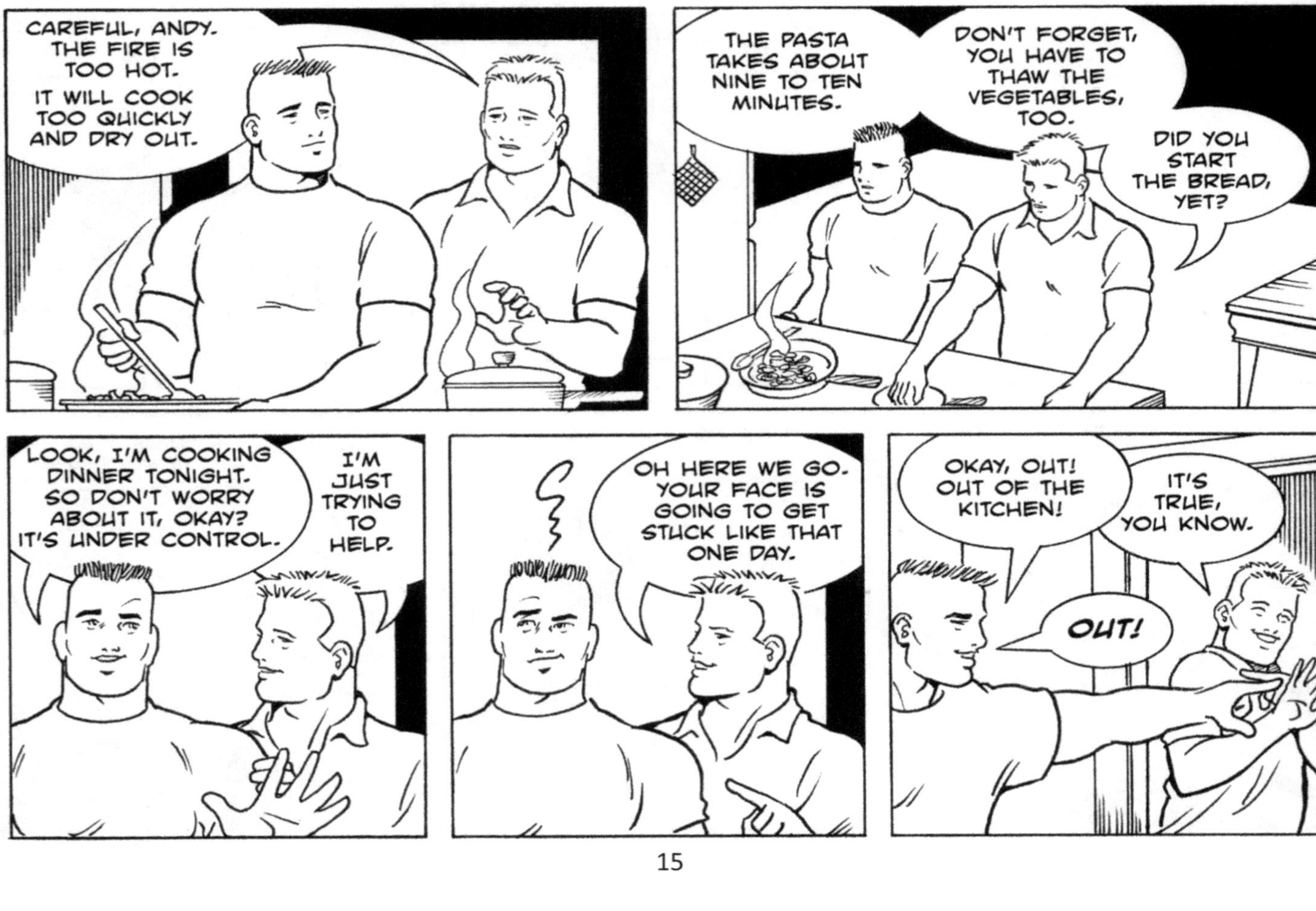
CAREFUL, ANDY. THE FIRE IS TOO HOT.
IT WILL COOK TOO QUICKLY AND DRY OUT.
THE PASTA TAKES ABOUT NINE TO TEN MINUTES.
DON'T FORGET, YOU HAVE TO THAW THE VEGETABLES, TOO.
DID YOU START THE BREAD, YET?
LOOK, I'M COOKING DINNER TONIGHT. SO DON'T WORRY ABOUT IT, OKAY? IT'S UNDER CONTROL.
I'M JUST TRYING TO HELP.
OH HERE WE GO. YOUR FACE IS GOING TO GET STUCK LIKE THAT ONE DAY.
OKAY, OUT! OUT OF THE KITCHEN!
IT'S TRUE, YOU KNOW.
OUT!

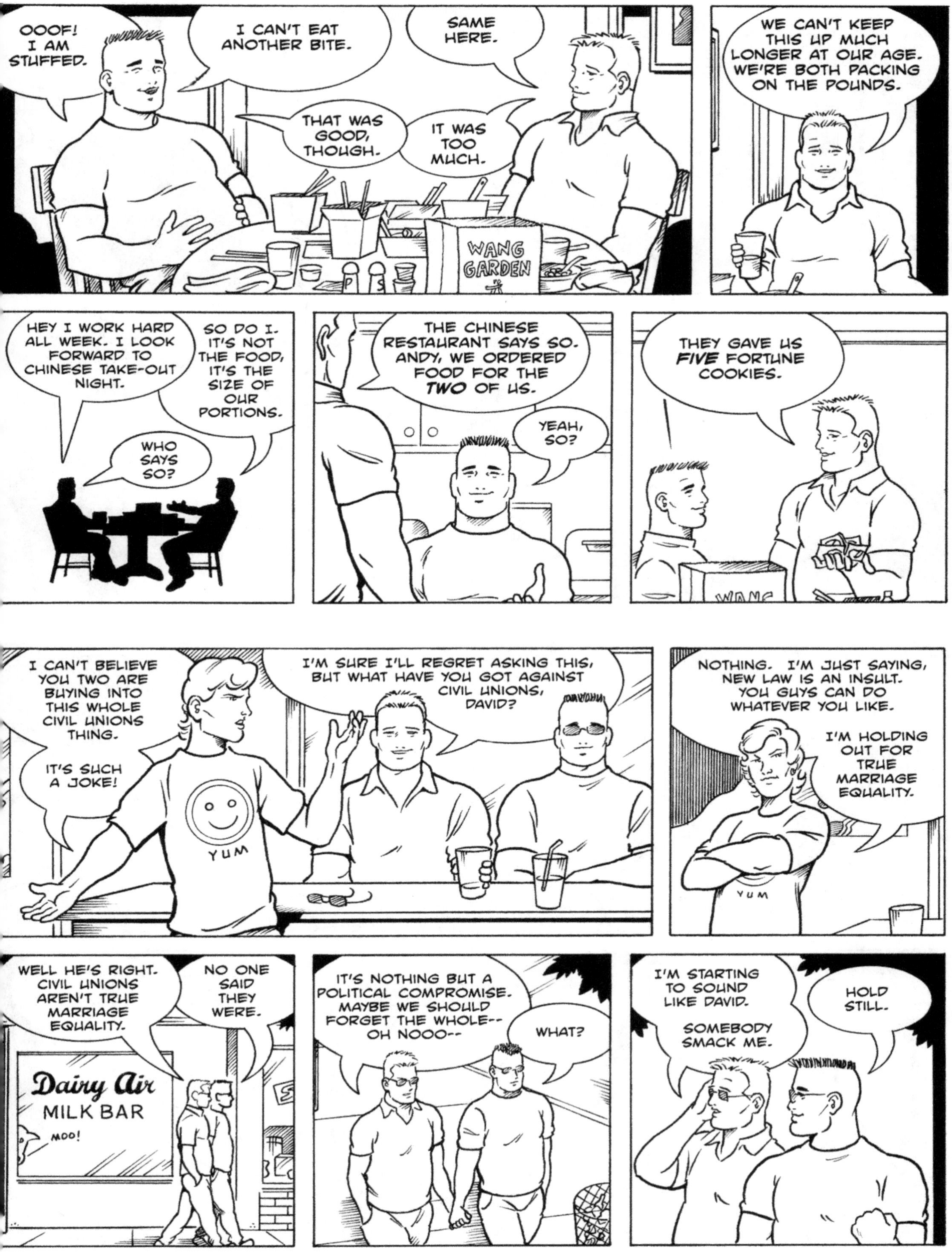

OOOF! I AM STUFFED.
I CAN'T EAT ANOTHER BITE.
SAME HERE.
THAT WAS GOOD, THOUGH.
IT WAS TOO MUCH.
WANG GARDEN
WE CAN'T KEEP THIS UP MUCH LONGER AT OUR AGE. WE'RE BOTH PACKING ON THE POUNDS.
HEY I WORK HARD ALL WEEK. I LOOK FORWARD TO CHINESE TAKE-OUT NIGHT.
SO DO I. IT'S NOT THE FOOD, IT'S THE SIZE OF OUR PORTIONS.
WHO SAYS SO?
THE CHINESE RESTAURANT SAYS SO. ANDY, WE ORDERED FOOD FOR THE TWO OF US.
YEAH, SO?
THEY GAVE US FIVE FORTUNE COOKIES.
I CAN'T BELIEVE YOU TWO ARE BUYING INTO THIS WHOLE CIVIL UNIONS THING.
IT'S SUCH A JOKE!
YUM
I'M SURE I'LL REGRET ASKING THIS, BUT WHAT HAVE YOU GOT AGAINST CIVIL UNIONS, DAVID?
NOTHING. I'M JUST SAYING, NEW LAW IS AN INSULT. YOU GUYS CAN DO WHATEVER YOU LIKE.
I'M HOLDING OUT FOR TRUE MARRIAGE EQUALITY.
YUM
WELL HE'S RIGHT. CIVIL UNIONS AREN'T TRUE MARRIAGE EQUALITY.
NO ONE SAID THEY WERE.
Dairy Air
MILK BAR
MOO!
IT'S NOTHING BUT A POLITICAL COMPROMISE. MAYBE WE SHOULD FORGET THE WHOLE-- OH NOOO--
WHAT?
I'M STARTING TO SOUND LIKE DAVID.
SOMEBODY SMACK ME.
HOLD STILL.

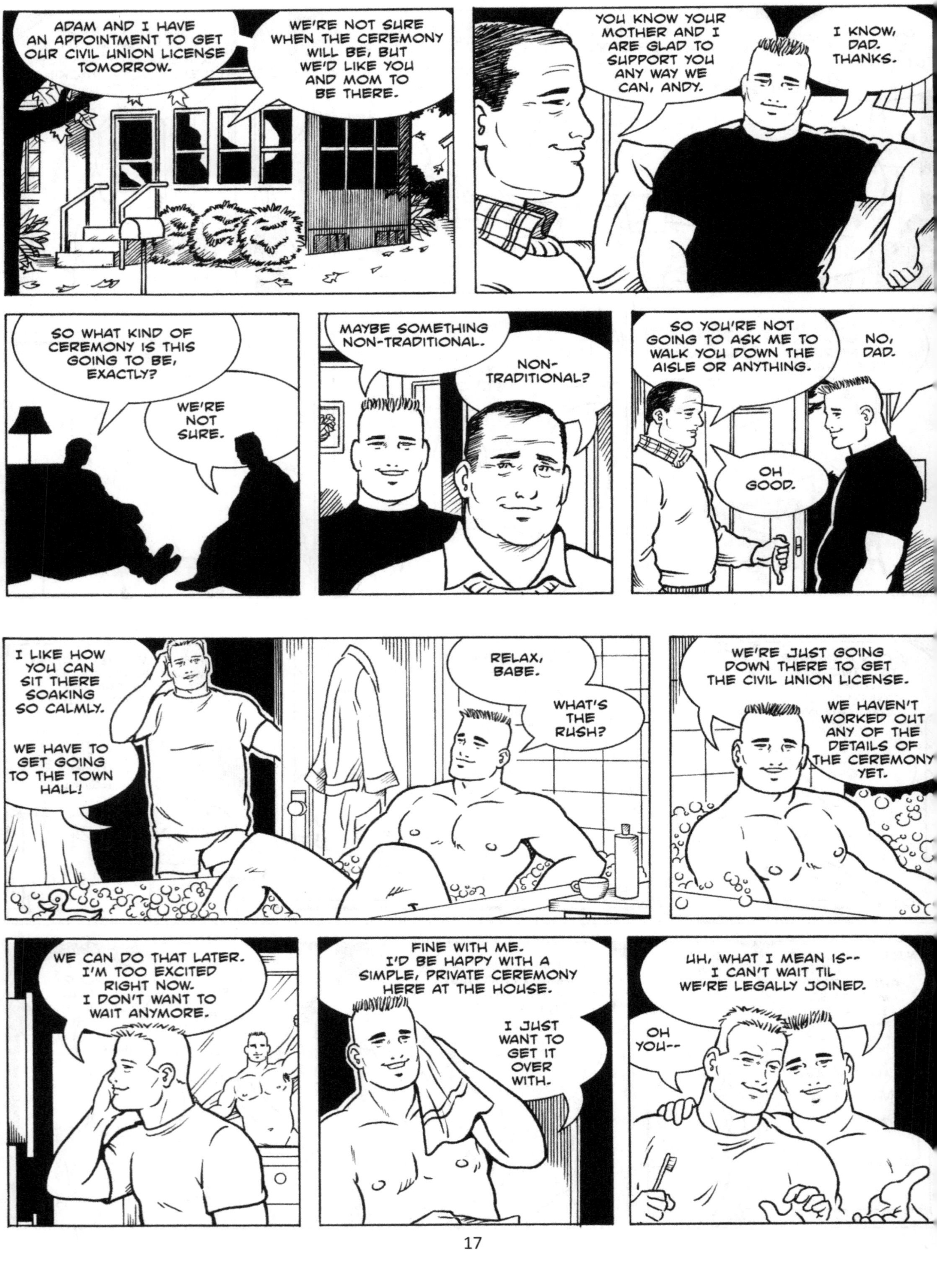
ADAM AND I HAVE AN APPOINTMENT TO GET OUR CIVIL UNION LICENSE TOMORROW.
WE'RE NOT SURE WHEN THE CEREMONY WILL BE, BUT WE'D LIKE YOU AND MOM TO BE THERE.
YOU KNOW YOUR MOTHER AND I ARE GLAD TO SUPPORT YOU ANY WAY WE CAN, ANDY.
I KNOW, DAD. THANKS.
SO WHAT KIND OF CEREMONY IS THIS GOING TO BE, EXACTLY?
WE'RE NOT SURE.
MAYBE SOMETHING NON-TRADITIONAL.
NON-TRADITIONAL?
SO YOU'RE NOT GOING TO ASK ME TO WALK YOU DOWN THE AISLE OR ANYTHING.
NO, DAD.
OH GOOD.
I LIKE HOW YOU CAN SIT THERE SOAKING SO CALMLY.
WE HAVE TO GET GOING TO THE TOWN HALL!
RELAX, BABE.
WHAT'S THE RUSH?
WE'RE JUST GOING DOWN THERE TO GET THE CIVIL UNION LICENSE.
WE HAVEN'T WORKED OUT ANY OF THE DETAILS OF THE CEREMONY YET.
WE CAN DO THAT LATER. I'M TOO EXCITED RIGHT NOW. I DON'T WANT TO WAIT ANYMORE.
FINE WITH ME. I'D BE HAPPY WITH A SIMPLE, PRIVATE CEREMONY HERE AT THE HOUSE.
I JUST WANT TO GET IT OVER WITH.
UH, WHAT I MEAN IS-- I CAN'T WAIT TIL WE'RE LEGALLY JOINED.
OH YOU--

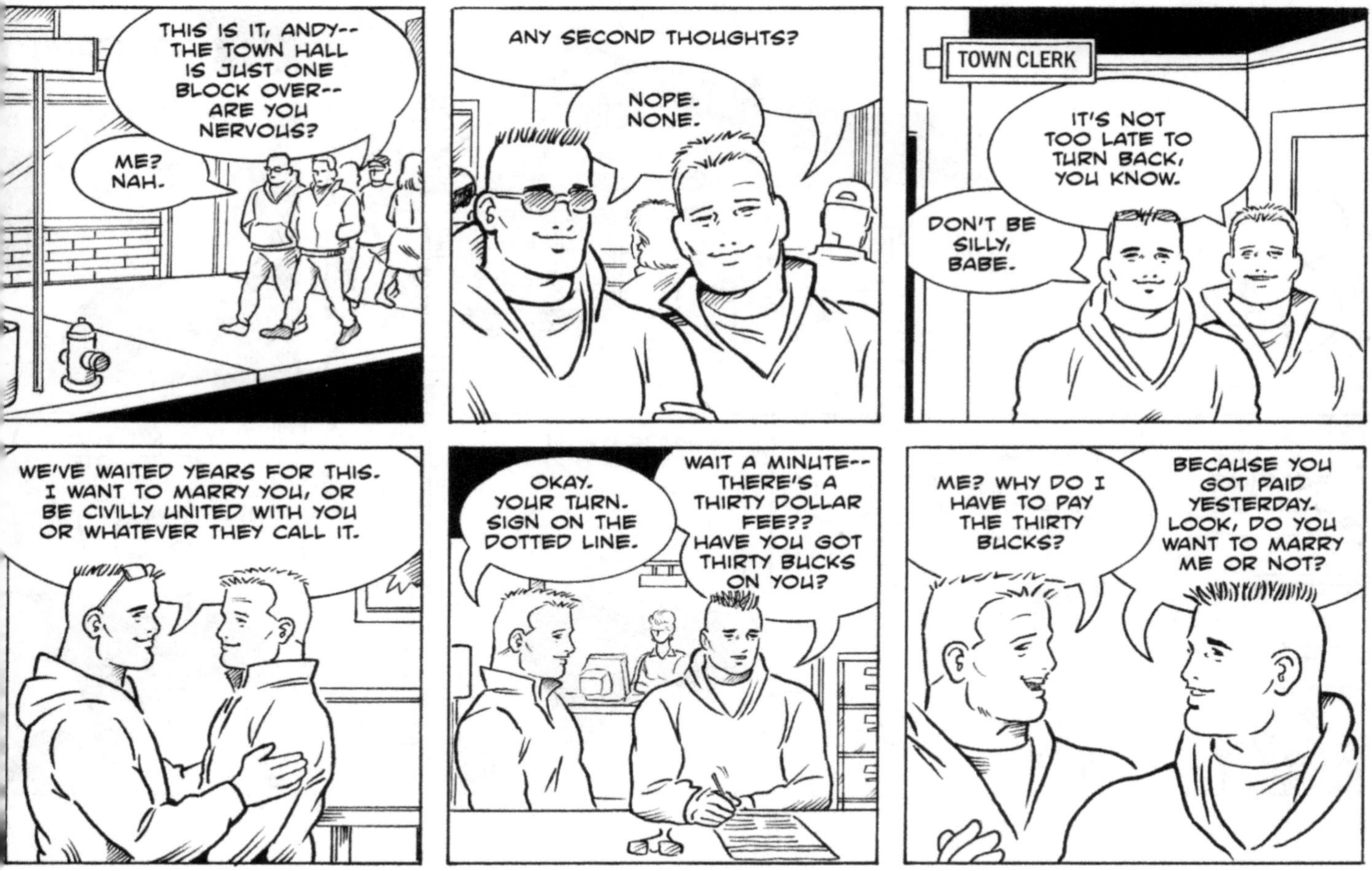
THIS IS IT, ANDY-- THE TOWN HALL IS JUST ONE BLOCK OVER-- ARE YOU NERVOUS?
ME? NAH.
ANY SECOND THOUGHTS?
NOPE. NONE.
TOWN CLERK
IT'S NOT TOO LATE TO TURN BACK, YOU KNOW.
DON'T BE SILLY, BABE.
WE'VE WAITED YEARS FOR THIS. I WANT TO MARRY YOU, OR BE CIVILLY UNITED WITH YOU OR WHATEVER THEY CALL IT.
OKAY. YOUR TURN. SIGN ON THE DOTTED LINE.
WAIT A MINUTE-- THERE'S A THIRTY DOLLAR FEE?? HAVE YOU GOT THIRTY BUCKS ON YOU?
ME? WHY DO I HAVE TO PAY THE THIRTY BUCKS?
BECAUSE YOU GOT PAID YESTERDAY. LOOK, DO YOU WANT TO MARRY ME OR NOT?

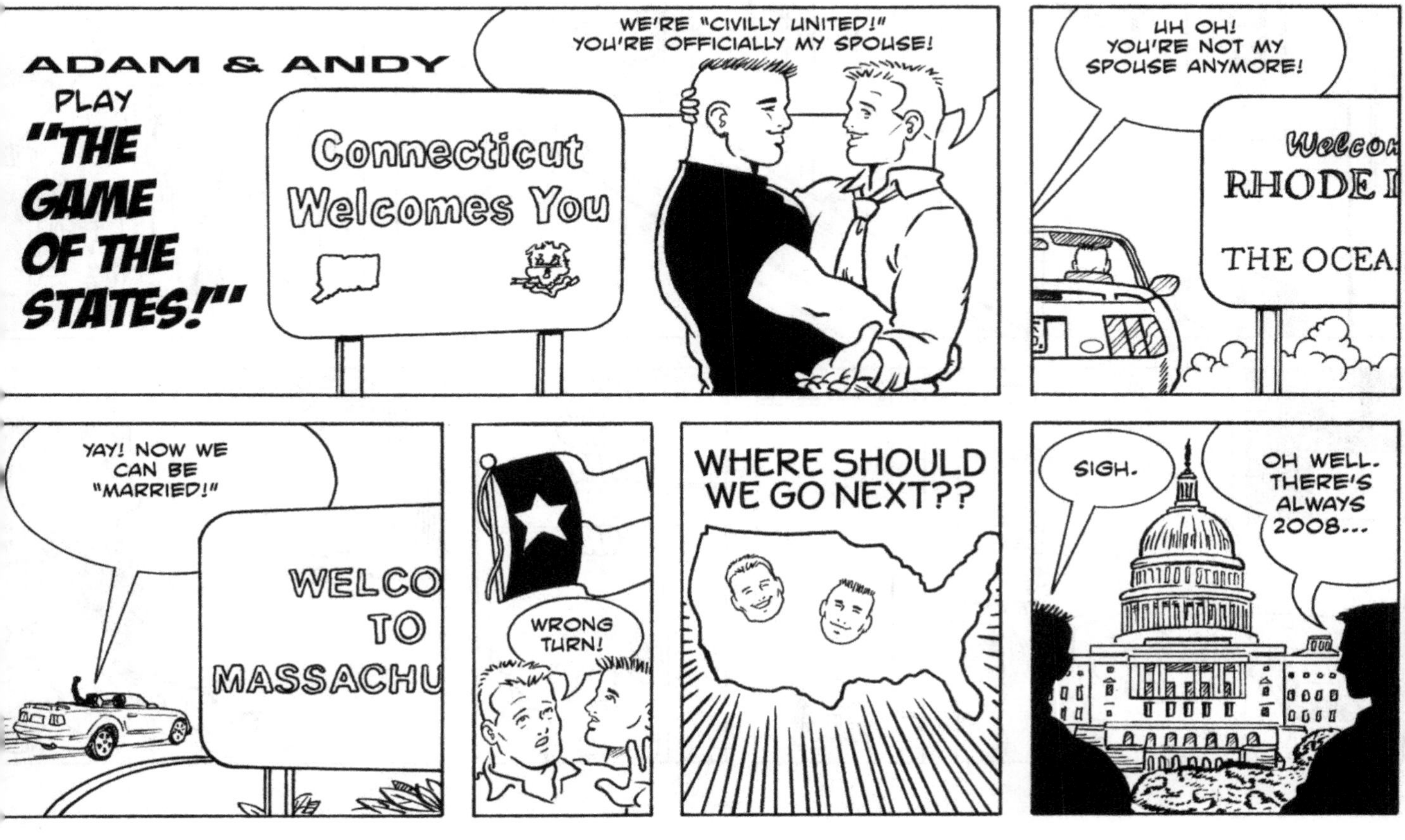
ADAM & ANDY
PLAY
"THE GAME OF THE STATES!"
Connecticut Welcomes You
WE'RE "CIVILLY UNITED!" YOU'RE OFFICIALLY MY SPOUSE!
UH OH! YOU'RE NOT MY SPOUSE ANYMORE!
Welcom
RHODE I
THE OCEA
YAY! NOW WE CAN BE "MARRIED!"
WELCO
TO
MASSACHU
WRONG TURN!
WHERE SHOULD WE GO NEXT??
SIGH.
OH WELL. THERE'S ALWAYS 2008...

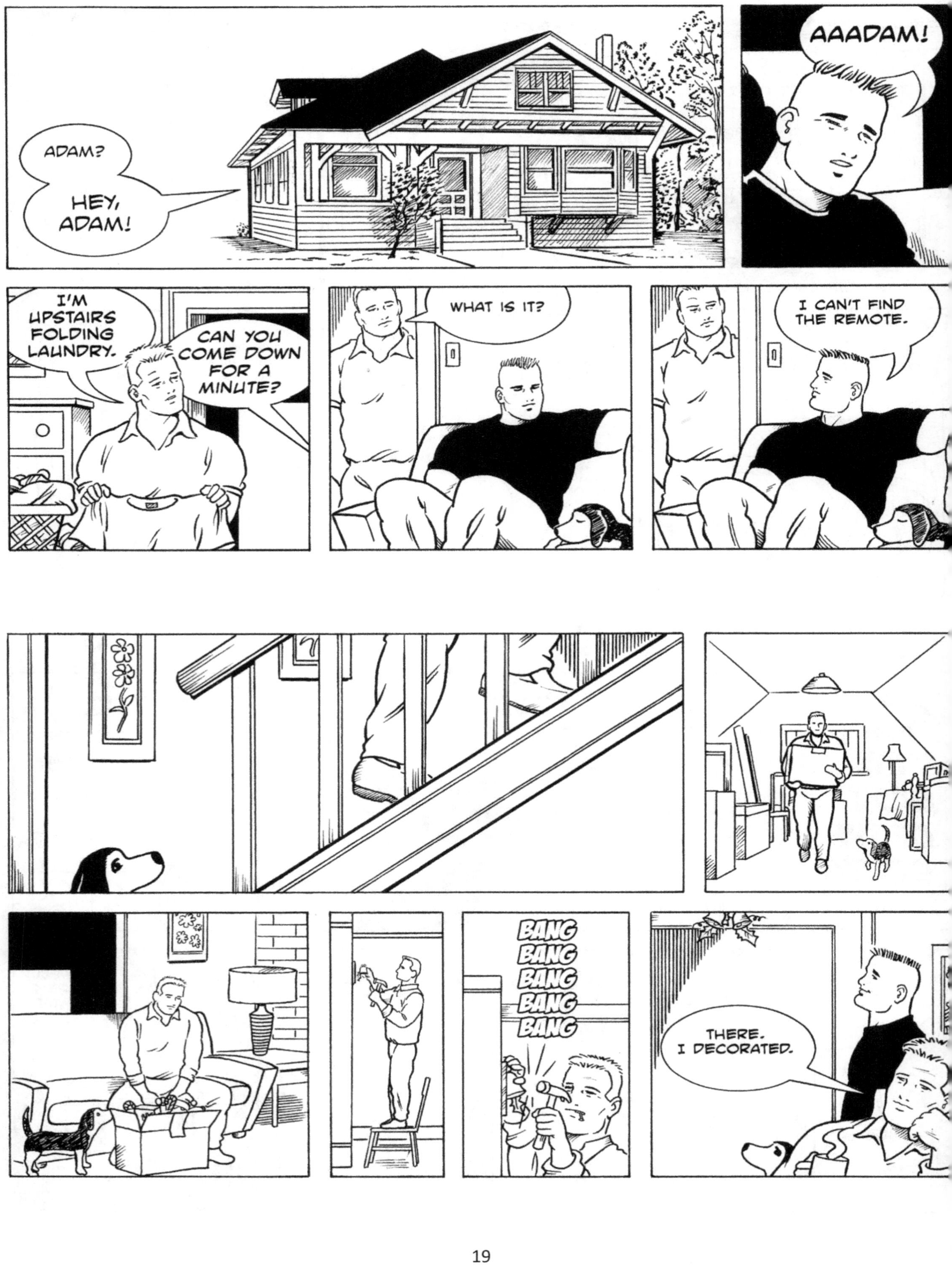
ADAM?
HEY, ADAM!
AAADAM!
I'M UPSTAIRS FOLDING LAUNDRY.
CAN YOU COME DOWN FOR A MINUTE?
WHAT IS IT?
I CAN'T FIND THE REMOTE.
BANG BANG BANG BANG BANG
THERE. I DECORATED.

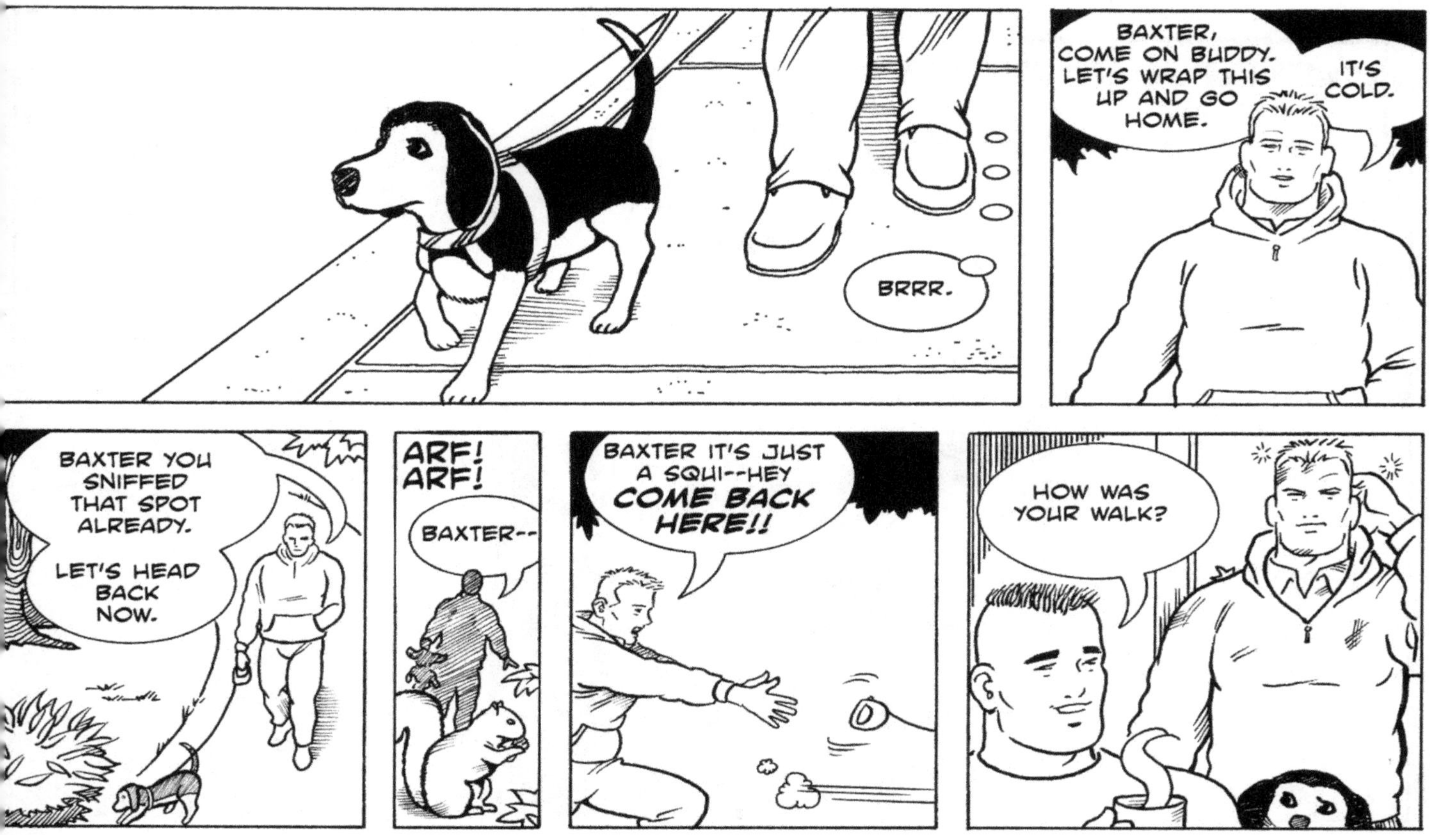
BRRR.
BAXTER, COME ON BUDDY. LET'S WRAP THIS UP AND GO HOME.
IT'S COLD.
BAXTER YOU SNIFFED THAT SPOT ALREADY.
LET'S HEAD BACK NOW.
ARF! ARF!
BAXTER--
BAXTER IT'S JUST A SQUI--HEY *COME BACK HERE!!*
HOW WAS YOUR WALK?

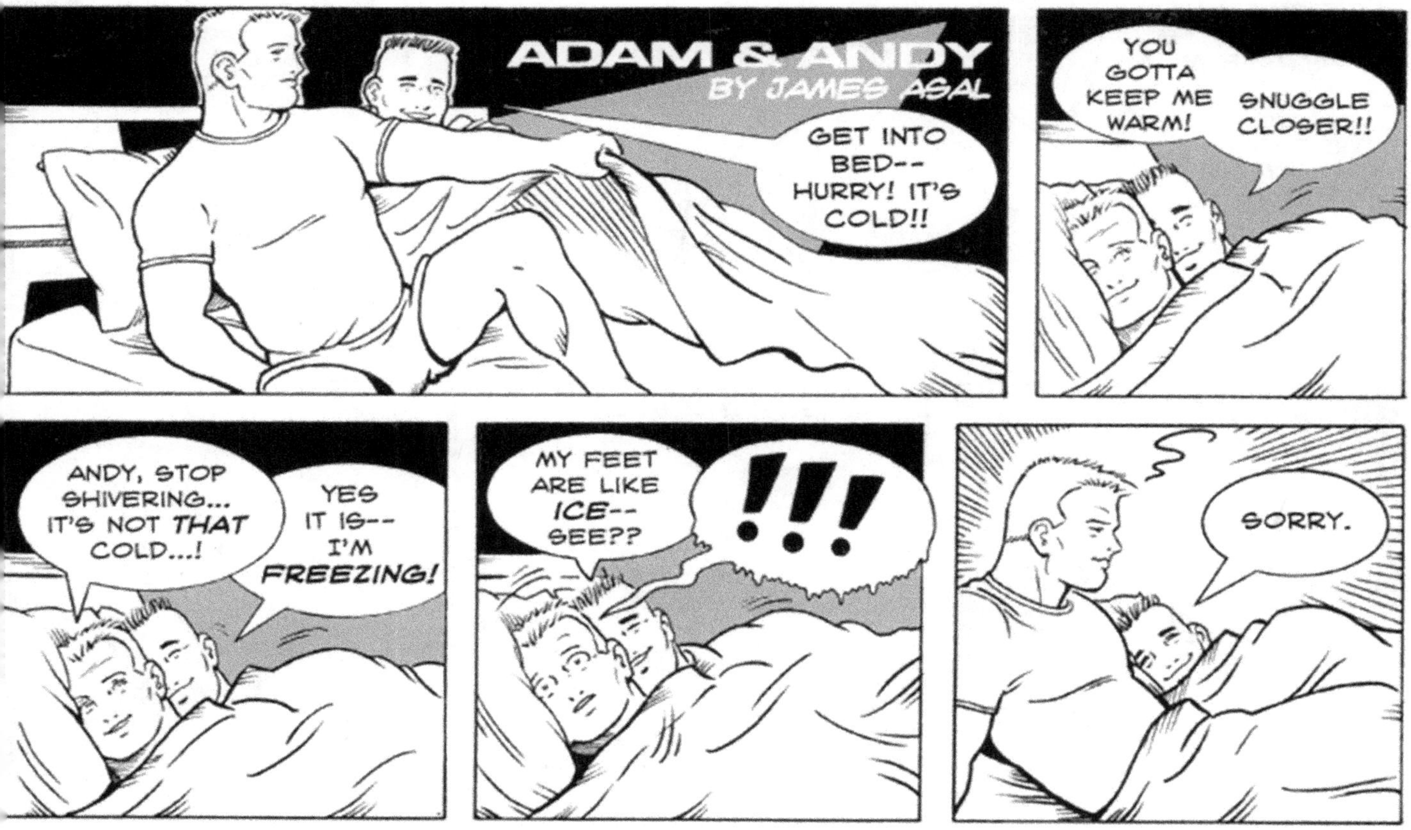
ADAM & ANDY
BY JAMES ASAL
GET INTO BED-- HURRY! IT'S COLD!!
YOU GOTTA KEEP ME WARM!
SNUGGLE CLOSER!!
ANDY, STOP SHIVERING... IT'S NOT *THAT* COLD...!
YES IT IS-- I'M *FREEZING!*
MY FEET ARE LIKE *ICE*-- SEE??
!!!
SORRY.

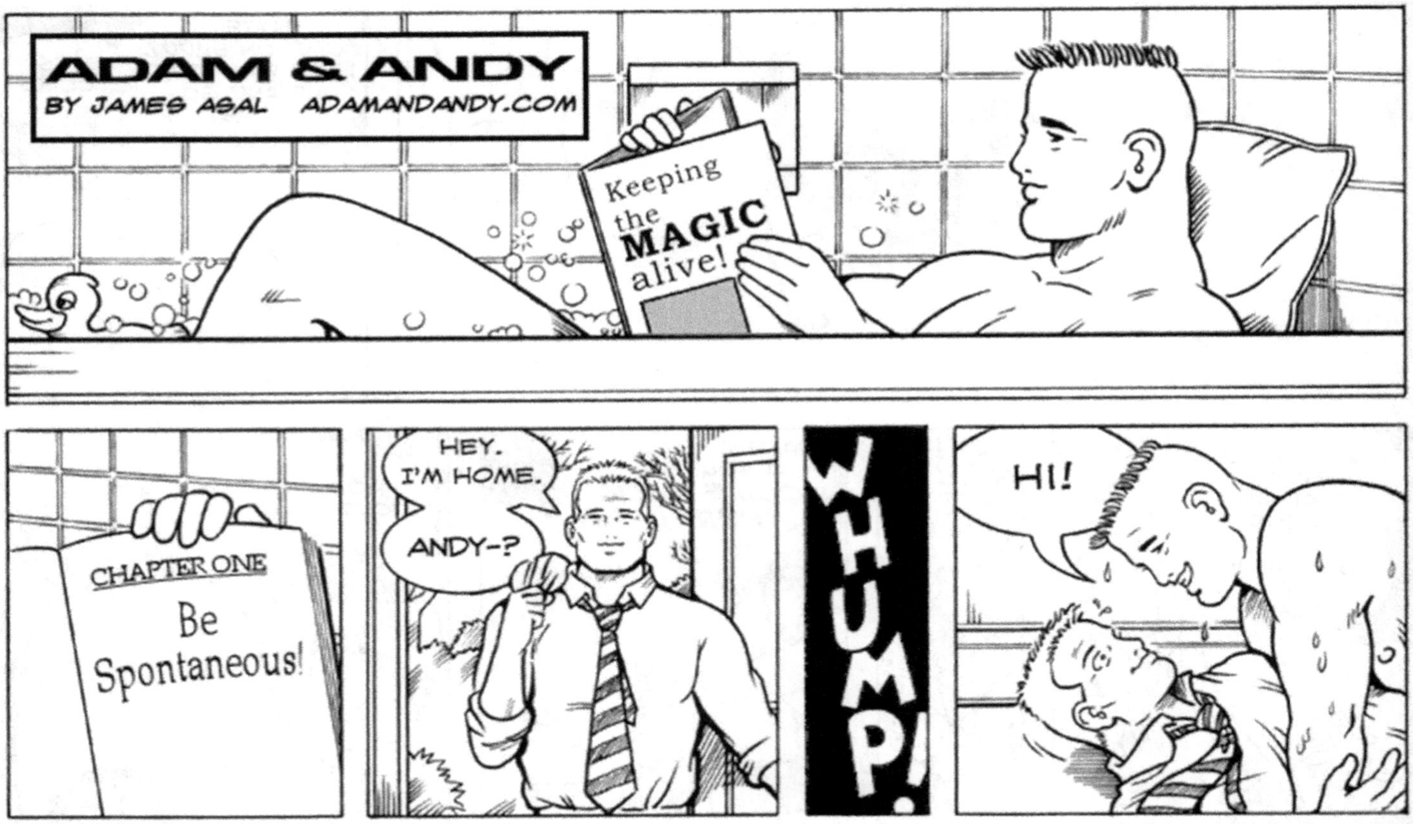
ADAM & ANDY
BY JAMES ASAL ADAMANDANDY.COM
Keeping the MAGIC alive!
CHAPTER ONE
Be Spontaneous!
HEY. I'M HOME.
ANDY–?
WHUMP!
HI!

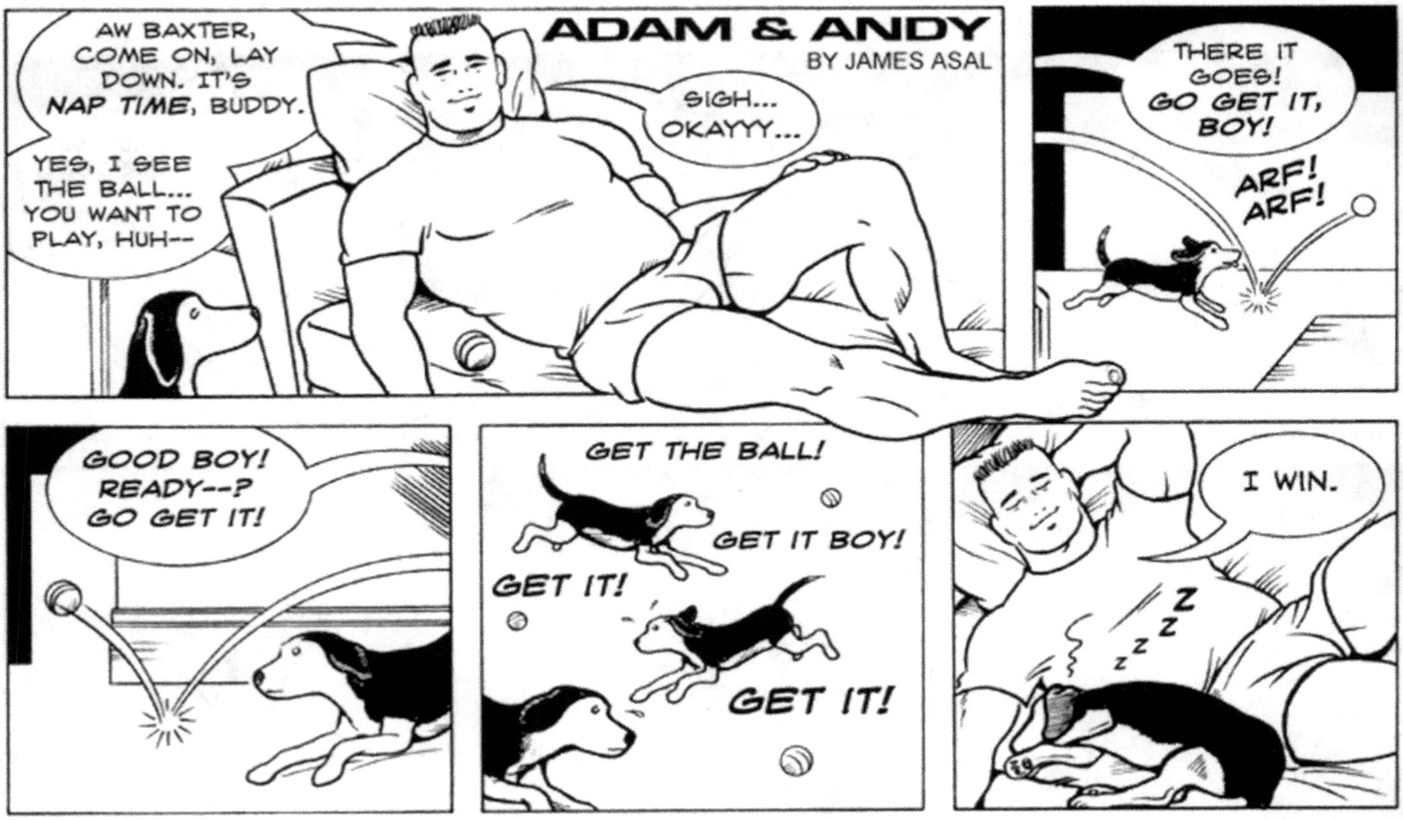
ADAM & ANDY
BY JAMES ASAL
AW BAXTER, COME ON, LAY DOWN. IT'S NAP TIME, BUDDY.
YES, I SEE THE BALL... YOU WANT TO PLAY, HUH--
SIGH... OKAYYY...
THERE IT GOES! GO GET IT, BOY!
ARF! ARF!
GOOD BOY! READY--? GO GET IT!
GET THE BALL!
GET IT BOY!
GET IT!
GET IT!
I WIN.
Z Z Z Z

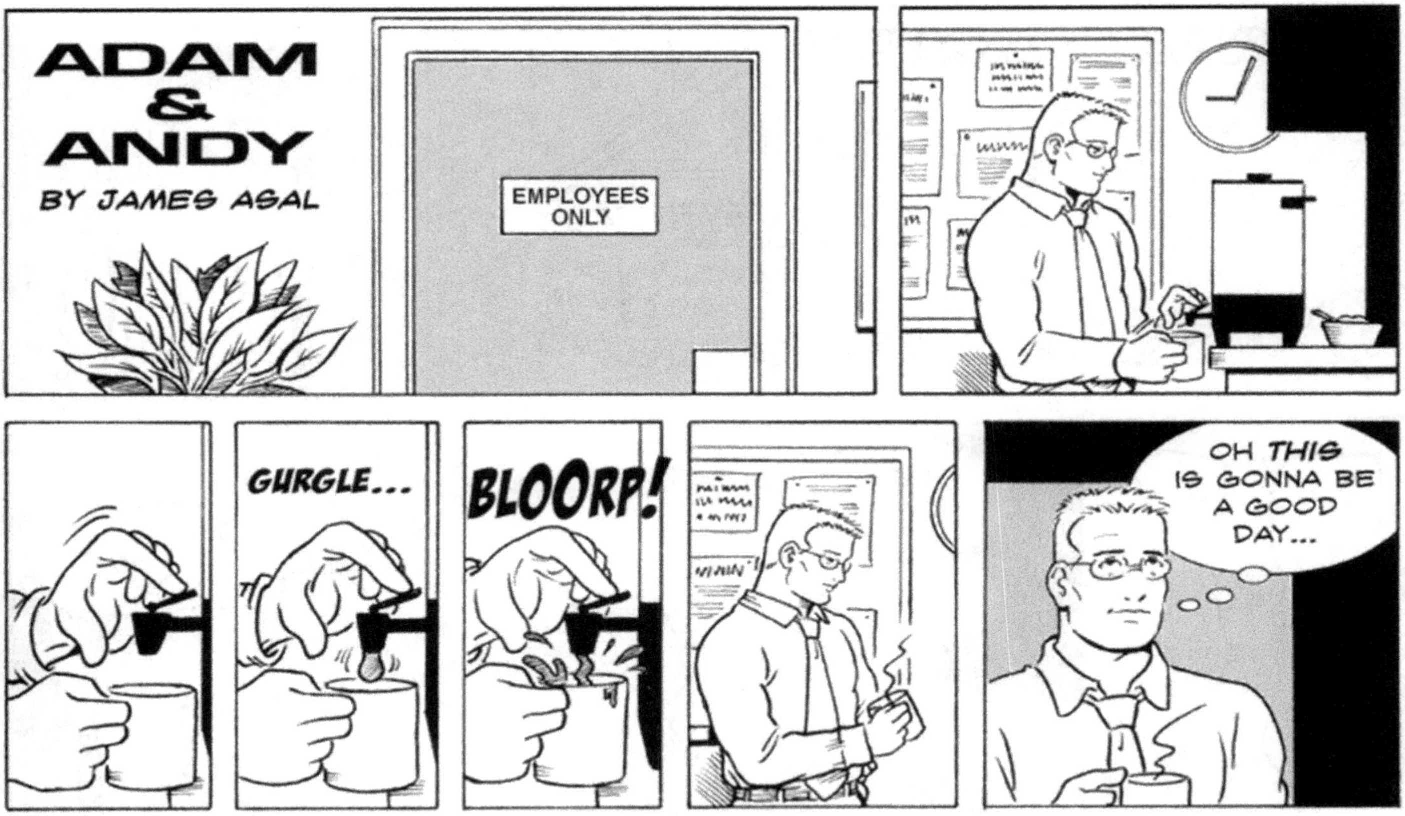
ADAM & ANDY
BY JAMES ASAL
EMPLOYEES ONLY
GURGLE...
BLOORP!
OH THIS IS GONNA BE A GOOD DAY...

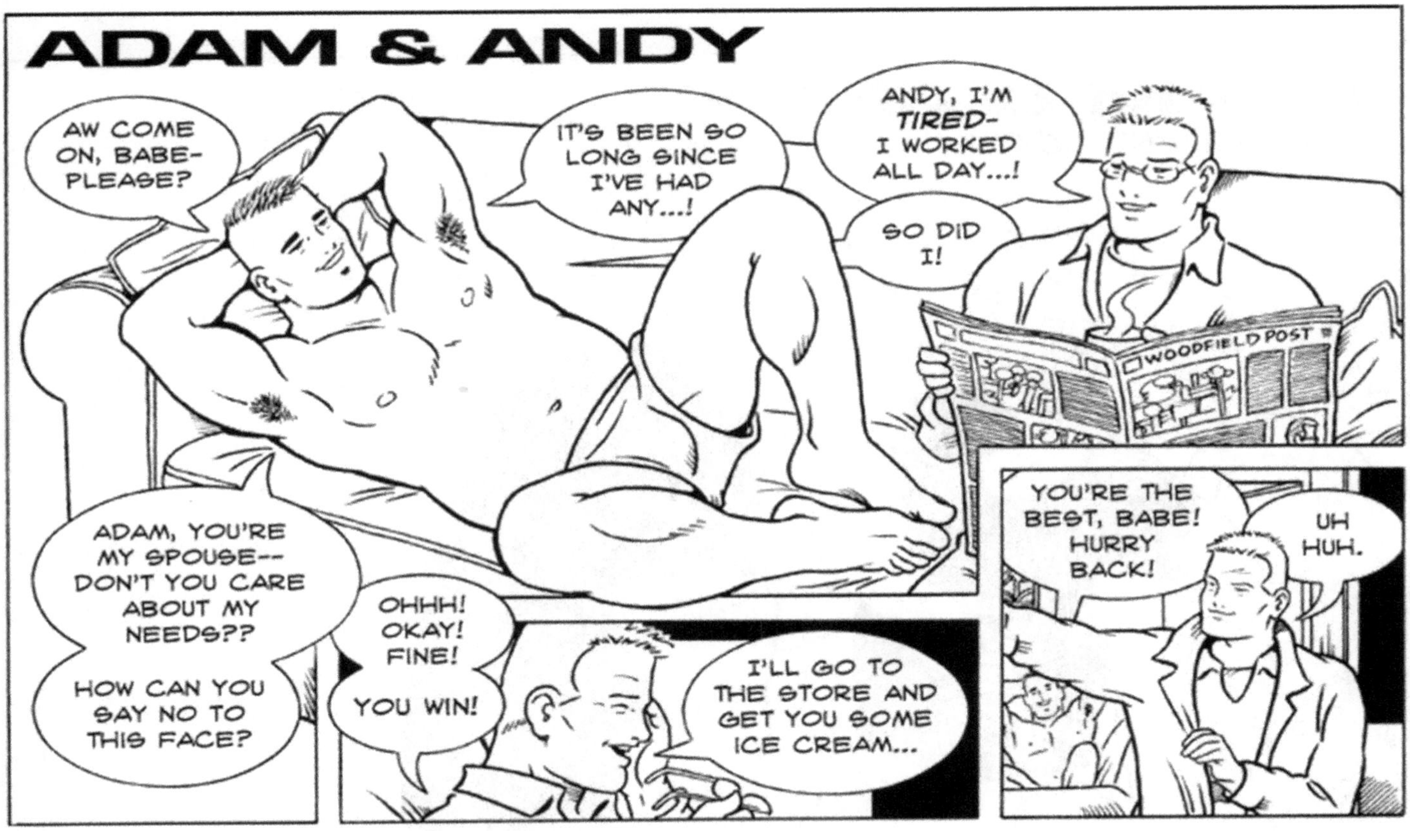
ADAM & ANDY
AW COME ON, BABE- PLEASE?
IT'S BEEN SO LONG SINCE I'VE HAD ANY...!
ANDY, I'M TIRED- I WORKED ALL DAY...!
SO DID I!
WOODFIELD POST
ADAM, YOU'RE MY SPOUSE-- DON'T YOU CARE ABOUT MY NEEDS??
HOW CAN YOU SAY NO TO THIS FACE?
OHHH! OKAY! FINE!
YOU WIN!
I'LL GO TO THE STORE AND GET YOU SOME ICE CREAM...
YOU'RE THE BEST, BABE! HURRY BACK!
UH HUH.

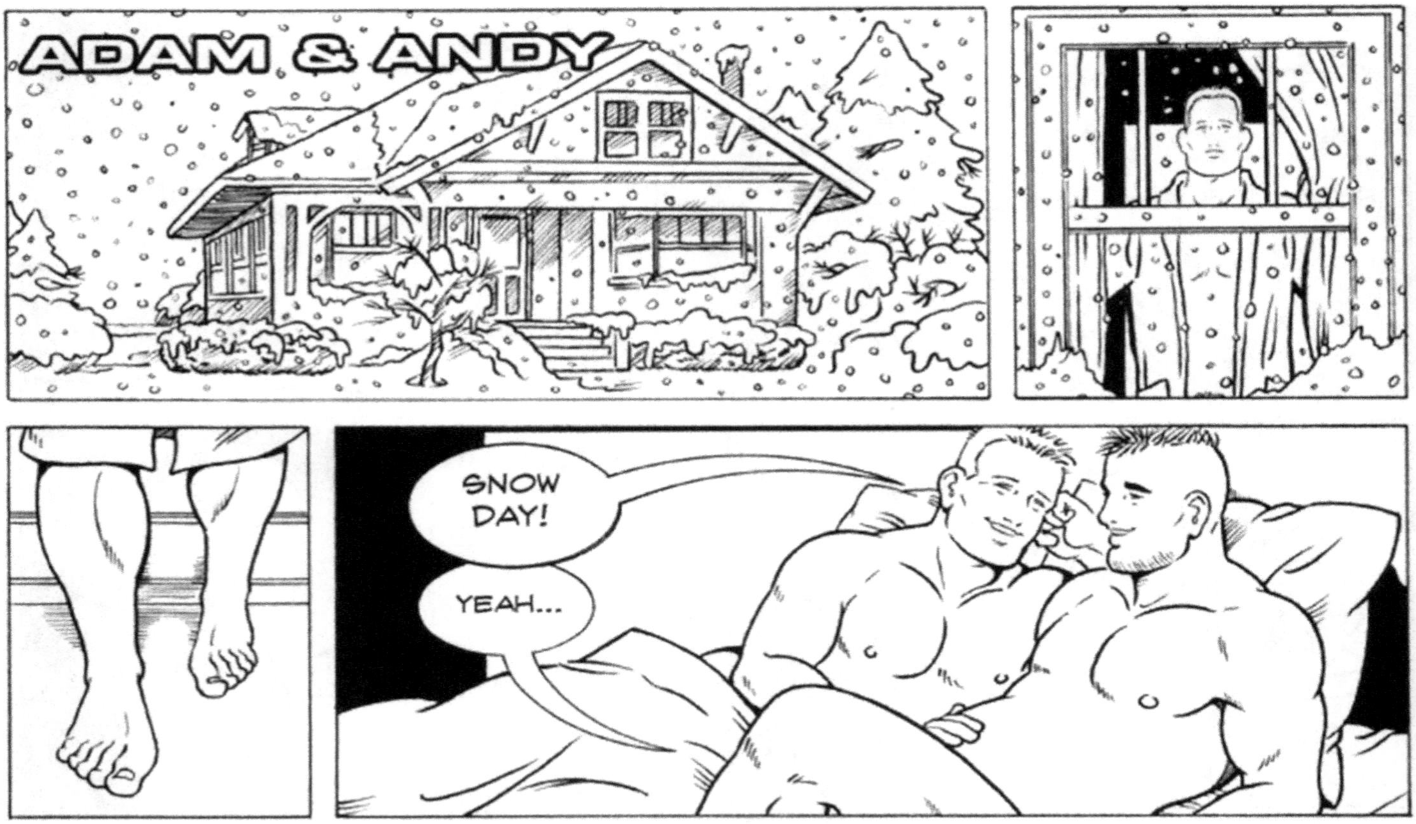
ADAM & ANDY
SNOW DAY!
YEAH...

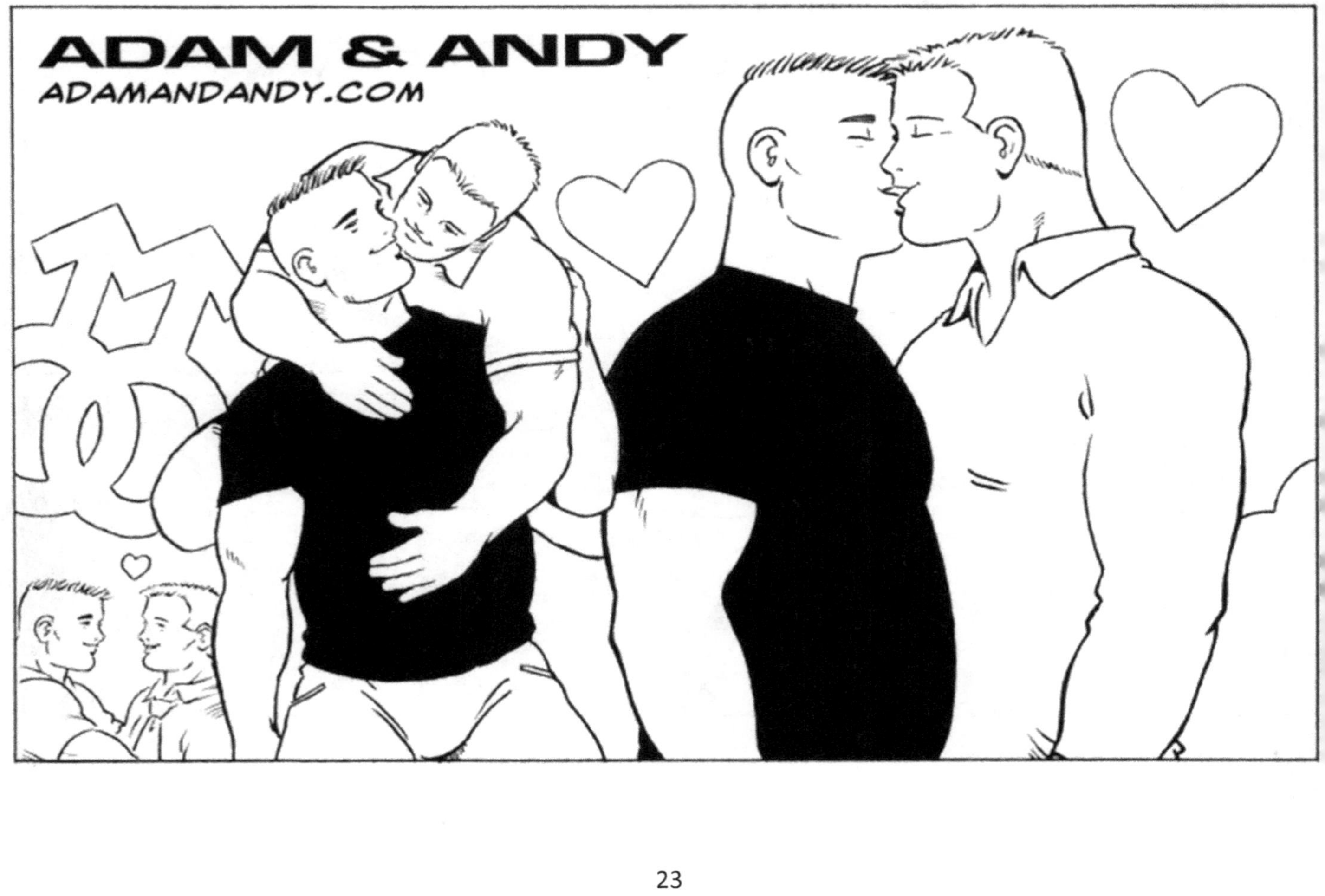
ADAM & ANDY
ADAMANDANDY.COM

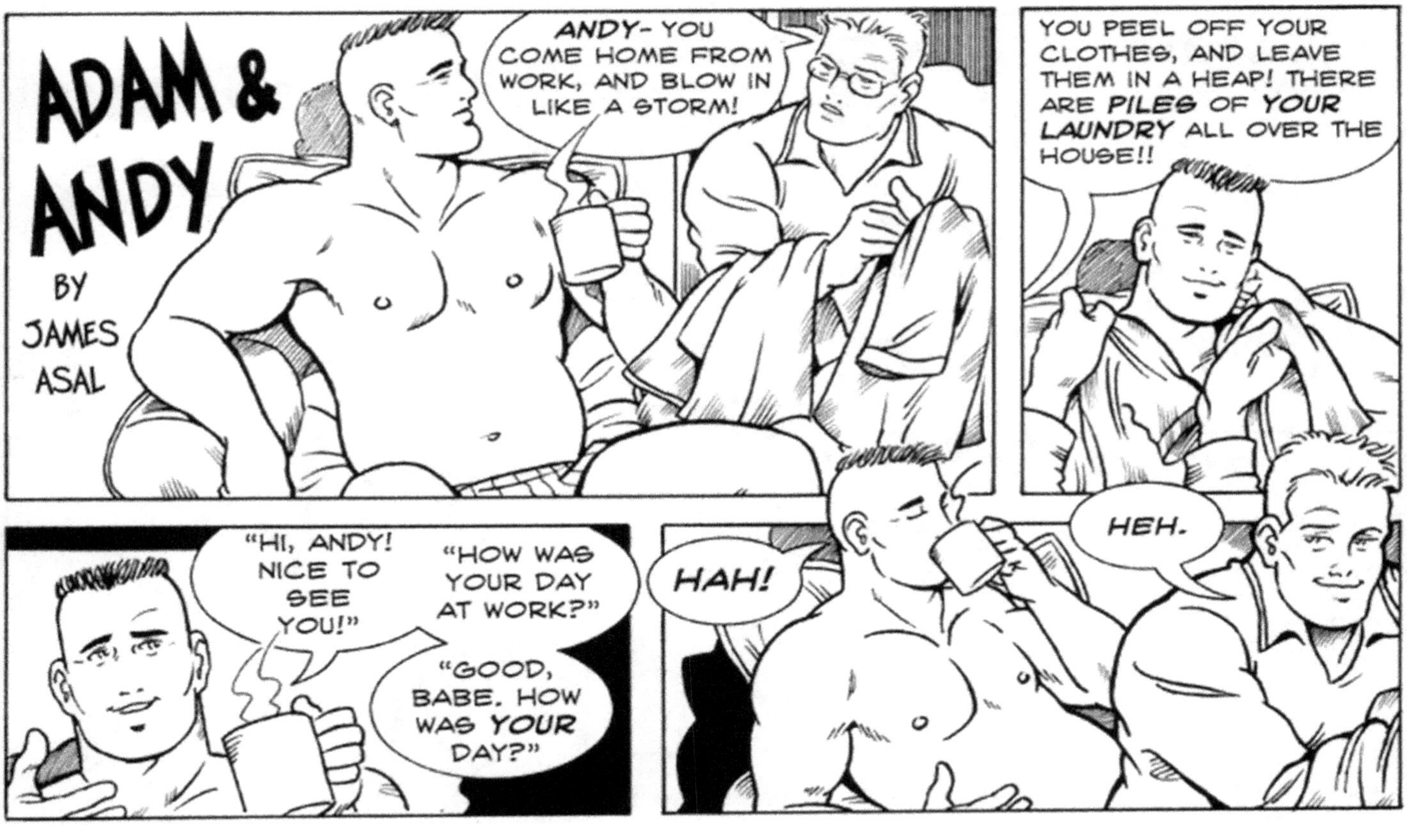
ADAM & ANDY
BY JAMES ASAL
ANDY- YOU COME HOME FROM WORK, AND BLOW IN LIKE A STORM!
YOU PEEL OFF YOUR CLOTHES, AND LEAVE THEM IN A HEAP! THERE ARE PILES OF YOUR LAUNDRY ALL OVER THE HOUSE!!
"HI, ANDY! NICE TO SEE YOU!"
"HOW WAS YOUR DAY AT WORK?"
"GOOD, BABE. HOW WAS YOUR DAY?"
HAH!
HEH.

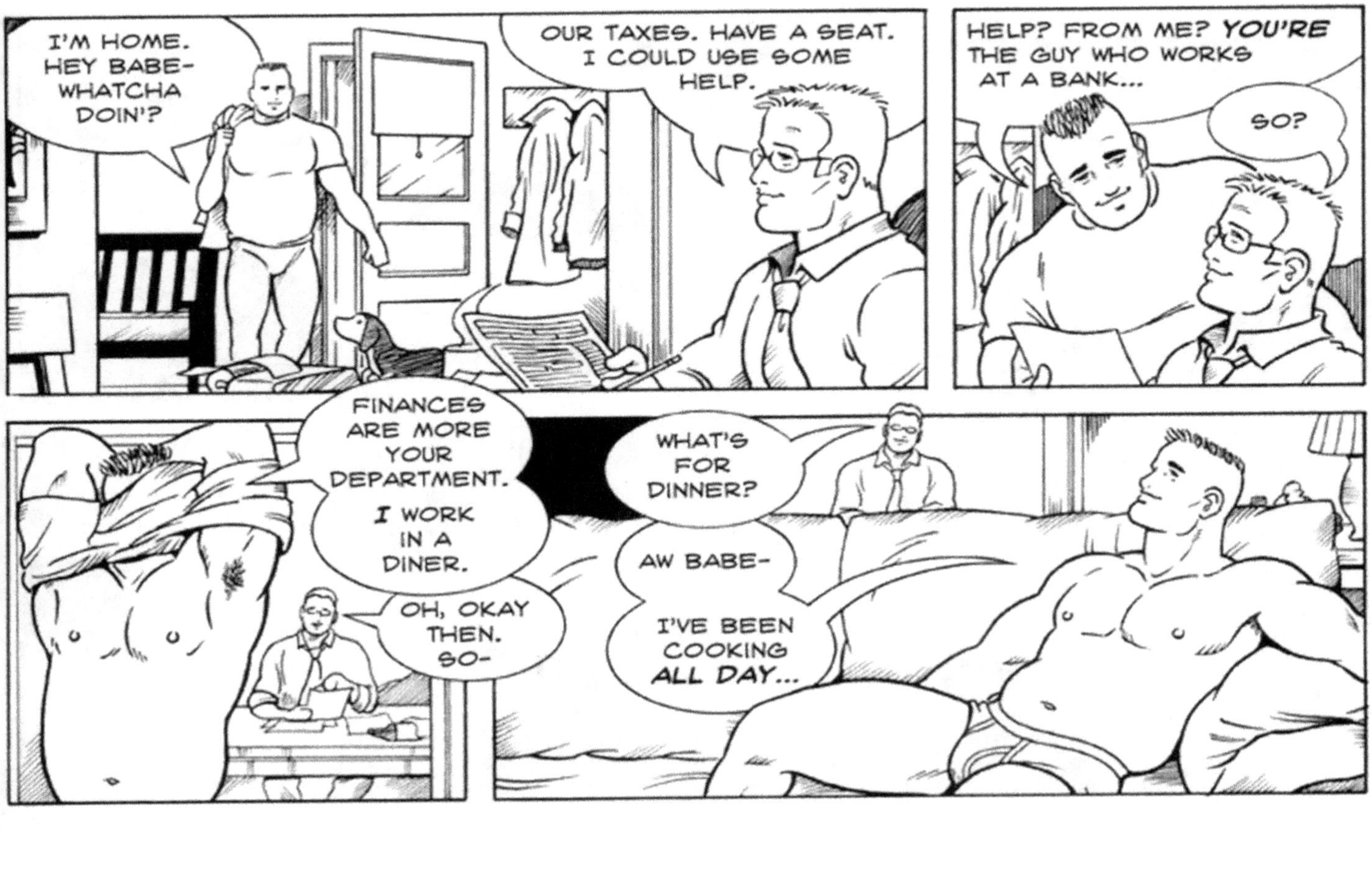
I'M HOME. HEY BABE- WHATCHA DOIN'?
OUR TAXES. HAVE A SEAT. I COULD USE SOME HELP.
HELP? FROM ME? YOU'RE THE GUY WHO WORKS AT A BANK...
SO?
FINANCES ARE MORE YOUR DEPARTMENT.
I WORK IN A DINER.
OH, OKAY THEN. SO-
WHAT'S FOR DINNER?
AW BABE-
I'VE BEEN COOKING ALL DAY...

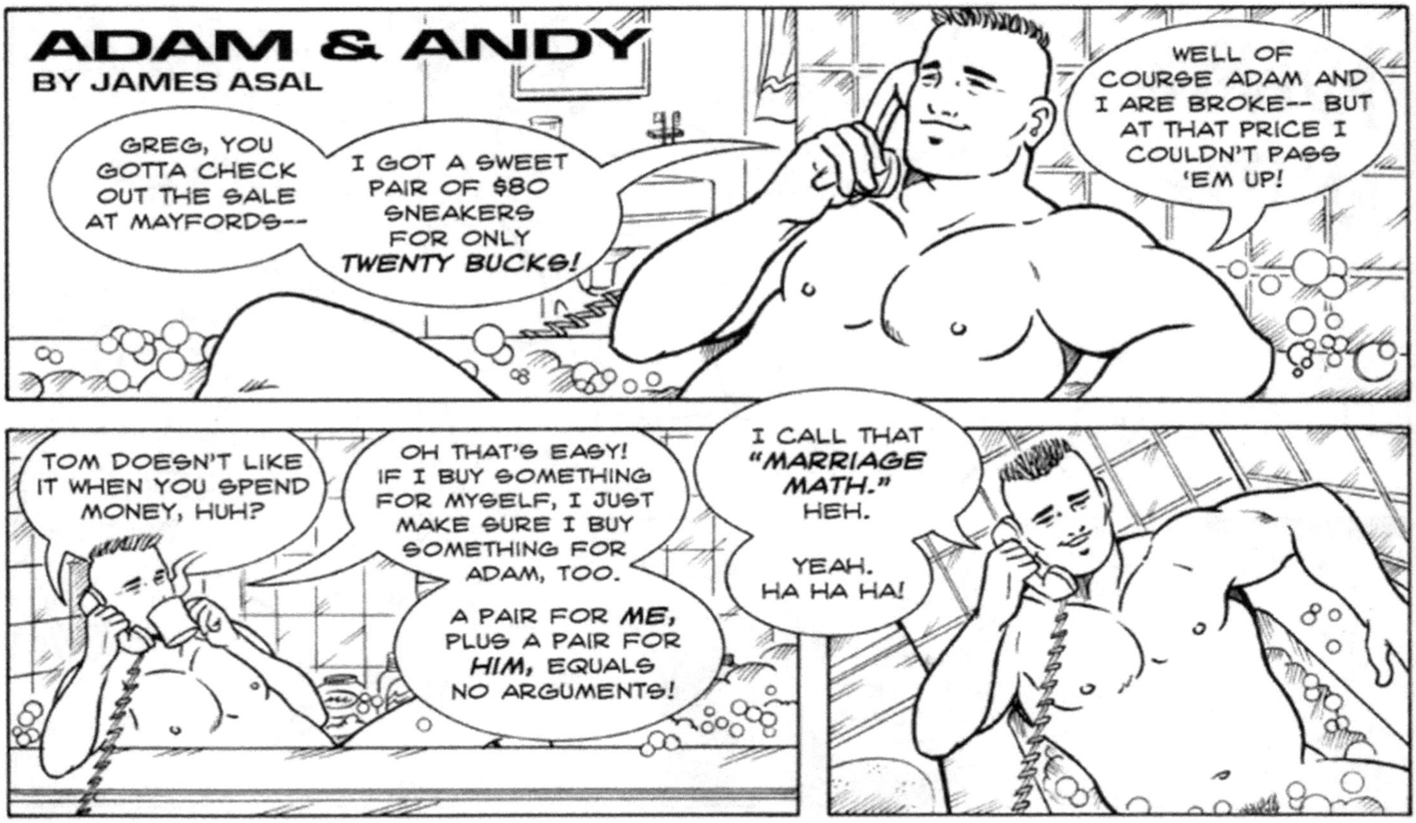
ADAM & ANDY
BY JAMES ASAL
GREG, YOU GOTTA CHECK OUT THE SALE AT MAYFORDS--
I GOT A SWEET PAIR OF $80 SNEAKERS FOR ONLY TWENTY BUCKS!
WELL OF COURSE ADAM AND I ARE BROKE-- BUT AT THAT PRICE I COULDN'T PASS 'EM UP!
TOM DOESN'T LIKE IT WHEN YOU SPEND MONEY, HUH?
OH THAT'S EASY! IF I BUY SOMETHING FOR MYSELF, I JUST MAKE SURE I BUY SOMETHING FOR ADAM, TOO.
A PAIR FOR ME, PLUS A PAIR FOR HIM, EQUALS NO ARGUMENTS!
I CALL THAT "MARRIAGE MATH." HEH.
YEAH. HA HA HA!

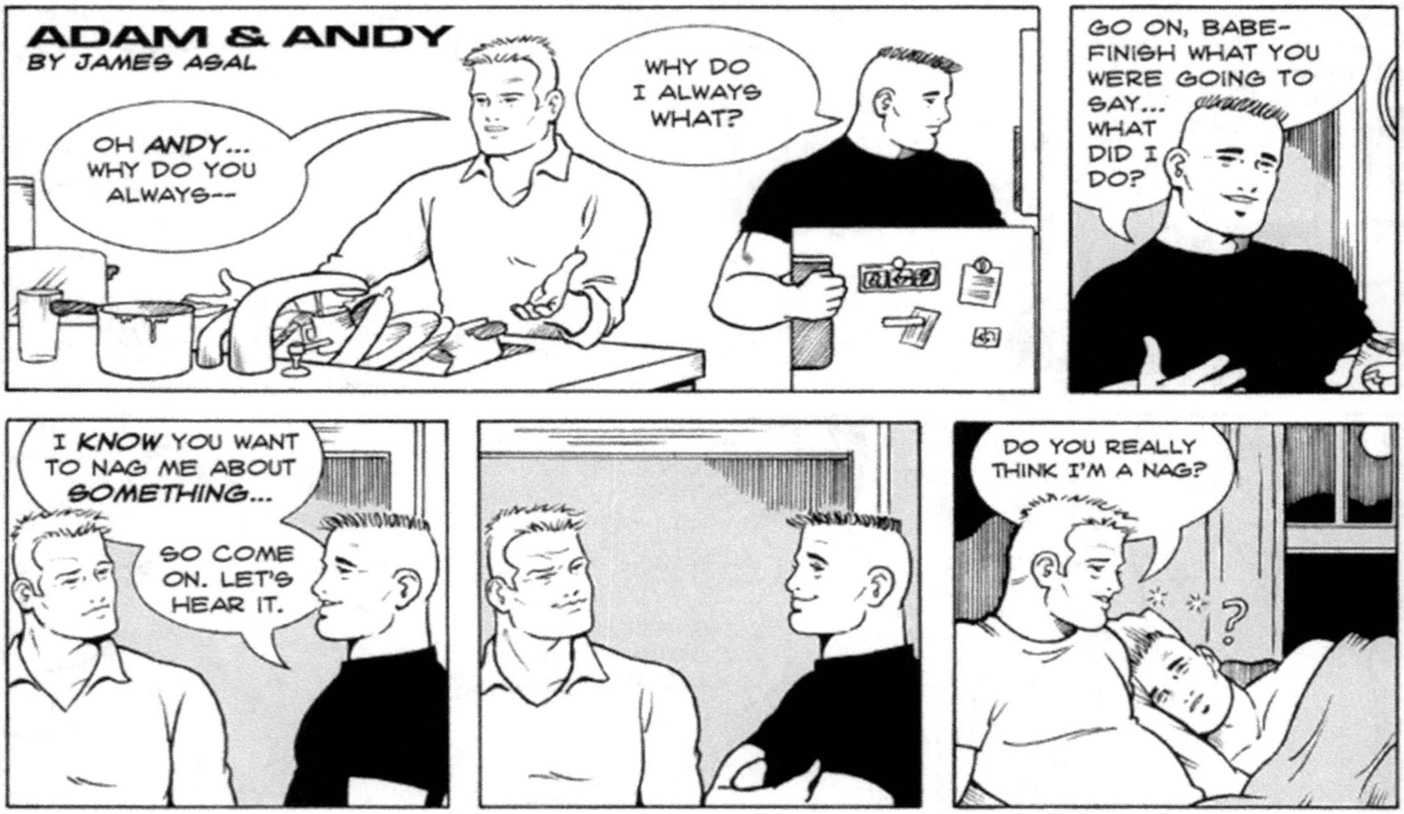
ADAM & ANDY
BY JAMES ASAL
OH ANDY... WHY DO YOU ALWAYS--
WHY DO I ALWAYS WHAT?
GO ON, BABE- FINISH WHAT YOU WERE GOING TO SAY... WHAT DID I DO?
I KNOW YOU WANT TO NAG ME ABOUT SOMETHING...
SO COME ON. LET'S HEAR IT.
DO YOU REALLY THINK I'M A NAG?
?

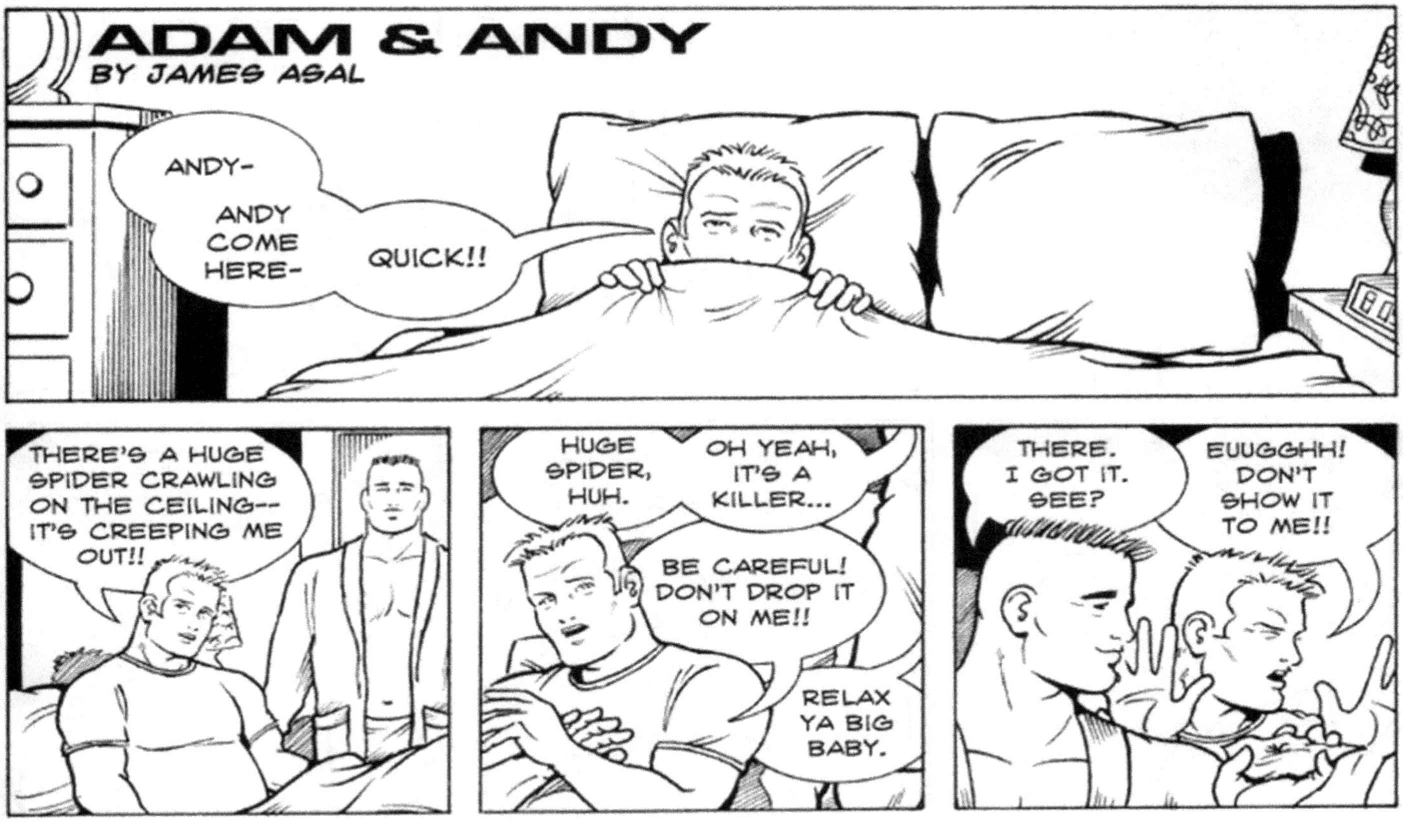
ADAM & ANDY
BY JAMES ASAL
ANDY-
ANDY COME HERE-
QUICK!!
THERE'S A HUGE SPIDER CRAWLING ON THE CEILING-- IT'S CREEPING ME OUT!!
HUGE SPIDER, HUH.
OH YEAH, IT'S A KILLER...
BE CAREFUL! DON'T DROP IT ON ME!!
RELAX YA BIG BABY.
THERE. I GOT IT. SEE?
EUUGGHH! DON'T SHOW IT TO ME!!

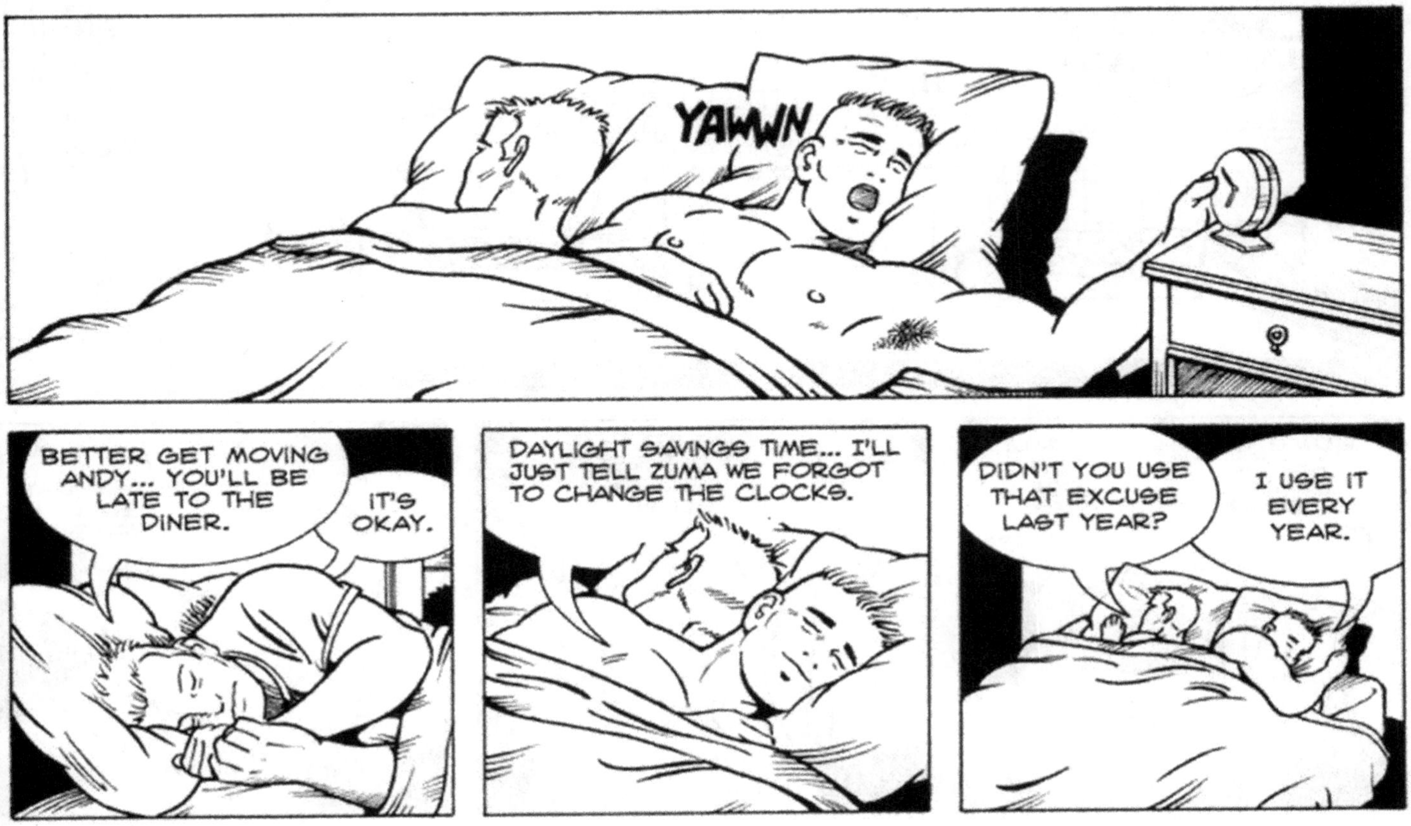
YAWWN
BETTER GET MOVING ANDY... YOU'LL BE LATE TO THE DINER.
IT'S OKAY.
DAYLIGHT SAVINGS TIME... I'LL JUST TELL ZUMA WE FORGOT TO CHANGE THE CLOCKS.
DIDN'T YOU USE THAT EXCUSE LAST YEAR?
I USE IT EVERY YEAR.

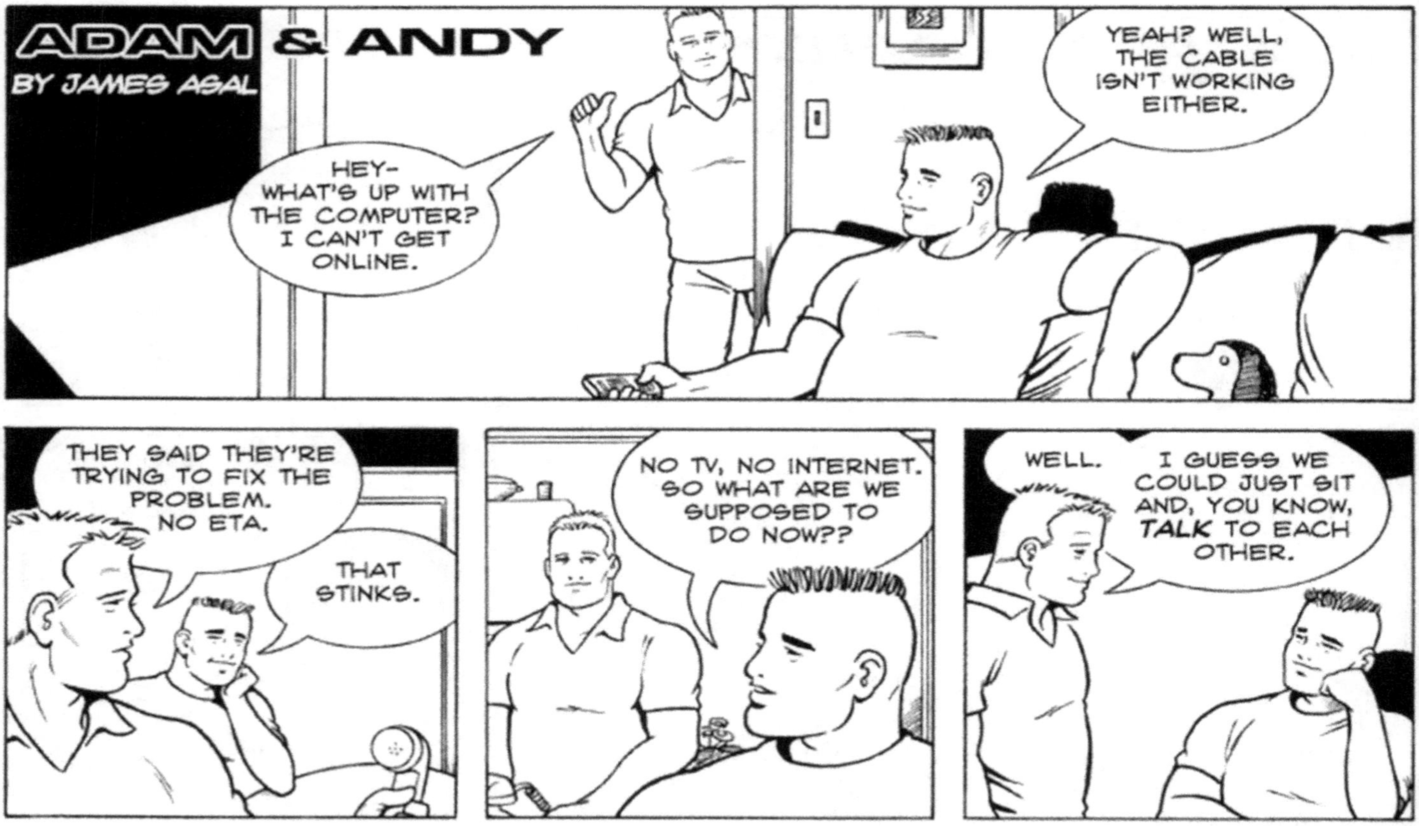
ADAM & ANDY
BY JAMES ASAL
HEY- WHAT'S UP WITH THE COMPUTER? I CAN'T GET ONLINE.
YEAH? WELL, THE CABLE ISN'T WORKING EITHER.
THEY SAID THEY'RE TRYING TO FIX THE PROBLEM. NO ETA.
THAT STINKS.
NO TV, NO INTERNET. SO WHAT ARE WE SUPPOSED TO DO NOW??
WELL.
I GUESS WE COULD JUST SIT AND, YOU KNOW, *TALK* TO EACH OTHER.

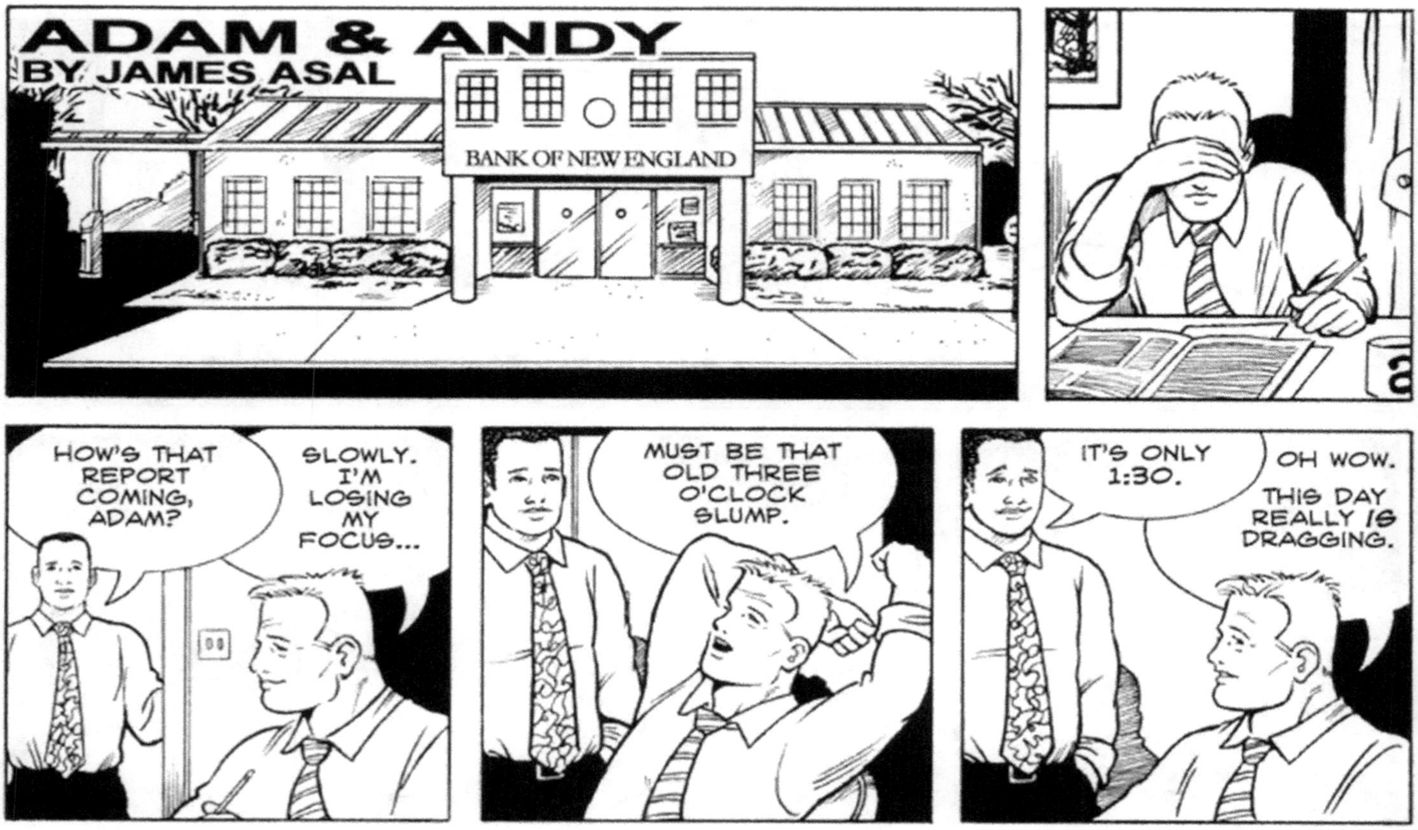
ADAM & ANDY
BY JAMES ASAL
BANK OF NEW ENGLAND
HOW'S THAT REPORT COMING, ADAM?
SLOWLY. I'M LOSING MY FOCUS...
MUST BE THAT OLD THREE O'CLOCK SLUMP.
IT'S ONLY 1:30.
OH WOW.
THIS DAY REALLY *IS* DRAGGING.

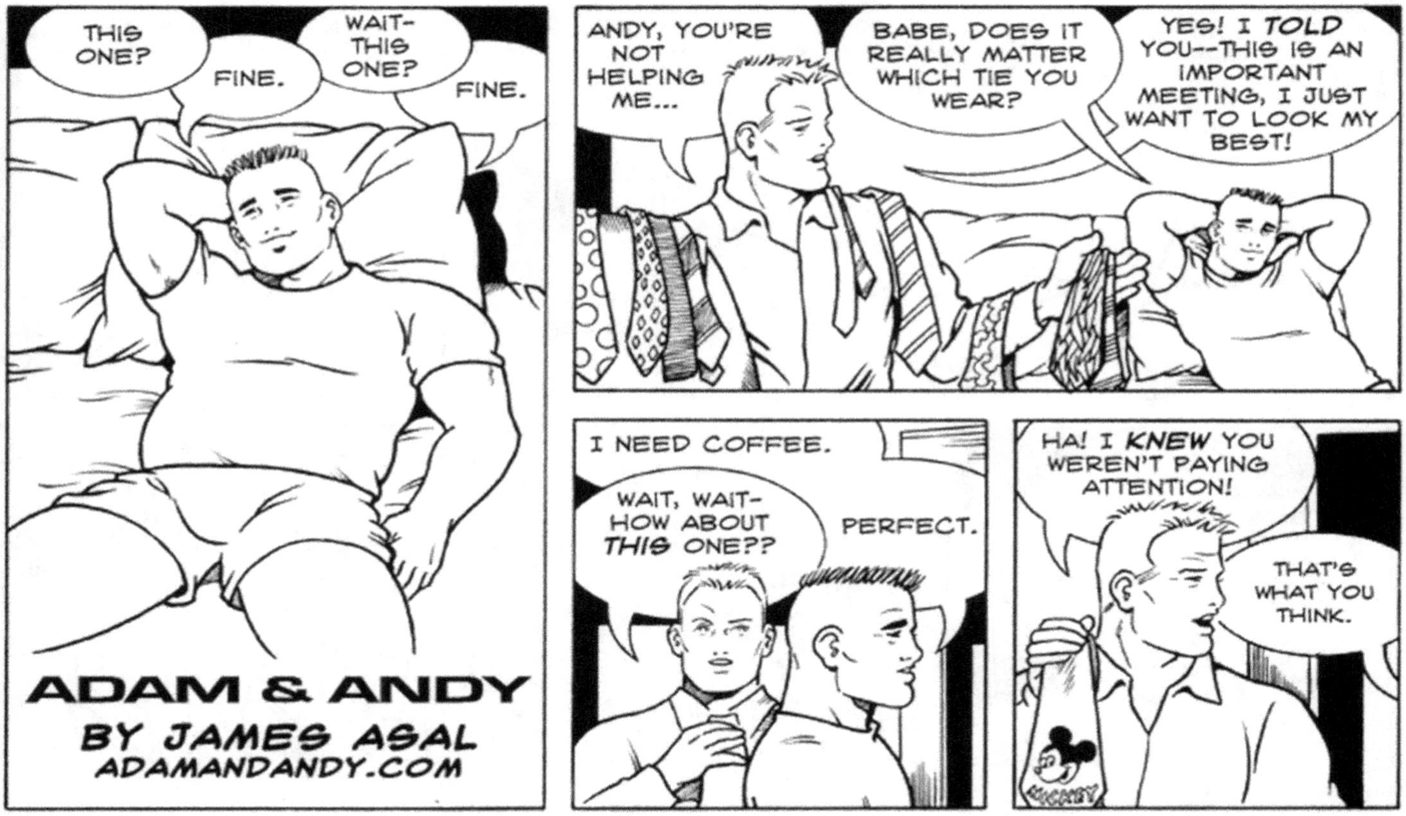

THIS ONE?
FINE.
WAIT- THIS ONE?
FINE.
ADAM & ANDY
BY JAMES ASAL
ADAMANDANDY.COM
ANDY, YOU'RE NOT HELPING ME...
BABE, DOES IT REALLY MATTER WHICH TIE YOU WEAR?
YES! I TOLD YOU--THIS IS AN IMPORTANT MEETING, I JUST WANT TO LOOK MY BEST!
I NEED COFFEE.
WAIT, WAIT- HOW ABOUT THIS ONE??
PERFECT.
HA! I KNEW YOU WEREN'T PAYING ATTENTION!
THAT'S WHAT YOU THINK.
MICKEY

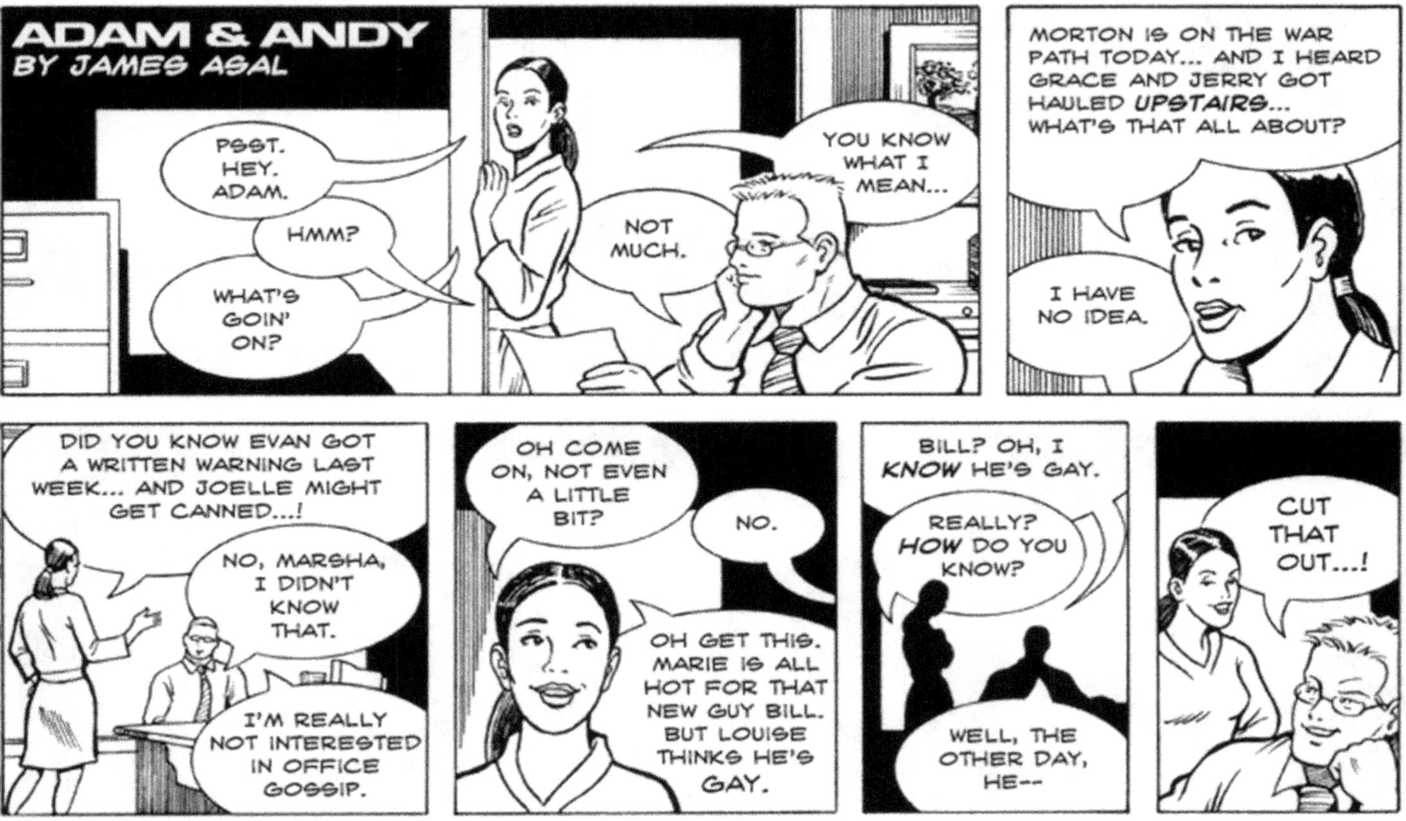

ADAM & ANDY
BY JAMES ASAL
PSST. HEY. ADAM.
HMM?
WHAT'S GOIN' ON?
NOT MUCH.
YOU KNOW WHAT I MEAN...
MORTON IS ON THE WAR PATH TODAY... AND I HEARD GRACE AND JERRY GOT HAULED UPSTAIRS... WHAT'S THAT ALL ABOUT?
I HAVE NO IDEA.
DID YOU KNOW EVAN GOT A WRITTEN WARNING LAST WEEK... AND JOELLE MIGHT GET CANNED...!
NO, MARSHA, I DIDN'T KNOW THAT.
I'M REALLY NOT INTERESTED IN OFFICE GOSSIP.
OH COME ON, NOT EVEN A LITTLE BIT?
NO.
OH GET THIS. MARIE IS ALL HOT FOR THAT NEW GUY BILL. BUT LOUISE THINKS HE'S GAY.
BILL? OH, I KNOW HE'S GAY.
REALLY? HOW DO YOU KNOW?
WELL, THE OTHER DAY, HE--
CUT THAT OUT...!

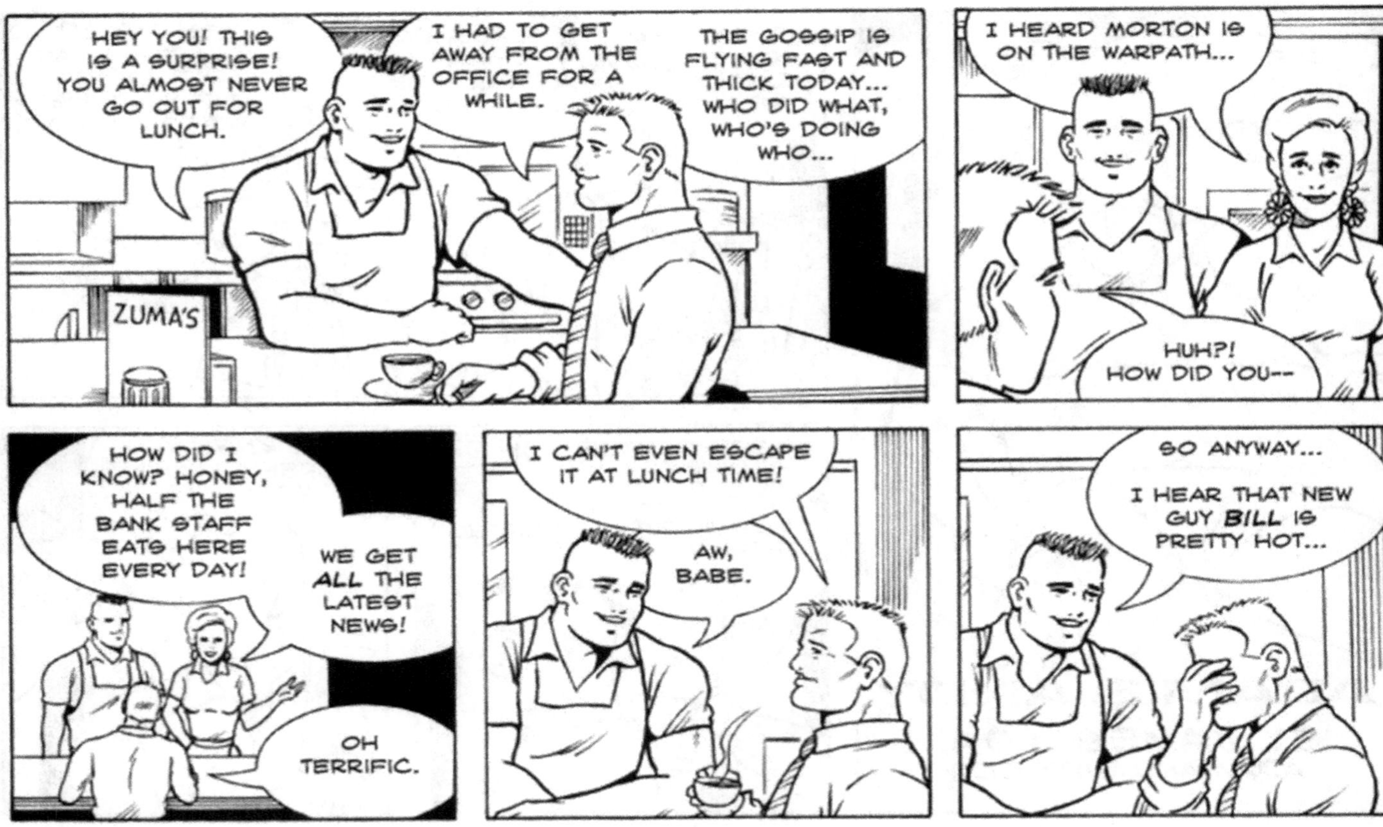

HEY YOU! THIS IS A SURPRISE! YOU ALMOST NEVER GO OUT FOR LUNCH.
I HAD TO GET AWAY FROM THE OFFICE FOR A WHILE.
THE GOSSIP IS FLYING FAST AND THICK TODAY... WHO DID WHAT, WHO'S DOING WHO...
ZUMA'S
I HEARD MORTON IS ON THE WARPATH...
HUH?! HOW DID YOU--
HOW DID I KNOW? HONEY, HALF THE BANK STAFF EATS HERE EVERY DAY!
WE GET ALL THE LATEST NEWS!
OH TERRIFIC.
I CAN'T EVEN ESCAPE IT AT LUNCH TIME!
AW, BABE.
SO ANYWAY...
I HEAR THAT NEW GUY BILL IS PRETTY HOT...

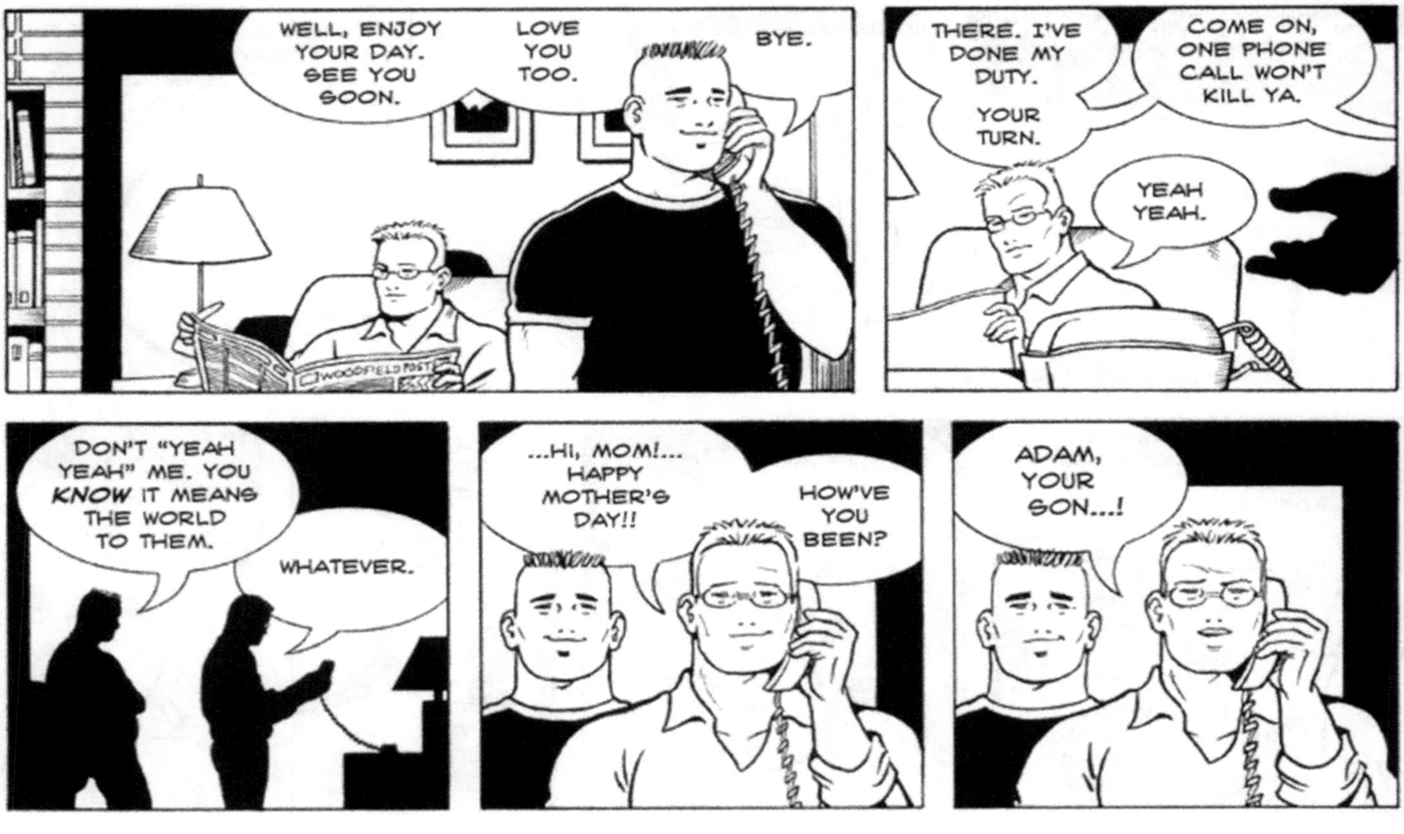

WELL, ENJOY YOUR DAY. SEE YOU SOON.
LOVE YOU TOO.
BYE.
WOODFIELD POST
THERE. I'VE DONE MY DUTY.
YOUR TURN.
COME ON, ONE PHONE CALL WON'T KILL YA.
YEAH YEAH.
DON'T "YEAH YEAH" ME. YOU KNOW IT MEANS THE WORLD TO THEM.
WHATEVER.
...HI, MOM!... HAPPY MOTHER'S DAY!!
HOW'VE YOU BEEN?
ADAM, YOUR SON...!

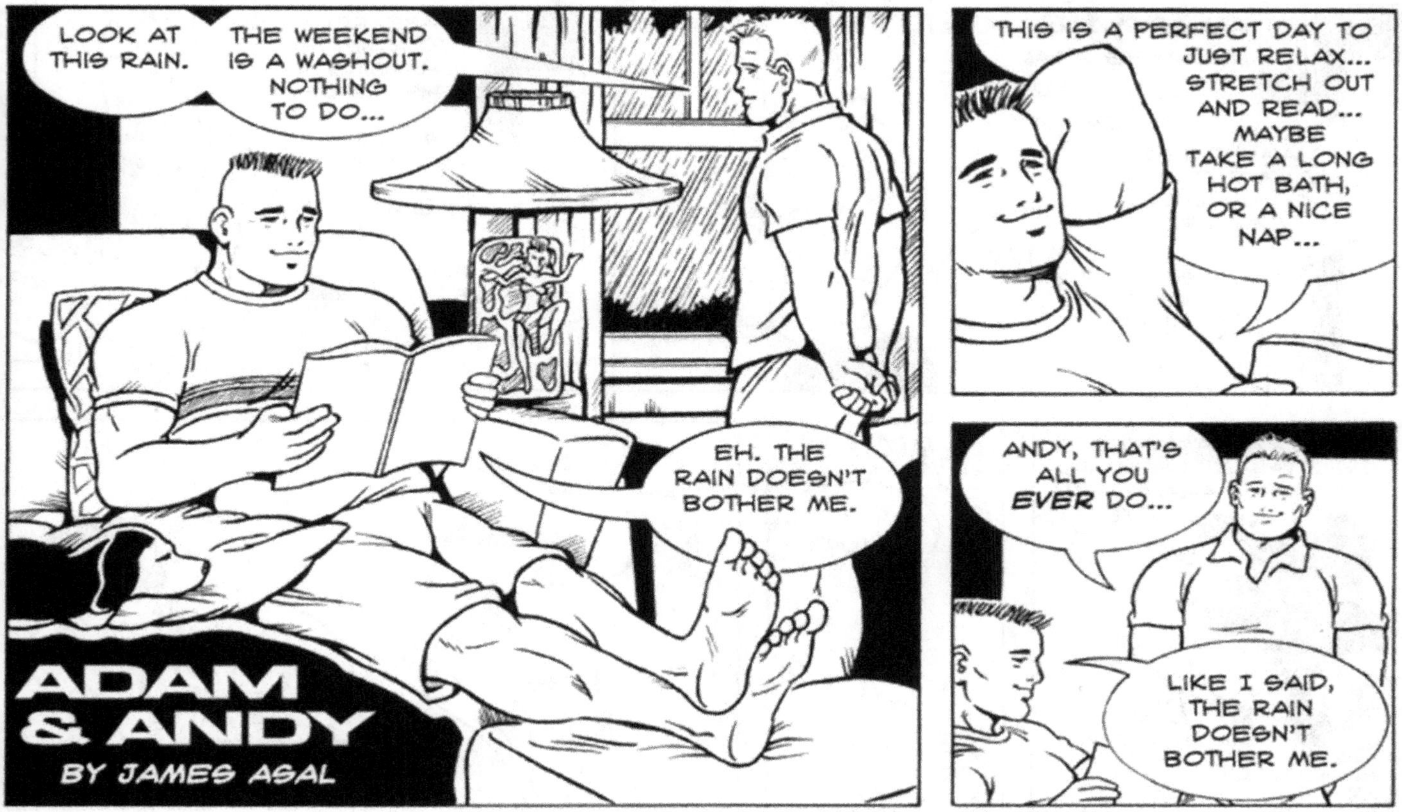
LOOK AT THIS RAIN.
THE WEEKEND IS A WASHOUT. NOTHING TO DO...
EH. THE RAIN DOESN'T BOTHER ME.
ADAM & ANDY
BY JAMES ASAL
THIS IS A PERFECT DAY TO JUST RELAX... STRETCH OUT AND READ... MAYBE TAKE A LONG HOT BATH, OR A NICE NAP...
ANDY, THAT'S ALL YOU EVER DO...
LIKE I SAID, THE RAIN DOESN'T BOTHER ME.

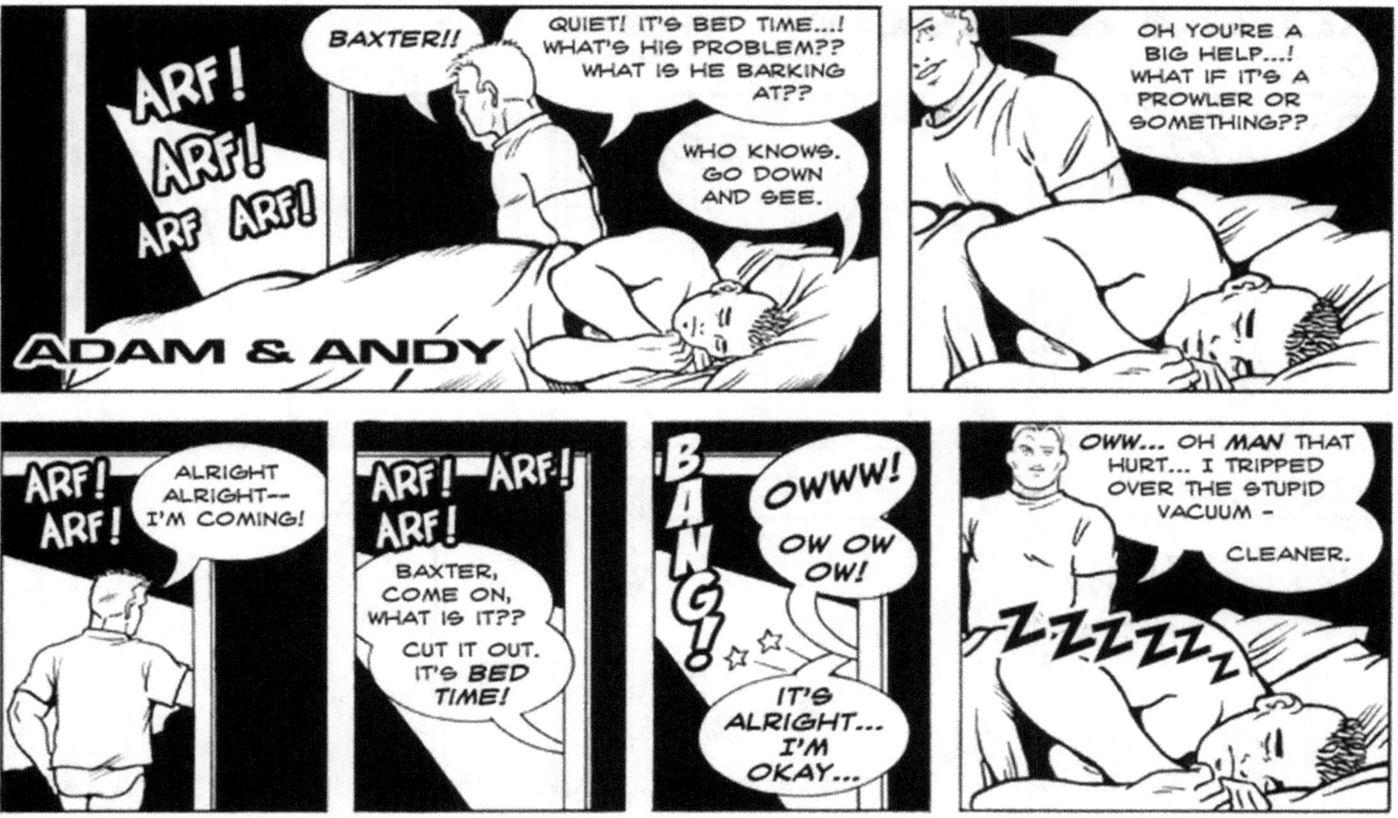
ARF! ARF! ARF ARF!
BAXTER!!
QUIET! IT'S BED TIME...! WHAT'S HIS PROBLEM?? WHAT IS HE BARKING AT??
WHO KNOWS. GO DOWN AND SEE.
ADAM & ANDY
OH YOU'RE A BIG HELP...! WHAT IF IT'S A PROWLER OR SOMETHING??
ARF! ARF!
ALRIGHT ALRIGHT-- I'M COMING!
ARF! ARF! ARF!
BAXTER, COME ON, WHAT IS IT??
CUT IT OUT. IT'S BED TIME!
BANG!
OWWW!
OW OW OW!
IT'S ALRIGHT... I'M OKAY...
OWW... OH MAN THAT HURT... I TRIPPED OVER THE STUPID VACUUM -
CLEANER.
ZZZZZZZ

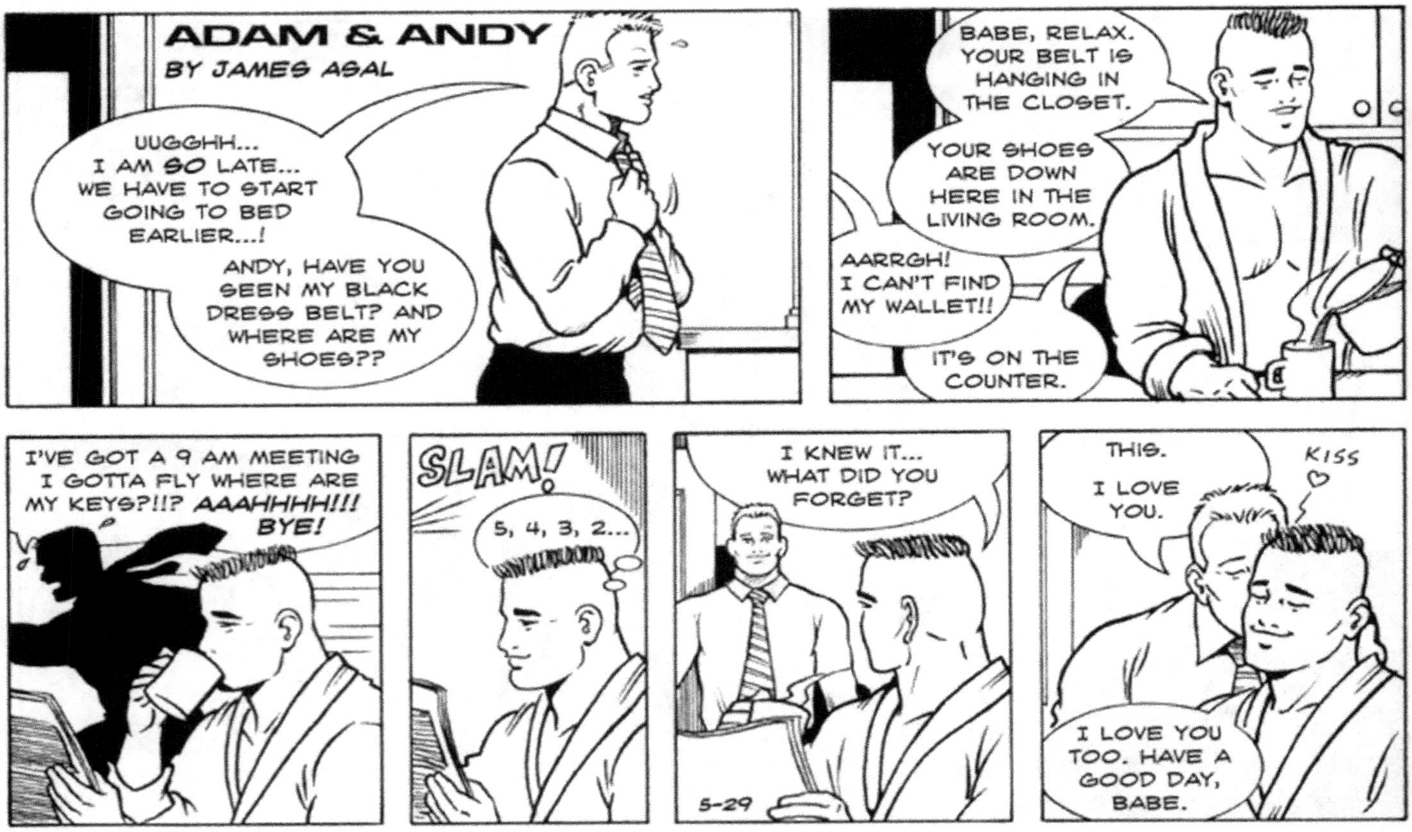
ADAM & ANDY
BY JAMES ASAL
UUGGHH... I AM SO LATE... WE HAVE TO START GOING TO BED EARLIER...!
ANDY, HAVE YOU SEEN MY BLACK DRESS BELT? AND WHERE ARE MY SHOES??
BABE, RELAX. YOUR BELT IS HANGING IN THE CLOSET.
YOUR SHOES ARE DOWN HERE IN THE LIVING ROOM.
AARRGH! I CAN'T FIND MY WALLET!!
IT'S ON THE COUNTER.
I'VE GOT A 9 AM MEETING I GOTTA FLY WHERE ARE MY KEYS?!!? AAAHHHH!!! BYE!
SLAM!
5, 4, 3, 2...
I KNEW IT... WHAT DID YOU FORGET?
5-29
THIS. I LOVE YOU.
KISS
I LOVE YOU TOO. HAVE A GOOD DAY, BABE.

ADAM & ANDY - THE DAILY GRIND

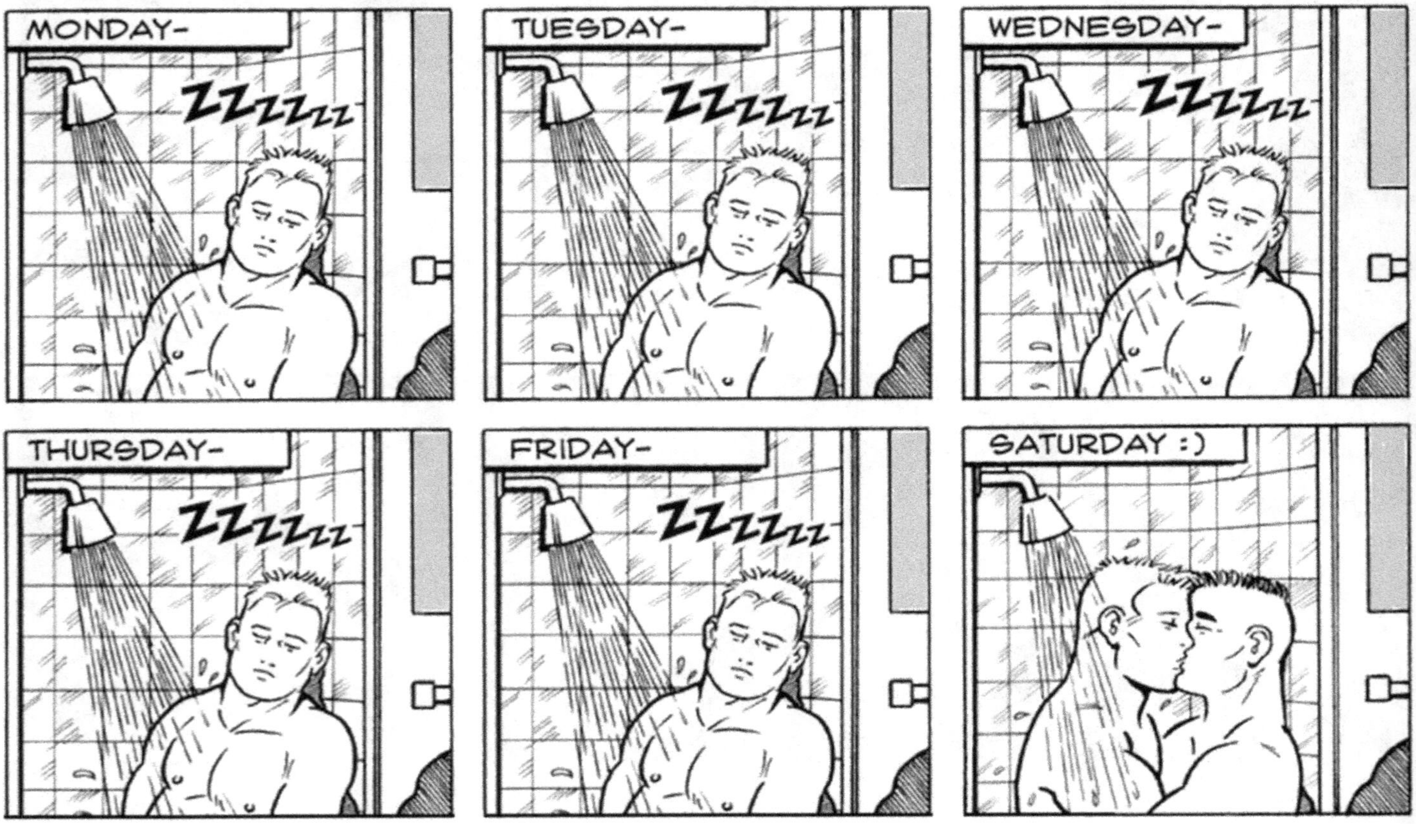
MONDAY-
ZZZZZZ
TUESDAY-
ZZZZZZ
WEDNESDAY-
ZZZZZZ
THURSDAY-
ZZZZZZ
FRIDAY-
ZZZZZZ
SATURDAY :)

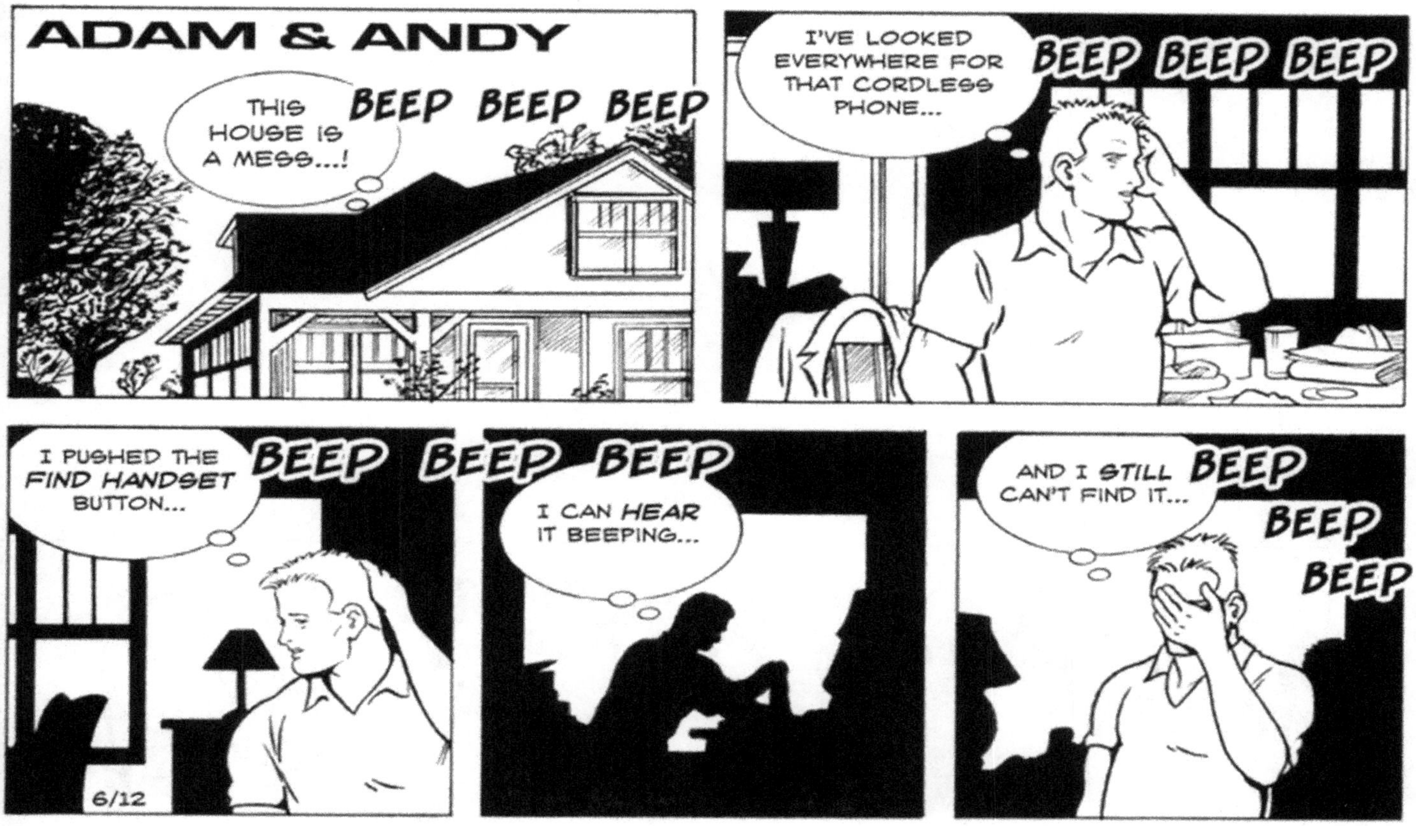
ADAM & ANDY
THIS HOUSE IS A MESS...!
BEEP BEEP BEEP
I'VE LOOKED EVERYWHERE FOR THAT CORDLESS PHONE...
BEEP BEEP BEEP
I PUSHED THE FIND HANDSET BUTTON...
BEEP BEEP BEEP
I CAN HEAR IT BEEPING...
AND I STILL CAN'T FIND IT...
BEEP
BEEP
BEEP
6/12

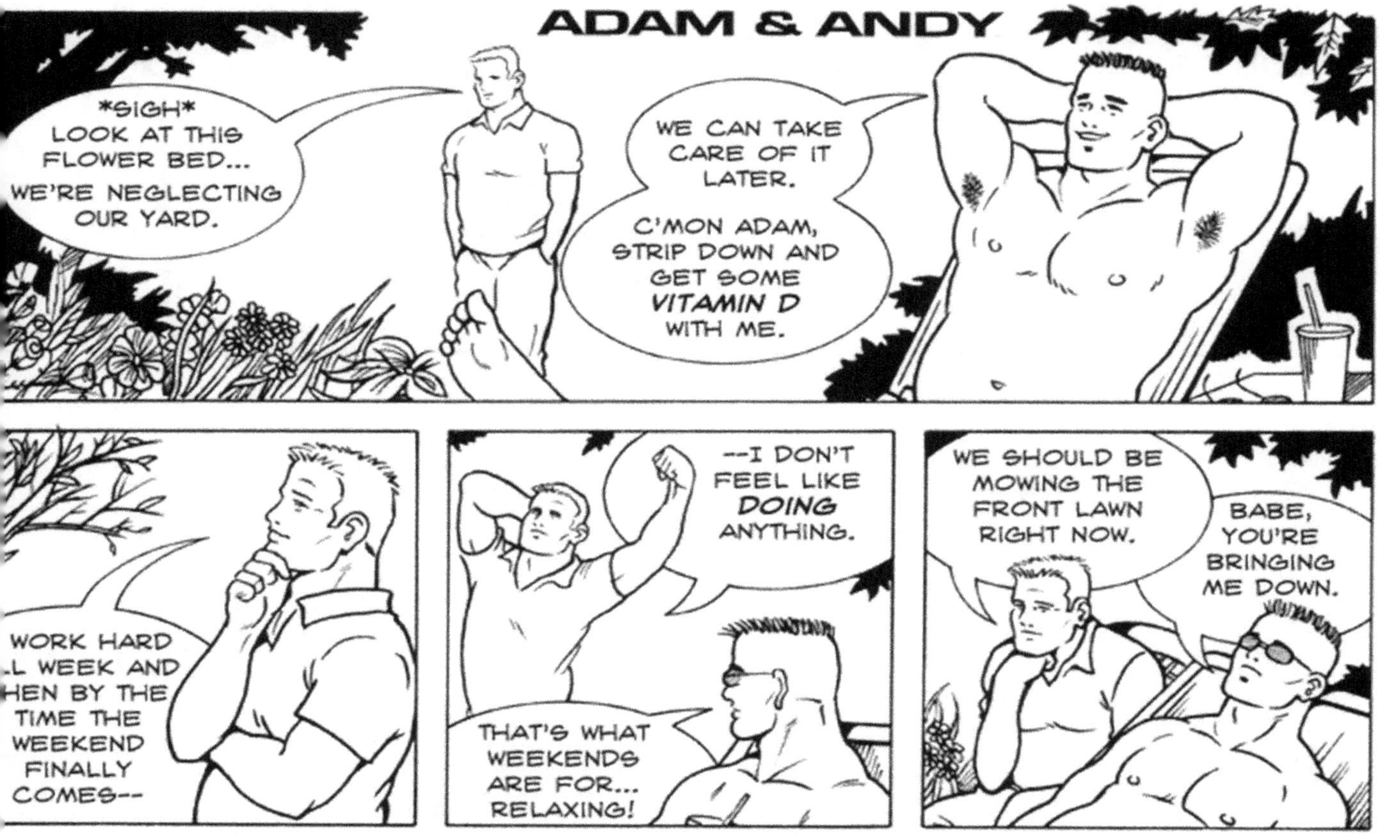
ADAM & ANDY
SIGH LOOK AT THIS FLOWER BED... WE'RE NEGLECTING OUR YARD.
WE CAN TAKE CARE OF IT LATER.
C'MON ADAM, STRIP DOWN AND GET SOME VITAMIN D WITH ME.
WORK HARD
L WEEK AND
HEN BY THE
TIME THE WEEKEND FINALLY COMES--
--I DON'T FEEL LIKE DOING ANYTHING.
THAT'S WHAT WEEKENDS ARE FOR... RELAXING!
WE SHOULD BE MOWING THE FRONT LAWN RIGHT NOW.
BABE, YOU'RE BRINGING ME DOWN.

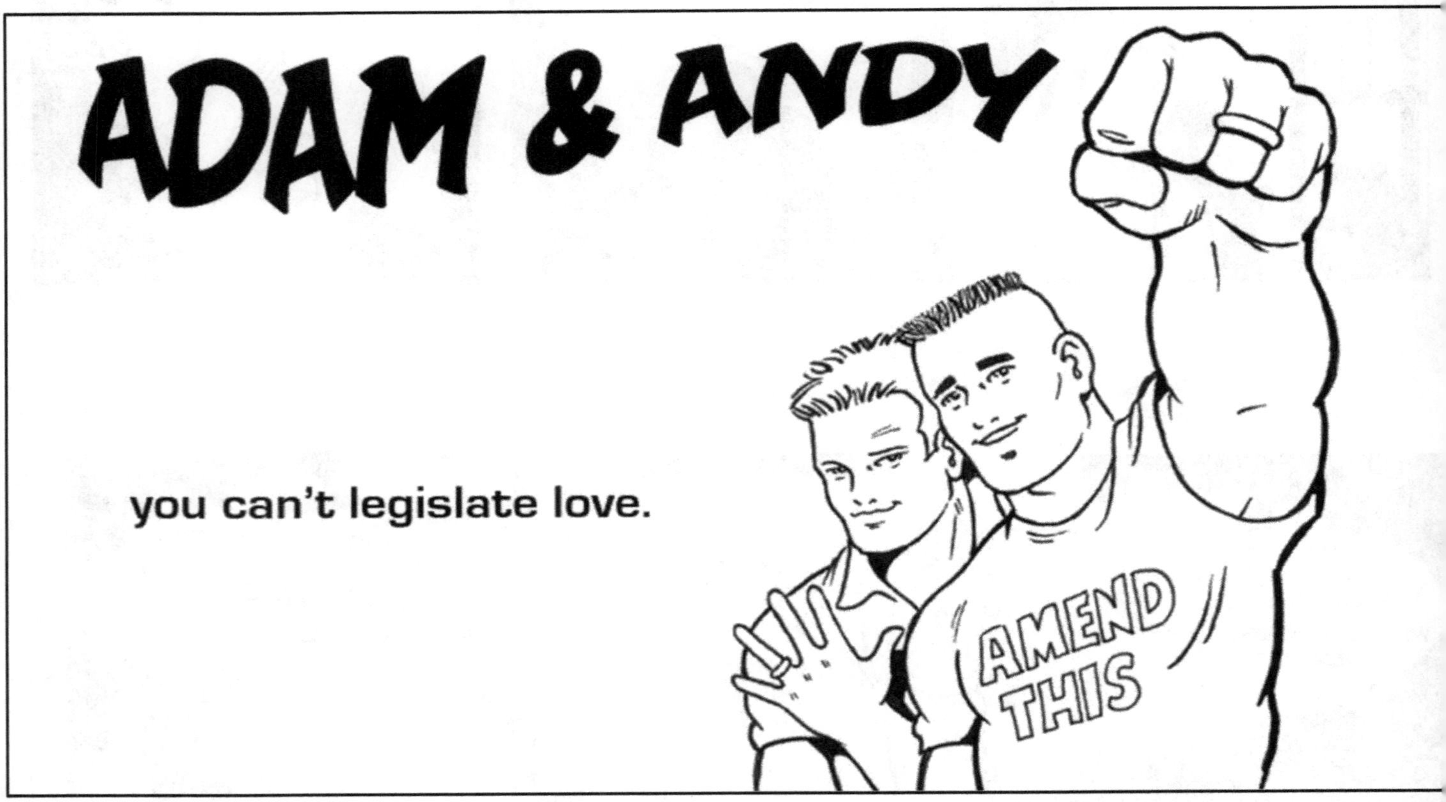
ADAM & ANDY
you can't legislate love.
AMEND THIS

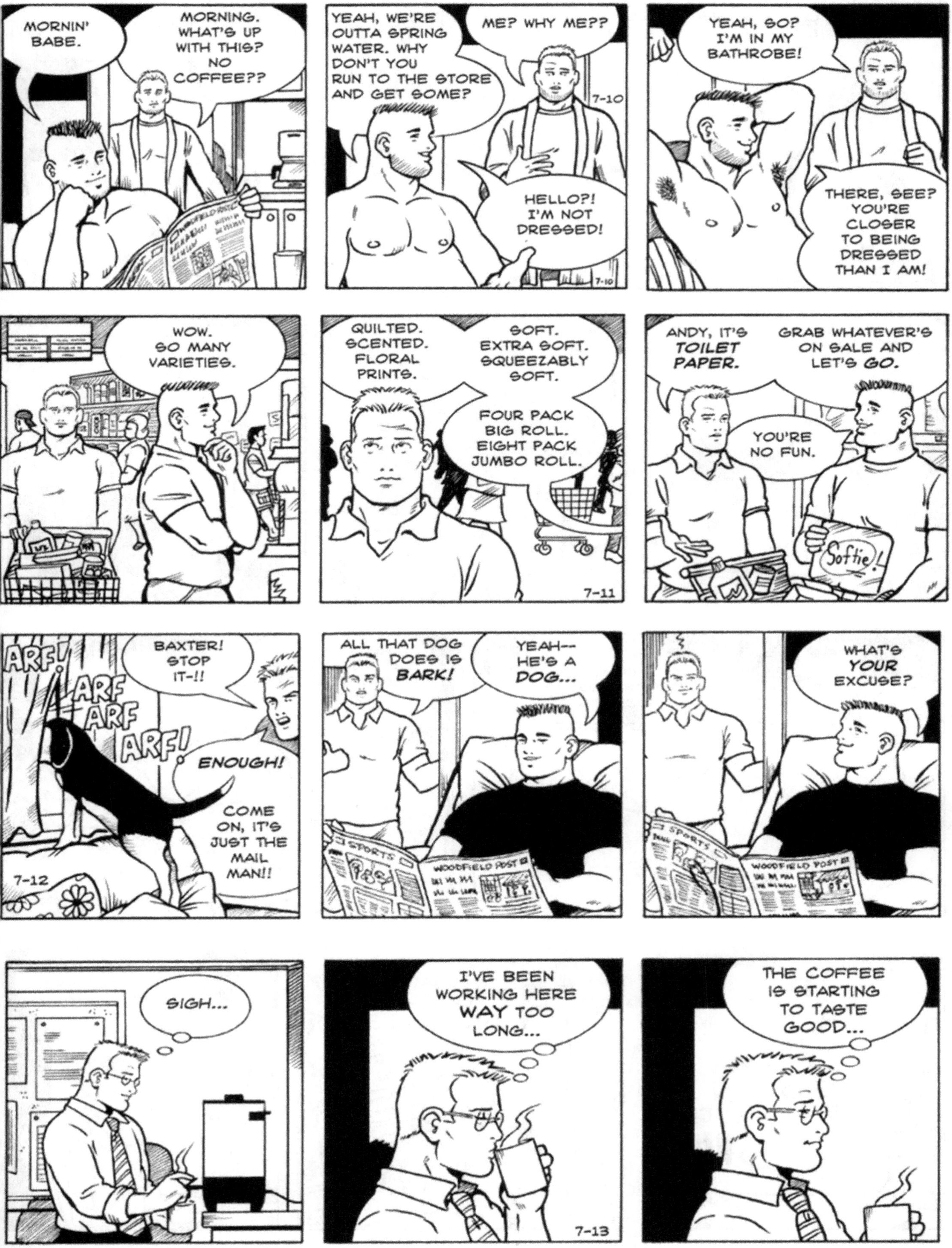
MORNIN' BABE.
MORNING. WHAT'S UP WITH THIS? NO COFFEE??
YEAH, WE'RE OUTTA SPRING WATER. WHY DON'T YOU RUN TO THE STORE AND GET SOME?
ME? WHY ME??
7-10
HELLO?! I'M NOT DRESSED!
YEAH, SO? I'M IN MY BATHROBE!
THERE, SEE? YOU'RE CLOSER TO BEING DRESSED THAN I AM!
WOW. SO MANY VARIETIES.
QUILTED. SCENTED. FLORAL PRINTS.
SOFT. EXTRA SOFT. SQUEEZABLY SOFT.
FOUR PACK BIG ROLL. EIGHT PACK JUMBO ROLL.
7-11
ANDY, IT'S *TOILET PAPER.*
GRAB WHATEVER'S ON SALE AND LET'S *GO.*
YOU'RE NO FUN.
Softie!
ARF!
ARF ARF ARF!
BAXTER! STOP IT-!!
ENOUGH!
COME ON, IT'S JUST THE MAIL MAN!!
7-12
ALL THAT DOG DOES IS *BARK!*
YEAH-- HE'S A *DOG...*
SPORTS
WOODFIELD POST
WHAT'S *YOUR* EXCUSE?
SIGH...
I'VE BEEN WORKING HERE **WAY** TOO LONG...
7-13
THE COFFEE IS STARTING TO TASTE GOOD...

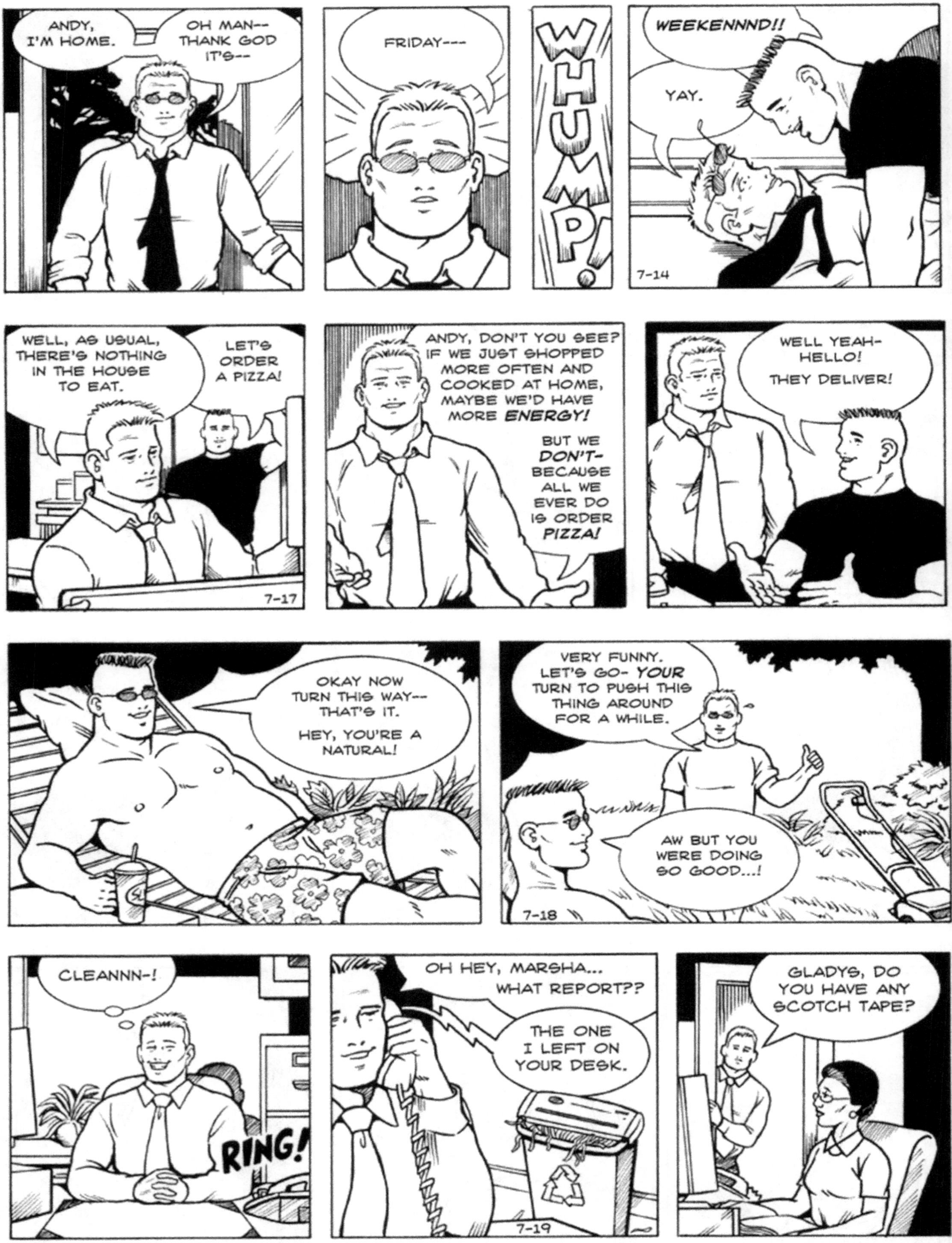
ANDY, I'M HOME.
OH MAN-- THANK GOD IT'S--
FRIDAY---
WHUMP!
WEEKENNND!!
YAY.
7-14
WELL, AS USUAL, THERE'S NOTHING IN THE HOUSE TO EAT.
LET'S ORDER A PIZZA!
7-17
ANDY, DON'T YOU SEE? IF WE JUST SHOPPED MORE OFTEN AND COOKED AT HOME, MAYBE WE'D HAVE MORE ENERGY!
BUT WE DON'T- BECAUSE ALL WE EVER DO IS ORDER PIZZA!
WELL YEAH- HELLO!
THEY DELIVER!
OKAY NOW TURN THIS WAY-- THAT'S IT.
HEY, YOU'RE A NATURAL!
VERY FUNNY. LET'S GO- YOUR TURN TO PUSH THIS THING AROUND FOR A WHILE.
AW BUT YOU WERE DOING SO GOOD...!
7-18
CLEANNN-!
RING!
OH HEY, MARSHA... WHAT REPORT??
THE ONE I LEFT ON YOUR DESK.
7-19
GLADYS, DO YOU HAVE ANY SCOTCH TAPE?

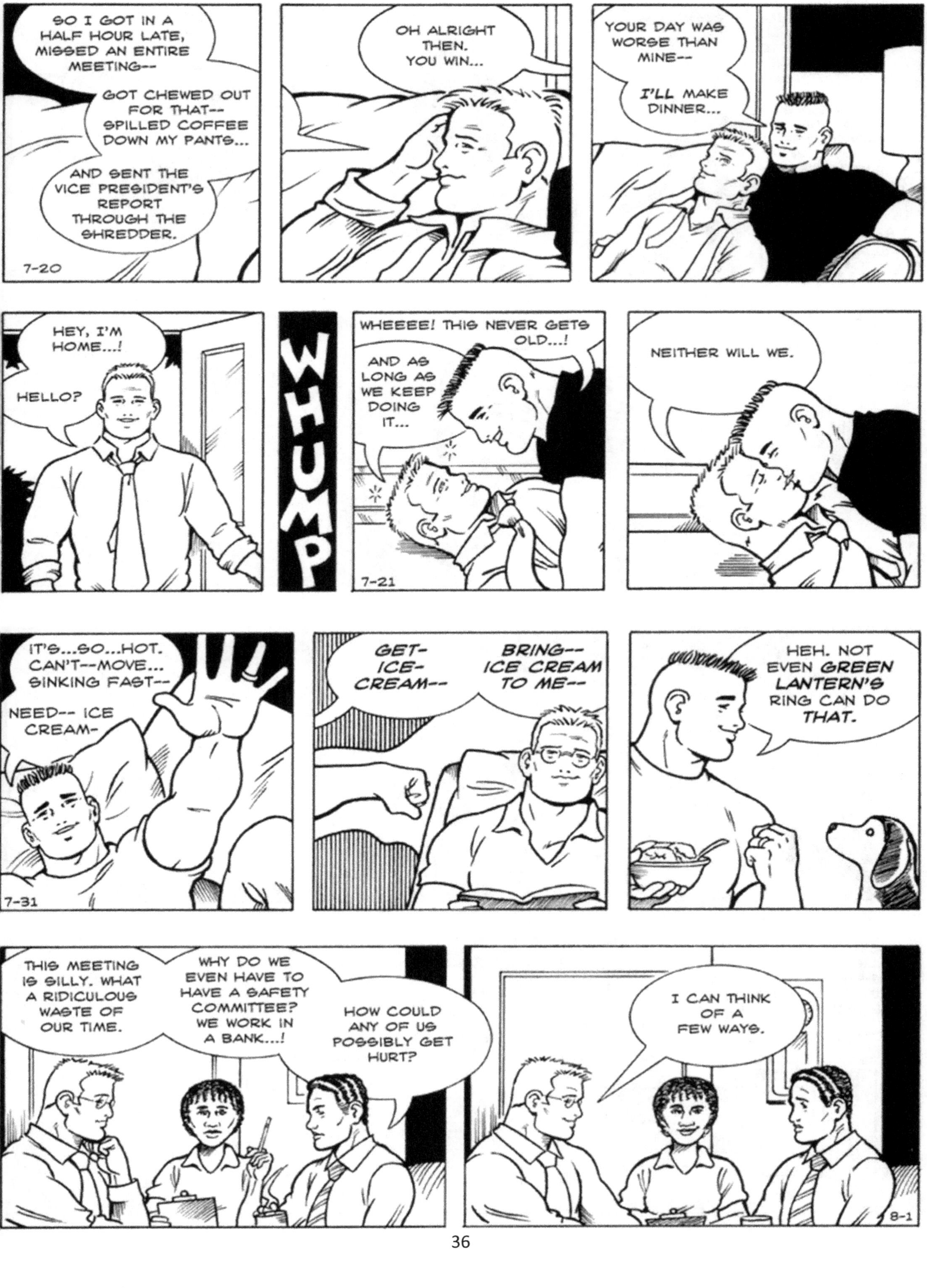
SO I GOT IN A HALF HOUR LATE, MISSED AN ENTIRE MEETING--
GOT CHEWED OUT FOR THAT-- SPILLED COFFEE DOWN MY PANTS...
AND SENT THE VICE PRESIDENT'S REPORT THROUGH THE SHREDDER.
7-20
OH ALRIGHT THEN. YOU WIN...
YOUR DAY WAS WORSE THAN MINE--
I'LL MAKE DINNER...
HEY, I'M HOME...!
HELLO?
WHUMP
WHEEEEE! THIS NEVER GETS OLD...!
AND AS LONG AS WE KEEP DOING IT...
7-21
NEITHER WILL WE.
IT'S...SO...HOT. CAN'T--MOVE... SINKING FAST--
NEED-- ICE CREAM-
7-31
GET-ICE-CREAM--
BRING-- ICE CREAM TO ME--
HEH. NOT EVEN **GREEN LANTERN'S** RING CAN DO *THAT.*
THIS MEETING IS SILLY. WHAT A RIDICULOUS WASTE OF OUR TIME.
WHY DO WE EVEN HAVE TO HAVE A SAFETY COMMITTEE? WE WORK IN A BANK...!
HOW COULD ANY OF US POSSIBLY GET HURT?
I CAN THINK OF A FEW WAYS.
8-1

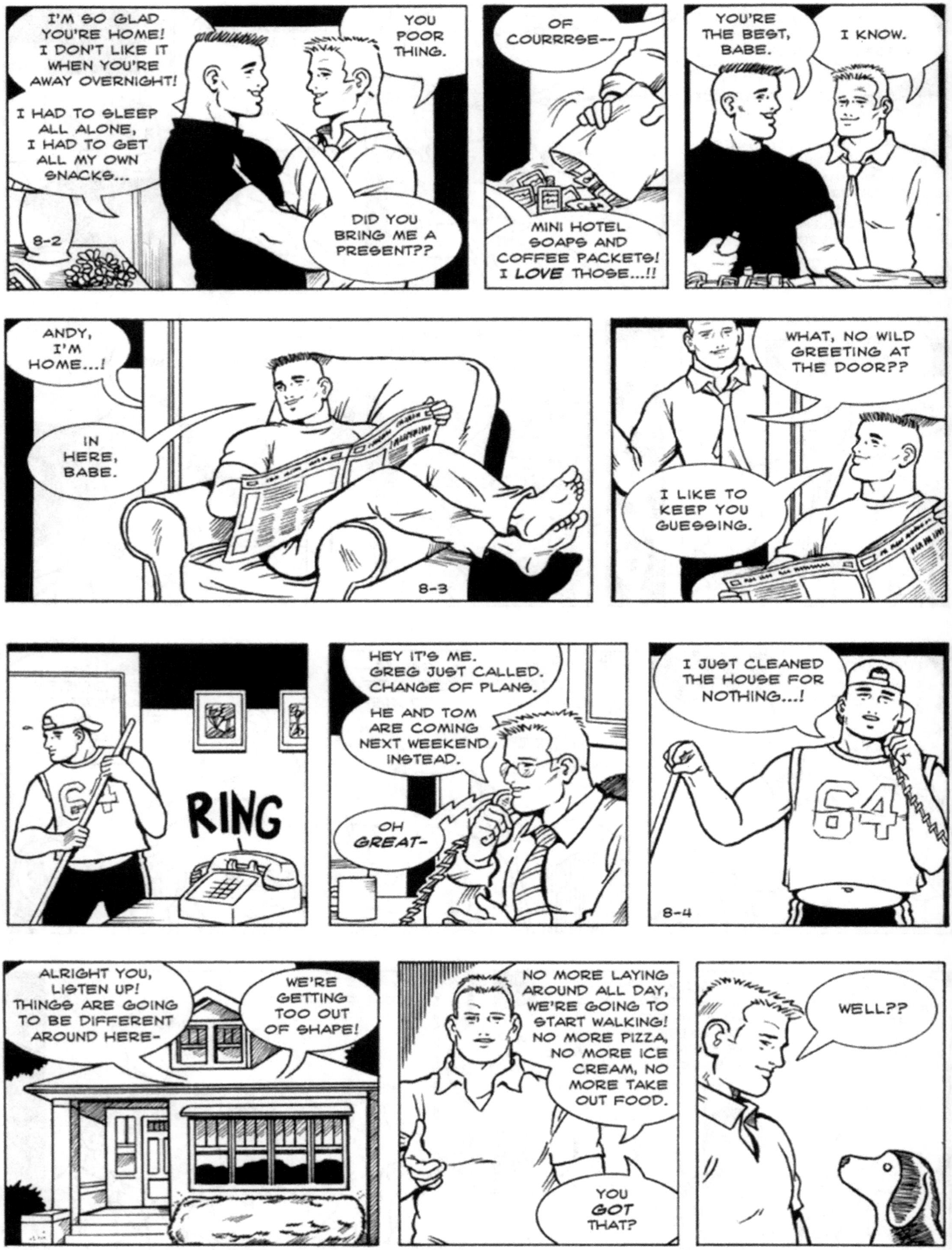

I'M SO GLAD YOU'RE HOME! I DON'T LIKE IT WHEN YOU'RE AWAY OVERNIGHT!
I HAD TO SLEEP ALL ALONE, I HAD TO GET ALL MY OWN SNACKS...
YOU POOR THING.
DID YOU BRING ME A PRESENT??
8-2
OF COURRRSE--
MINI HOTEL SOAPS AND COFFEE PACKETS! I *LOVE* THOSE...!!
YOU'RE THE BEST, BABE.
I KNOW.
ANDY, I'M HOME...!
IN HERE, BABE.
8-3
WHAT, NO WILD GREETING AT THE DOOR??
I LIKE TO KEEP YOU GUESSING.
RING
HEY IT'S ME. GREG JUST CALLED. CHANGE OF PLANS.
HE AND TOM ARE COMING NEXT WEEKEND INSTEAD.
OH *GREAT*-
I JUST CLEANED THE HOUSE FOR NOTHING...!
8-4
ALRIGHT YOU, LISTEN UP! THINGS ARE GOING TO BE DIFFERENT AROUND HERE-
WE'RE GETTING TOO OUT OF SHAPE!
NO MORE LAYING AROUND ALL DAY, WE'RE GOING TO START WALKING! NO MORE PIZZA, NO MORE ICE CREAM, NO MORE TAKE OUT FOOD.
YOU *GOT* THAT?
WELL??

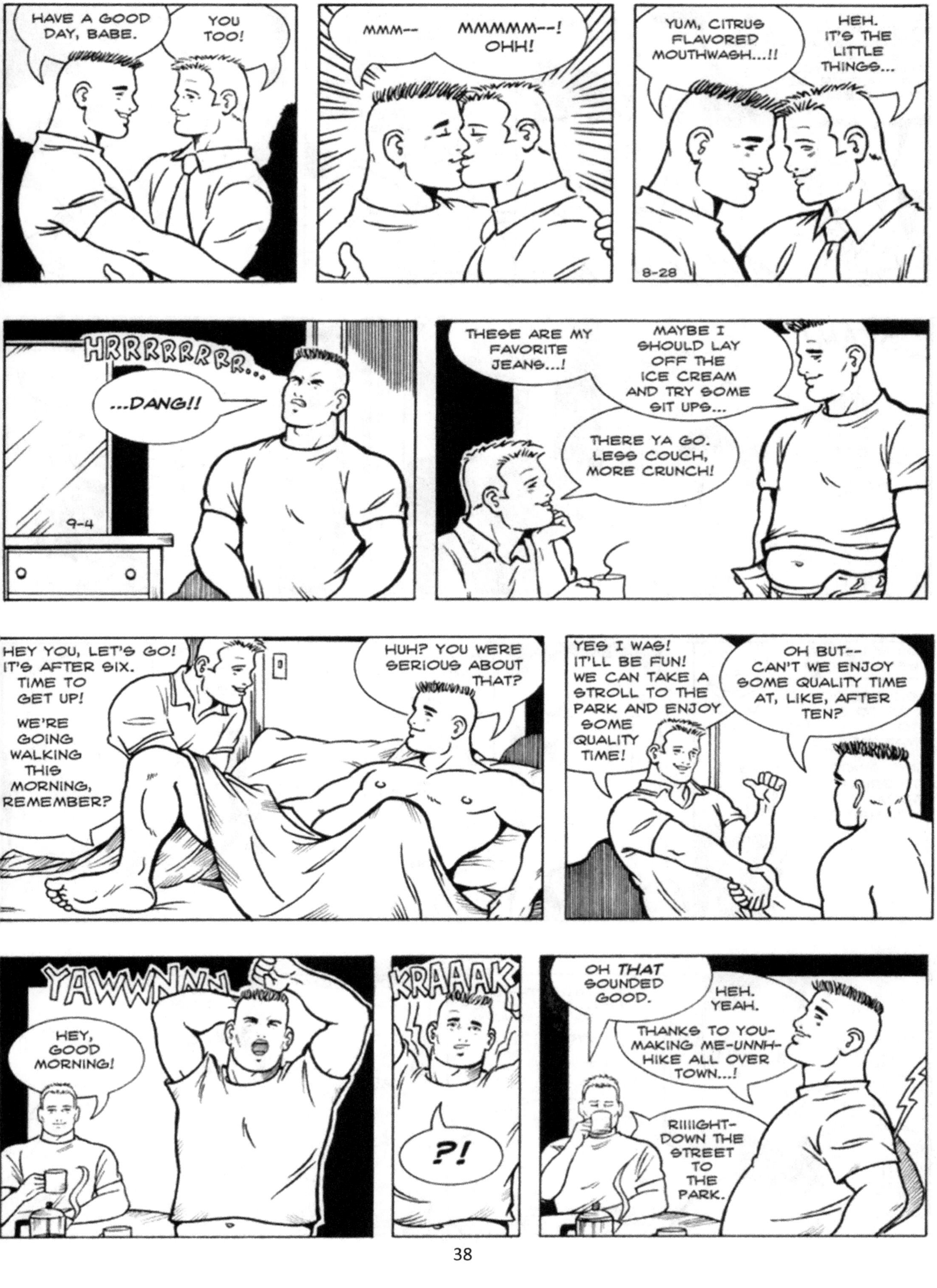
HAVE A GOOD DAY, BABE.
YOU TOO!
MMM--
MMMMM--! OHH!
YUM, CITRUS FLAVORED MOUTHWASH...!!
HEH. IT'S THE LITTLE THINGS...
8-28
HRRRRRRRRR...
...DANG!!
9-4
THESE ARE MY FAVORITE JEANS...!
MAYBE I SHOULD LAY OFF THE ICE CREAM AND TRY SOME SIT UPS...
THERE YA GO. LESS COUCH, MORE CRUNCH!
HEY YOU, LET'S GO! IT'S AFTER SIX. TIME TO GET UP!
WE'RE GOING WALKING THIS MORNING, REMEMBER?
HUH? YOU WERE SERIOUS ABOUT THAT?
YES I WAS! IT'LL BE FUN! WE CAN TAKE A STROLL TO THE PARK AND ENJOY SOME QUALITY TIME!
OH BUT-- CAN'T WE ENJOY SOME QUALITY TIME AT, LIKE, AFTER TEN?
YAWWNNN
HEY, GOOD MORNING!
KRAAAK
?!
OH THAT SOUNDED GOOD.
HEH. YEAH.
THANKS TO YOU-MAKING ME-UNNH-HIKE ALL OVER TOWN...!
RIIIIGHT-DOWN THE STREET TO THE PARK.

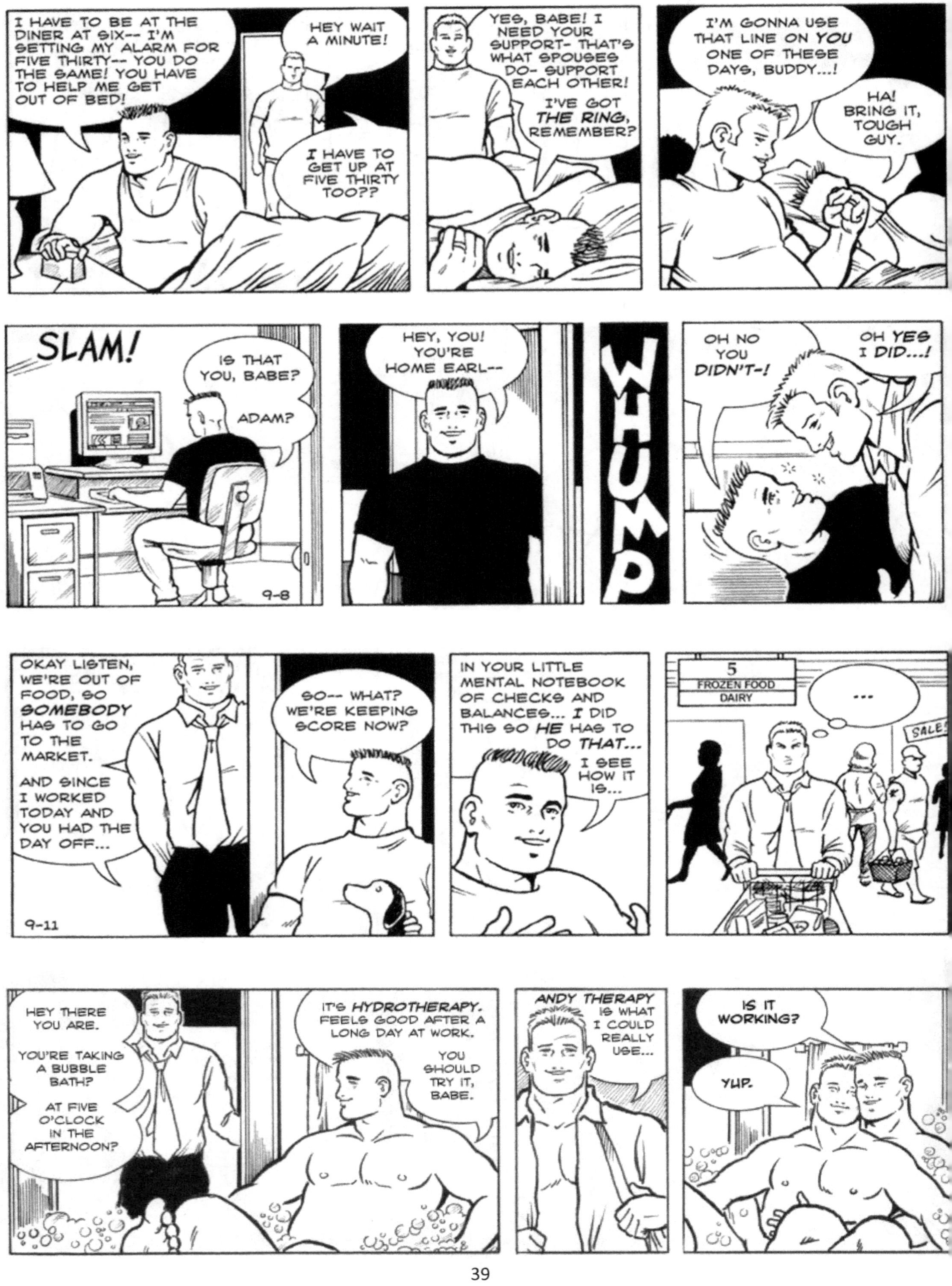
I HAVE TO BE AT THE DINER AT SIX-- I'M SETTING MY ALARM FOR FIVE THIRTY-- YOU DO THE SAME! YOU HAVE TO HELP ME GET OUT OF BED!
HEY WAIT A MINUTE!
I HAVE TO GET UP AT FIVE THIRTY TOO??
YES, BABE! I NEED YOUR SUPPORT- THAT'S WHAT SPOUSES DO- SUPPORT EACH OTHER!
I'VE GOT THE RING, REMEMBER?
I'M GONNA USE THAT LINE ON YOU ONE OF THESE DAYS, BUDDY...!
HA! BRING IT, TOUGH GUY.
SLAM!
IS THAT YOU, BABE?
ADAM?
9-8
HEY, YOU! YOU'RE HOME EARL--
WHUMP
OH NO YOU DIDN'T-!
OH YES I DID...!
OKAY LISTEN, WE'RE OUT OF FOOD, SO SOMEBODY HAS TO GO TO THE MARKET.
AND SINCE I WORKED TODAY AND YOU HAD THE DAY OFF...
9-11
SO-- WHAT? WE'RE KEEPING SCORE NOW?
IN YOUR LITTLE MENTAL NOTEBOOK OF CHECKS AND BALANCES... I DID THIS SO HE HAS TO DO THAT...
I SEE HOW IT IS...
5
FROZEN FOOD
DAIRY
SALE
...
HEY THERE YOU ARE.
YOU'RE TAKING A BUBBLE BATH?
AT FIVE O'CLOCK IN THE AFTERNOON?
IT'S HYDROTHERAPY. FEELS GOOD AFTER A LONG DAY AT WORK.
YOU SHOULD TRY IT, BABE.
ANDY THERAPY IS WHAT I COULD REALLY USE...
IS IT WORKING?
YUP.

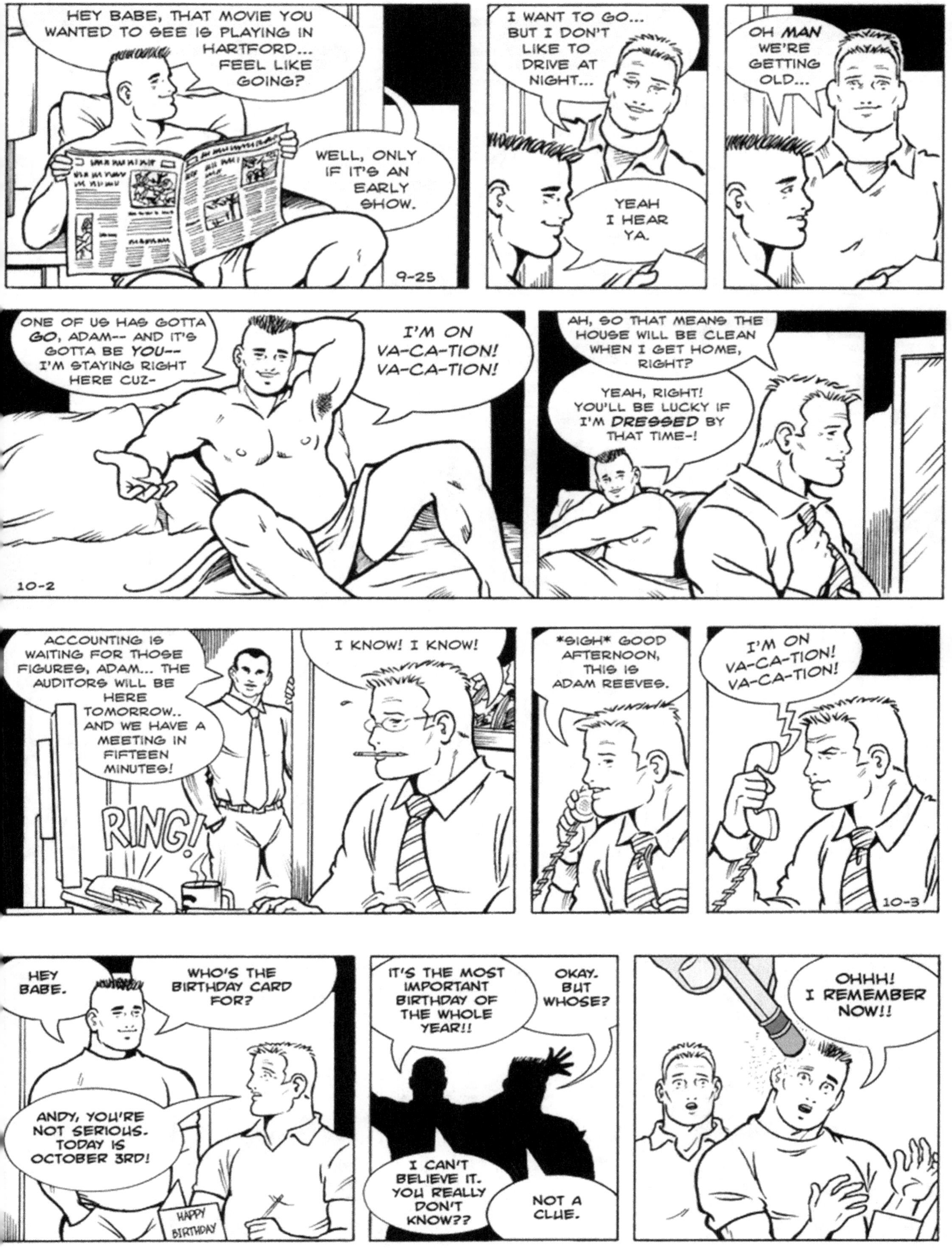
HEY BABE, THAT MOVIE YOU WANTED TO SEE IS PLAYING IN HARTFORD... FEEL LIKE GOING?
WELL, ONLY IF IT'S AN EARLY SHOW.
9-25
I WANT TO GO... BUT I DON'T LIKE TO DRIVE AT NIGHT...
YEAH I HEAR YA.
OH MAN WE'RE GETTING OLD...
ONE OF US HAS GOTTA GO, ADAM-- AND IT'S GOTTA BE YOU-- I'M STAYING RIGHT HERE CUZ-
I'M ON VA-CA-TION! VA-CA-TION!
10-2
AH, SO THAT MEANS THE HOUSE WILL BE CLEAN WHEN I GET HOME, RIGHT?
YEAH, RIGHT! YOU'LL BE LUCKY IF I'M DRESSED BY THAT TIME-!
ACCOUNTING IS WAITING FOR THOSE FIGURES, ADAM... THE AUDITORS WILL BE HERE TOMORROW.. AND WE HAVE A MEETING IN FIFTEEN MINUTES!
RING!
I KNOW! I KNOW!
SIGH GOOD AFTERNOON, THIS IS ADAM REEVES.
I'M ON VA-CA-TION! VA-CA-TION!
10-3
HEY BABE.
WHO'S THE BIRTHDAY CARD FOR?
ANDY, YOU'RE NOT SERIOUS. TODAY IS OCTOBER 3RD!
HAPPY BIRTHDAY
IT'S THE MOST IMPORTANT BIRTHDAY OF THE WHOLE YEAR!!
OKAY. BUT WHOSE?
I CAN'T BELIEVE IT. YOU REALLY DON'T KNOW??
NOT A CLUE.
OHHH! I REMEMBER NOW!!

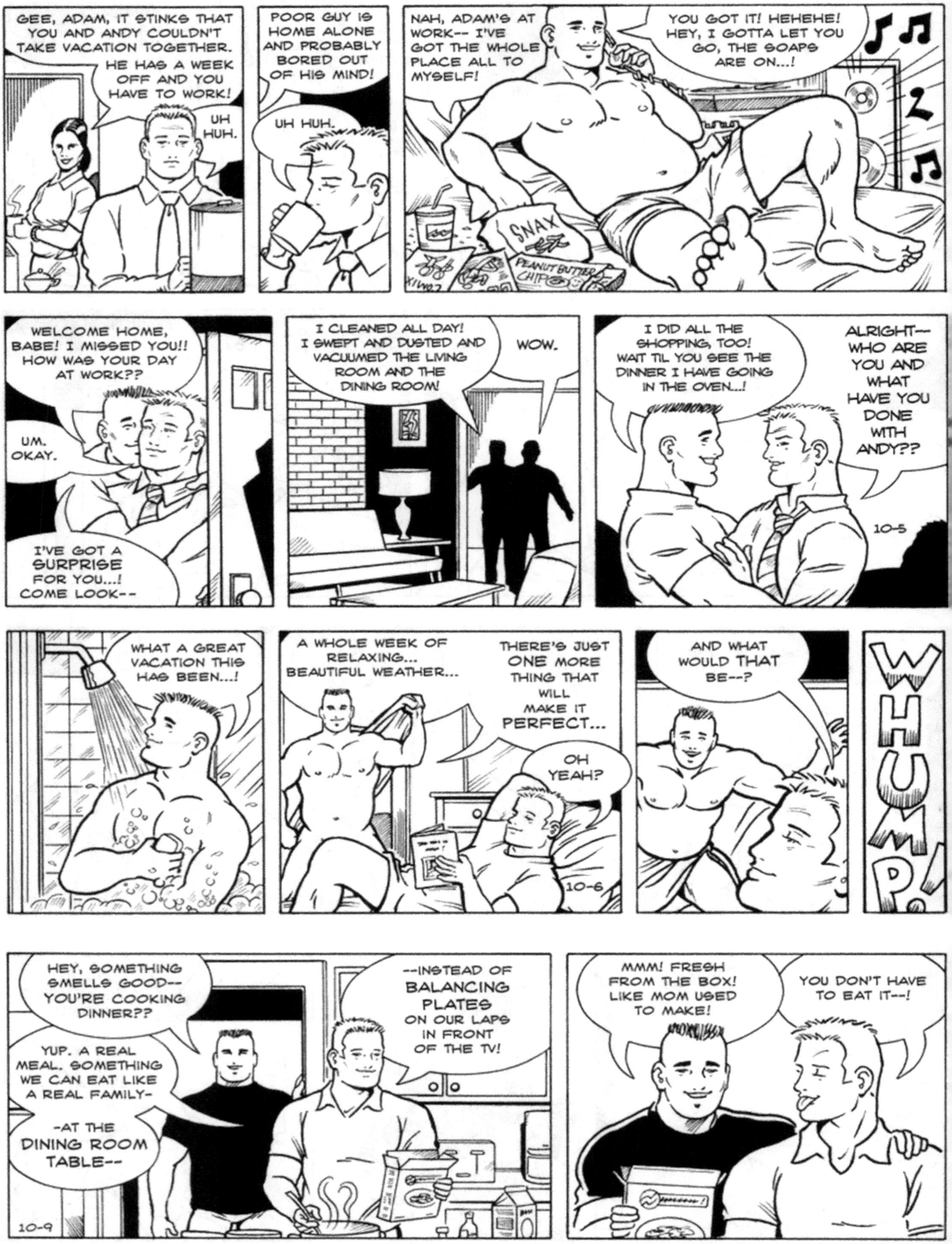
GEE, ADAM, IT STINKS THAT YOU AND ANDY COULDN'T TAKE VACATION TOGETHER.
HE HAS A WEEK OFF AND YOU HAVE TO WORK!
UH HUH.
POOR GUY IS HOME ALONE AND PROBABLY BORED OUT OF HIS MIND!
UH HUH.
NAH, ADAM'S AT WORK-- I'VE GOT THE WHOLE PLACE ALL TO MYSELF!
YOU GOT IT! HEHEHE! HEY, I GOTTA LET YOU GO, THE SOAPS ARE ON...!
SNAX
PEANUT BUTTER CHIPS
WELCOME HOME, BABE! I MISSED YOU!! HOW WAS YOUR DAY AT WORK??
UM. OKAY.
I'VE GOT A SURPRISE FOR YOU...! COME LOOK--
I CLEANED ALL DAY! I SWEPT AND DUSTED AND VACUUMED THE LIVING ROOM AND THE DINING ROOM!
WOW.
I DID ALL THE SHOPPING, TOO! WAIT TIL YOU SEE THE DINNER I HAVE GOING IN THE OVEN...!
ALRIGHT-- WHO ARE YOU AND WHAT HAVE YOU DONE WITH ANDY??
10-5
WHAT A GREAT VACATION THIS HAS BEEN...!
A WHOLE WEEK OF RELAXING... BEAUTIFUL WEATHER...
THERE'S JUST ONE MORE THING THAT WILL MAKE IT PERFECT...
OH YEAH?
10-6
AND WHAT WOULD THAT BE--?
WHUMP!
HEY, SOMETHING SMELLS GOOD-- YOU'RE COOKING DINNER??
YUP. A REAL MEAL. SOMETHING WE CAN EAT LIKE A REAL FAMILY-
-AT THE DINING ROOM TABLE--
--INSTEAD OF BALANCING PLATES ON OUR LAPS IN FRONT OF THE TV!
10-9
MMM! FRESH FROM THE BOX! LIKE MOM USED TO MAKE!
YOU DON'T HAVE TO EAT IT--!

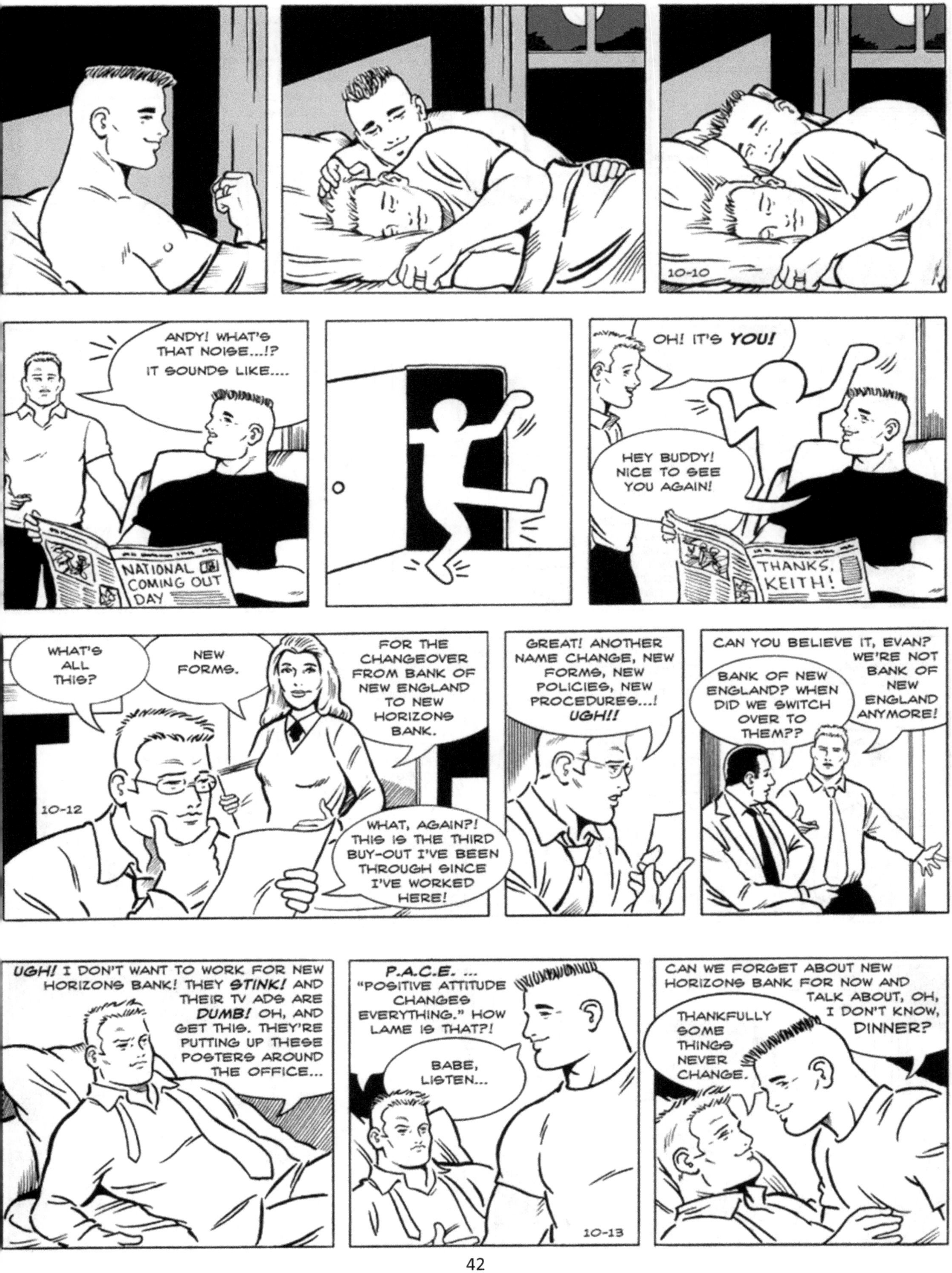
10-10
ANDY! WHAT'S THAT NOISE...!? IT SOUNDS LIKE....
NATIONAL COMING OUT DAY
OH! IT'S *YOU!*
HEY BUDDY! NICE TO SEE YOU AGAIN!
THANKS, KEITH!
WHAT'S ALL THIS?
NEW FORMS.
FOR THE CHANGEOVER FROM BANK OF NEW ENGLAND TO NEW HORIZONS BANK.
10-12
WHAT, AGAIN?! THIS IS THE THIRD BUY-OUT I'VE BEEN THROUGH SINCE I'VE WORKED HERE!
GREAT! ANOTHER NAME CHANGE, NEW FORMS, NEW POLICIES, NEW PROCEDURES...! *UGH!!*
CAN YOU BELIEVE IT, EVAN?
WE'RE NOT BANK OF NEW ENGLAND ANYMORE!
BANK OF NEW ENGLAND? WHEN DID WE SWITCH OVER TO THEM??
UGH! I DON'T WANT TO WORK FOR NEW HORIZONS BANK! THEY *STINK!* AND THEIR TV ADS ARE *DUMB!* OH, AND GET THIS. THEY'RE PUTTING UP THESE POSTERS AROUND THE OFFICE...
P.A.C.E. ... "POSITIVE ATTITUDE CHANGES EVERYTHING." HOW LAME IS THAT?!
BABE, LISTEN...
10-13
CAN WE FORGET ABOUT NEW HORIZONS BANK FOR NOW AND TALK ABOUT, OH, I DON'T KNOW, DINNER?
THANKFULLY SOME THINGS NEVER CHANGE.

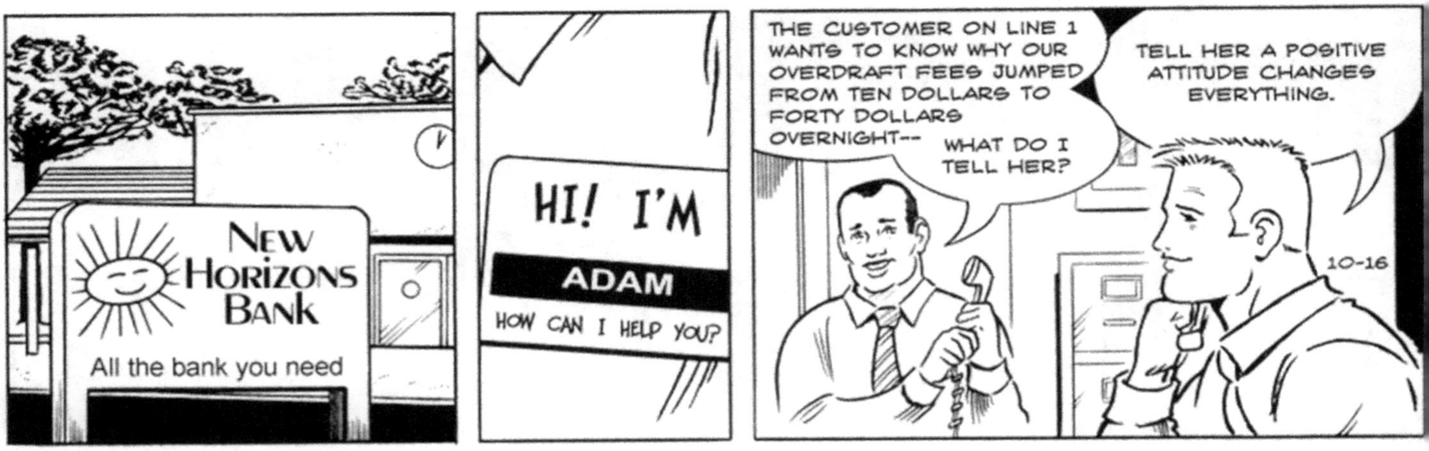
NEW HORIZONS BANK
All the bank you need
HI! I'M
ADAM
HOW CAN I HELP YOU?
THE CUSTOMER ON LINE 1 WANTS TO KNOW WHY OUR OVERDRAFT FEES JUMPED FROM TEN DOLLARS TO FORTY DOLLARS OVERNIGHT--
WHAT DO I TELL HER?
TELL HER A POSITIVE ATTITUDE CHANGES EVERYTHING.
10-16

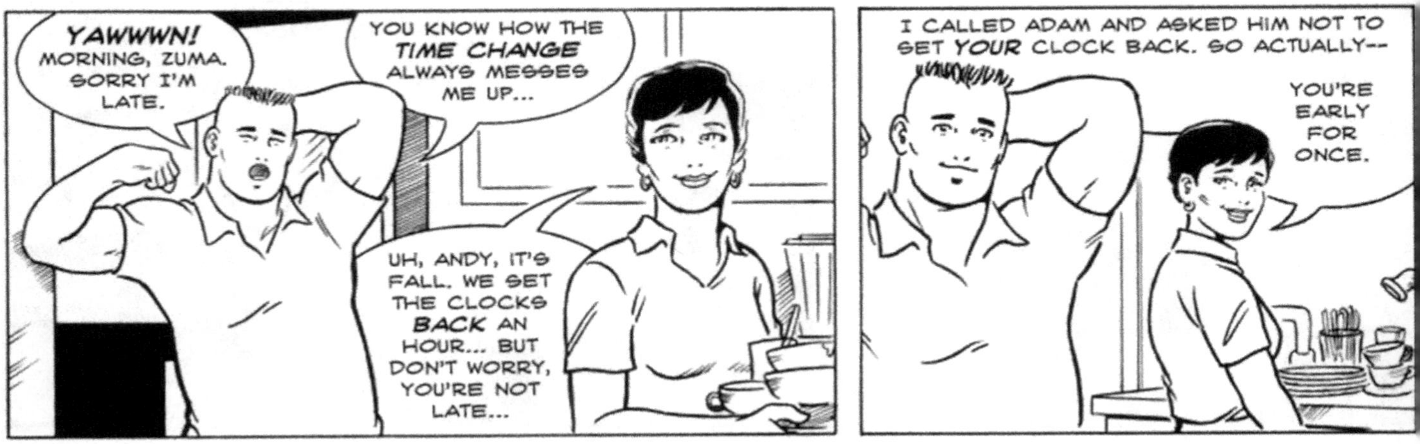
YAWWWN! MORNING, ZUMA. SORRY I'M LATE.
YOU KNOW HOW THE TIME CHANGE ALWAYS MESSES ME UP...
UH, ANDY, IT'S FALL. WE SET THE CLOCKS BACK AN HOUR... BUT DON'T WORRY, YOU'RE NOT LATE...
I CALLED ADAM AND ASKED HIM NOT TO SET YOUR CLOCK BACK. SO ACTUALLY--
YOU'RE EARLY FOR ONCE.

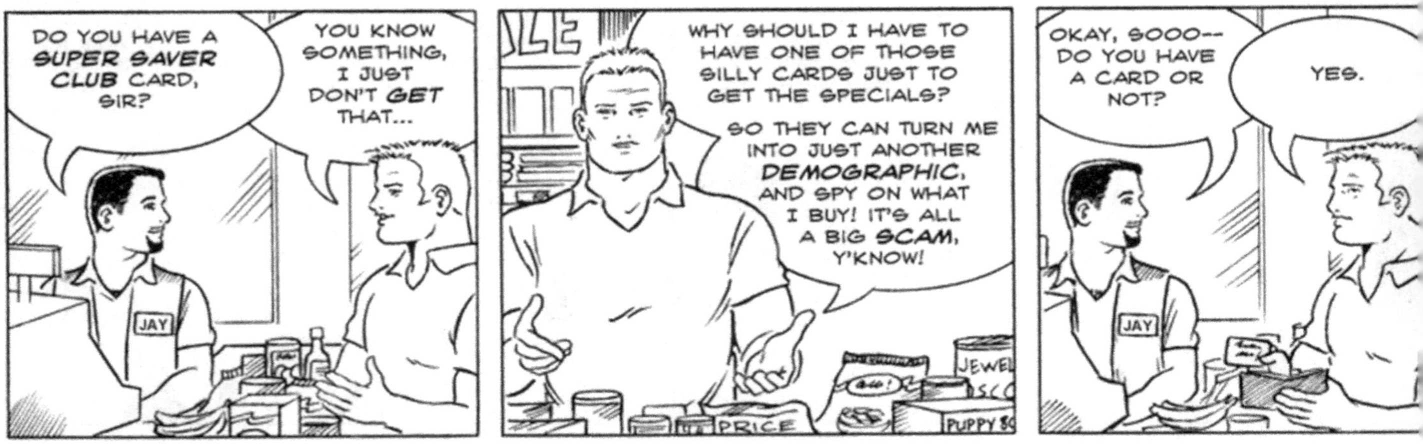
DO YOU HAVE A SUPER SAVER CLUB CARD, SIR?
YOU KNOW SOMETHING, I JUST DON'T GET THAT...
JAY
WHY SHOULD I HAVE TO HAVE ONE OF THOSE SILLY CARDS JUST TO GET THE SPECIALS?
SO THEY CAN TURN ME INTO JUST ANOTHER DEMOGRAPHIC, AND SPY ON WHAT I BUY! IT'S ALL A BIG SCAM, Y'KNOW!
OKAY, SOOO-- DO YOU HAVE A CARD OR NOT?
YES.
JAY

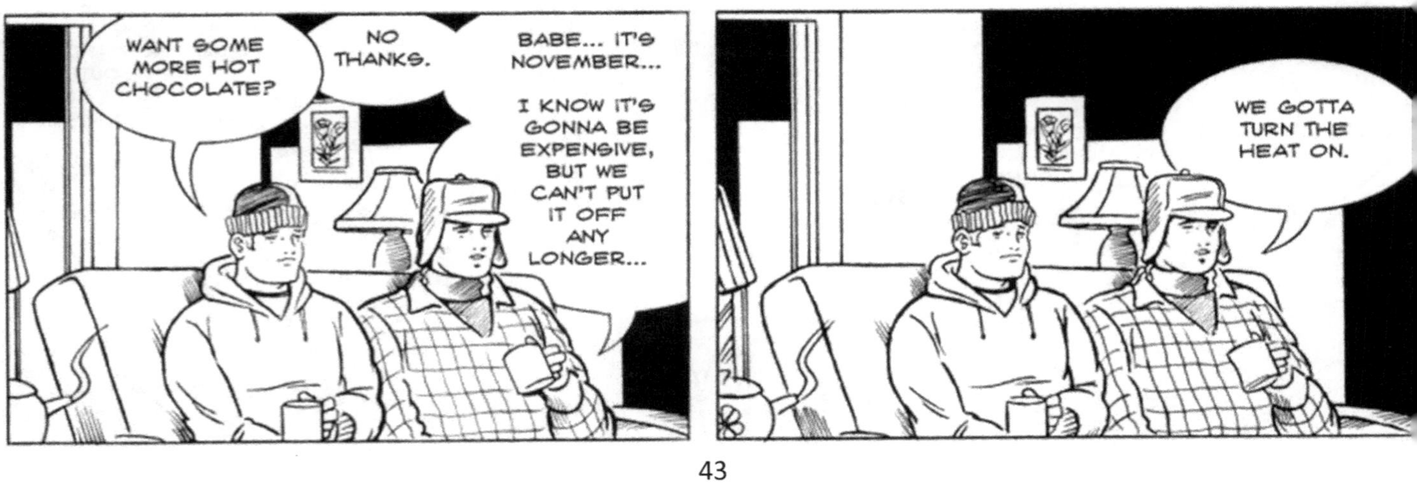
WANT SOME MORE HOT CHOCOLATE?
NO THANKS.
BABE... IT'S NOVEMBER...
I KNOW IT'S GONNA BE EXPENSIVE, BUT WE CAN'T PUT IT OFF ANY LONGER...
WE GOTTA TURN THE HEAT ON.

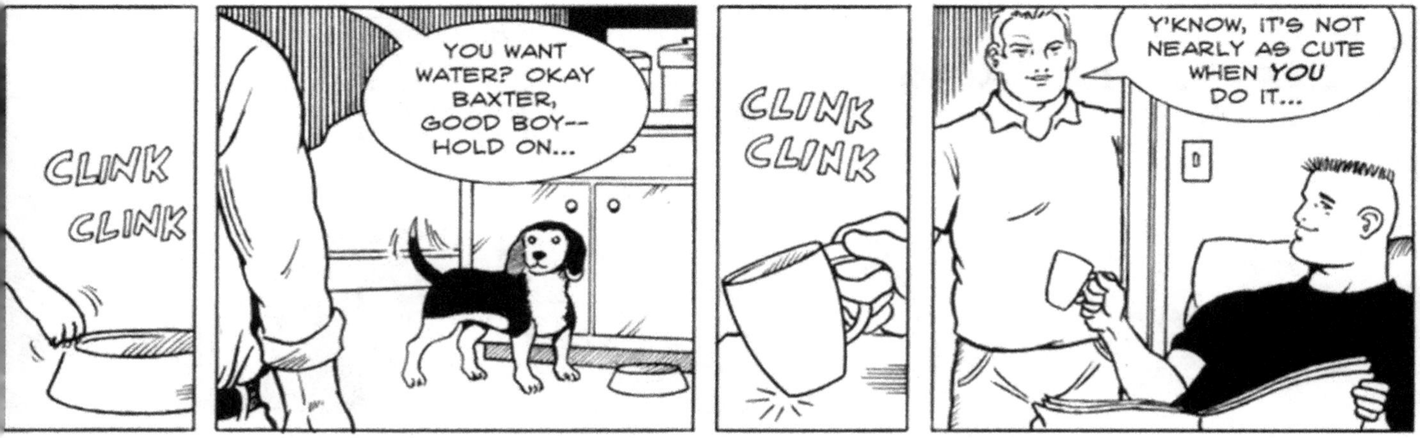

CLINK
CLINK
YOU WANT WATER? OKAY BAXTER, GOOD BOY-- HOLD ON...
CLINK
CLINK
Y'KNOW, IT'S NOT NEARLY AS CUTE WHEN *YOU* DO IT...

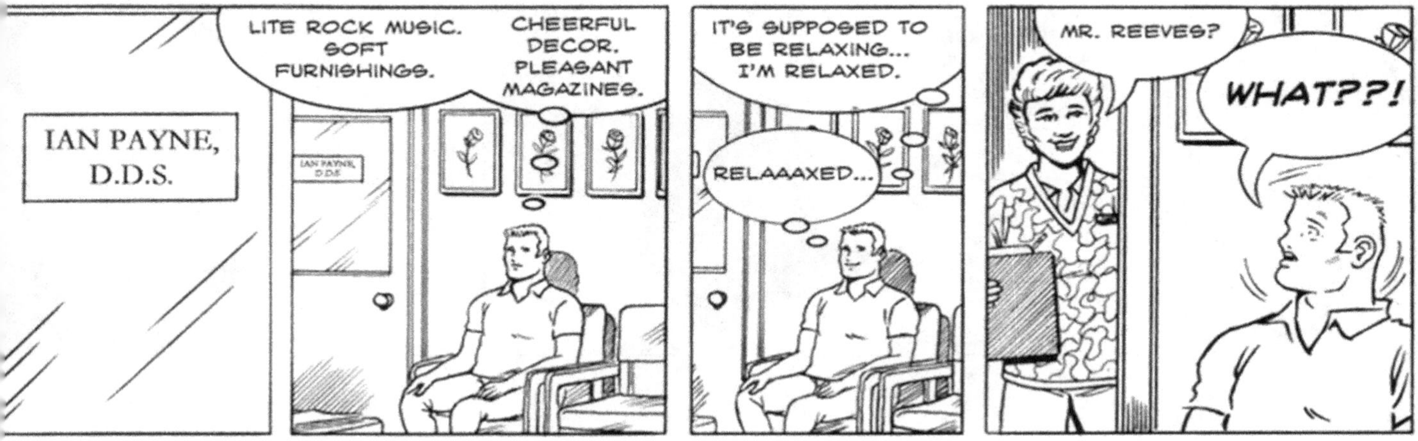

IAN PAYNE, D.D.S.
LITE ROCK MUSIC. SOFT FURNISHINGS.
CHEERFUL DECOR. PLEASANT MAGAZINES.
IT'S SUPPOSED TO BE RELAXING... I'M RELAXED.
RELAAAXED...
MR. REEVES?
WHAT??!

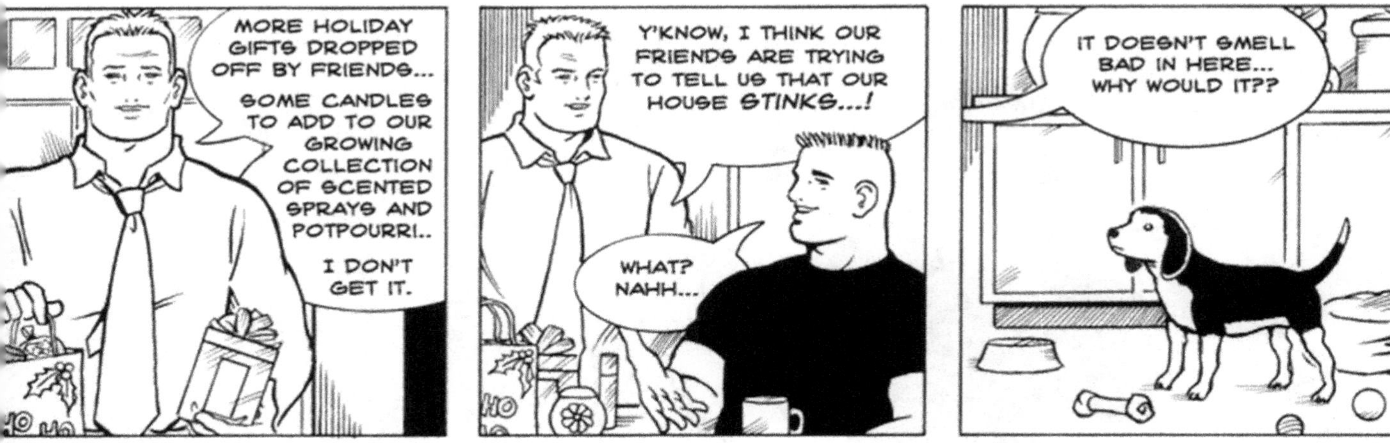

MORE HOLIDAY GIFTS DROPPED OFF BY FRIENDS...
SOME CANDLES TO ADD TO OUR GROWING COLLECTION OF SCENTED SPRAYS AND POTPOURRI..
I DON'T GET IT.
Y'KNOW, I THINK OUR FRIENDS ARE TRYING TO TELL US THAT OUR HOUSE *STINKS...!*
WHAT? NAHH...
IT DOESN'T SMELL BAD IN HERE... WHY WOULD IT??

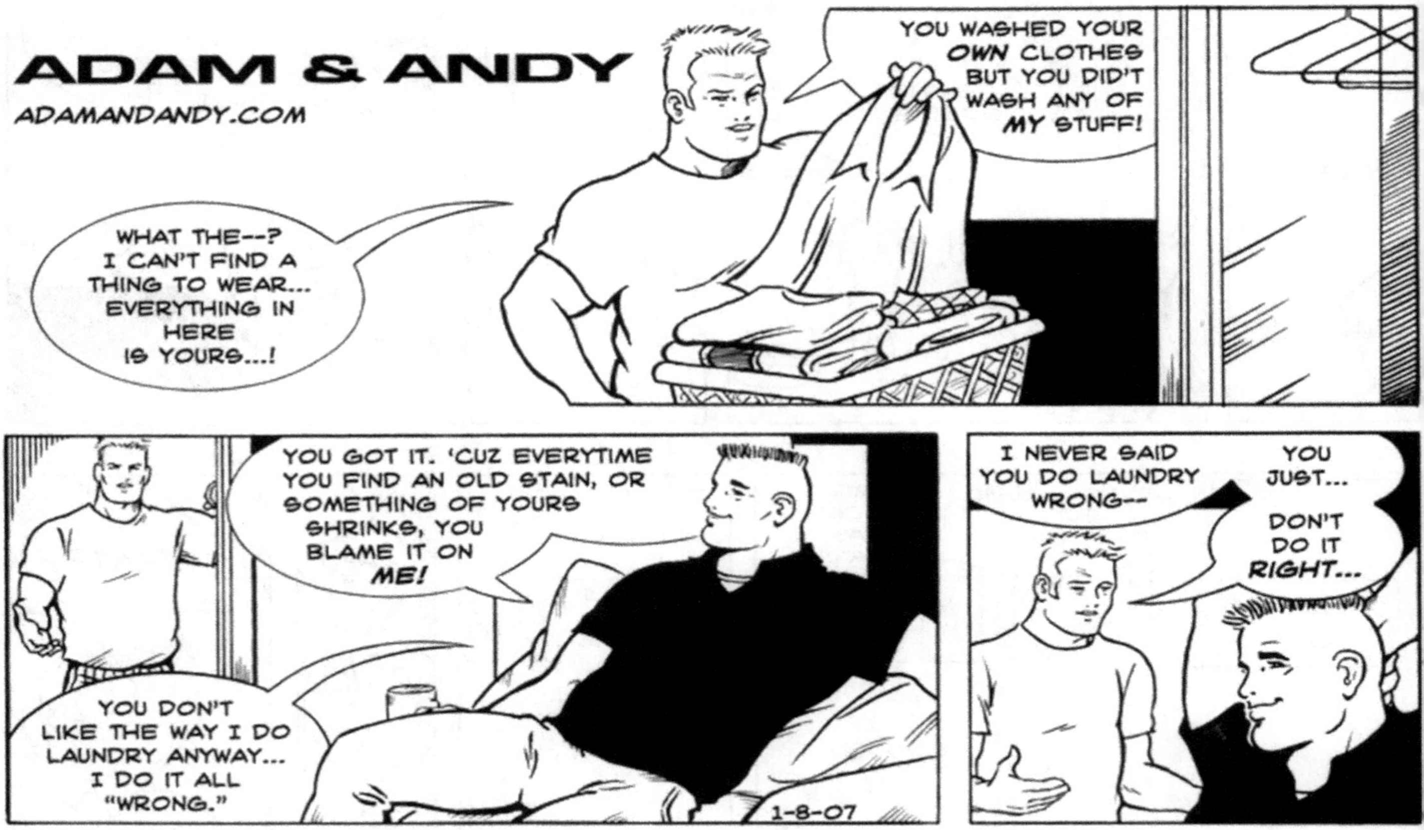
ADAM & ANDY
ADAMANDANDY.COM
WHAT THE--? I CAN'T FIND A THING TO WEAR... EVERYTHING IN HERE IS YOURS...!
YOU WASHED YOUR *OWN* CLOTHES BUT YOU DID'T WASH ANY OF *MY* STUFF!
YOU DON'T LIKE THE WAY I DO LAUNDRY ANYWAY... I DO IT ALL "WRONG."
YOU GOT IT. 'CUZ EVERYTIME YOU FIND AN OLD STAIN, OR SOMETHING OF YOURS SHRINKS, YOU BLAME IT ON *ME!*
1-8-07
I NEVER SAID YOU DO LAUNDRY WRONG--
YOU JUST...
DON'T DO IT *RIGHT...*

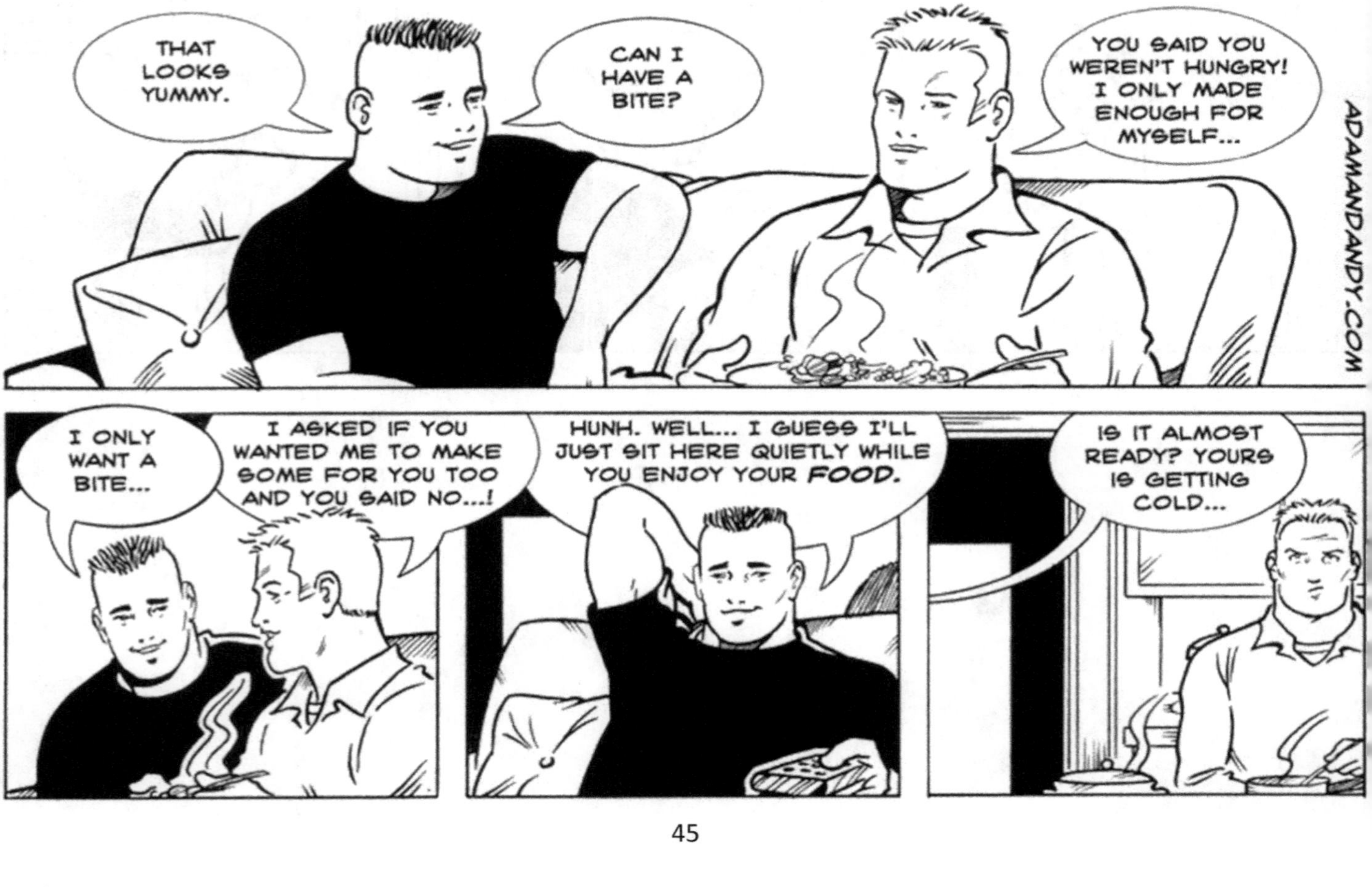
THAT LOOKS YUMMY.
CAN I HAVE A BITE?
YOU SAID YOU WEREN'T HUNGRY! I ONLY MADE ENOUGH FOR MYSELF...
ADAMANDANDY.COM
I ONLY WANT A BITE...
I ASKED IF YOU WANTED ME TO MAKE SOME FOR YOU TOO AND YOU SAID NO...!
HUNH. WELL... I GUESS I'LL JUST SIT HERE QUIETLY WHILE YOU ENJOY YOUR *FOOD.*
IS IT ALMOST READY? YOURS IS GETTING COLD...

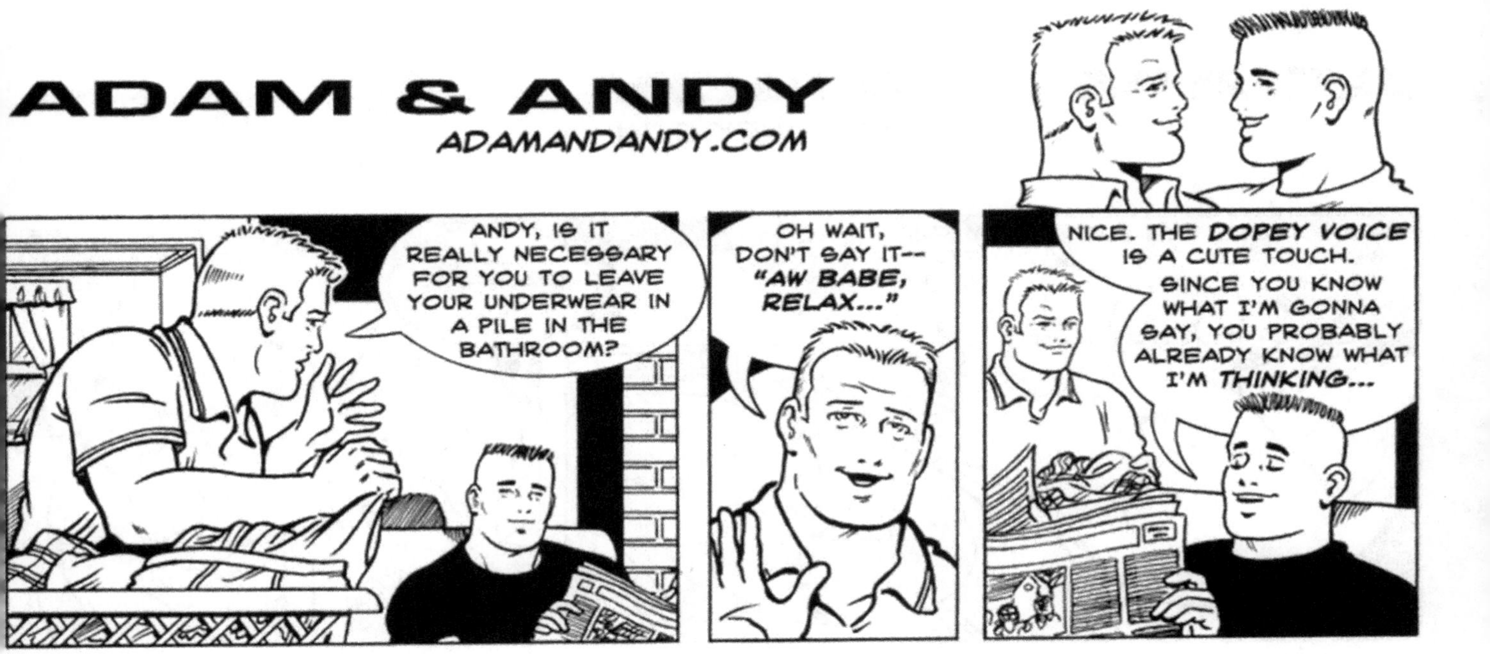
ADAM & ANDY
ADAMANDANDY.COM
ANDY, IS IT REALLY NECESSARY FOR YOU TO LEAVE YOUR UNDERWEAR IN A PILE IN THE BATHROOM?
OH WAIT, DON'T SAY IT-- "AW BABE, RELAX..."
NICE. THE DOPEY VOICE IS A CUTE TOUCH.
SINCE YOU KNOW WHAT I'M GONNA SAY, YOU PROBABLY ALREADY KNOW WHAT I'M THINKING...

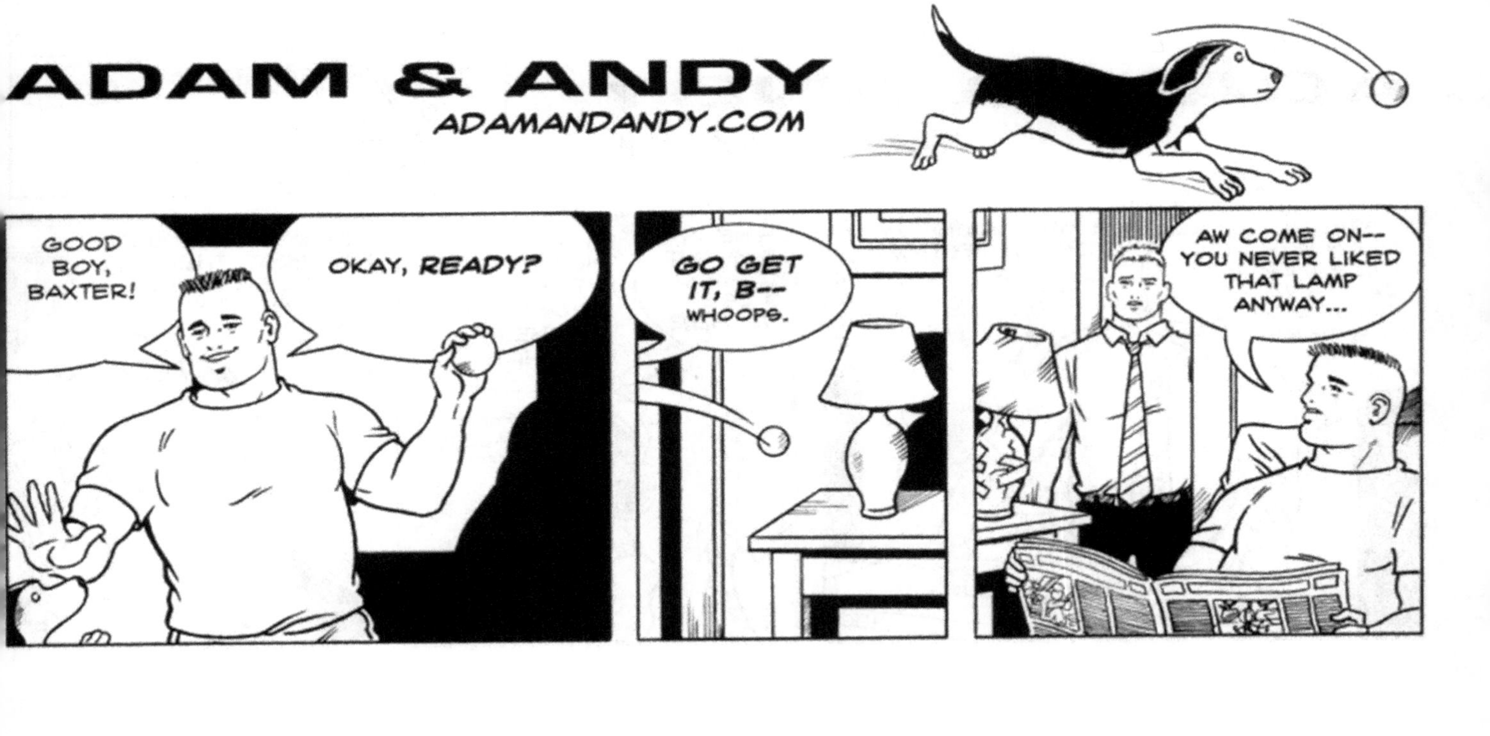
ADAM & ANDY
ADAMANDANDY.COM
GOOD BOY, BAXTER!
OKAY, READY?
GO GET IT, B-- WHOOPS.
AW COME ON-- YOU NEVER LIKED THAT LAMP ANYWAY...

ADAM & ANDY

ADAMANDANDY.COM

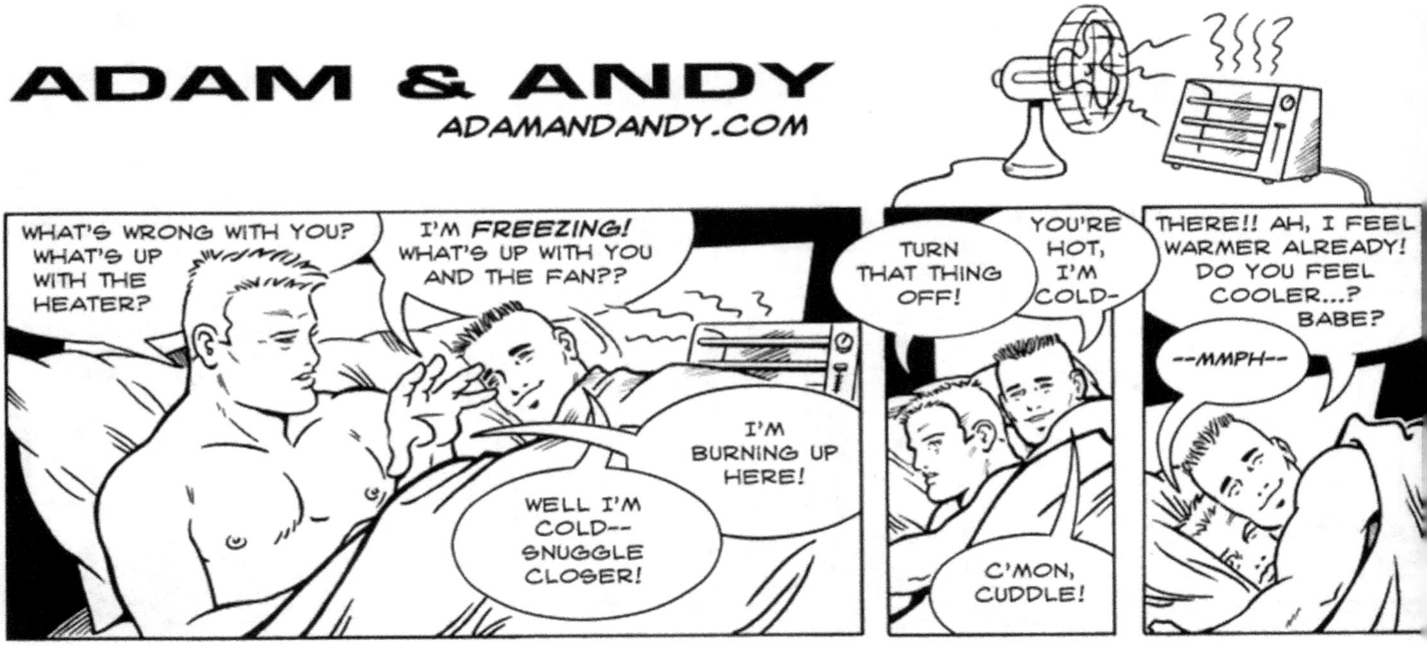
WHAT'S WRONG WITH YOU? WHAT'S UP WITH THE HEATER?
I'M *FREEZING!* WHAT'S UP WITH YOU AND THE FAN??
I'M BURNING UP HERE!
WELL I'M COLD-- SNUGGLE CLOSER!
TURN THAT THING OFF!
YOU'RE HOT, I'M COLD-
C'MON, CUDDLE!
THERE!! AH, I FEEL WARMER ALREADY! DO YOU FEEL COOLER...? BABE?
--MMPH--

ADAM & ANDY

ADAMANDANDY.COM

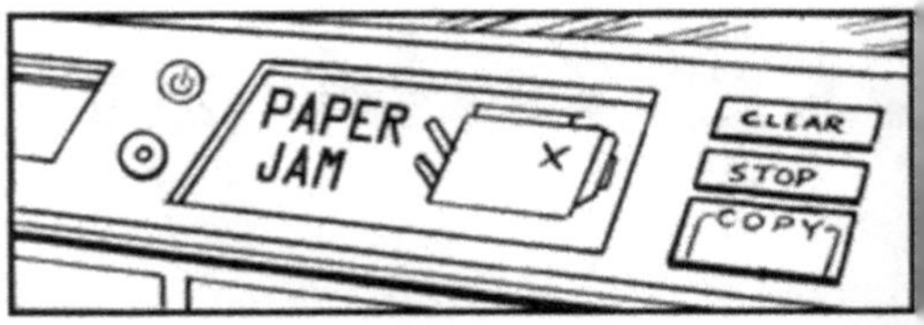
PAPER JAM
CLEAR
STOP
COPY

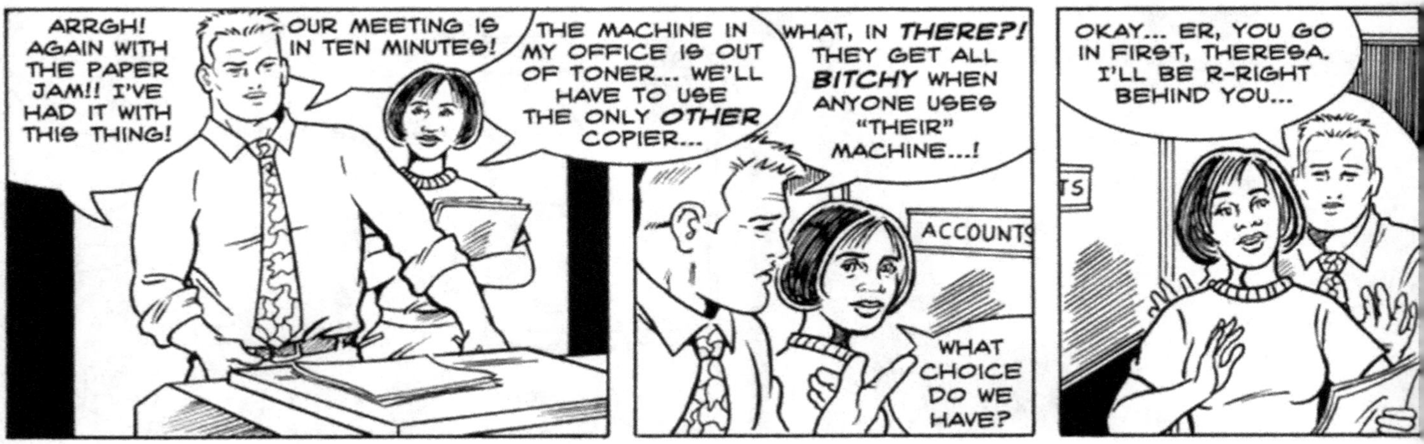
ARRGH! AGAIN WITH THE PAPER JAM!! I'VE HAD IT WITH THIS THING!
OUR MEETING IS IN TEN MINUTES!
THE MACHINE IN MY OFFICE IS OUT OF TONER... WE'LL HAVE TO USE THE ONLY *OTHER* COPIER...
WHAT, IN *THERE?!* THEY GET ALL *BITCHY* WHEN ANYONE USES "THEIR" MACHINE...!
ACCOUNTS
WHAT CHOICE DO WE HAVE?
OKAY... ER, YOU GO IN FIRST, THERESA. I'LL BE R-RIGHT BEHIND YOU...

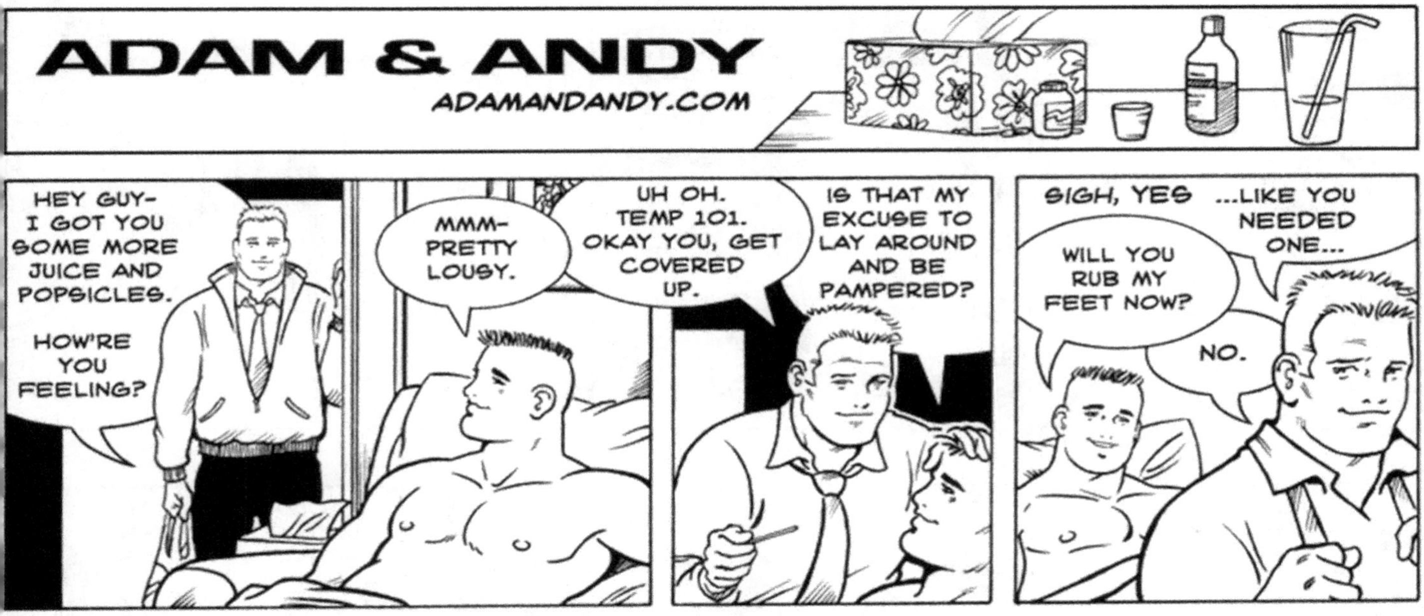
ADAM & ANDY
ADAMANDANDY.COM
HEY GUY- I GOT YOU SOME MORE JUICE AND POPSICLES.
HOW'RE YOU FEELING?
MMM- PRETTY LOUSY.
UH OH. TEMP 101. OKAY YOU, GET COVERED UP.
IS THAT MY EXCUSE TO LAY AROUND AND BE PAMPERED?
SIGH, YES
...LIKE YOU NEEDED ONE...
WILL YOU RUB MY FEET NOW?
NO.

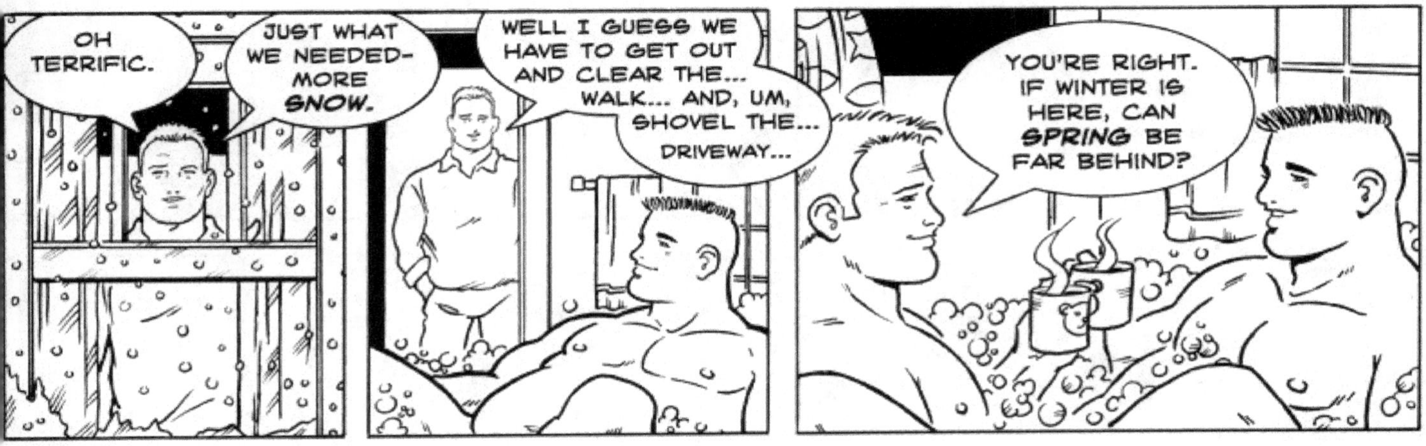
OH TERRIFIC.
JUST WHAT WE NEEDED- MORE SNOW.
WELL I GUESS WE HAVE TO GET OUT AND CLEAR THE... WALK... AND, UM,
SHOVEL THE... DRIVEWAY...
YOU'RE RIGHT. IF WINTER IS HERE, CAN SPRING BE FAR BEHIND?

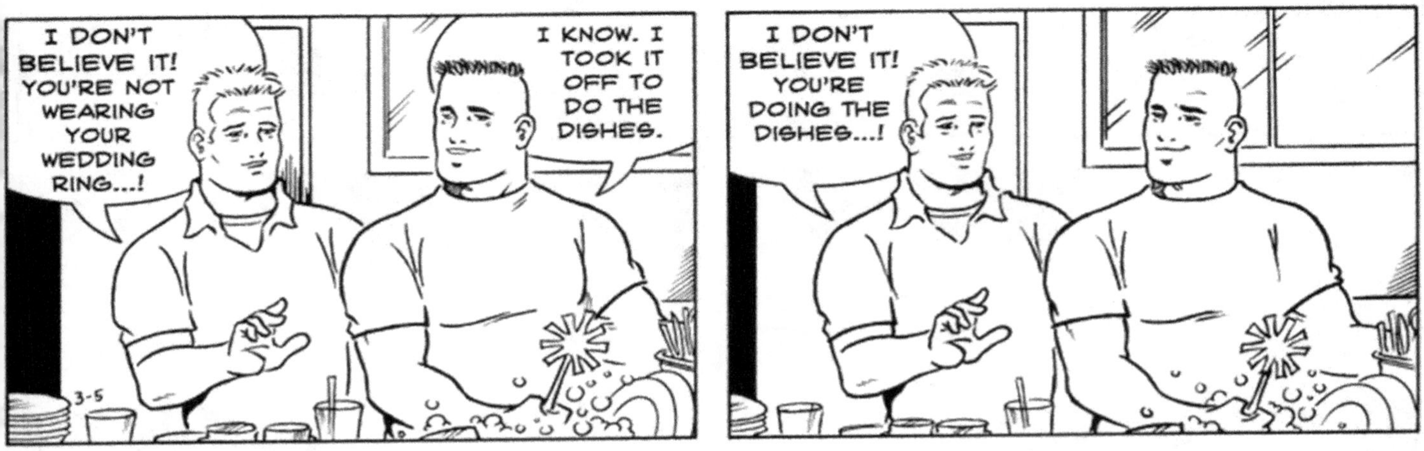
I DON'T BELIEVE IT! YOU'RE NOT WEARING YOUR WEDDING RING...!
I KNOW. I TOOK IT OFF TO DO THE DISHES.
3-5
I DON'T BELIEVE IT! YOU'RE DOING THE DISHES...!

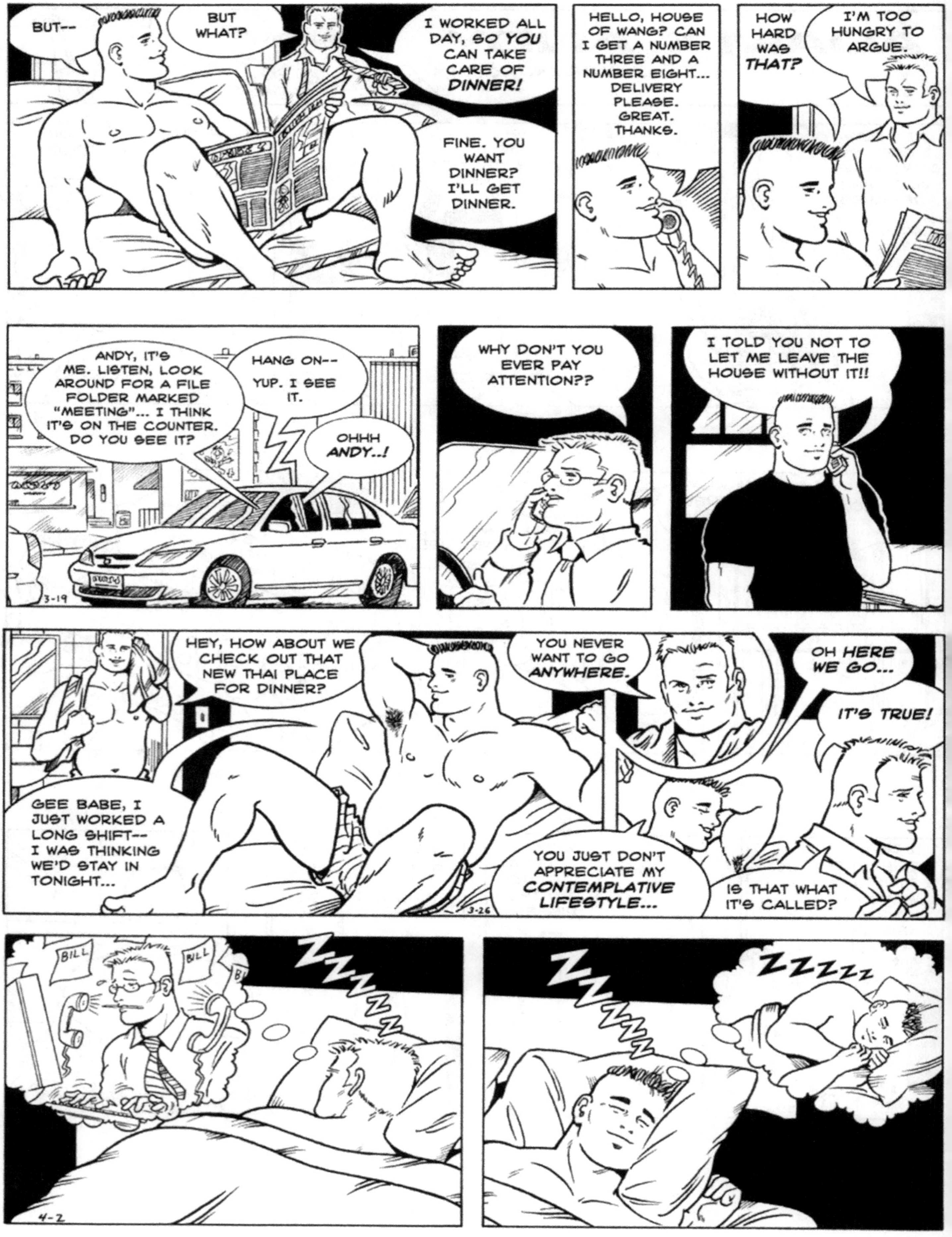
BUT--
BUT WHAT?
I WORKED ALL DAY, SO *YOU* CAN TAKE CARE OF ***DINNER!***
FINE. YOU WANT DINNER? I'LL GET DINNER.
HELLO, HOUSE OF WANG? CAN I GET A NUMBER THREE AND A NUMBER EIGHT... DELIVERY PLEASE. GREAT. THANKS.
HOW HARD WAS ***THAT?***
I'M TOO HUNGRY TO ARGUE.
ANDY, IT'S ME. LISTEN, LOOK AROUND FOR A FILE FOLDER MARKED "MEETING"... I THINK IT'S ON THE COUNTER. DO YOU SEE IT?
HANG ON-- YUP. I SEE IT.
OHHH ***ANDY..!***
3-19
WHY DON'T YOU EVER PAY ATTENTION??
I TOLD YOU NOT TO LET ME LEAVE THE HOUSE WITHOUT IT!!
HEY, HOW ABOUT WE CHECK OUT THAT NEW THAI PLACE FOR DINNER?
GEE BABE, I JUST WORKED A LONG SHIFT-- I WAS THINKING WE'D STAY IN TONIGHT...
3-26
YOU NEVER WANT TO GO ***ANYWHERE.***
YOU JUST DON'T APPRECIATE MY ***CONTEMPLATIVE LIFESTYLE...***
OH ***HERE WE GO...***
IT'S TRUE!
IS THAT WHAT IT'S CALLED?
BILL
BILL
ZZZZZ
4-2
ZZZZZ
ZZZZZ

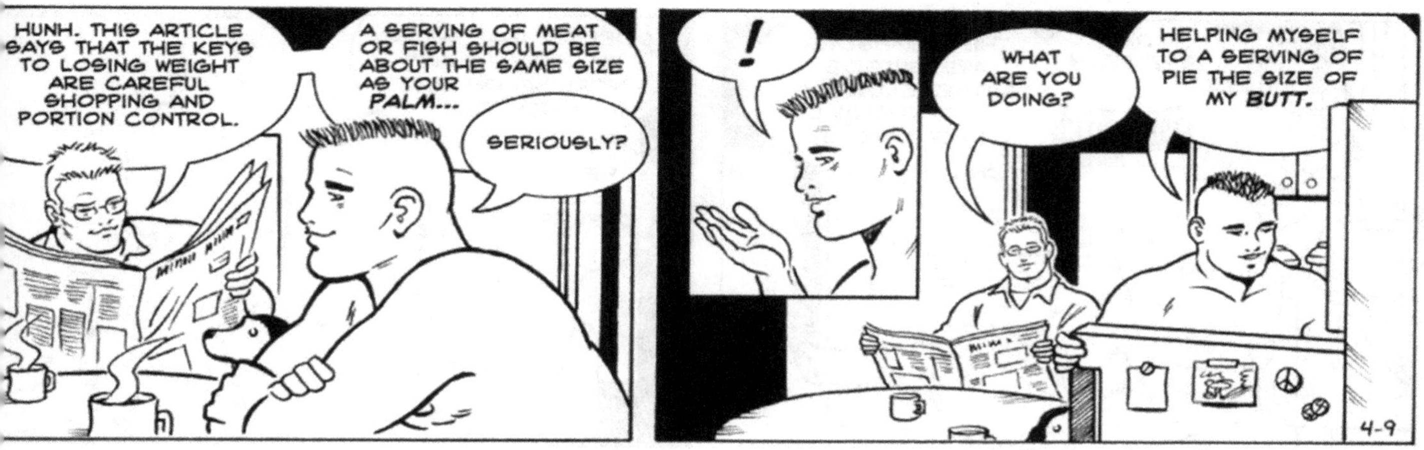
HUNH. THIS ARTICLE SAYS THAT THE KEYS TO LOSING WEIGHT ARE CAREFUL SHOPPING AND PORTION CONTROL.
A SERVING OF MEAT OR FISH SHOULD BE ABOUT THE SAME SIZE AS YOUR *PALM...*
SERIOUSLY?
!
WHAT ARE YOU DOING?
HELPING MYSELF TO A SERVING OF PIE THE SIZE OF MY *BUTT.*
4-9

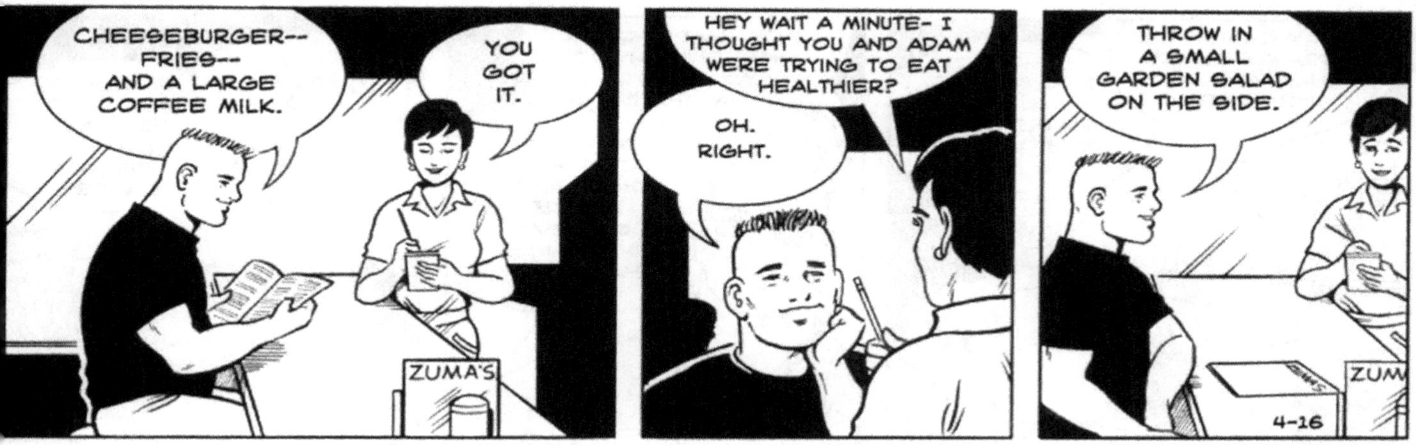
CHEESEBURGER-- FRIES-- AND A LARGE COFFEE MILK.
YOU GOT IT.
ZUMA'S
HEY WAIT A MINUTE- I THOUGHT YOU AND ADAM WERE TRYING TO EAT HEALTHIER?
OH. RIGHT.
THROW IN A SMALL GARDEN SALAD ON THE SIDE.
4-16

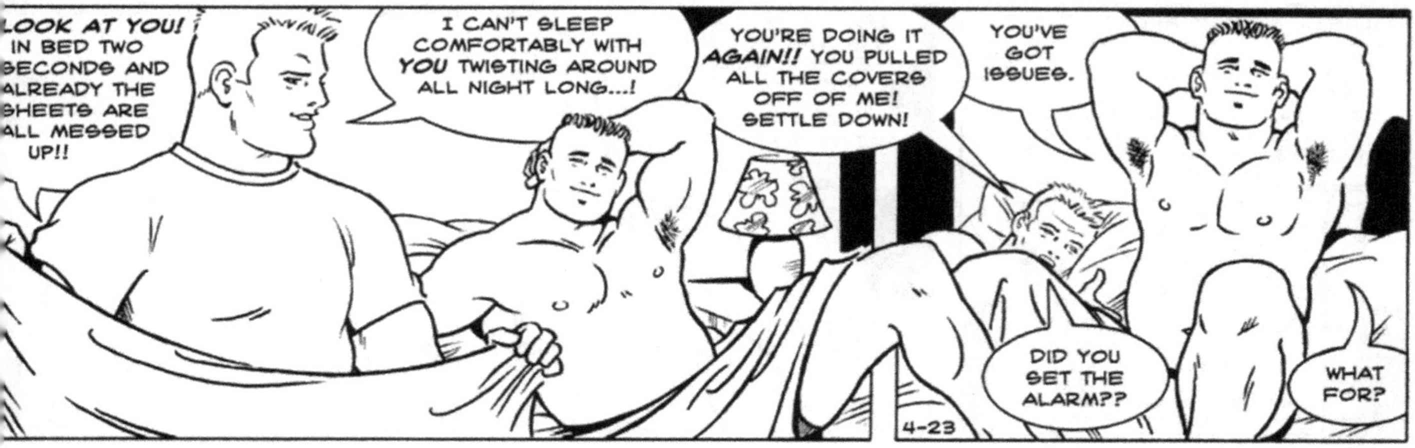
LOOK AT YOU! IN BED TWO SECONDS AND ALREADY THE SHEETS ARE ALL MESSED UP!!
I CAN'T SLEEP COMFORTABLY WITH *YOU* TWISTING AROUND ALL NIGHT LONG...!
YOU'RE DOING IT *AGAIN!!* YOU PULLED ALL THE COVERS OFF OF ME! SETTLE DOWN!
YOU'VE GOT ISSUES.
DID YOU SET THE ALARM??
WHAT FOR?
4-23

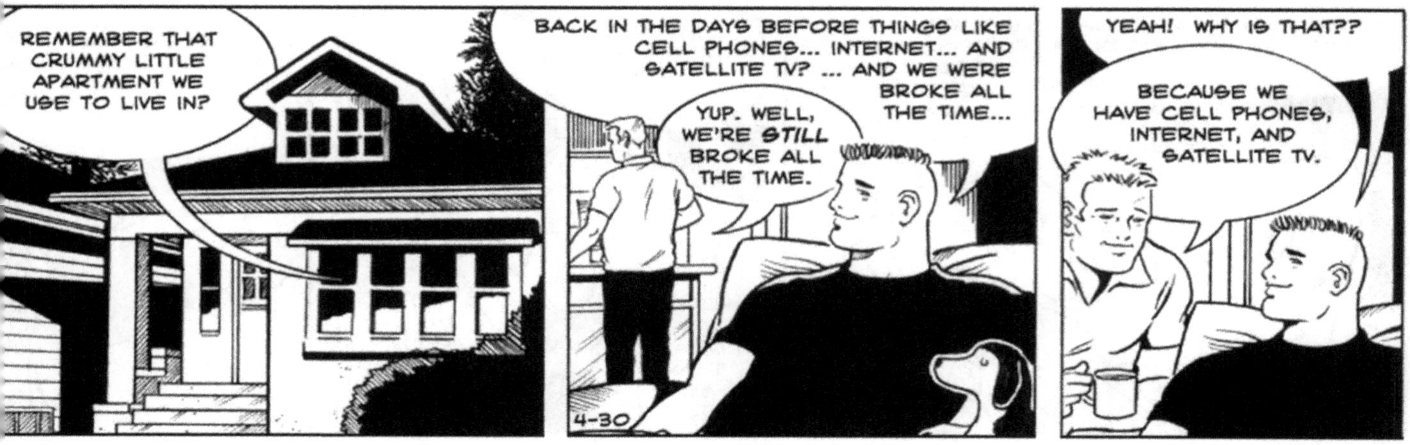
REMEMBER THAT CRUMMY LITTLE APARTMENT WE USE TO LIVE IN?
BACK IN THE DAYS BEFORE THINGS LIKE CELL PHONES... INTERNET... AND SATELLITE TV? ... AND WE WERE BROKE ALL THE TIME...
YUP. WELL, WE'RE *STILL* BROKE ALL THE TIME.
4-30
YEAH! WHY IS THAT??
BECAUSE WE HAVE CELL PHONES, INTERNET, AND SATELLITE TV.

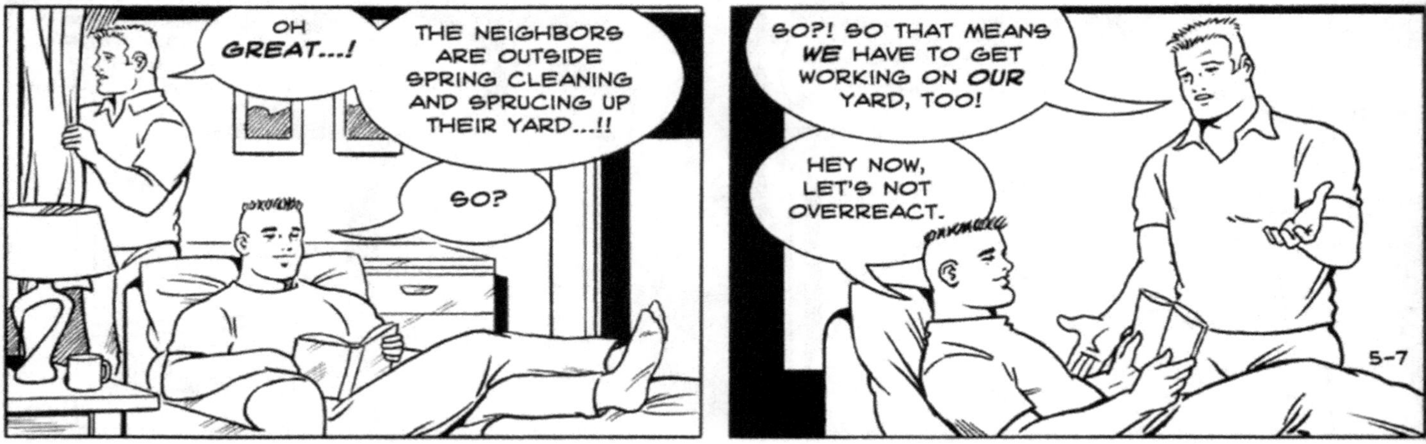
OH GREAT...!
THE NEIGHBORS ARE OUTSIDE SPRING CLEANING AND SPRUCING UP THEIR YARD...!!
SO?
SO?! SO THAT MEANS WE HAVE TO GET WORKING ON OUR YARD, TOO!
HEY NOW, LET'S NOT OVERREACT.
5-7

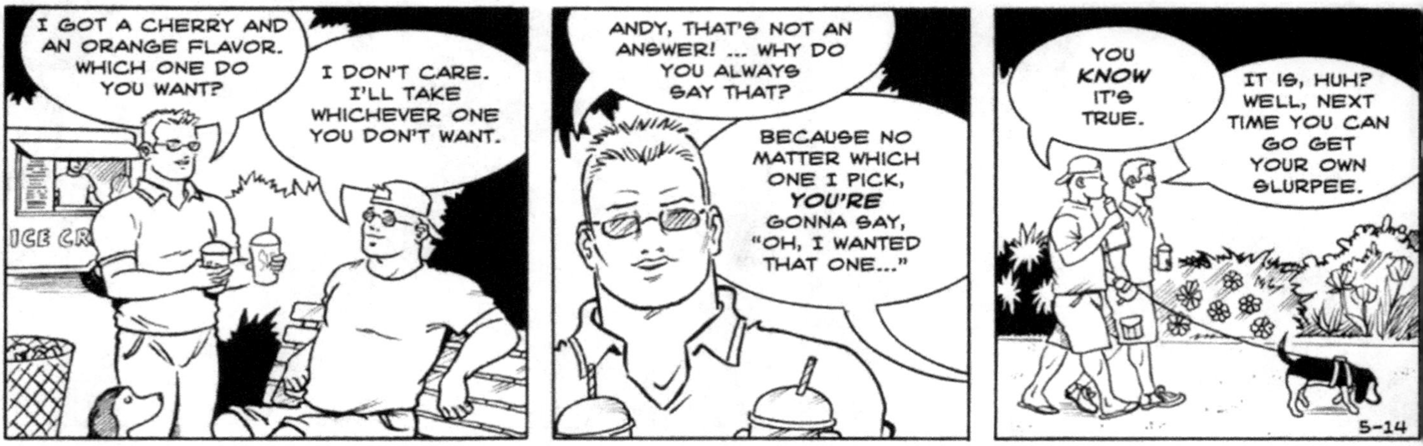
I GOT A CHERRY AND AN ORANGE FLAVOR. WHICH ONE DO YOU WANT?
I DON'T CARE. I'LL TAKE WHICHEVER ONE YOU DON'T WANT.
ICE CR
ANDY, THAT'S NOT AN ANSWER! ... WHY DO YOU ALWAYS SAY THAT?
BECAUSE NO MATTER WHICH ONE I PICK, YOU'RE GONNA SAY, "OH, I WANTED THAT ONE..."
YOU KNOW IT'S TRUE.
IT IS, HUH? WELL, NEXT TIME YOU CAN GO GET YOUR OWN SLURPEE.
5-14

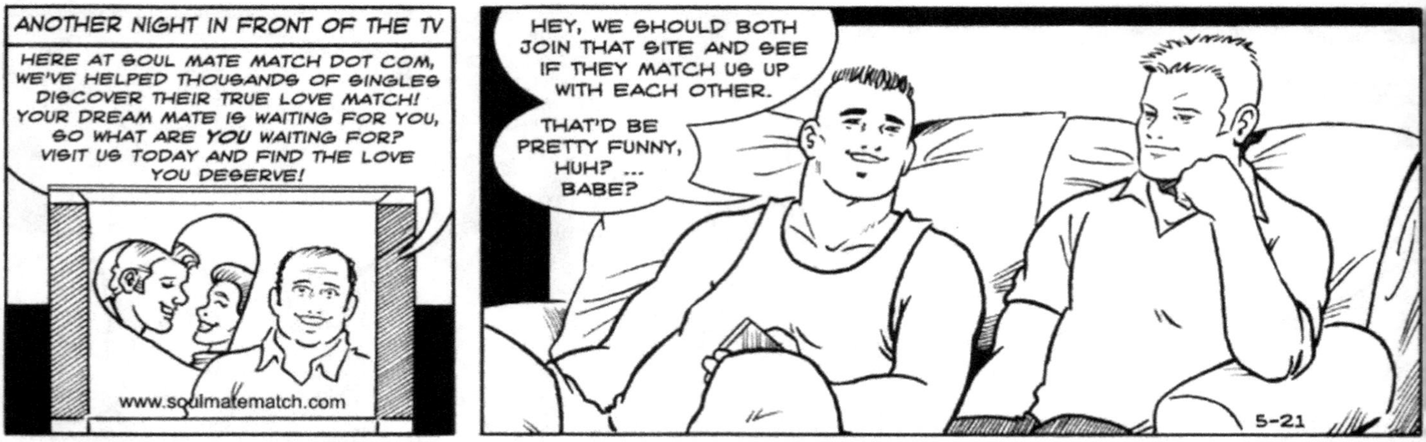
ANOTHER NIGHT IN FRONT OF THE TV
HERE AT SOUL MATE MATCH DOT COM, WE'VE HELPED THOUSANDS OF SINGLES DISCOVER THEIR TRUE LOVE MATCH! YOUR DREAM MATE IS WAITING FOR YOU, SO WHAT ARE YOU WAITING FOR? VISIT US TODAY AND FIND THE LOVE YOU DESERVE!
www.soulmatematch.com
HEY, WE SHOULD BOTH JOIN THAT SITE AND SEE IF THEY MATCH US UP WITH EACH OTHER.
THAT'D BE PRETTY FUNNY, HUH? ... BABE?
5-21

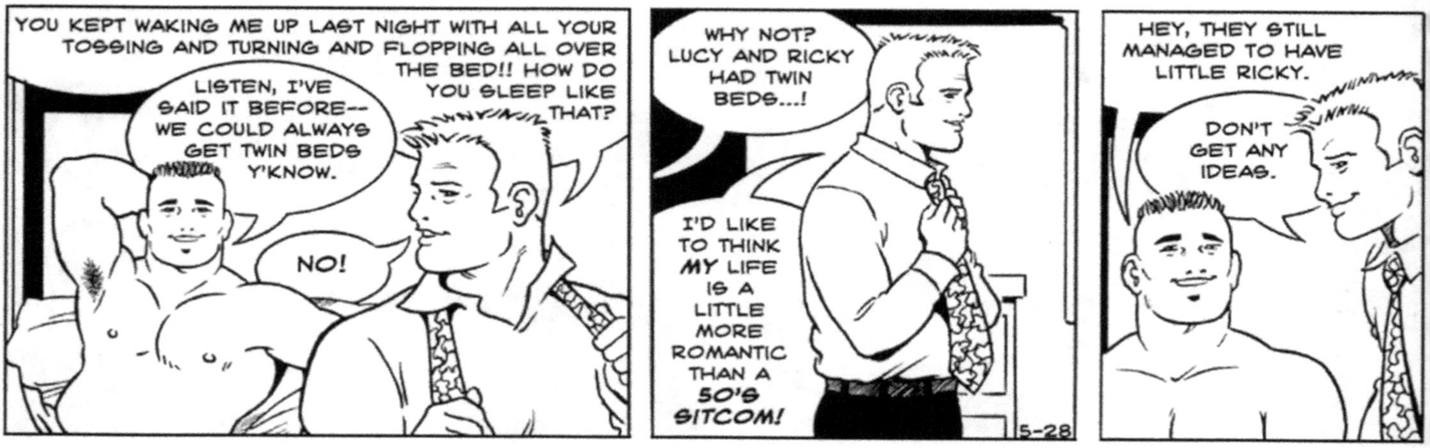
YOU KEPT WAKING ME UP LAST NIGHT WITH ALL YOUR TOSSING AND TURNING AND FLOPPING ALL OVER THE BED!! HOW DO YOU SLEEP LIKE THAT?
LISTEN, I'VE SAID IT BEFORE-- WE COULD ALWAYS GET TWIN BEDS Y'KNOW.
NO!
WHY NOT? LUCY AND RICKY HAD TWIN BEDS...!
I'D LIKE TO THINK MY LIFE IS A LITTLE MORE ROMANTIC THAN A 50'S SITCOM!
5-28
HEY, THEY STILL MANAGED TO HAVE LITTLE RICKY.
DON'T GET ANY IDEAS.

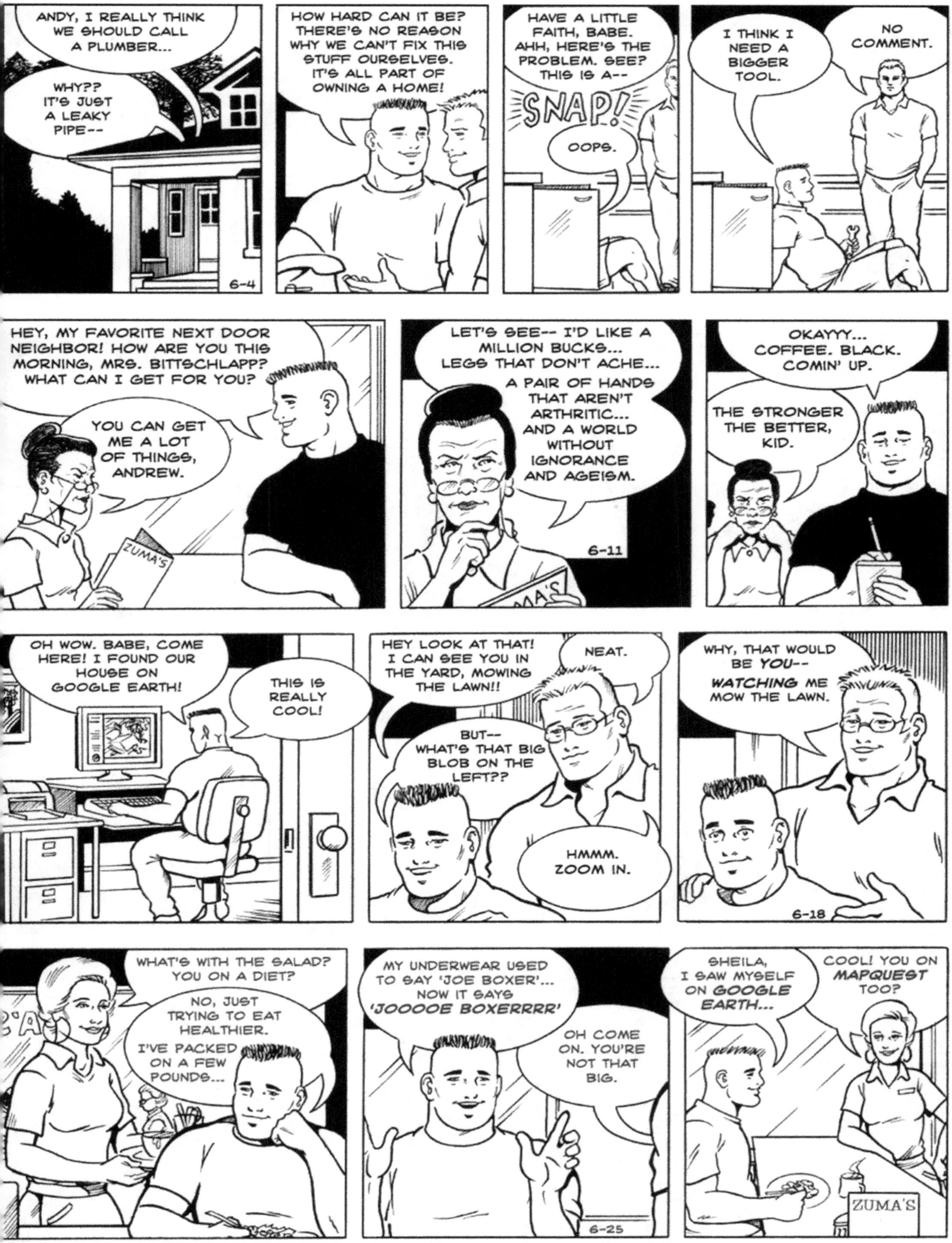
ANDY, I REALLY THINK WE SHOULD CALL A PLUMBER...
WHY?? IT'S JUST A LEAKY PIPE--
6-4
HOW HARD CAN IT BE? THERE'S NO REASON WHY WE CAN'T FIX THIS STUFF OURSELVES. IT'S ALL PART OF OWNING A HOME!
HAVE A LITTLE FAITH, BABE. AHH, HERE'S THE PROBLEM. SEE? THIS IS A--
SNAP!
OOPS.
I THINK I NEED A BIGGER TOOL.
NO COMMENT.
HEY, MY FAVORITE NEXT DOOR NEIGHBOR! HOW ARE YOU THIS MORNING, MRS. BITTSCHLAPP? WHAT CAN I GET FOR YOU?
YOU CAN GET ME A LOT OF THINGS, ANDREW.
ZUMA'S
LET'S SEE-- I'D LIKE A MILLION BUCKS... LEGS THAT DON'T ACHE...
A PAIR OF HANDS THAT AREN'T ARTHRITIC... AND A WORLD WITHOUT IGNORANCE AND AGEISM.
6-11
OKAYYY... COFFEE. BLACK. COMIN' UP.
THE STRONGER THE BETTER, KID.
OH WOW. BABE, COME HERE! I FOUND OUR HOUSE ON GOOGLE EARTH!
THIS IS REALLY COOL!
HEY LOOK AT THAT! I CAN SEE YOU IN THE YARD, MOWING THE LAWN!!
NEAT.
BUT-- WHAT'S THAT BIG BLOB ON THE LEFT??
HMMM. ZOOM IN.
WHY, THAT WOULD BE *YOU--* *WATCHING* ME MOW THE LAWN.
6-18
WHAT'S WITH THE SALAD? YOU ON A DIET?
NO, JUST TRYING TO EAT HEALTHIER.
I'VE PACKED ON A FEW POUNDS...
MY UNDERWEAR USED TO SAY 'JOE BOXER'... NOW IT SAYS *'JOOOOE BOXERRRR'*
OH COME ON. YOU'RE NOT THAT BIG.
6-25
SHEILA, I SAW MYSELF ON *GOOGLE EARTH...*
COOL! YOU ON *MAPQUEST* TOO?
ZUMA'S

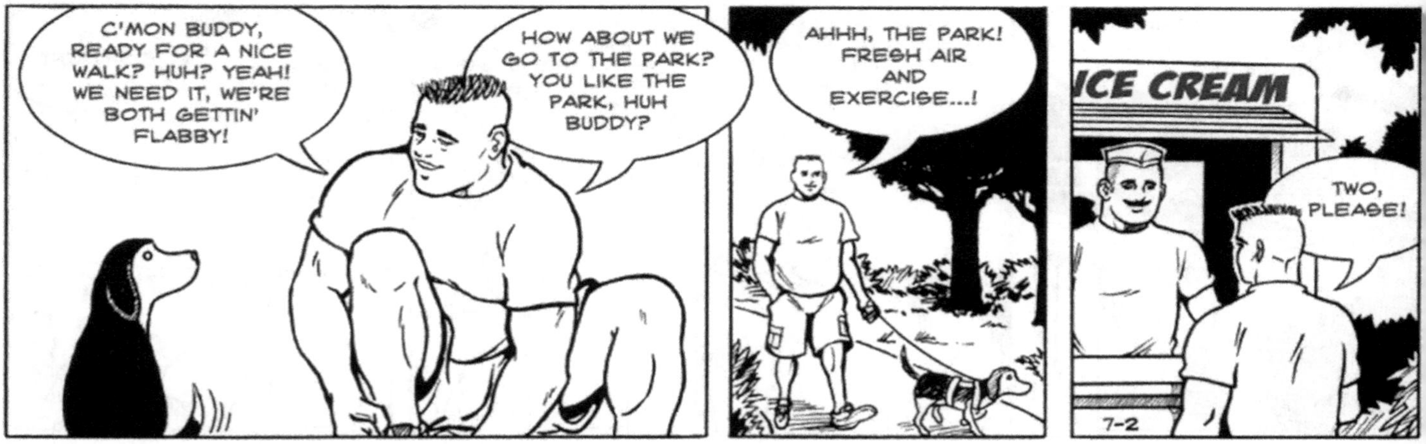
C'MON BUDDY, READY FOR A NICE WALK? HUH? YEAH! WE NEED IT, WE'RE BOTH GETTIN' FLABBY!
HOW ABOUT WE GO TO THE PARK? YOU LIKE THE PARK, HUH BUDDY?
AHHH, THE PARK! FRESH AIR AND EXERCISE...!
ICE CREAM
TWO, PLEASE!
7-2

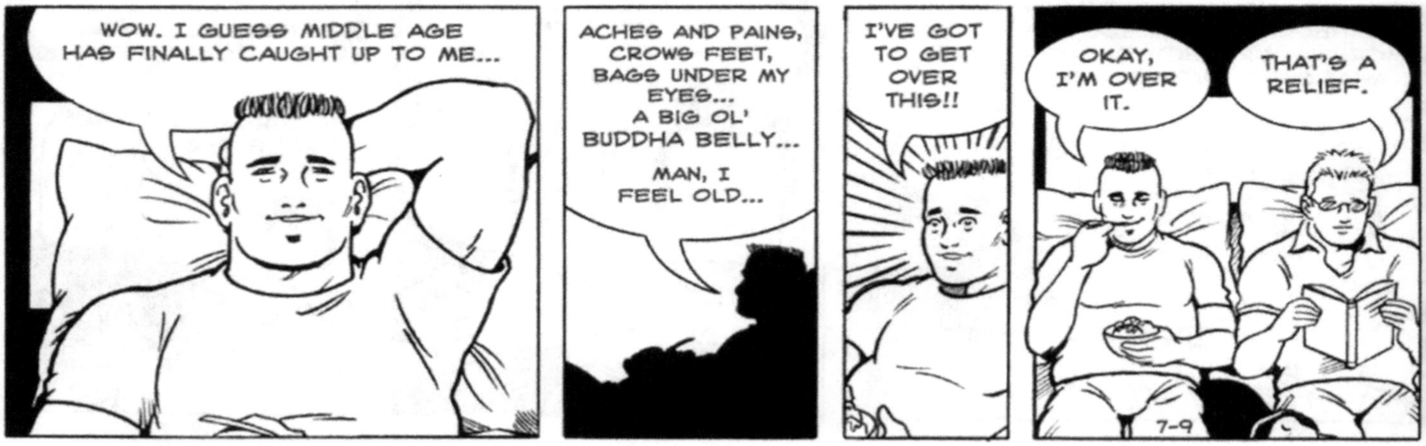
WOW. I GUESS MIDDLE AGE HAS FINALLY CAUGHT UP TO ME...
ACHES AND PAINS, CROWS FEET, BAGS UNDER MY EYES... A BIG OL' BUDDHA BELLY...
MAN, I FEEL OLD...
I'VE GOT TO GET OVER THIS!!
OKAY, I'M OVER IT.
THAT'S A RELIEF.
7-9

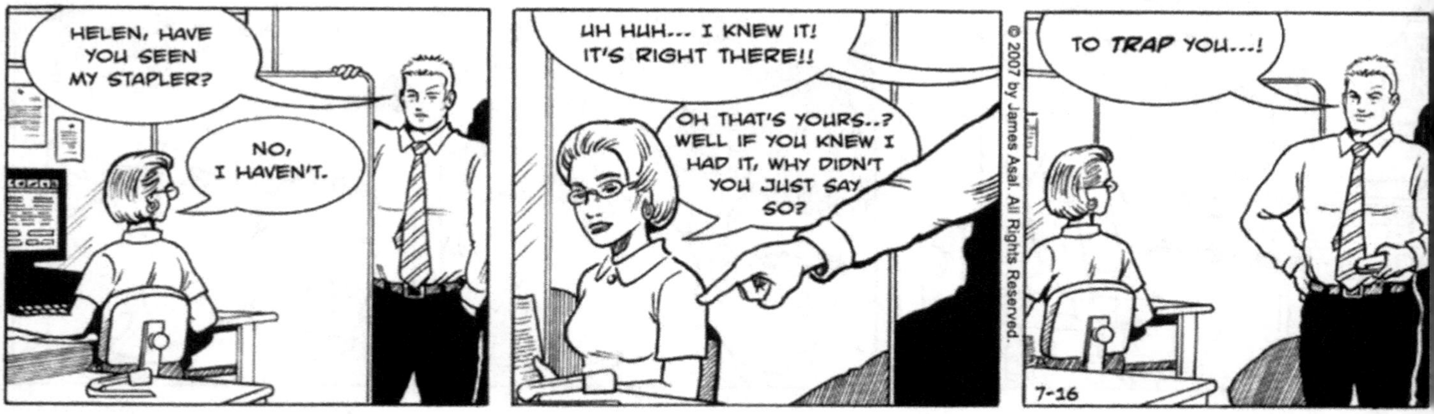
HELEN, HAVE YOU SEEN MY STAPLER?
NO, I HAVEN'T.
UH HUH... I KNEW IT! IT'S RIGHT THERE!!
OH THAT'S YOURS..? WELL IF YOU KNEW I HAD IT, WHY DIDN'T YOU JUST SAY SO?
© 2007 by James Asal. All Rights Reserved.
TO TRAP YOU...!
7-16

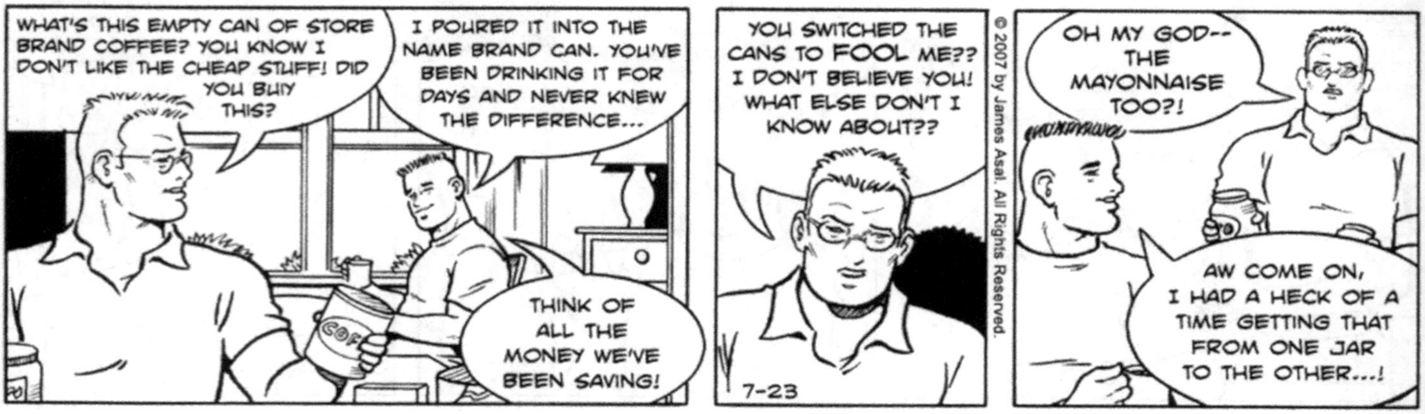
WHAT'S THIS EMPTY CAN OF STORE BRAND COFFEE? YOU KNOW I DON'T LIKE THE CHEAP STUFF! DID YOU BUY THIS?
I POURED IT INTO THE NAME BRAND CAN. YOU'VE BEEN DRINKING IT FOR DAYS AND NEVER KNEW THE DIFFERENCE...
THINK OF ALL THE MONEY WE'VE BEEN SAVING!
YOU SWITCHED THE CANS TO FOOL ME?? I DON'T BELIEVE YOU! WHAT ELSE DON'T I KNOW ABOUT??
7-23
© 2007 by James Asal. All Rights Reserved.
OH MY GOD-- THE MAYONNAISE TOO?!
AW COME ON, I HAD A HECK OF A TIME GETTING THAT FROM ONE JAR TO THE OTHER...!

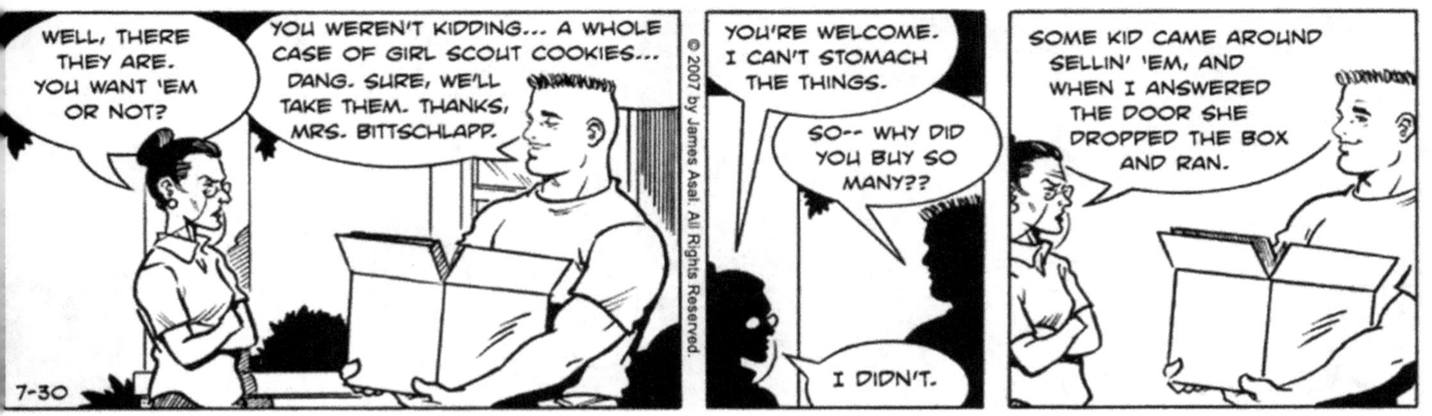
WELL, THERE THEY ARE. YOU WANT 'EM OR NOT?
YOU WEREN'T KIDDING... A WHOLE CASE OF GIRL SCOUT COOKIES... DANG. SURE, WE'LL TAKE THEM. THANKS, MRS. BITTSCHLAPP.
7-30
© 2007 by James Asal. All Rights Reserved.
YOU'RE WELCOME. I CAN'T STOMACH THE THINGS.
SO-- WHY DID YOU BUY SO MANY??
I DIDN'T.
SOME KID CAME AROUND SELLIN' 'EM, AND WHEN I ANSWERED THE DOOR SHE DROPPED THE BOX AND RAN.

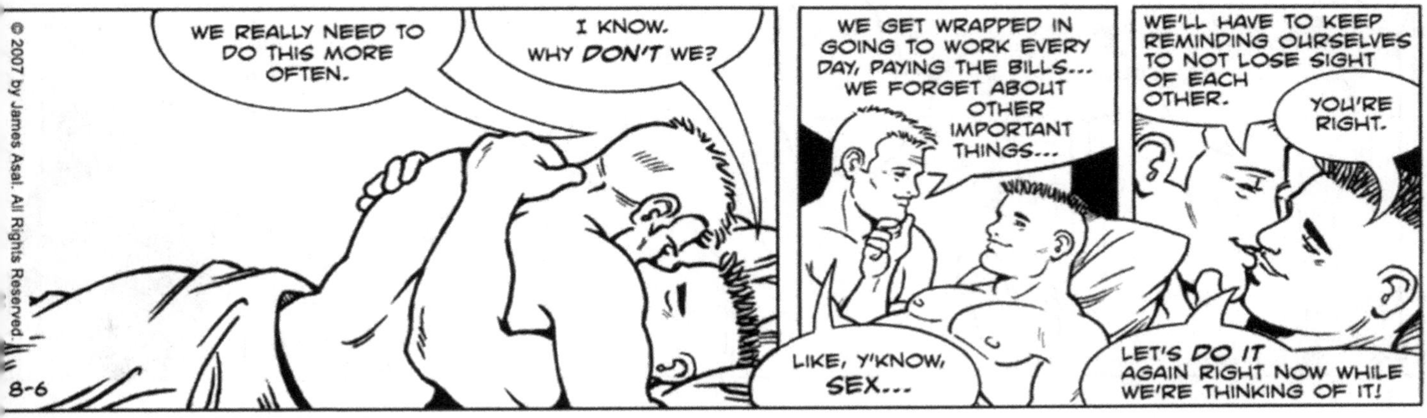
© 2007 by James Asal. All Rights Reserved.
8-6
WE REALLY NEED TO DO THIS MORE OFTEN.
I KNOW. WHY DON'T WE?
WE GET WRAPPED IN GOING TO WORK EVERY DAY, PAYING THE BILLS... WE FORGET ABOUT OTHER IMPORTANT THINGS...
LIKE, Y'KNOW, SEX...
WE'LL HAVE TO KEEP REMINDING OURSELVES TO NOT LOSE SIGHT OF EACH OTHER.
YOU'RE RIGHT.
LET'S DO IT AGAIN RIGHT NOW WHILE WE'RE THINKING OF IT!

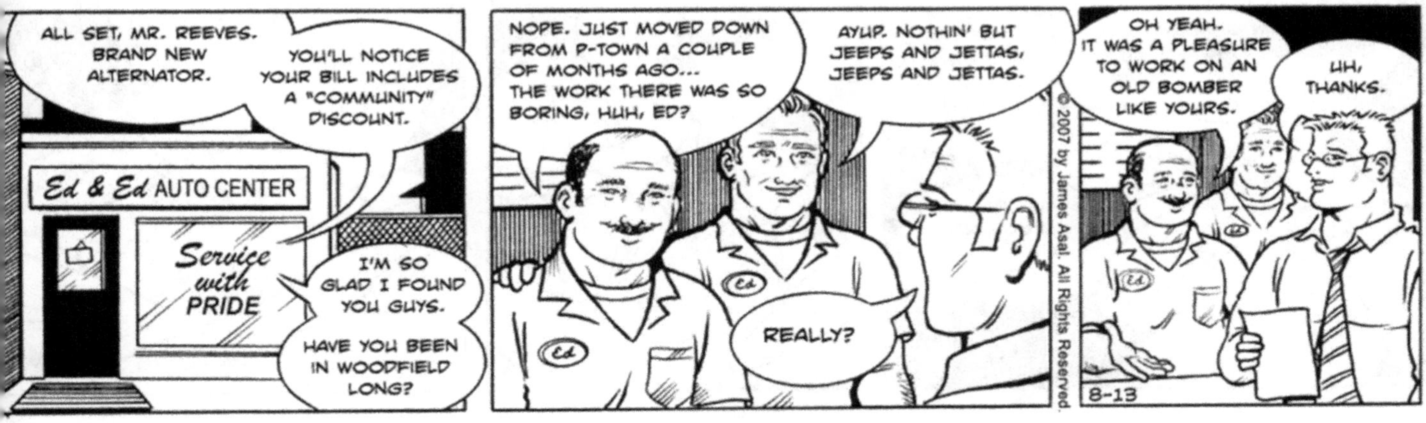
ALL SET, MR. REEVES. BRAND NEW ALTERNATOR.
YOU'LL NOTICE YOUR BILL INCLUDES A "COMMUNITY" DISCOUNT.
Ed & Ed AUTO CENTER
Service with PRIDE
I'M SO GLAD I FOUND YOU GUYS.
HAVE YOU BEEN IN WOODFIELD LONG?
NOPE. JUST MOVED DOWN FROM P-TOWN A COUPLE OF MONTHS AGO... THE WORK THERE WAS SO BORING, HUH, ED?
AYUP. NOTHIN' BUT JEEPS AND JETTAS. JEEPS AND JETTAS.
REALLY?
© 2007 by James Asal. All Rights Reserved.
OH YEAH. IT WAS A PLEASURE TO WORK ON AN OLD BOMBER LIKE YOURS.
UH, THANKS.
8-13

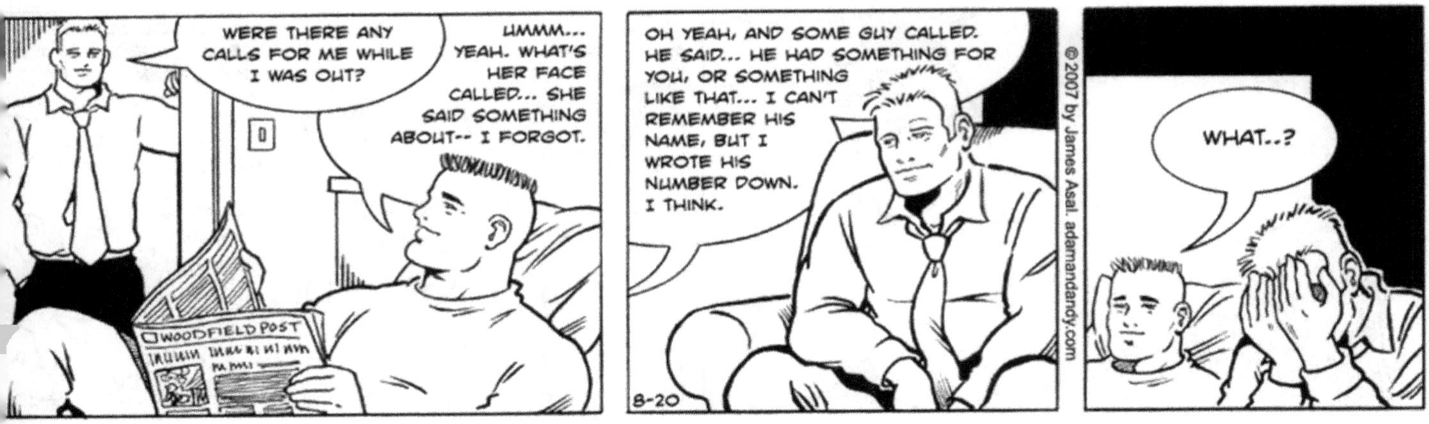
WERE THERE ANY CALLS FOR ME WHILE I WAS OUT?
UMMM... YEAH. WHAT'S HER FACE CALLED... SHE SAID SOMETHING ABOUT-- I FORGOT.
WOODFIELD POST
OH YEAH, AND SOME GUY CALLED. HE SAID... HE HAD SOMETHING FOR YOU, OR SOMETHING LIKE THAT... I CAN'T REMEMBER HIS NAME, BUT I WROTE HIS NUMBER DOWN. I THINK.
8-20
© 2007 by James Asal. adamandandy.com
WHAT..?

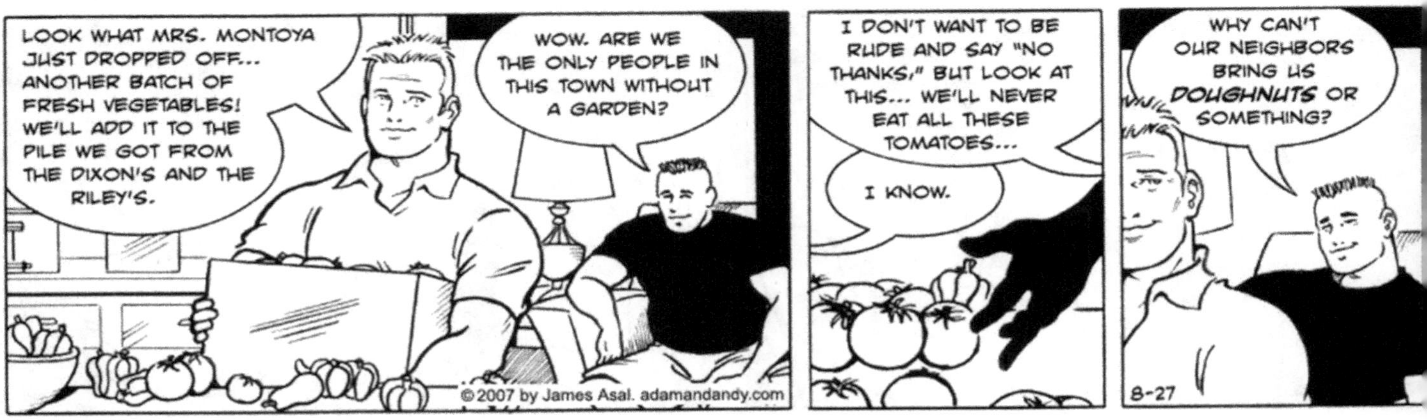
LOOK WHAT MRS. MONTOYA JUST DROPPED OFF... ANOTHER BATCH OF FRESH VEGETABLES! WE'LL ADD IT TO THE PILE WE GOT FROM THE DIXON'S AND THE RILEY'S.
WOW. ARE WE THE ONLY PEOPLE IN THIS TOWN WITHOUT A GARDEN?
© 2007 by James Asal. adamandandy.com
I DON'T WANT TO BE RUDE AND SAY "NO THANKS," BUT LOOK AT THIS... WE'LL NEVER EAT ALL THESE TOMATOES...
I KNOW.
WHY CAN'T OUR NEIGHBORS BRING US DOUGHNUTS OR SOMETHING?
8-27

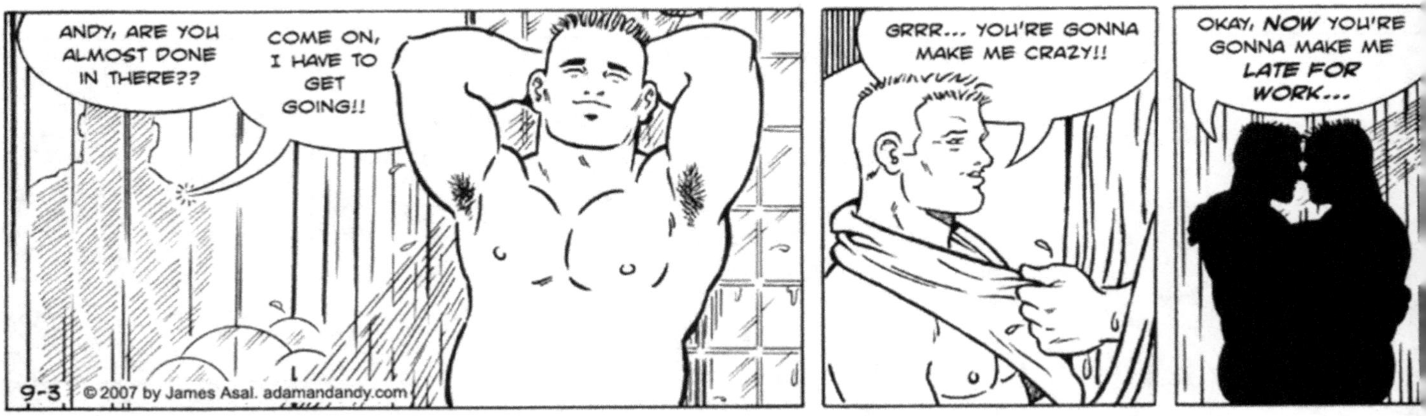
ANDY, ARE YOU ALMOST DONE IN THERE??
COME ON, I HAVE TO GET GOING!!
9-3
© 2007 by James Asal. adamandandy.com
GRRR... YOU'RE GONNA MAKE ME CRAZY!!
OKAY, NOW YOU'RE GONNA MAKE ME LATE FOR WORK...

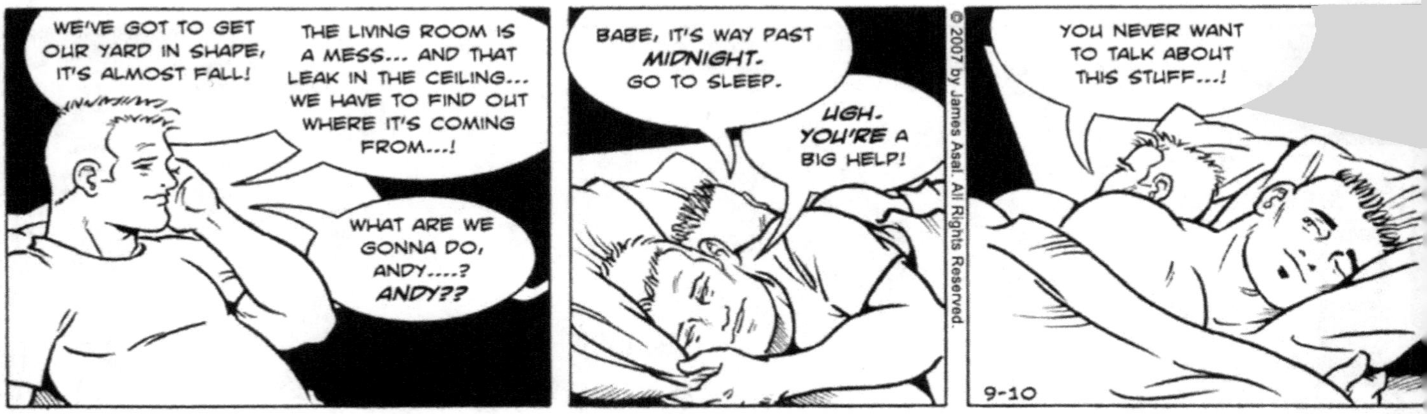
WE'VE GOT TO GET OUR YARD IN SHAPE, IT'S ALMOST FALL!
THE LIVING ROOM IS A MESS... AND THAT LEAK IN THE CEILING... WE HAVE TO FIND OUT WHERE IT'S COMING FROM...!
WHAT ARE WE GONNA DO, ANDY....? ANDY??
BABE, IT'S WAY PAST MIDNIGHT. GO TO SLEEP.
UGH. YOU'RE A BIG HELP!
© 2007 by James Asal. All Rights Reserved.
YOU NEVER WANT TO TALK ABOUT THIS STUFF...!
9-10

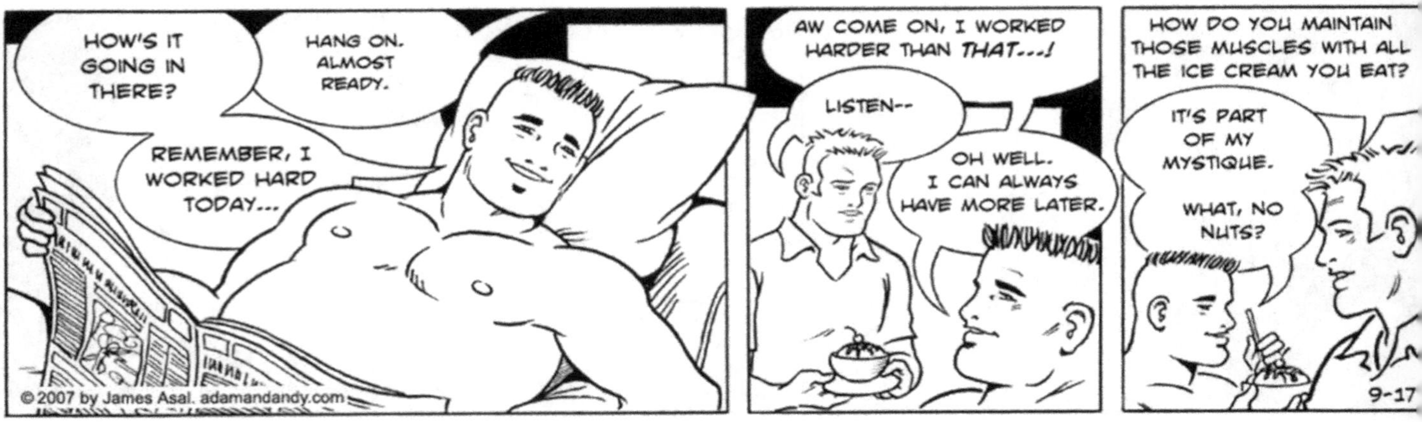
HOW'S IT GOING IN THERE?
HANG ON. ALMOST READY.
REMEMBER, I WORKED HARD TODAY...
© 2007 by James Asal. adamandandy.com
AW COME ON, I WORKED HARDER THAN THAT...!
LISTEN--
OH WELL. I CAN ALWAYS HAVE MORE LATER.
HOW DO YOU MAINTAIN THOSE MUSCLES WITH ALL THE ICE CREAM YOU EAT?
IT'S PART OF MY MYSTIQUE.
WHAT, NO NUTS?
9-17

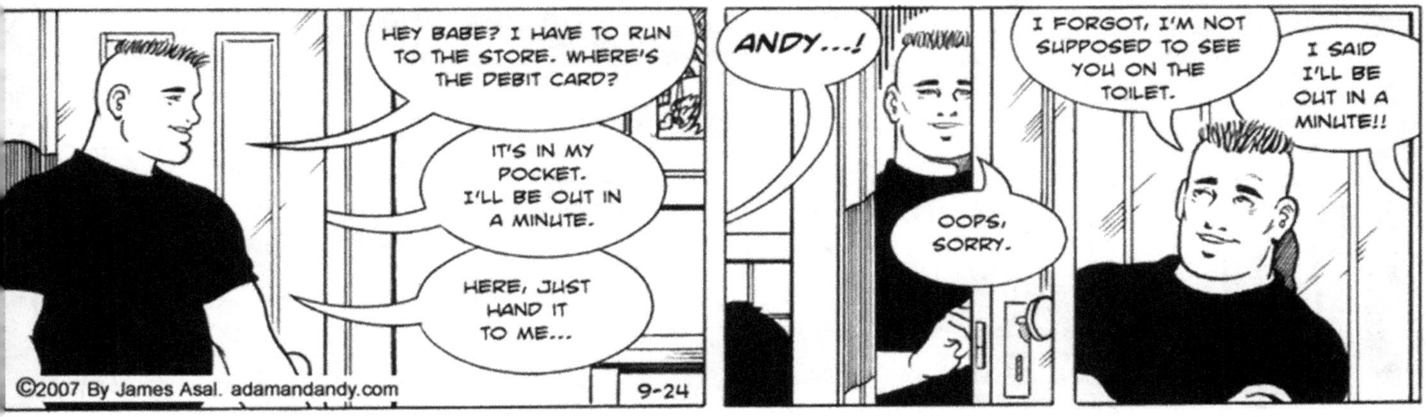
HEY BABE? I HAVE TO RUN TO THE STORE. WHERE'S THE DEBIT CARD?
IT'S IN MY POCKET. I'LL BE OUT IN A MINUTE.
HERE, JUST HAND IT TO ME...
©2007 By James Asal. adamandandy.com
9-24
ANDY...!
OOPS, SORRY.
I FORGOT, I'M NOT SUPPOSED TO SEE YOU ON THE TOILET.
I SAID I'LL BE OUT IN A MINUTE!!

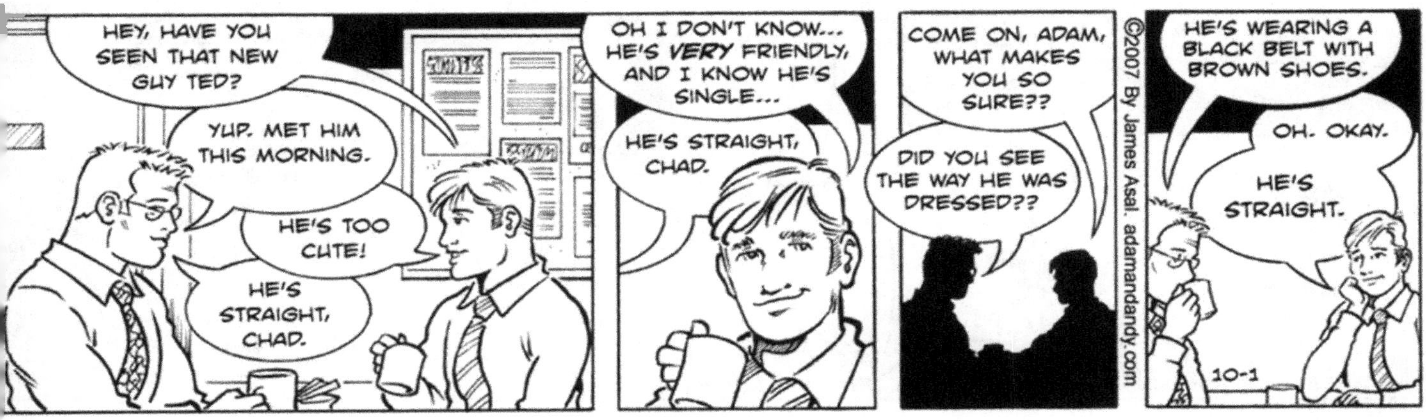
HEY, HAVE YOU SEEN THAT NEW GUY TED?
YUP. MET HIM THIS MORNING.
HE'S TOO CUTE!
HE'S STRAIGHT, CHAD.
OH I DON'T KNOW... HE'S VERY FRIENDLY, AND I KNOW HE'S SINGLE...
HE'S STRAIGHT, CHAD.
COME ON, ADAM, WHAT MAKES YOU SO SURE??
DID YOU SEE THE WAY HE WAS DRESSED??
©2007 By James Asal. adamandandy.com
HE'S WEARING A BLACK BELT WITH BROWN SHOES.
OH. OKAY.
HE'S STRAIGHT.
10-1

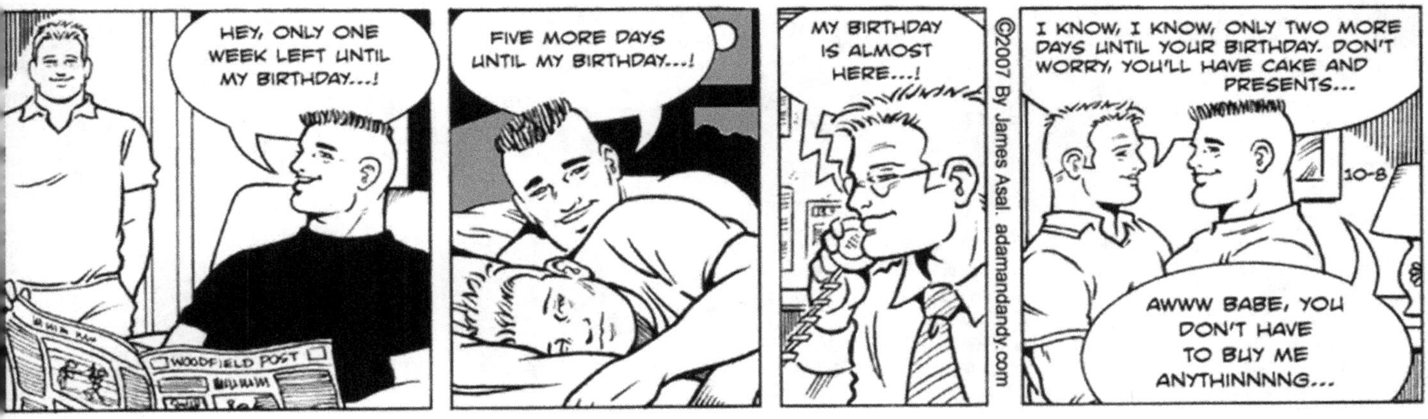
HEY, ONLY ONE WEEK LEFT UNTIL MY BIRTHDAY...!
WOODFIELD POST
FIVE MORE DAYS UNTIL MY BIRTHDAY...!
MY BIRTHDAY IS ALMOST HERE...!
©2007 By James Asal. adamandandy.com
I KNOW, I KNOW, ONLY TWO MORE DAYS UNTIL YOUR BIRTHDAY. DON'T WORRY, YOU'LL HAVE CAKE AND PRESENTS...
10-8
AWWW BABE, YOU DON'T HAVE TO BUY ME ANYTHINNNNG...

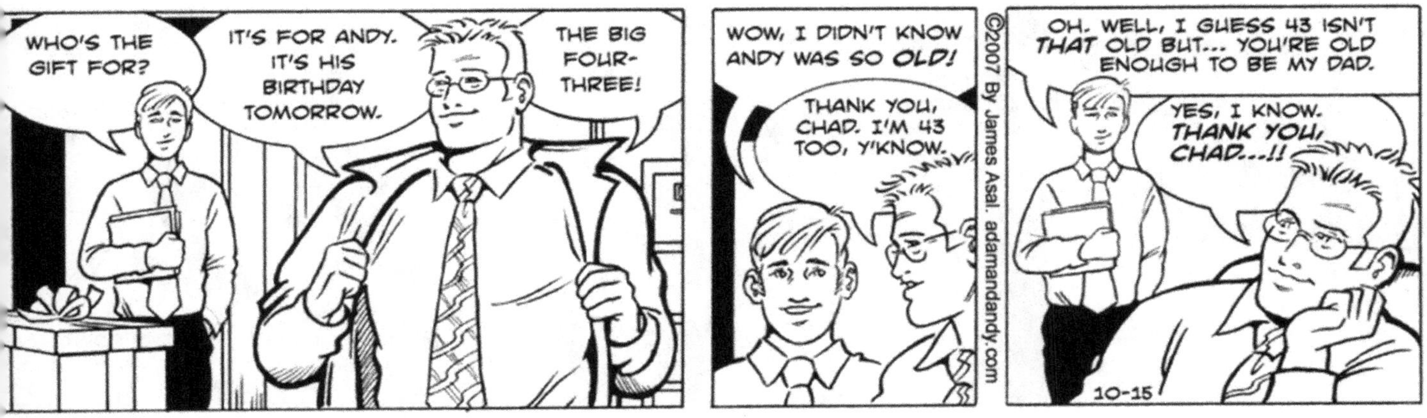
WHO'S THE GIFT FOR?
IT'S FOR ANDY. IT'S HIS BIRTHDAY TOMORROW.
THE BIG FOUR-THREE!
WOW, I DIDN'T KNOW ANDY WAS SO OLD!
THANK YOU, CHAD. I'M 43 TOO, Y'KNOW.
©2007 By James Asal. adamandandy.com
OH. WELL, I GUESS 43 ISN'T THAT OLD BUT... YOU'RE OLD ENOUGH TO BE MY DAD.
YES, I KNOW. THANK YOU, CHAD...!!
10-15

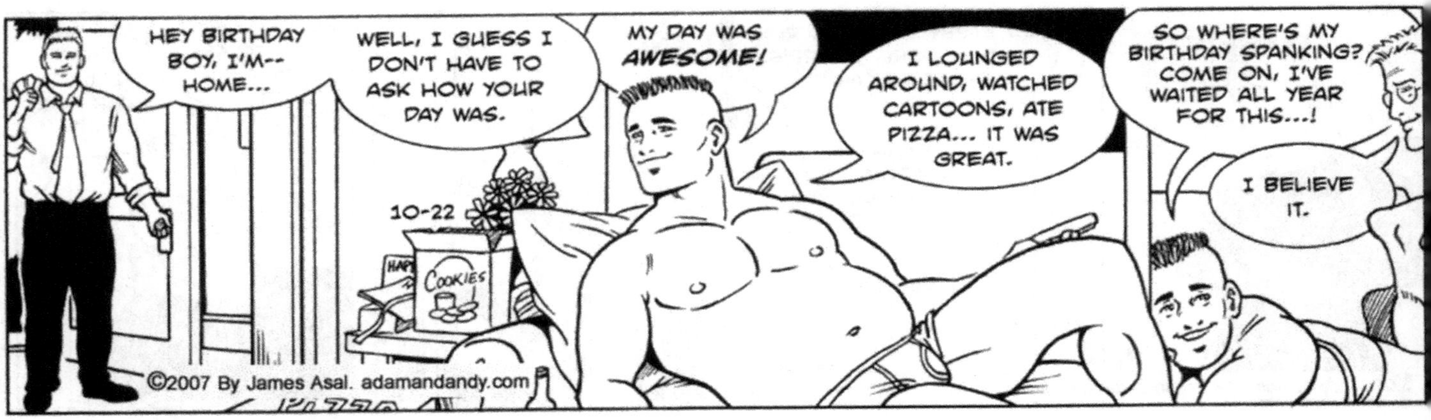
HEY BIRTHDAY BOY, I'M-- HOME...
WELL, I GUESS I DON'T HAVE TO ASK HOW YOUR DAY WAS.
10-22
COOKIES
©2007 By James Asal. adamandandy.com
MY DAY WAS AWESOME!
I LOUNGED AROUND, WATCHED CARTOONS, ATE PIZZA... IT WAS GREAT.
SO WHERE'S MY BIRTHDAY SPANKING? COME ON, I'VE WAITED ALL YEAR FOR THIS...!
I BELIEVE IT.

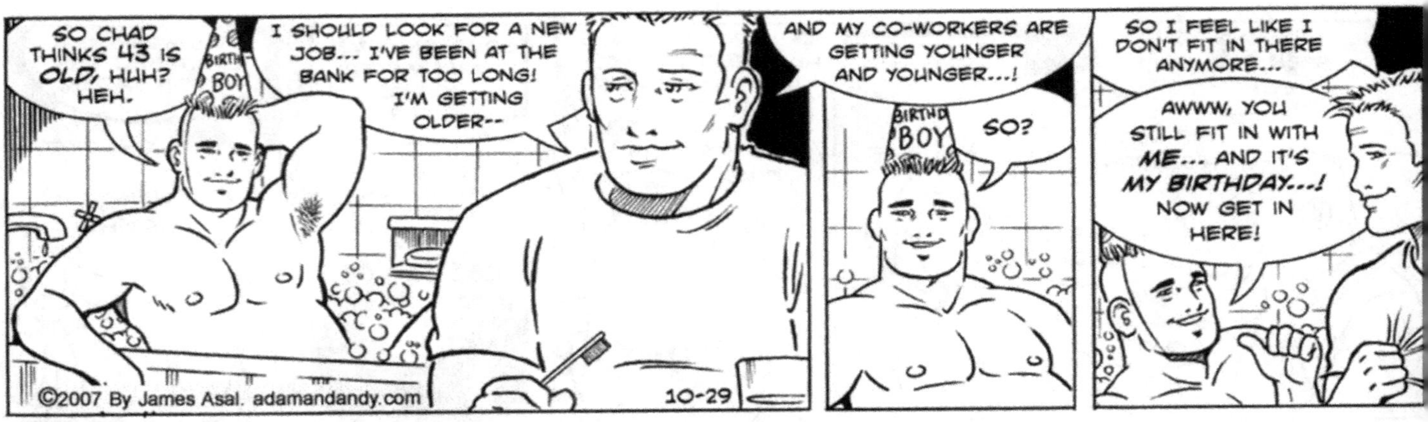
SO CHAD THINKS 43 IS OLD, HUH? HEH.
I SHOULD LOOK FOR A NEW JOB... I'VE BEEN AT THE BANK FOR TOO LONG! I'M GETTING OLDER--
©2007 By James Asal. adamandandy.com
10-29
AND MY CO-WORKERS ARE GETTING YOUNGER AND YOUNGER...!
SO?
SO I FEEL LIKE I DON'T FIT IN THERE ANYMORE...
AWWW, YOU STILL FIT IN WITH ME... AND IT'S MY BIRTHDAY...! NOW GET IN HERE!

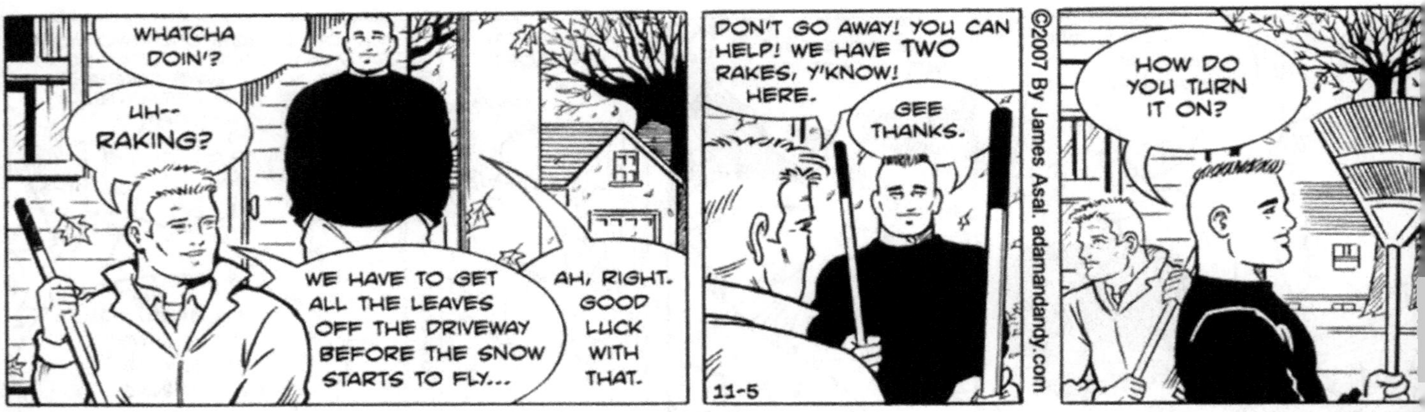
WHATCHA DOIN'?
UH-- RAKING?
WE HAVE TO GET ALL THE LEAVES OFF THE DRIVEWAY BEFORE THE SNOW STARTS TO FLY...
AH, RIGHT. GOOD LUCK WITH THAT.
DON'T GO AWAY! YOU CAN HELP! WE HAVE TWO RAKES, Y'KNOW! HERE.
GEE THANKS.
11-5
©2007 By James Asal. adamandandy.com
HOW DO YOU TURN IT ON?

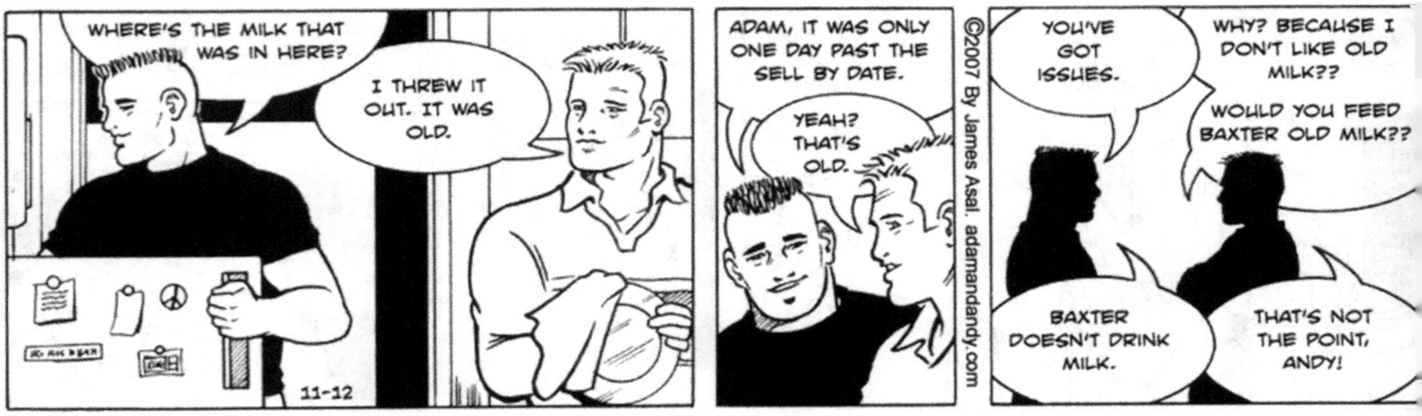
WHERE'S THE MILK THAT WAS IN HERE?
I THREW IT OUT. IT WAS OLD.
11-12
ADAM, IT WAS ONLY ONE DAY PAST THE SELL BY DATE.
YEAH? THAT'S OLD.
©2007 By James Asal. adamandandy.com
YOU'VE GOT ISSUES.
WHY? BECAUSE I DON'T LIKE OLD MILK?? WOULD YOU FEED BAXTER OLD MILK??
BAXTER DOESN'T DRINK MILK.
THAT'S NOT THE POINT, ANDY!

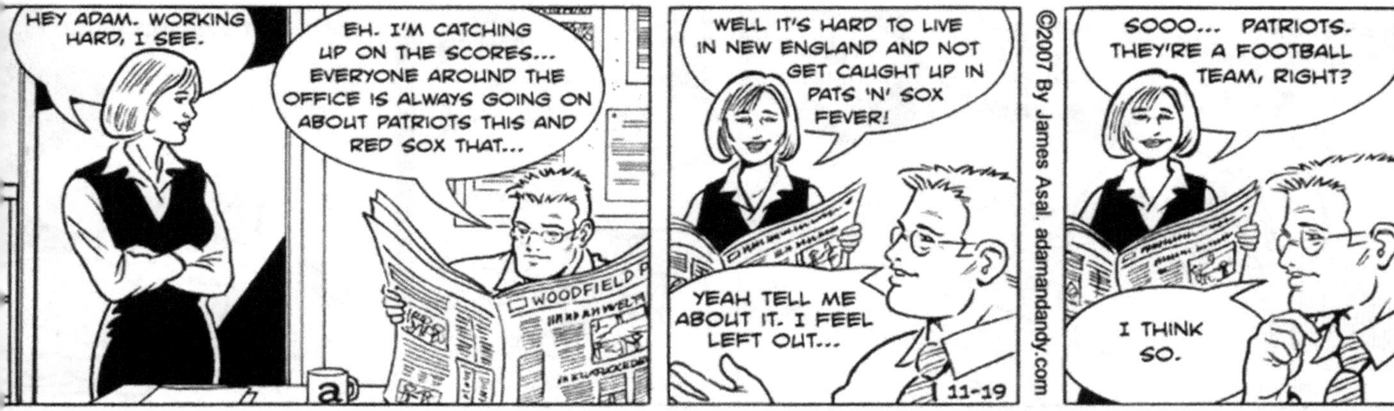
HEY ADAM. WORKING HARD, I SEE.
EH. I'M CATCHING UP ON THE SCORES... EVERYONE AROUND THE OFFICE IS ALWAYS GOING ON ABOUT PATRIOTS THIS AND RED SOX THAT...
WELL IT'S HARD TO LIVE IN NEW ENGLAND AND NOT GET CAUGHT UP IN PATS 'N' SOX FEVER!
YEAH TELL ME ABOUT IT. I FEEL LEFT OUT...
11-19
©2007 By James Asal. adamandandy.com
SOOO... PATRIOTS. THEY'RE A FOOTBALL TEAM, RIGHT?
I THINK SO.

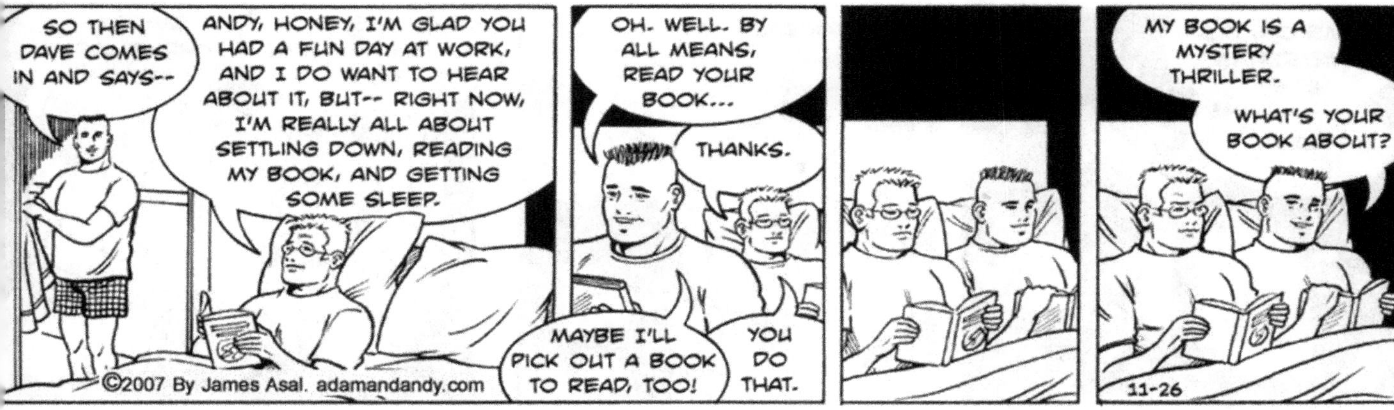
SO THEN DAVE COMES IN AND SAYS--
ANDY, HONEY, I'M GLAD YOU HAD A FUN DAY AT WORK, AND I DO WANT TO HEAR ABOUT IT, BUT-- RIGHT NOW, I'M REALLY ALL ABOUT SETTLING DOWN, READING MY BOOK, AND GETTING SOME SLEEP.
©2007 By James Asal. adamandandy.com
OH. WELL. BY ALL MEANS, READ YOUR BOOK...
THANKS.
MAYBE I'LL PICK OUT A BOOK TO READ, TOO!
YOU DO THAT.
MY BOOK IS A MYSTERY THRILLER.
WHAT'S YOUR BOOK ABOUT?
11-26

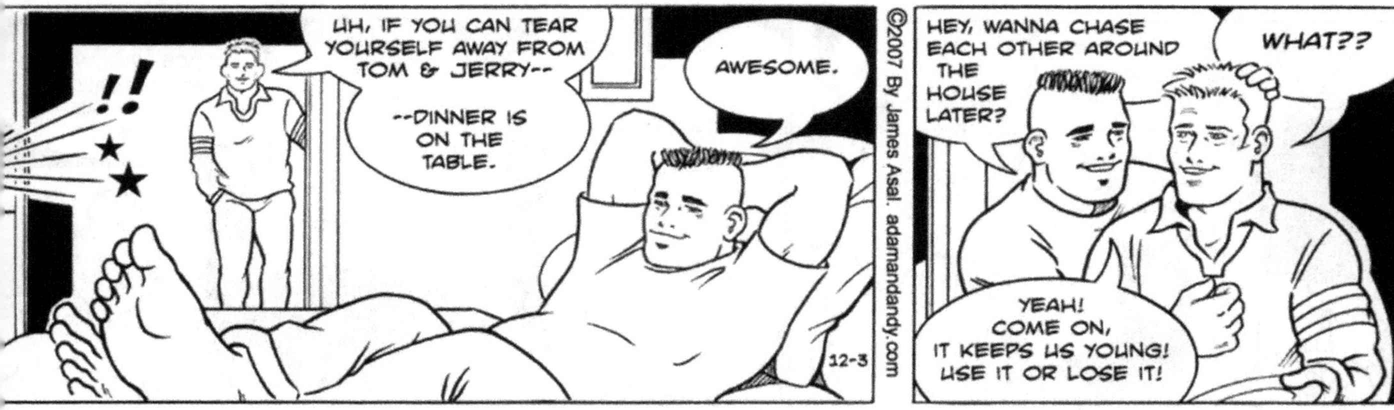
UH, IF YOU CAN TEAR YOURSELF AWAY FROM TOM & JERRY--
--DINNER IS ON THE TABLE.
AWESOME.
12-3
©2007 By James Asal. adamandandy.com
HEY, WANNA CHASE EACH OTHER AROUND THE HOUSE LATER?
WHAT??
YEAH! COME ON, IT KEEPS US YOUNG! USE IT OR LOSE IT!

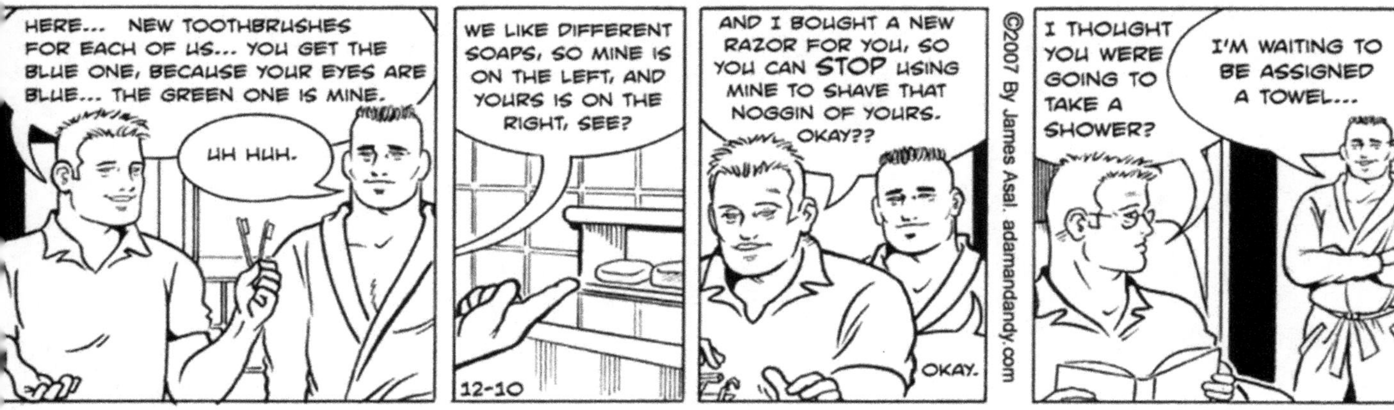
HERE... NEW TOOTHBRUSHES FOR EACH OF US... YOU GET THE BLUE ONE, BECAUSE YOUR EYES ARE BLUE... THE GREEN ONE IS MINE.
UH HUH.
WE LIKE DIFFERENT SOAPS, SO MINE IS ON THE LEFT, AND YOURS IS ON THE RIGHT, SEE?
12-10
AND I BOUGHT A NEW RAZOR FOR YOU, SO YOU CAN STOP USING MINE TO SHAVE THAT NOGGIN OF YOURS. OKAY??
OKAY.
©2007 By James Asal. adamandandy.com
I THOUGHT YOU WERE GOING TO TAKE A SHOWER?
I'M WAITING TO BE ASSIGNED A TOWEL...

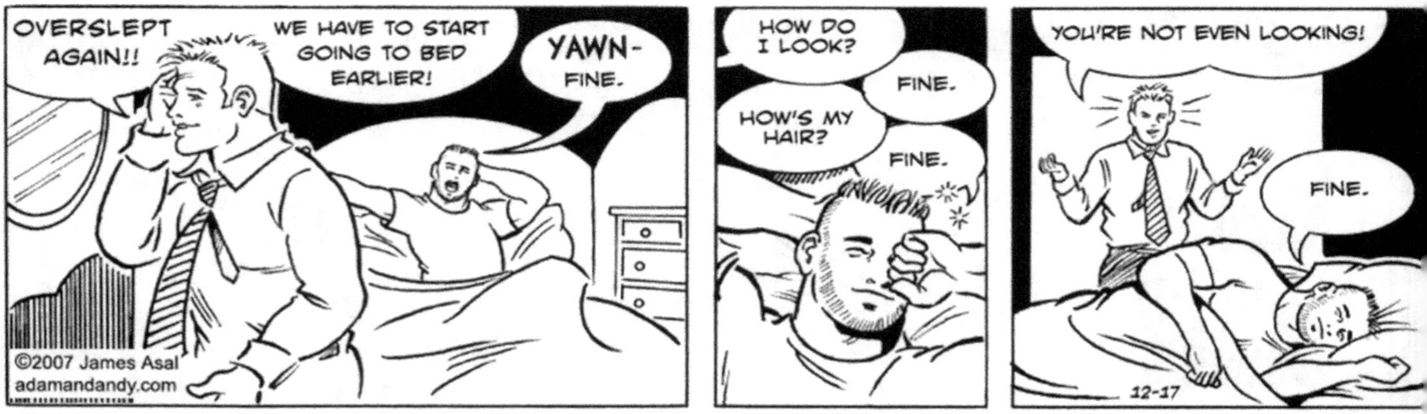
OVERSLEPT AGAIN!!
WE HAVE TO START GOING TO BED EARLIER!
YAWN- FINE.
©2007 James Asal
adamandandy.com
HOW DO I LOOK?
FINE.
HOW'S MY HAIR?
FINE.
YOU'RE NOT EVEN LOOKING!
FINE.
12-17

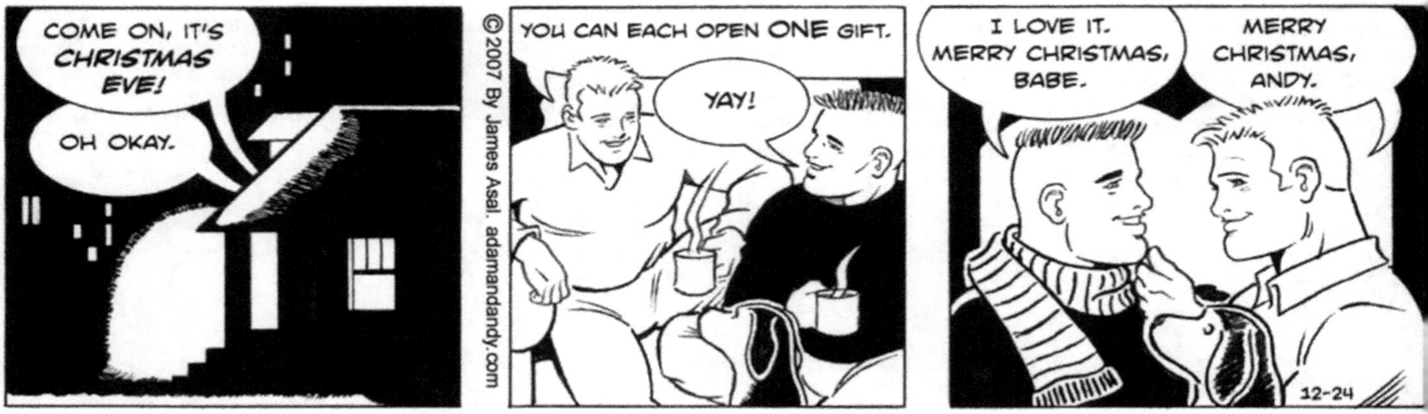
COME ON, IT'S CHRISTMAS EVE!
OH OKAY.
© 2007 By James Asal. adamandandy.com
YOU CAN EACH OPEN ONE GIFT.
YAY!
I LOVE IT. MERRY CHRISTMAS, BABE.
MERRY CHRISTMAS, ANDY.
12-24

Merry Christmas AND Happy Holidays TO ALL FROM ADAM, ANDY, AND BAXTER!

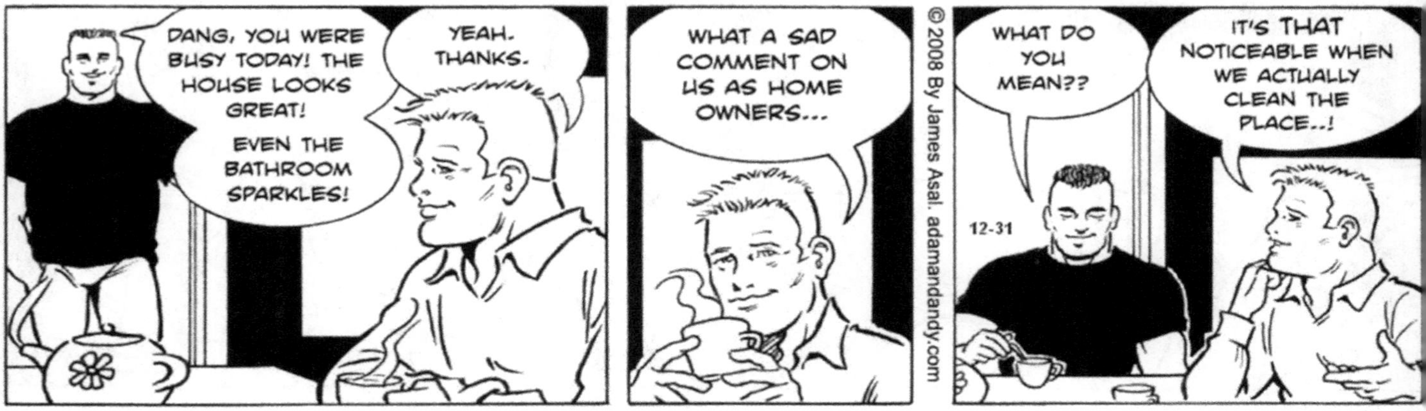
DANG, YOU WERE BUSY TODAY! THE HOUSE LOOKS GREAT!
EVEN THE BATHROOM SPARKLES!
YEAH. THANKS.
WHAT A SAD COMMENT ON US AS HOME OWNERS...
© 2008 By James Asal. adamandandy.com
WHAT DO YOU MEAN??
IT'S THAT NOTICEABLE WHEN WE ACTUALLY CLEAN THE PLACE..!
12-31

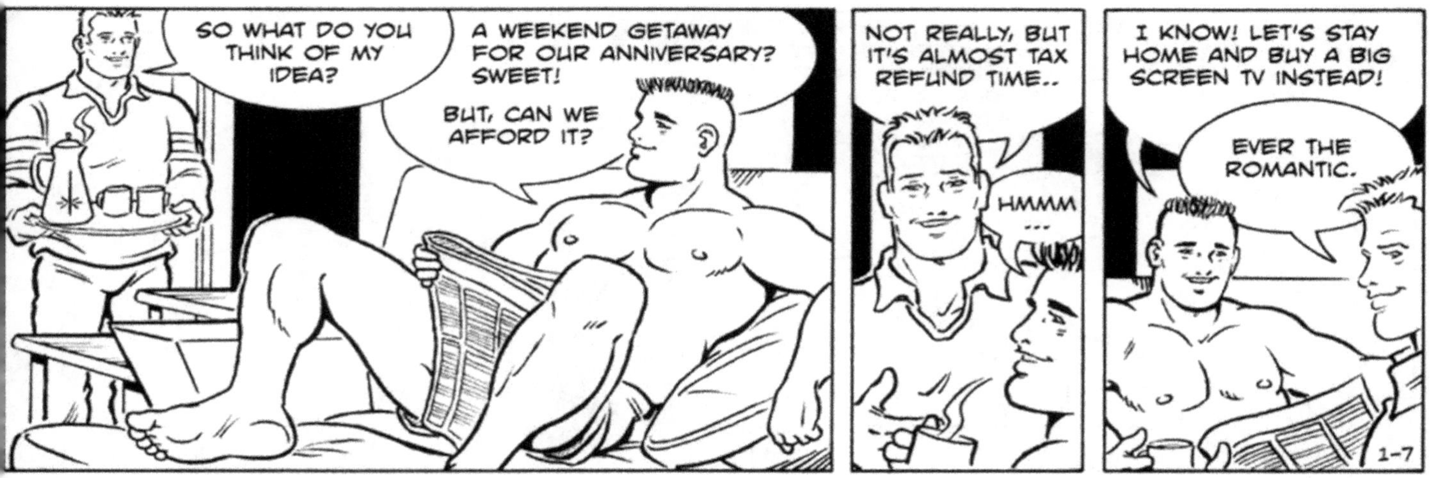
SO WHAT DO YOU THINK OF MY IDEA?
A WEEKEND GETAWAY FOR OUR ANNIVERSARY? SWEET!
BUT, CAN WE AFFORD IT?
NOT REALLY, BUT IT'S ALMOST TAX REFUND TIME..
HMMM ...
I KNOW! LET'S STAY HOME AND BUY A BIG SCREEN TV INSTEAD!
EVER THE ROMANTIC.
1-7

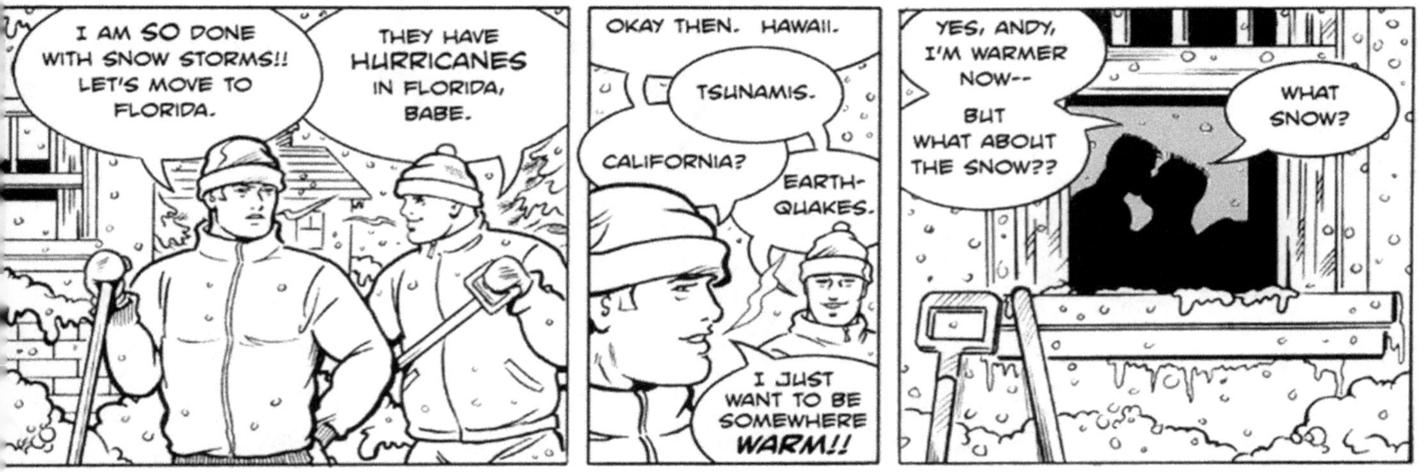
I AM SO DONE WITH SNOW STORMS!! LET'S MOVE TO FLORIDA.
THEY HAVE HURRICANES IN FLORIDA, BABE.
OKAY THEN. HAWAII.
TSUNAMIS.
CALIFORNIA?
EARTH-QUAKES.
I JUST WANT TO BE SOMEWHERE WARM!!
YES, ANDY, I'M WARMER NOW--
BUT WHAT ABOUT THE SNOW??
WHAT SNOW?

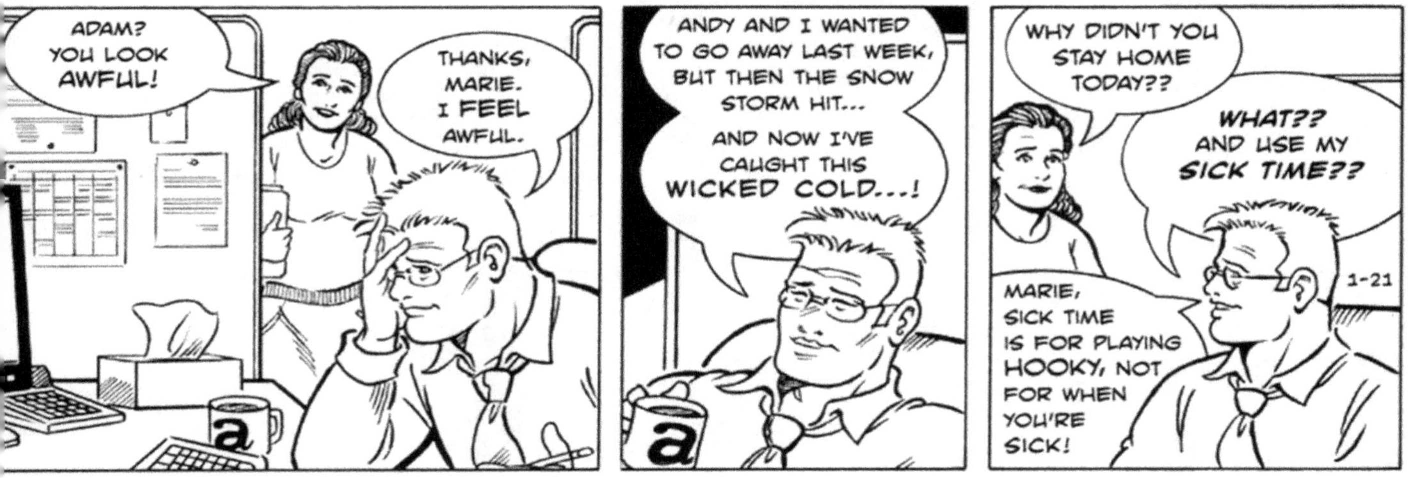
ADAM? YOU LOOK AWFUL!
THANKS, MARIE. I FEEL AWFUL.
ANDY AND I WANTED TO GO AWAY LAST WEEK, BUT THEN THE SNOW STORM HIT...
AND NOW I'VE CAUGHT THIS WICKED COLD...!
WHY DIDN'T YOU STAY HOME TODAY??
WHAT?? AND USE MY SICK TIME??
MARIE, SICK TIME IS FOR PLAYING HOOKY, NOT FOR WHEN YOU'RE SICK!
1-21

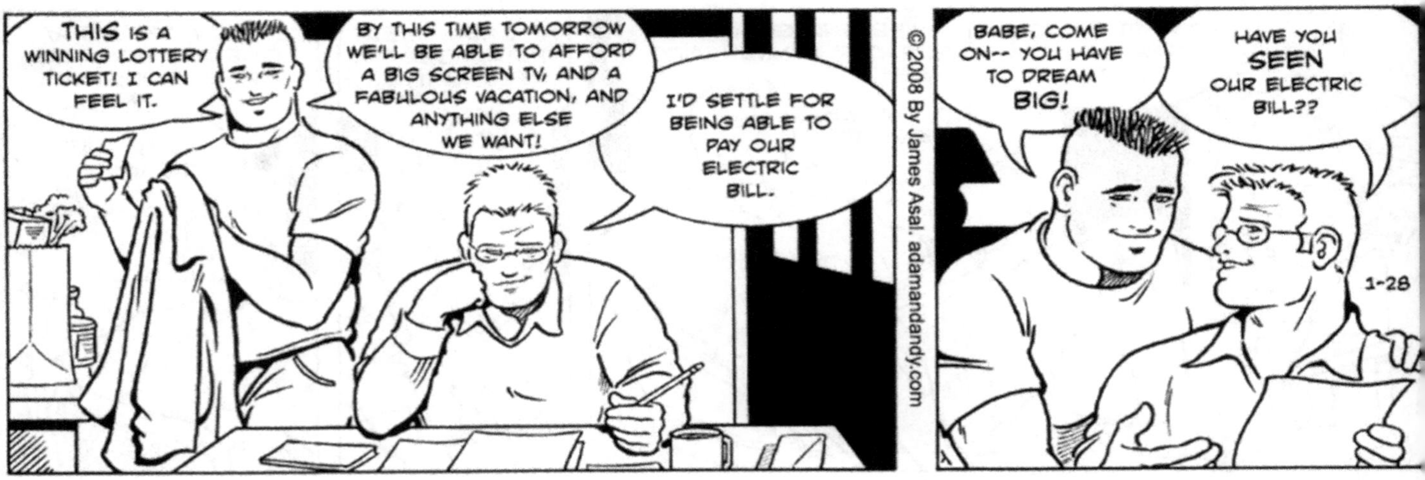
THIS IS A WINNING LOTTERY TICKET! I CAN FEEL IT.
BY THIS TIME TOMORROW WE'LL BE ABLE TO AFFORD A BIG SCREEN TV, AND A FABULOUS VACATION, AND ANYTHING ELSE WE WANT!
I'D SETTLE FOR BEING ABLE TO PAY OUR ELECTRIC BILL.
© 2008 By James Asal. adamandandy.com
BABE, COME ON-- YOU HAVE TO DREAM BIG!
HAVE YOU SEEN OUR ELECTRIC BILL??
1-28

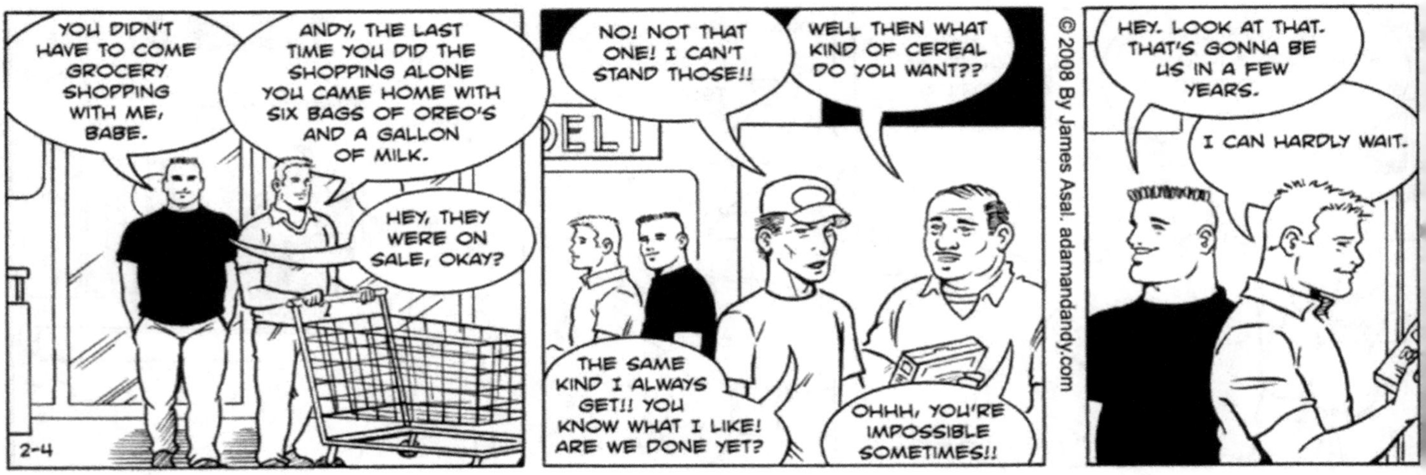
YOU DIDN'T HAVE TO COME GROCERY SHOPPING WITH ME, BABE.
ANDY, THE LAST TIME YOU DID THE SHOPPING ALONE YOU CAME HOME WITH SIX BAGS OF OREO'S AND A GALLON OF MILK.
HEY, THEY WERE ON SALE, OKAY?
2-4
NO! NOT THAT ONE! I CAN'T STAND THOSE!!
WELL THEN WHAT KIND OF CEREAL DO YOU WANT??
DELI
THE SAME KIND I ALWAYS GET!! YOU KNOW WHAT I LIKE! ARE WE DONE YET?
OHHH, YOU'RE IMPOSSIBLE SOMETIMES!!
© 2008 By James Asal. adamandandy.com
HEY. LOOK AT THAT. THAT'S GONNA BE US IN A FEW YEARS.
I CAN HARDLY WAIT.

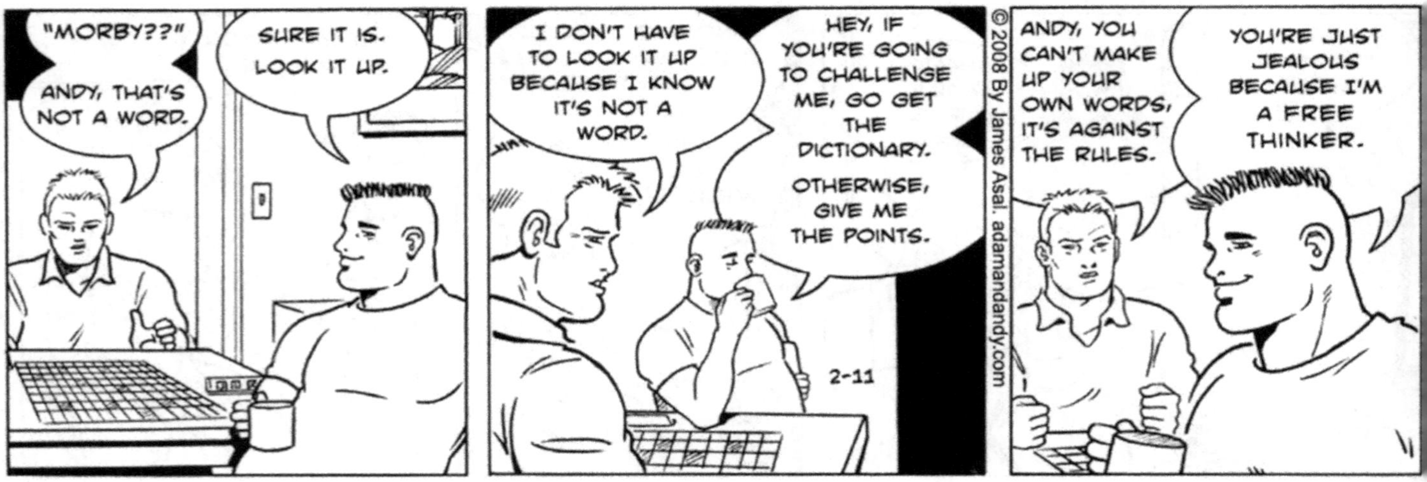
"MORBY??"
ANDY, THAT'S NOT A WORD.
SURE IT IS. LOOK IT UP.
I DON'T HAVE TO LOOK IT UP BECAUSE I KNOW IT'S NOT A WORD.
HEY, IF YOU'RE GOING TO CHALLENGE ME, GO GET THE DICTIONARY.
OTHERWISE, GIVE ME THE POINTS.
2-11
© 2008 By James Asal. adamandandy.com
ANDY, YOU CAN'T MAKE UP YOUR OWN WORDS, IT'S AGAINST THE RULES.
YOU'RE JUST JEALOUS BECAUSE I'M A FREE THINKER.

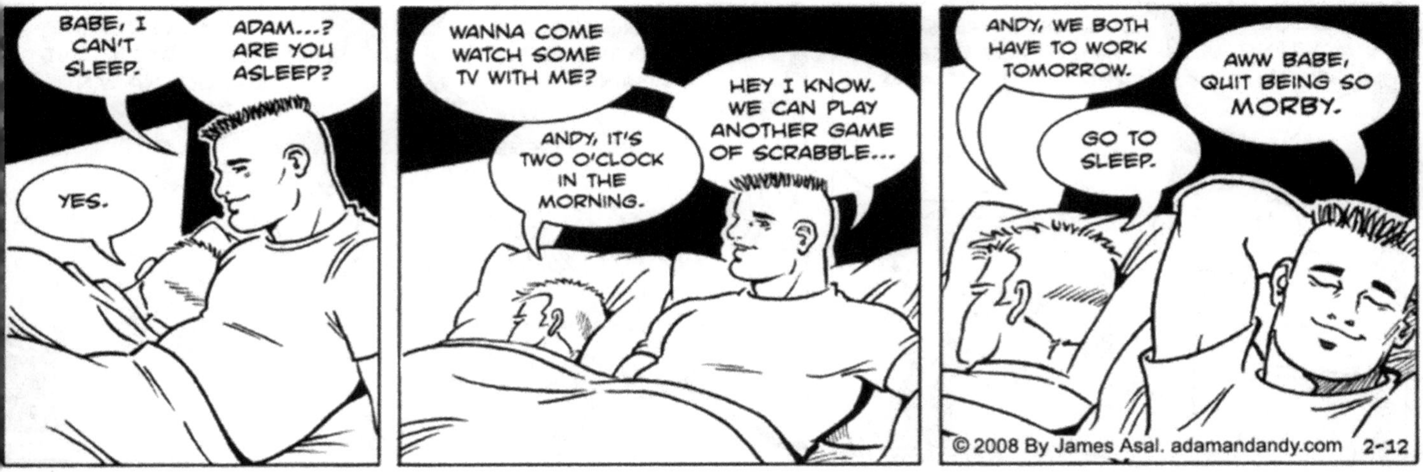
BABE, I CAN'T SLEEP.
ADAM...? ARE YOU ASLEEP?
YES.
WANNA COME WATCH SOME TV WITH ME?
ANDY, IT'S TWO O'CLOCK IN THE MORNING.
HEY I KNOW. WE CAN PLAY ANOTHER GAME OF SCRABBLE...
ANDY, WE BOTH HAVE TO WORK TOMORROW.
GO TO SLEEP.
AWW BABE, QUIT BEING SO MORBY.
© 2008 By James Asal. adamandandy.com 2-12

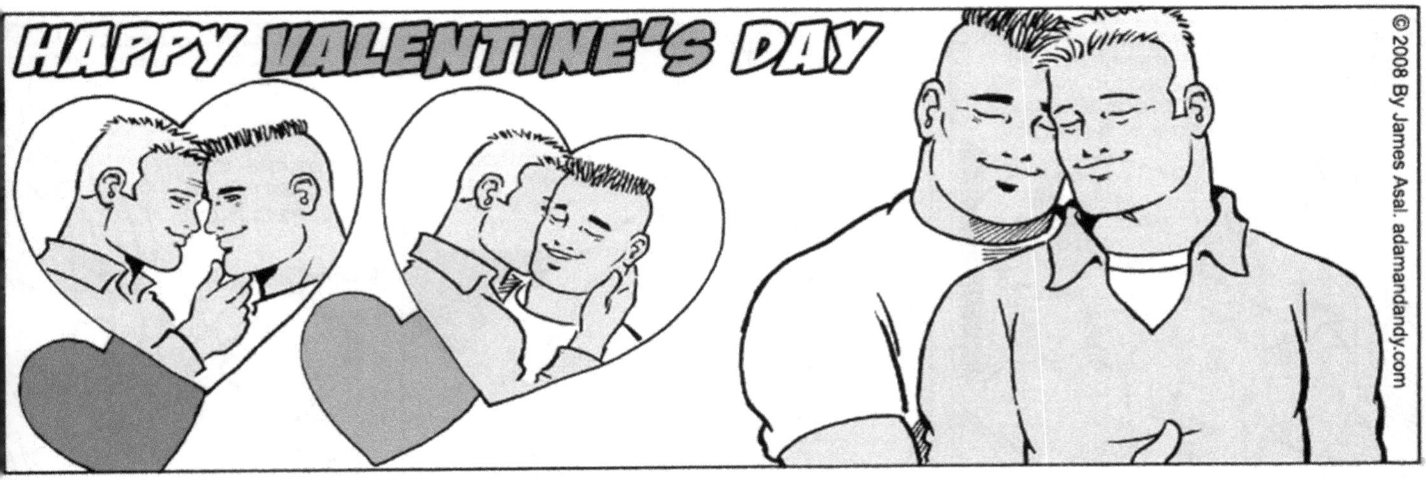
HAPPY VALENTINE'S DAY
© 2008 By James Asal. adamandandy.com

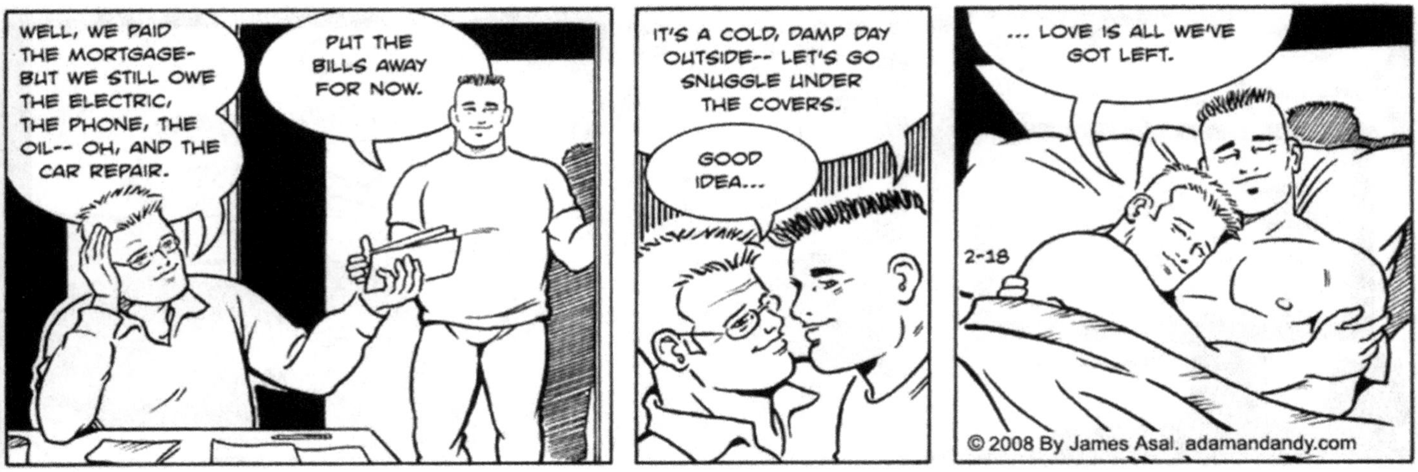
WELL, WE PAID THE MORTGAGE- BUT WE STILL OWE THE ELECTRIC, THE PHONE, THE OIL-- OH, AND THE CAR REPAIR.
PUT THE BILLS AWAY FOR NOW.
IT'S A COLD, DAMP DAY OUTSIDE-- LET'S GO SNUGGLE UNDER THE COVERS.
GOOD IDEA...
... LOVE IS ALL WE'VE GOT LEFT.
2-18
© 2008 By James Asal. adamandandy.com

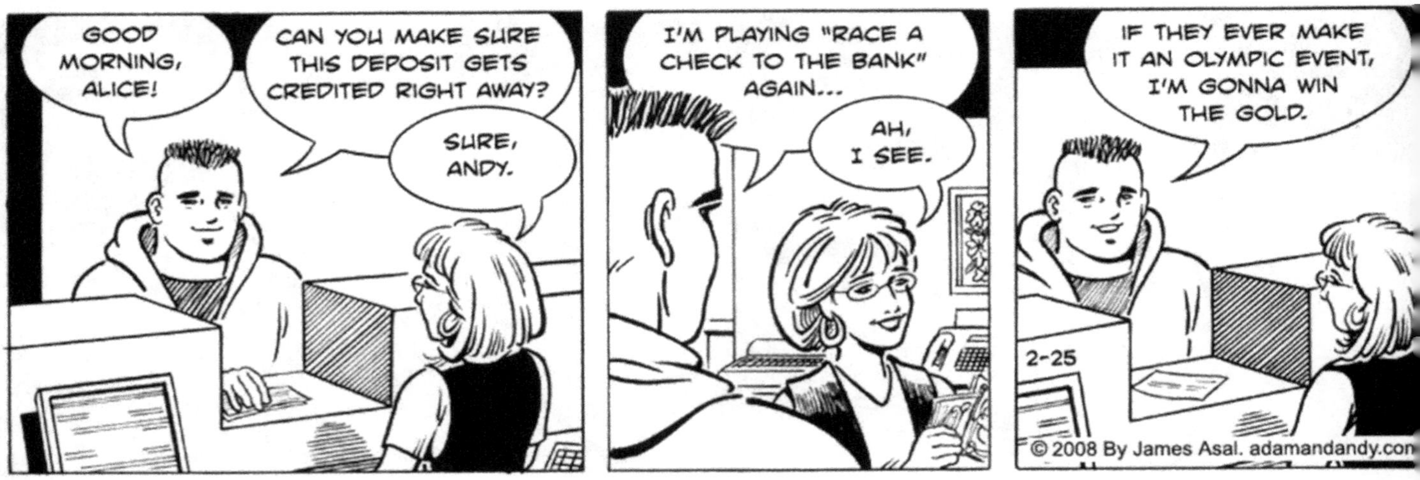
GOOD MORNING, ALICE!
CAN YOU MAKE SURE THIS DEPOSIT GETS CREDITED RIGHT AWAY?
SURE, ANDY.
I'M PLAYING "RACE A CHECK TO THE BANK" AGAIN...
AH, I SEE.
IF THEY EVER MAKE IT AN OLYMPIC EVENT, I'M GONNA WIN THE GOLD.
2-25
© 2008 By James Asal. adamandandy.com

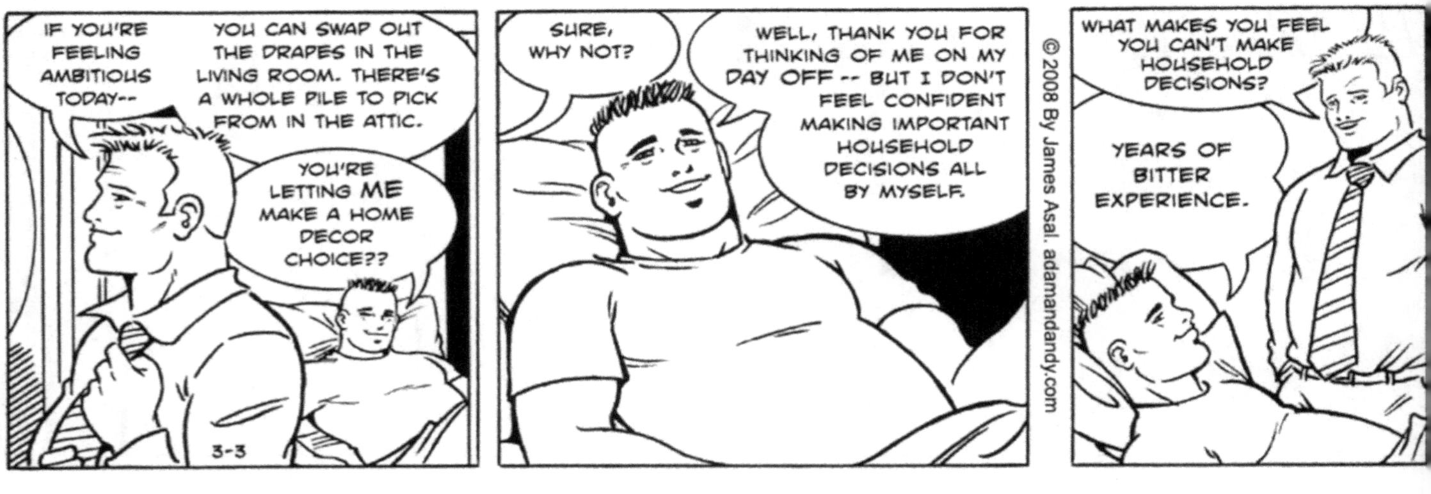
IF YOU'RE FEELING AMBITIOUS TODAY--
YOU CAN SWAP OUT THE DRAPES IN THE LIVING ROOM. THERE'S A WHOLE PILE TO PICK FROM IN THE ATTIC.
YOU'RE LETTING ME MAKE A HOME DECOR CHOICE??
3-3
SURE, WHY NOT?
WELL, THANK YOU FOR THINKING OF ME ON MY DAY OFF -- BUT I DON'T FEEL CONFIDENT MAKING IMPORTANT HOUSEHOLD DECISIONS ALL BY MYSELF.
© 2008 By James Asal. adamandandy.com
WHAT MAKES YOU FEEL YOU CAN'T MAKE HOUSEHOLD DECISIONS?
YEARS OF BITTER EXPERIENCE.

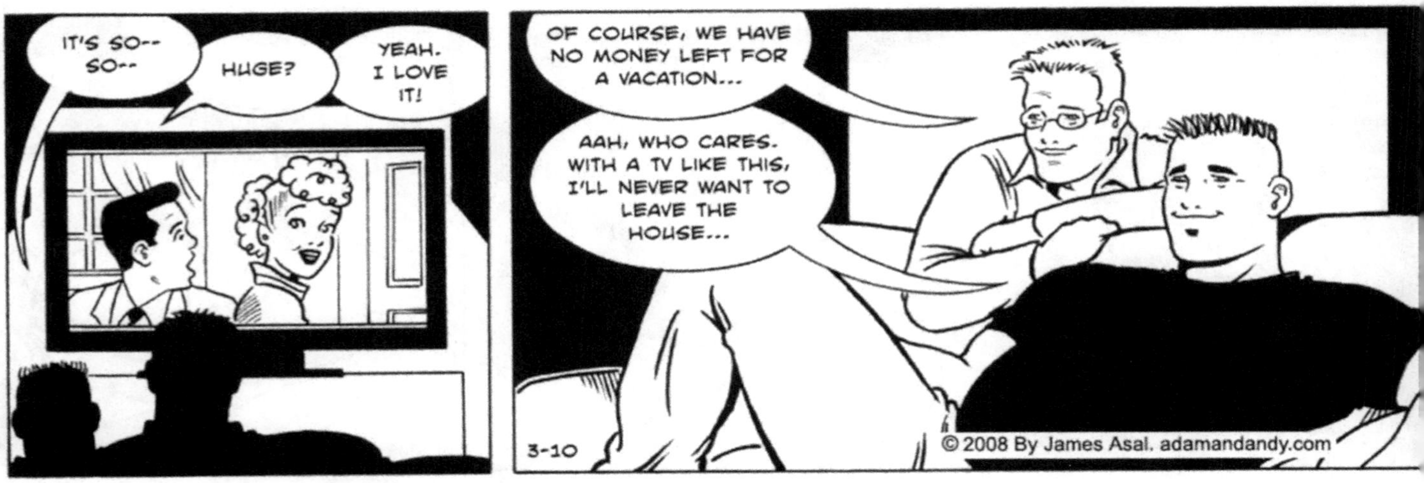
IT'S SO-- SO--
HUGE?
YEAH. I LOVE IT!
OF COURSE, WE HAVE NO MONEY LEFT FOR A VACATION...
AAH, WHO CARES. WITH A TV LIKE THIS, I'LL NEVER WANT TO LEAVE THE HOUSE...
3-10
© 2008 By James Asal. adamandandy.com

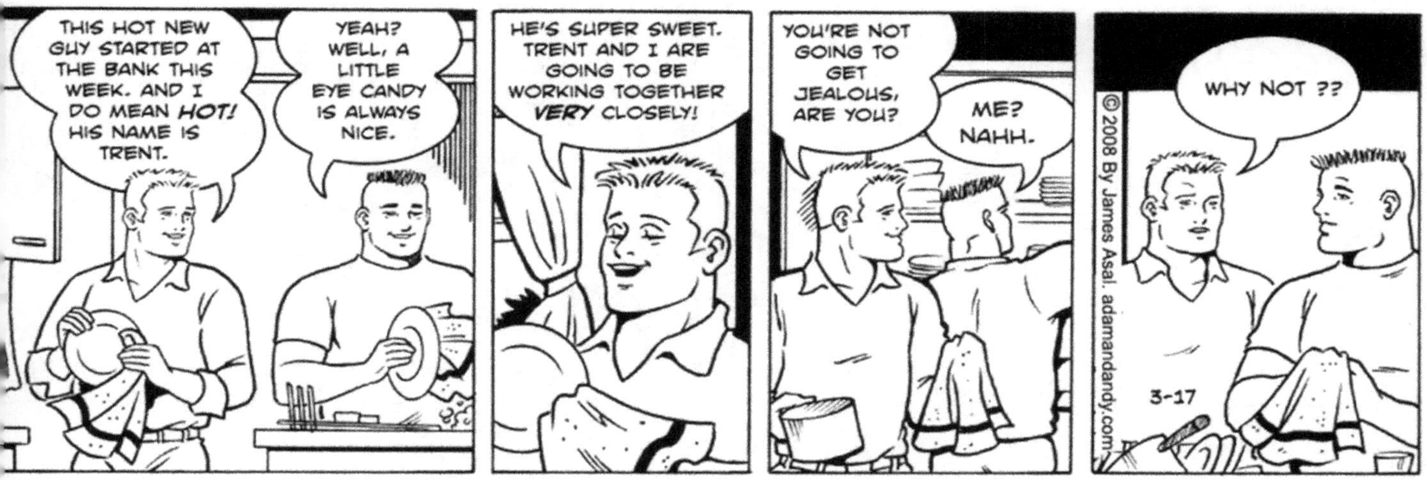
THIS HOT NEW GUY STARTED AT THE BANK THIS WEEK. AND I DO MEAN HOT! HIS NAME IS TRENT.
YEAH? WELL, A LITTLE EYE CANDY IS ALWAYS NICE.
HE'S SUPER SWEET. TRENT AND I ARE GOING TO BE WORKING TOGETHER VERY CLOSELY!
YOU'RE NOT GOING TO GET JEALOUS, ARE YOU?
ME? NAHH.
© 2008 By James Asal. adamandandy.com
WHY NOT ??
3-17

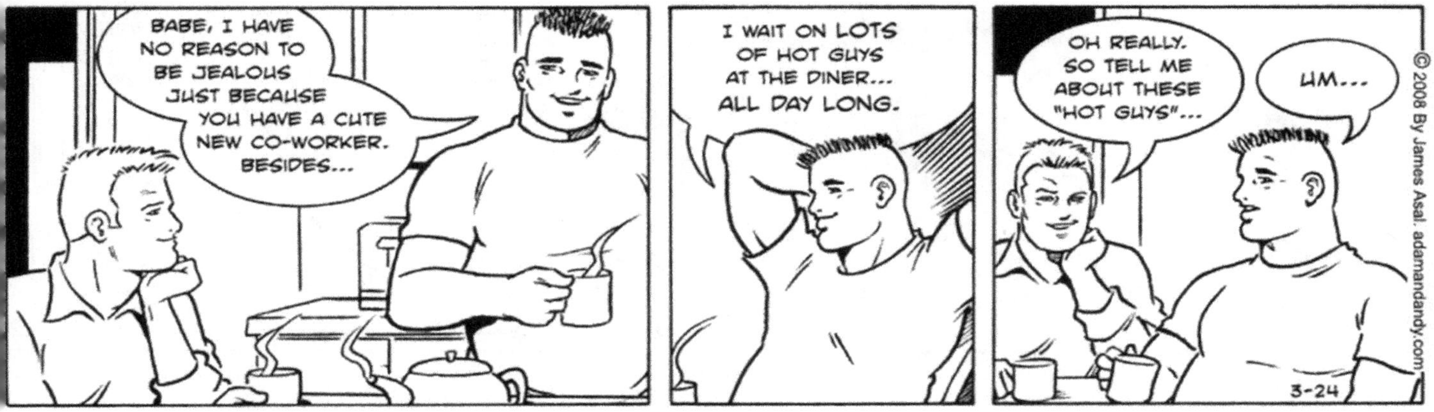
BABE, I HAVE NO REASON TO BE JEALOUS JUST BECAUSE YOU HAVE A CUTE NEW CO-WORKER. BESIDES...
I WAIT ON LOTS OF HOT GUYS AT THE DINER... ALL DAY LONG.
OH REALLY. SO TELL ME ABOUT THESE "HOT GUYS"...
UM...
© 2008 By James Asal. adamandandy.com
3-24

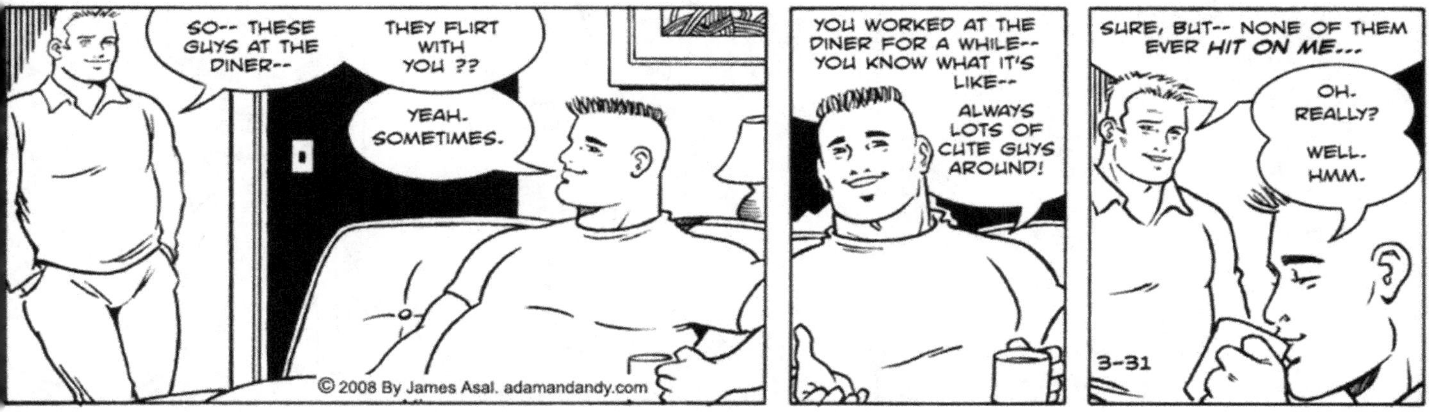
SO-- THESE GUYS AT THE DINER--
THEY FLIRT WITH YOU ??
YEAH. SOMETIMES.
© 2008 By James Asal. adamandandy.com
YOU WORKED AT THE DINER FOR A WHILE-- YOU KNOW WHAT IT'S LIKE--
ALWAYS LOTS OF CUTE GUYS AROUND!
SURE, BUT-- NONE OF THEM EVER HIT ON ME...
OH. REALLY?
WELL. HMM.
3-31

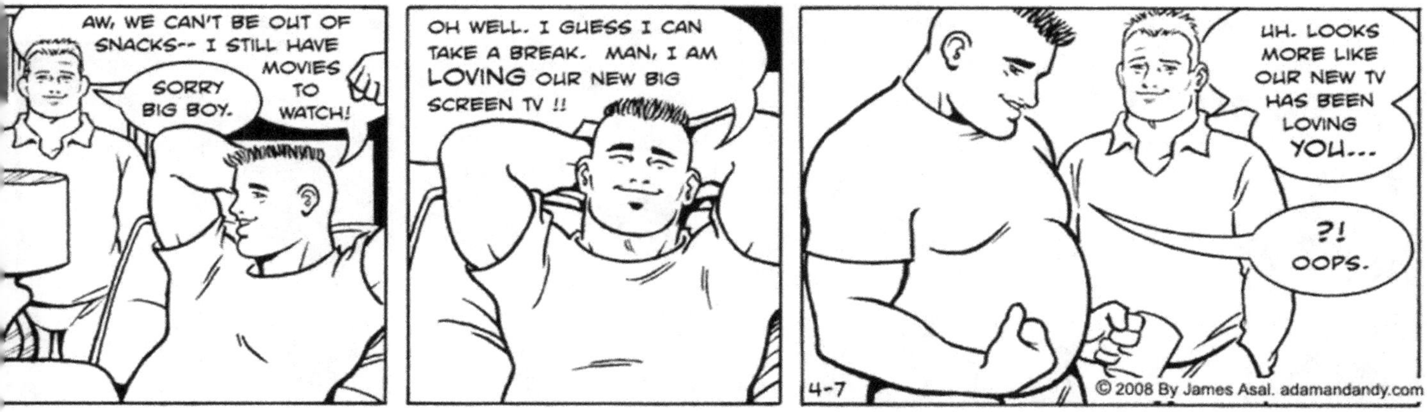
AW, WE CAN'T BE OUT OF SNACKS-- I STILL HAVE MOVIES TO WATCH!
SORRY BIG BOY.
OH WELL. I GUESS I CAN TAKE A BREAK. MAN, I AM LOVING OUR NEW BIG SCREEN TV !!
UH. LOOKS MORE LIKE OUR NEW TV HAS BEEN LOVING YOU...
?! OOPS.
4-7
© 2008 By James Asal. adamandandy.com

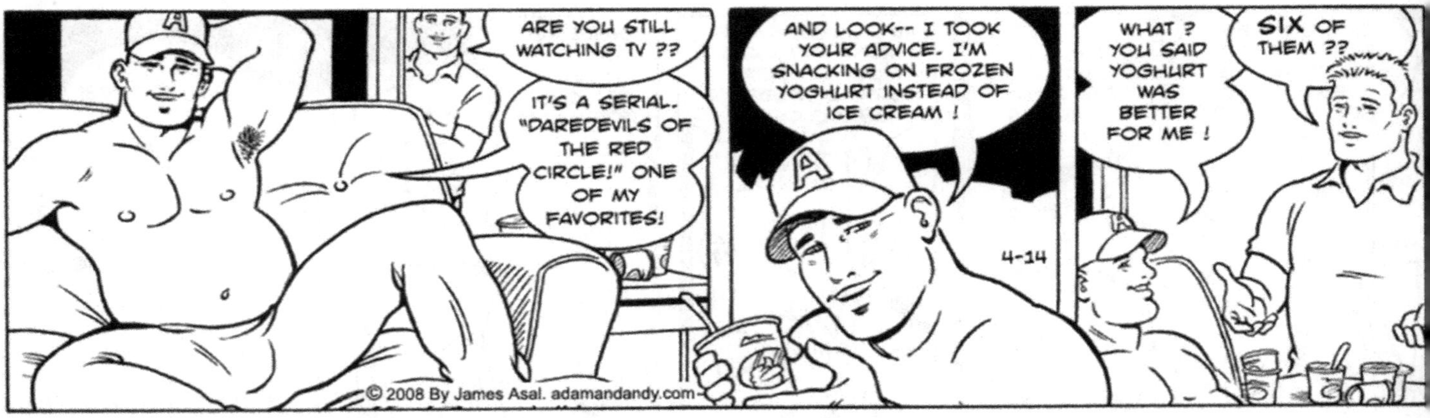
ARE YOU STILL WATCHING TV ??
IT'S A SERIAL. "DAREDEVILS OF THE RED CIRCLE!" ONE OF MY FAVORITES!
© 2008 By James Asal. adamandandy.com
AND LOOK-- I TOOK YOUR ADVICE. I'M SNACKING ON FROZEN YOGHURT INSTEAD OF ICE CREAM !
4-14
WHAT ? YOU SAID YOGHURT WAS BETTER FOR ME !
SIX OF THEM ??

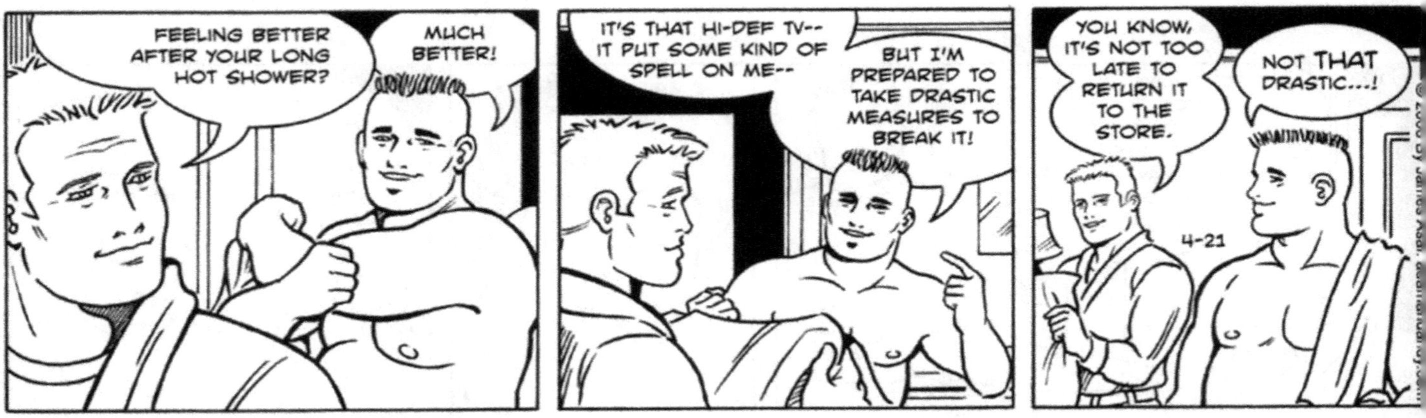
FEELING BETTER AFTER YOUR LONG HOT SHOWER?
MUCH BETTER!
IT'S THAT HI-DEF TV-- IT PUT SOME KIND OF SPELL ON ME--
BUT I'M PREPARED TO TAKE DRASTIC MEASURES TO BREAK IT!
YOU KNOW, IT'S NOT TOO LATE TO RETURN IT TO THE STORE.
NOT THAT DRASTIC...!
4-21

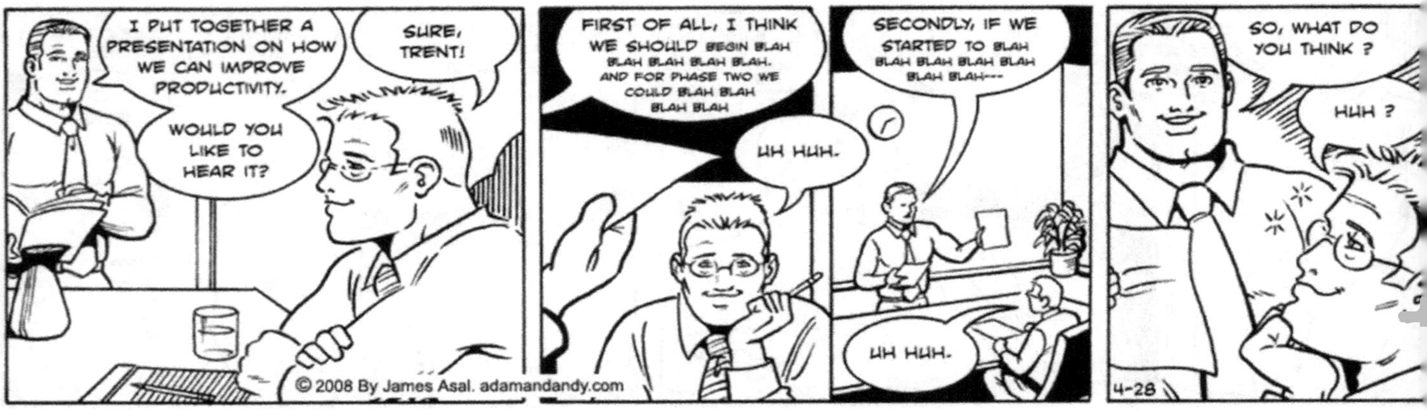
I PUT TOGETHER A PRESENTATION ON HOW WE CAN IMPROVE PRODUCTIVITY.
WOULD YOU LIKE TO HEAR IT?
SURE, TRENT!
© 2008 By James Asal. adamandandy.com
FIRST OF ALL, I THINK WE SHOULD BEGIN BLAH BLAH BLAH BLAH BLAH. AND FOR PHASE TWO WE COULD BLAH BLAH BLAH BLAH
UH HUH.
SECONDLY, IF WE STARTED TO BLAH BLAH BLAH BLAH BLAH BLAH BLAH---
UH HUH.
SO, WHAT DO YOU THINK ?
HUH ?
4-28

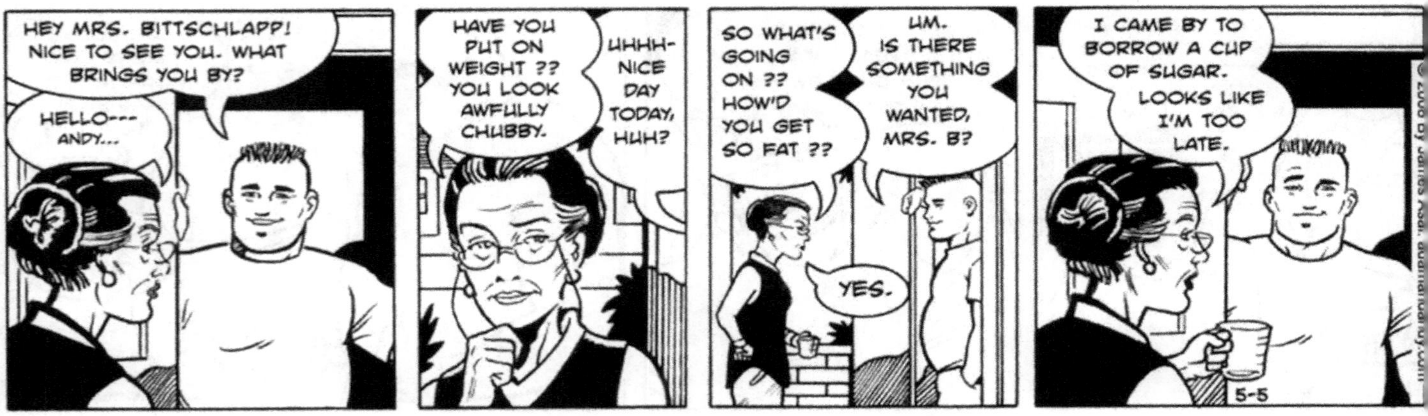
HEY MRS. BITTSCHLAPP! NICE TO SEE YOU. WHAT BRINGS YOU BY?
HELLO--- ANDY...
HAVE YOU PUT ON WEIGHT ?? YOU LOOK AWFULLY CHUBBY.
UHHH- NICE DAY TODAY, HUH?
SO WHAT'S GOING ON ?? HOW'D YOU GET SO FAT ??
UM. IS THERE SOMETHING YOU WANTED, MRS. B?
YES.
I CAME BY TO BORROW A CUP OF SUGAR.
LOOKS LIKE I'M TOO LATE.
5-5

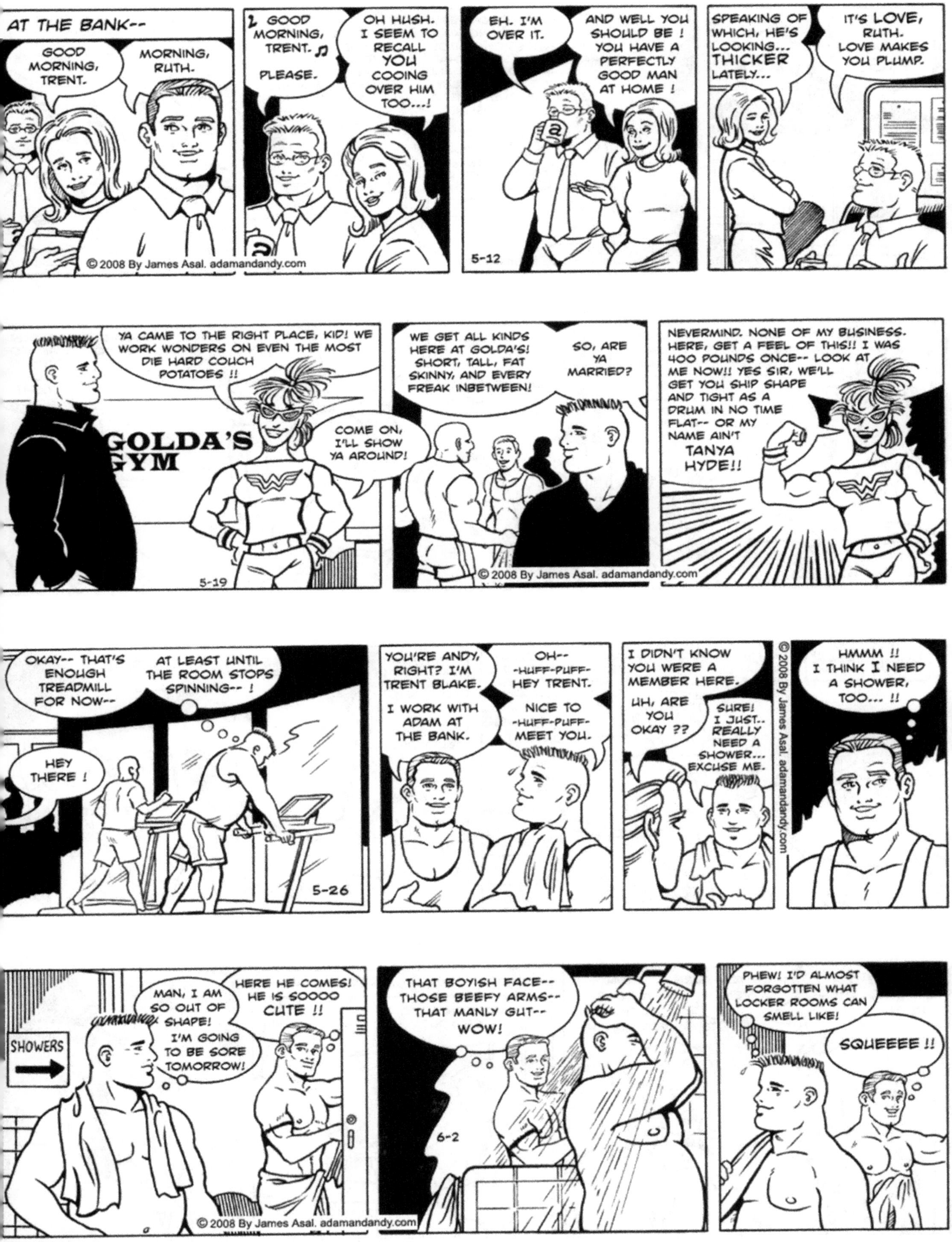
AT THE BANK--
GOOD MORNING, TRENT.
MORNING, RUTH.
© 2008 By James Asal. adamandandy.com
GOOD MORNING, TRENT. ♫
PLEASE.
OH HUSH. I SEEM TO RECALL YOU COOING OVER HIM TOO...!
EH. I'M OVER IT.
AND WELL YOU SHOULD BE ! YOU HAVE A PERFECTLY GOOD MAN AT HOME !
5-12
SPEAKING OF WHICH, HE'S LOOKING... THICKER LATELY...
IT'S LOVE, RUTH. LOVE MAKES YOU PLUMP.
YA CAME TO THE RIGHT PLACE, KID! WE WORK WONDERS ON EVEN THE MOST DIE HARD COUCH POTATOES !!
GOLDA'S GYM
COME ON, I'LL SHOW YA AROUND!
5-19
WE GET ALL KINDS HERE AT GOLDA'S! SHORT, TALL, FAT SKINNY, AND EVERY FREAK INBETWEEN!
SO, ARE YA MARRIED?
© 2008 By James Asal. adamandandy.com
NEVERMIND. NONE OF MY BUSINESS. HERE, GET A FEEL OF THIS!! I WAS 400 POUNDS ONCE-- LOOK AT ME NOW!! YES SIR, WE'LL GET YOU SHIP SHAPE AND TIGHT AS A DRUM IN NO TIME FLAT-- OR MY NAME AIN'T TANYA HYDE!!
OKAY-- THAT'S ENOUGH TREADMILL FOR NOW--
AT LEAST UNTIL THE ROOM STOPS SPINNING-- !
HEY THERE !
5-26
YOU'RE ANDY, RIGHT? I'M TRENT BLAKE.
OH-- -HUFF-PUFF- HEY TRENT.
I WORK WITH ADAM AT THE BANK.
NICE TO -HUFF-PUFF- MEET YOU.
I DIDN'T KNOW YOU WERE A MEMBER HERE.
UH, ARE YOU OKAY ??
SURE! I JUST.. REALLY NEED A SHOWER... EXCUSE ME.
© 2008 By James Asal. adamandandy.com
HMMM !! I THINK I NEED A SHOWER, TOO... !!
SHOWERS
MAN, I AM SO OUT OF SHAPE! I'M GOING TO BE SORE TOMORROW!
HERE HE COMES! HE IS SOOOO CUTE !!
© 2008 By James Asal. adamandandy.com
THAT BOYISH FACE-- THOSE BEEFY ARMS-- THAT MANLY GUT-- WOW!
6-2
PHEW! I'D ALMOST FORGOTTEN WHAT LOCKER ROOMS CAN SMELL LIKE!
SQUEEEE !!

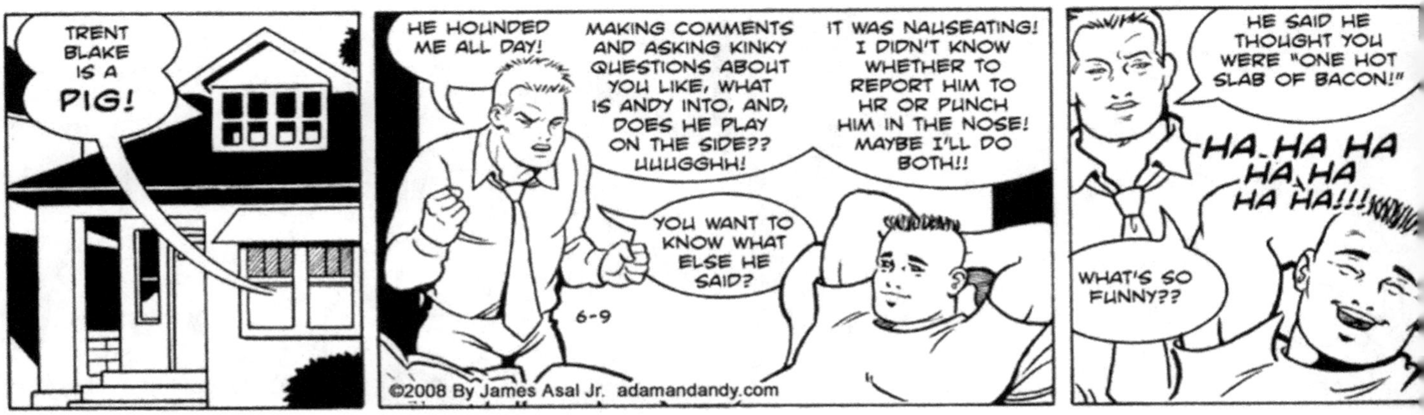
TRENT BLAKE IS A PIG!
HE HOUNDED ME ALL DAY!
MAKING COMMENTS AND ASKING KINKY QUESTIONS ABOUT YOU LIKE, WHAT IS ANDY INTO, AND, DOES HE PLAY ON THE SIDE?? UUUGGHH!
IT WAS NAUSEATING! I DIDN'T KNOW WHETHER TO REPORT HIM TO HR OR PUNCH HIM IN THE NOSE! MAYBE I'LL DO BOTH!!
YOU WANT TO KNOW WHAT ELSE HE SAID?
6-9
©2008 By James Asal Jr. adamandandy.com
HE SAID HE THOUGHT YOU WERE "ONE HOT SLAB OF BACON!"
HA HA HA HA HA HA HA!!!
WHAT'S SO FUNNY??

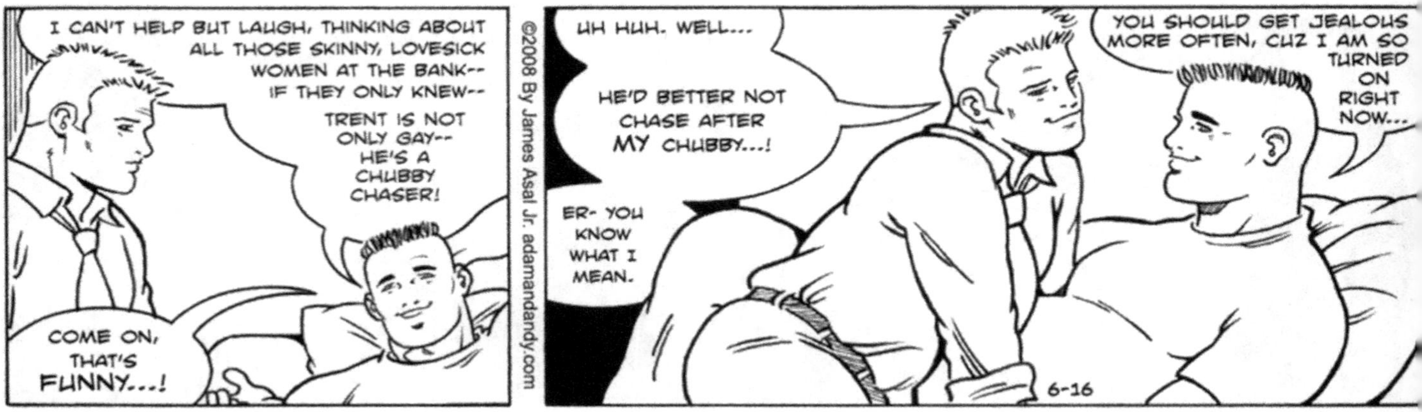
I CAN'T HELP BUT LAUGH, THINKING ABOUT ALL THOSE SKINNY, LOVESICK WOMEN AT THE BANK-- IF THEY ONLY KNEW--
TRENT IS NOT ONLY GAY-- HE'S A CHUBBY CHASER!
COME ON, THAT'S FUNNY...!
©2008 By James Asal Jr. adamandandy.com
UH HUH. WELL...
HE'D BETTER NOT CHASE AFTER MY CHUBBY...!
ER- YOU KNOW WHAT I MEAN.
YOU SHOULD GET JEALOUS MORE OFTEN, CUZ I AM SO TURNED ON RIGHT NOW...
6-16

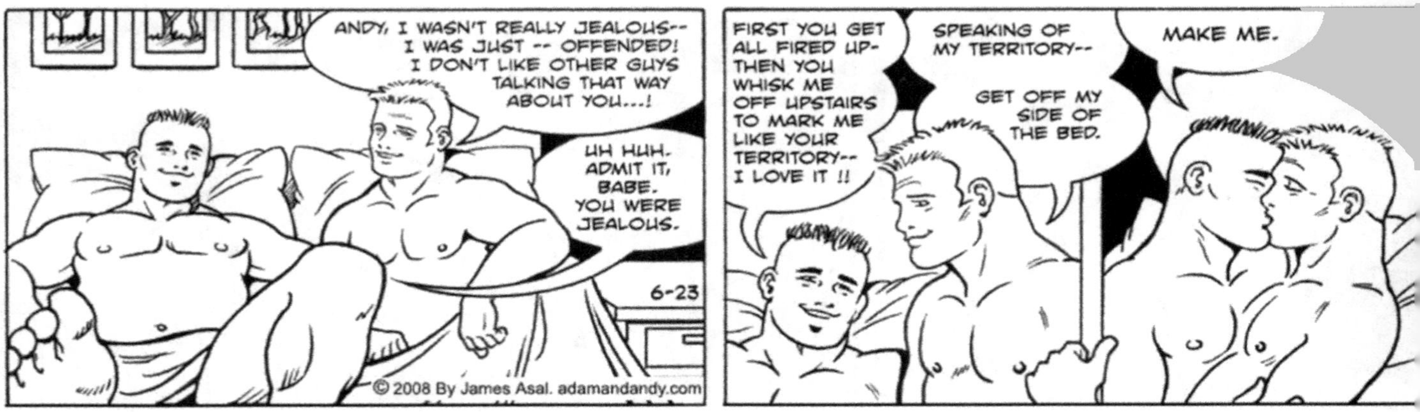
ANDY, I WASN'T REALLY JEALOUS-- I WAS JUST -- OFFENDED! I DON'T LIKE OTHER GUYS TALKING THAT WAY ABOUT YOU...!
UH HUH. ADMIT IT, BABE. YOU WERE JEALOUS.
6-23
© 2008 By James Asal. adamandandy.com
FIRST YOU GET ALL FIRED UP- THEN YOU WHISK ME OFF UPSTAIRS TO MARK ME LIKE YOUR TERRITORY-- I LOVE IT !!
SPEAKING OF MY TERRITORY--
GET OFF MY SIDE OF THE BED.
MAKE ME.

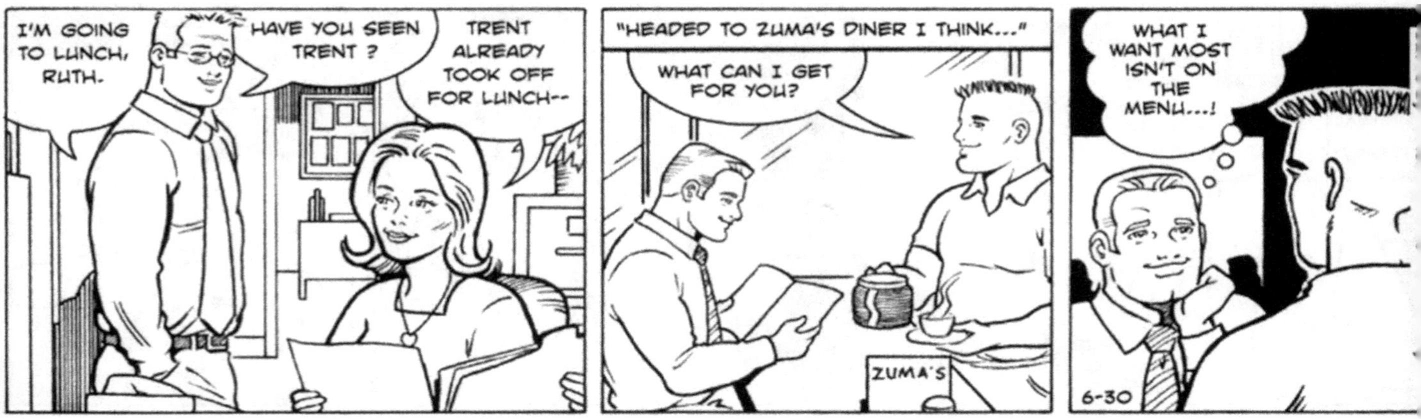
I'M GOING TO LUNCH, RUTH.
HAVE YOU SEEN TRENT ?
TRENT ALREADY TOOK OFF FOR LUNCH--
"HEADED TO ZUMA'S DINER I THINK..."
WHAT CAN I GET FOR YOU?
ZUMA'S
WHAT I WANT MOST ISN'T ON THE MENU...!
6-30

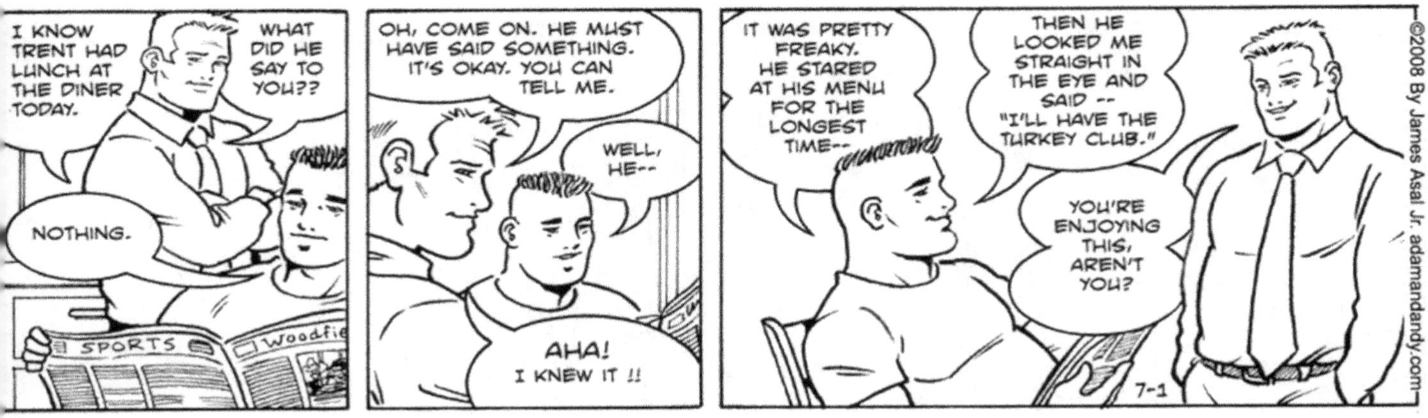
I KNOW TRENT HAD LUNCH AT THE DINER TODAY.
WHAT DID HE SAY TO YOU??
NOTHING.
SPORTS
OH, COME ON. HE MUST HAVE SAID SOMETHING. IT'S OKAY. YOU CAN TELL ME.
WELL, HE--
AHA! I KNEW IT !!
IT WAS PRETTY FREAKY. HE STARED AT HIS MENU FOR THE LONGEST TIME--
THEN HE LOOKED ME STRAIGHT IN THE EYE AND SAID -- "I'LL HAVE THE TURKEY CLUB."
YOU'RE ENJOYING THIS, AREN'T YOU?
7-1
©2008 By James Asal Jr. adamandandy.com

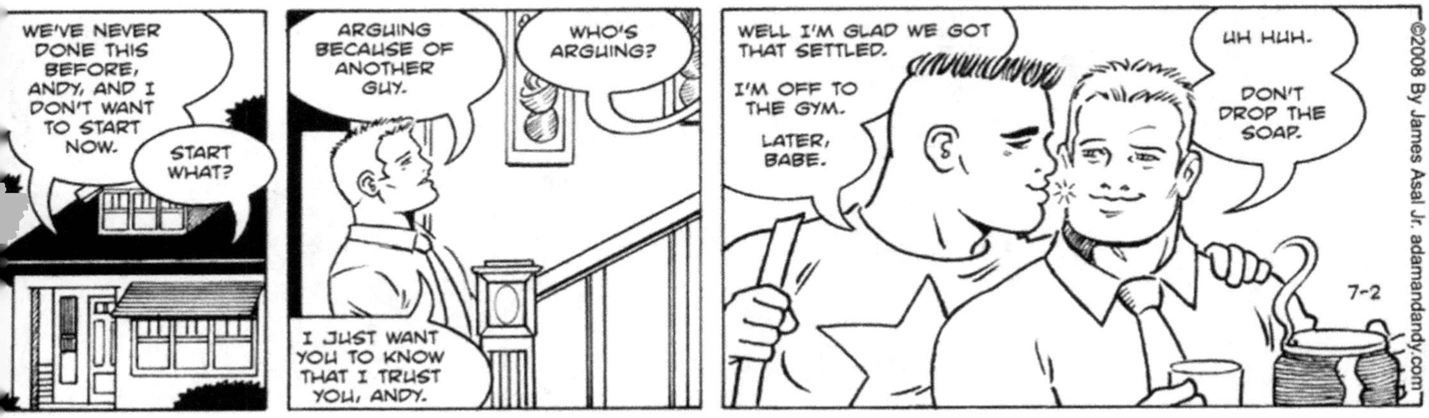
WE'VE NEVER DONE THIS BEFORE, ANDY, AND I DON'T WANT TO START NOW.
START WHAT?
ARGUING BECAUSE OF ANOTHER GUY.
WHO'S ARGUING?
I JUST WANT YOU TO KNOW THAT I TRUST YOU, ANDY.
WELL I'M GLAD WE GOT THAT SETTLED.
I'M OFF TO THE GYM.
LATER, BABE.
UH HUH.
DON'T DROP THE SOAP.
7-2
©2008 By James Asal Jr. adamandandy.com

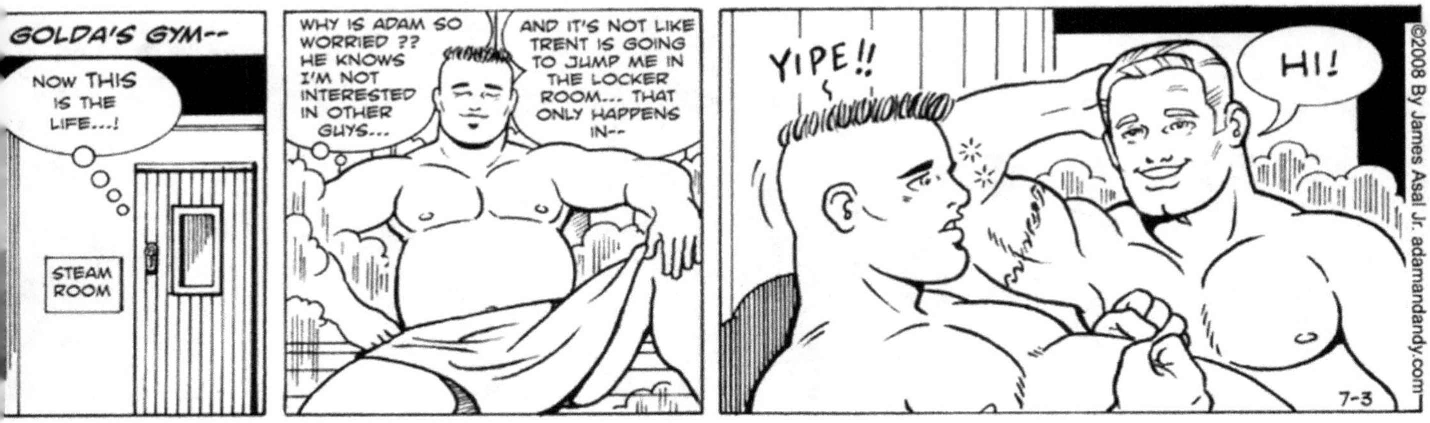
GOLDA'S GYM--
NOW THIS IS THE LIFE...!
STEAM ROOM
WHY IS ADAM SO WORRIED ?? HE KNOWS I'M NOT INTERESTED IN OTHER GUYS...
AND IT'S NOT LIKE TRENT IS GOING TO JUMP ME IN THE LOCKER ROOM... THAT ONLY HAPPENS IN--
YIPE!!
HI!
7-3
©2008 By James Asal Jr. adamandandy.com

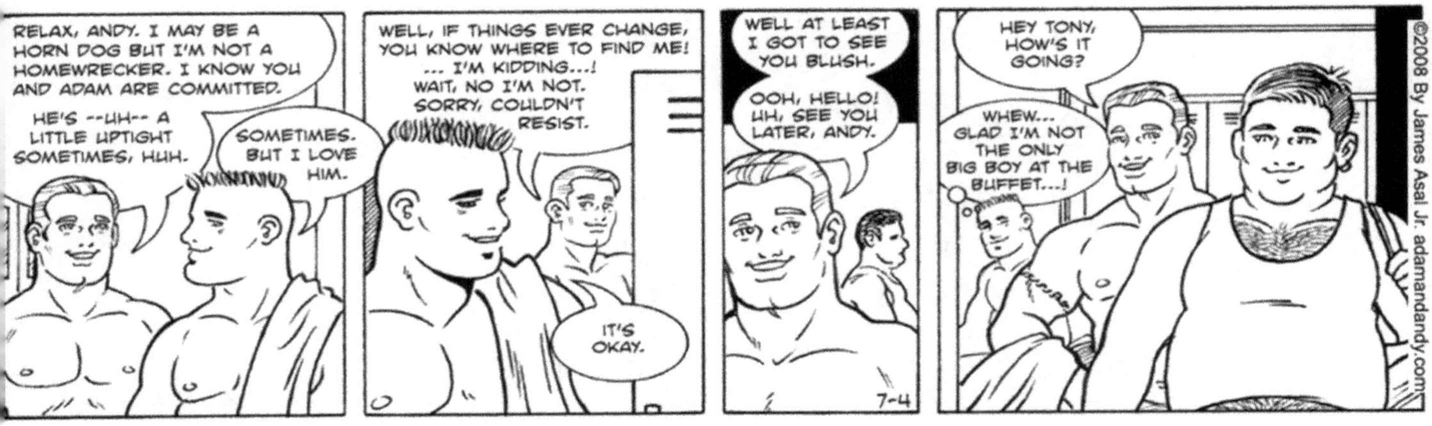
RELAX, ANDY. I MAY BE A HORN DOG BUT I'M NOT A HOMEWRECKER. I KNOW YOU AND ADAM ARE COMMITTED.
HE'S --UH-- A LITTLE UPTIGHT SOMETIMES, HUH.
SOMETIMES. BUT I LOVE HIM.
WELL, IF THINGS EVER CHANGE, YOU KNOW WHERE TO FIND ME! ... I'M KIDDING...! WAIT, NO I'M NOT. SORRY, COULDN'T RESIST.
IT'S OKAY.
WELL AT LEAST I GOT TO SEE YOU BLUSH.
OOH, HELLO! UH, SEE YOU LATER, ANDY.
7-4
HEY TONY, HOW'S IT GOING?
WHEW... GLAD I'M NOT THE ONLY BIG BOY AT THE BUFFET...!
©2008 By James Asal Jr. adamandandy.com

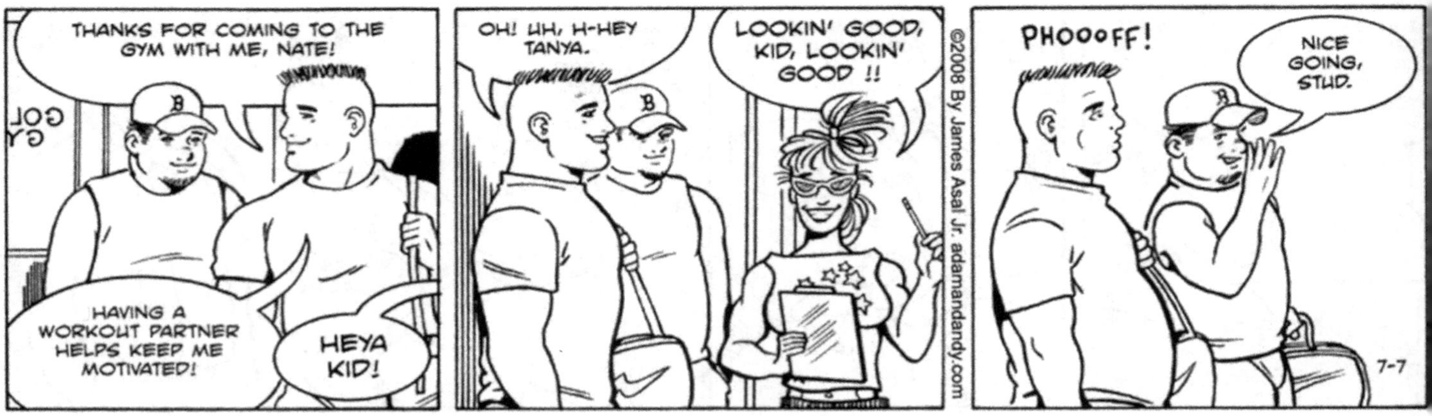
THANKS FOR COMING TO THE GYM WITH ME, NATE!
HAVING A WORKOUT PARTNER HELPS KEEP ME MOTIVATED!
HEYA KID!
OH! UH, H-HEY TANYA.
LOOKIN' GOOD, KID, LOOKIN' GOOD !!
©2008 By James Asal Jr. adamandandy.com
PHOOOFF!
NICE GOING, STUD.
7-7

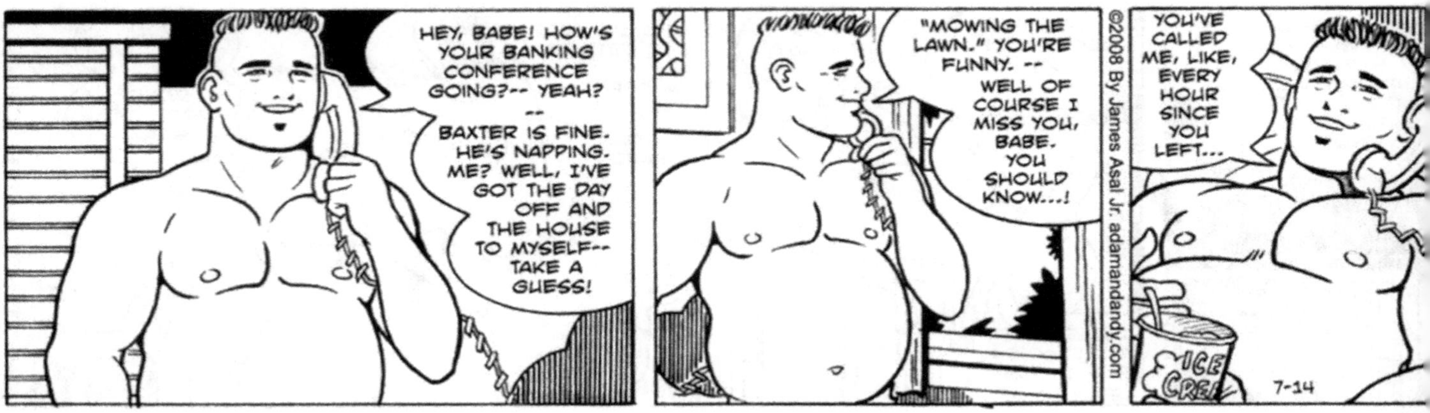
HEY, BABE! HOW'S YOUR BANKING CONFERENCE GOING?-- YEAH? -- BAXTER IS FINE. HE'S NAPPING. ME? WELL, I'VE GOT THE DAY OFF AND THE HOUSE TO MYSELF-- TAKE A GUESS!
"MOWING THE LAWN." YOU'RE FUNNY. -- WELL OF COURSE I MISS YOU, BABE. YOU SHOULD KNOW...!
©2008 By James Asal Jr. adamandandy.com
YOU'VE CALLED ME, LIKE, EVERY HOUR SINCE YOU LEFT...
ICE CRE
7-14

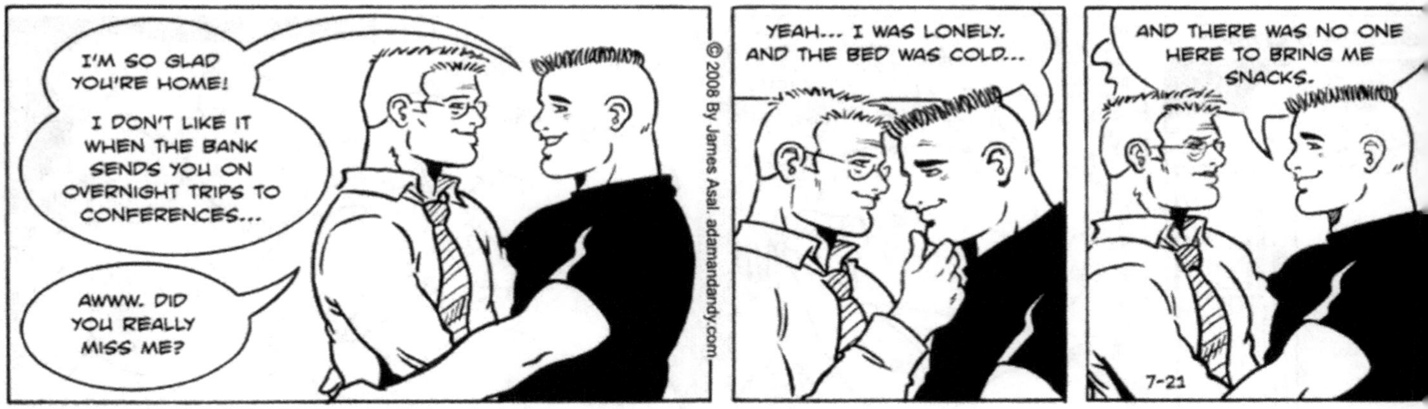
I'M SO GLAD YOU'RE HOME!
I DON'T LIKE IT WHEN THE BANK SENDS YOU ON OVERNIGHT TRIPS TO CONFERENCES...
AWWW. DID YOU REALLY MISS ME?
© 2008 By James Asal. adamandandy.com
YEAH... I WAS LONELY. AND THE BED WAS COLD...
AND THERE WAS NO ONE HERE TO BRING ME SNACKS.
7-21

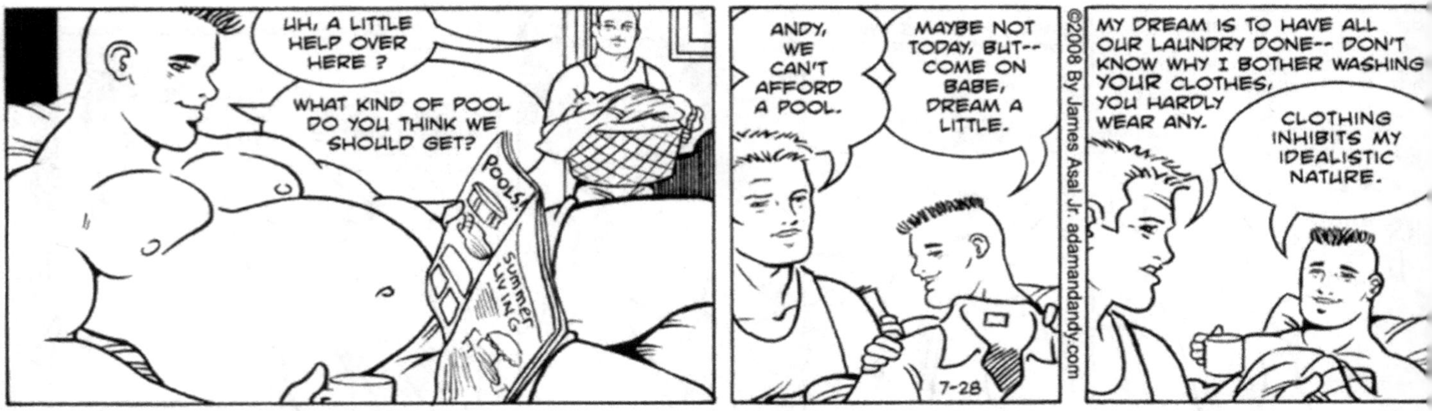
UH, A LITTLE HELP OVER HERE ?
WHAT KIND OF POOL DO YOU THINK WE SHOULD GET?
POOLS!
SUMMER LIVING
ANDY, WE CAN'T AFFORD A POOL.
MAYBE NOT TODAY, BUT-- COME ON BABE, DREAM A LITTLE.
7-28
©2008 By James Asal Jr. adamandandy.com
MY DREAM IS TO HAVE ALL OUR LAUNDRY DONE-- DON'T KNOW WHY I BOTHER WASHING YOUR CLOTHES, YOU HARDLY WEAR ANY.
CLOTHING INHIBITS MY IDEALISTIC NATURE.

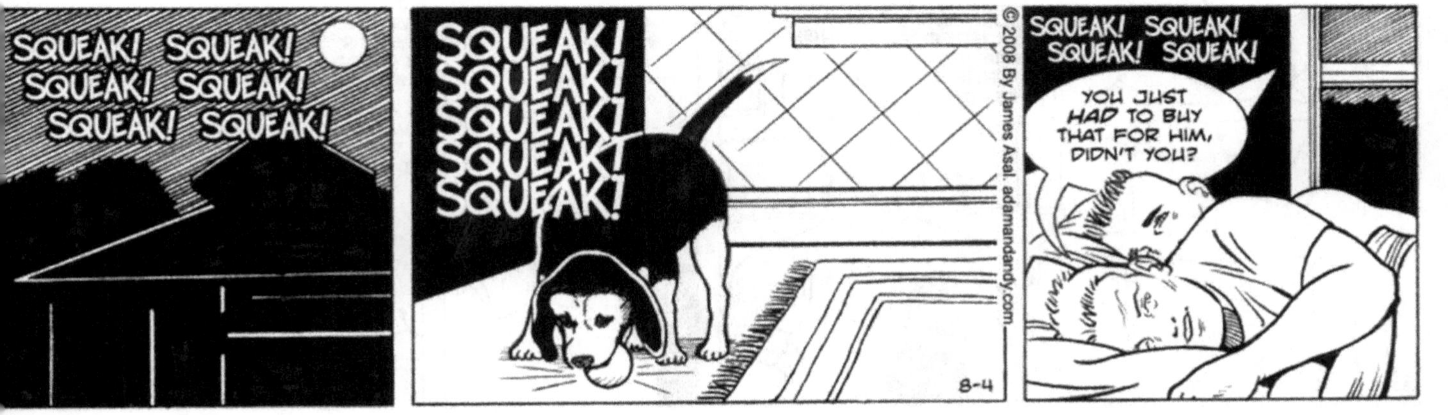
SQUEAK! SQUEAK! SQUEAK! SQUEAK! SQUEAK! SQUEAK!
SQUEAK! SQUEAK! SQUEAK! SQUEAK! SQUEAK!
© 2008 By James Asal. adamandandy.com
8-4
SQUEAK! SQUEAK! SQUEAK! SQUEAK!
YOU JUST HAD TO BUY THAT FOR HIM, DIDN'T YOU?

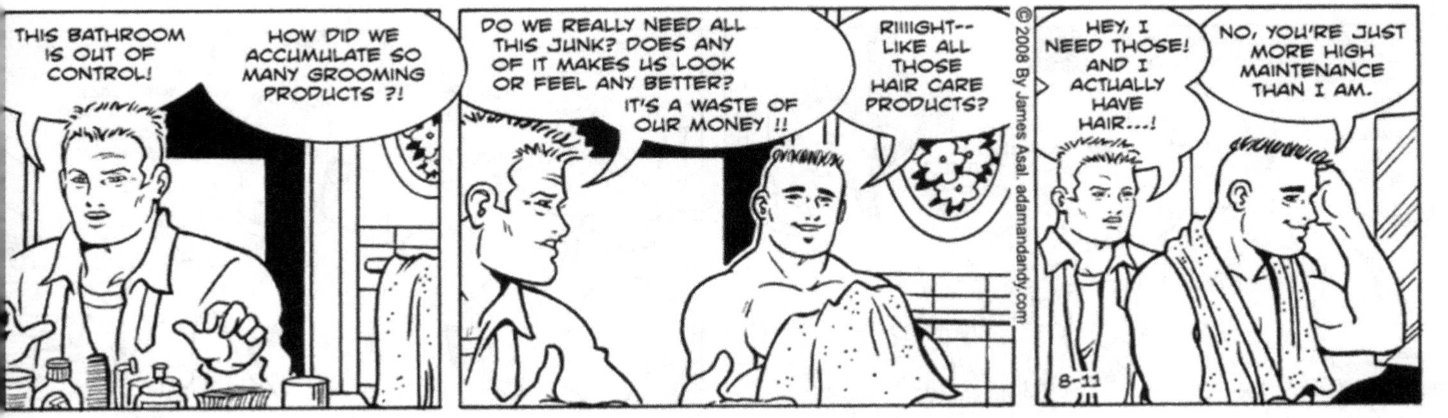
THIS BATHROOM IS OUT OF CONTROL!
HOW DID WE ACCUMULATE SO MANY GROOMING PRODUCTS ?!
DO WE REALLY NEED ALL THIS JUNK? DOES ANY OF IT MAKES US LOOK OR FEEL ANY BETTER?
IT'S A WASTE OF OUR MONEY !!
RIIIGHT-- LIKE ALL THOSE HAIR CARE PRODUCTS?
© 2008 By James Asal. adamandandy.com
HEY, I NEED THOSE! AND I ACTUALLY HAVE HAIR...!
NO, YOU'RE JUST MORE HIGH MAINTENANCE THAN I AM.
8-11

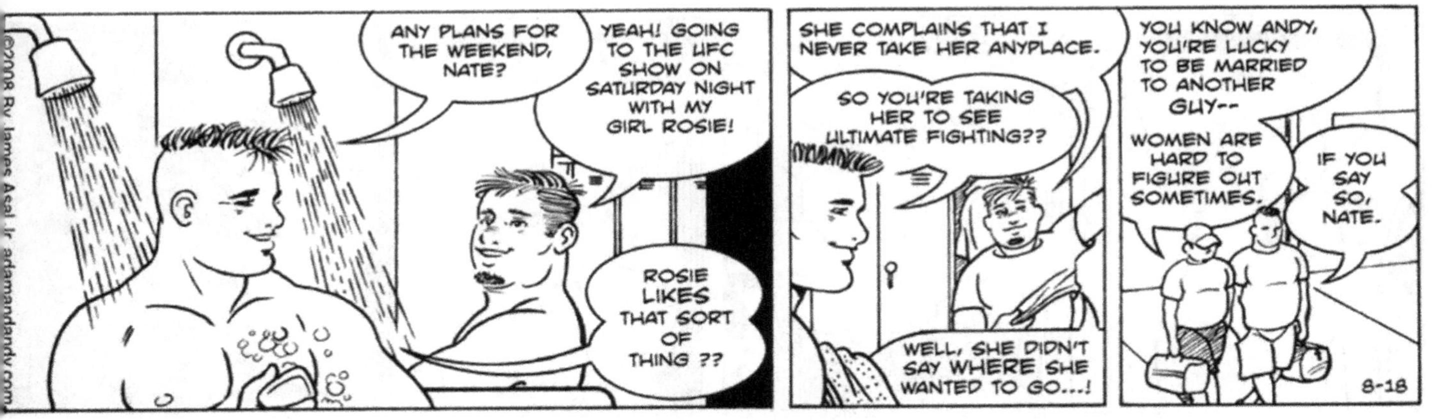
ANY PLANS FOR THE WEEKEND, NATE?
YEAH! GOING TO THE UFC SHOW ON SATURDAY NIGHT WITH MY GIRL ROSIE!
ROSIE LIKES THAT SORT OF THING ??
SHE COMPLAINS THAT I NEVER TAKE HER ANYPLACE.
SO YOU'RE TAKING HER TO SEE ULTIMATE FIGHTING??
WELL, SHE DIDN'T SAY WHERE SHE WANTED TO GO...!
YOU KNOW ANDY, YOU'RE LUCKY TO BE MARRIED TO ANOTHER GUY--
WOMEN ARE HARD TO FIGURE OUT SOMETIMES.
IF YOU SAY SO, NATE.
8-18

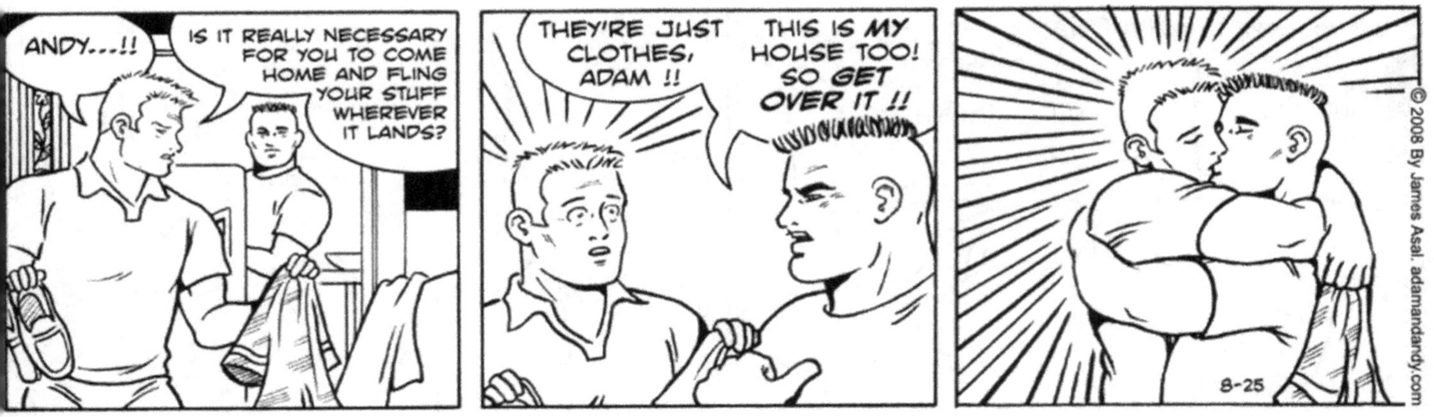
ANDY...!!
IS IT REALLY NECESSARY FOR YOU TO COME HOME AND FLING YOUR STUFF WHEREVER IT LANDS?
THEY'RE JUST CLOTHES, ADAM !!
THIS IS MY HOUSE TOO! SO GET OVER IT !!
© 2008 By James Asal. adamandandy.com
8-25

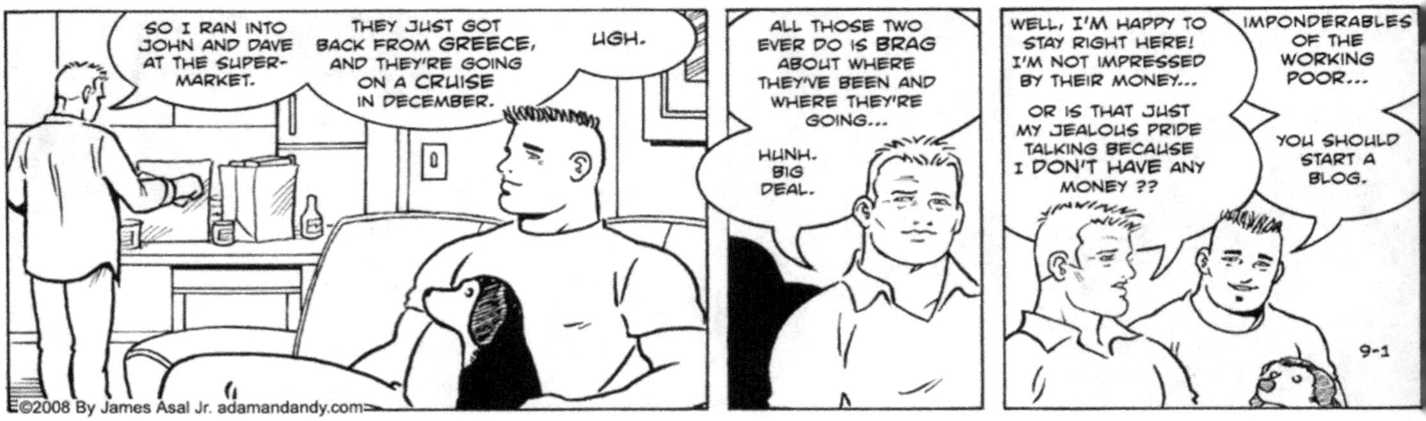
SO I RAN INTO JOHN AND DAVE AT THE SUPER-MARKET.
THEY JUST GOT BACK FROM GREECE, AND THEY'RE GOING ON A CRUISE IN DECEMBER.
UGH.
ALL THOSE TWO EVER DO IS BRAG ABOUT WHERE THEY'VE BEEN AND WHERE THEY'RE GOING...
HUNH. BIG DEAL.
WELL, I'M HAPPY TO STAY RIGHT HERE! I'M NOT IMPRESSED BY THEIR MONEY...
OR IS THAT JUST MY JEALOUS PRIDE TALKING BECAUSE I DON'T HAVE ANY MONEY ??
IMPONDERABLES OF THE WORKING POOR...
YOU SHOULD START A BLOG.
9-1
©2008 By James Asal Jr. adamandandy.com

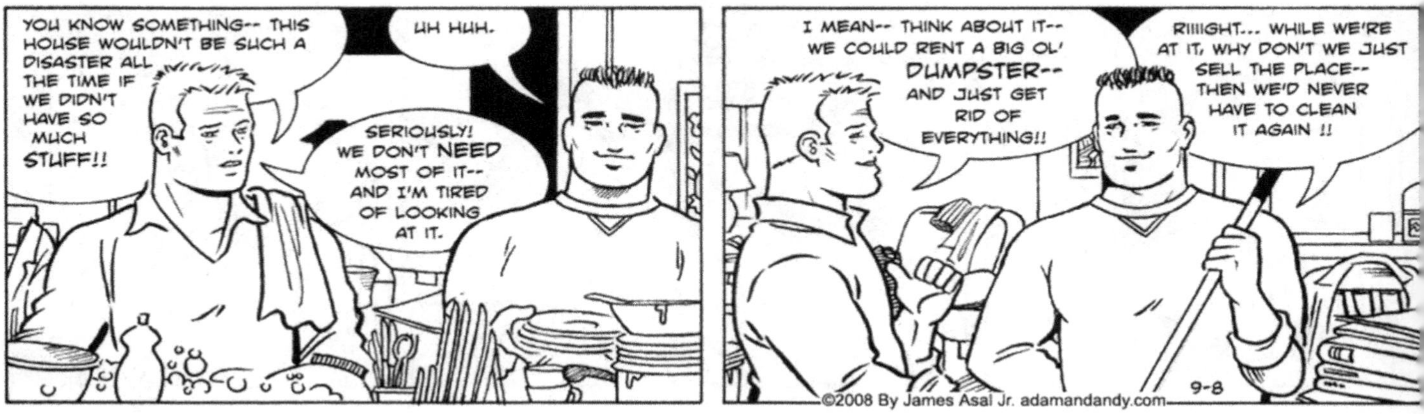
YOU KNOW SOMETHING-- THIS HOUSE WOULDN'T BE SUCH A DISASTER ALL THE TIME IF WE DIDN'T HAVE SO MUCH STUFF!!
UH HUH.
SERIOUSLY! WE DON'T NEED MOST OF IT-- AND I'M TIRED OF LOOKING AT IT.
I MEAN-- THINK ABOUT IT-- WE COULD RENT A BIG OL' DUMPSTER-- AND JUST GET RID OF EVERYTHING!!
RIIIGHT... WHILE WE'RE AT IT, WHY DON'T WE JUST SELL THE PLACE-- THEN WE'D NEVER HAVE TO CLEAN IT AGAIN !!
9-8
©2008 By James Asal Jr. adamandandy.com

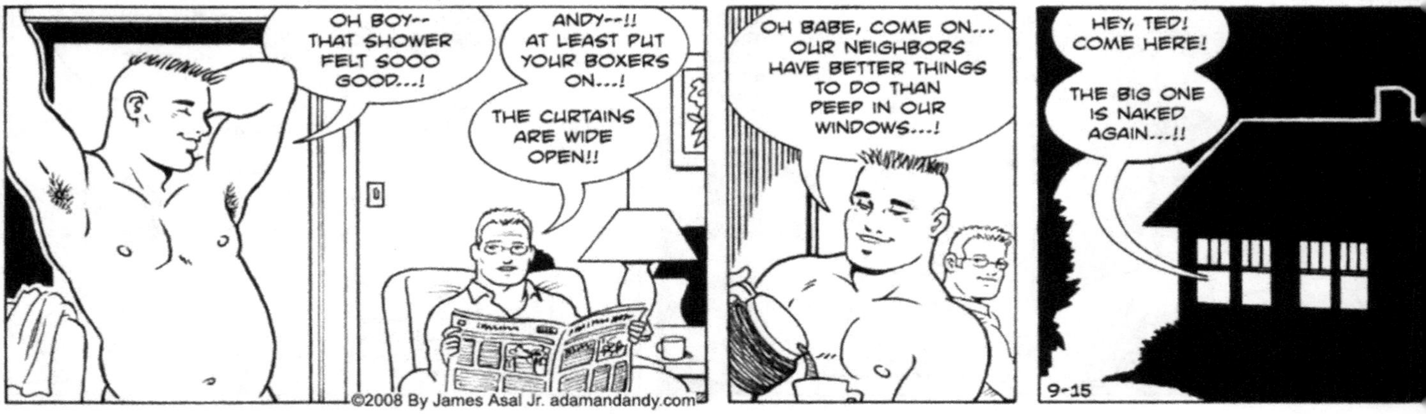
OH BOY-- THAT SHOWER FELT SOOO GOOD...!
ANDY--!! AT LEAST PUT YOUR BOXERS ON...!
THE CURTAINS ARE WIDE OPEN!!
OH BABE, COME ON... OUR NEIGHBORS HAVE BETTER THINGS TO DO THAN PEEP IN OUR WINDOWS...!
HEY, TED! COME HERE!
THE BIG ONE IS NAKED AGAIN...!!
9-15
©2008 By James Asal Jr. adamandandy.com

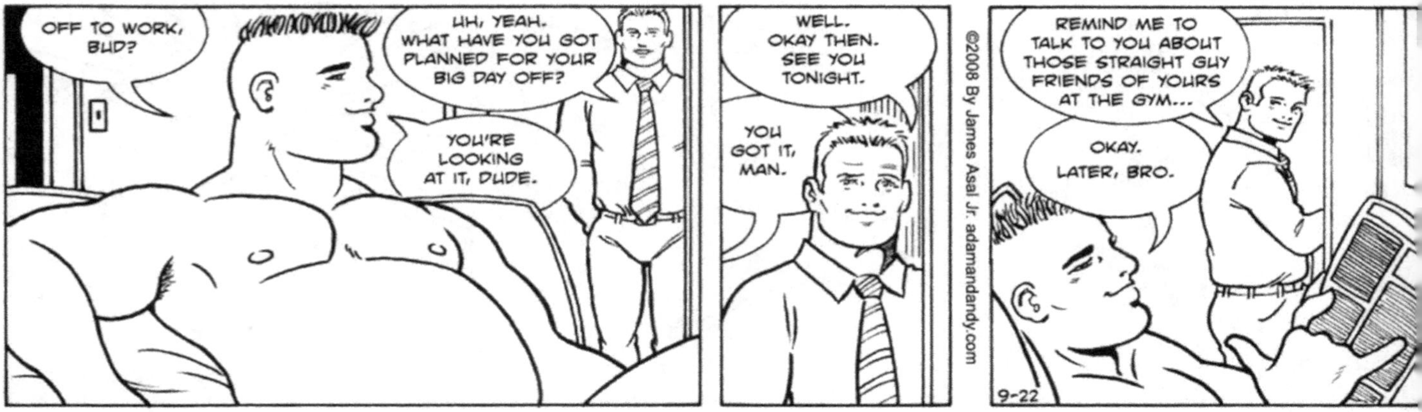
OFF TO WORK, BUD?
UH, YEAH. WHAT HAVE YOU GOT PLANNED FOR YOUR BIG DAY OFF?
YOU'RE LOOKING AT IT, DUDE.
WELL. OKAY THEN. SEE YOU TONIGHT.
YOU GOT IT, MAN.
REMIND ME TO TALK TO YOU ABOUT THOSE STRAIGHT GUY FRIENDS OF YOURS AT THE GYM...
OKAY. LATER, BRO.
9-22
©2008 By James Asal Jr. adamandandy.com

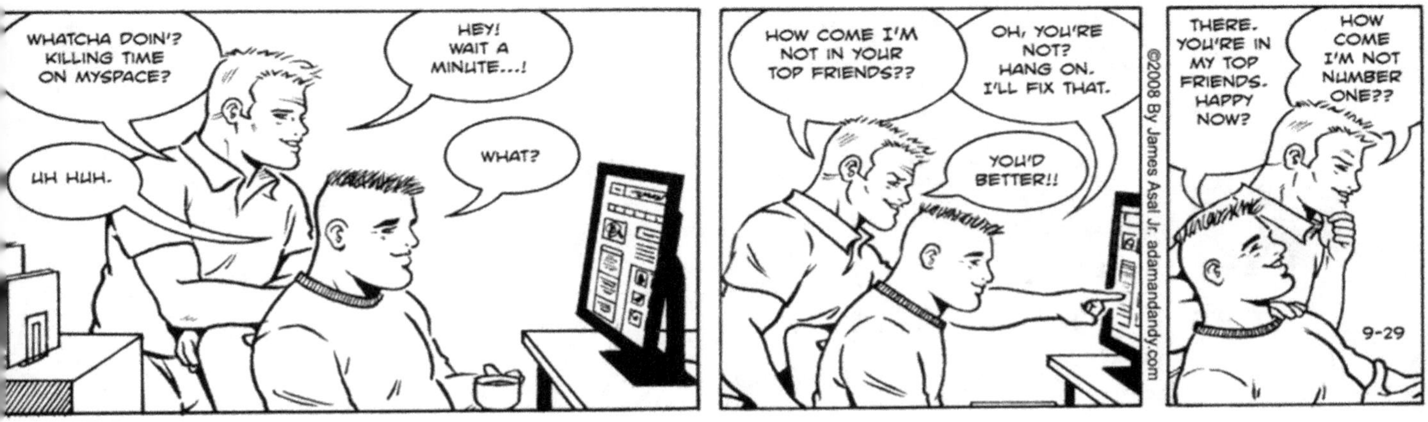
WHATCHA DOIN'? KILLING TIME ON MYSPACE?
UH HUH.
HEY! WAIT A MINUTE...!
WHAT?
HOW COME I'M NOT IN YOUR TOP FRIENDS??
OH, YOU'RE NOT? HANG ON. I'LL FIX THAT.
YOU'D BETTER!!
THERE. YOU'RE IN MY TOP FRIENDS. HAPPY NOW?
HOW COME I'M NOT NUMBER ONE??
9-29
©2008 By James Asal Jr. adamandandy.com

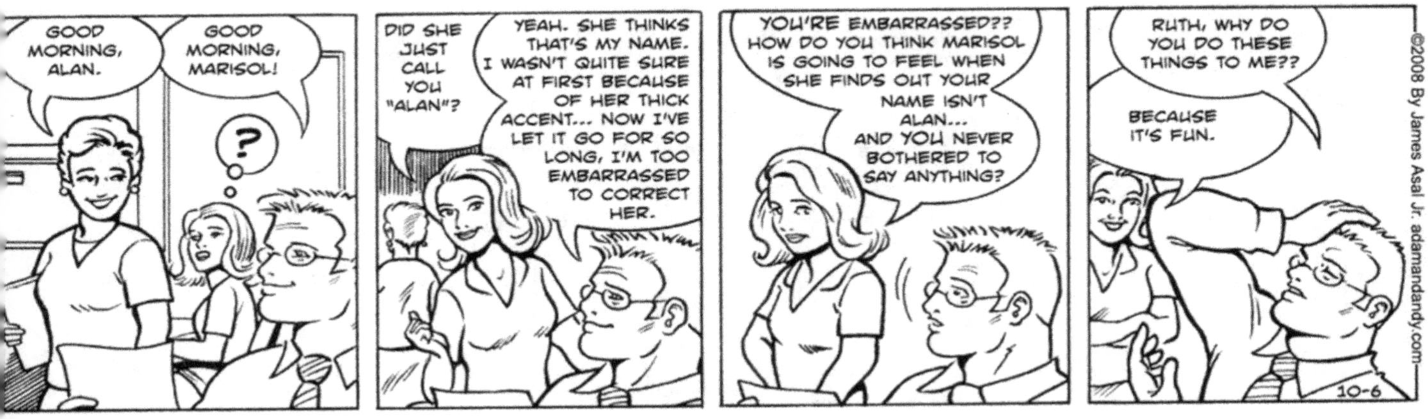
GOOD MORNING, ALAN.
GOOD MORNING, MARISOL!
?
DID SHE JUST CALL YOU "ALAN"?
YEAH. SHE THINKS THAT'S MY NAME. I WASN'T QUITE SURE AT FIRST BECAUSE OF HER THICK ACCENT... NOW I'VE LET IT GO FOR SO LONG, I'M TOO EMBARRASSED TO CORRECT HER.
YOU'RE EMBARRASSED?? HOW DO YOU THINK MARISOL IS GOING TO FEEL WHEN SHE FINDS OUT YOUR NAME ISN'T ALAN... AND YOU NEVER BOTHERED TO SAY ANYTHING?
RUTH, WHY DO YOU DO THESE THINGS TO ME??
BECAUSE IT'S FUN.
10-6
©2008 By James Asal Jr. adamandandy.com

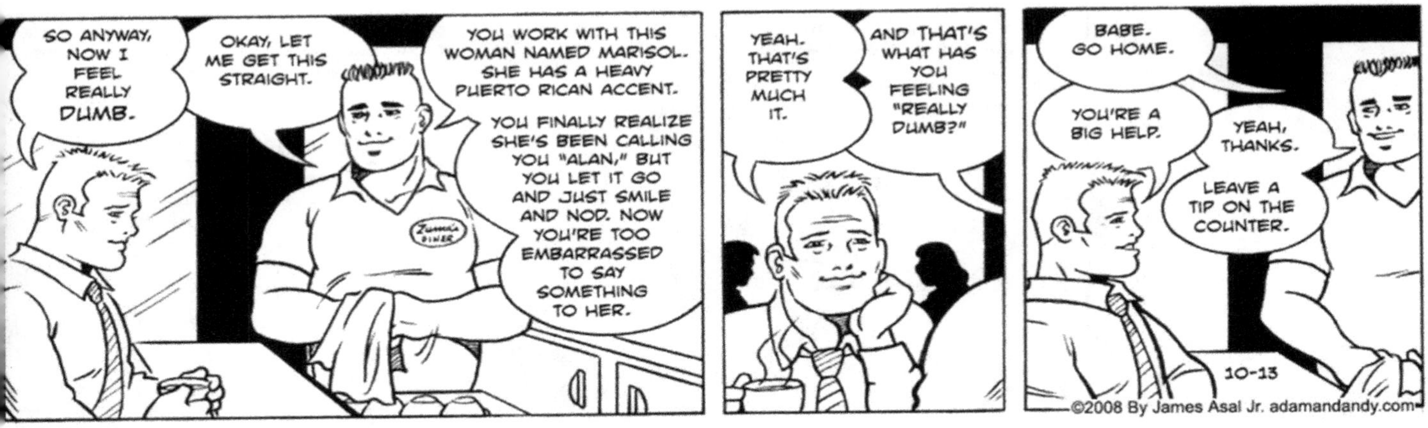
SO ANYWAY, NOW I FEEL REALLY DUMB.
OKAY, LET ME GET THIS STRAIGHT.
YOU WORK WITH THIS WOMAN NAMED MARISOL. SHE HAS A HEAVY PUERTO RICAN ACCENT.
YOU FINALLY REALIZE SHE'S BEEN CALLING YOU "ALAN," BUT YOU LET IT GO AND JUST SMILE AND NOD. NOW YOU'RE TOO EMBARRASSED TO SAY SOMETHING TO HER.
YEAH. THAT'S PRETTY MUCH IT.
AND THAT'S WHAT HAS YOU FEELING "REALLY DUMB?"
BABE. GO HOME.
YOU'RE A BIG HELP.
YEAH, THANKS.
LEAVE A TIP ON THE COUNTER.
10-13
©2008 By James Asal Jr. adamandandy.com

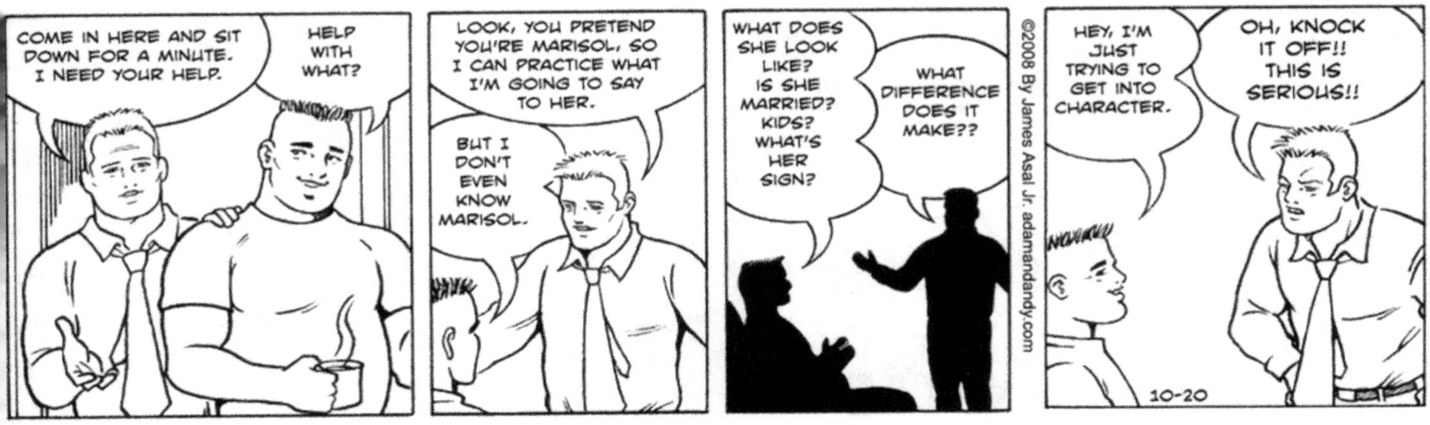
COME IN HERE AND SIT DOWN FOR A MINUTE. I NEED YOUR HELP.
HELP WITH WHAT?
LOOK, YOU PRETEND YOU'RE MARISOL, SO I CAN PRACTICE WHAT I'M GOING TO SAY TO HER.
BUT I DON'T EVEN KNOW MARISOL.
WHAT DOES SHE LOOK LIKE? IS SHE MARRIED? KIDS? WHAT'S HER SIGN?
WHAT DIFFERENCE DOES IT MAKE??
HEY, I'M JUST TRYING TO GET INTO CHARACTER.
OH, KNOCK IT OFF!! THIS IS SERIOUS!!
10-20
©2008 By James Asal Jr. adamandandy.com

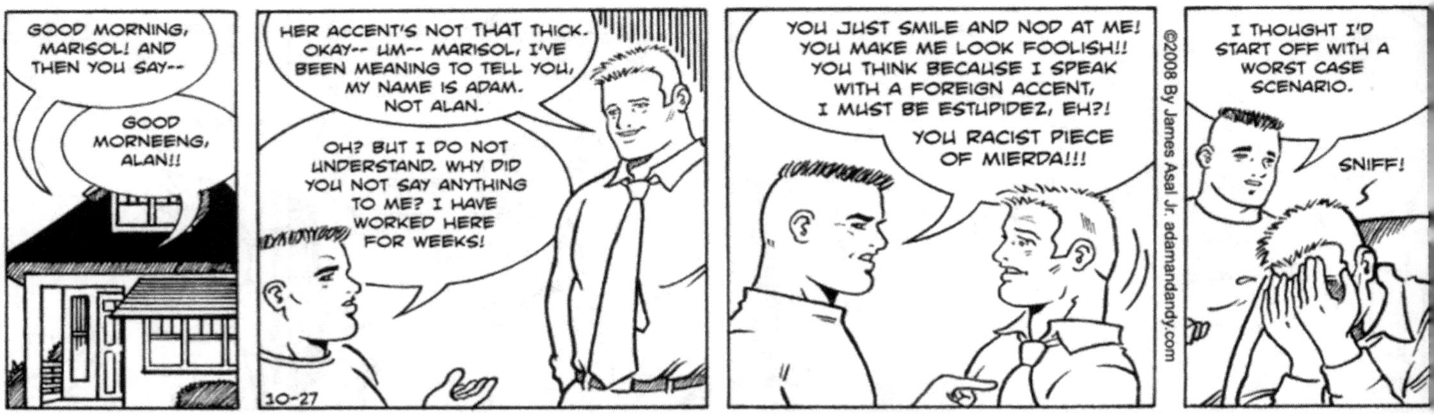
GOOD MORNING, MARISOL! AND THEN YOU SAY--
GOOD MORNEENG, ALAN!!
10-27
HER ACCENT'S NOT THAT THICK. OKAY-- UM-- MARISOL, I'VE BEEN MEANING TO TELL YOU, MY NAME IS ADAM. NOT ALAN.
OH? BUT I DO NOT UNDERSTAND. WHY DID YOU NOT SAY ANYTHING TO ME? I HAVE WORKED HERE FOR WEEKS!
YOU JUST SMILE AND NOD AT ME! YOU MAKE ME LOOK FOOLISH!! YOU THINK BECAUSE I SPEAK WITH A FOREIGN ACCENT, I MUST BE ESTUPIDEZ, EH?!
YOU RACIST PIECE OF MIERDA!!!
©2008 By James Asal Jr. adamandandy.com
I THOUGHT I'D START OFF WITH A WORST CASE SCENARIO.
SNIFF!

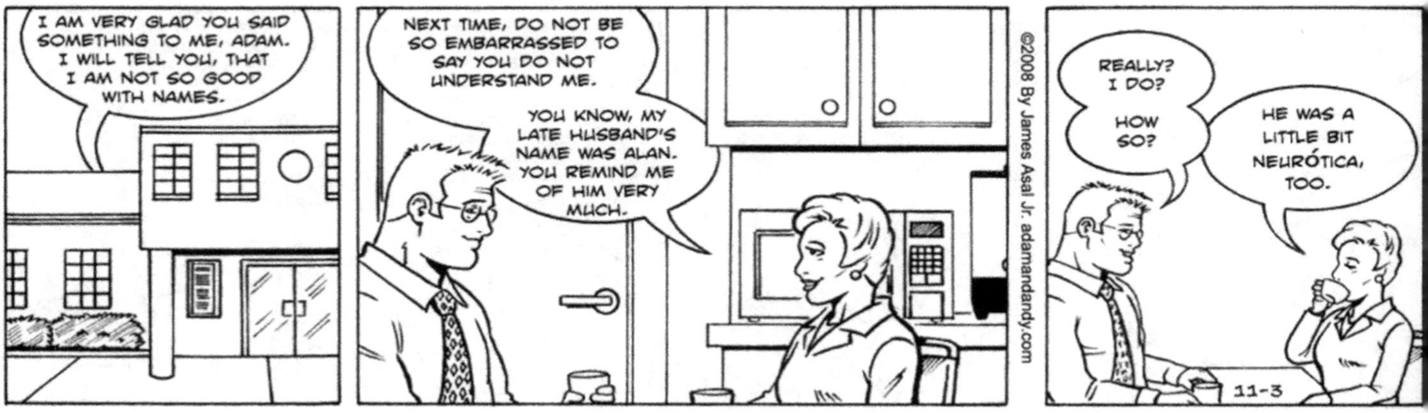
I AM VERY GLAD YOU SAID SOMETHING TO ME, ADAM. I WILL TELL YOU, THAT I AM NOT SO GOOD WITH NAMES.
NEXT TIME, DO NOT BE SO EMBARRASSED TO SAY YOU DO NOT UNDERSTAND ME.
YOU KNOW, MY LATE HUSBAND'S NAME WAS ALAN. YOU REMIND ME OF HIM VERY MUCH.
©2008 By James Asal Jr. adamandandy.com
REALLY? I DO?
HOW SO?
HE WAS A LITTLE BIT NEURÓTICA, TOO.
11-3

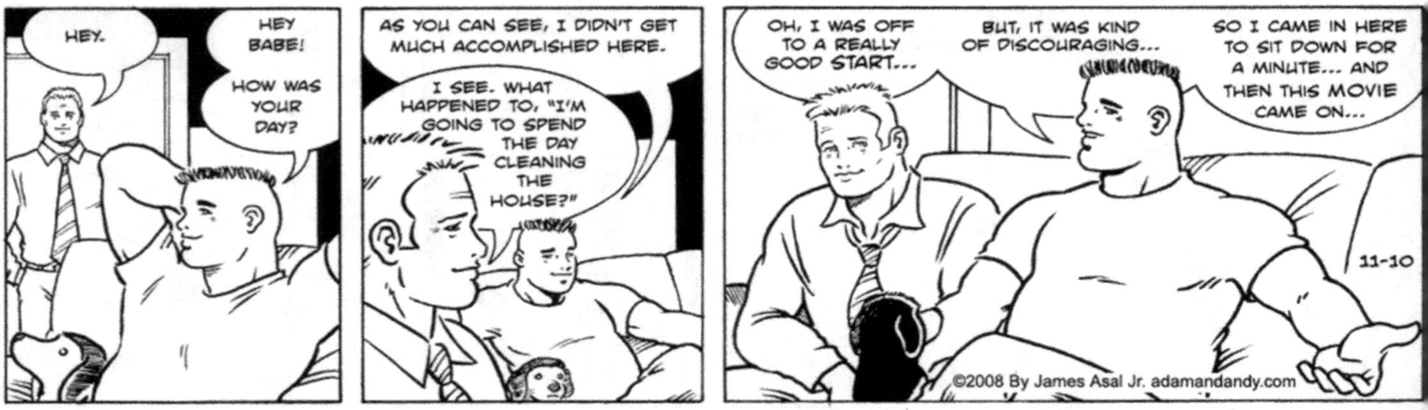
HEY.
HEY BABE!
HOW WAS YOUR DAY?
AS YOU CAN SEE, I DIDN'T GET MUCH ACCOMPLISHED HERE.
I SEE. WHAT HAPPENED TO, "I'M GOING TO SPEND THE DAY CLEANING THE HOUSE?"
OH, I WAS OFF TO A REALLY GOOD START...
BUT, IT WAS KIND OF DISCOURAGING...
SO I CAME IN HERE TO SIT DOWN FOR A MINUTE... AND THEN THIS MOVIE CAME ON...
11-10
©2008 By James Asal Jr. adamandandy.com

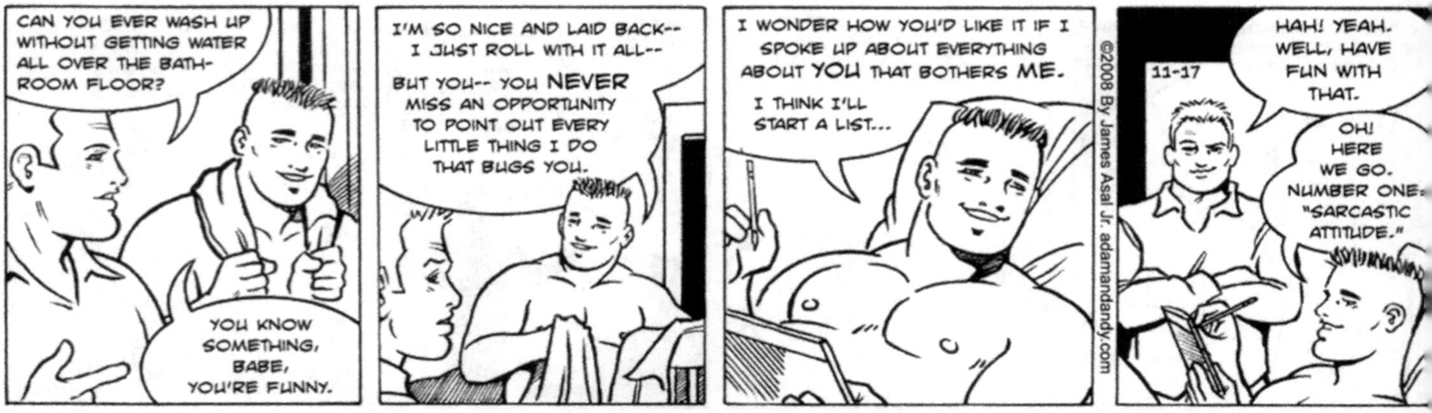
CAN YOU EVER WASH UP WITHOUT GETTING WATER ALL OVER THE BATH-ROOM FLOOR?
YOU KNOW SOMETHING, BABE, YOU'RE FUNNY.
I'M SO NICE AND LAID BACK-- I JUST ROLL WITH IT ALL--
BUT YOU-- YOU NEVER MISS AN OPPORTUNITY TO POINT OUT EVERY LITTLE THING I DO THAT BUGS YOU.
I WONDER HOW YOU'D LIKE IT IF I SPOKE UP ABOUT EVERYTHING ABOUT YOU THAT BOTHERS ME.
I THINK I'LL START A LIST...
©2008 By James Asal Jr. adamandandy.com
11-17
HAH! YEAH. WELL, HAVE FUN WITH THAT.
OH! HERE WE GO. NUMBER ONE: "SARCASTIC ATTITUDE."

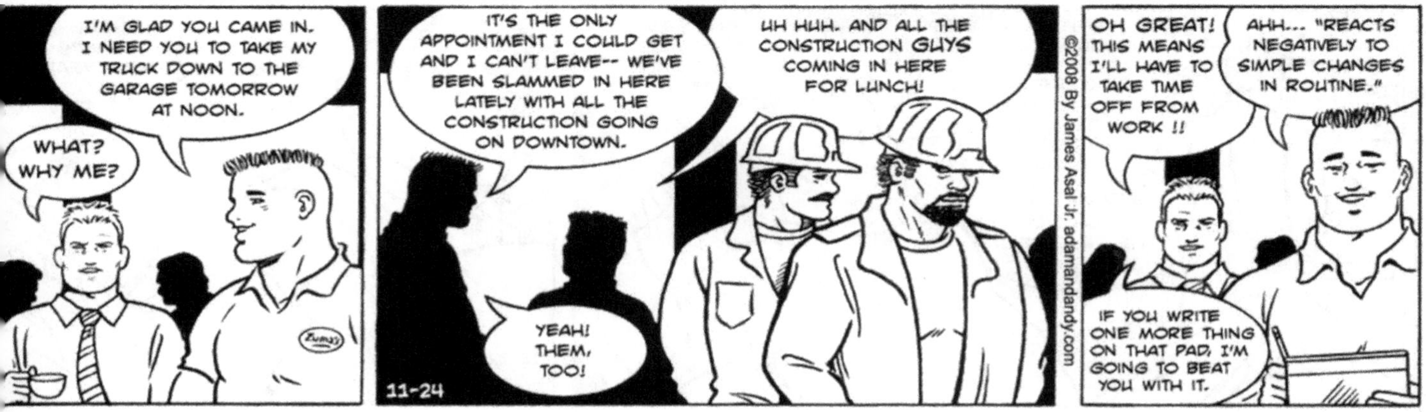
I'M GLAD YOU CAME IN. I NEED YOU TO TAKE MY TRUCK DOWN TO THE GARAGE TOMORROW AT NOON.
WHAT? WHY ME?
IT'S THE ONLY APPOINTMENT I COULD GET AND I CAN'T LEAVE-- WE'VE BEEN SLAMMED IN HERE LATELY WITH ALL THE CONSTRUCTION GOING ON DOWNTOWN.
UH HUH. AND ALL THE CONSTRUCTION GUYS COMING IN HERE FOR LUNCH!
YEAH! THEM, TOO!
11-24
OH GREAT! THIS MEANS I'LL HAVE TO TAKE TIME OFF FROM WORK !!
AHH... "REACTS NEGATIVELY TO SIMPLE CHANGES IN ROUTINE."
IF YOU WRITE ONE MORE THING ON THAT PAD, I'M GOING TO BEAT YOU WITH IT.
©2008 By James Asal Jr. adamandandy.com

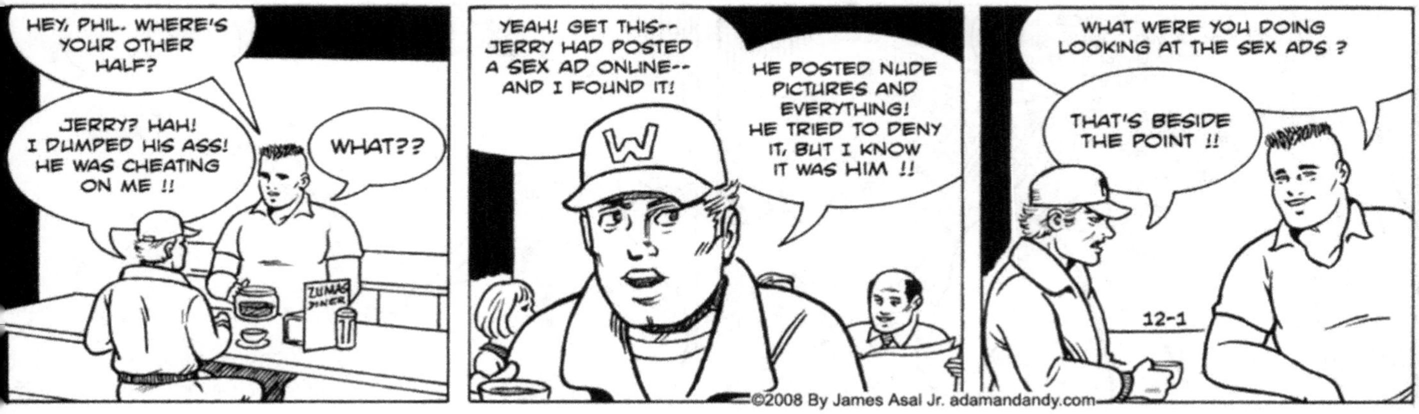
HEY, PHIL. WHERE'S YOUR OTHER HALF?
JERRY? HAH! I DUMPED HIS ASS! HE WAS CHEATING ON ME !!
WHAT??
YEAH! GET THIS-- JERRY HAD POSTED A SEX AD ONLINE-- AND I FOUND IT!
HE POSTED NUDE PICTURES AND EVERYTHING! HE TRIED TO DENY IT, BUT I KNOW IT WAS HIM !!
WHAT WERE YOU DOING LOOKING AT THE SEX ADS ?
THAT'S BESIDE THE POINT !!
12-1
©2008 By James Asal Jr. adamandandy.com

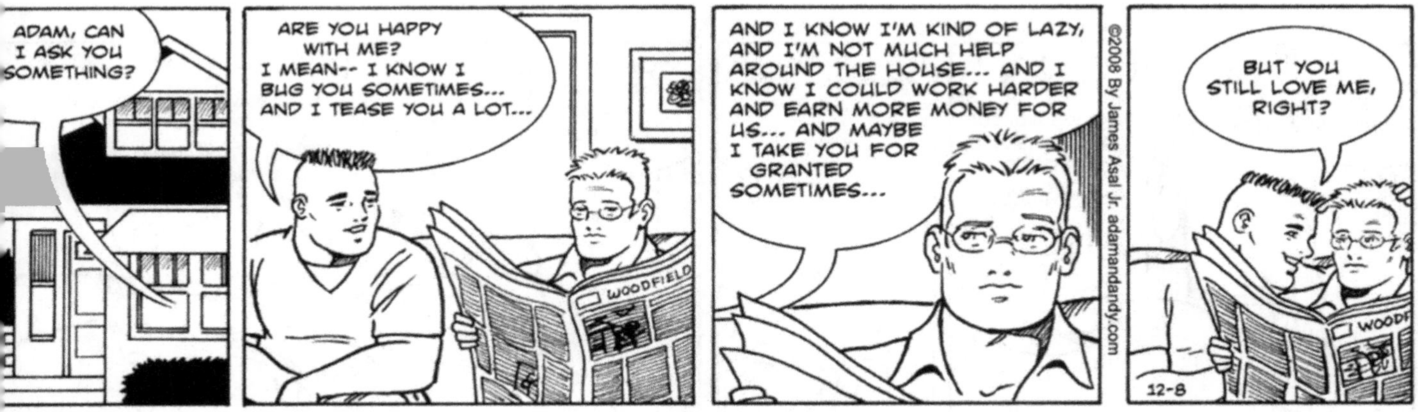
ADAM, CAN I ASK YOU SOMETHING?
ARE YOU HAPPY WITH ME? I MEAN-- I KNOW I BUG YOU SOMETIMES... AND I TEASE YOU A LOT...
WOODFIELD
AND I KNOW I'M KIND OF LAZY, AND I'M NOT MUCH HELP AROUND THE HOUSE... AND I KNOW I COULD WORK HARDER AND EARN MORE MONEY FOR US... AND MAYBE I TAKE YOU FOR GRANTED SOMETIMES...
©2008 By James Asal Jr. adamandandy.com
BUT YOU STILL LOVE ME, RIGHT?
12-8

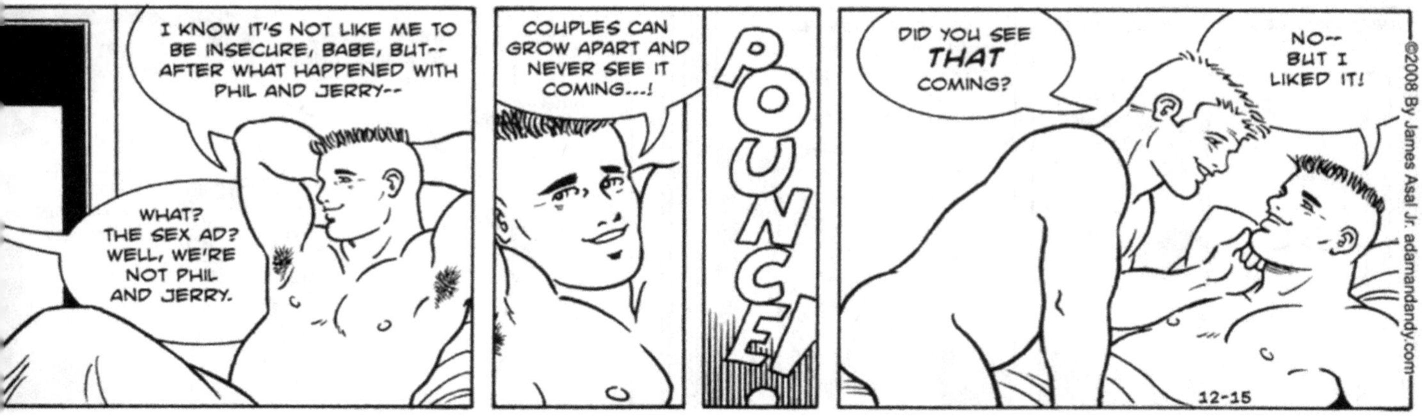
I KNOW IT'S NOT LIKE ME TO BE INSECURE, BABE, BUT-- AFTER WHAT HAPPENED WITH PHIL AND JERRY--
WHAT? THE SEX AD? WELL, WE'RE NOT PHIL AND JERRY.
COUPLES CAN GROW APART AND NEVER SEE IT COMING...!
POUNCE!
DID YOU SEE THAT COMING?
NO-- BUT I LIKED IT!
12-15
©2008 By James Asal Jr. adamandandy.com

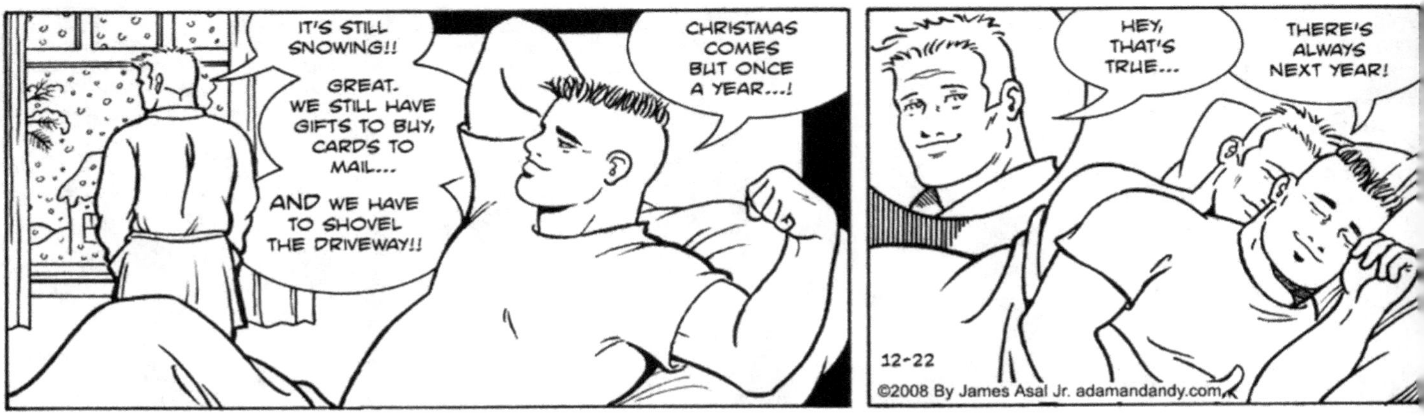
IT'S STILL SNOWING!!
GREAT. WE STILL HAVE GIFTS TO BUY, CARDS TO MAIL...
AND WE HAVE TO SHOVEL THE DRIVEWAY!!
CHRISTMAS COMES BUT ONCE A YEAR...!
HEY, THAT'S TRUE...
THERE'S ALWAYS NEXT YEAR!
12-22
©2008 By James Asal Jr. adamandandy.com

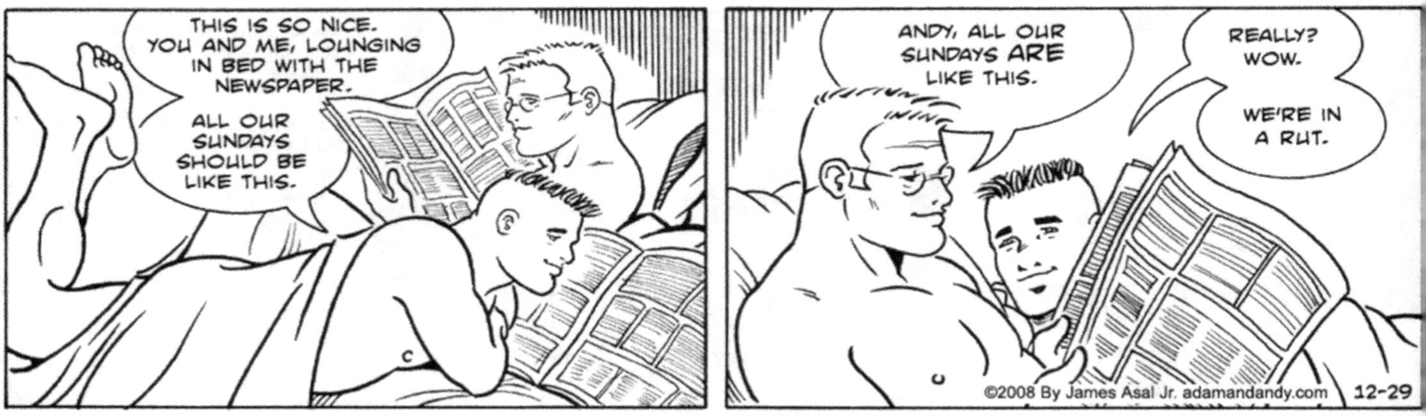
THIS IS SO NICE. YOU AND ME, LOUNGING IN BED WITH THE NEWSPAPER.
ALL OUR SUNDAYS SHOULD BE LIKE THIS.
ANDY, ALL OUR SUNDAYS ARE LIKE THIS.
REALLY? WOW.
WE'RE IN A RUT.
©2008 By James Asal Jr. adamandandy.com
12-29

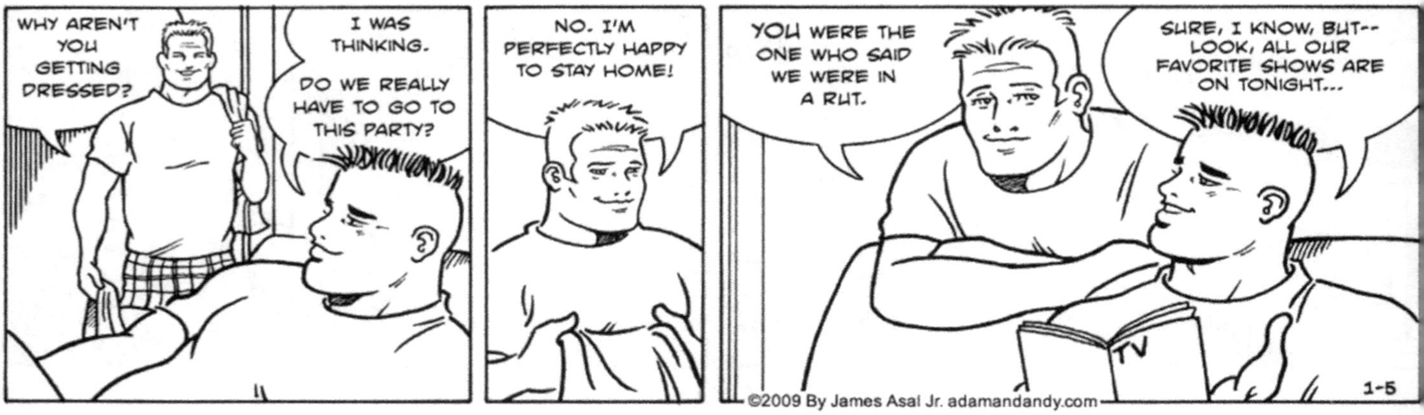
WHY AREN'T YOU GETTING DRESSED?
I WAS THINKING.
DO WE REALLY HAVE TO GO TO THIS PARTY?
NO. I'M PERFECTLY HAPPY TO STAY HOME!
YOU WERE THE ONE WHO SAID WE WERE IN A RUT.
SURE, I KNOW, BUT-- LOOK, ALL OUR FAVORITE SHOWS ARE ON TONIGHT...
TV
©2009 By James Asal Jr. adamandandy.com
1-5

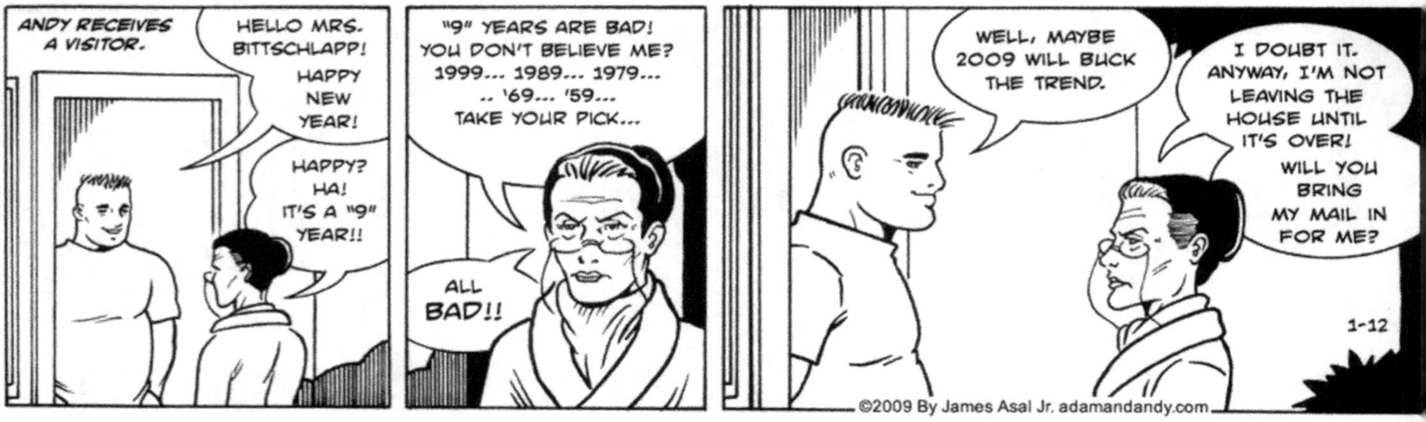
ANDY RECEIVES A VISITOR.
HELLO MRS. BITTSCHLAPP!
HAPPY NEW YEAR!
HAPPY? HA! IT'S A "9" YEAR!!
"9" YEARS ARE BAD! YOU DON'T BELIEVE ME? 1999... 1989... 1979... .. '69... '59... TAKE YOUR PICK...
ALL BAD!!
WELL, MAYBE 2009 WILL BUCK THE TREND.
I DOUBT IT. ANYWAY, I'M NOT LEAVING THE HOUSE UNTIL IT'S OVER!
WILL YOU BRING MY MAIL IN FOR ME?
1-12
©2009 By James Asal Jr. adamandandy.com

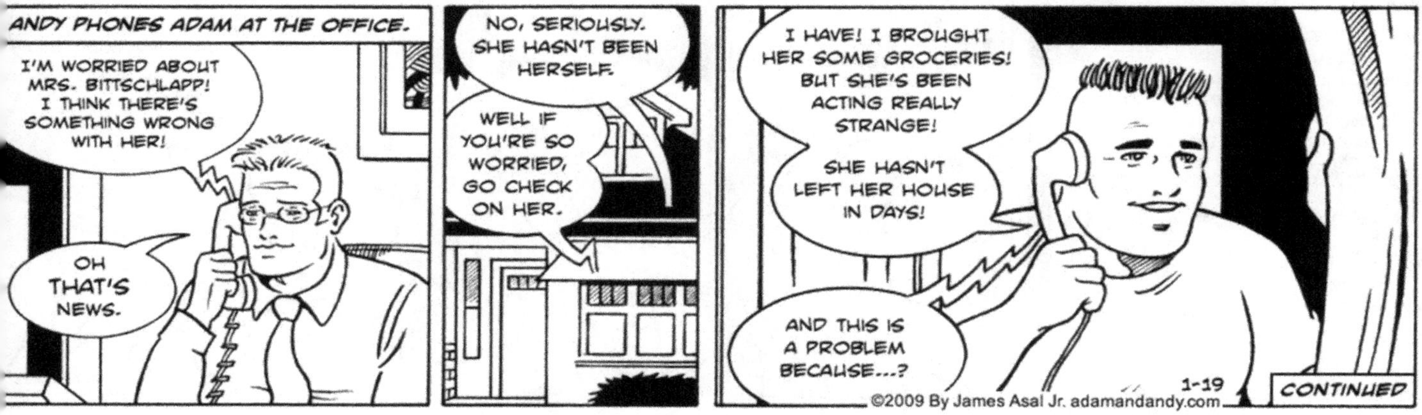
ANDY PHONES ADAM AT THE OFFICE.
I'M WORRIED ABOUT MRS. BITTSCHLAPP! I THINK THERE'S SOMETHING WRONG WITH HER!
OH THAT'S NEWS.
NO, SERIOUSLY. SHE HASN'T BEEN HERSELF.
WELL IF YOU'RE SO WORRIED, GO CHECK ON HER.
I HAVE! I BROUGHT HER SOME GROCERIES! BUT SHE'S BEEN ACTING REALLY STRANGE!
SHE HASN'T LEFT HER HOUSE IN DAYS!
AND THIS IS A PROBLEM BECAUSE...?
1-19
©2009 By James Asal Jr. adamandandy.com
CONTINUED

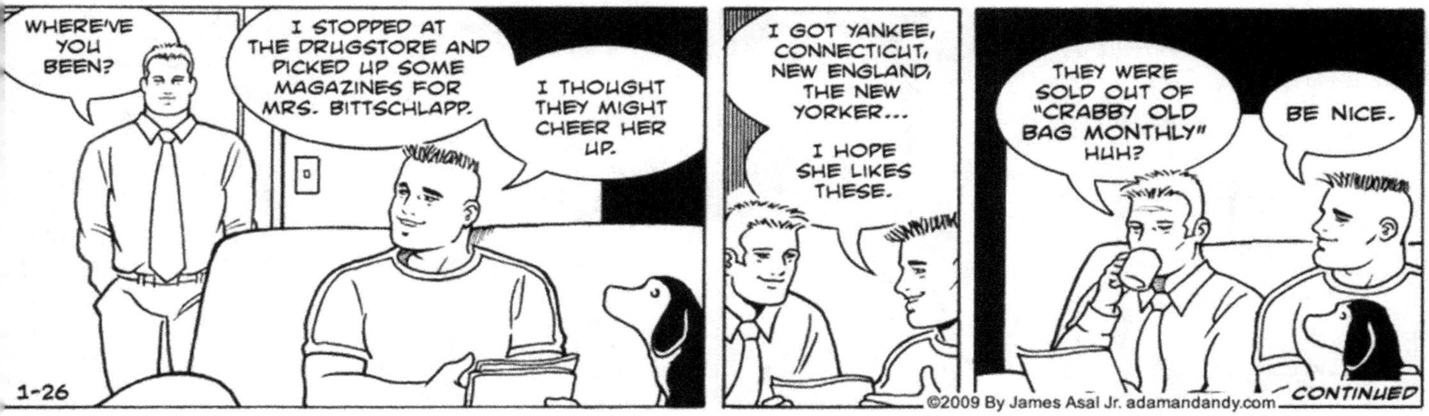
WHERE'VE YOU BEEN?
I STOPPED AT THE DRUGSTORE AND PICKED UP SOME MAGAZINES FOR MRS. BITTSCHLAPP.
I THOUGHT THEY MIGHT CHEER HER UP.
1-26
I GOT YANKEE, CONNECTICUT, NEW ENGLAND, THE NEW YORKER...
I HOPE SHE LIKES THESE.
THEY WERE SOLD OUT OF "CRABBY OLD BAG MONTHLY" HUH?
BE NICE.
©2009 By James Asal Jr. adamandandy.com
CONTINUED

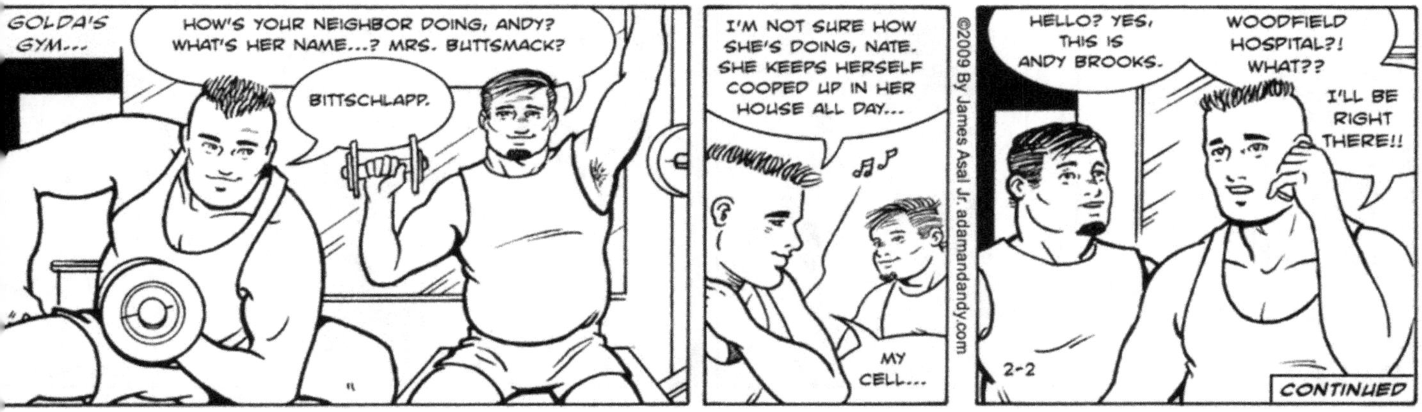
GOLDA'S GYM...
HOW'S YOUR NEIGHBOR DOING, ANDY? WHAT'S HER NAME...? MRS. BUTTSMACK?
BITTSCHLAPP.
I'M NOT SURE HOW SHE'S DOING, NATE. SHE KEEPS HERSELF COOPED UP IN HER HOUSE ALL DAY...
MY CELL...
©2009 By James Asal Jr. adamandandy.com
HELLO? YES, THIS IS ANDY BROOKS.
WOODFIELD HOSPITAL?! WHAT??
I'LL BE RIGHT THERE!!
2-2
CONTINUED

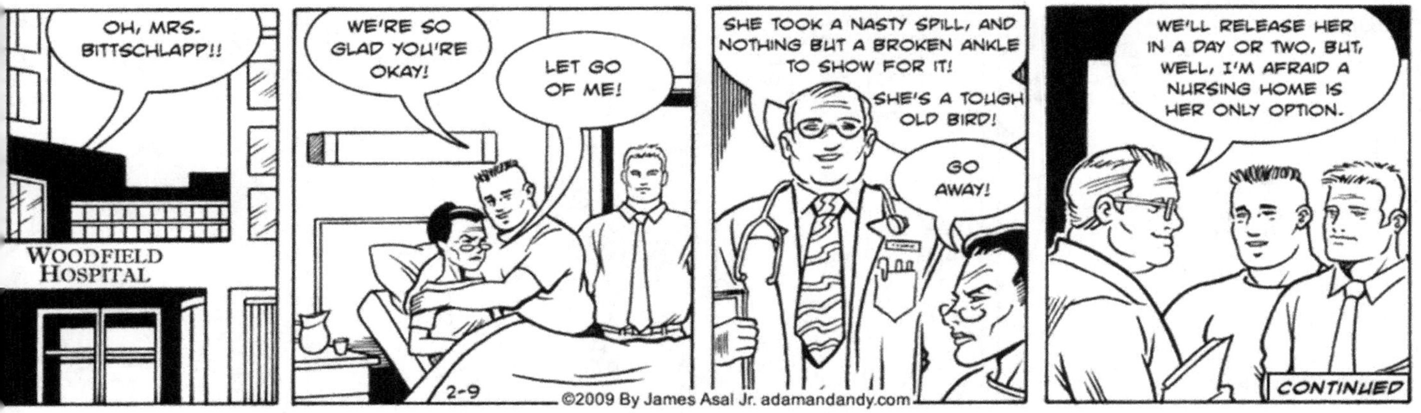
OH, MRS. BITTSCHLAPP!!
WOODFIELD HOSPITAL
WE'RE SO GLAD YOU'RE OKAY!
LET GO OF ME!
2-9
SHE TOOK A NASTY SPILL, AND NOTHING BUT A BROKEN ANKLE TO SHOW FOR IT!
SHE'S A TOUGH OLD BIRD!
GO AWAY!
WE'LL RELEASE HER IN A DAY OR TWO, BUT, WELL, I'M AFRAID A NURSING HOME IS HER ONLY OPTION.
©2009 By James Asal Jr. adamandandy.com
CONTINUED

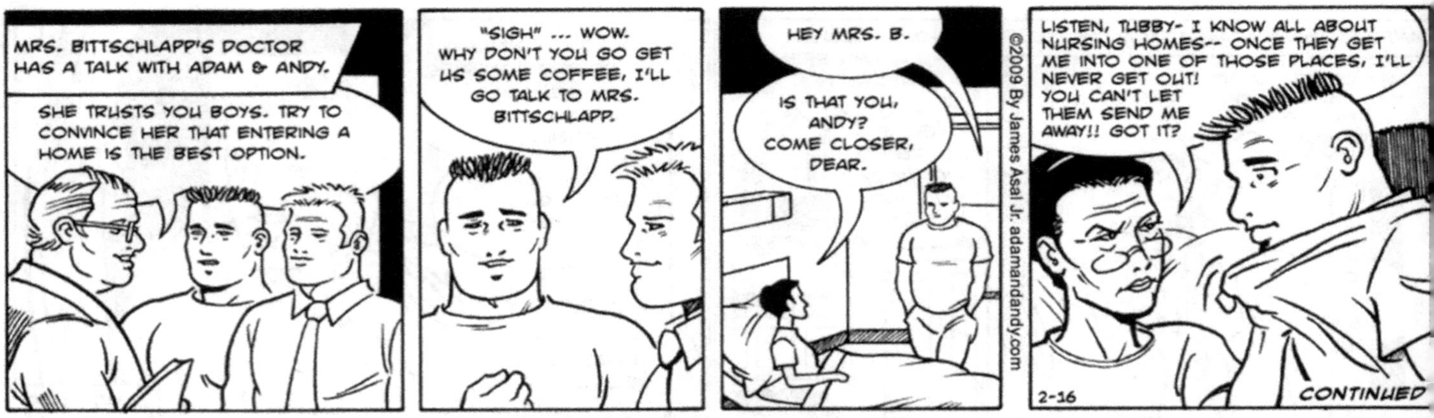
MRS. BITTSCHLAPP'S DOCTOR HAS A TALK WITH ADAM & ANDY.
SHE TRUSTS YOU BOYS. TRY TO CONVINCE HER THAT ENTERING A HOME IS THE BEST OPTION.
"SIGH" ... WOW. WHY DON'T YOU GO GET US SOME COFFEE, I'LL GO TALK TO MRS. BITTSCHLAPP.
HEY MRS. B.
IS THAT YOU, ANDY? COME CLOSER, DEAR.
©2009 By James Asal Jr. adamandandy.com
LISTEN, TUBBY- I KNOW ALL ABOUT NURSING HOMES-- ONCE THEY GET ME INTO ONE OF THOSE PLACES, I'LL NEVER GET OUT! YOU CAN'T LET THEM SEND ME AWAY!! GOT IT?
2-16
CONTINUED

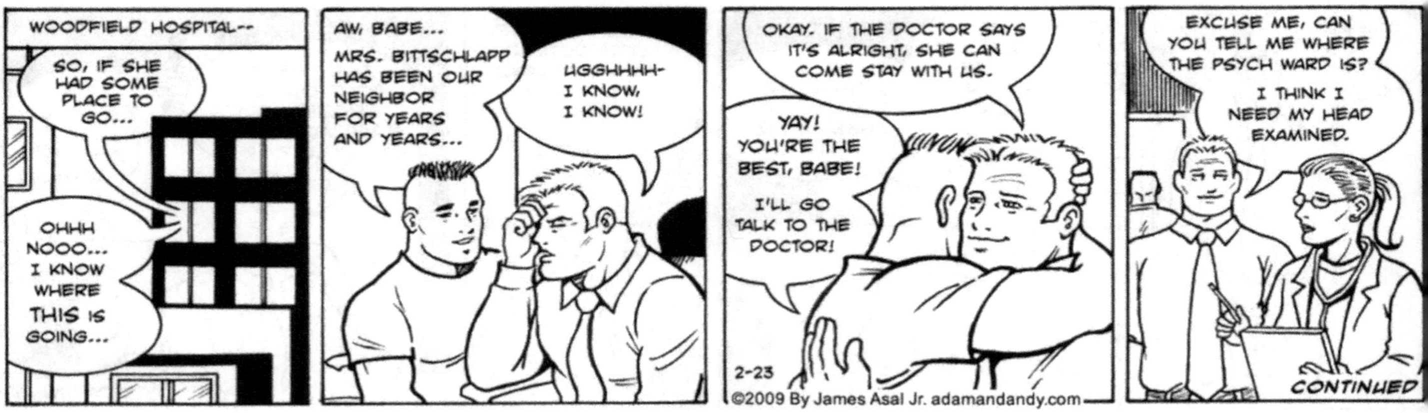
WOODFIELD HOSPITAL--
SO, IF SHE HAD SOME PLACE TO GO...
OHHH NOOO... I KNOW WHERE THIS IS GOING...
AW, BABE...
MRS. BITTSCHLAPP HAS BEEN OUR NEIGHBOR FOR YEARS AND YEARS...
UGGHHHH- I KNOW, I KNOW!
OKAY. IF THE DOCTOR SAYS IT'S ALRIGHT, SHE CAN COME STAY WITH US.
YAY! YOU'RE THE BEST, BABE!
I'LL GO TALK TO THE DOCTOR!
2-23
©2009 By James Asal Jr. adamandandy.com
EXCUSE ME, CAN YOU TELL ME WHERE THE PSYCH WARD IS?
I THINK I NEED MY HEAD EXAMINED.
CONTINUED

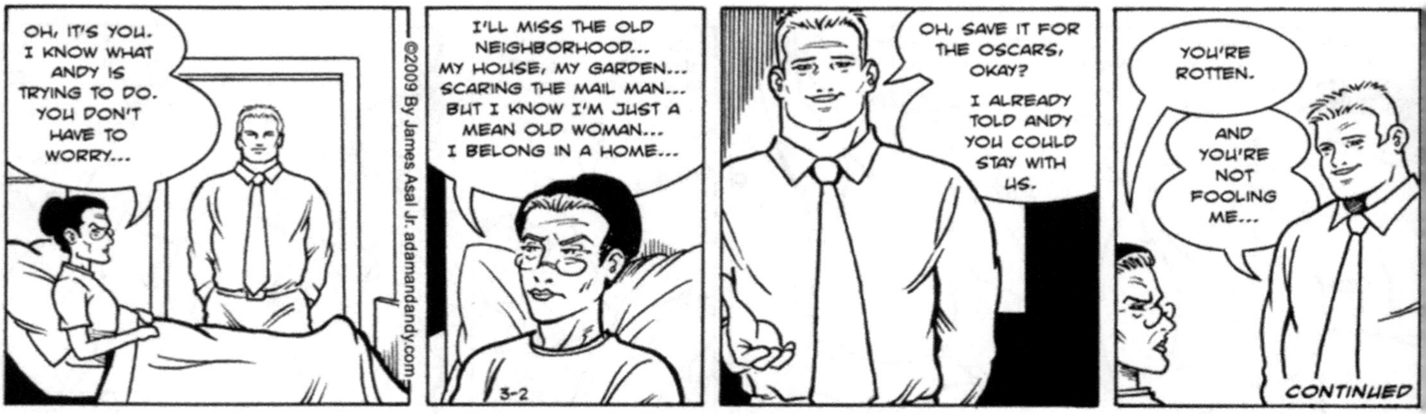
OH, IT'S YOU. I KNOW WHAT ANDY IS TRYING TO DO. YOU DON'T HAVE TO WORRY...
©2009 By James Asal Jr. adamandandy.com
I'LL MISS THE OLD NEIGHBORHOOD... MY HOUSE, MY GARDEN... SCARING THE MAIL MAN... BUT I KNOW I'M JUST A MEAN OLD WOMAN... I BELONG IN A HOME...
3-2
OH, SAVE IT FOR THE OSCARS, OKAY?
I ALREADY TOLD ANDY YOU COULD STAY WITH US.
YOU'RE ROTTEN.
AND YOU'RE NOT FOOLING ME...
CONTINUED

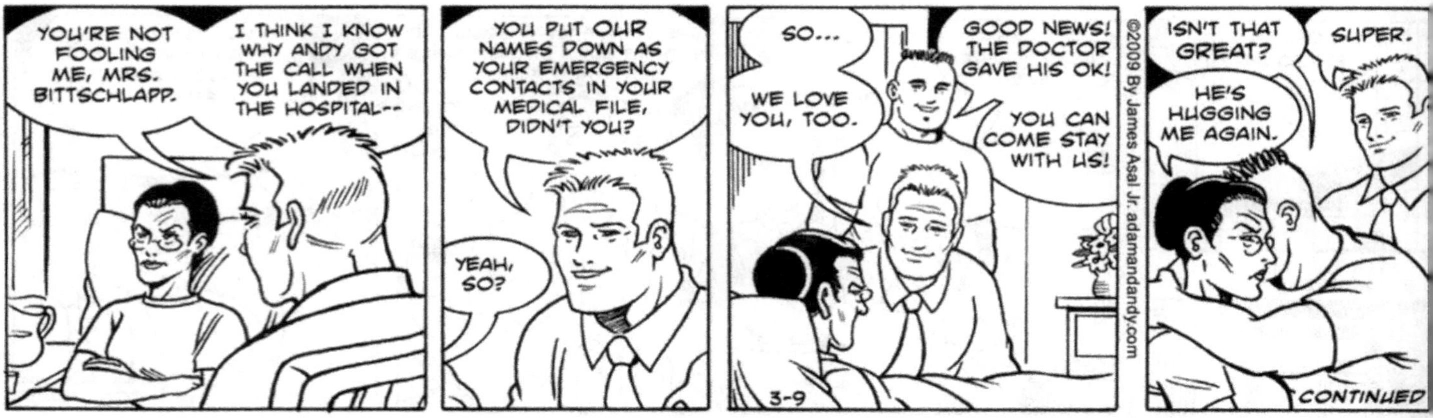
YOU'RE NOT FOOLING ME, MRS. BITTSCHLAPP.
I THINK I KNOW WHY ANDY GOT THE CALL WHEN YOU LANDED IN THE HOSPITAL--
YOU PUT OUR NAMES DOWN AS YOUR EMERGENCY CONTACTS IN YOUR MEDICAL FILE, DIDN'T YOU?
YEAH, SO?
SO...
WE LOVE YOU, TOO.
GOOD NEWS! THE DOCTOR GAVE HIS OK!
YOU CAN COME STAY WITH US!
3-9
©2009 By James Asal Jr. adamandandy.com
ISN'T THAT GREAT?
SUPER.
HE'S HUGGING ME AGAIN.
CONTINUED

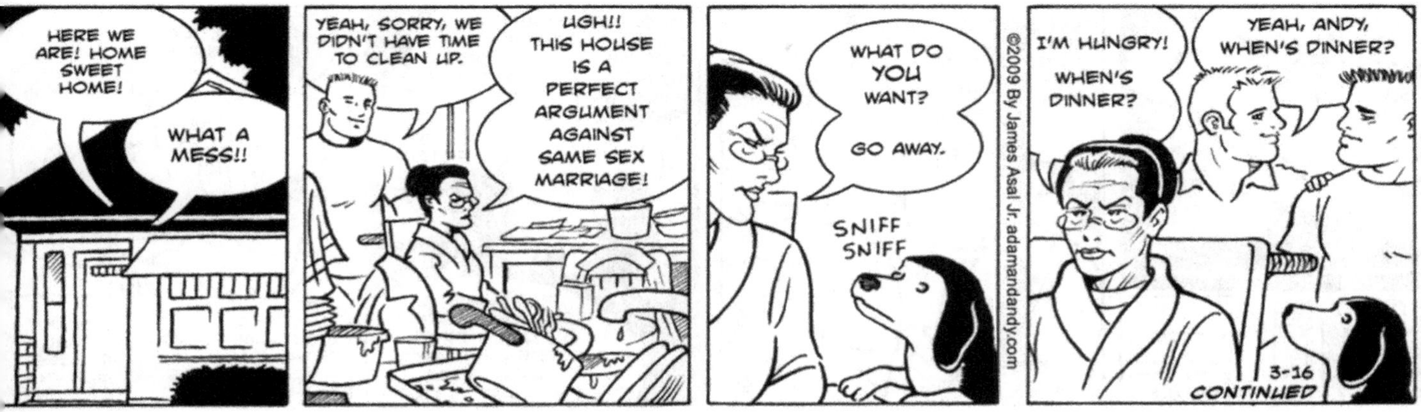
HERE WE ARE! HOME SWEET HOME!
WHAT A MESS!!
YEAH, SORRY, WE DIDN'T HAVE TIME TO CLEAN UP.
UGH!! THIS HOUSE IS A PERFECT ARGUMENT AGAINST SAME SEX MARRIAGE!
WHAT DO YOU WANT?
GO AWAY.
SNIFF SNIFF
©2009 By James Asal Jr. adamandandy.com
I'M HUNGRY!
WHEN'S DINNER?
YEAH, ANDY, WHEN'S DINNER?
3-16
CONTINUED

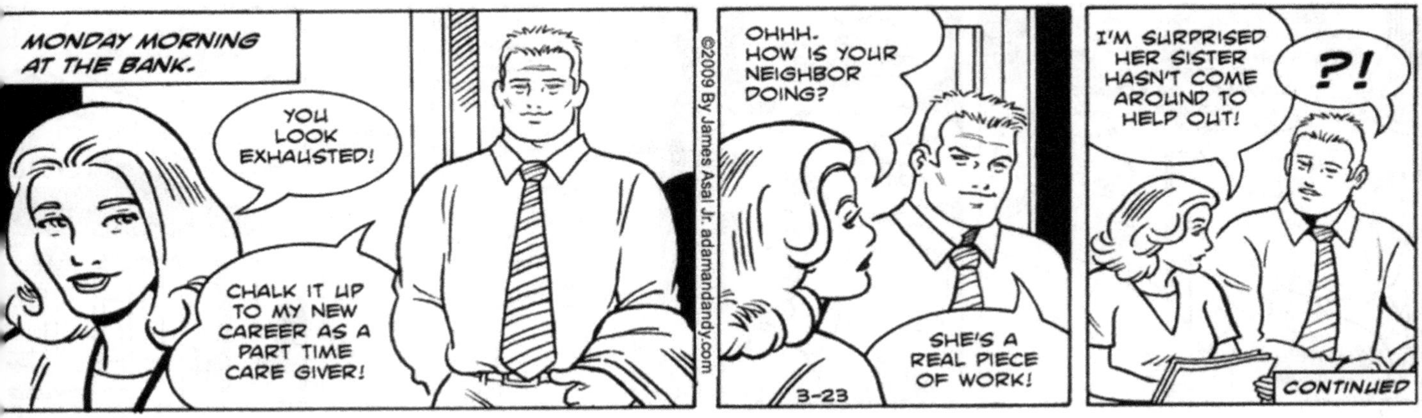
MONDAY MORNING AT THE BANK.
YOU LOOK EXHAUSTED!
CHALK IT UP TO MY NEW CAREER AS A PART TIME CARE GIVER!
©2009 By James Asal Jr. adamandandy.com
OHHH. HOW IS YOUR NEIGHBOR DOING?
SHE'S A REAL PIECE OF WORK!
3-23
I'M SURPRISED HER SISTER HASN'T COME AROUND TO HELP OUT!
?!
CONTINUED

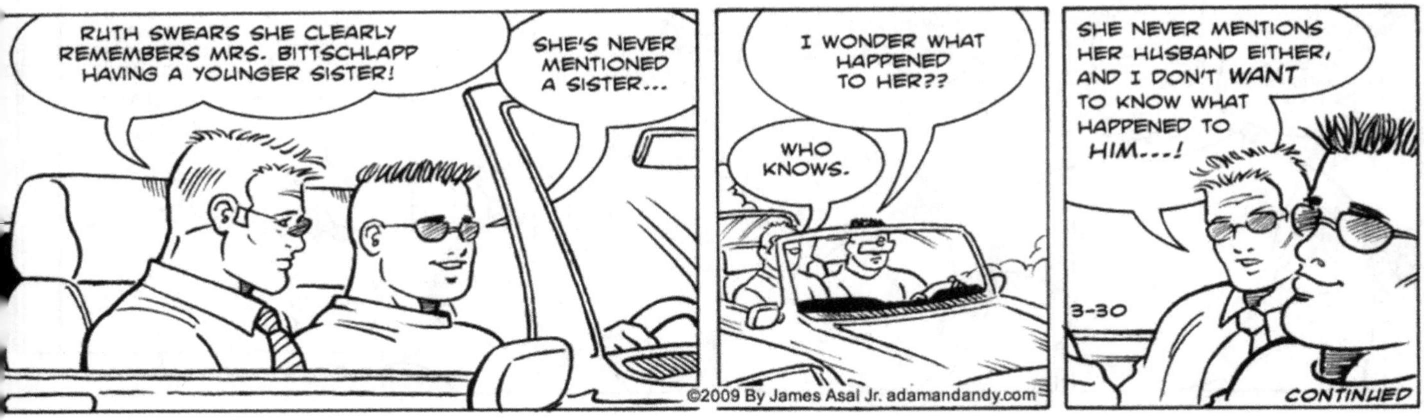
RUTH SWEARS SHE CLEARLY REMEMBERS MRS. BITTSCHLAPP HAVING A YOUNGER SISTER!
SHE'S NEVER MENTIONED A SISTER...
I WONDER WHAT HAPPENED TO HER??
WHO KNOWS.
©2009 By James Asal Jr. adamandandy.com
SHE NEVER MENTIONS HER HUSBAND EITHER, AND I DON'T WANT TO KNOW WHAT HAPPENED TO HIM...!
3-30
CONTINUED

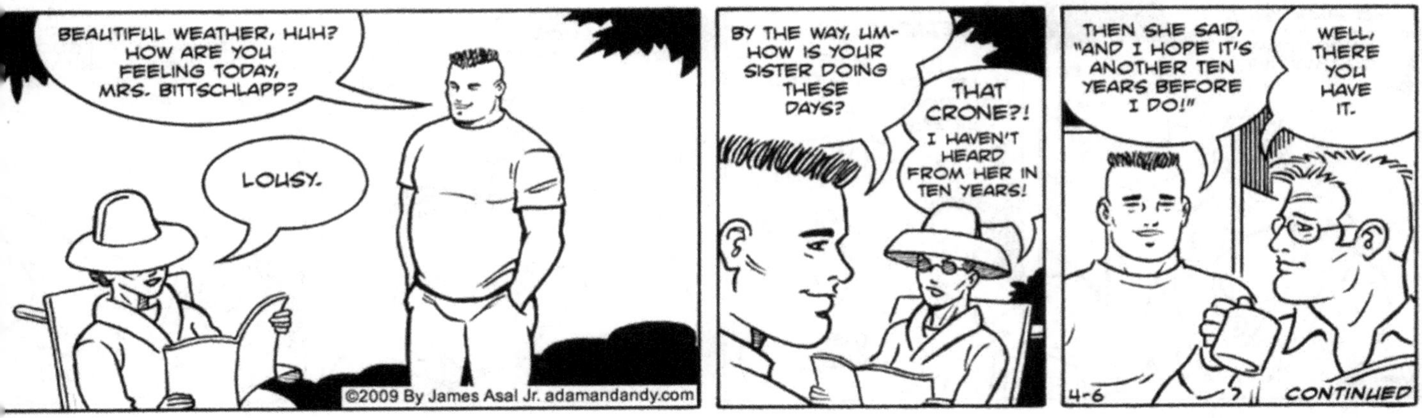
BEAUTIFUL WEATHER, HUH? HOW ARE YOU FEELING TODAY, MRS. BITTSCHLAPP?
LOUSY.
©2009 By James Asal Jr. adamandandy.com
BY THE WAY, UM- HOW IS YOUR SISTER DOING THESE DAYS?
THAT CRONE?!
I HAVEN'T HEARD FROM HER IN TEN YEARS!
THEN SHE SAID, "AND I HOPE IT'S ANOTHER TEN YEARS BEFORE I DO!"
WELL, THERE YOU HAVE IT.
4-6
CONTINUED

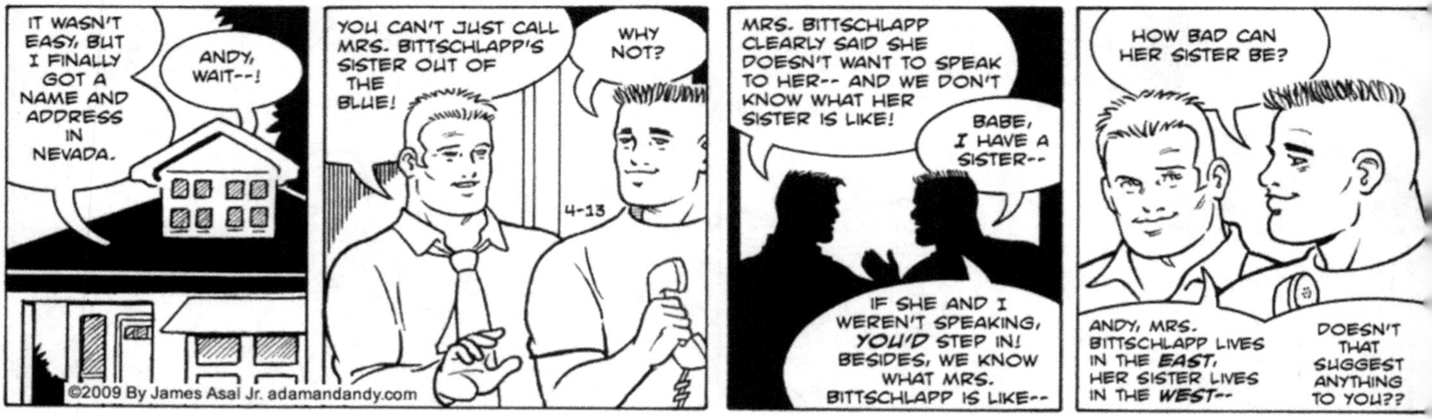
IT WASN'T EASY, BUT I FINALLY GOT A NAME AND ADDRESS IN NEVADA.
ANDY, WAIT--!
©2009 By James Asal Jr. adamandandy.com
YOU CAN'T JUST CALL MRS. BITTSCHLAPP'S SISTER OUT OF THE BLUE!
WHY NOT?
4-13
MRS. BITTSCHLAPP CLEARLY SAID SHE DOESN'T WANT TO SPEAK TO HER-- AND WE DON'T KNOW WHAT HER SISTER IS LIKE!
BABE, I HAVE A SISTER--
IF SHE AND I WEREN'T SPEAKING, YOU'D STEP IN! BESIDES, WE KNOW WHAT MRS. BITTSCHLAPP IS LIKE--
HOW BAD CAN HER SISTER BE?
ANDY, MRS. BITTSCHLAPP LIVES IN THE EAST, HER SISTER LIVES IN THE WEST--
DOESN'T THAT SUGGEST ANYTHING TO YOU??

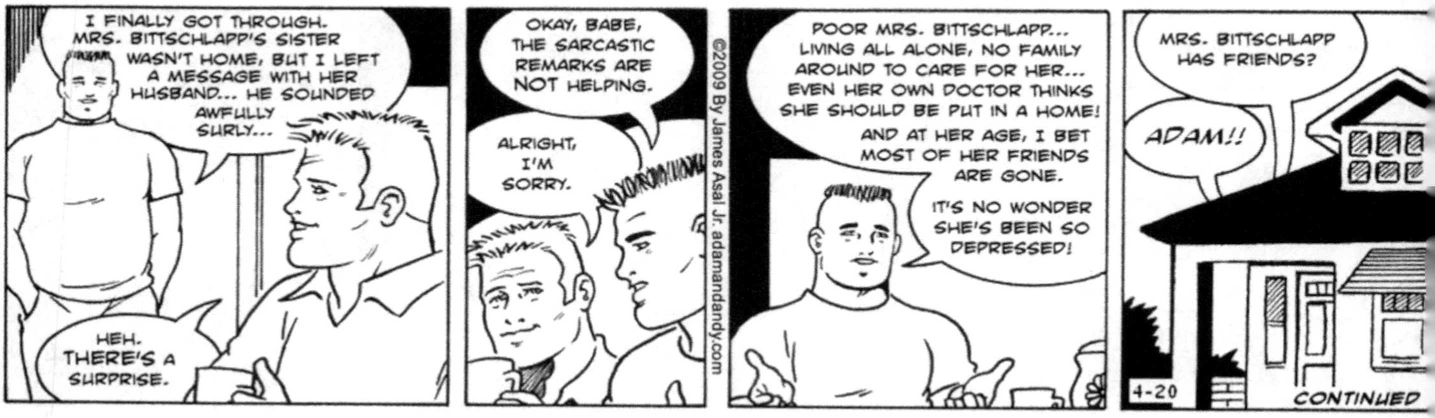
I FINALLY GOT THROUGH. MRS. BITTSCHLAPP'S SISTER WASN'T HOME, BUT I LEFT A MESSAGE WITH HER HUSBAND... HE SOUNDED AWFULLY SURLY...
HEH. THERE'S A SURPRISE.
OKAY, BABE, THE SARCASTIC REMARKS ARE NOT HELPING.
ALRIGHT, I'M SORRY.
©2009 By James Asal Jr. adamandandy.com
POOR MRS. BITTSCHLAPP... LIVING ALL ALONE, NO FAMILY AROUND TO CARE FOR HER... EVEN HER OWN DOCTOR THINKS SHE SHOULD BE PUT IN A HOME!
AND AT HER AGE, I BET MOST OF HER FRIENDS ARE GONE.
IT'S NO WONDER SHE'S BEEN SO DEPRESSED!
MRS. BITTSCHLAPP HAS FRIENDS?
ADAM!!
4-20
CONTINUED

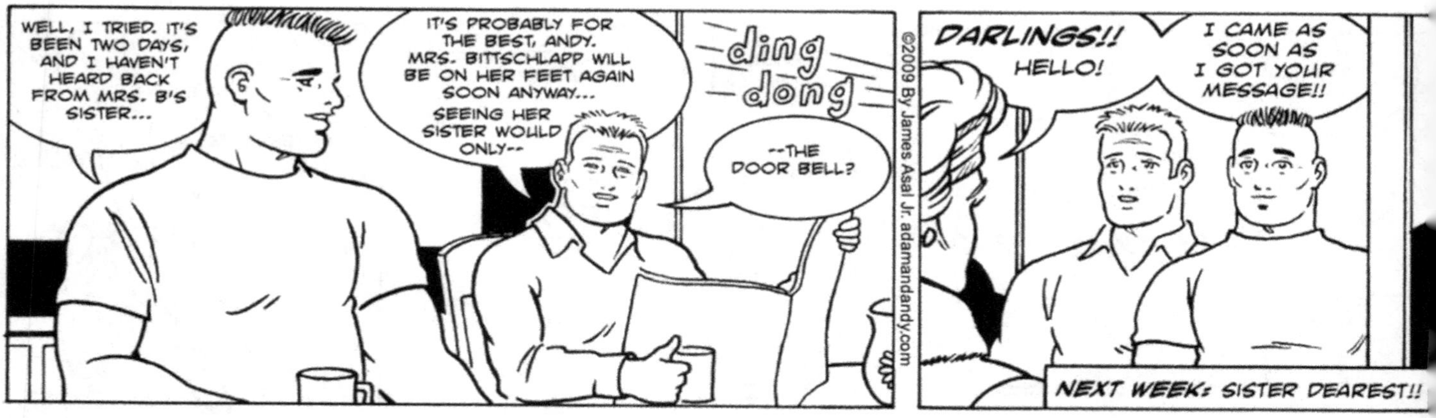
WELL, I TRIED. IT'S BEEN TWO DAYS, AND I HAVEN'T HEARD BACK FROM MRS. B'S SISTER...
IT'S PROBABLY FOR THE BEST, ANDY. MRS. BITTSCHLAPP WILL BE ON HER FEET AGAIN SOON ANYWAY... SEEING HER SISTER WOULD ONLY--
ding dong
--THE DOOR BELL?
©2009 By James Asal Jr. adamandandy.com
DARLINGS!! HELLO!
I CAME AS SOON AS I GOT YOUR MESSAGE!!
NEXT WEEK: SISTER DEAREST!!

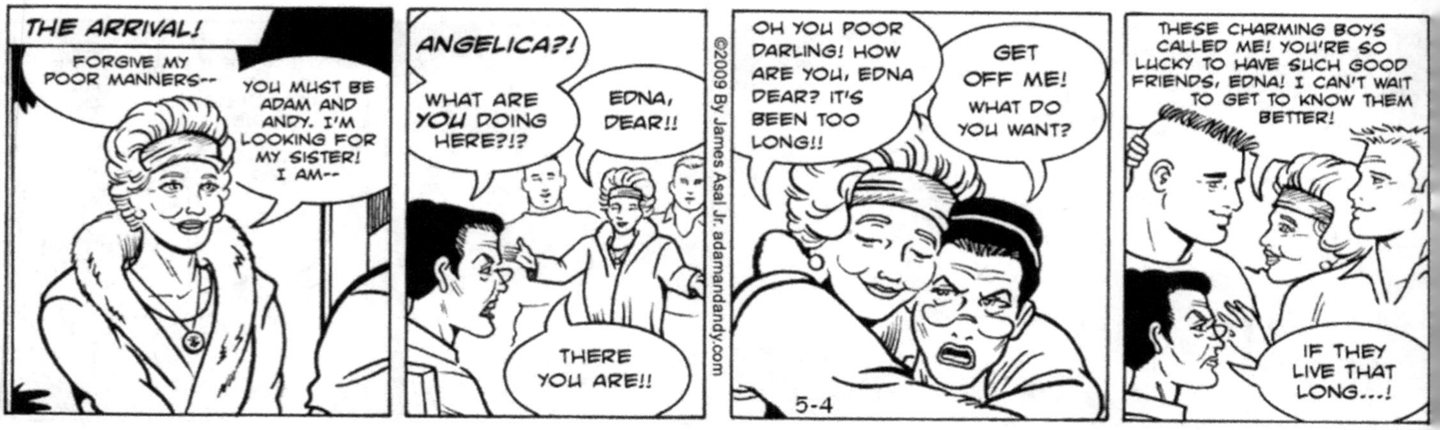
THE ARRIVAL!
FORGIVE MY POOR MANNERS--
YOU MUST BE ADAM AND ANDY. I'M LOOKING FOR MY SISTER! I AM--
ANGELICA?!
WHAT ARE YOU DOING HERE?!?
EDNA, DEAR!!
THERE YOU ARE!!
©2009 By James Asal Jr. adamandandy.com
OH YOU POOR DARLING! HOW ARE YOU, EDNA DEAR? IT'S BEEN TOO LONG!!
GET OFF ME! WHAT DO YOU WANT?
5-4
THESE CHARMING BOYS CALLED ME! YOU'RE SO LUCKY TO HAVE SUCH GOOD FRIENDS, EDNA! I CAN'T WAIT TO GET TO KNOW THEM BETTER!
IF THEY LIVE THAT LONG...!

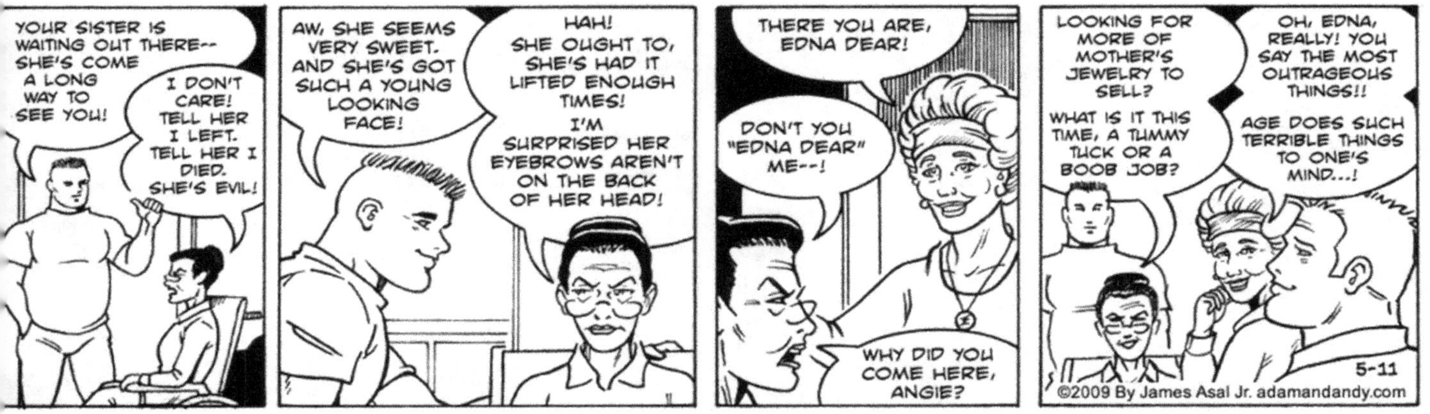

YOUR SISTER IS WAITING OUT THERE-- SHE'S COME A LONG WAY TO SEE YOU!
I DON'T CARE! TELL HER I LEFT. TELL HER I DIED. SHE'S EVIL!
AW, SHE SEEMS VERY SWEET. AND SHE'S GOT SUCH A YOUNG LOOKING FACE!
HAH! SHE OUGHT TO, SHE'S HAD IT LIFTED ENOUGH TIMES!
I'M SURPRISED HER EYEBROWS AREN'T ON THE BACK OF HER HEAD!
THERE YOU ARE, EDNA DEAR!
DON'T YOU "EDNA DEAR" ME--!
WHY DID YOU COME HERE, ANGIE?
LOOKING FOR MORE OF MOTHER'S JEWELRY TO SELL?
WHAT IS IT THIS TIME, A TUMMY TUCK OR A BOOB JOB?
OH, EDNA, REALLY! YOU SAY THE MOST OUTRAGEOUS THINGS!!
AGE DOES SUCH TERRIBLE THINGS TO ONE'S MIND...!
5-11
©2009 By James Asal Jr. adamandandy.com

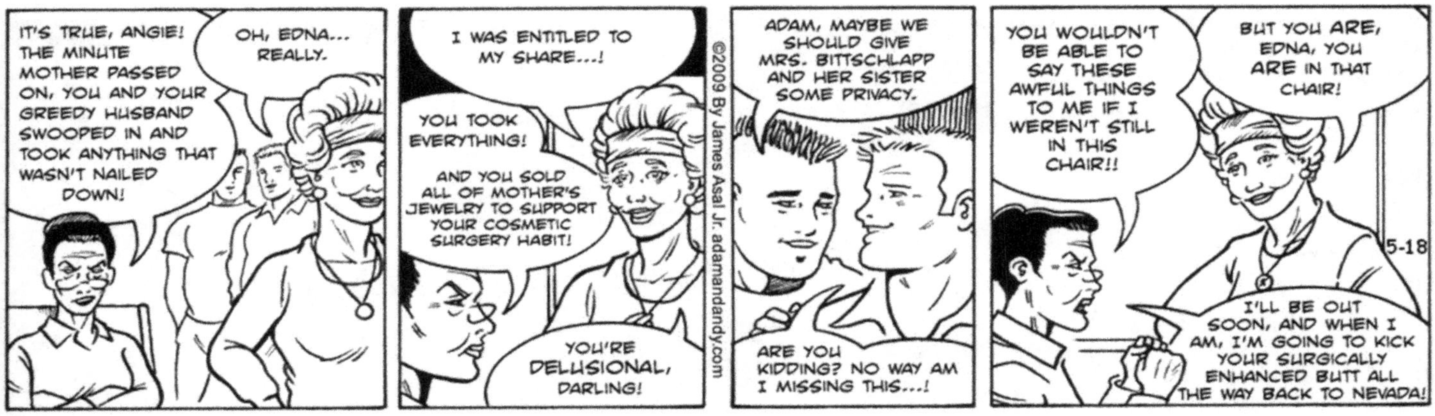

IT'S TRUE, ANGIE! THE MINUTE MOTHER PASSED ON, YOU AND YOUR GREEDY HUSBAND SWOOPED IN AND TOOK ANYTHING THAT WASN'T NAILED DOWN!
OH, EDNA... REALLY.
I WAS ENTITLED TO MY SHARE...!
YOU TOOK EVERYTHING!
AND YOU SOLD ALL OF MOTHER'S JEWELRY TO SUPPORT YOUR COSMETIC SURGERY HABIT!
YOU'RE DELUSIONAL, DARLING!
©2009 By James Asal Jr. adamandandy.com
ADAM, MAYBE WE SHOULD GIVE MRS. BITTSCHLAPP AND HER SISTER SOME PRIVACY.
ARE YOU KIDDING? NO WAY AM I MISSING THIS...!
YOU WOULDN'T BE ABLE TO SAY THESE AWFUL THINGS TO ME IF I WEREN'T STILL IN THIS CHAIR!!
BUT YOU ARE, EDNA, YOU ARE IN THAT CHAIR!
I'LL BE OUT SOON, AND WHEN I AM, I'M GOING TO KICK YOUR SURGICALLY ENHANCED BUTT ALL THE WAY BACK TO NEVADA!
5-18

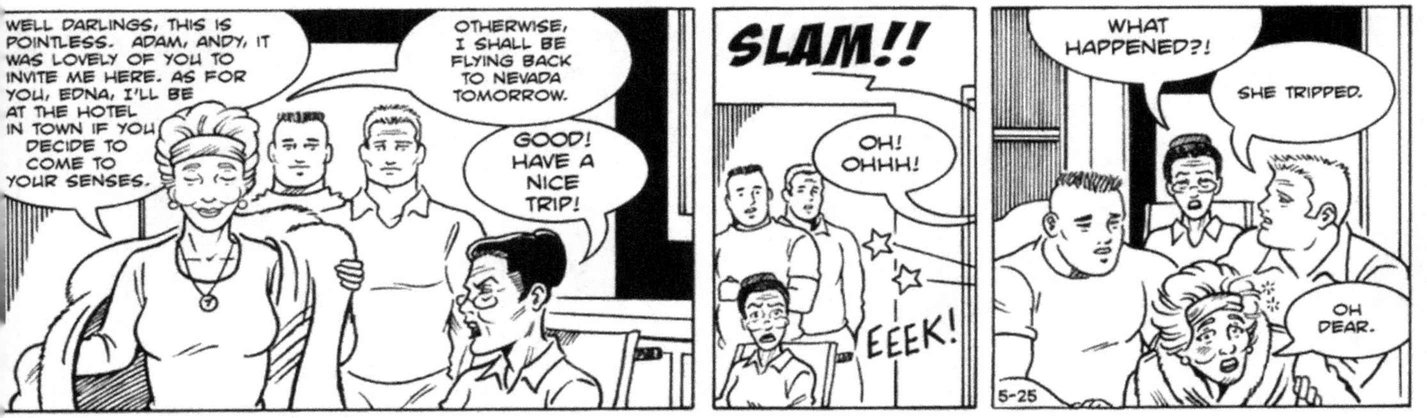

WELL DARLINGS, THIS IS POINTLESS. ADAM, ANDY, IT WAS LOVELY OF YOU TO INVITE ME HERE. AS FOR YOU, EDNA, I'LL BE AT THE HOTEL IN TOWN IF YOU DECIDE TO COME TO YOUR SENSES.
OTHERWISE, I SHALL BE FLYING BACK TO NEVADA TOMORROW.
GOOD! HAVE A NICE TRIP!
SLAM!!
OH! OHHH!
EEEK!
5-25
WHAT HAPPENED?!
SHE TRIPPED.
OH DEAR.

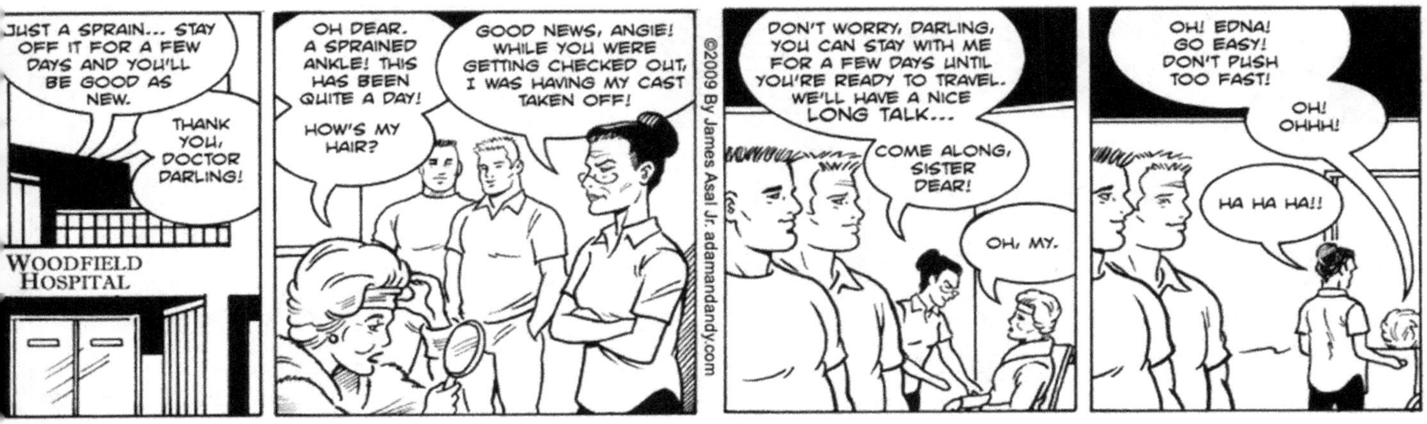

JUST A SPRAIN... STAY OFF IT FOR A FEW DAYS AND YOU'LL BE GOOD AS NEW.
THANK YOU, DOCTOR DARLING!
WOODFIELD HOSPITAL
OH DEAR. A SPRAINED ANKLE! THIS HAS BEEN QUITE A DAY!
HOW'S MY HAIR?
GOOD NEWS, ANGIE! WHILE YOU WERE GETTING CHECKED OUT, I WAS HAVING MY CAST TAKEN OFF!
©2009 By James Asal Jr. adamandandy.com
DON'T WORRY, DARLING, YOU CAN STAY WITH ME FOR A FEW DAYS UNTIL YOU'RE READY TO TRAVEL. WE'LL HAVE A NICE LONG TALK...
COME ALONG, SISTER DEAR!
OH, MY.
OH! EDNA! GO EASY! DON'T PUSH TOO FAST!
OH! OHHH!
HA HA HA!!

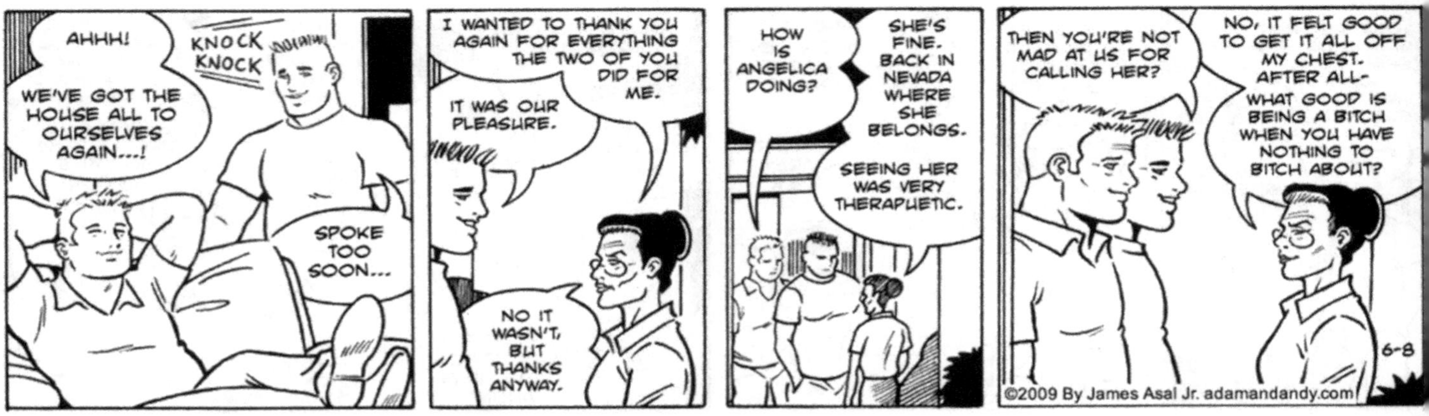
AHHH!
WE'VE GOT THE HOUSE ALL TO OURSELVES AGAIN...!
KNOCK KNOCK
SPOKE TOO SOON...
I WANTED TO THANK YOU AGAIN FOR EVERYTHING THE TWO OF YOU DID FOR ME.
IT WAS OUR PLEASURE.
NO IT WASN'T, BUT THANKS ANYWAY.
HOW IS ANGELICA DOING?
SHE'S FINE. BACK IN NEVADA WHERE SHE BELONGS.
SEEING HER WAS VERY THERAPUETIC.
THEN YOU'RE NOT MAD AT US FOR CALLING HER?
NO, IT FELT GOOD TO GET IT ALL OFF MY CHEST. AFTER ALL- WHAT GOOD IS BEING A BITCH WHEN YOU HAVE NOTHING TO BITCH ABOUT?
6-8
©2009 By James Asal Jr. adamandandy.com

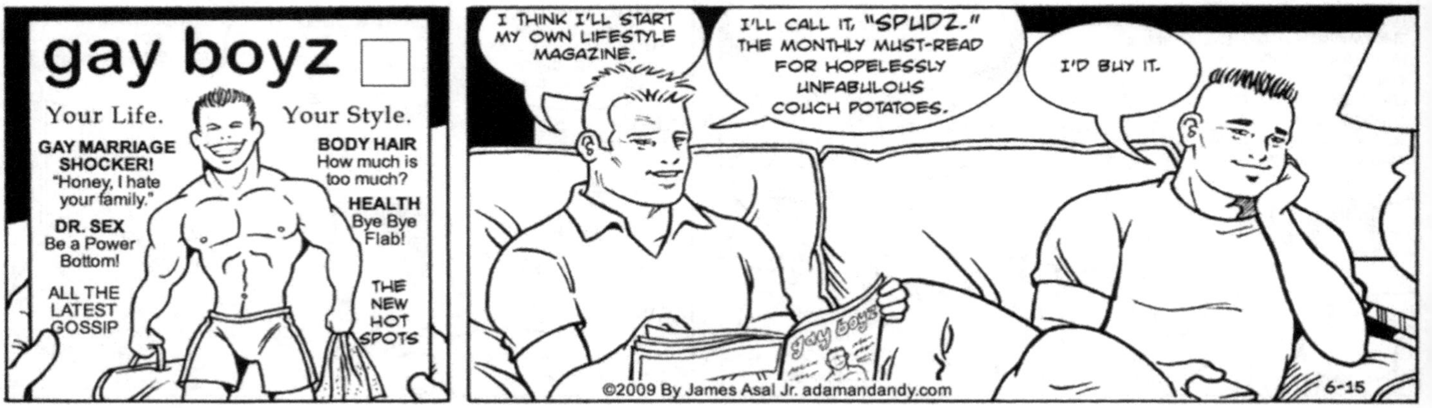
gay boyz
Your Life. Your Style.
GAY MARRIAGE SHOCKER! "Honey, I hate your family."
DR. SEX Be a Power Bottom!
ALL THE LATEST GOSSIP
BODY HAIR How much is too much?
HEALTH Bye Bye Flab!
THE NEW HOT SPOTS
I THINK I'LL START MY OWN LIFESTYLE MAGAZINE.
I'LL CALL IT, "SPUDZ." THE MONTHLY MUST-READ FOR HOPELESSLY UNFABULOUS COUCH POTATOES.
I'D BUY IT.
gay boyz
©2009 By James Asal Jr. adamandandy.com
6-15

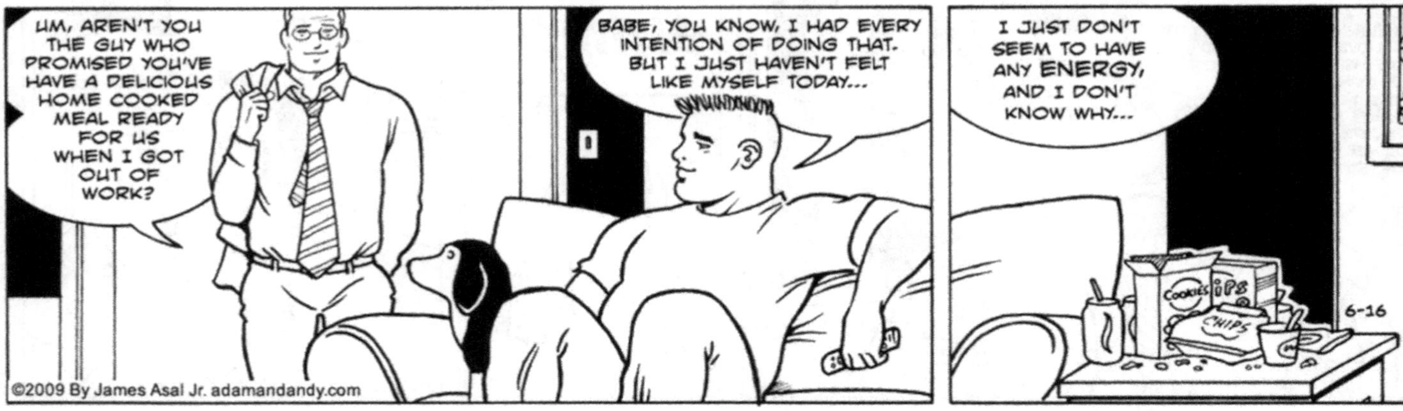
UM, AREN'T YOU THE GUY WHO PROMISED YOU'VE HAVE A DELICIOUS HOME COOKED MEAL READY FOR US WHEN I GOT OUT OF WORK?
BABE, YOU KNOW, I HAD EVERY INTENTION OF DOING THAT. BUT I JUST HAVEN'T FELT LIKE MYSELF TODAY...
I JUST DON'T SEEM TO HAVE ANY ENERGY, AND I DON'T KNOW WHY...
COOKIES
CHIPS
6-16
©2009 By James Asal Jr. adamandandy.com

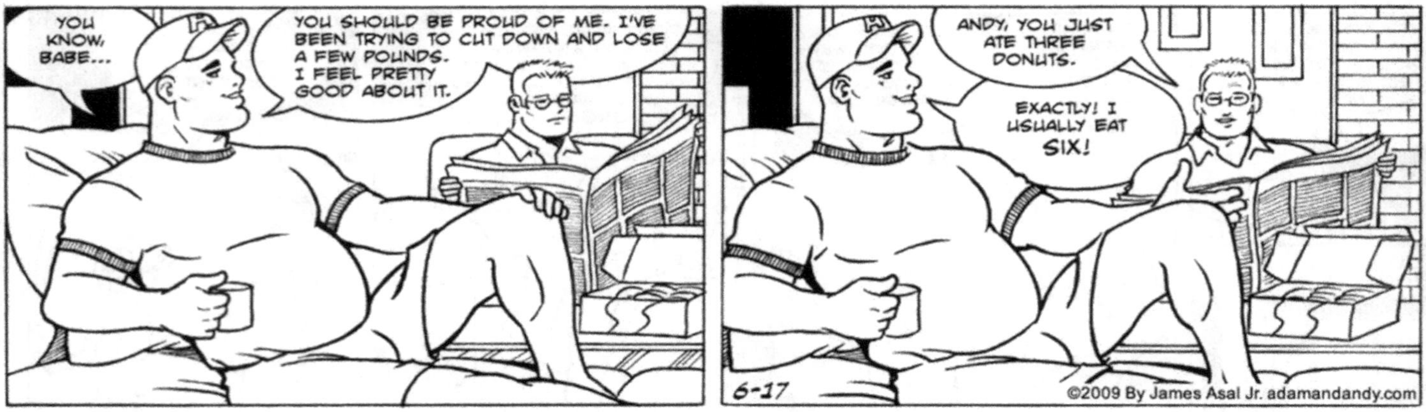
YOU KNOW, BABE...
YOU SHOULD BE PROUD OF ME. I'VE BEEN TRYING TO CUT DOWN AND LOSE A FEW POUNDS. I FEEL PRETTY GOOD ABOUT IT.
ANDY, YOU JUST ATE THREE DONUTS.
EXACTLY! I USUALLY EAT SIX!
6-17
©2009 By James Asal Jr. adamandandy.com

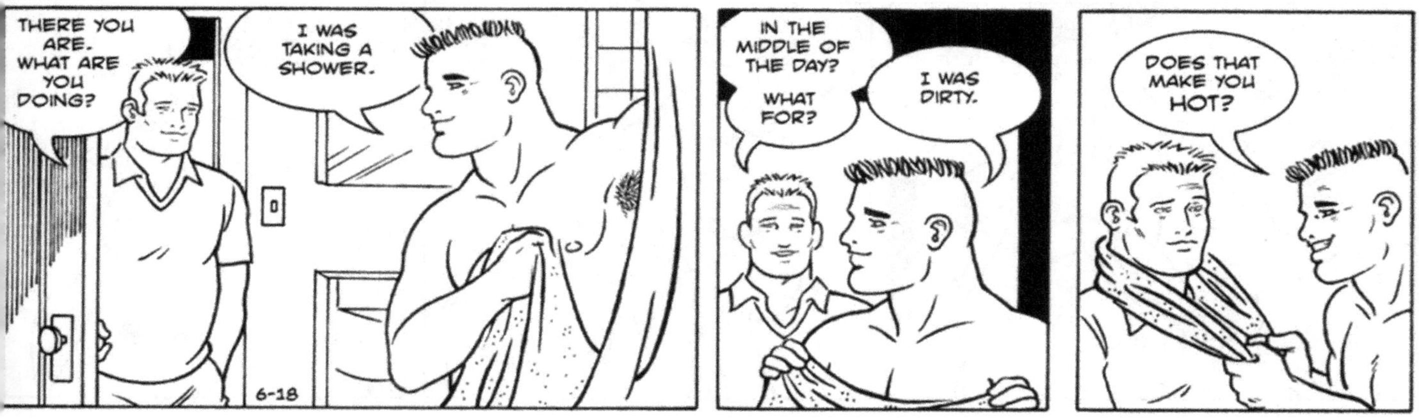
THERE YOU ARE. WHAT ARE YOU DOING?
I WAS TAKING A SHOWER.
6-18
IN THE MIDDLE OF THE DAY?
WHAT FOR?
I WAS DIRTY.
DOES THAT MAKE YOU HOT?

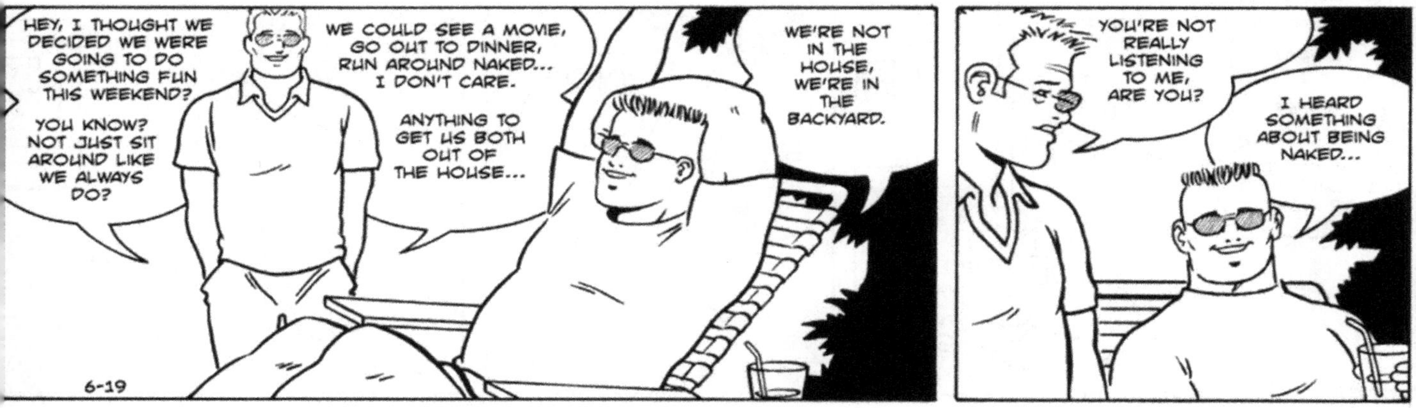
HEY, I THOUGHT WE DECIDED WE WERE GOING TO DO SOMETHING FUN THIS WEEKEND?
YOU KNOW? NOT JUST SIT AROUND LIKE WE ALWAYS DO?
WE COULD SEE A MOVIE, GO OUT TO DINNER, RUN AROUND NAKED... I DON'T CARE.
ANYTHING TO GET US BOTH OUT OF THE HOUSE...
WE'RE NOT IN THE HOUSE, WE'RE IN THE BACKYARD.
6-19
YOU'RE NOT REALLY LISTENING TO ME, ARE YOU?
I HEARD SOMETHING ABOUT BEING NAKED...

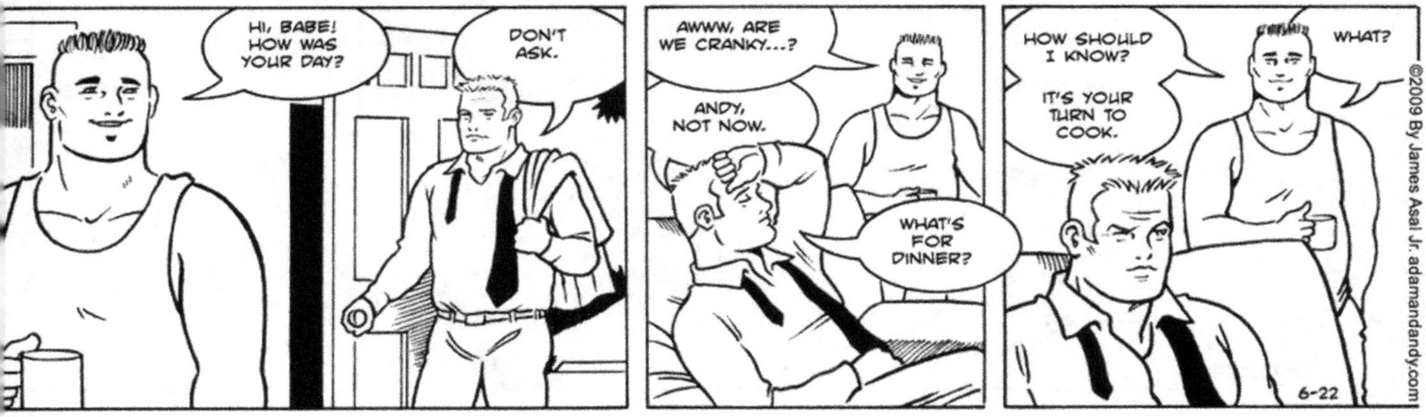
HI, BABE! HOW WAS YOUR DAY?
DON'T ASK.
AWWW, ARE WE CRANKY...?
ANDY, NOT NOW.
WHAT'S FOR DINNER?
HOW SHOULD I KNOW?
IT'S YOUR TURN TO COOK.
WHAT?
6-22
©2009 By James Asal Jr. adamandandy.com

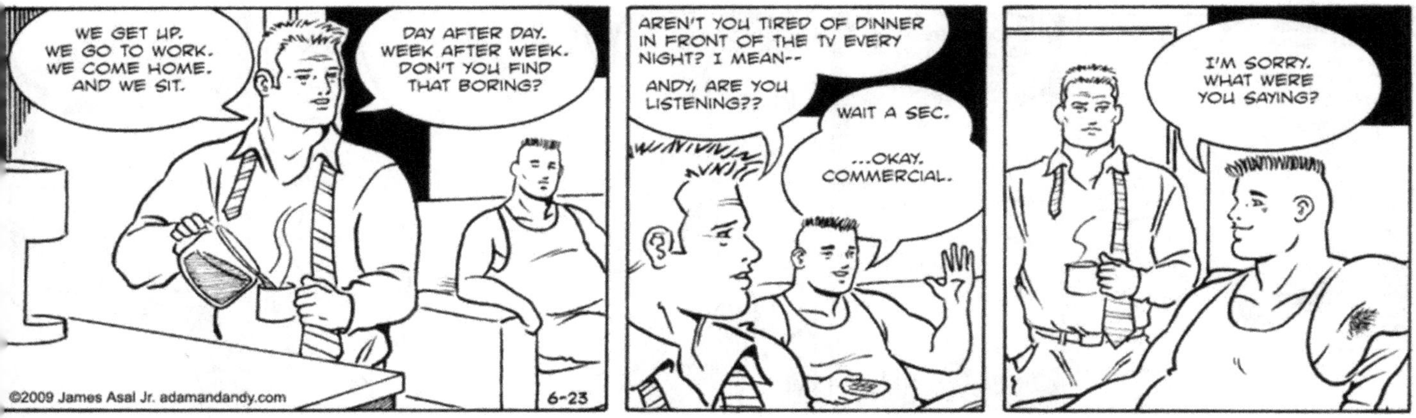
WE GET UP. WE GO TO WORK. WE COME HOME. AND WE SIT.
DAY AFTER DAY. WEEK AFTER WEEK. DON'T YOU FIND THAT BORING?
©2009 James Asal Jr. adamandandy.com
6-23
AREN'T YOU TIRED OF DINNER IN FRONT OF THE TV EVERY NIGHT? I MEAN--
ANDY, ARE YOU LISTENING??
WAIT A SEC.
...OKAY. COMMERCIAL.
I'M SORRY. WHAT WERE YOU SAYING?

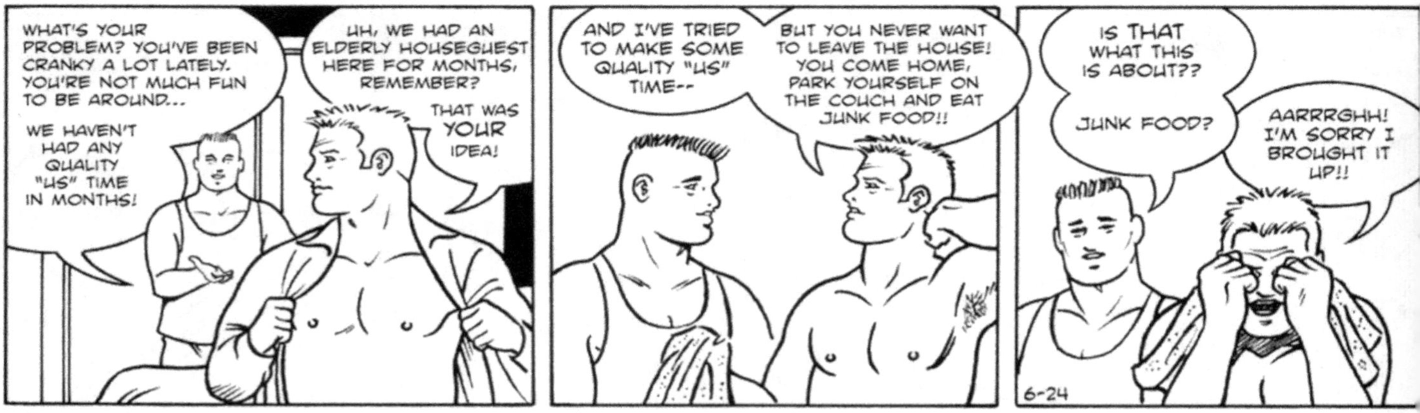
WHAT'S YOUR PROBLEM? YOU'VE BEEN CRANKY A LOT LATELY. YOU'RE NOT MUCH FUN TO BE AROUND...
WE HAVEN'T HAD ANY QUALITY "US" TIME IN MONTHS!
UH, WE HAD AN ELDERLY HOUSEGUEST HERE FOR MONTHS, REMEMBER?
THAT WAS YOUR IDEA!
AND I'VE TRIED TO MAKE SOME QUALITY "US" TIME--
BUT YOU NEVER WANT TO LEAVE THE HOUSE! YOU COME HOME, PARK YOURSELF ON THE COUCH AND EAT JUNK FOOD!!
IS THAT WHAT THIS IS ABOUT??
JUNK FOOD?
AARRRGHH! I'M SORRY I BROUGHT IT UP!!
6-24

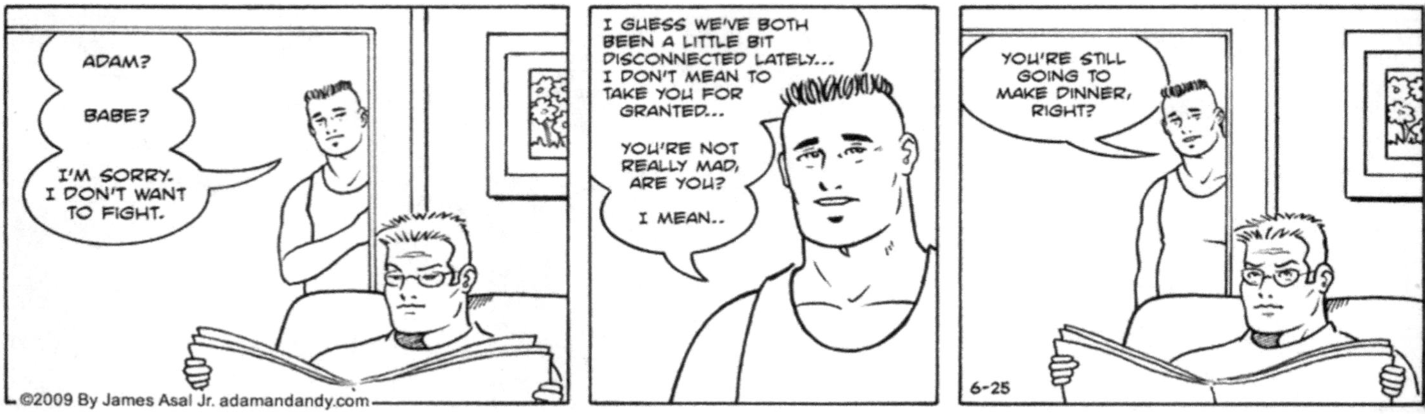
ADAM?
BABE?
I'M SORRY. I DON'T WANT TO FIGHT.
I GUESS WE'VE BOTH BEEN A LITTLE BIT DISCONNECTED LATELY... I DON'T MEAN TO TAKE YOU FOR GRANTED...
YOU'RE NOT REALLY MAD, ARE YOU?
I MEAN..
YOU'RE STILL GOING TO MAKE DINNER, RIGHT?
6-25

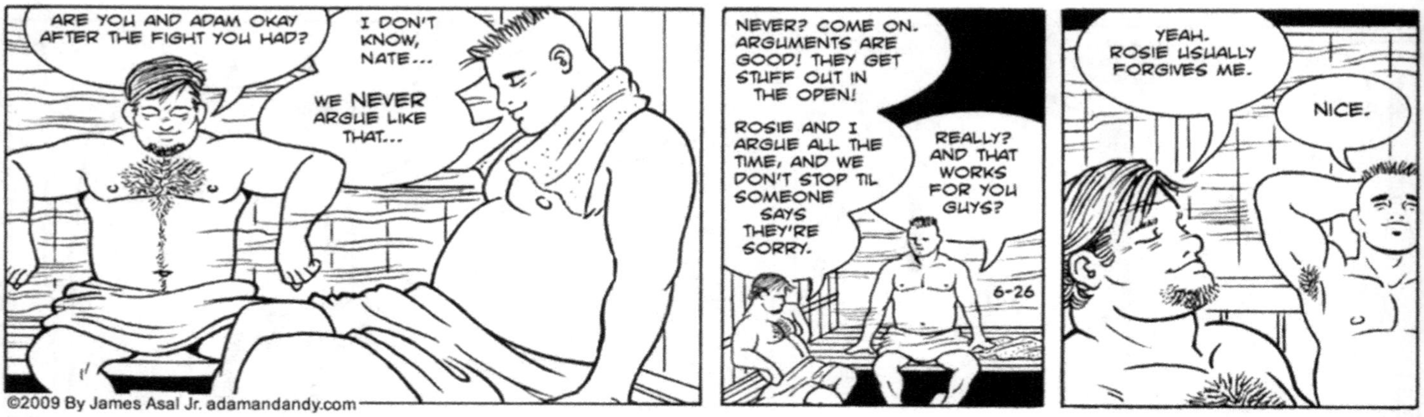
ARE YOU AND ADAM OKAY AFTER THE FIGHT YOU HAD?
I DON'T KNOW, NATE...
WE NEVER ARGUE LIKE THAT...
NEVER? COME ON. ARGUMENTS ARE GOOD! THEY GET STUFF OUT IN THE OPEN!
ROSIE AND I ARGUE ALL THE TIME, AND WE DON'T STOP TIL SOMEONE SAYS THEY'RE SORRY.
REALLY? AND THAT WORKS FOR YOU GUYS?
6-26
YEAH. ROSIE USUALLY FORGIVES ME.
NICE.

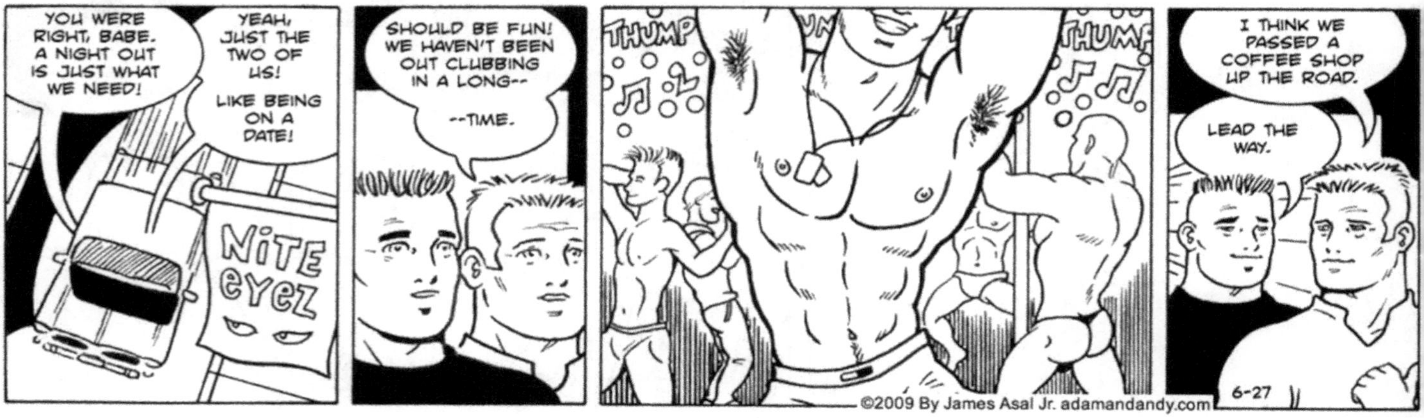
YOU WERE RIGHT, BABE. A NIGHT OUT IS JUST WHAT WE NEED!
YEAH, JUST THE TWO OF US!
LIKE BEING ON A DATE!
NiTE eYeZ
SHOULD BE FUN! WE HAVEN'T BEEN OUT CLUBBING IN A LONG--
--TIME.
THUMP
THUMP
I THINK WE PASSED A COFFEE SHOP UP THE ROAD.
LEAD THE WAY.
6-27

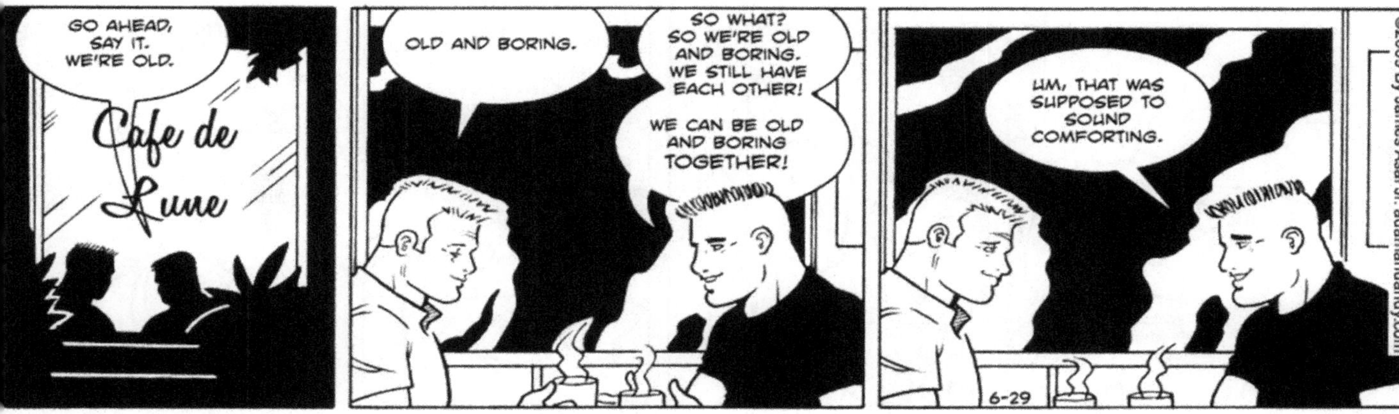
GO AHEAD, SAY IT. WE'RE OLD.
Cafe de Lune
OLD AND BORING.
SO WHAT? SO WE'RE OLD AND BORING. WE STILL HAVE EACH OTHER!
WE CAN BE OLD AND BORING TOGETHER!
UM, THAT WAS SUPPOSED TO SOUND COMFORTING.
6-29
©2009 By James Asal Jr. adamandandy.com

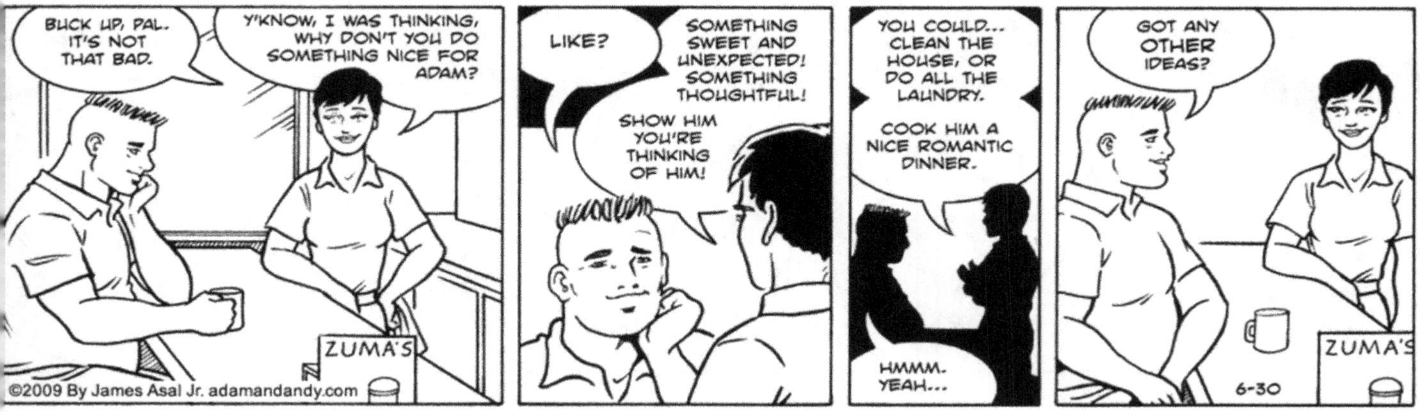
BUCK UP, PAL. IT'S NOT THAT BAD.
Y'KNOW, I WAS THINKING, WHY DON'T YOU DO SOMETHING NICE FOR ADAM?
ZUMA'S
©2009 By James Asal Jr. adamandandy.com
LIKE?
SOMETHING SWEET AND UNEXPECTED! SOMETHING THOUGHTFUL!
SHOW HIM YOU'RE THINKING OF HIM!
YOU COULD... CLEAN THE HOUSE, OR DO ALL THE LAUNDRY.
COOK HIM A NICE ROMANTIC DINNER.
HMMM. YEAH...
GOT ANY OTHER IDEAS?
ZUMA'S
6-30

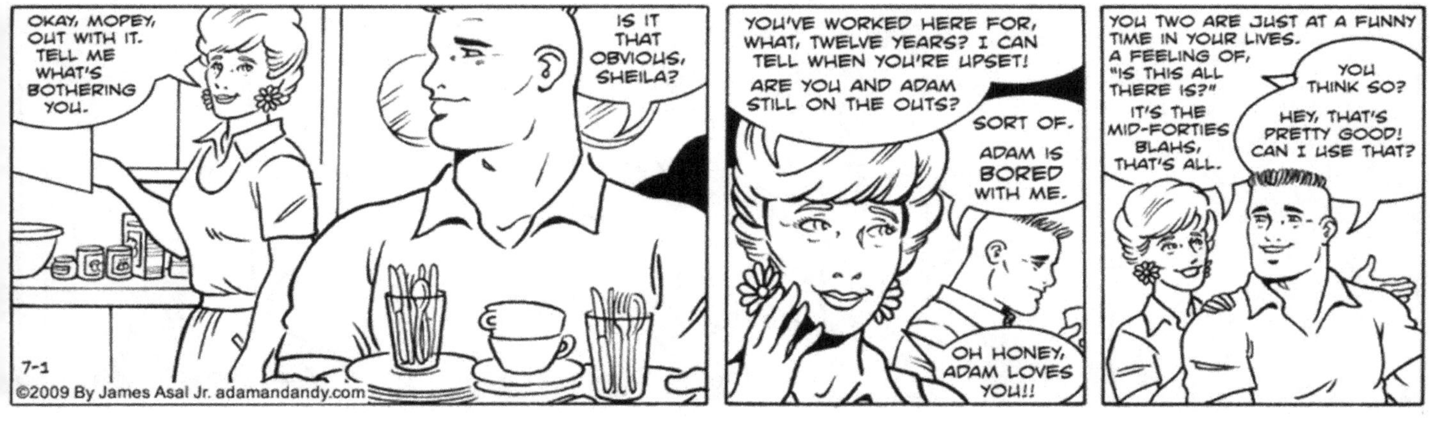
OKAY, MOPEY, OUT WITH IT. TELL ME WHAT'S BOTHERING YOU.
IS IT THAT OBVIOUS, SHEILA?
7-1
©2009 By James Asal Jr. adamandandy.com
YOU'VE WORKED HERE FOR, WHAT, TWELVE YEARS? I CAN TELL WHEN YOU'RE UPSET!
ARE YOU AND ADAM STILL ON THE OUTS?
SORT OF.
ADAM IS BORED WITH ME.
OH HONEY, ADAM LOVES YOU!!
YOU TWO ARE JUST AT A FUNNY TIME IN YOUR LIVES. A FEELING OF, "IS THIS ALL THERE IS?"
IT'S THE MID-FORTIES BLAHS, THAT'S ALL.
YOU THINK SO?
HEY, THAT'S PRETTY GOOD! CAN I USE THAT?

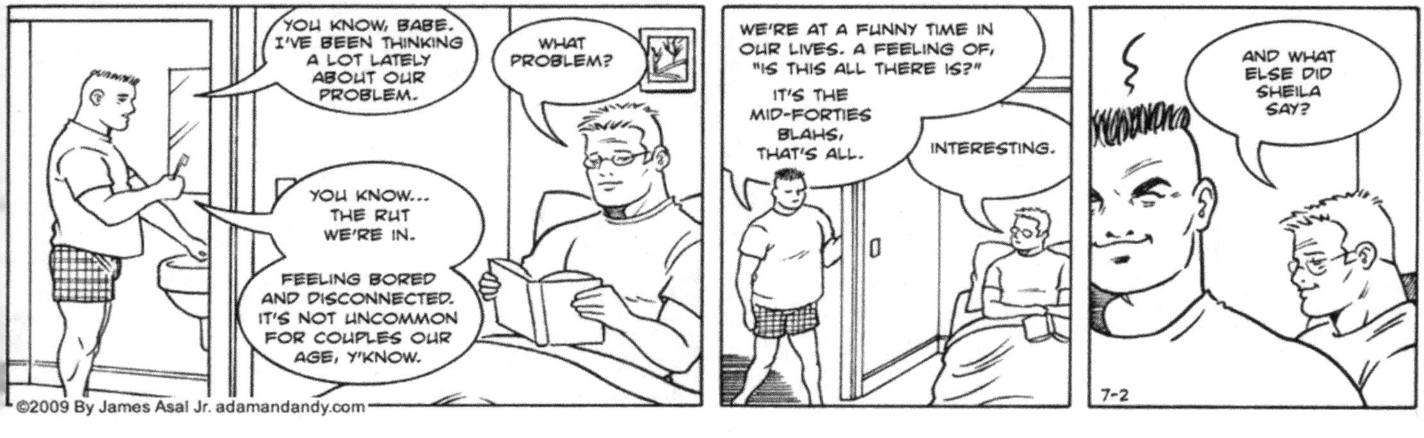
YOU KNOW, BABE. I'VE BEEN THINKING A LOT LATELY ABOUT OUR PROBLEM.
WHAT PROBLEM?
YOU KNOW... THE RUT WE'RE IN.
FEELING BORED AND DISCONNECTED. IT'S NOT UNCOMMON FOR COUPLES OUR AGE, Y'KNOW.
©2009 By James Asal Jr. adamandandy.com
WE'RE AT A FUNNY TIME IN OUR LIVES. A FEELING OF, "IS THIS ALL THERE IS?"
IT'S THE MID-FORTIES BLAHS, THAT'S ALL.
INTERESTING.
AND WHAT ELSE DID SHEILA SAY?
7-2

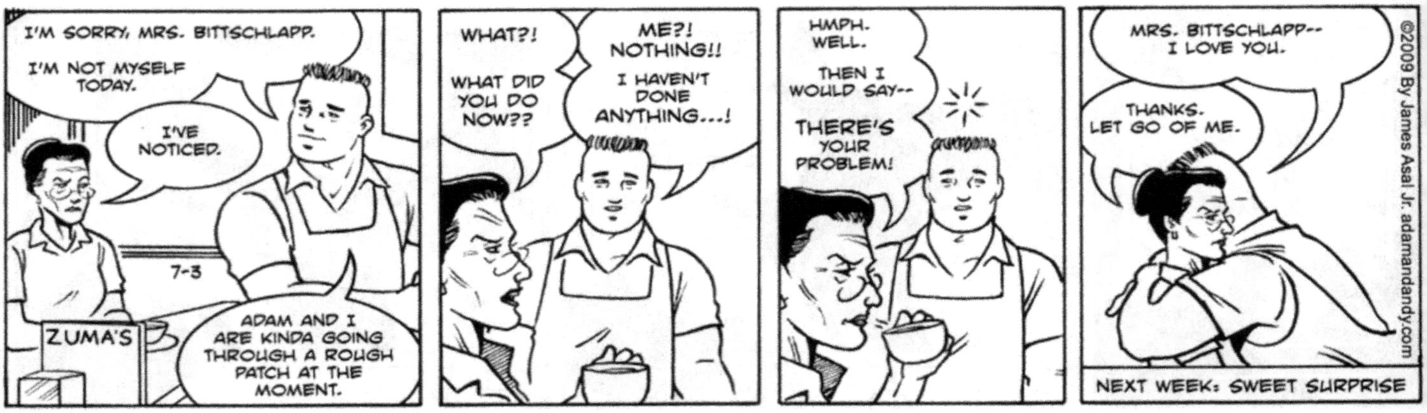
I'M SORRY, MRS. BITTSCHLAPP.
I'M NOT MYSELF TODAY.
I'VE NOTICED.
ZUMA'S
7-3
ADAM AND I ARE KINDA GOING THROUGH A ROUGH PATCH AT THE MOMENT.
WHAT?!
WHAT DID YOU DO NOW??
ME?! NOTHING!!
I HAVEN'T DONE ANYTHING...!
HMPH. WELL.
THEN I WOULD SAY--
THERE'S YOUR PROBLEM!
MRS. BITTSCHLAPP-- I LOVE YOU.
THANKS. LET GO OF ME.
NEXT WEEK: SWEET SURPRISE
©2009 By James Asal Jr. adamandandy.com

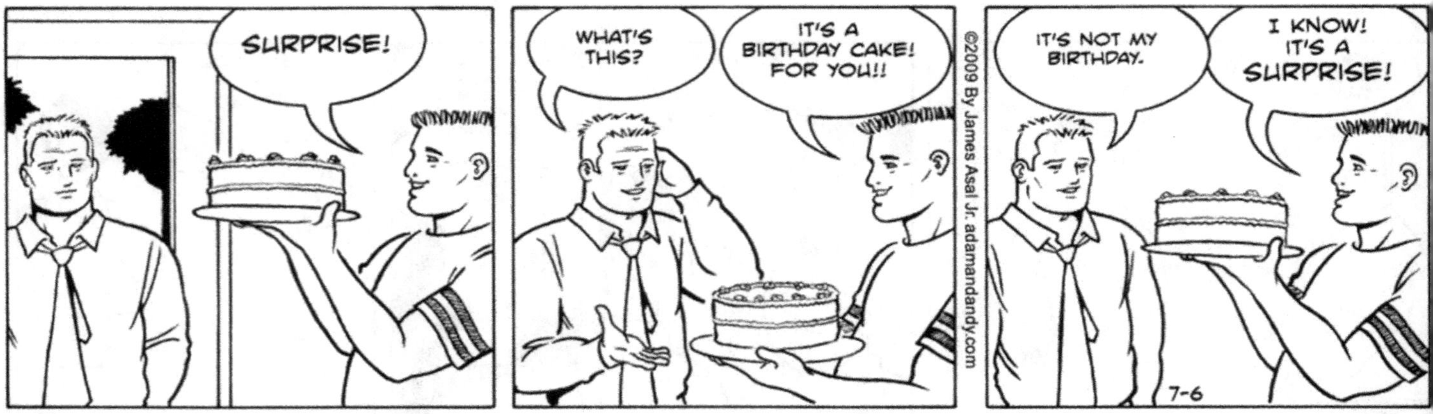
SURPRISE!
WHAT'S THIS?
IT'S A BIRTHDAY CAKE! FOR YOU!!
©2009 By James Asal Jr. adamandandy.com
IT'S NOT MY BIRTHDAY.
I KNOW! IT'S A SURPRISE!
7-6

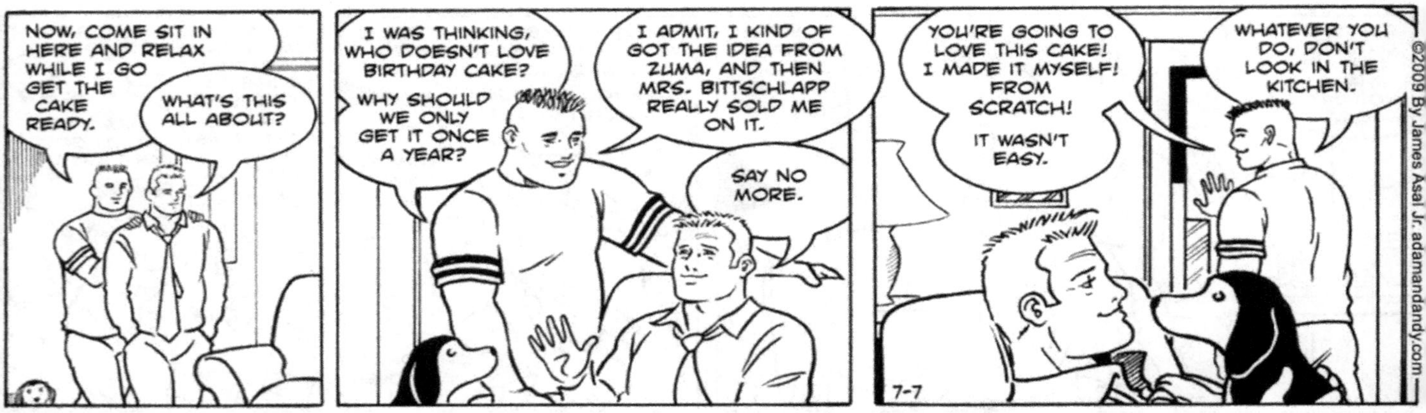
NOW, COME SIT IN HERE AND RELAX WHILE I GO GET THE CAKE READY.
WHAT'S THIS ALL ABOUT?
I WAS THINKING, WHO DOESN'T LOVE BIRTHDAY CAKE?
WHY SHOULD WE ONLY GET IT ONCE A YEAR?
I ADMIT, I KIND OF GOT THE IDEA FROM ZUMA, AND THEN MRS. BITTSCHLAPP REALLY SOLD ME ON IT.
SAY NO MORE.
YOU'RE GOING TO LOVE THIS CAKE! I MADE IT MYSELF! FROM SCRATCH!
IT WASN'T EASY.
WHATEVER YOU DO, DON'T LOOK IN THE KITCHEN.
7-7
©2009 By James Asal Jr. adamandandy.com

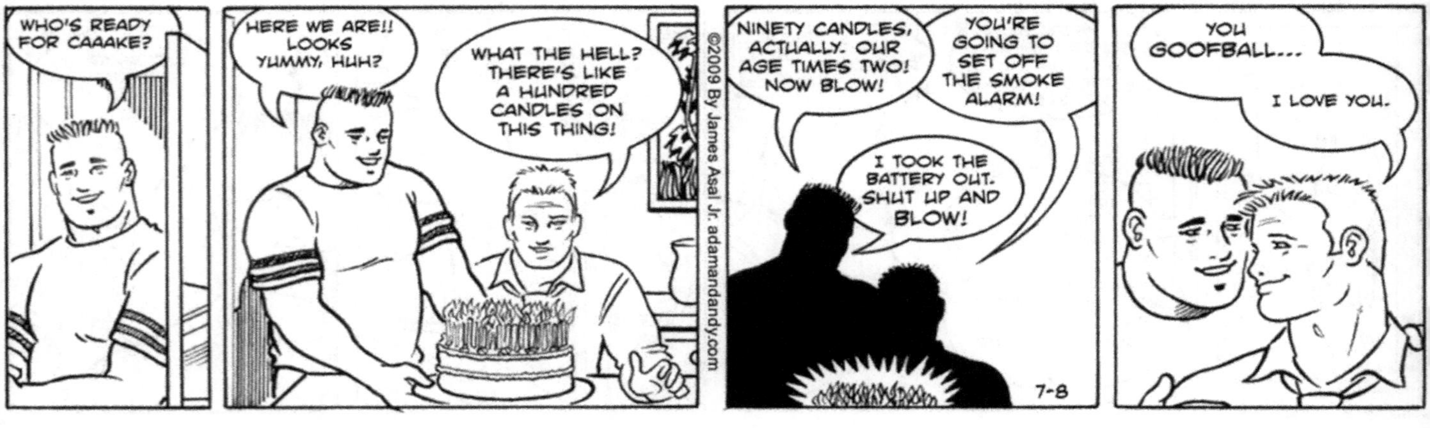
WHO'S READY FOR CAAAKE?
HERE WE ARE!! LOOKS YUMMY, HUH?
WHAT THE HELL? THERE'S LIKE A HUNDRED CANDLES ON THIS THING!
©2009 By James Asal Jr. adamandandy.com
NINETY CANDLES, ACTUALLY. OUR AGE TIMES TWO! NOW BLOW!
YOU'RE GOING TO SET OFF THE SMOKE ALARM!
I TOOK THE BATTERY OUT. SHUT UP AND BLOW!
7-8
YOU GOOFBALL...
I LOVE YOU.

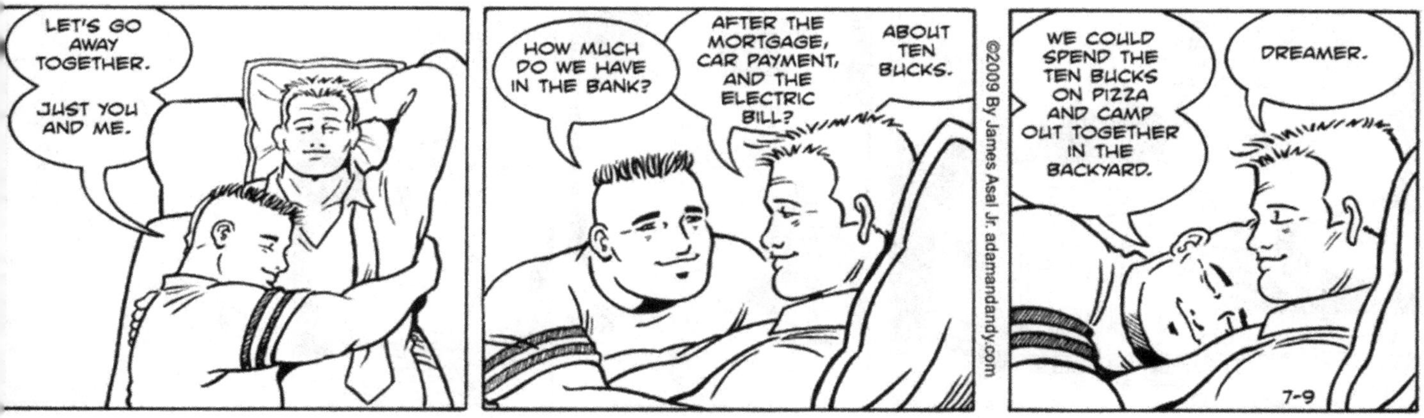
LET'S GO AWAY TOGETHER.
JUST YOU AND ME.
HOW MUCH DO WE HAVE IN THE BANK?
AFTER THE MORTGAGE, CAR PAYMENT, AND THE ELECTRIC BILL?
ABOUT TEN BUCKS.
©2009 By James Asal Jr. adamandandy.com
WE COULD SPEND THE TEN BUCKS ON PIZZA AND CAMP OUT TOGETHER IN THE BACKYARD.
DREAMER.
7-9

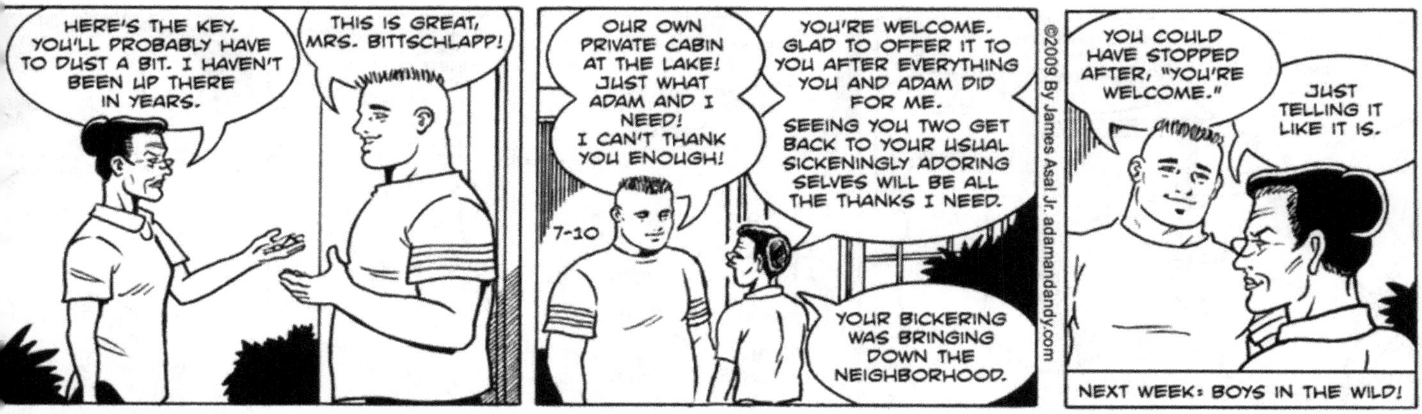
HERE'S THE KEY. YOU'LL PROBABLY HAVE TO DUST A BIT. I HAVEN'T BEEN UP THERE IN YEARS.
THIS IS GREAT, MRS. BITTSCHLAPP!
OUR OWN PRIVATE CABIN AT THE LAKE! JUST WHAT ADAM AND I NEED! I CAN'T THANK YOU ENOUGH!
YOU'RE WELCOME. GLAD TO OFFER IT TO YOU AFTER EVERYTHING YOU AND ADAM DID FOR ME.
SEEING YOU TWO GET BACK TO YOUR USUAL SICKENINGLY ADORING SELVES WILL BE ALL THE THANKS I NEED.
7-10
YOUR BICKERING WAS BRINGING DOWN THE NEIGHBORHOOD.
©2009 By James Asal Jr. adamandandy.com
YOU COULD HAVE STOPPED AFTER, "YOU'RE WELCOME."
JUST TELLING IT LIKE IT IS.
NEXT WEEK: BOYS IN THE WILD!

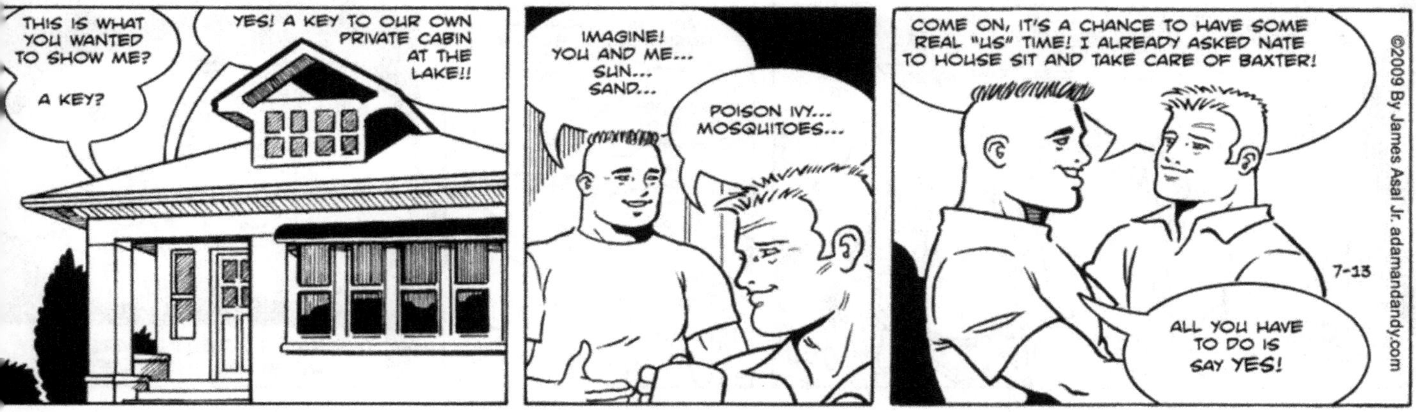
THIS IS WHAT YOU WANTED TO SHOW ME?
A KEY?
YES! A KEY TO OUR OWN PRIVATE CABIN AT THE LAKE!!
IMAGINE! YOU AND ME... SUN... SAND...
POISON IVY... MOSQUITOES...
COME ON, IT'S A CHANCE TO HAVE SOME REAL "US" TIME! I ALREADY ASKED NATE TO HOUSE SIT AND TAKE CARE OF BAXTER!
ALL YOU HAVE TO DO IS SAY YES!
7-13
©2009 By James Asal Jr. adamandandy.com

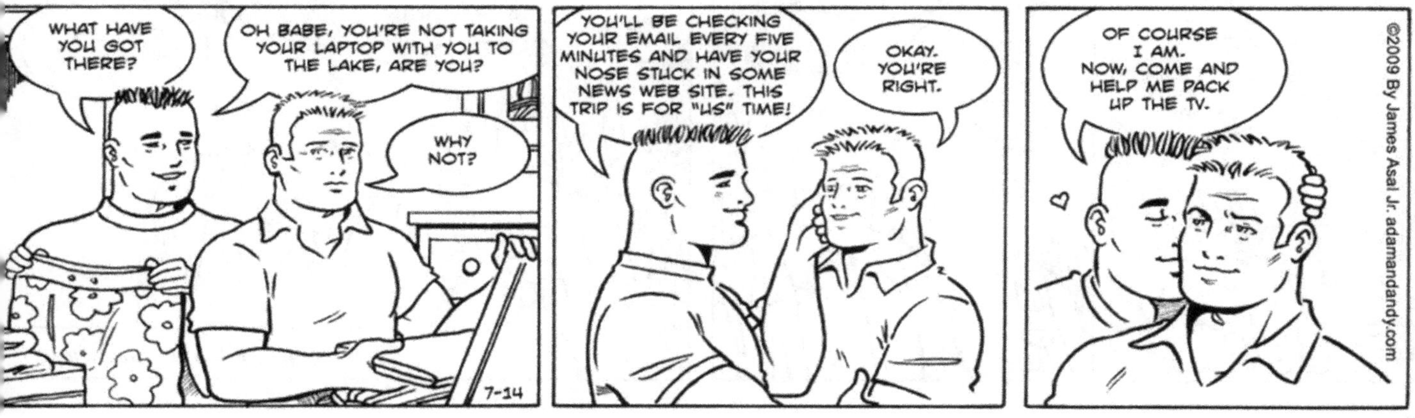
WHAT HAVE YOU GOT THERE?
OH BABE, YOU'RE NOT TAKING YOUR LAPTOP WITH YOU TO THE LAKE, ARE YOU?
WHY NOT?
7-14
YOU'LL BE CHECKING YOUR EMAIL EVERY FIVE MINUTES AND HAVE YOUR NOSE STUCK IN SOME NEWS WEB SITE. THIS TRIP IS FOR "US" TIME!
OKAY. YOU'RE RIGHT.
OF COURSE I AM. NOW, COME AND HELP ME PACK UP THE TV.
©2009 By James Asal Jr. adamandandy.com

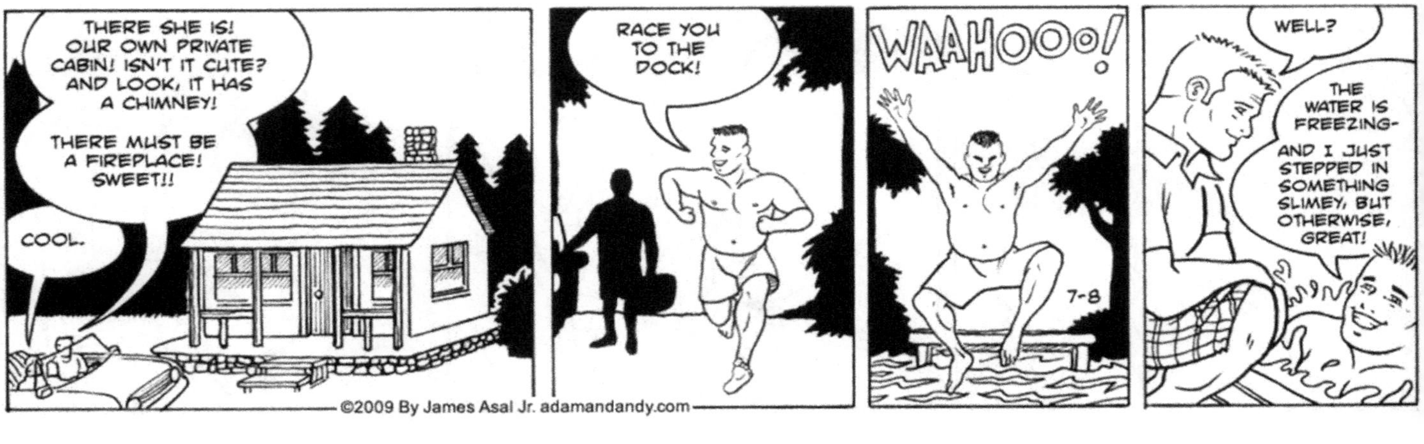
THERE SHE IS! OUR OWN PRIVATE CABIN! ISN'T IT CUTE? AND LOOK, IT HAS A CHIMNEY!
THERE MUST BE A FIREPLACE! SWEET!!
COOL.
©2009 By James Asal Jr. adamandandy.com
RACE YOU TO THE DOCK!
WAAHOOOo!
7-8
WELL?
THE WATER IS FREEZING-
AND I JUST STEPPED IN SOMETHING SLIMEY, BUT OTHERWISE, GREAT!

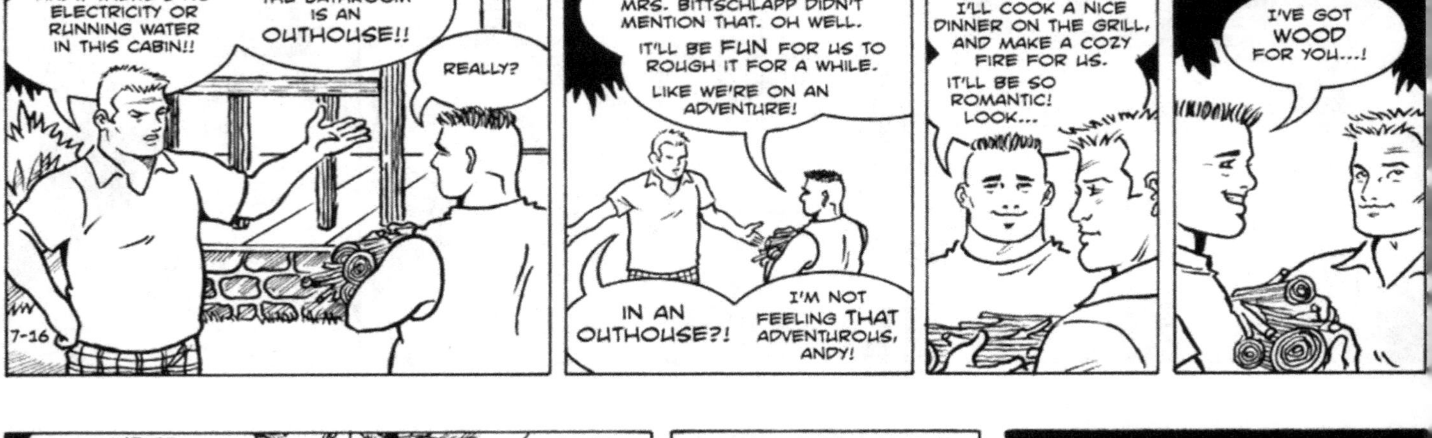
ANDY, THERE'S NO ELECTRICITY OR RUNNING WATER IN THIS CABIN!!
THE BATHROOM IS AN OUTHOUSE!!
REALLY?
7-16
THAT'S FUNNY. MRS. BITTSCHLAPP DIDN'T MENTION THAT. OH WELL.
IT'LL BE FUN FOR US TO ROUGH IT FOR A WHILE.
LIKE WE'RE ON AN ADVENTURE!
IN AN OUTHOUSE?!
I'M NOT FEELING THAT ADVENTUROUS, ANDY!
IT'LL BE OKAY, BABE. I'LL COOK A NICE DINNER ON THE GRILL, AND MAKE A COZY FIRE FOR US.
IT'LL BE SO ROMANTIC! LOOK...
I'VE GOT WOOD FOR YOU...!

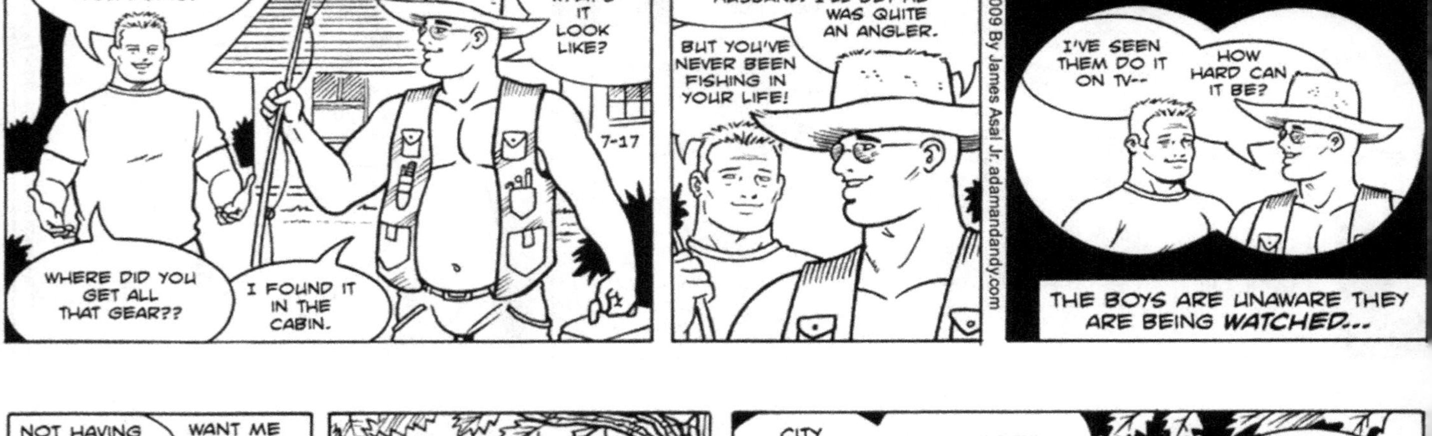
ANDY?? WHAT THE HECK ARE YOU DOING?
GOING FISHING, WHAT'S IT LOOK LIKE?
7-17
WHERE DID YOU GET ALL THAT GEAR??
I FOUND IT IN THE CABIN.
IT MUST HAVE BELONGED TO MRS. BITTSCHLAPP'S HUSBAND. I'LL BET HE WAS QUITE AN ANGLER.
BUT YOU'VE NEVER BEEN FISHING IN YOUR LIFE!
©2009 By James Asal Jr. adamandandy.com
I'VE SEEN THEM DO IT ON TV--
HOW HARD CAN IT BE?
THE BOYS ARE UNAWARE THEY ARE BEING WATCHED...

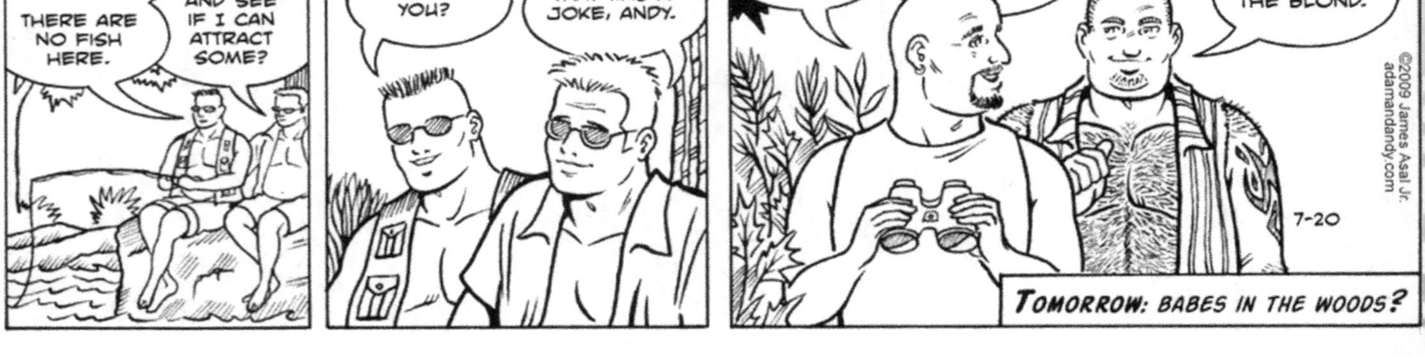
NOT HAVING MUCH LUCK WITH THIS.
THERE ARE NO FISH HERE.
WANT ME TO SWIM AROUND AND SEE IF I CAN ATTRACT SOME?
WOULD YOU?
THAT WAS A JOKE, ANDY.
CITY BOYS!
MY FAVORITE...!
DIBS ON THE BLOND.
7-20
©2009 James Asal Jr. adamandandy.com
TOMORROW: BABES IN THE WOODS?

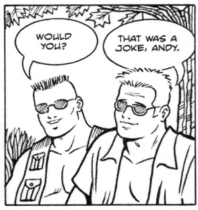

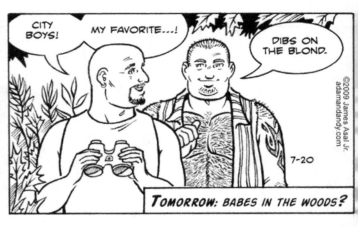

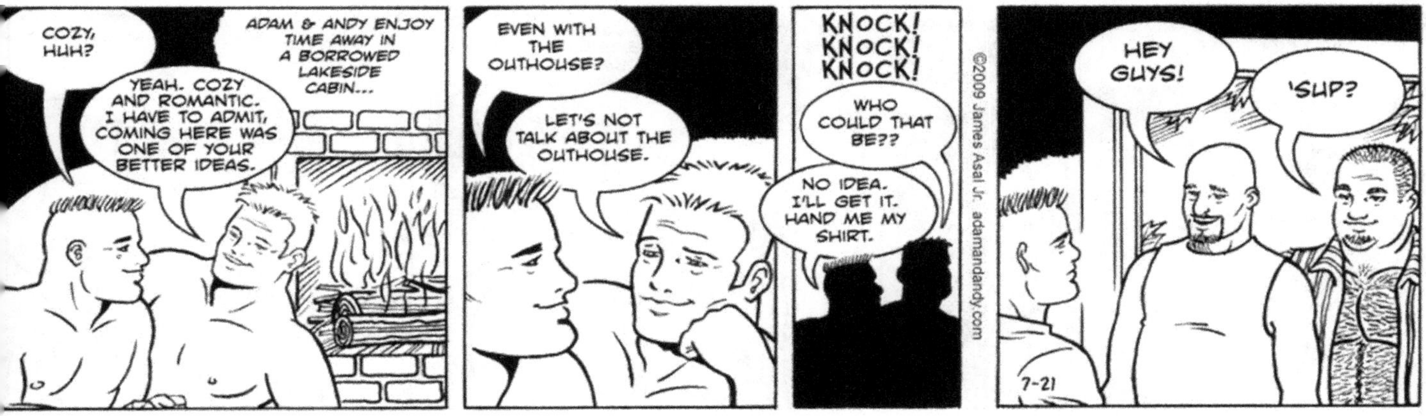
ADAM & ANDY ENJOY TIME AWAY IN A BORROWED LAKESIDE CABIN...
COZY, HUH?
YEAH. COZY AND ROMANTIC. I HAVE TO ADMIT, COMING HERE WAS ONE OF YOUR BETTER IDEAS.
EVEN WITH THE OUTHOUSE?
LET'S NOT TALK ABOUT THE OUTHOUSE.
KNOCK! KNOCK! KNOCK!
WHO COULD THAT BE??
NO IDEA. I'LL GET IT. HAND ME MY SHIRT.
©2009 James Asal Jr. adamandandy.com
HEY GUYS!
'SUP?
7-21

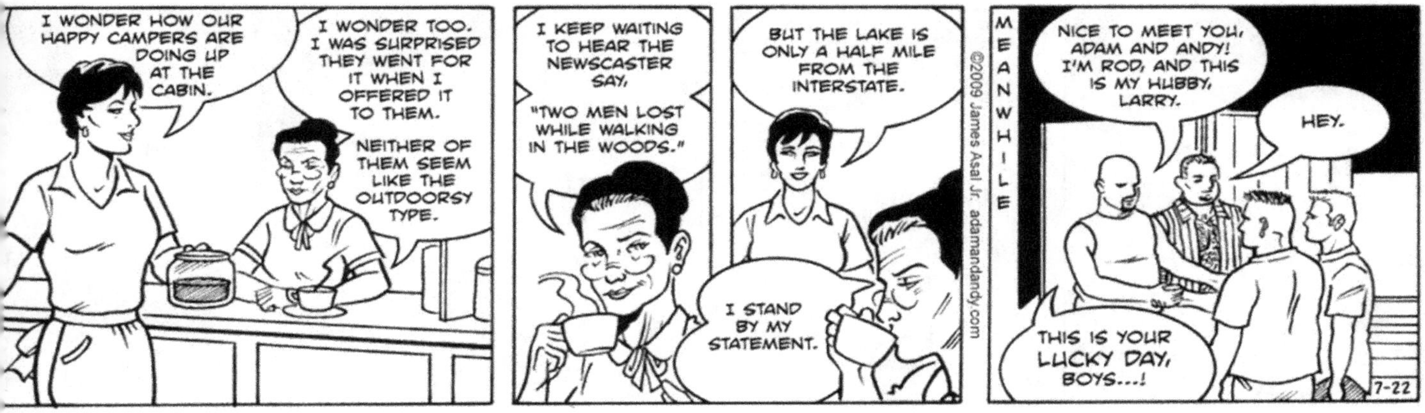
I WONDER HOW OUR HAPPY CAMPERS ARE DOING UP AT THE CABIN.
I WONDER TOO. I WAS SURPRISED THEY WENT FOR IT WHEN I OFFERED IT TO THEM.
NEITHER OF THEM SEEM LIKE THE OUTDOORSY TYPE.
I KEEP WAITING TO HEAR THE NEWSCASTER SAY, "TWO MEN LOST WHILE WALKING IN THE WOODS."
BUT THE LAKE IS ONLY A HALF MILE FROM THE INTERSTATE.
I STAND BY MY STATEMENT.
©2009 James Asal Jr. adamandandy.com
MEANWHILE
NICE TO MEET YOU, ADAM AND ANDY! I'M ROD, AND THIS IS MY HUBBY, LARRY.
HEY.
THIS IS YOUR LUCKY DAY, BOYS...!
7-22

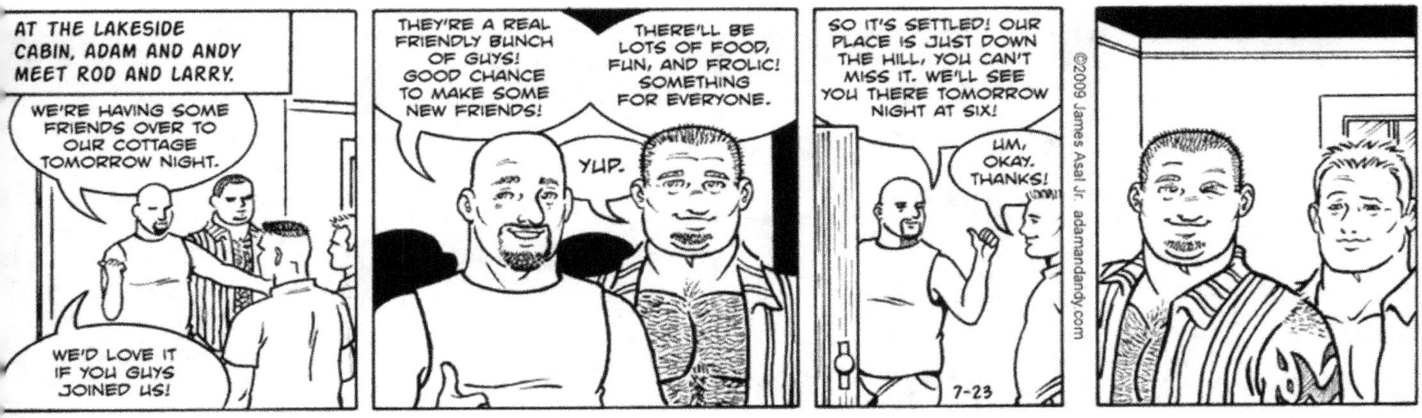
AT THE LAKESIDE CABIN, ADAM AND ANDY MEET ROD AND LARRY.
WE'RE HAVING SOME FRIENDS OVER TO OUR COTTAGE TOMORROW NIGHT.
WE'D LOVE IT IF YOU GUYS JOINED US!
THEY'RE A REAL FRIENDLY BUNCH OF GUYS! GOOD CHANCE TO MAKE SOME NEW FRIENDS!
THERE'LL BE LOTS OF FOOD, FUN, AND FROLIC! SOMETHING FOR EVERYONE.
YUP.
SO IT'S SETTLED! OUR PLACE IS JUST DOWN THE HILL, YOU CAN'T MISS IT. WE'LL SEE YOU THERE TOMORROW NIGHT AT SIX!
UM, OKAY. THANKS!
7-23
©2009 James Asal Jr. adamandandy.com

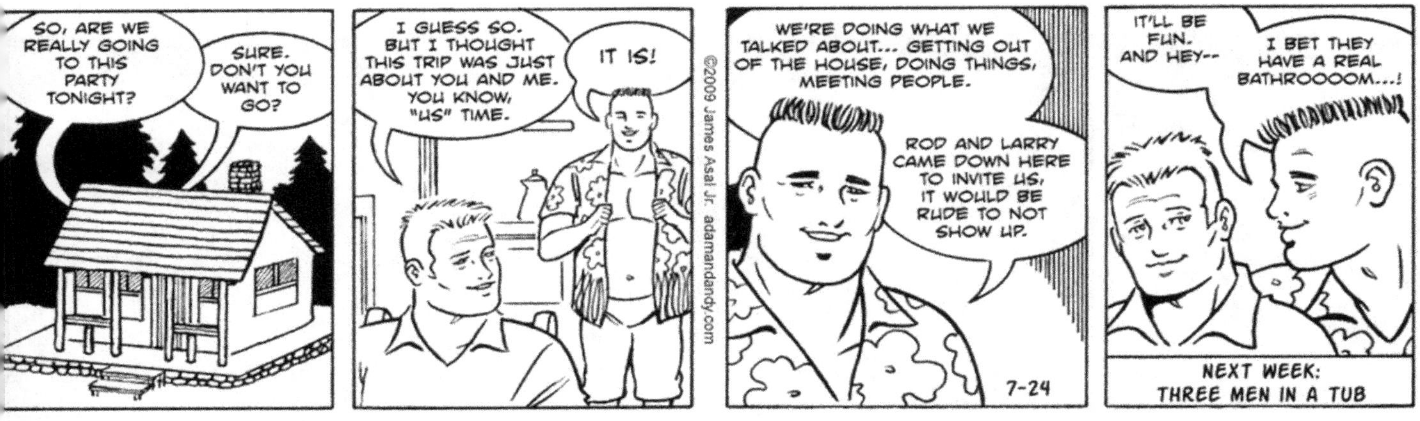
SO, ARE WE REALLY GOING TO THIS PARTY TONIGHT?
SURE. DON'T YOU WANT TO GO?
I GUESS SO. BUT I THOUGHT THIS TRIP WAS JUST ABOUT YOU AND ME. YOU KNOW, "US" TIME.
IT IS!
©2009 James Asal Jr. adamandandy.com
WE'RE DOING WHAT WE TALKED ABOUT... GETTING OUT OF THE HOUSE, DOING THINGS, MEETING PEOPLE.
ROD AND LARRY CAME DOWN HERE TO INVITE US, IT WOULD BE RUDE TO NOT SHOW UP.
7-24
IT'LL BE FUN. AND HEY--
I BET THEY HAVE A REAL BATHROOOOM...!
NEXT WEEK: THREE MEN IN A TUB

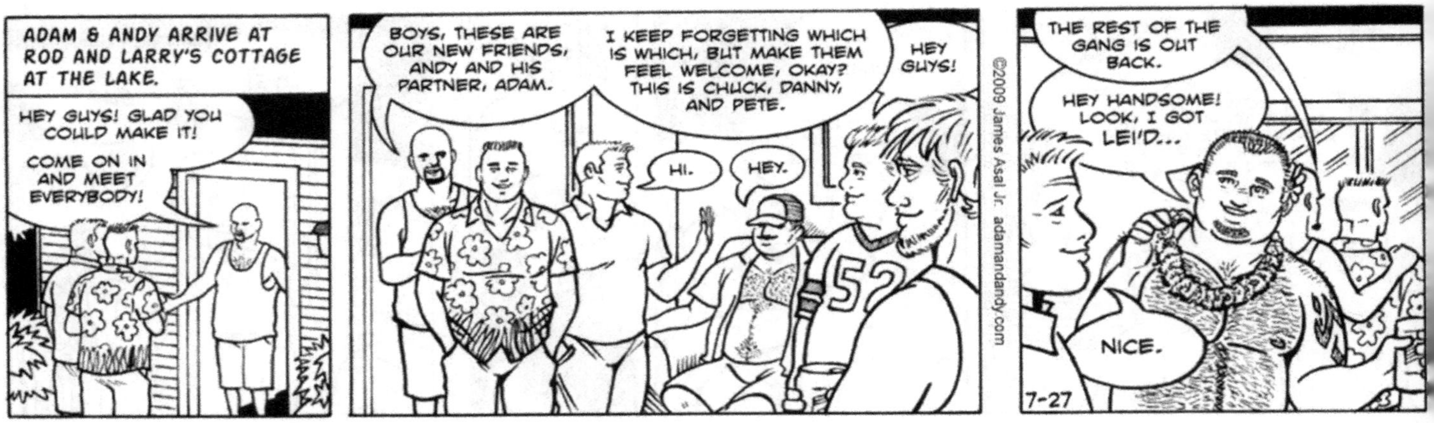
ADAM & ANDY ARRIVE AT ROD AND LARRY'S COTTAGE AT THE LAKE.
HEY GUYS! GLAD YOU COULD MAKE IT!
COME ON IN AND MEET EVERYBODY!
BOYS, THESE ARE OUR NEW FRIENDS, ANDY AND HIS PARTNER, ADAM.
I KEEP FORGETTING WHICH IS WHICH, BUT MAKE THEM FEEL WELCOME, OKAY? THIS IS CHUCK, DANNY, AND PETE.
HI.
HEY.
HEY GUYS!
©2009 James Asal Jr. adamandandy.com
THE REST OF THE GANG IS OUT BACK.
HEY HANDSOME! LOOK, I GOT LEI'D...
NICE.
7-27

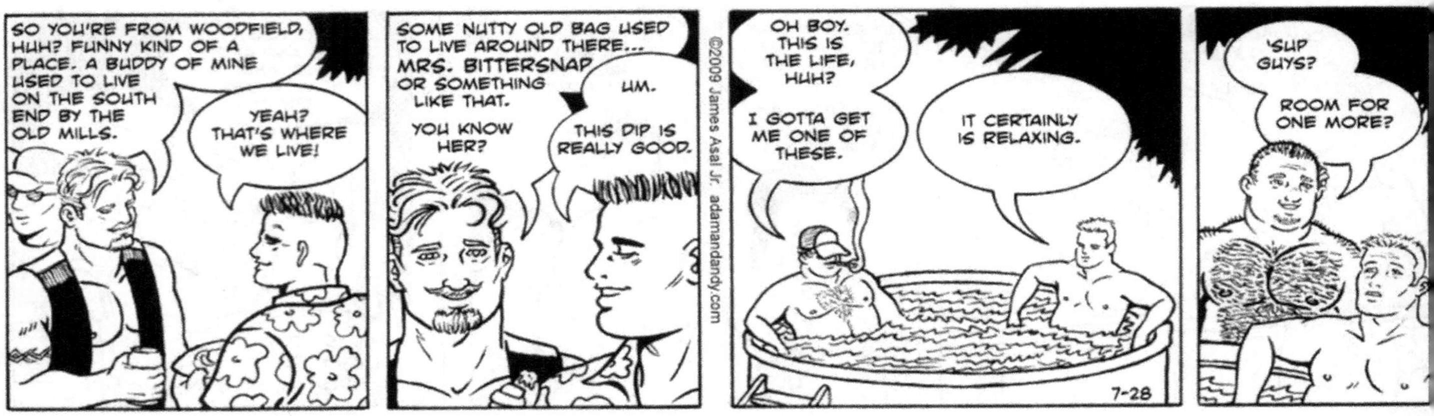
SO YOU'RE FROM WOODFIELD, HUH? FUNNY KIND OF A PLACE. A BUDDY OF MINE USED TO LIVE ON THE SOUTH END BY THE OLD MILLS.
YEAH? THAT'S WHERE WE LIVE!
SOME NUTTY OLD BAG USED TO LIVE AROUND THERE... MRS. BITTERSNAP OR SOMETHING LIKE THAT.
YOU KNOW HER?
UM.
THIS DIP IS REALLY GOOD.
©2009 James Asal Jr. adamandandy.com
OH BOY. THIS IS THE LIFE, HUH?
I GOTTA GET ME ONE OF THESE.
IT CERTAINLY IS RELAXING.
7-28
'SUP GUYS?
ROOM FOR ONE MORE?

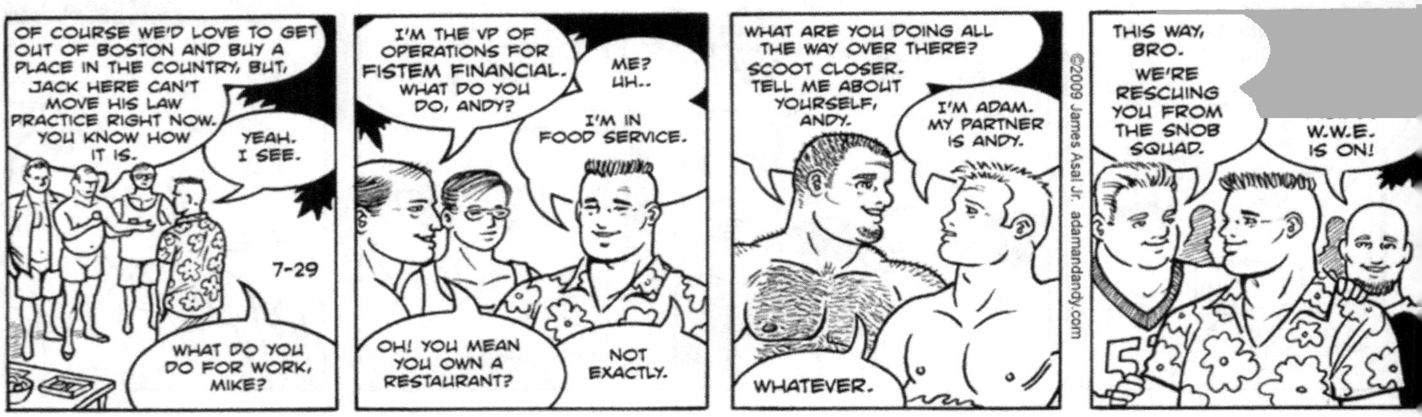
OF COURSE WE'D LOVE TO GET OUT OF BOSTON AND BUY A PLACE IN THE COUNTRY, BUT, JACK HERE CAN'T MOVE HIS LAW PRACTICE RIGHT NOW. YOU KNOW HOW IT IS.
YEAH. I SEE.
7-29
WHAT DO YOU DO FOR WORK, MIKE?
I'M THE VP OF OPERATIONS FOR FISTEM FINANCIAL. WHAT DO YOU DO, ANDY?
ME? UH..
I'M IN FOOD SERVICE.
OH! YOU MEAN YOU OWN A RESTAURANT?
NOT EXACTLY.
WHAT ARE YOU DOING ALL THE WAY OVER THERE? SCOOT CLOSER. TELL ME ABOUT YOURSELF, ANDY.
I'M ADAM. MY PARTNER IS ANDY.
WHATEVER.
©2009 James Asal Jr. adamandandy.com
THIS WAY, BRO.
WE'RE RESCUING YOU FROM THE SNOB SQUAD.
W.W.E. IS ON!

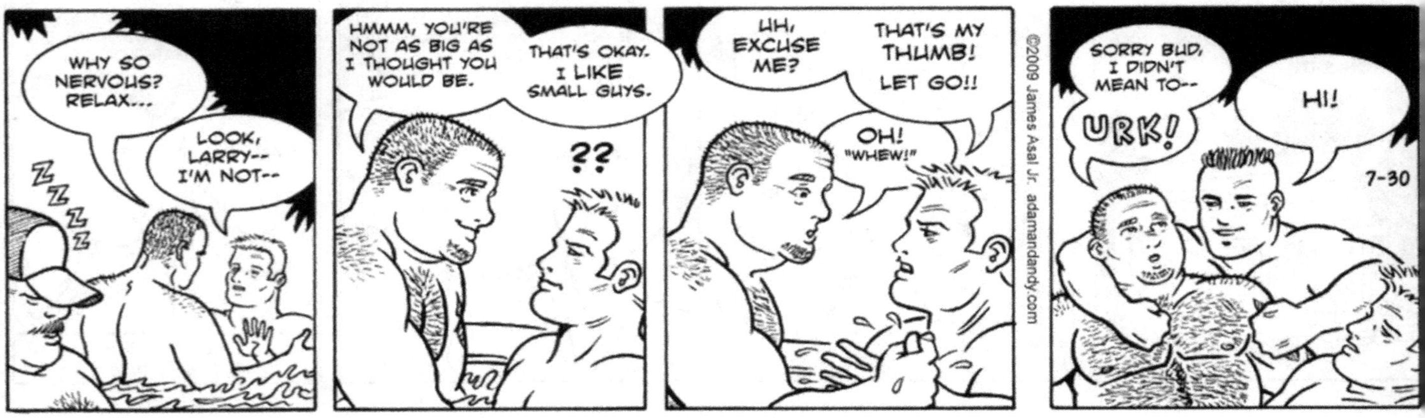
WHY SO NERVOUS? RELAX...
LOOK, LARRY-- I'M NOT--
Z Z Z Z
HMMM, YOU'RE NOT AS BIG AS I THOUGHT YOU WOULD BE.
THAT'S OKAY. I LIKE SMALL GUYS.
??
UH, EXCUSE ME?
THAT'S MY THUMB! LET GO!!
OH! "WHEW!"
©2009 James Asal Jr. adamandandy.com
SORRY BUD, I DIDN'T MEAN TO--
URK!
HI!
7-30

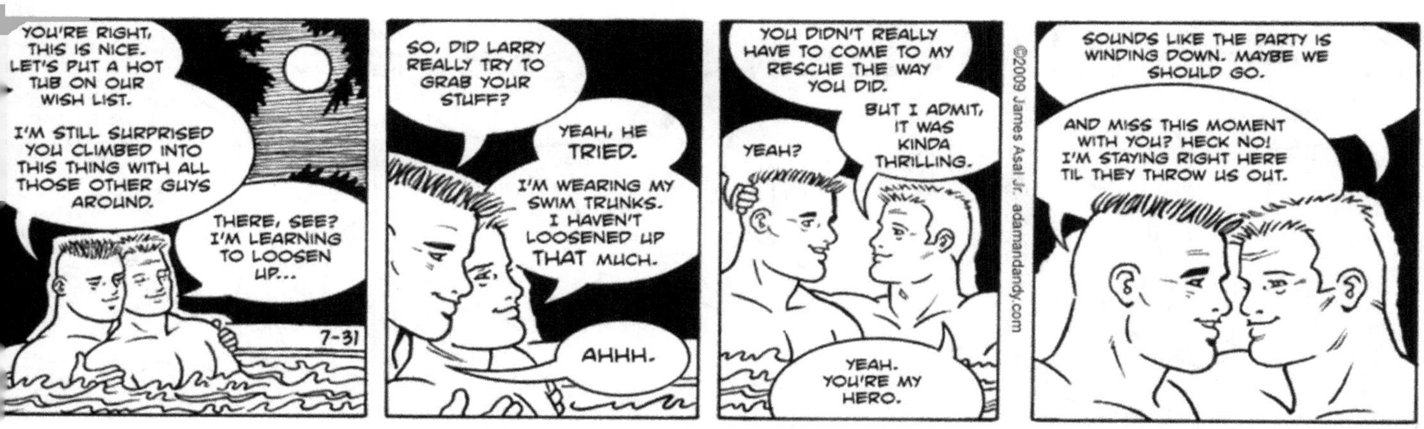
YOU'RE RIGHT, THIS IS NICE. LET'S PUT A HOT TUB ON OUR WISH LIST.
I'M STILL SURPRISED YOU CLIMBED INTO THIS THING WITH ALL THOSE OTHER GUYS AROUND.
THERE, SEE? I'M LEARNING TO LOOSEN UP...
7-31
SO, DID LARRY REALLY TRY TO GRAB YOUR STUFF?
YEAH, HE TRIED.
I'M WEARING MY SWIM TRUNKS. I HAVEN'T LOOSENED UP THAT MUCH.
AHHH.
YOU DIDN'T REALLY HAVE TO COME TO MY RESCUE THE WAY YOU DID.
YEAH?
BUT I ADMIT, IT WAS KINDA THRILLING.
YEAH. YOU'RE MY HERO.
©2009 James Asal Jr. adamandandy.com
SOUNDS LIKE THE PARTY IS WINDING DOWN. MAYBE WE SHOULD GO.
AND MISS THIS MOMENT WITH YOU? HECK NO! I'M STAYING RIGHT HERE TIL THEY THROW US OUT.

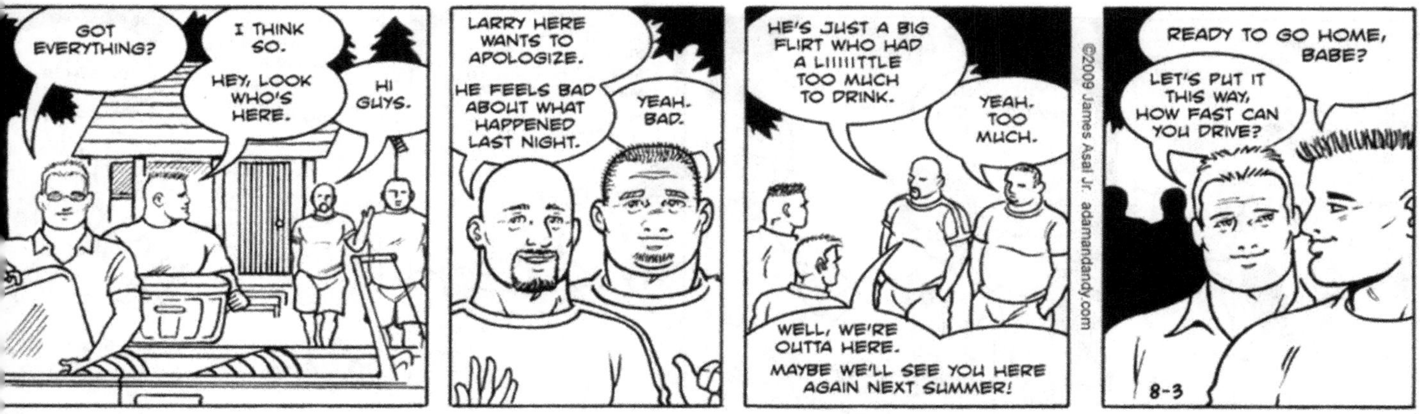
GOT EVERYTHING?
I THINK SO.
HEY, LOOK WHO'S HERE.
HI GUYS.
LARRY HERE WANTS TO APOLOGIZE.
HE FEELS BAD ABOUT WHAT HAPPENED LAST NIGHT.
YEAH. BAD.
HE'S JUST A BIG FLIRT WHO HAD A LIIIIITTLE TOO MUCH TO DRINK.
YEAH. TOO MUCH.
WELL, WE'RE OUTTA HERE.
MAYBE WE'LL SEE YOU HERE AGAIN NEXT SUMMER!
©2009 James Asal Jr. adamandandy.com
READY TO GO HOME, BABE?
LET'S PUT IT THIS WAY, HOW FAST CAN YOU DRIVE?
8-3

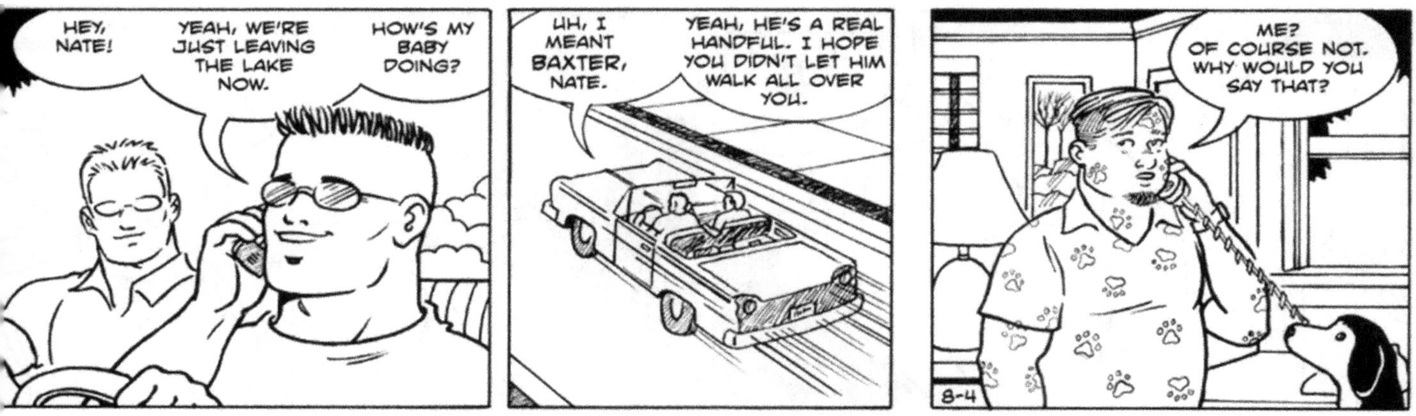
HEY, NATE!
YEAH, WE'RE JUST LEAVING THE LAKE NOW.
HOW'S MY BABY DOING?
UH, I MEANT BAXTER, NATE.
YEAH, HE'S A REAL HANDFUL. I HOPE YOU DIDN'T LET HIM WALK ALL OVER YOU.
ME? OF COURSE NOT. WHY WOULD YOU SAY THAT?
8-4

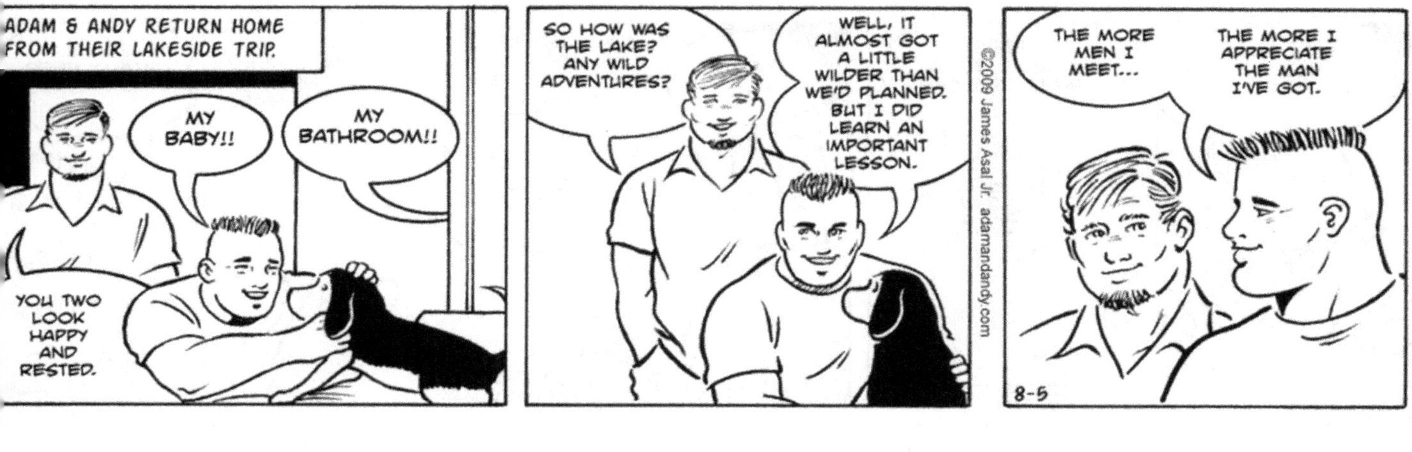
ADAM & ANDY RETURN HOME FROM THEIR LAKESIDE TRIP.
MY BABY!!
MY BATHROOM!!
YOU TWO LOOK HAPPY AND RESTED.
SO HOW WAS THE LAKE? ANY WILD ADVENTURES?
WELL, IT ALMOST GOT A LITTLE WILDER THAN WE'D PLANNED. BUT I DID LEARN AN IMPORTANT LESSON.
©2009 James Asal Jr. adamandandy.com
THE MORE MEN I MEET...
THE MORE I APPRECIATE THE MAN I'VE GOT.
8-5

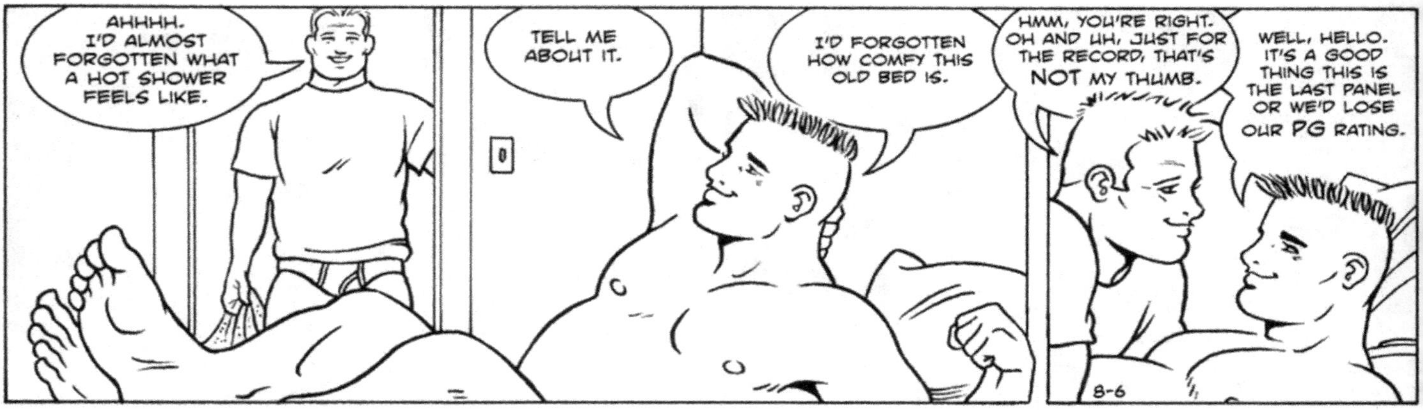
AHHHH. I'D ALMOST FORGOTTEN WHAT A HOT SHOWER FEELS LIKE.
TELL ME ABOUT IT.
I'D FORGOTTEN HOW COMFY THIS OLD BED IS.
HMM, YOU'RE RIGHT. OH AND UH, JUST FOR THE RECORD, THAT'S NOT MY THUMB.
WELL, HELLO. IT'S A GOOD THING THIS IS THE LAST PANEL OR WE'D LOSE OUR PG RATING.
8-6

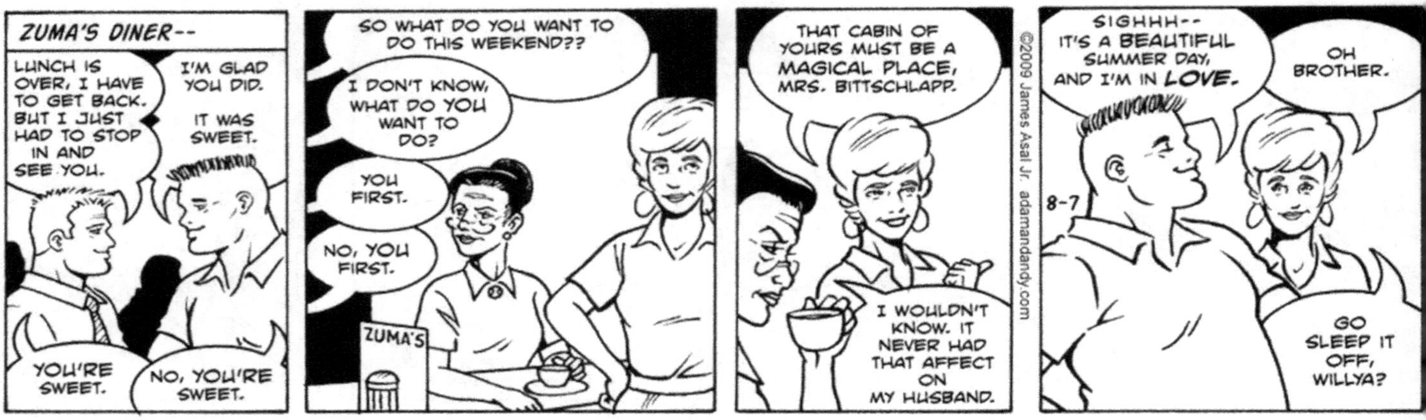
ZUMA'S DINER--
LUNCH IS OVER, I HAVE TO GET BACK. BUT I JUST HAD TO STOP IN AND SEE YOU.
I'M GLAD YOU DID. IT WAS SWEET.
YOU'RE SWEET.
NO, YOU'RE SWEET.
SO WHAT DO YOU WANT TO DO THIS WEEKEND??
I DON'T KNOW, WHAT DO YOU WANT TO DO?
YOU FIRST.
NO, YOU FIRST.
ZUMA'S
THAT CABIN OF YOURS MUST BE A MAGICAL PLACE, MRS. BITTSCHLAPP.
I WOULDN'T KNOW. IT NEVER HAD THAT AFFECT ON MY HUSBAND.
©2009 James Asal Jr. adamandandy.com
SIGHHH-- IT'S A BEAUTIFUL SUMMER DAY, AND I'M IN LOVE.
OH BROTHER.
GO SLEEP IT OFF, WILLYA?
8-7

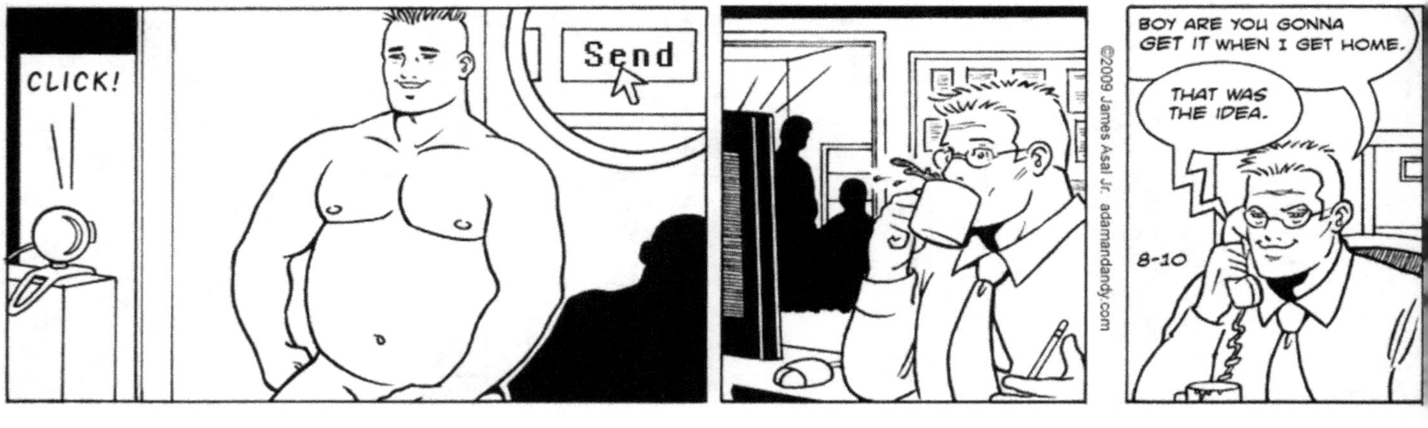
CLICK!
Send
©2009 James Asal Jr. adamandandy.com
BOY ARE YOU GONNA GET IT WHEN I GET HOME.
THAT WAS THE IDEA.
8-10

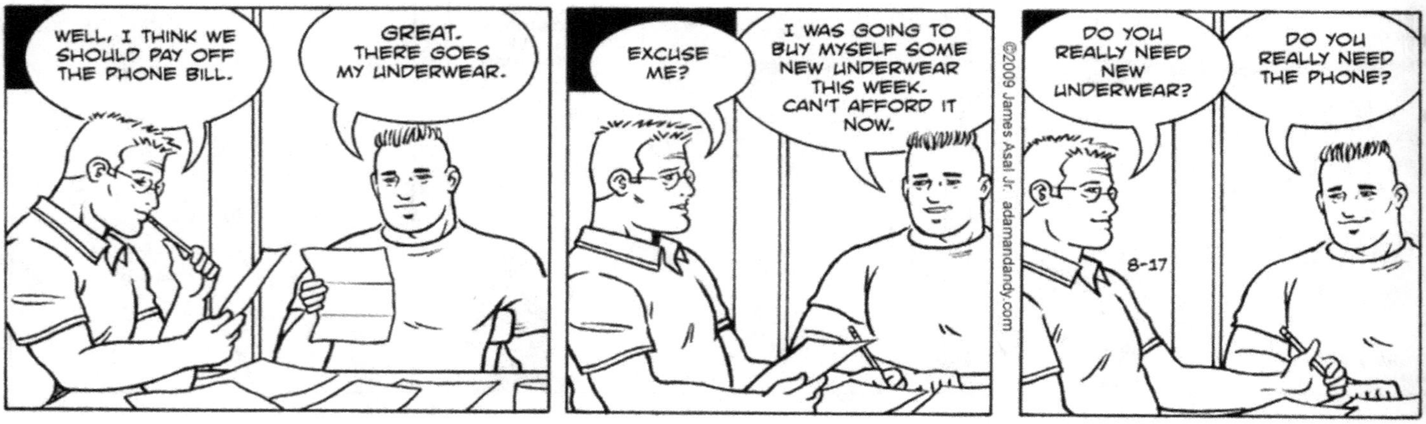
WELL, I THINK WE SHOULD PAY OFF THE PHONE BILL.
GREAT. THERE GOES MY UNDERWEAR.
EXCUSE ME?
I WAS GOING TO BUY MYSELF SOME NEW UNDERWEAR THIS WEEK. CAN'T AFFORD IT NOW.
©2009 James Asal Jr. adamandandy.com
DO YOU REALLY NEED NEW UNDERWEAR?
DO YOU REALLY NEED THE PHONE?
8-17

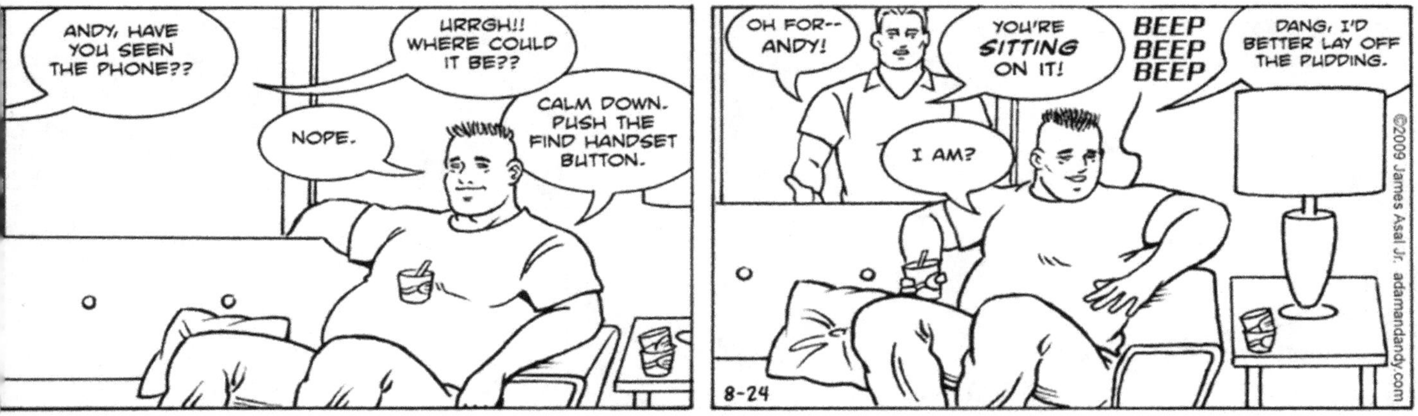
ANDY, HAVE YOU SEEN THE PHONE??
NOPE.
URRGH!! WHERE COULD IT BE??
CALM DOWN. PUSH THE FIND HANDSET BUTTON.
OH FOR-- ANDY!
YOU'RE SITTING ON IT!
I AM?
BEEP BEEP BEEP
DANG, I'D BETTER LAY OFF THE PUDDING.
8-24
©2009 James Asal Jr. adamandandy.com

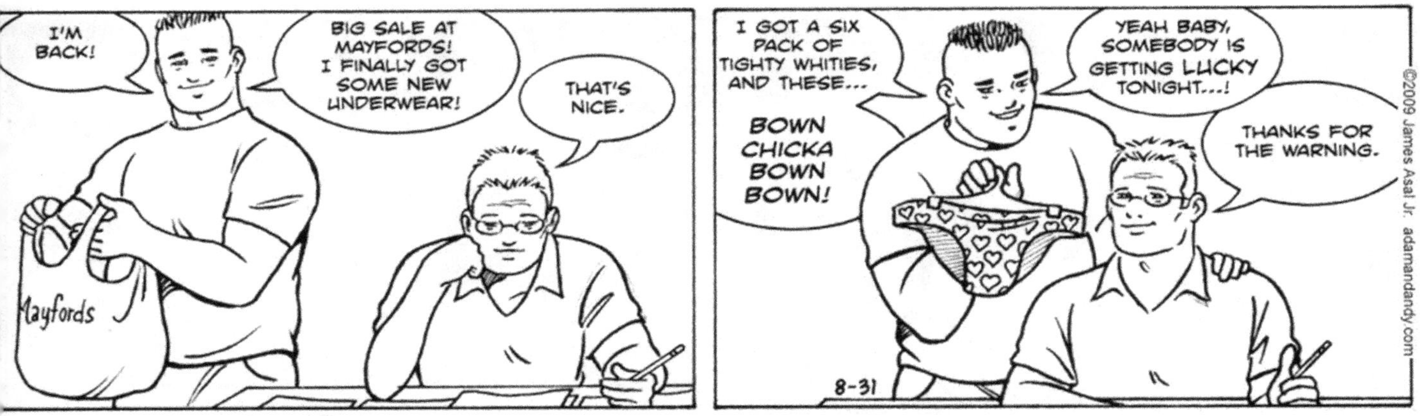
I'M BACK!
BIG SALE AT MAYFORDS! I FINALLY GOT SOME NEW UNDERWEAR!
Mayfords
THAT'S NICE.
I GOT A SIX PACK OF TIGHTY WHITIES, AND THESE...
BOWN CHICKA BOWN BOWN!
YEAH BABY, SOMEBODY IS GETTING LUCKY TONIGHT...!
THANKS FOR THE WARNING.
8-31
©2009 James Asal Jr. adamandandy.com

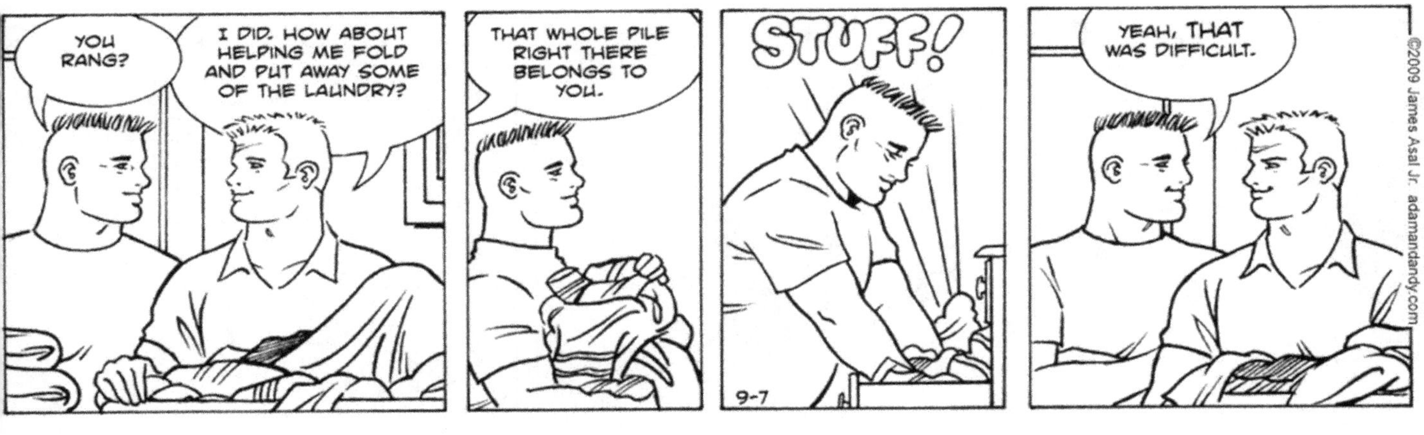
YOU RANG?
I DID. HOW ABOUT HELPING ME FOLD AND PUT AWAY SOME OF THE LAUNDRY?
THAT WHOLE PILE RIGHT THERE BELONGS TO YOU.
STUFF!
9-7
YEAH, THAT WAS DIFFICULT.
©2009 James Asal Jr. adamandandy.com

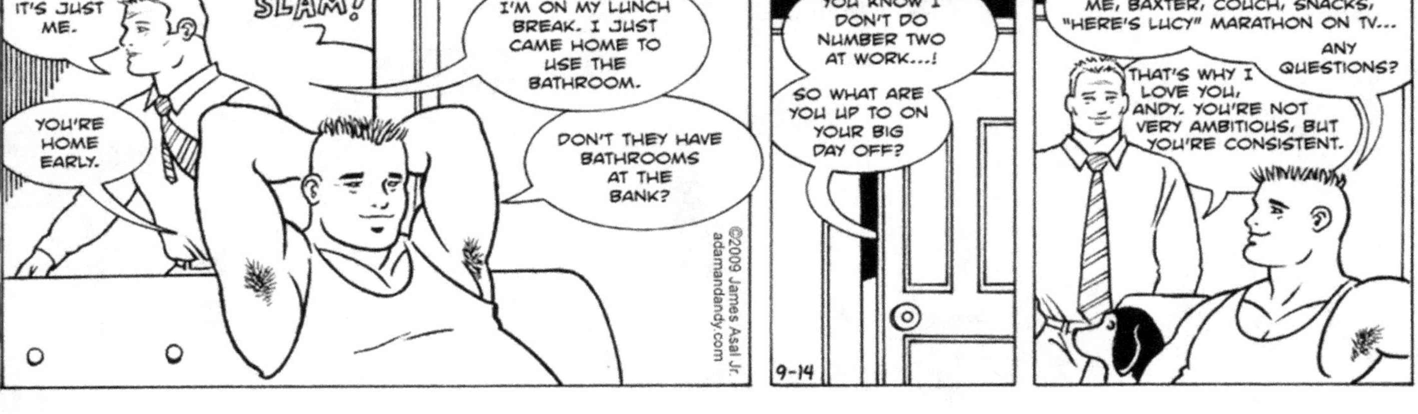
IT'S JUST ME.
SLAM!
YOU'RE HOME EARLY.
I'M ON MY LUNCH BREAK. I JUST CAME HOME TO USE THE BATHROOM.
DON'T THEY HAVE BATHROOMS AT THE BANK?
©2009 James Asal Jr. adamandandy.com
YOU KNOW I DON'T DO NUMBER TWO AT WORK...!
SO WHAT ARE YOU UP TO ON YOUR BIG DAY OFF?
9-14
ME, BAXTER, COUCH, SNACKS, "HERE'S LUCY" MARATHON ON TV... ANY QUESTIONS?
THAT'S WHY I LOVE YOU, ANDY. YOU'RE NOT VERY AMBITIOUS, BUT YOU'RE CONSISTENT.

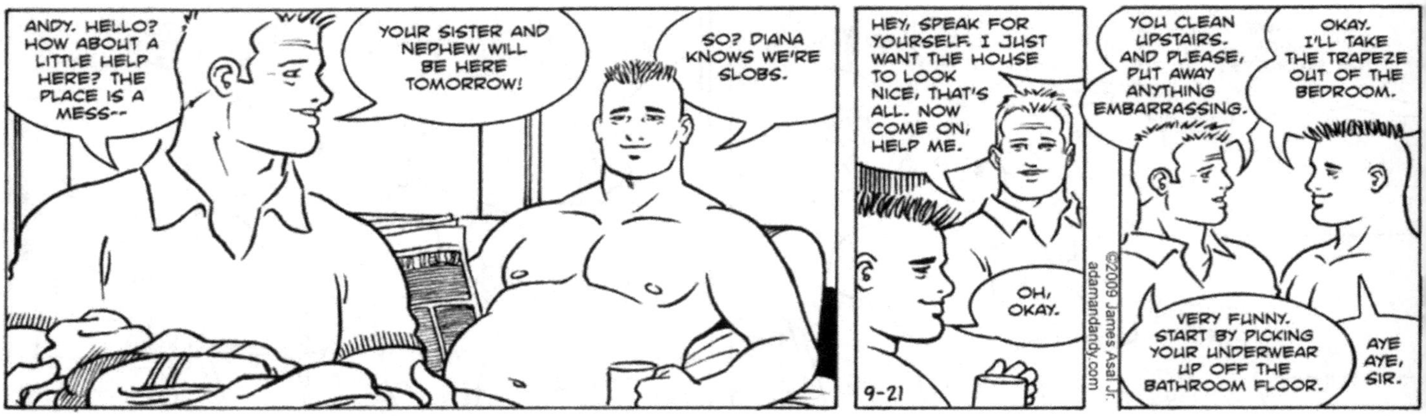
ANDY. HELLO? HOW ABOUT A LITTLE HELP HERE? THE PLACE IS A MESS--
YOUR SISTER AND NEPHEW WILL BE HERE TOMORROW!
SO? DIANA KNOWS WE'RE SLOBS.
HEY, SPEAK FOR YOURSELF. I JUST WANT THE HOUSE TO LOOK NICE, THAT'S ALL. NOW COME ON, HELP ME.
OH, OKAY.
YOU CLEAN UPSTAIRS. AND PLEASE, PUT AWAY ANYTHING EMBARRASSING.
OKAY. I'LL TAKE THE TRAPEZE OUT OF THE BEDROOM.
VERY FUNNY. START BY PICKING YOUR UNDERWEAR UP OFF THE BATHROOM FLOOR.
AYE AYE, SIR.
9-21
©2009 James Asal Jr. adamandandy.com

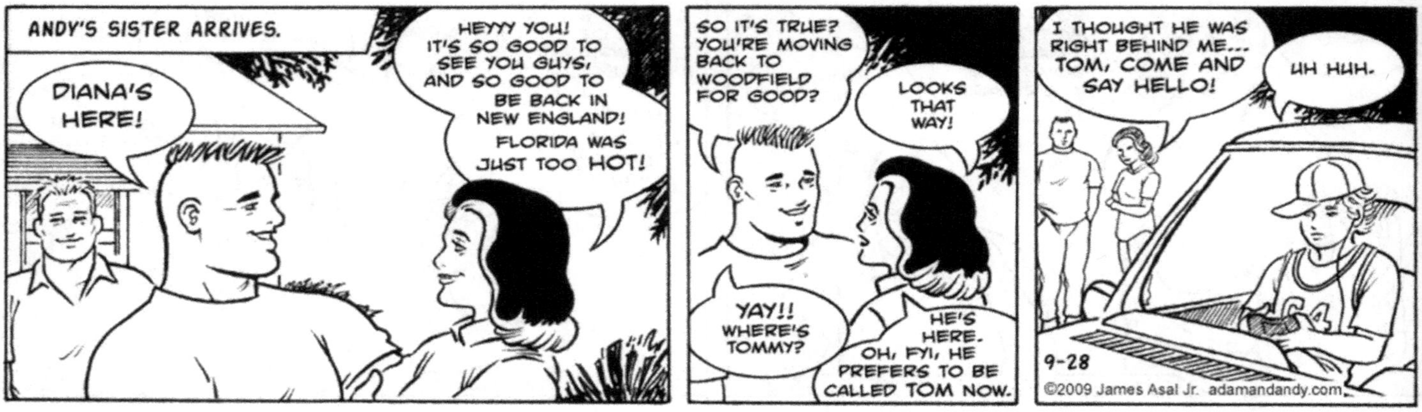
ANDY'S SISTER ARRIVES.
DIANA'S HERE!
HEYYY YOU! IT'S SO GOOD TO SEE YOU GUYS, AND SO GOOD TO BE BACK IN NEW ENGLAND! FLORIDA WAS JUST TOO HOT!
SO IT'S TRUE? YOU'RE MOVING BACK TO WOODFIELD FOR GOOD?
LOOKS THAT WAY!
YAY!! WHERE'S TOMMY?
HE'S HERE. OH, FYI, HE PREFERS TO BE CALLED TOM NOW.
I THOUGHT HE WAS RIGHT BEHIND ME... TOM, COME AND SAY HELLO!
UH HUH.
9-28
©2009 James Asal Jr. adamandandy.com

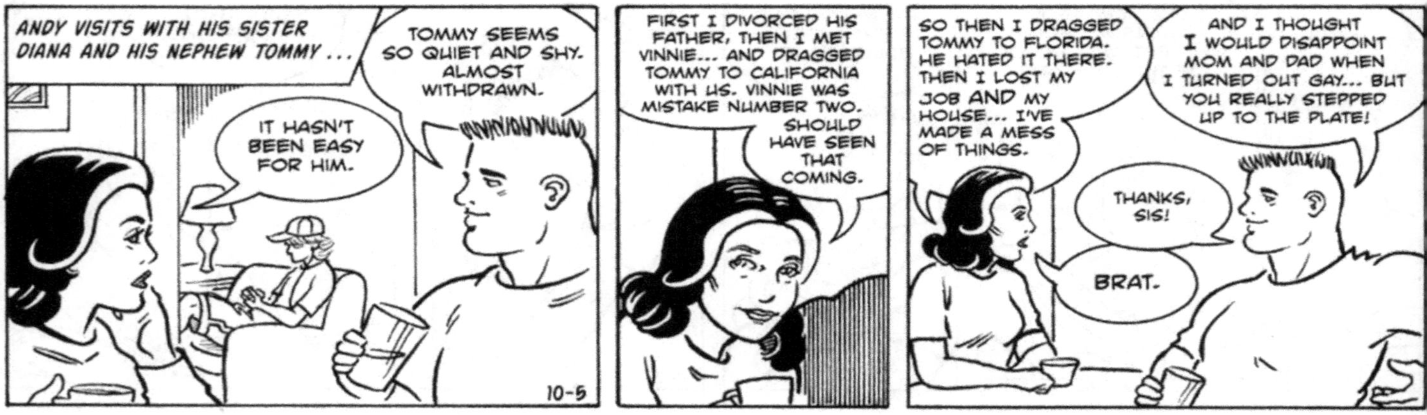
ANDY VISITS WITH HIS SISTER DIANA AND HIS NEPHEW TOMMY ...
TOMMY SEEMS SO QUIET AND SHY. ALMOST WITHDRAWN.
IT HASN'T BEEN EASY FOR HIM.
10-5
FIRST I DIVORCED HIS FATHER, THEN I MET VINNIE... AND DRAGGED TOMMY TO CALIFORNIA WITH US. VINNIE WAS MISTAKE NUMBER TWO.
SHOULD HAVE SEEN THAT COMING.
SO THEN I DRAGGED TOMMY TO FLORIDA. HE HATED IT THERE. THEN I LOST MY JOB AND MY HOUSE... I'VE MADE A MESS OF THINGS.
AND I THOUGHT I WOULD DISAPPOINT MOM AND DAD WHEN I TURNED OUT GAY... BUT YOU REALLY STEPPED UP TO THE PLATE!
THANKS, SIS!
BRAT.

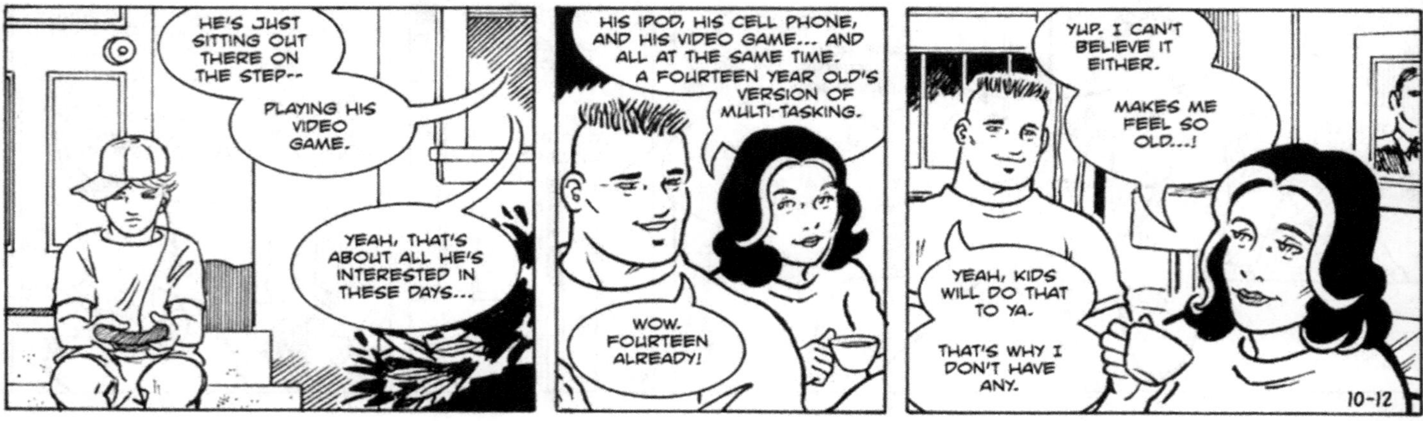
HE'S JUST SITTING OUT THERE ON THE STEP--
PLAYING HIS VIDEO GAME.
YEAH, THAT'S ABOUT ALL HE'S INTERESTED IN THESE DAYS...
HIS IPOD, HIS CELL PHONE, AND HIS VIDEO GAME... AND ALL AT THE SAME TIME.
A FOURTEEN YEAR OLD'S VERSION OF MULTI-TASKING.
WOW. FOURTEEN ALREADY!
YUP. I CAN'T BELIEVE IT EITHER.
MAKES ME FEEL SO OLD...!
YEAH, KIDS WILL DO THAT TO YA.
THAT'S WHY I DON'T HAVE ANY.
10-12

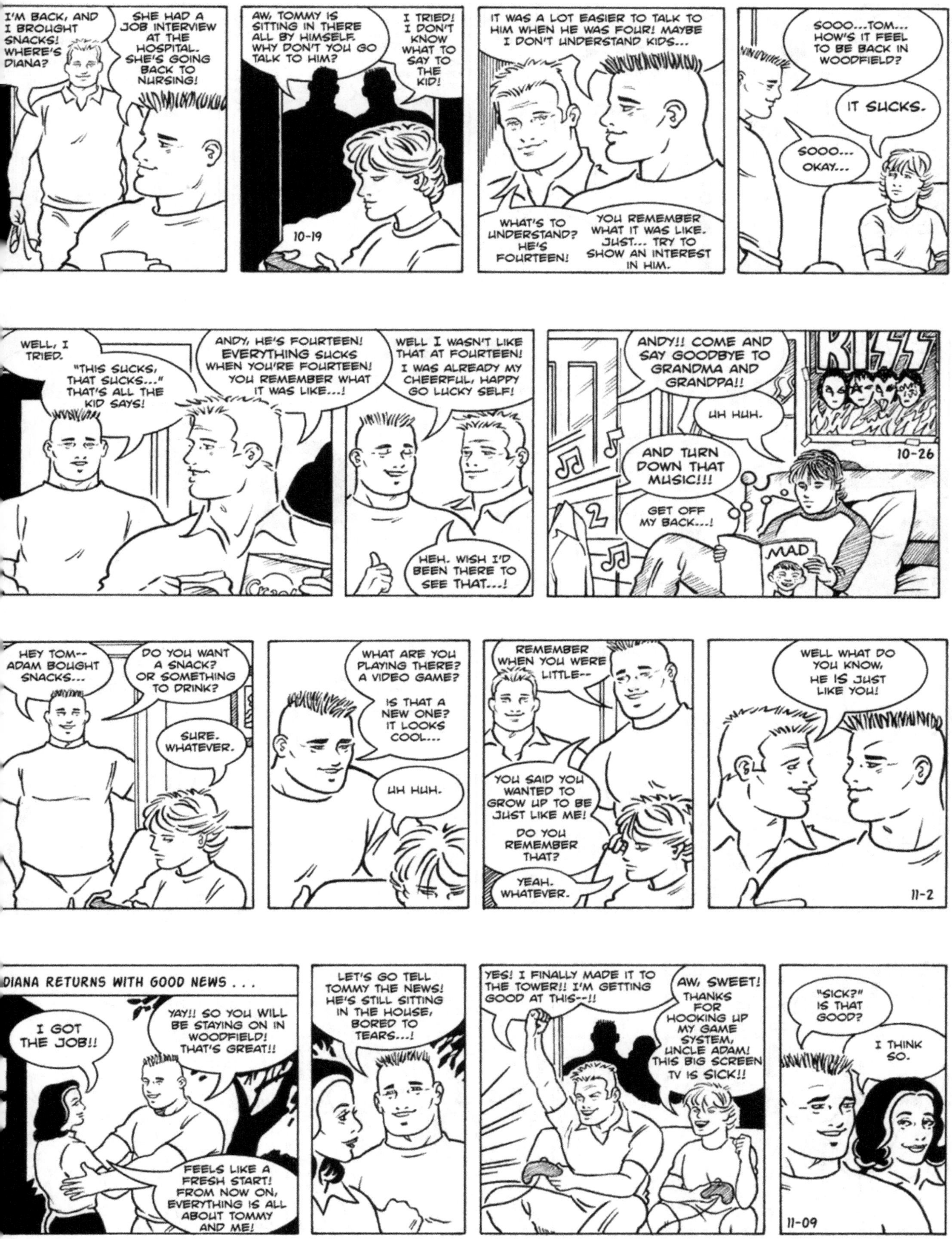

I'M BACK, AND I BROUGHT SNACKS! WHERE'S DIANA?
SHE HAD A JOB INTERVIEW AT THE HOSPITAL. SHE'S GOING BACK TO NURSING!
AW, TOMMY IS SITTING IN THERE ALL BY HIMSELF. WHY DON'T YOU GO TALK TO HIM?
I TRIED! I DON'T KNOW WHAT TO SAY TO THE KID!
10-19
IT WAS A LOT EASIER TO TALK TO HIM WHEN HE WAS FOUR! MAYBE I DON'T UNDERSTAND KIDS...
WHAT'S TO UNDERSTAND? HE'S FOURTEEN!
YOU REMEMBER WHAT IT WAS LIKE. JUST... TRY TO SHOW AN INTEREST IN HIM.
SOOO...TOM... HOW'S IT FEEL TO BE BACK IN WOODFIELD?
IT SUCKS.
SOOO... OKAY...
WELL, I TRIED.
"THIS SUCKS, THAT SUCKS..." THAT'S ALL THE KID SAYS!
ANDY, HE'S FOURTEEN! EVERYTHING SUCKS WHEN YOU'RE FOURTEEN! YOU REMEMBER WHAT IT WAS LIKE...!
WELL I WASN'T LIKE THAT AT FOURTEEN! I WAS ALREADY MY CHEERFUL, HAPPY GO LUCKY SELF!
HEH. WISH I'D BEEN THERE TO SEE THAT...!
ANDY!! COME AND SAY GOODBYE TO GRANDMA AND GRANDPA!!
UH HUH.
AND TURN DOWN THAT MUSIC!!!
GET OFF MY BACK...!
MAD
10-26
HEY TOM-- ADAM BOUGHT SNACKS...
DO YOU WANT A SNACK? OR SOMETHING TO DRINK?
SURE. WHATEVER.
WHAT ARE YOU PLAYING THERE? A VIDEO GAME?
IS THAT A NEW ONE? IT LOOKS COOL...
UH HUH.
REMEMBER WHEN YOU WERE LITTLE--
YOU SAID YOU WANTED TO GROW UP TO BE JUST LIKE ME!
DO YOU REMEMBER THAT?
YEAH. WHATEVER.
WELL WHAT DO YOU KNOW, HE IS JUST LIKE YOU!
11-2
DIANA RETURNS WITH GOOD NEWS . . .
I GOT THE JOB!!
YAY!! SO YOU WILL BE STAYING ON IN WOODFIELD! THAT'S GREAT!!
FEELS LIKE A FRESH START! FROM NOW ON, EVERYTHING IS ALL ABOUT TOMMY AND ME!
LET'S GO TELL TOMMY THE NEWS! HE'S STILL SITTING IN THE HOUSE, BORED TO TEARS...!
YES! I FINALLY MADE IT TO THE TOWER!! I'M GETTING GOOD AT THIS--!!
AW, SWEET! THANKS FOR HOOKING UP MY GAME SYSTEM, UNCLE ADAM! THIS BIG SCREEN TV IS SICK!!
"SICK?" IS THAT GOOD?
I THINK SO.
11-09

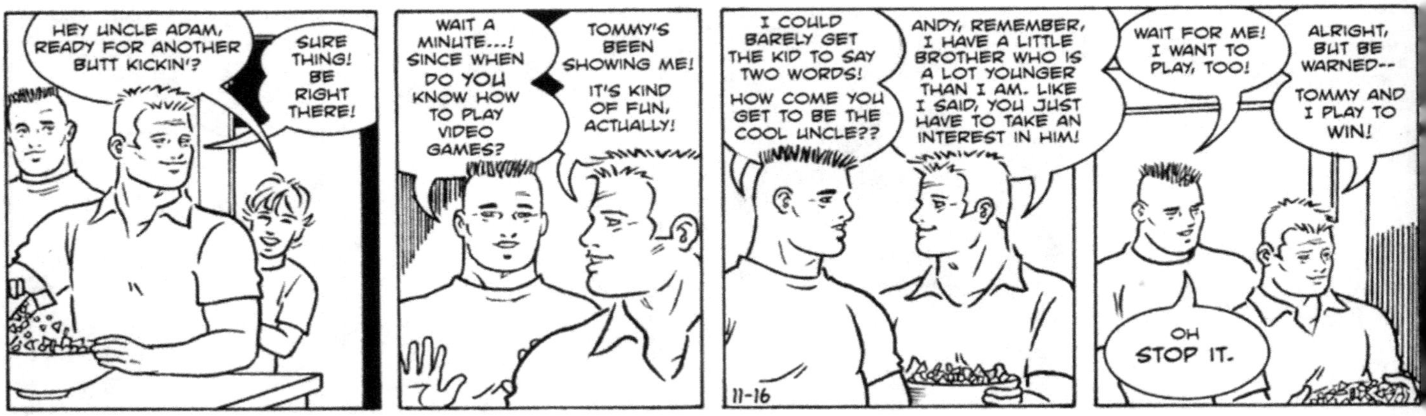
HEY UNCLE ADAM, READY FOR ANOTHER BUTT KICKIN'?
SURE THING! BE RIGHT THERE!
WAIT A MINUTE...! SINCE WHEN DO YOU KNOW HOW TO PLAY VIDEO GAMES?
TOMMY'S BEEN SHOWING ME!
IT'S KIND OF FUN, ACTUALLY!
I COULD BARELY GET THE KID TO SAY TWO WORDS!
HOW COME YOU GET TO BE THE COOL UNCLE??
ANDY, REMEMBER, I HAVE A LITTLE BROTHER WHO IS A LOT YOUNGER THAN I AM. LIKE I SAID, YOU JUST HAVE TO TAKE AN INTEREST IN HIM!
11-16
WAIT FOR ME! I WANT TO PLAY, TOO!
ALRIGHT, BUT BE WARNED--
TOMMY AND I PLAY TO WIN!
OH STOP IT.

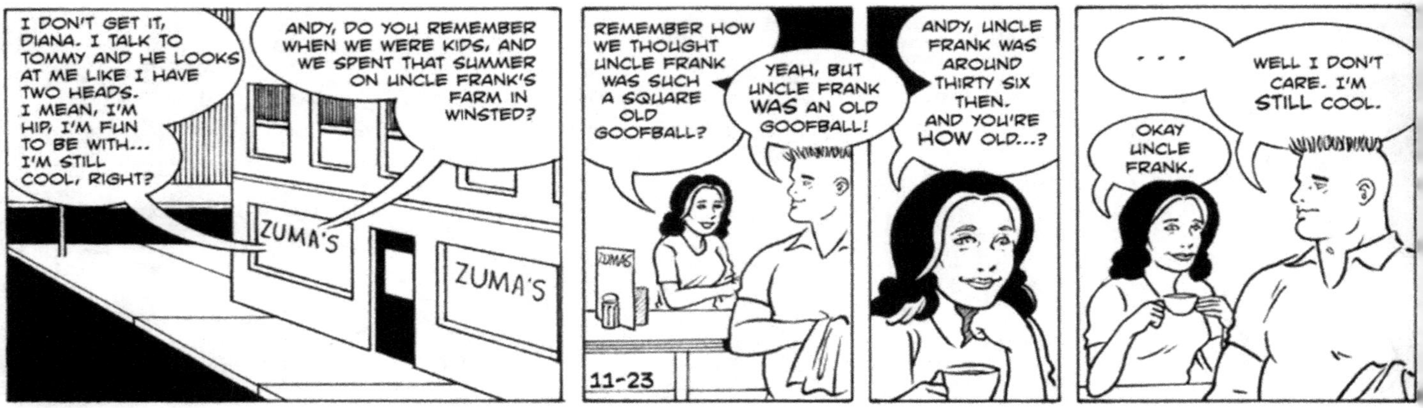
I DON'T GET IT, DIANA. I TALK TO TOMMY AND HE LOOKS AT ME LIKE I HAVE TWO HEADS. I MEAN, I'M HIP, I'M FUN TO BE WITH... I'M STILL COOL, RIGHT?
ANDY, DO YOU REMEMBER WHEN WE WERE KIDS, AND WE SPENT THAT SUMMER ON UNCLE FRANK'S FARM IN WINSTED?
ZUMA'S
ZUMA'S
REMEMBER HOW WE THOUGHT UNCLE FRANK WAS SUCH A SQUARE OLD GOOFBALL?
YEAH, BUT UNCLE FRANK WAS AN OLD GOOFBALL!
11-23
ANDY, UNCLE FRANK WAS AROUND THIRTY SIX THEN.
AND YOU'RE HOW OLD...?
. . .
WELL I DON'T CARE. I'M STILL COOL.
OKAY UNCLE FRANK.

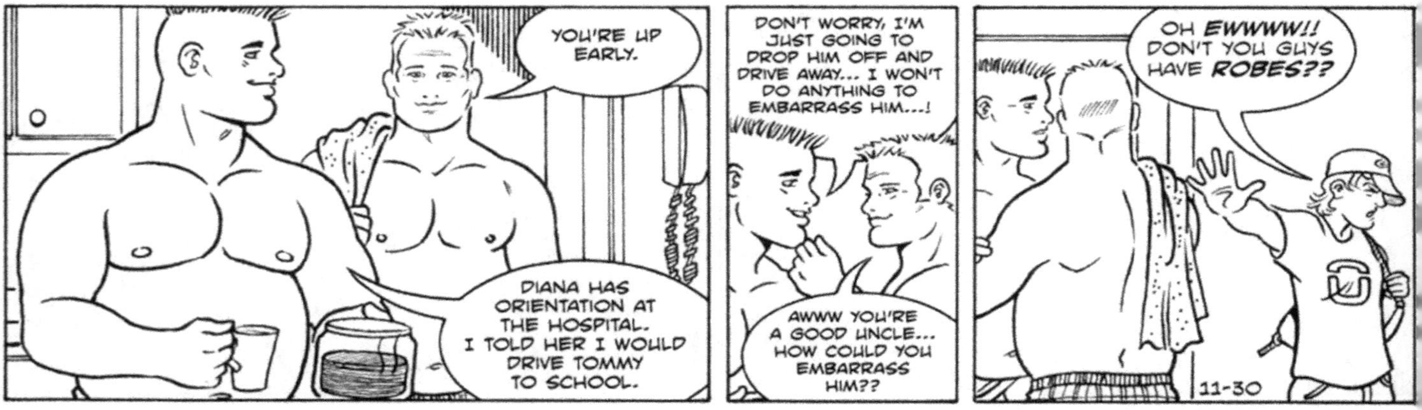
YOU'RE UP EARLY.
DIANA HAS ORIENTATION AT THE HOSPITAL. I TOLD HER I WOULD DRIVE TOMMY TO SCHOOL.
DON'T WORRY, I'M JUST GOING TO DROP HIM OFF AND DRIVE AWAY... I WON'T DO ANYTHING TO EMBARRASS HIM...!
AWWW YOU'RE A GOOD UNCLE... HOW COULD YOU EMBARRASS HIM??
OH EWWWW!! DON'T YOU GUYS HAVE ROBES??
11-30

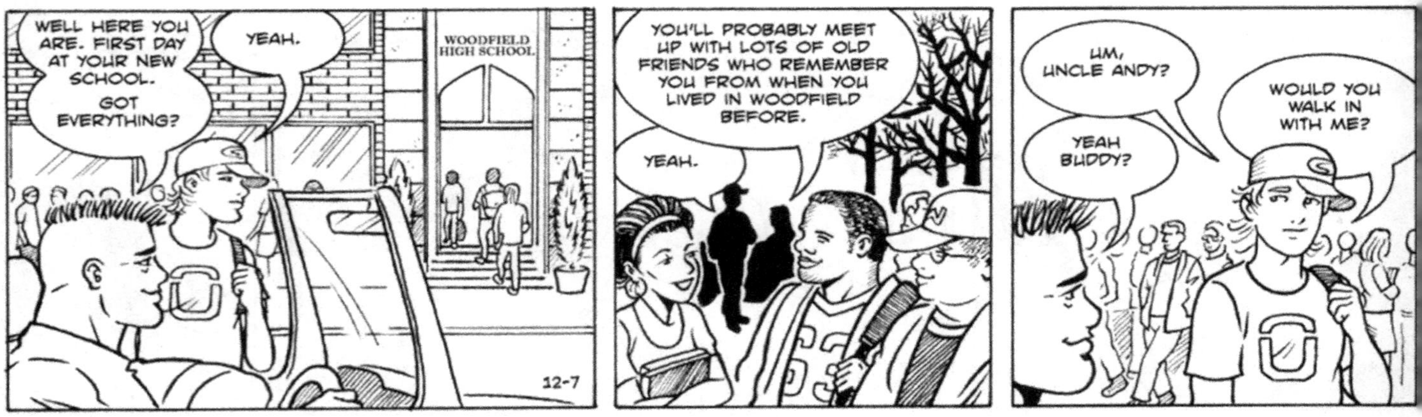
WELL HERE YOU ARE. FIRST DAY AT YOUR NEW SCHOOL.
GOT EVERYTHING?
YEAH.
WOODFIELD HIGH SCHOOL
12-7
YOU'LL PROBABLY MEET UP WITH LOTS OF OLD FRIENDS WHO REMEMBER YOU FROM WHEN YOU LIVED IN WOODFIELD BEFORE.
YEAH.
UM, UNCLE ANDY?
YEAH BUDDY?
WOULD YOU WALK IN WITH ME?

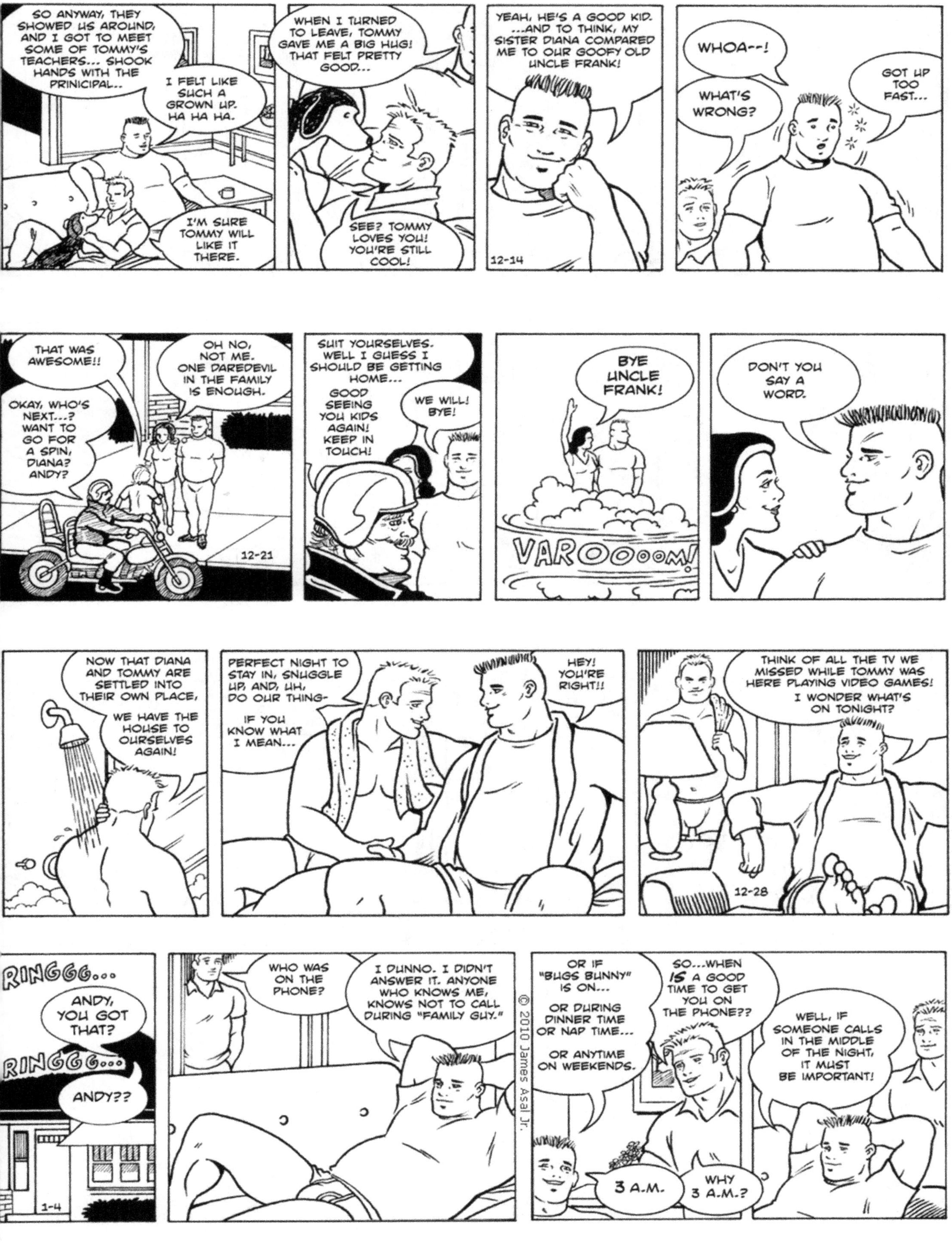

SO ANYWAY, THEY SHOWED US AROUND, AND I GOT TO MEET SOME OF TOMMY'S TEACHERS... SHOOK HANDS WITH THE PRINCIPAL...
I FELT LIKE SUCH A GROWN UP. HA HA HA.
I'M SURE TOMMY WILL LIKE IT THERE.
WHEN I TURNED TO LEAVE, TOMMY GAVE ME A BIG HUG! THAT FELT PRETTY GOOD...
SEE? TOMMY LOVES YOU! YOU'RE STILL COOL!
YEAH, HE'S A GOOD KID. ...AND TO THINK, MY SISTER DIANA COMPARED ME TO OUR GOOFY OLD UNCLE FRANK!
12-14
WHOA--!
WHAT'S WRONG?
GOT UP TOO FAST...
THAT WAS AWESOME!!
OH NO, NOT ME. ONE DAREDEVIL IN THE FAMILY IS ENOUGH.
OKAY, WHO'S NEXT...? WANT TO GO FOR A SPIN, DIANA? ANDY?
12-21
SUIT YOURSELVES. WELL I GUESS I SHOULD BE GETTING HOME...
GOOD SEEING YOU KIDS AGAIN! KEEP IN TOUCH!
WE WILL! BYE!
BYE UNCLE FRANK!
VAROOoom!
DON'T YOU SAY A WORD.
NOW THAT DIANA AND TOMMY ARE SETTLED INTO THEIR OWN PLACE,
WE HAVE THE HOUSE TO OURSELVES AGAIN!
PERFECT NIGHT TO STAY IN, SNUGGLE UP, AND, UH, DO OUR THING-
IF YOU KNOW WHAT I MEAN...
HEY! YOU'RE RIGHT!!
THINK OF ALL THE TV WE MISSED WHILE TOMMY WAS HERE PLAYING VIDEO GAMES!
I WONDER WHAT'S ON TONIGHT?
12-28
RINGGG...
ANDY, YOU GOT THAT?
RINGGG...
ANDY??
1-4
WHO WAS ON THE PHONE?
I DUNNO. I DIDN'T ANSWER IT. ANYONE WHO KNOWS ME, KNOWS NOT TO CALL DURING "FAMILY GUY."
© 2010 James Asal Jr.
OR IF "BUGS BUNNY" IS ON...
OR DURING DINNER TIME OR NAP TIME...
OR ANYTIME ON WEEKENDS.
SO...WHEN IS A GOOD TIME TO GET YOU ON THE PHONE??
3 A.M.
WHY 3 A.M.?
WELL, IF SOMEONE CALLS IN THE MIDDLE OF THE NIGHT, IT MUST BE IMPORTANT!

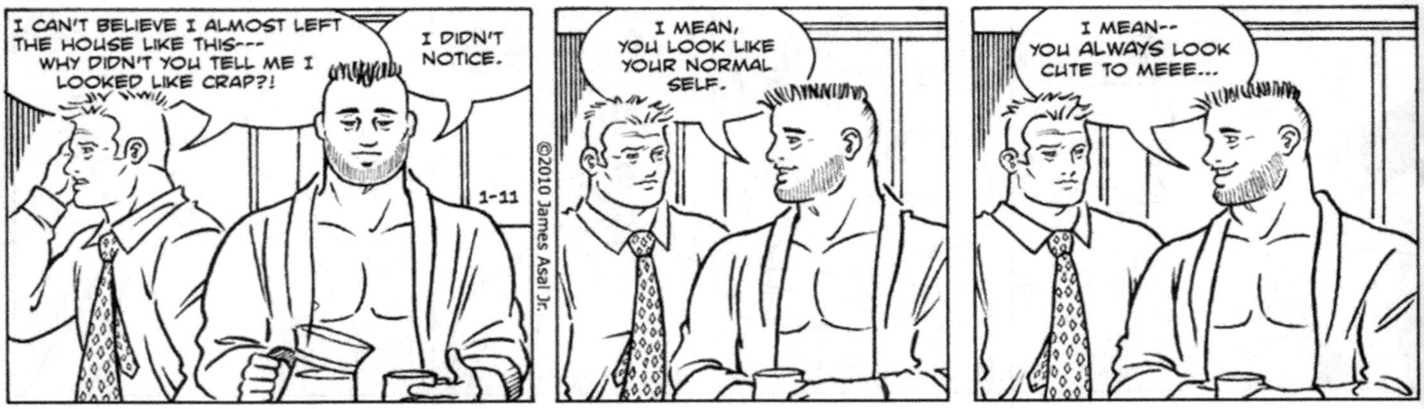
I CAN'T BELIEVE I ALMOST LEFT THE HOUSE LIKE THIS--- WHY DIDN'T YOU TELL ME I LOOKED LIKE CRAP?!
I DIDN'T NOTICE.
©2010 James Asal Jr.
1-11
I MEAN, YOU LOOK LIKE YOUR NORMAL SELF.
I MEAN-- YOU ALWAYS LOOK CUTE TO MEEE...

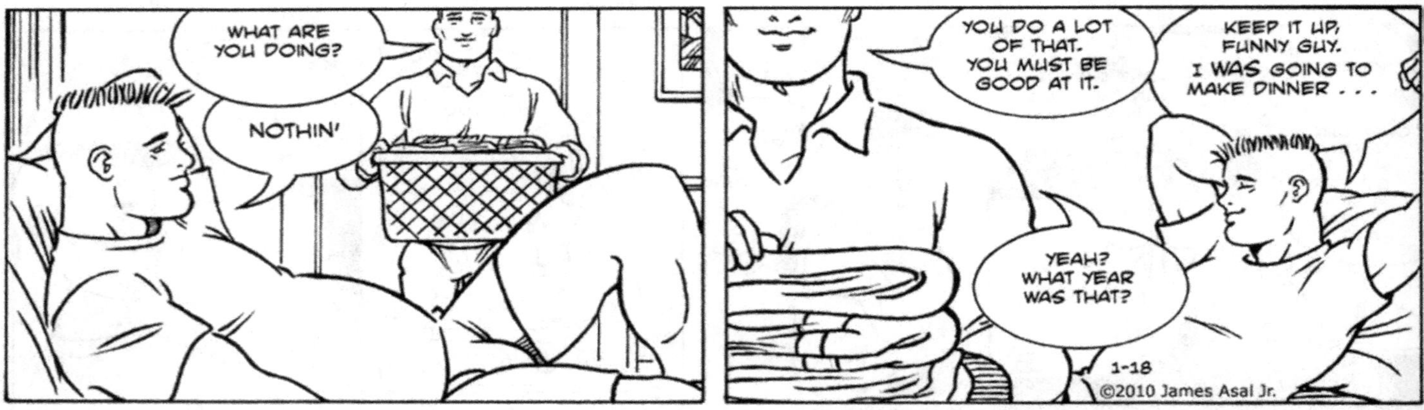
WHAT ARE YOU DOING?
NOTHIN'
YOU DO A LOT OF THAT. YOU MUST BE GOOD AT IT.
KEEP IT UP, FUNNY GUY. I WAS GOING TO MAKE DINNER . . .
YEAH? WHAT YEAR WAS THAT?
1-18
©2010 James Asal Jr.

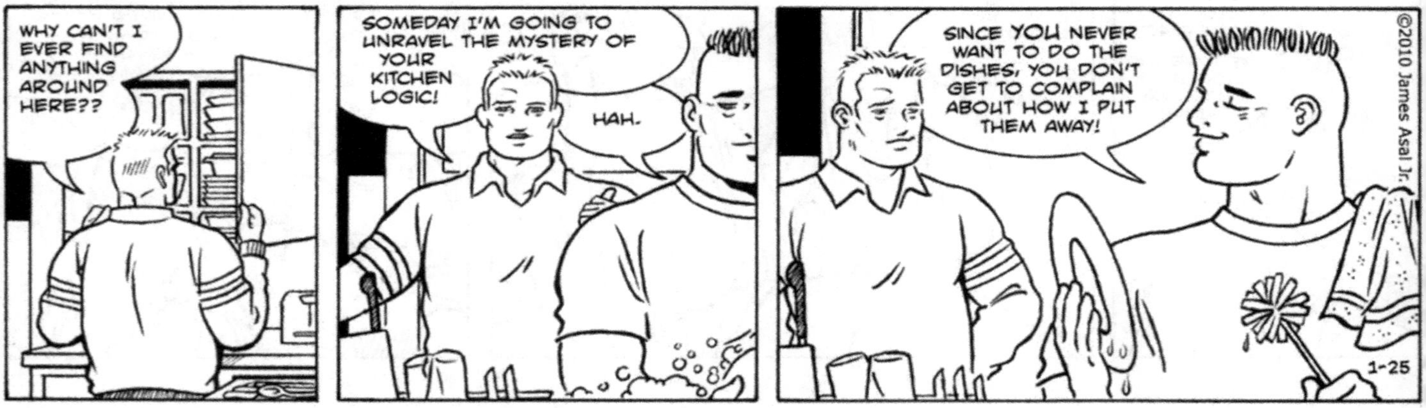
WHY CAN'T I EVER FIND ANYTHING AROUND HERE??
SOMEDAY I'M GOING TO UNRAVEL THE MYSTERY OF YOUR KITCHEN LOGIC!
HAH.
SINCE YOU NEVER WANT TO DO THE DISHES, YOU DON'T GET TO COMPLAIN ABOUT HOW I PUT THEM AWAY!
©2010 James Asal Jr.
1-25

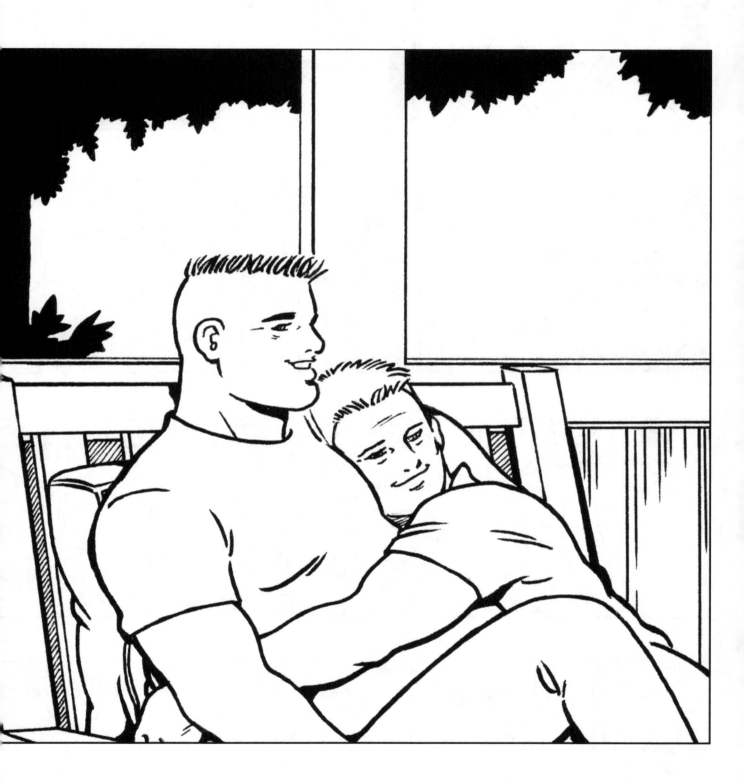

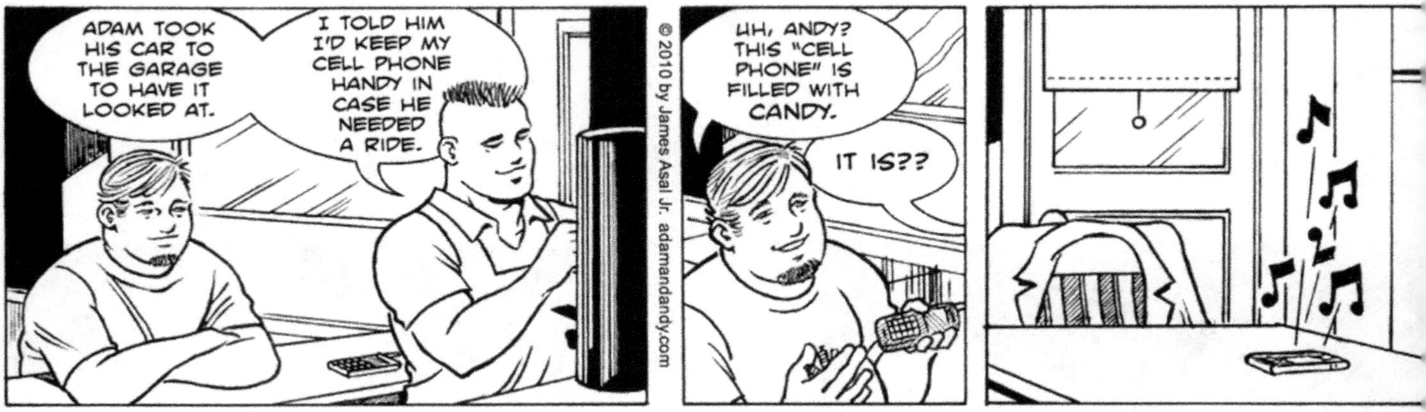
ADAM TOOK HIS CAR TO THE GARAGE TO HAVE IT LOOKED AT.
I TOLD HIM I'D KEEP MY CELL PHONE HANDY IN CASE HE NEEDED A RIDE.
© 2010 by James Asal Jr. adamandandy.com
UH, ANDY? THIS "CELL PHONE" IS FILLED WITH CANDY.
IT IS??

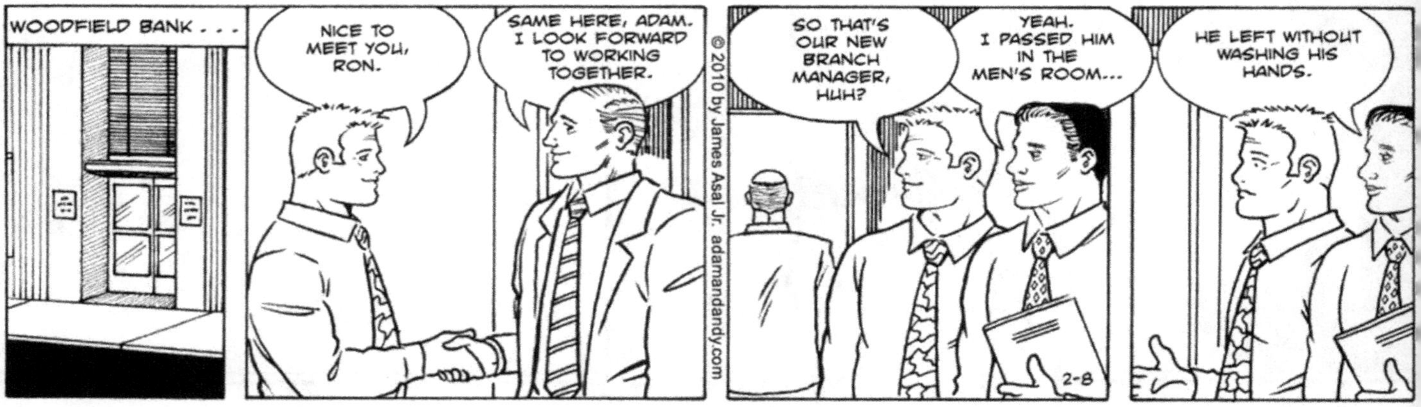
WOODFIELD BANK . . .
NICE TO MEET YOU, RON.
SAME HERE, ADAM. I LOOK FORWARD TO WORKING TOGETHER.
© 2010 by James Asal Jr. adamandandy.com
SO THAT'S OUR NEW BRANCH MANAGER, HUH?
YEAH. I PASSED HIM IN THE MEN'S ROOM...
2-8
HE LEFT WITHOUT WASHING HIS HANDS.

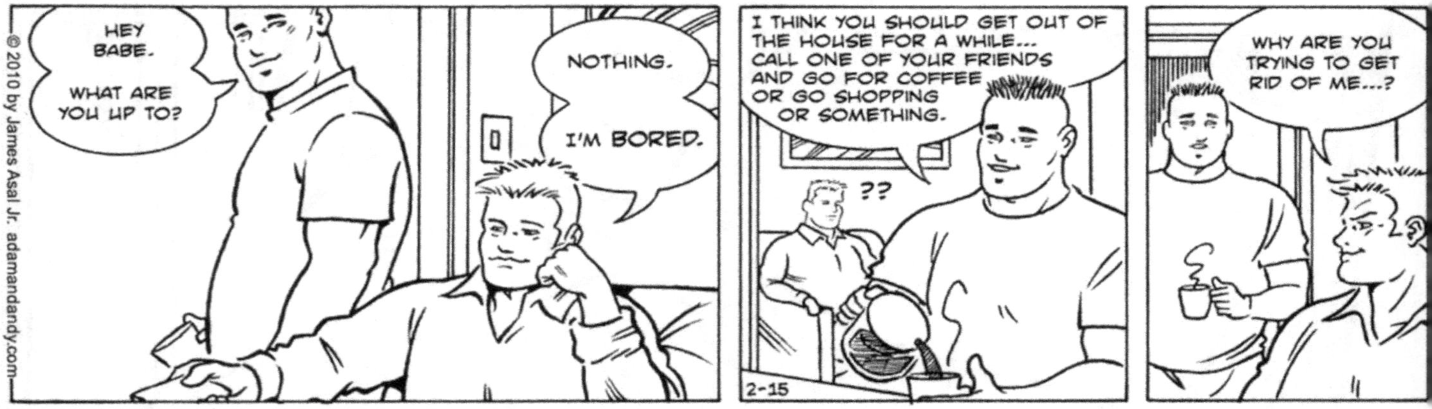
© 2010 by James Asal Jr. adamandandy.com
HEY BABE.
WHAT ARE YOU UP TO?
NOTHING.
I'M BORED.
I THINK YOU SHOULD GET OUT OF THE HOUSE FOR A WHILE... CALL ONE OF YOUR FRIENDS AND GO FOR COFFEE OR GO SHOPPING OR SOMETHING.
??
2-15
WHY ARE YOU TRYING TO GET RID OF ME...?

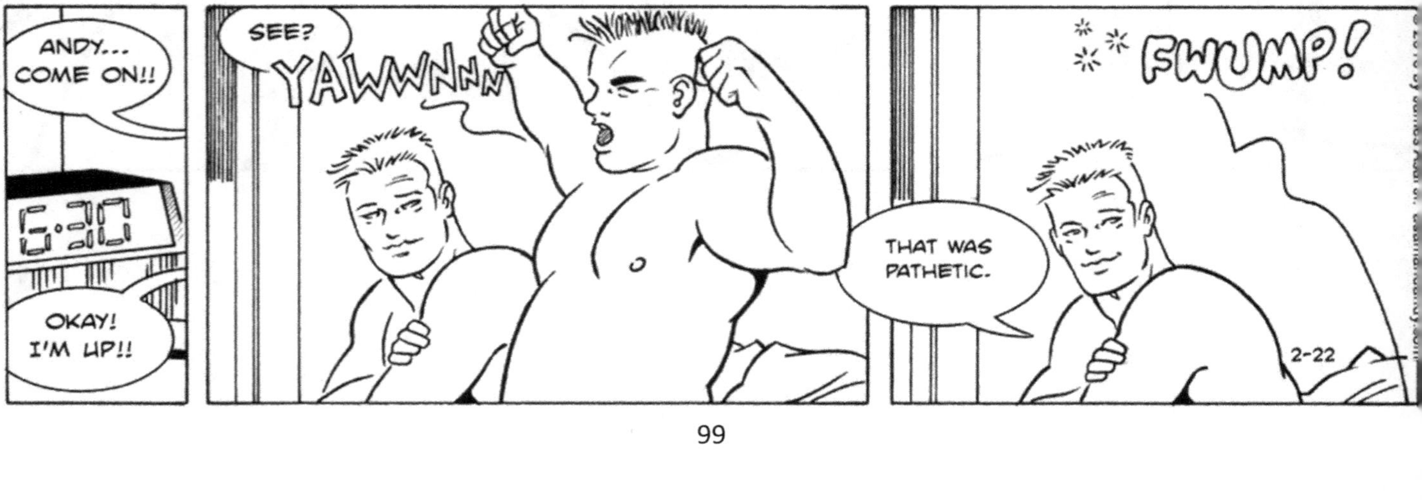
ANDY... COME ON!!
OKAY! I'M UP!!
SEE?
YAWWNNN
THAT WAS PATHETIC.
FWUMP!
2-22

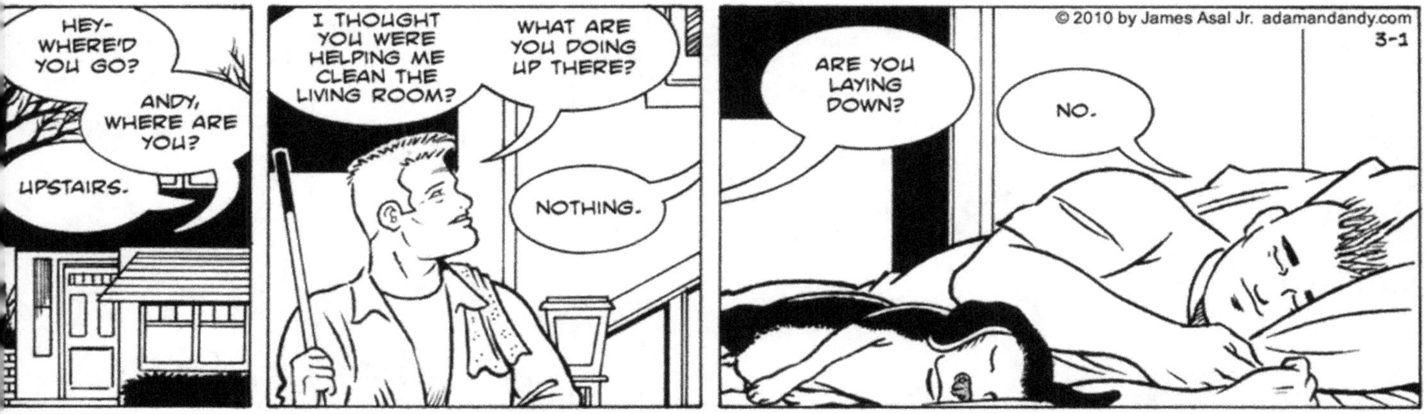
HEY- WHERE'D YOU GO?
ANDY, WHERE ARE YOU?
UPSTAIRS.
I THOUGHT YOU WERE HELPING ME CLEAN THE LIVING ROOM?
WHAT ARE YOU DOING UP THERE?
NOTHING.
© 2010 by James Asal Jr. adamandandy.com
3-1
ARE YOU LAYING DOWN?
NO.

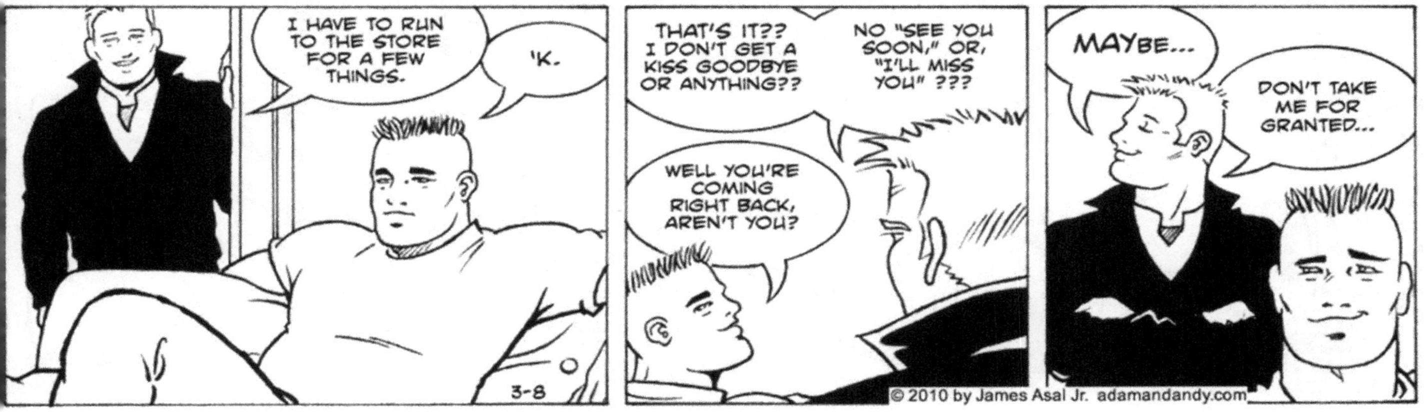
I HAVE TO RUN TO THE STORE FOR A FEW THINGS.
'K.
3-8
THAT'S IT?? I DON'T GET A KISS GOODBYE OR ANYTHING??
NO "SEE YOU SOON," OR, "I'LL MISS YOU" ???
WELL YOU'RE COMING RIGHT BACK, AREN'T YOU?
MAYBE...
DON'T TAKE ME FOR GRANTED...
© 2010 by James Asal Jr. adamandandy.com

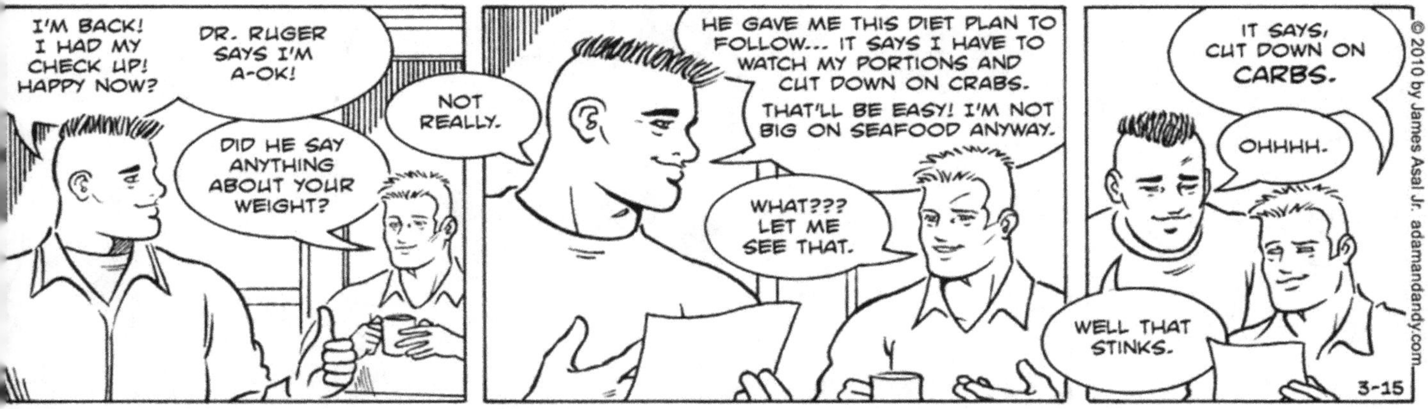
I'M BACK! I HAD MY CHECK UP! HAPPY NOW?
DR. RUGER SAYS I'M A-OK!
NOT REALLY.
DID HE SAY ANYTHING ABOUT YOUR WEIGHT?
HE GAVE ME THIS DIET PLAN TO FOLLOW... IT SAYS I HAVE TO WATCH MY PORTIONS AND CUT DOWN ON CRABS.
THAT'LL BE EASY! I'M NOT BIG ON SEAFOOD ANYWAY.
WHAT??? LET ME SEE THAT.
IT SAYS, CUT DOWN ON CARBS.
OHHHH.
WELL THAT STINKS.
© 2010 by James Asal Jr. adamandandy.com
3-15

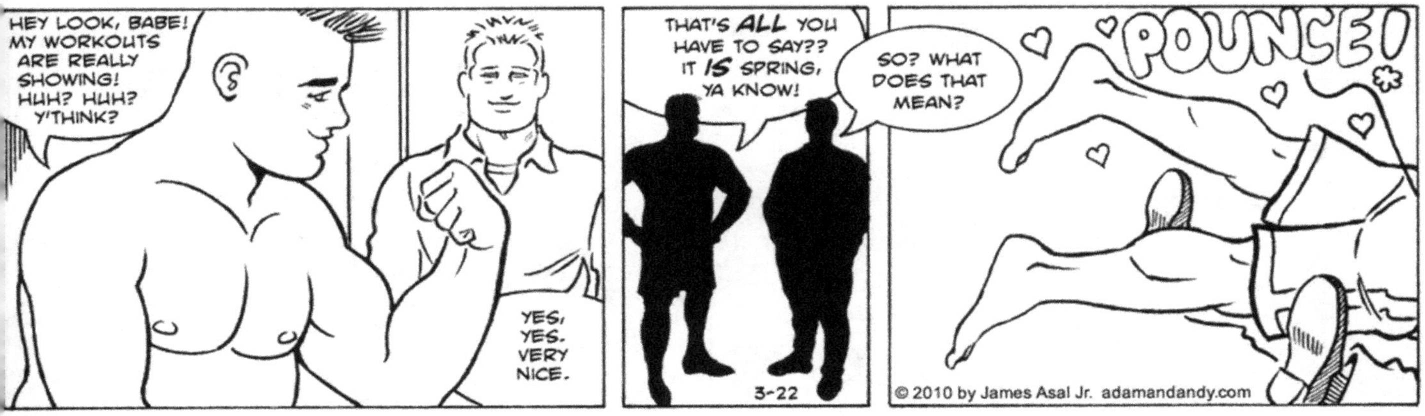
HEY LOOK, BABE! MY WORKOUTS ARE REALLY SHOWING! HUH? HUH? Y'THINK?
YES, YES. VERY NICE.
THAT'S ALL YOU HAVE TO SAY?? IT IS SPRING, YA KNOW!
SO? WHAT DOES THAT MEAN?
3-22
POUNCE!
© 2010 by James Asal Jr. adamandandy.com

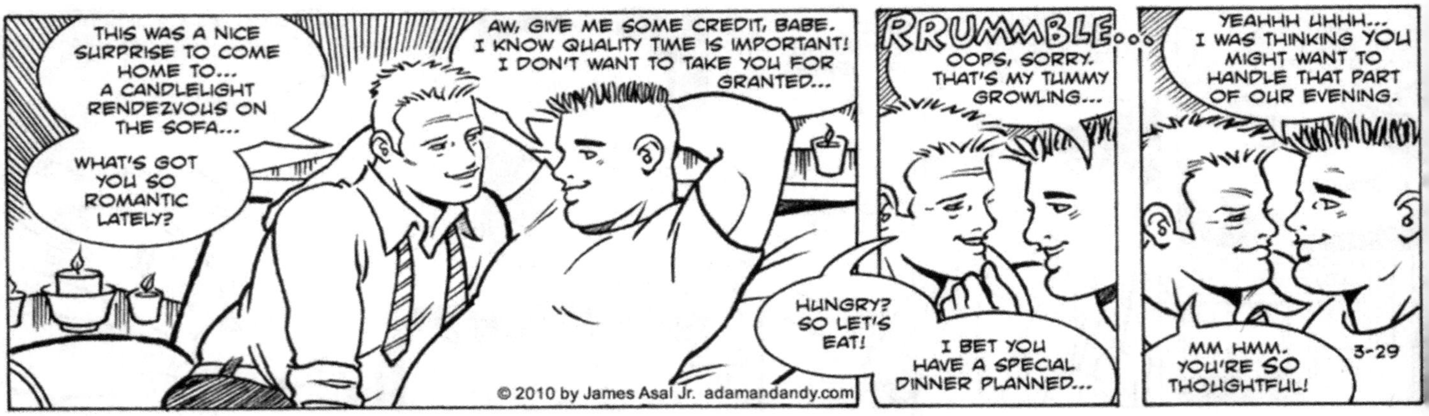
THIS WAS A NICE SURPRISE TO COME HOME TO... A CANDLELIGHT RENDEZVOUS ON THE SOFA...
WHAT'S GOT YOU SO ROMANTIC LATELY?
AW, GIVE ME SOME CREDIT, BABE. I KNOW QUALITY TIME IS IMPORTANT! I DON'T WANT TO TAKE YOU FOR GRANTED...
© 2010 by James Asal Jr. adamandandy.com
RRUMMBLE...
OOPS, SORRY. THAT'S MY TUMMY GROWLING...
HUNGRY? SO LET'S EAT!
I BET YOU HAVE A SPECIAL DINNER PLANNED...
YEAHHH UHHH... I WAS THINKING YOU MIGHT WANT TO HANDLE THAT PART OF OUR EVENING.
MM HMM. YOU'RE SO THOUGHTFUL!
3-29

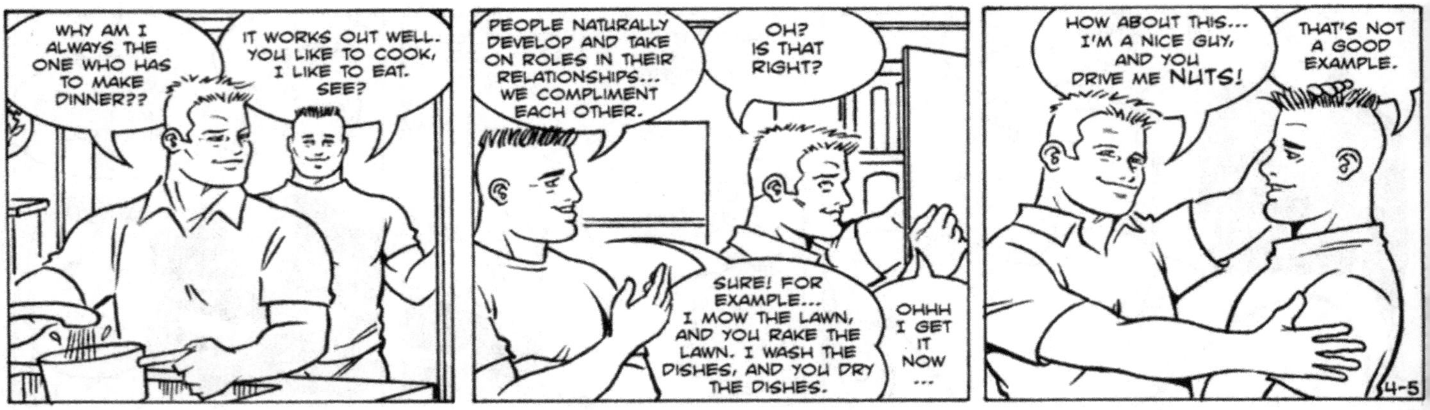
WHY AM I ALWAYS THE ONE WHO HAS TO MAKE DINNER??
IT WORKS OUT WELL. YOU LIKE TO COOK, I LIKE TO EAT. SEE?
PEOPLE NATURALLY DEVELOP AND TAKE ON ROLES IN THEIR RELATIONSHIPS... WE COMPLIMENT EACH OTHER.
OH? IS THAT RIGHT?
SURE! FOR EXAMPLE... I MOW THE LAWN, AND YOU RAKE THE LAWN. I WASH THE DISHES, AND YOU DRY THE DISHES.
OHHH I GET IT NOW ...
HOW ABOUT THIS... I'M A NICE GUY, AND YOU DRIVE ME NUTS!
THAT'S NOT A GOOD EXAMPLE.
4-5

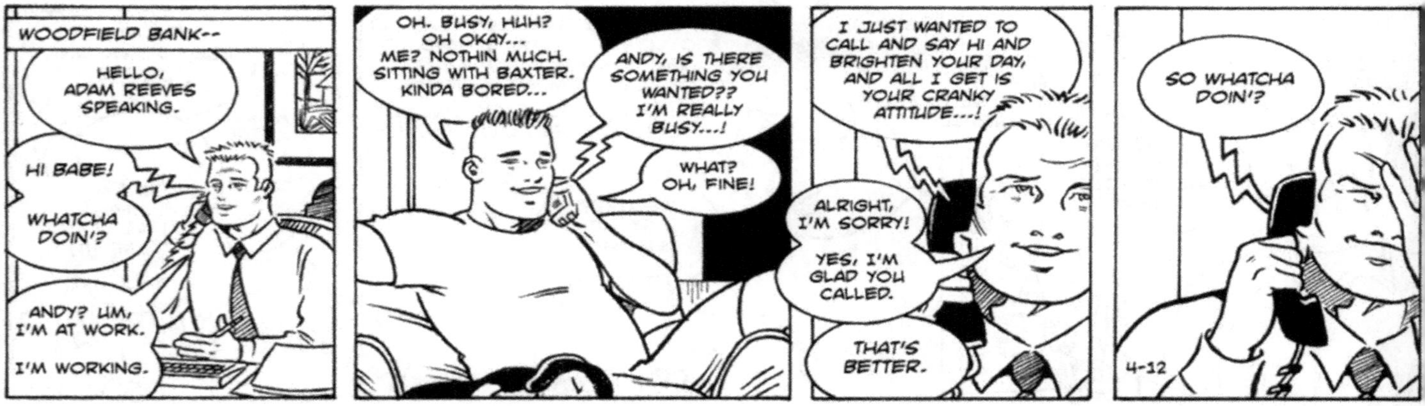
WOODFIELD BANK--
HELLO, ADAM REEVES SPEAKING.
HI BABE!
WHATCHA DOIN'?
ANDY? UM, I'M AT WORK.
I'M WORKING.
OH. BUSY, HUH? OH OKAY... ME? NOTHIN MUCH. SITTING WITH BAXTER. KINDA BORED...
ANDY, IS THERE SOMETHING YOU WANTED?? I'M REALLY BUSY...!
WHAT? OH, FINE!
I JUST WANTED TO CALL AND SAY HI AND BRIGHTEN YOUR DAY, AND ALL I GET IS YOUR CRANKY ATTITUDE...!
ALRIGHT, I'M SORRY!
YES, I'M GLAD YOU CALLED.
THAT'S BETTER.
SO WHATCHA DOIN'?
4-12

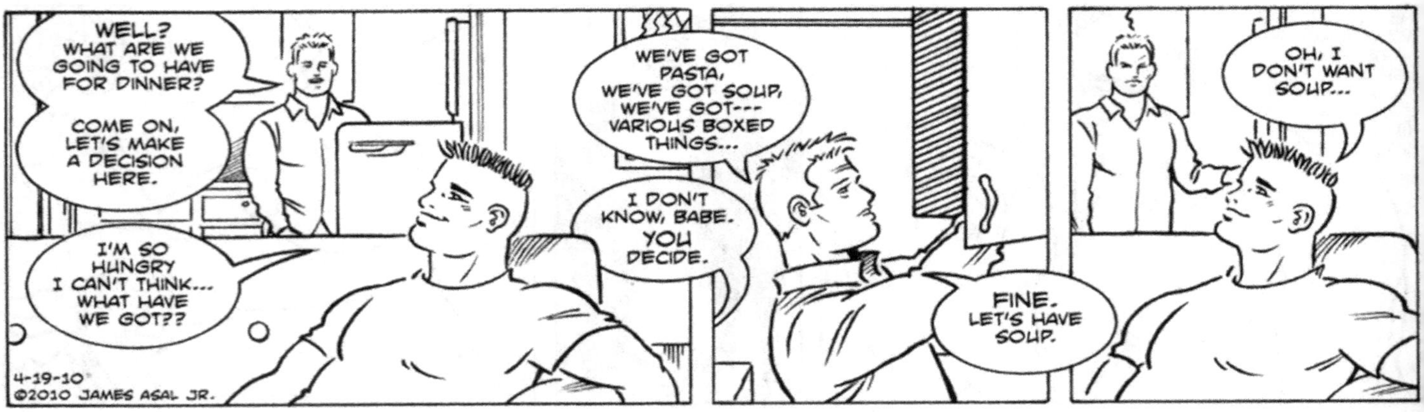
WELL? WHAT ARE WE GOING TO HAVE FOR DINNER?
COME ON, LET'S MAKE A DECISION HERE.
I'M SO HUNGRY I CAN'T THINK... WHAT HAVE WE GOT??
4-19-10
©2010 JAMES ASAL JR.
WE'VE GOT PASTA, WE'VE GOT SOUP, WE'VE GOT--- VARIOUS BOXED THINGS...
I DON'T KNOW, BABE. YOU DECIDE.
FINE. LET'S HAVE SOUP.
OH, I DON'T WANT SOUP...

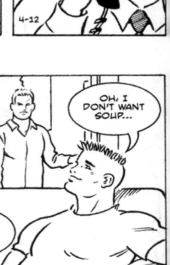

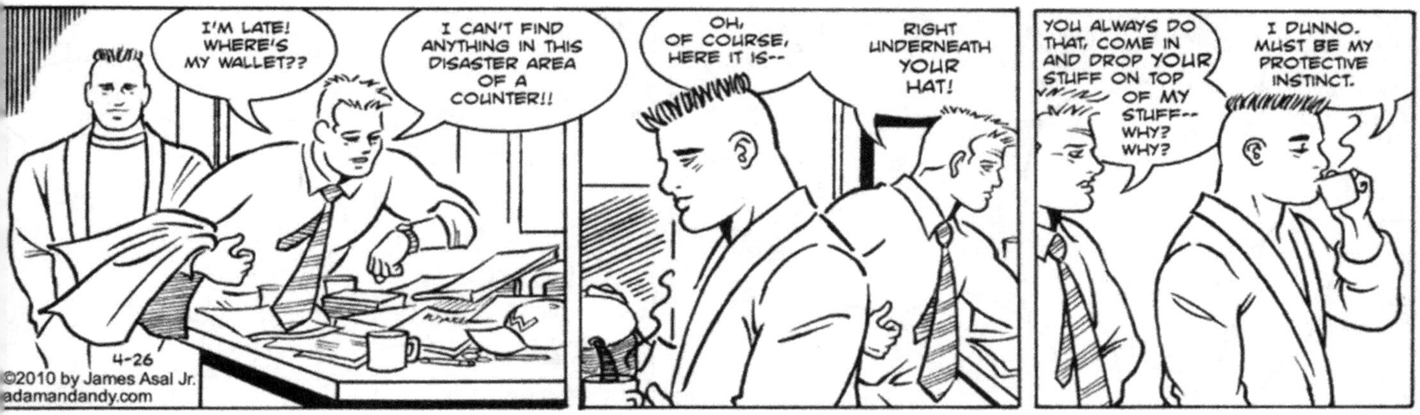
I'M LATE! WHERE'S MY WALLET??
I CAN'T FIND ANYTHING IN THIS DISASTER AREA OF A COUNTER!!
4-26
©2010 by James Asal Jr.
adamandandy.com
OH, OF COURSE, HERE IT IS--
RIGHT UNDERNEATH YOUR HAT!
YOU ALWAYS DO THAT, COME IN AND DROP YOUR STUFF ON TOP OF MY STUFF-- WHY? WHY?
I DUNNO. MUST BE MY PROTECTIVE INSTINCT.

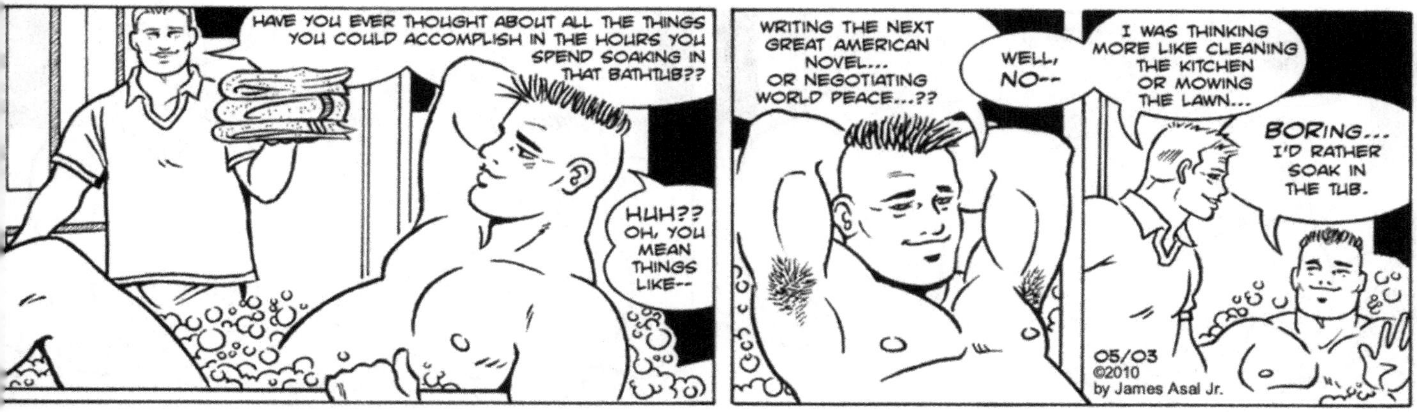
HAVE YOU EVER THOUGHT ABOUT ALL THE THINGS YOU COULD ACCOMPLISH IN THE HOURS YOU SPEND SOAKING IN THAT BATHTUB??
HUH?? OH, YOU MEAN THINGS LIKE--
WRITING THE NEXT GREAT AMERICAN NOVEL... OR NEGOTIATING WORLD PEACE...??
WELL, NO--
I WAS THINKING MORE LIKE CLEANING THE KITCHEN OR MOWING THE LAWN...
BORING... I'D RATHER SOAK IN THE TUB.
05/03
©2010
by James Asal Jr.

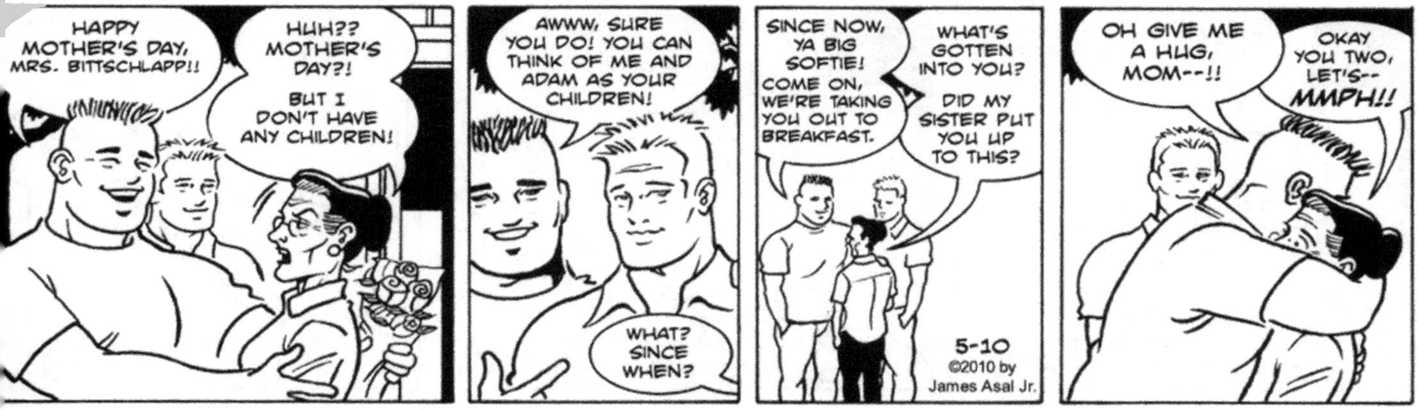
HAPPY MOTHER'S DAY, MRS. BITTSCHLAPP!!
HUH?? MOTHER'S DAY?! BUT I DON'T HAVE ANY CHILDREN!
AWWW, SURE YOU DO! YOU CAN THINK OF ME AND ADAM AS YOUR CHILDREN!
WHAT? SINCE WHEN?
SINCE NOW, YA BIG SOFTIE! COME ON, WE'RE TAKING YOU OUT TO BREAKFAST.
WHAT'S GOTTEN INTO YOU? DID MY SISTER PUT YOU UP TO THIS?
5-10
©2010 by
James Asal Jr.
OH GIVE ME A HUG, MOM--!!
OKAY YOU TWO, LET'S-- MMPH!!

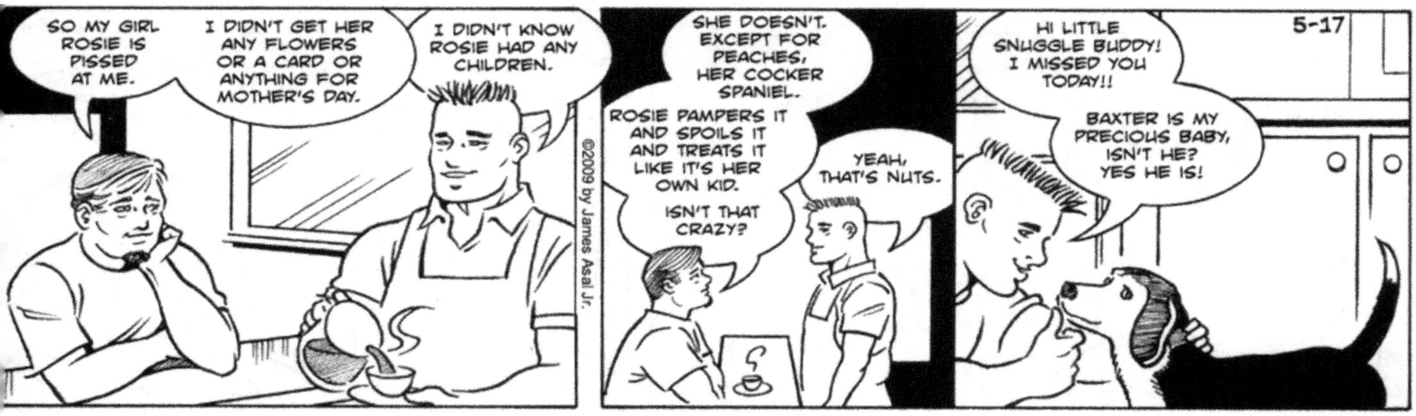
SO MY GIRL ROSIE IS PISSED AT ME.
I DIDN'T GET HER ANY FLOWERS OR A CARD OR ANYTHING FOR MOTHER'S DAY.
I DIDN'T KNOW ROSIE HAD ANY CHILDREN.
©2009 by James Asal Jr.
SHE DOESN'T. EXCEPT FOR PEACHES, HER COCKER SPANIEL.
ROSIE PAMPERS IT AND SPOILS IT AND TREATS IT LIKE IT'S HER OWN KID.
ISN'T THAT CRAZY?
YEAH, THAT'S NUTS.
5-17
HI LITTLE SNUGGLE BUDDY! I MISSED YOU TODAY!!
BAXTER IS MY PRECIOUS BABY, ISN'T HE? YES HE IS!

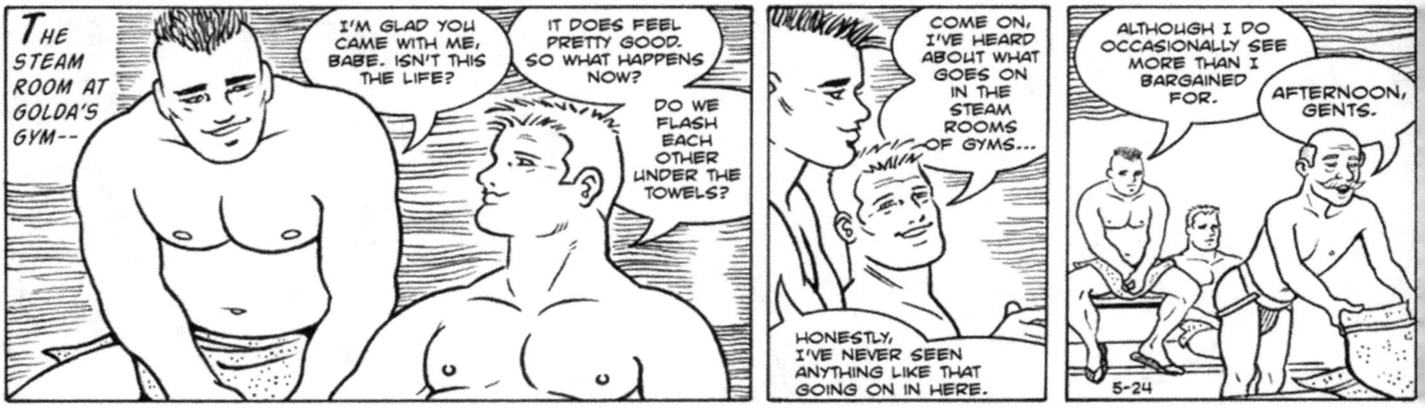
THE STEAM ROOM AT GOLDA'S GYM--
I'M GLAD YOU CAME WITH ME, BABE. ISN'T THIS THE LIFE?
IT DOES FEEL PRETTY GOOD. SO WHAT HAPPENS NOW?
DO WE FLASH EACH OTHER UNDER THE TOWELS?
COME ON, I'VE HEARD ABOUT WHAT GOES ON IN THE STEAM ROOMS OF GYMS...
HONESTLY, I'VE NEVER SEEN ANYTHING LIKE THAT GOING ON IN HERE.
ALTHOUGH I DO OCCASIONALLY SEE MORE THAN I BARGAINED FOR.
AFTERNOON, GENTS.
5-24

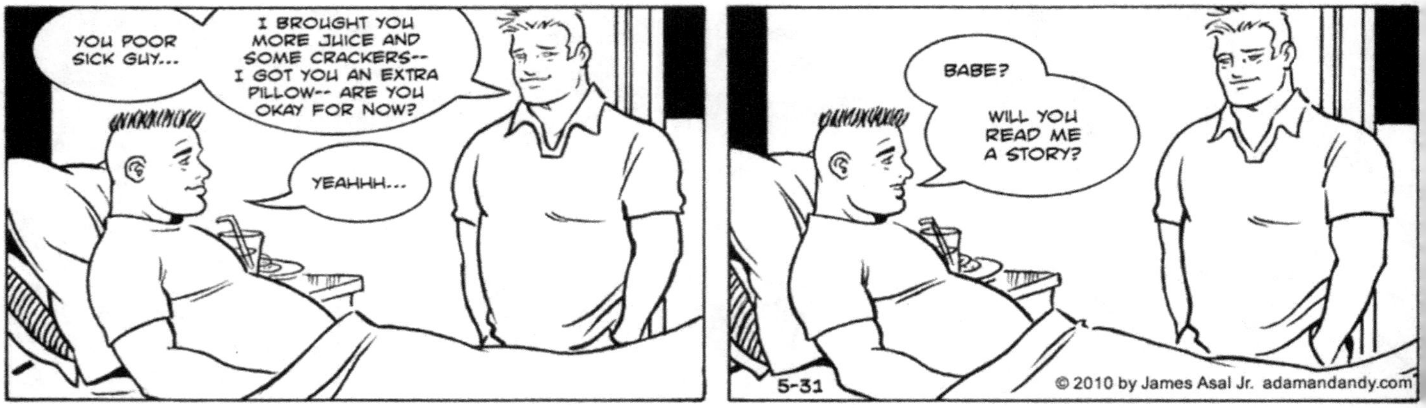
YOU POOR SICK GUY...
I BROUGHT YOU MORE JUICE AND SOME CRACKERS-- I GOT YOU AN EXTRA PILLOW-- ARE YOU OKAY FOR NOW?
YEAHHH...
BABE?
WILL YOU READ ME A STORY?
5-31
© 2010 by James Asal Jr. adamandandy.com

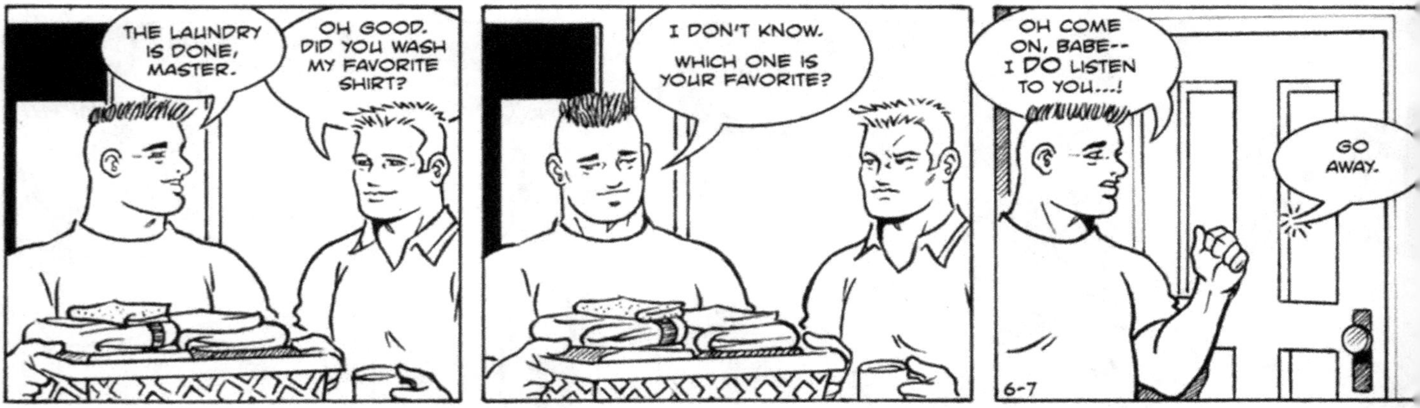
THE LAUNDRY IS DONE, MASTER.
OH GOOD. DID YOU WASH MY FAVORITE SHIRT?
I DON'T KNOW.
WHICH ONE IS YOUR FAVORITE?
OH COME ON, BABE-- I DO LISTEN TO YOU...!
GO AWAY.
6-7

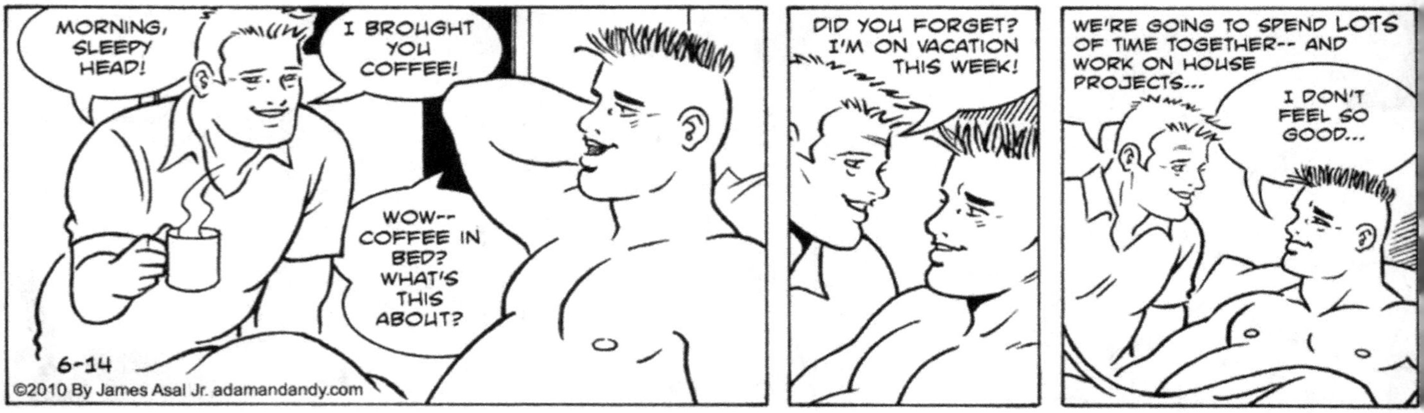
MORNING, SLEEPY HEAD!
I BROUGHT YOU COFFEE!
WOW-- COFFEE IN BED? WHAT'S THIS ABOUT?
6-14
©2010 By James Asal Jr. adamandandy.com
DID YOU FORGET? I'M ON VACATION THIS WEEK!
WE'RE GOING TO SPEND LOTS OF TIME TOGETHER-- AND WORK ON HOUSE PROJECTS...
I DON'T FEEL SO GOOD...

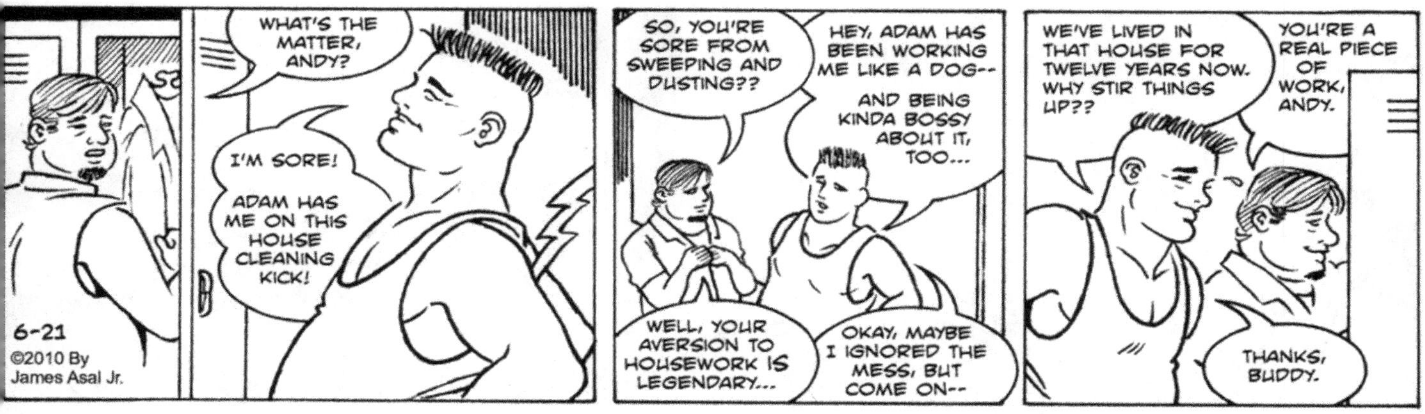
WHAT'S THE MATTER, ANDY?
I'M SORE!
ADAM HAS ME ON THIS HOUSE CLEANING KICK!
6-21
©2010 By James Asal Jr.
SO, YOU'RE SORE FROM SWEEPING AND DUSTING??
HEY, ADAM HAS BEEN WORKING ME LIKE A DOG--
AND BEING KINDA BOSSY ABOUT IT, TOO...
WELL, YOUR AVERSION TO HOUSEWORK IS LEGENDARY...
OKAY, MAYBE I IGNORED THE MESS, BUT COME ON--
WE'VE LIVED IN THAT HOUSE FOR TWELVE YEARS NOW. WHY STIR THINGS UP??
YOU'RE A REAL PIECE OF WORK, ANDY.
THANKS, BUDDY.

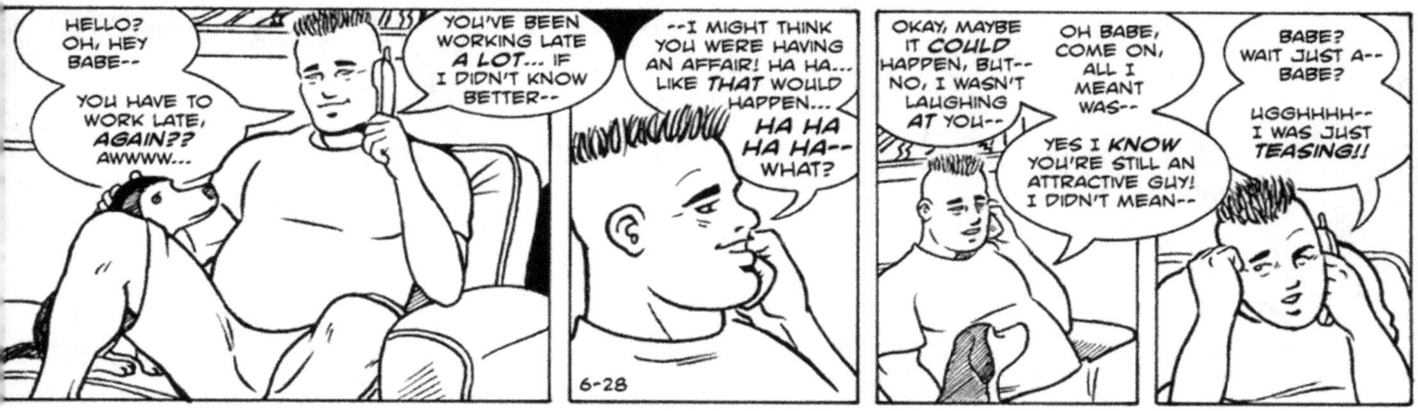
HELLO? OH, HEY BABE--
YOU HAVE TO WORK LATE, AGAIN?? AWWWW...
YOU'VE BEEN WORKING LATE A LOT... IF I DIDN'T KNOW BETTER--
--I MIGHT THINK YOU WERE HAVING AN AFFAIR! HA HA... LIKE THAT WOULD HAPPEN...
HA HA HA HA-- WHAT?
6-28
OKAY, MAYBE IT COULD HAPPEN, BUT-- NO, I WASN'T LAUGHING AT YOU--
OH BABE, COME ON, ALL I MEANT WAS--
YES I KNOW YOU'RE STILL AN ATTRACTIVE GUY! I DIDN'T MEAN--
BABE? WAIT JUST A-- BABE?
UGGHHHH-- I WAS JUST TEASING!!

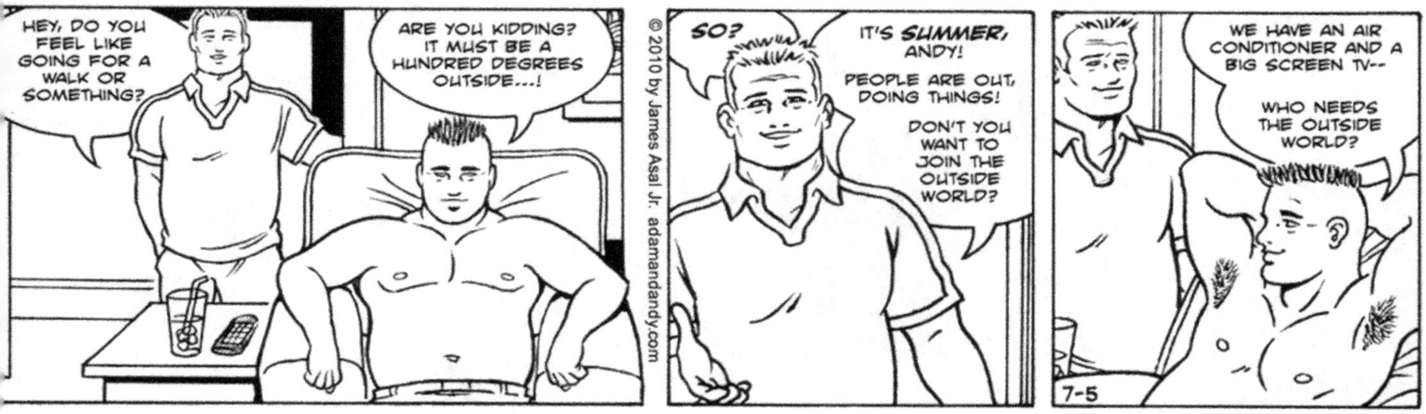
HEY, DO YOU FEEL LIKE GOING FOR A WALK OR SOMETHING?
ARE YOU KIDDING? IT MUST BE A HUNDRED DEGREES OUTSIDE...!
© 2010 by James Asal Jr. adamandandy.com
SO?
IT'S SUMMER, ANDY!
PEOPLE ARE OUT, DOING THINGS!
DON'T YOU WANT TO JOIN THE OUTSIDE WORLD?
WE HAVE AN AIR CONDITIONER AND A BIG SCREEN TV--
WHO NEEDS THE OUTSIDE WORLD?
7-5

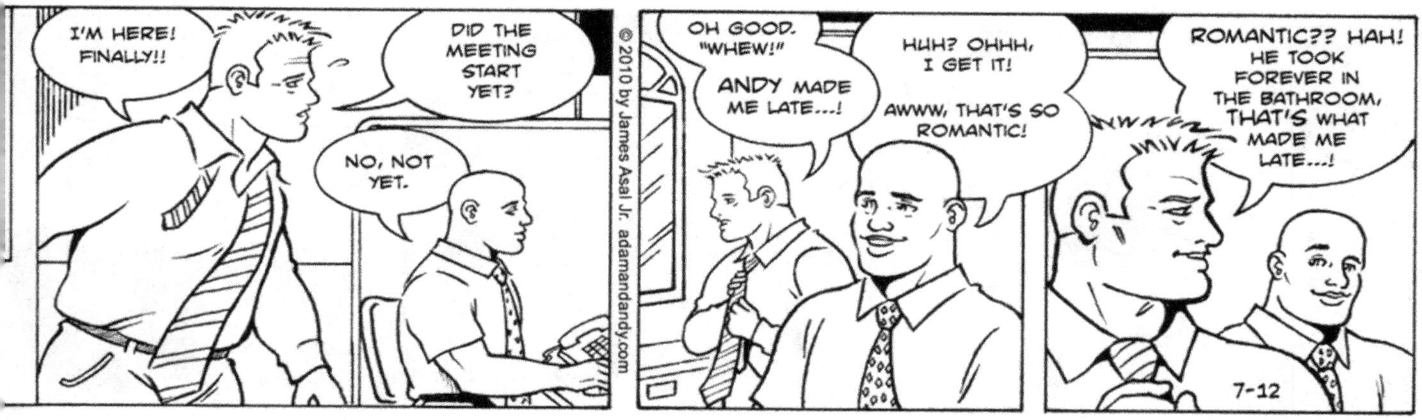
I'M HERE! FINALLY!!
DID THE MEETING START YET?
NO, NOT YET.
© 2010 by James Asal Jr. adamandandy.com
OH GOOD. "WHEW!"
ANDY MADE ME LATE...!
HUH? OHHH, I GET IT!
AWWW, THAT'S SO ROMANTIC!
ROMANTIC?? HAH! HE TOOK FOREVER IN THE BATHROOM, THAT'S WHAT MADE ME LATE...!
7-12

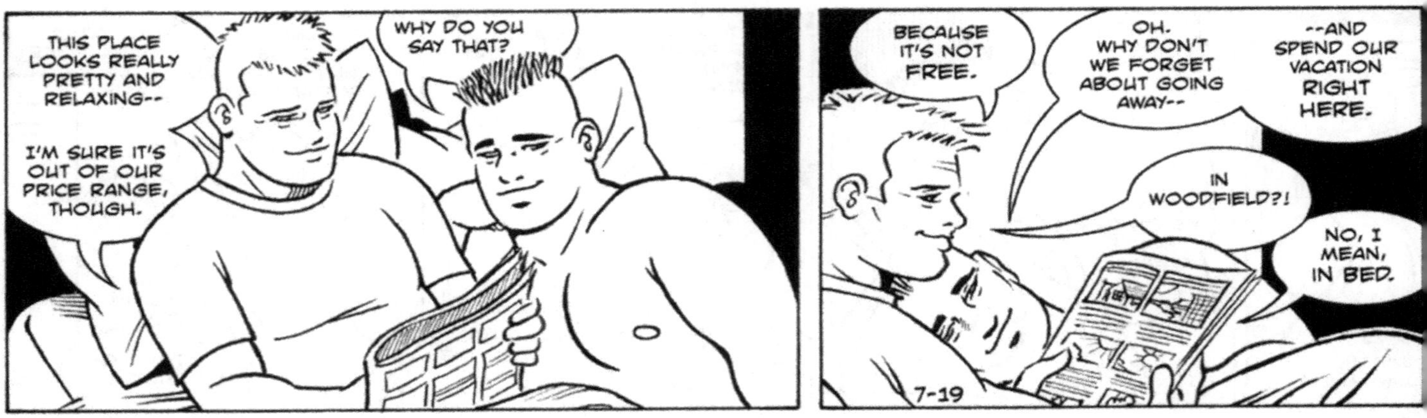
THIS PLACE LOOKS REALLY PRETTY AND RELAXING--
I'M SURE IT'S OUT OF OUR PRICE RANGE, THOUGH.
WHY DO YOU SAY THAT?
BECAUSE IT'S NOT FREE.
OH. WHY DON'T WE FORGET ABOUT GOING AWAY--
--AND SPEND OUR VACATION RIGHT HERE.
IN WOODFIELD?!
NO, I MEAN, IN BED.
7-19

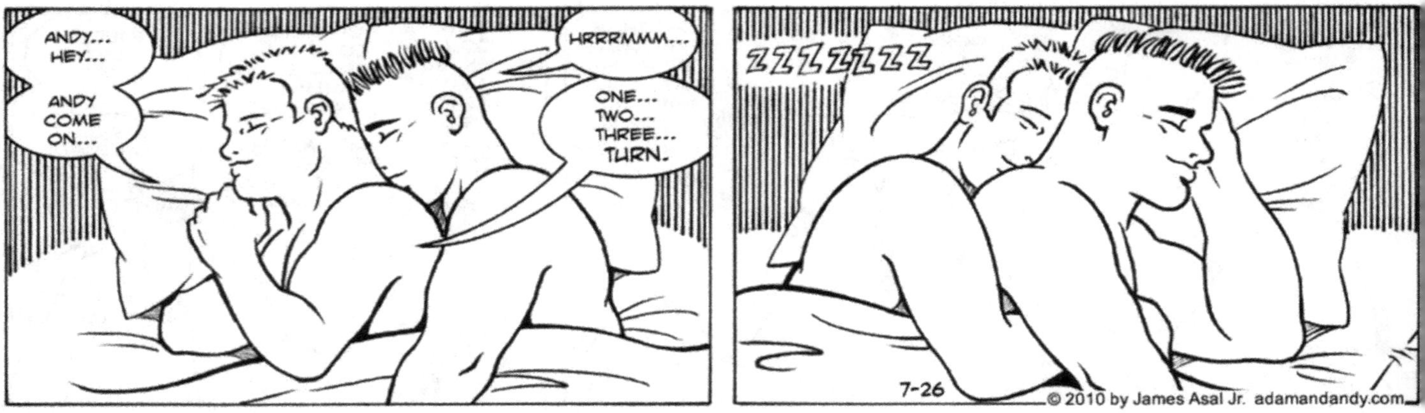
ANDY... HEY...
ANDY COME ON...
HRRRMMM...
ONE... TWO... THREE... TURN.
ZZZZZZZ
7-26
© 2010 by James Asal Jr. adamandandy.com

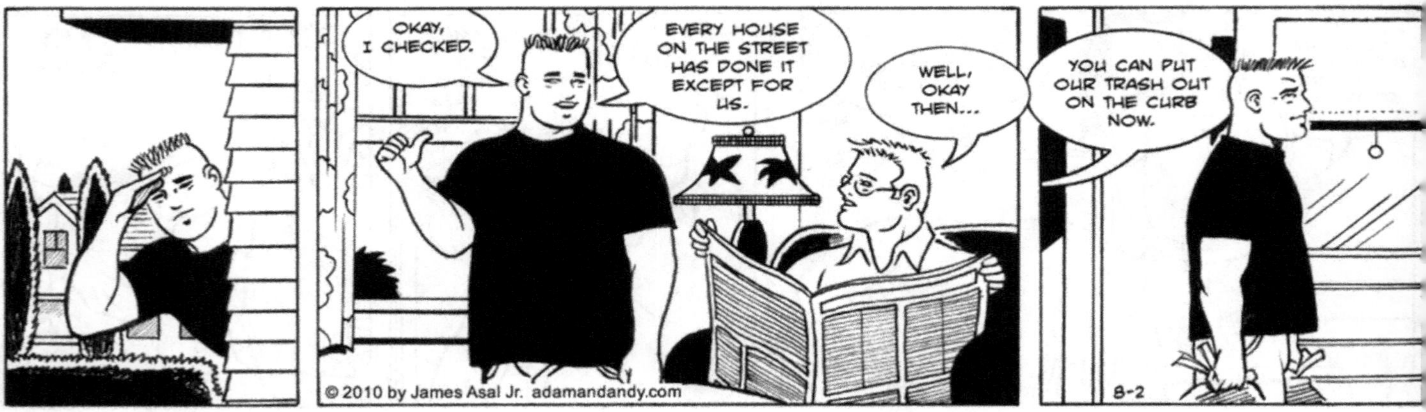
OKAY, I CHECKED.
EVERY HOUSE ON THE STREET HAS DONE IT EXCEPT FOR US.
WELL, OKAY THEN...
© 2010 by James Asal Jr. adamandandy.com
YOU CAN PUT OUR TRASH OUT ON THE CURB NOW.
8-2

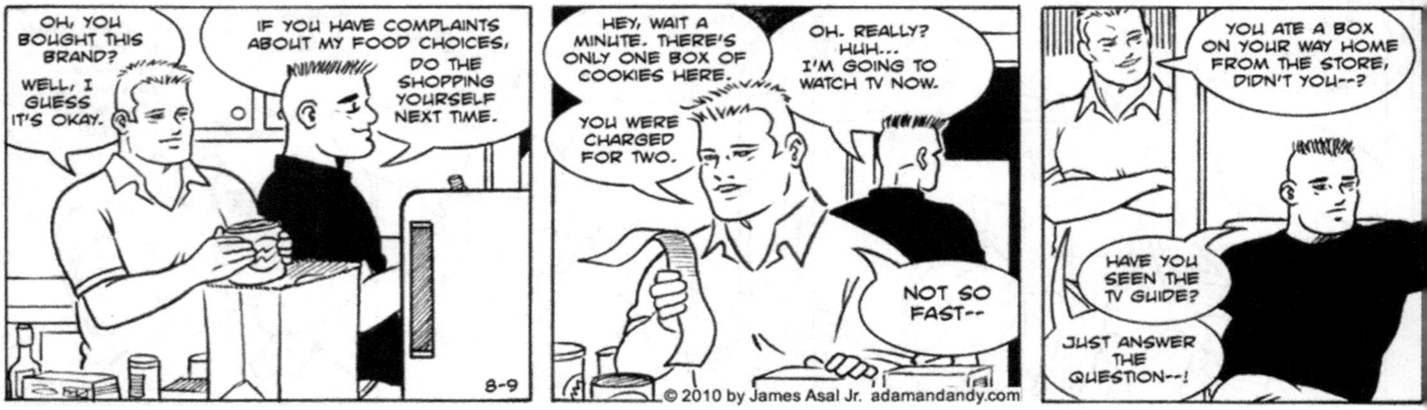
OH, YOU BOUGHT THIS BRAND?
WELL, I GUESS IT'S OKAY.
IF YOU HAVE COMPLAINTS ABOUT MY FOOD CHOICES, DO THE SHOPPING YOURSELF NEXT TIME.
8-9
HEY, WAIT A MINUTE. THERE'S ONLY ONE BOX OF COOKIES HERE.
YOU WERE CHARGED FOR TWO.
OH. REALLY? HUH... I'M GOING TO WATCH TV NOW.
NOT SO FAST--
© 2010 by James Asal Jr. adamandandy.com
YOU ATE A BOX ON YOUR WAY HOME FROM THE STORE, DIDN'T YOU--?
HAVE YOU SEEN THE TV GUIDE?
JUST ANSWER THE QUESTION--!

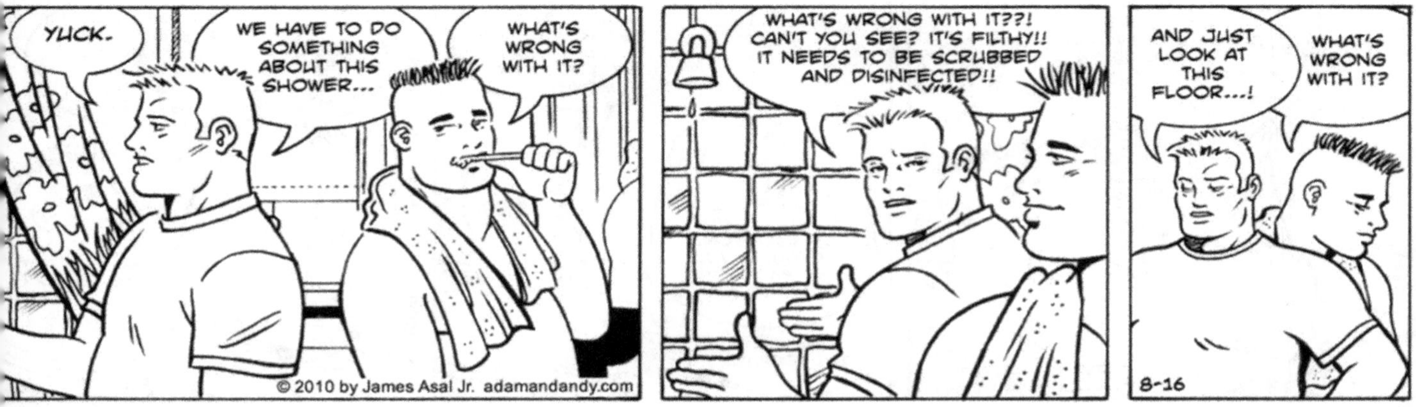
YUCK.
WE HAVE TO DO SOMETHING ABOUT THIS SHOWER...
WHAT'S WRONG WITH IT?
© 2010 by James Asal Jr. adamandandy.com
WHAT'S WRONG WITH IT??! CAN'T YOU SEE? IT'S FILTHY!! IT NEEDS TO BE SCRUBBED AND DISINFECTED!!
AND JUST LOOK AT THIS FLOOR...!
WHAT'S WRONG WITH IT?
8-16

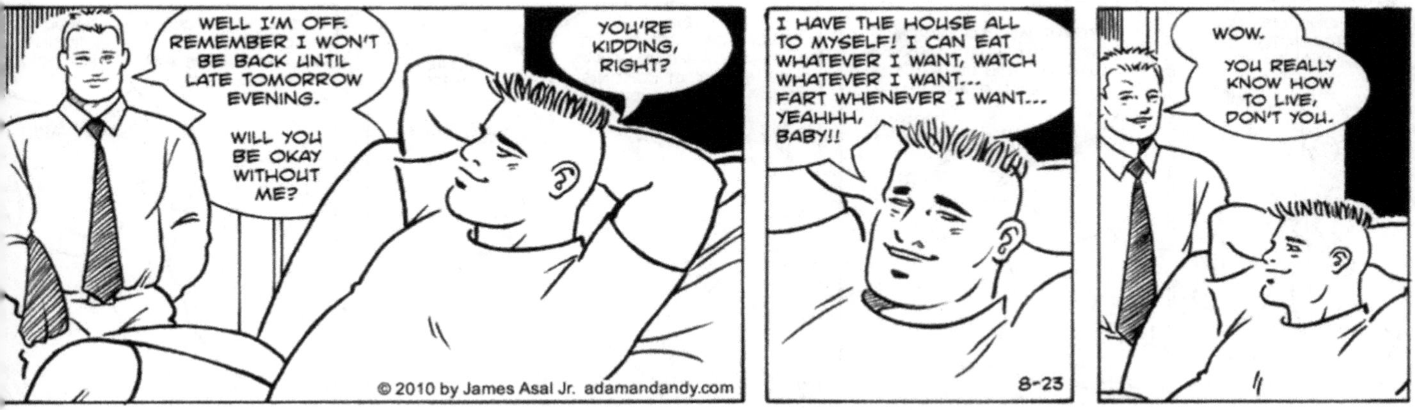
WELL I'M OFF. REMEMBER I WON'T BE BACK UNTIL LATE TOMORROW EVENING.
WILL YOU BE OKAY WITHOUT ME?
YOU'RE KIDDING, RIGHT?
© 2010 by James Asal Jr. adamandandy.com
I HAVE THE HOUSE ALL TO MYSELF! I CAN EAT WHATEVER I WANT, WATCH WHATEVER I WANT... FART WHENEVER I WANT... YEAHHH, BABY!!
8-23
WOW.
YOU REALLY KNOW HOW TO LIVE, DON'T YOU.

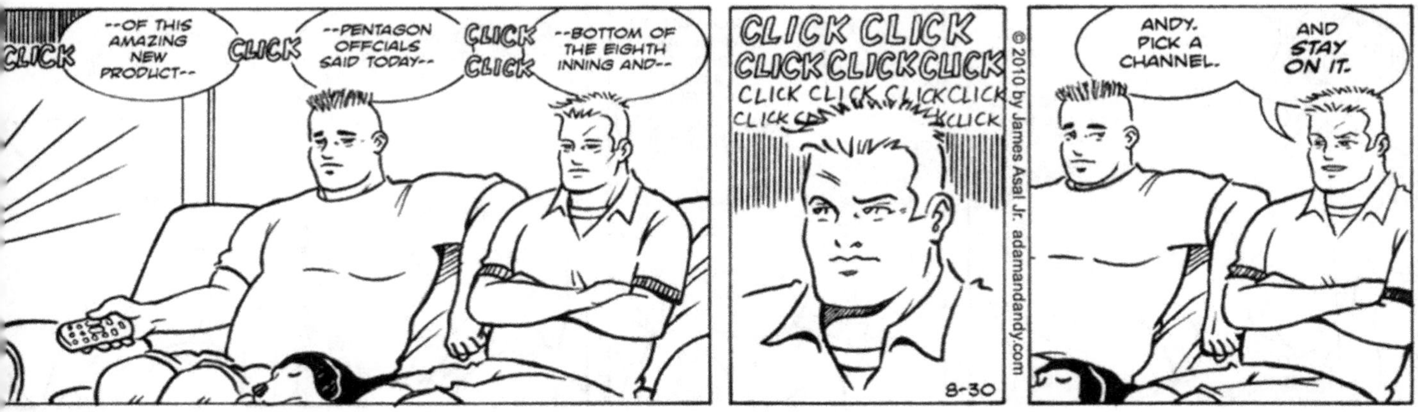
CLICK
--OF THIS AMAZING NEW PRODUCT--
CLICK
--PENTAGON OFFCIALS SAID TODAY--
CLICK CLICK
--BOTTOM OF THE EIGHTH INNING AND--
CLICK CLICK
CLICK CLICK CLICK
CLICK CLICK CLICK CLICK
8-30
© 2010 by James Asal Jr. adamandandy.com
ANDY. PICK A CHANNEL.
AND STAY ON IT.

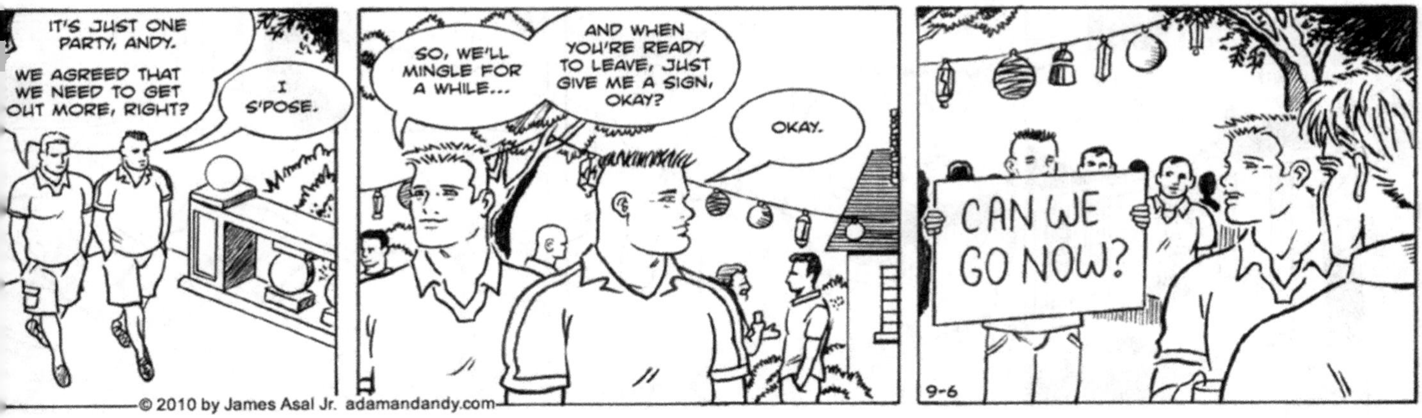
IT'S JUST ONE PARTY, ANDY.
WE AGREED THAT WE NEED TO GET OUT MORE, RIGHT?
I S'POSE.
SO, WE'LL MINGLE FOR A WHILE...
AND WHEN YOU'RE READY TO LEAVE, JUST GIVE ME A SIGN, OKAY?
OKAY.
CAN WE GO NOW?
9-6
© 2010 by James Asal Jr. adamandandy.com

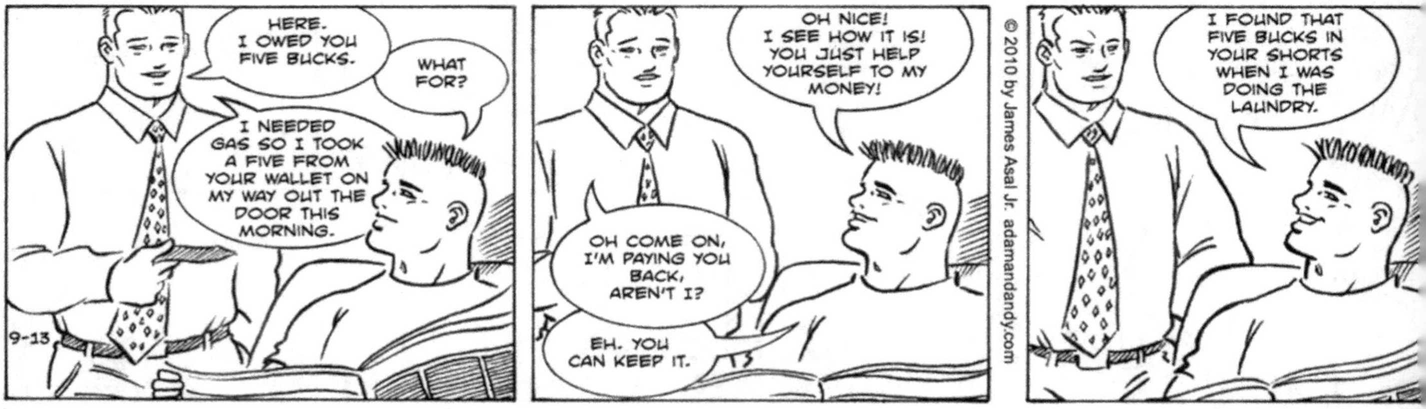
9-13
HERE. I OWED YOU FIVE BUCKS.
WHAT FOR?
I NEEDED GAS SO I TOOK A FIVE FROM YOUR WALLET ON MY WAY OUT THE DOOR THIS MORNING.
OH NICE! I SEE HOW IT IS! YOU JUST HELP YOURSELF TO MY MONEY!
OH COME ON, I'M PAYING YOU BACK, AREN'T I?
EH. YOU CAN KEEP IT.
© 2010 by James Asal Jr. adamandandy.com
I FOUND THAT FIVE BUCKS IN YOUR SHORTS WHEN I WAS DOING THE LAUNDRY.

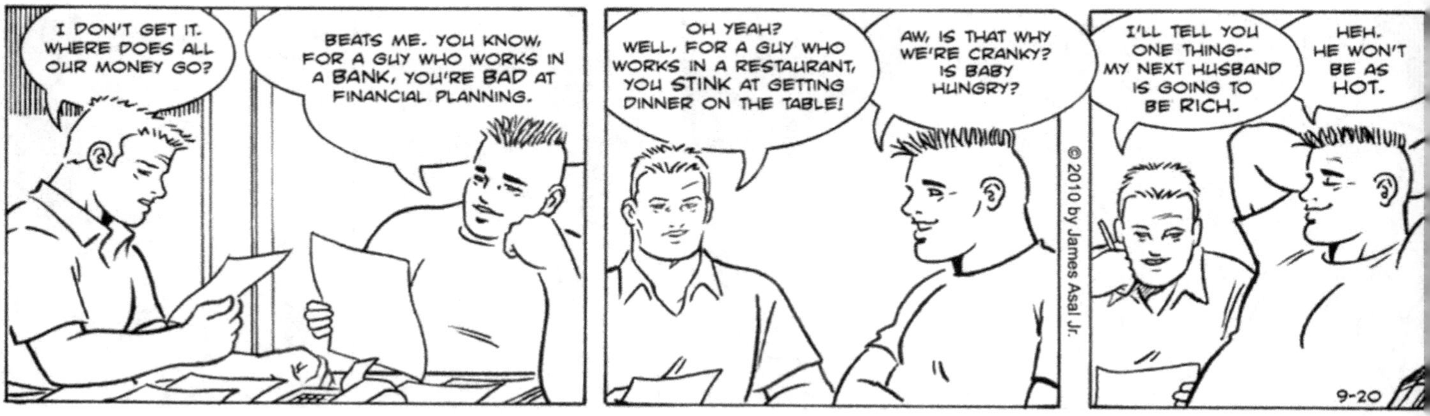
I DON'T GET IT. WHERE DOES ALL OUR MONEY GO?
BEATS ME. YOU KNOW, FOR A GUY WHO WORKS IN A BANK, YOU'RE BAD AT FINANCIAL PLANNING.
OH YEAH? WELL, FOR A GUY WHO WORKS IN A RESTAURANT, YOU STINK AT GETTING DINNER ON THE TABLE!
AW, IS THAT WHY WE'RE CRANKY? IS BABY HUNGRY?
© 2010 by James Asal Jr.
I'LL TELL YOU ONE THING-- MY NEXT HUSBAND IS GOING TO BE RICH.
HEH. HE WON'T BE AS HOT.
9-20

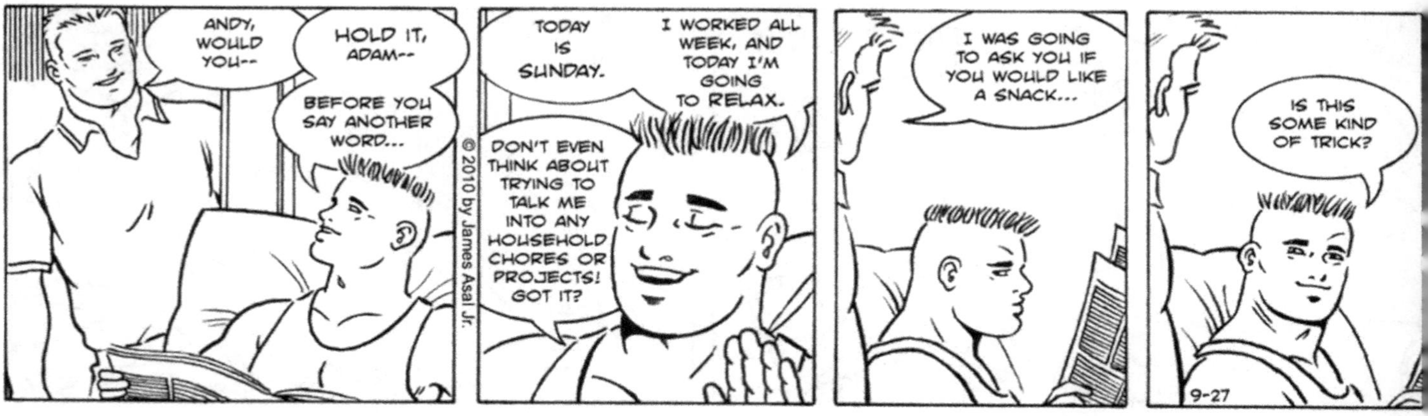
ANDY, WOULD YOU--
HOLD IT, ADAM--
BEFORE YOU SAY ANOTHER WORD...
© 2010 by James Asal Jr.
TODAY IS SUNDAY.
I WORKED ALL WEEK, AND TODAY I'M GOING TO RELAX.
DON'T EVEN THINK ABOUT TRYING TO TALK ME INTO ANY HOUSEHOLD CHORES OR PROJECTS! GOT IT?
I WAS GOING TO ASK YOU IF YOU WOULD LIKE A SNACK...
IS THIS SOME KIND OF TRICK?
9-27

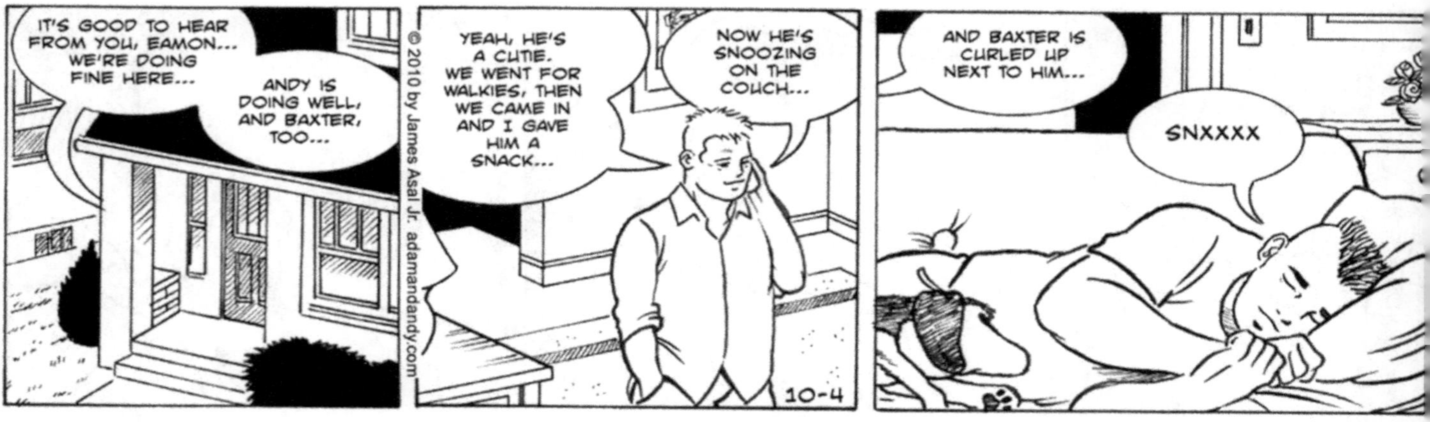
IT'S GOOD TO HEAR FROM YOU, EAMON... WE'RE DOING FINE HERE...
ANDY IS DOING WELL, AND BAXTER, TOO...
© 2010 by James Asal Jr. adamandandy.com
YEAH, HE'S A CUTIE. WE WENT FOR WALKIES, THEN WE CAME IN AND I GAVE HIM A SNACK...
NOW HE'S SNOOZING ON THE COUCH...
10-4
AND BAXTER IS CURLED UP NEXT TO HIM...
SNXXXX

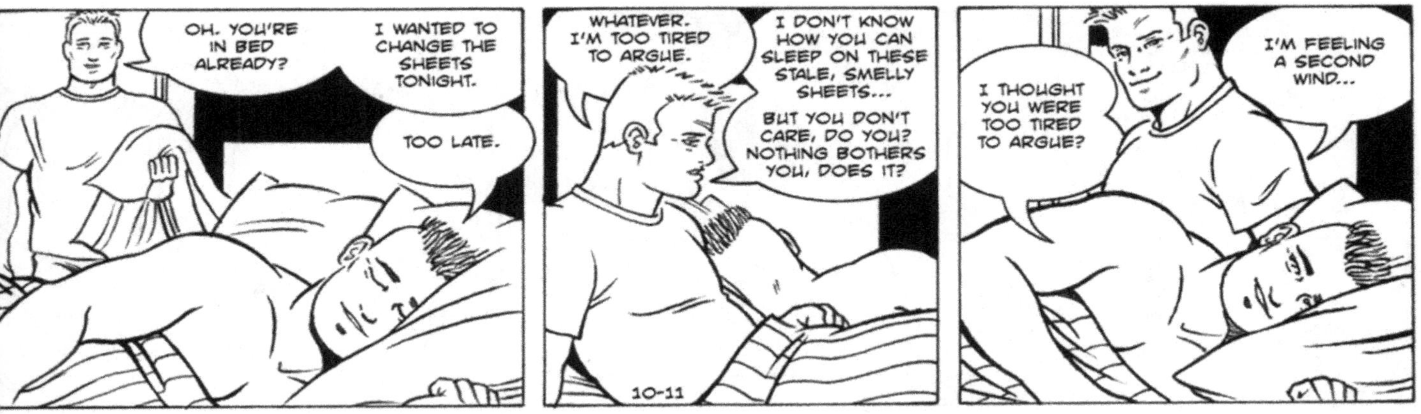
OH. YOU'RE IN BED ALREADY?
I WANTED TO CHANGE THE SHEETS TONIGHT.
TOO LATE.
WHATEVER. I'M TOO TIRED TO ARGUE.
I DON'T KNOW HOW YOU CAN SLEEP ON THESE STALE, SMELLY SHEETS...
BUT YOU DON'T CARE, DO YOU? NOTHING BOTHERS YOU, DOES IT?
10-11
I THOUGHT YOU WERE TOO TIRED TO ARGUE?
I'M FEELING A SECOND WIND...

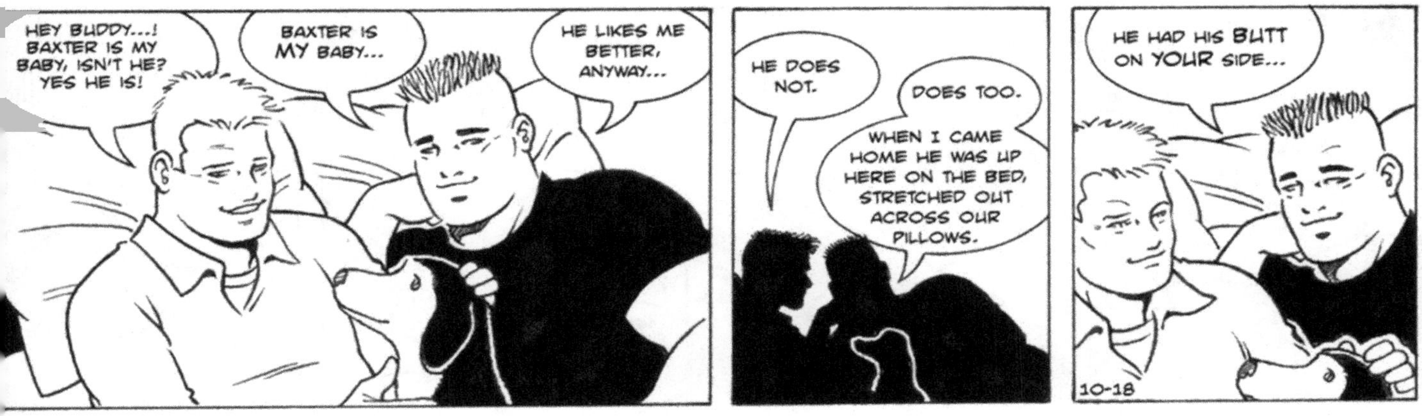
HEY BUDDY...! BAXTER IS MY BABY, ISN'T HE? YES HE IS!
BAXTER IS MY BABY...
HE LIKES ME BETTER, ANYWAY...
HE DOES NOT.
DOES TOO.
WHEN I CAME HOME HE WAS UP HERE ON THE BED, STRETCHED OUT ACROSS OUR PILLOWS.
HE HAD HIS BUTT ON YOUR SIDE...
10-18

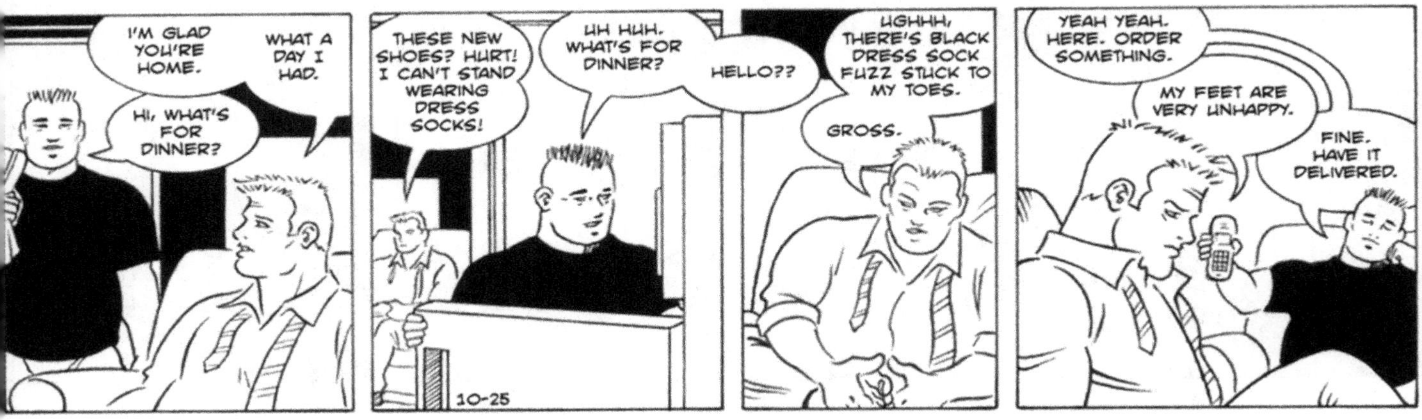
I'M GLAD YOU'RE HOME.
WHAT A DAY I HAD.
HI, WHAT'S FOR DINNER?
THESE NEW SHOES? HURT! I CAN'T STAND WEARING DRESS SOCKS!
UH HUH. WHAT'S FOR DINNER?
HELLO??
10-25
UGHHH, THERE'S BLACK DRESS SOCK FUZZ STUCK TO MY TOES.
GROSS.
YEAH YEAH. HERE. ORDER SOMETHING.
MY FEET ARE VERY UNHAPPY.
FINE. HAVE IT DELIVERED.

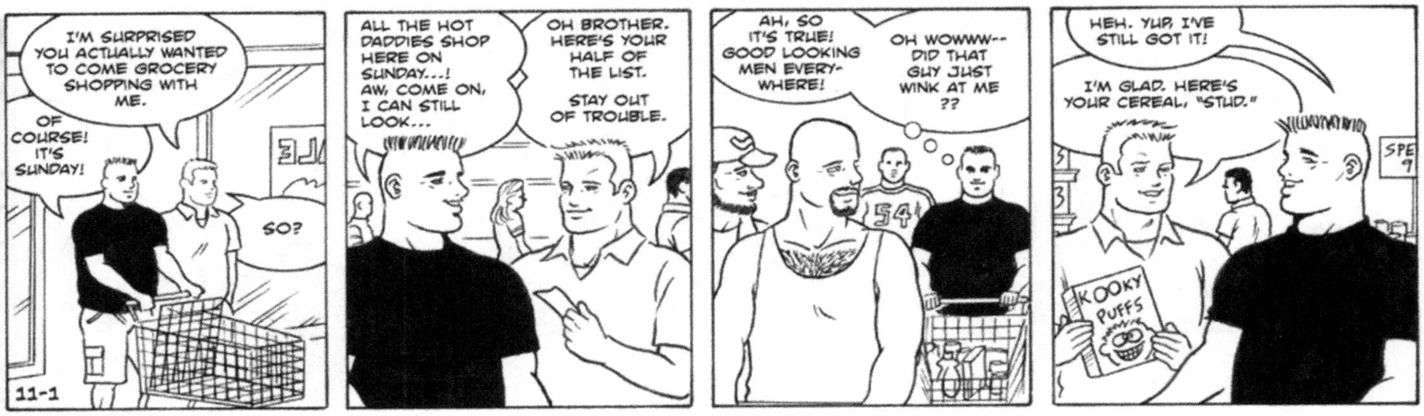
I'M SURPRISED YOU ACTUALLY WANTED TO COME GROCERY SHOPPING WITH ME.
OF COURSE! IT'S SUNDAY!
SO?
11-1
ALL THE HOT DADDIES SHOP HERE ON SUNDAY...! AW, COME ON, I CAN STILL LOOK...
OH BROTHER. HERE'S YOUR HALF OF THE LIST.
STAY OUT OF TROUBLE.
AH, SO IT'S TRUE! GOOD LOOKING MEN EVERY-WHERE!
OH WOWWW-- DID THAT GUY JUST WINK AT ME ??
54
HEH. YUP, I'VE STILL GOT IT!
I'M GLAD. HERE'S YOUR CEREAL, "STUD."
KOOKY PUFFS

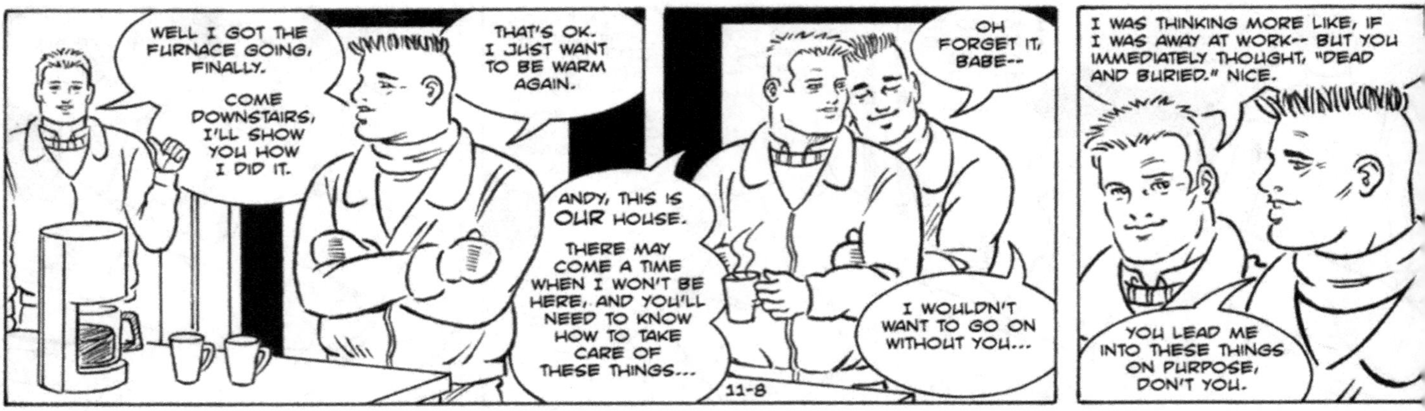
WELL I GOT THE FURNACE GOING, FINALLY.
COME DOWNSTAIRS, I'LL SHOW YOU HOW I DID IT.
THAT'S OK. I JUST WANT TO BE WARM AGAIN.
ANDY, THIS IS OUR HOUSE.
THERE MAY COME A TIME WHEN I WON'T BE HERE, AND YOU'LL NEED TO KNOW HOW TO TAKE CARE OF THESE THINGS...
OH FORGET IT, BABE--
I WOULDN'T WANT TO GO ON WITHOUT YOU...
I WAS THINKING MORE LIKE, IF I WAS AWAY AT WORK-- BUT YOU IMMEDIATELY THOUGHT, "DEAD AND BURIED." NICE.
YOU LEAD ME INTO THESE THINGS ON PURPOSE, DON'T YOU.
11-8

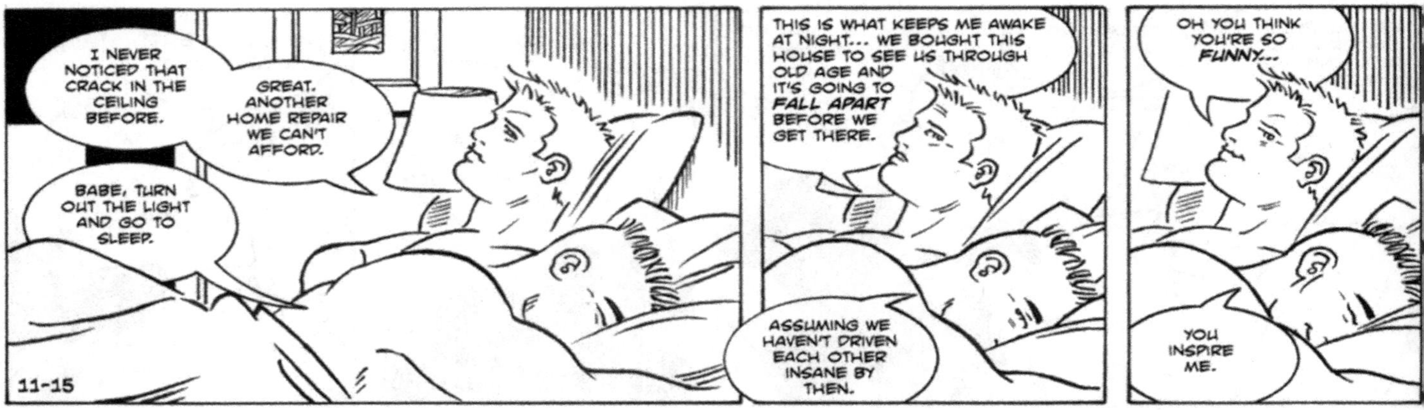
I NEVER NOTICED THAT CRACK IN THE CEILING BEFORE.
GREAT. ANOTHER HOME REPAIR WE CAN'T AFFORD.
BABE, TURN OUT THE LIGHT AND GO TO SLEEP.
THIS IS WHAT KEEPS ME AWAKE AT NIGHT... WE BOUGHT THIS HOUSE TO SEE US THROUGH OLD AGE AND IT'S GOING TO FALL APART BEFORE WE GET THERE.
ASSUMING WE HAVEN'T DRIVEN EACH OTHER INSANE BY THEN.
OH YOU THINK YOU'RE SO FUNNY...
YOU INSPIRE ME.
11-15

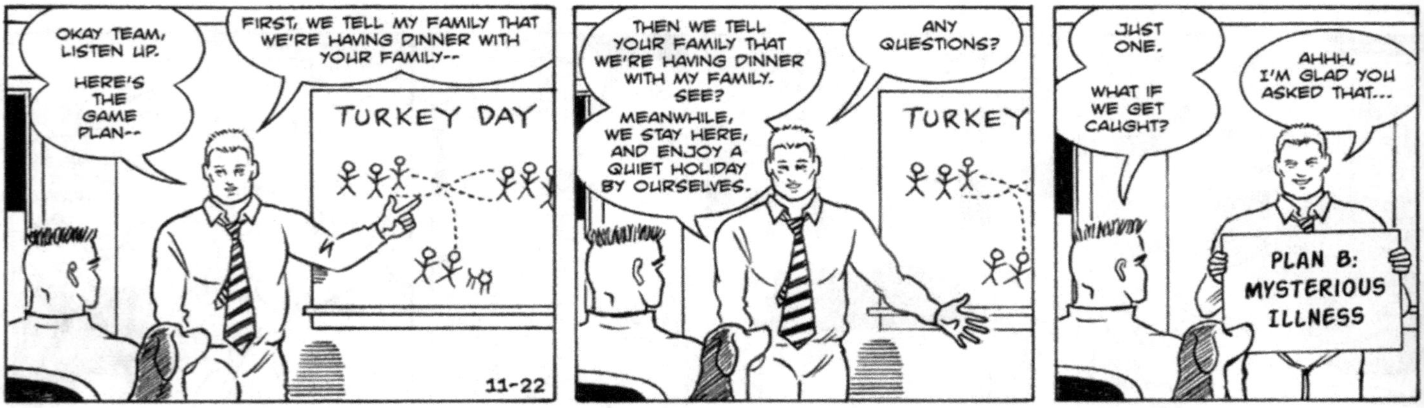
OKAY TEAM, LISTEN UP.
HERE'S THE GAME PLAN--
FIRST, WE TELL MY FAMILY THAT WE'RE HAVING DINNER WITH YOUR FAMILY--
TURKEY DAY
THEN WE TELL YOUR FAMILY THAT WE'RE HAVING DINNER WITH MY FAMILY. SEE?
MEANWHILE, WE STAY HERE, AND ENJOY A QUIET HOLIDAY BY OURSELVES.
ANY QUESTIONS?
TURKEY
JUST ONE.
WHAT IF WE GET CAUGHT?
AHHH, I'M GLAD YOU ASKED THAT...
PLAN B: MYSTERIOUS ILLNESS
11-22

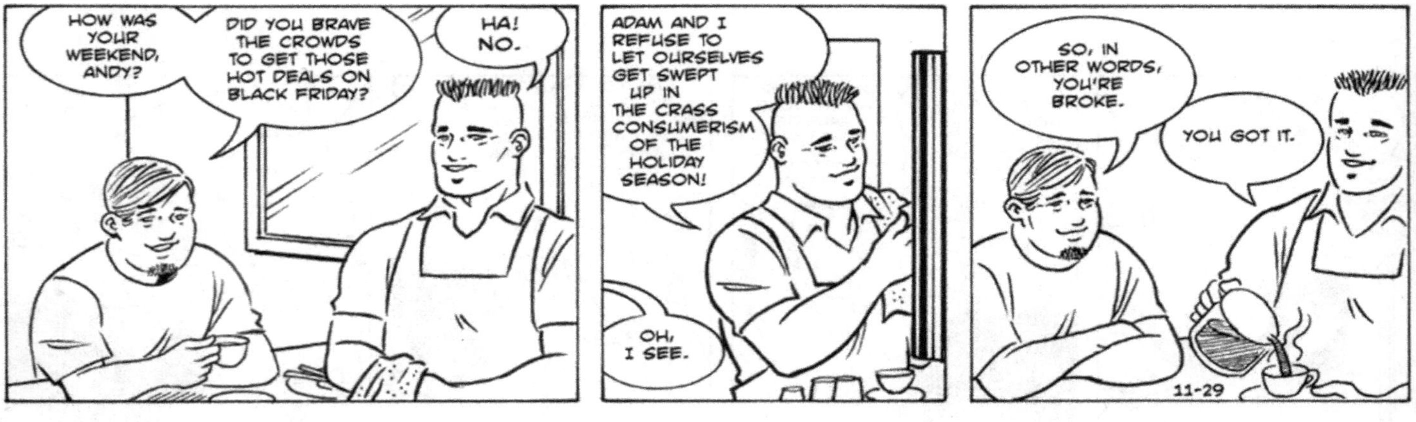
HOW WAS YOUR WEEKEND, ANDY?
DID YOU BRAVE THE CROWDS TO GET THOSE HOT DEALS ON BLACK FRIDAY?
HA! NO.
ADAM AND I REFUSE TO LET OURSELVES GET SWEPT UP IN THE CRASS CONSUMERISM OF THE HOLIDAY SEASON!
OH, I SEE.
SO, IN OTHER WORDS, YOU'RE BROKE.
YOU GOT IT.
11-29

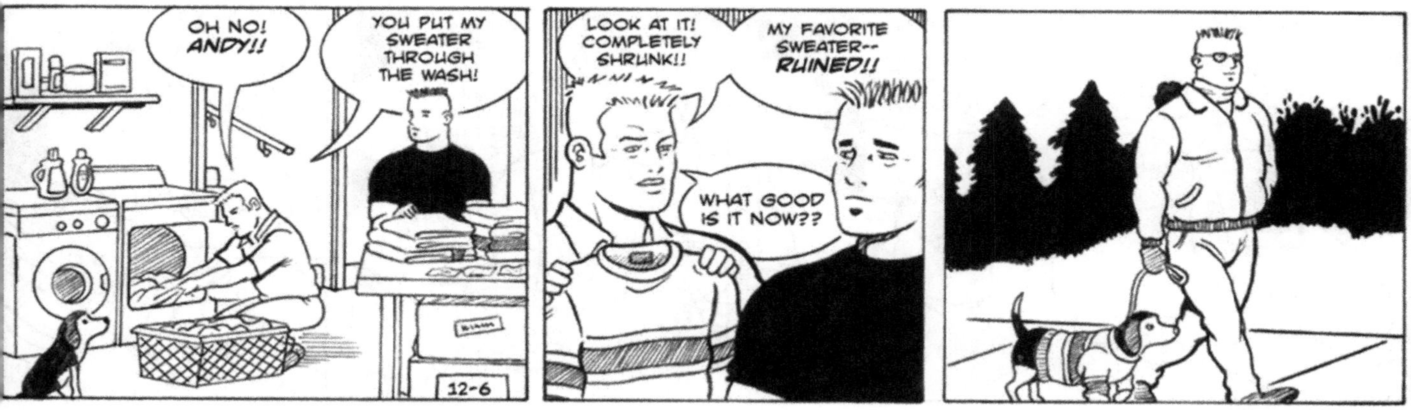
OH NO! ANDY!!
YOU PUT MY SWEATER THROUGH THE WASH!
12-6
LOOK AT IT! COMPLETELY SHRUNK!!
MY FAVORITE SWEATER-- RUINED!!
WHAT GOOD IS IT NOW??

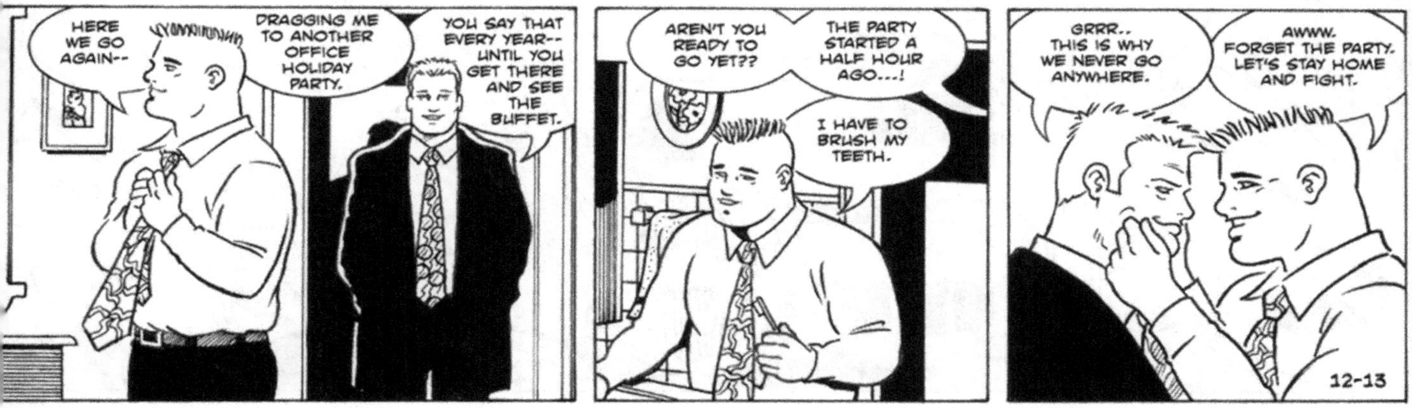
HERE WE GO AGAIN--
DRAGGING ME TO ANOTHER OFFICE HOLIDAY PARTY.
YOU SAY THAT EVERY YEAR-- UNTIL YOU GET THERE AND SEE THE BUFFET.
AREN'T YOU READY TO GO YET??
THE PARTY STARTED A HALF HOUR AGO...!
I HAVE TO BRUSH MY TEETH.
GRRR.. THIS IS WHY WE NEVER GO ANYWHERE.
AWWW. FORGET THE PARTY. LET'S STAY HOME AND FIGHT.
12-13

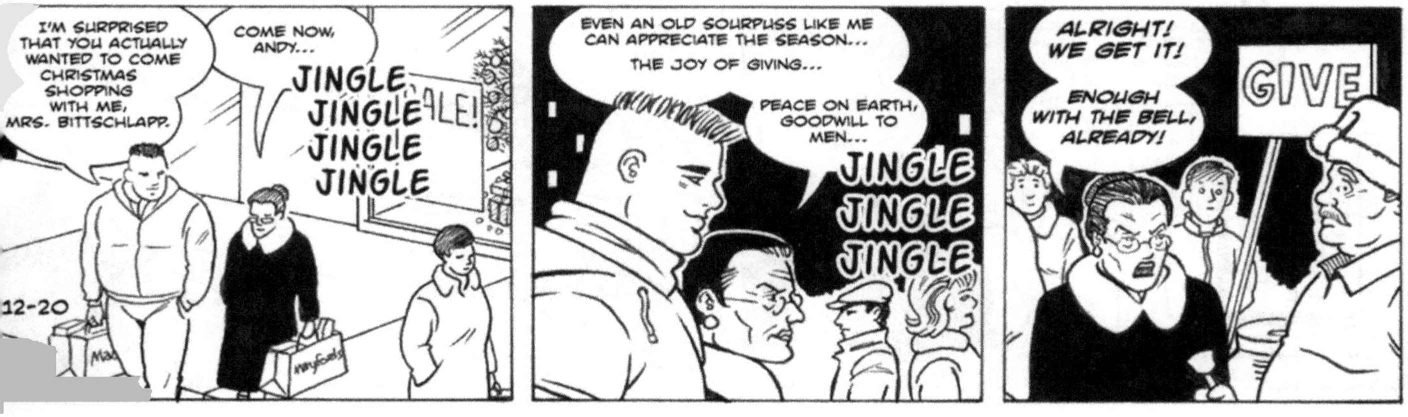
I'M SURPRISED THAT YOU ACTUALLY WANTED TO COME CHRISTMAS SHOPPING WITH ME, MRS. BITTSCHLAPP.
COME NOW, ANDY...
JINGLE JINGLE JINGLE JINGLE
12-20
EVEN AN OLD SOURPUSS LIKE ME CAN APPRECIATE THE SEASON...
THE JOY OF GIVING...
PEACE ON EARTH, GOODWILL TO MEN...
JINGLE JINGLE JINGLE
ALRIGHT! WE GET IT!
ENOUGH WITH THE BELL, ALREADY!
GIVE

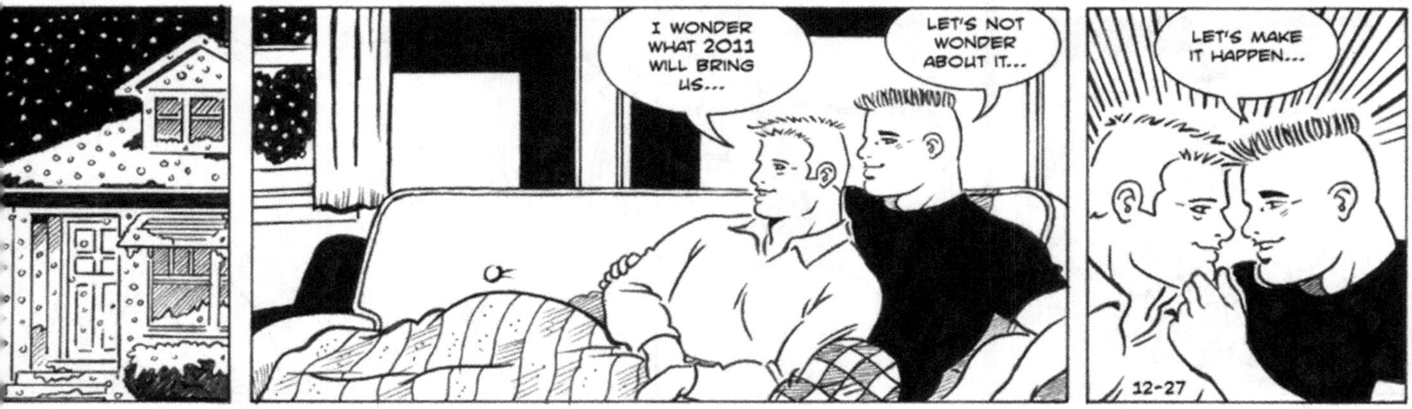
I WONDER WHAT 2011 WILL BRING US...
LET'S NOT WONDER ABOUT IT...
LET'S MAKE IT HAPPEN...
12-27

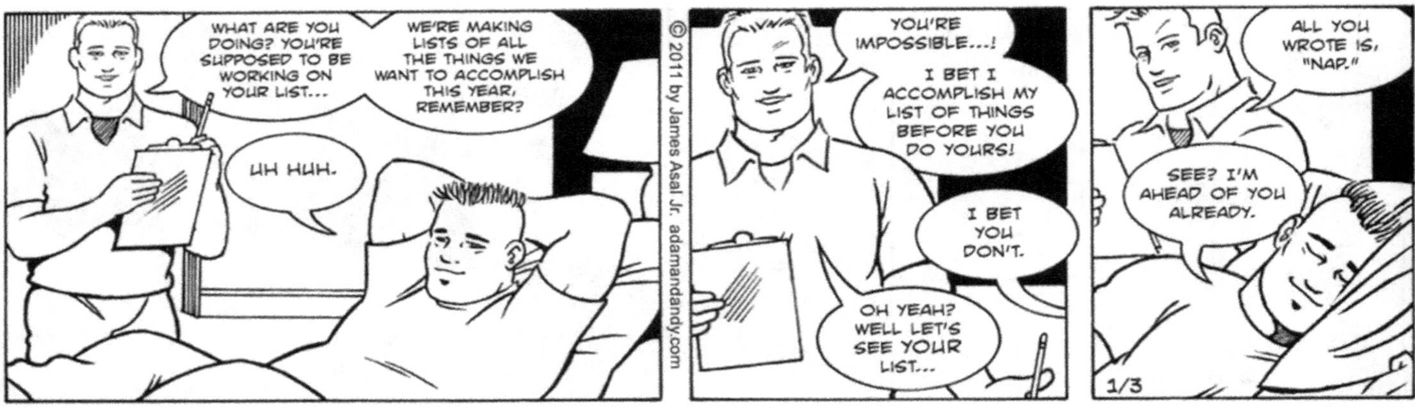
WHAT ARE YOU DOING? YOU'RE SUPPOSED TO BE WORKING ON YOUR LIST...
WE'RE MAKING LISTS OF ALL THE THINGS WE WANT TO ACCOMPLISH THIS YEAR, REMEMBER?
UH HUH.
© 2011 by James Asal Jr. adamandandy.com
YOU'RE IMPOSSIBLE...!
I BET I ACCOMPLISH MY LIST OF THINGS BEFORE YOU DO YOURS!
I BET YOU DON'T.
OH YEAH? WELL LET'S SEE YOUR LIST...
ALL YOU WROTE IS, "NAP."
SEE? I'M AHEAD OF YOU ALREADY.
1/3

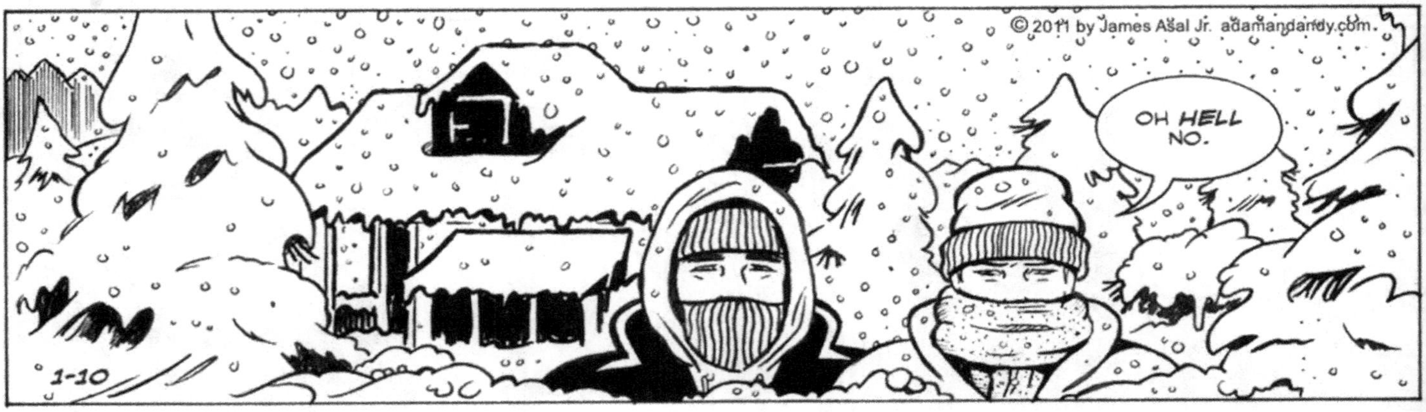
© 2011 by James Asal Jr. adamandandy.com
OH HELL NO.
1-10

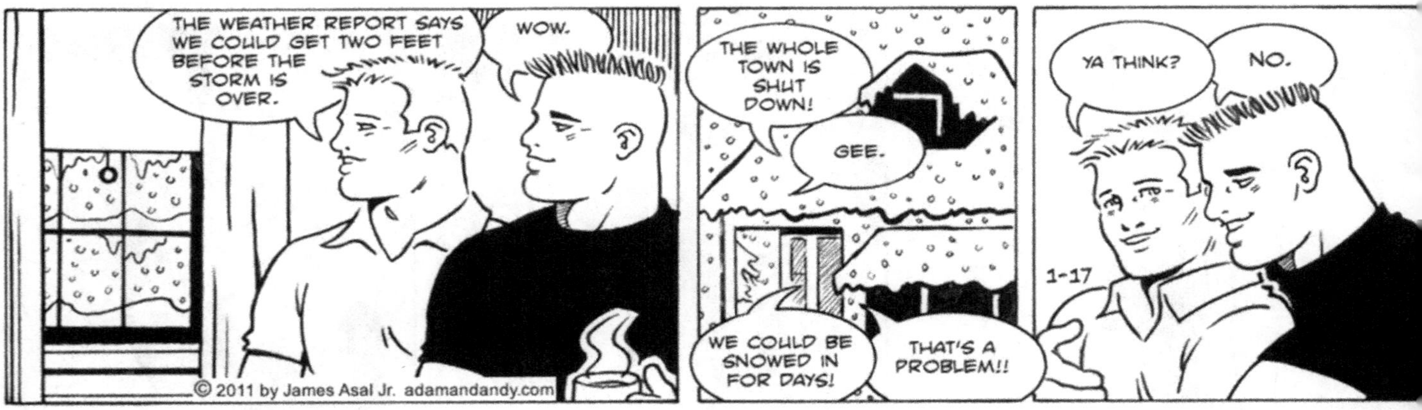
THE WEATHER REPORT SAYS WE COULD GET TWO FEET BEFORE THE STORM IS OVER.
WOW.
© 2011 by James Asal Jr. adamandandy.com
THE WHOLE TOWN IS SHUT DOWN!
GEE.
WE COULD BE SNOWED IN FOR DAYS!
THAT'S A PROBLEM!!
YA THINK?
NO.
1-17

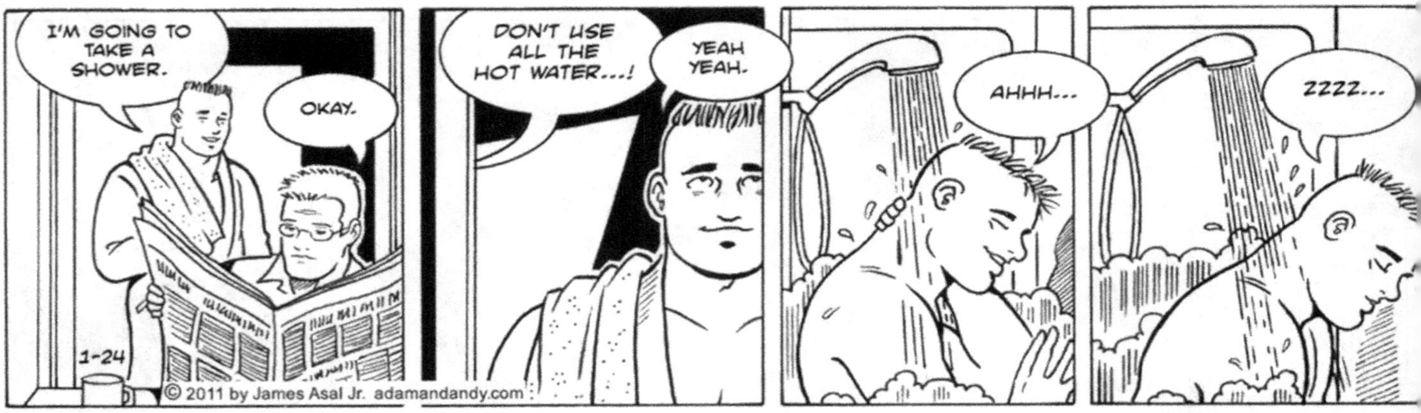
I'M GOING TO TAKE A SHOWER.
OKAY.
1-24
© 2011 by James Asal Jr. adamandandy.com
DON'T USE ALL THE HOT WATER...!
YEAH YEAH.
AHHH...
ZZZZ...

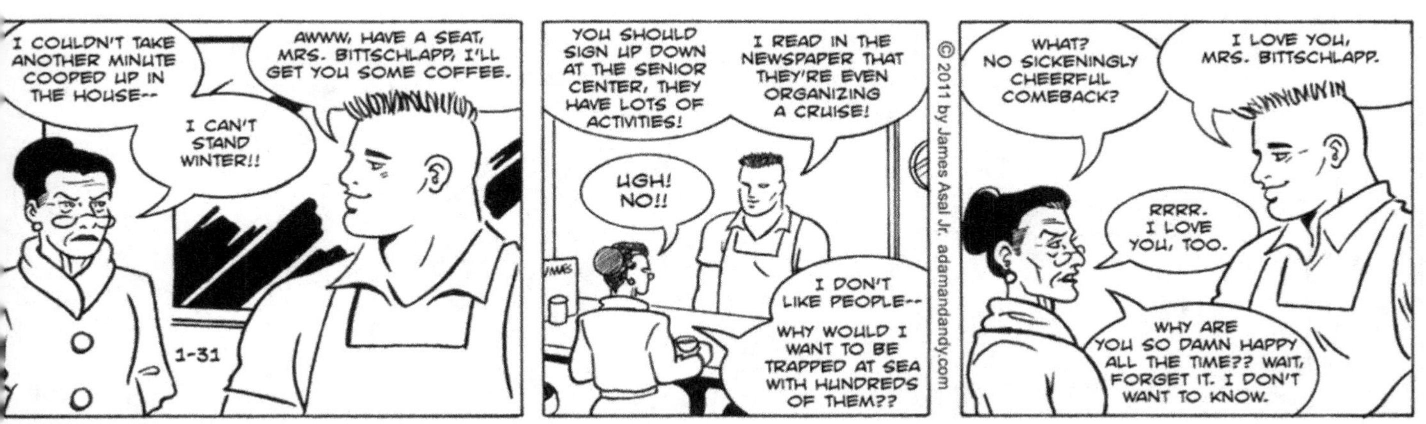
I COULDN'T TAKE ANOTHER MINUTE COOPED UP IN THE HOUSE--
I CAN'T STAND WINTER!!
AWWW, HAVE A SEAT, MRS. BITTSCHLAPP, I'LL GET YOU SOME COFFEE.
1-31
YOU SHOULD SIGN UP DOWN AT THE SENIOR CENTER, THEY HAVE LOTS OF ACTIVITIES!
I READ IN THE NEWSPAPER THAT THEY'RE EVEN ORGANIZING A CRUISE!
UGH! NO!!
I DON'T LIKE PEOPLE--
WHY WOULD I WANT TO BE TRAPPED AT SEA WITH HUNDREDS OF THEM??
© 2011 by James Asal Jr. adamandandy.com
WHAT? NO SICKENINGLY CHEERFUL COMEBACK?
I LOVE YOU, MRS. BITTSCHLAPP.
RRRR. I LOVE YOU, TOO.
WHY ARE YOU SO DAMN HAPPY ALL THE TIME?? WAIT, FORGET IT. I DON'T WANT TO KNOW.

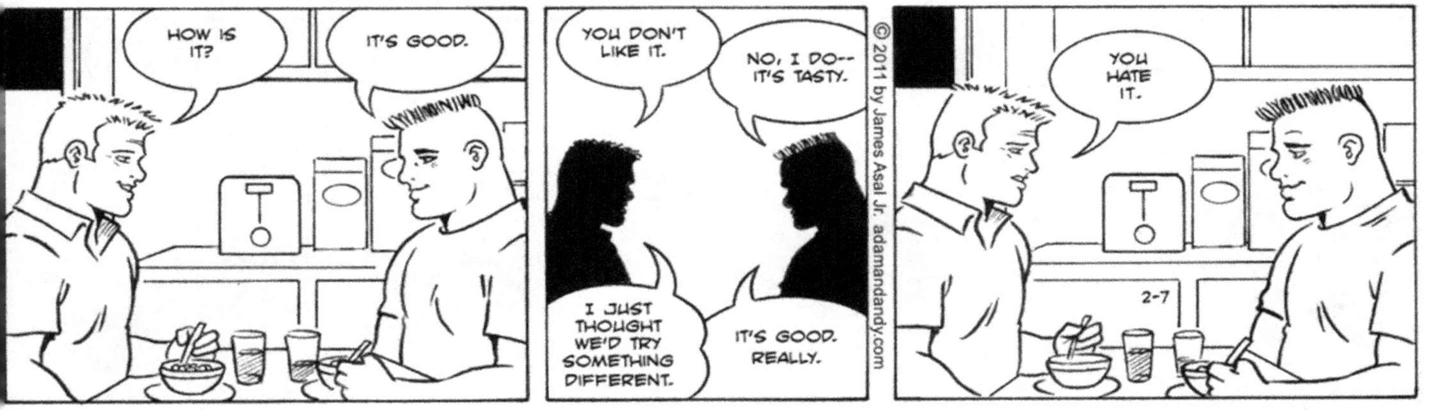
HOW IS IT?
IT'S GOOD.
YOU DON'T LIKE IT.
NO, I DO-- IT'S TASTY.
I JUST THOUGHT WE'D TRY SOMETHING DIFFERENT.
IT'S GOOD. REALLY.
© 2011 by James Asal Jr. adamandandy.com
YOU HATE IT.
2-7

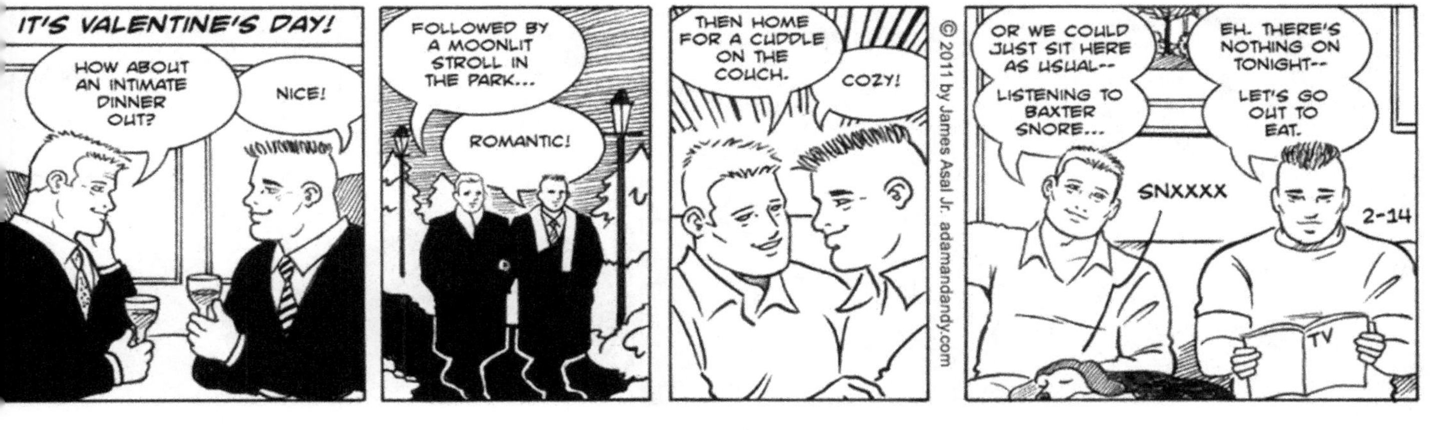
IT'S VALENTINE'S DAY!
HOW ABOUT AN INTIMATE DINNER OUT?
NICE!
FOLLOWED BY A MOONLIT STROLL IN THE PARK...
ROMANTIC!
THEN HOME FOR A CUDDLE ON THE COUCH.
COZY!
© 2011 by James Asal Jr. adamandandy.com
OR WE COULD JUST SIT HERE AS USUAL--
LISTENING TO BAXTER SNORE...
EH. THERE'S NOTHING ON TONIGHT--
LET'S GO OUT TO EAT.
SNXXXX
2-14
TV

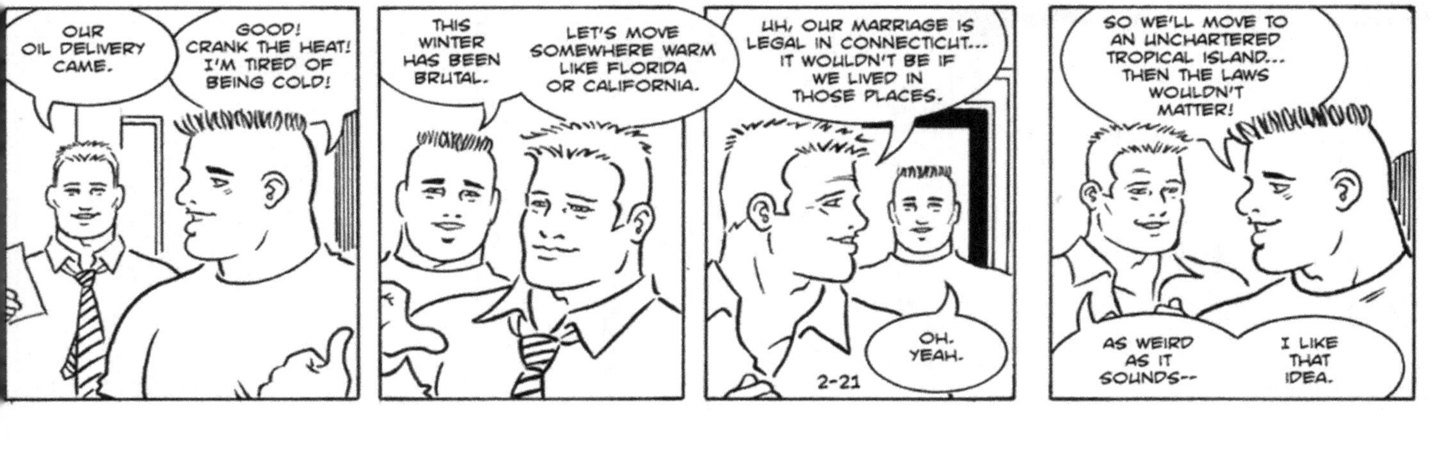
OUR OIL DELIVERY CAME.
GOOD! CRANK THE HEAT! I'M TIRED OF BEING COLD!
THIS WINTER HAS BEEN BRUTAL.
LET'S MOVE SOMEWHERE WARM LIKE FLORIDA OR CALIFORNIA.
UH, OUR MARRIAGE IS LEGAL IN CONNECTICUT... IT WOULDN'T BE IF WE LIVED IN THOSE PLACES.
OH. YEAH.
2-21
SO WE'LL MOVE TO AN UNCHARTERED TROPICAL ISLAND... THEN THE LAWS WOULDN'T MATTER!
AS WEIRD AS IT SOUNDS--
I LIKE THAT IDEA.

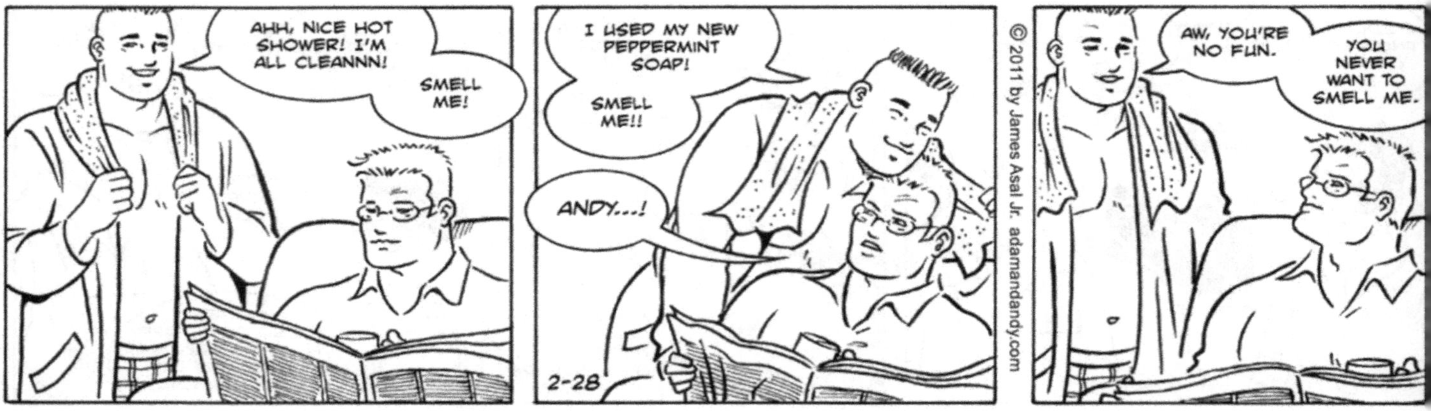
AHH, NICE HOT SHOWER! I'M ALL CLEANNN!
SMELL ME!
I USED MY NEW PEPPERMINT SOAP!
SMELL ME!!
ANDY...!
2-28
© 2011 by James Asal Jr. adamandandy.com
AW, YOU'RE NO FUN.
YOU NEVER WANT TO SMELL ME.

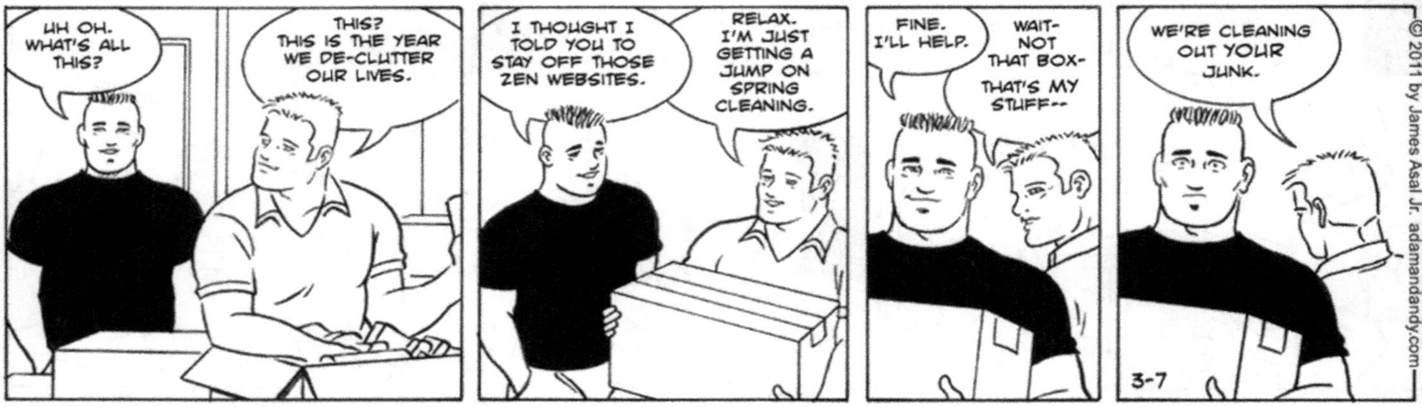
UH OH. WHAT'S ALL THIS?
THIS? THIS IS THE YEAR WE DE-CLUTTER OUR LIVES.
I THOUGHT I TOLD YOU TO STAY OFF THOSE ZEN WEBSITES.
RELAX. I'M JUST GETTING A JUMP ON SPRING CLEANING.
FINE. I'LL HELP.
WAIT- NOT THAT BOX- THAT'S MY STUFF--
WE'RE CLEANING OUT YOUR JUNK.
3-7
© 2011 by James Asal Jr. adamandandy.com

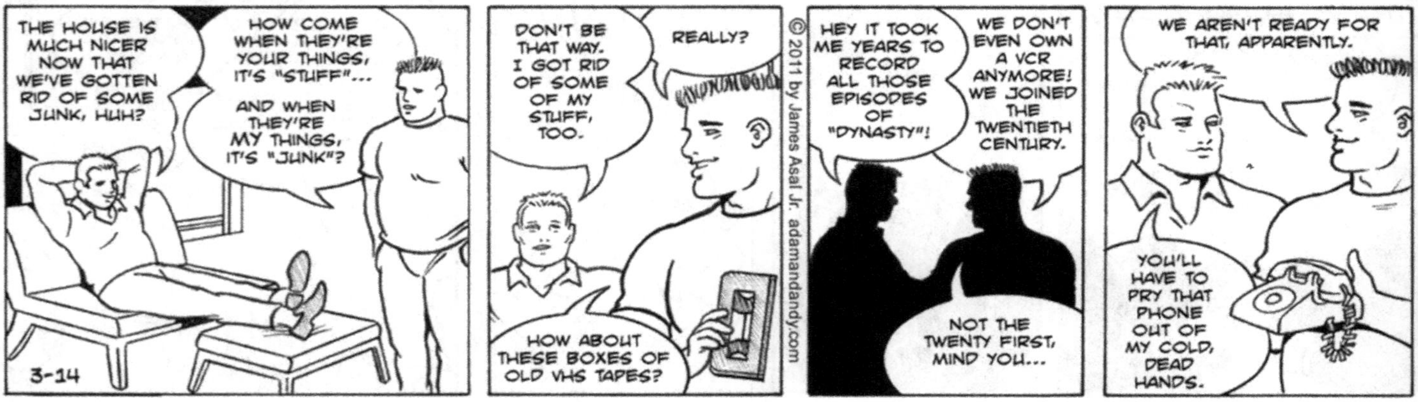
THE HOUSE IS MUCH NICER NOW THAT WE'VE GOTTEN RID OF SOME JUNK, HUH?
HOW COME WHEN THEY'RE YOUR THINGS, IT'S "STUFF"...
AND WHEN THEY'RE MY THINGS, IT'S "JUNK"?
3-14
DON'T BE THAT WAY. I GOT RID OF SOME OF MY STUFF, TOO.
REALLY?
HOW ABOUT THESE BOXES OF OLD VHS TAPES?
© 2011 by James Asal Jr. adamandandy.com
HEY IT TOOK ME YEARS TO RECORD ALL THOSE EPISODES OF "DYNASTY"!
WE DON'T EVEN OWN A VCR ANYMORE! WE JOINED THE TWENTIETH CENTURY.
NOT THE TWENTY FIRST, MIND YOU...
WE AREN'T READY FOR THAT, APPARENTLY.
YOU'LL HAVE TO PRY THAT PHONE OUT OF MY COLD, DEAD HANDS.

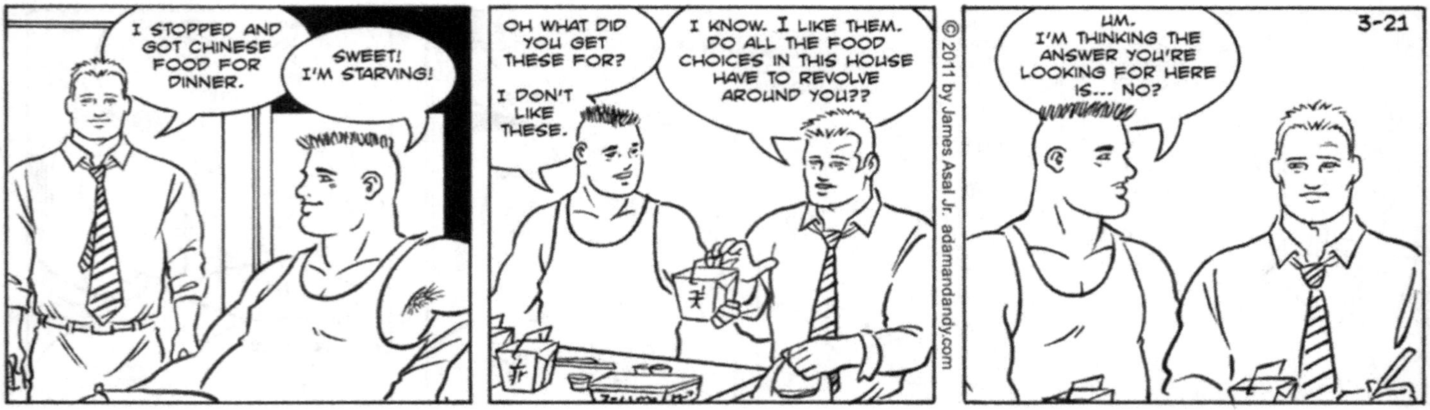
I STOPPED AND GOT CHINESE FOOD FOR DINNER.
SWEET! I'M STARVING!
OH WHAT DID YOU GET THESE FOR?
I DON'T LIKE THESE.
I KNOW. I LIKE THEM. DO ALL THE FOOD CHOICES IN THIS HOUSE HAVE TO REVOLVE AROUND YOU??
© 2011 by James Asal Jr. adamandandy.com
3-21
UM. I'M THINKING THE ANSWER YOU'RE LOOKING FOR HERE IS... NO?

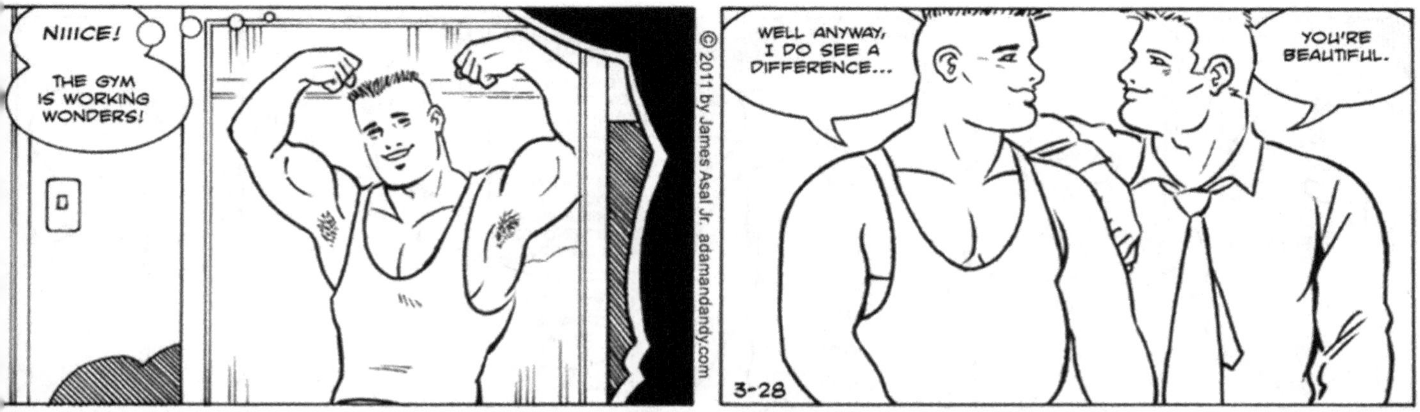
NIIICE!
THE GYM IS WORKING WONDERS!
© 2011 by James Asal Jr. adamandandy.com
WELL ANYWAY, I DO SEE A DIFFERENCE...
YOU'RE BEAUTIFUL.
3-28

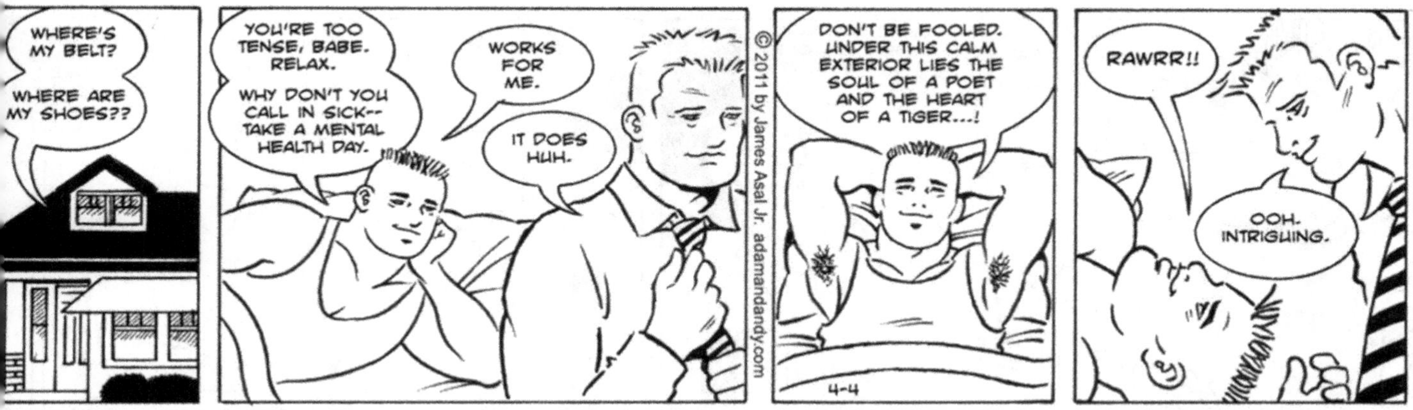
WHERE'S MY BELT?
WHERE ARE MY SHOES??
YOU'RE TOO TENSE, BABE. RELAX.
WHY DON'T YOU CALL IN SICK-- TAKE A MENTAL HEALTH DAY.
WORKS FOR ME.
IT DOES HUH.
© 2011 by James Asal Jr. adamandandy.com
DON'T BE FOOLED. UNDER THIS CALM EXTERIOR LIES THE SOUL OF A POET AND THE HEART OF A TIGER...!
4-4
RAWRR!!
OOH. INTRIGUING.

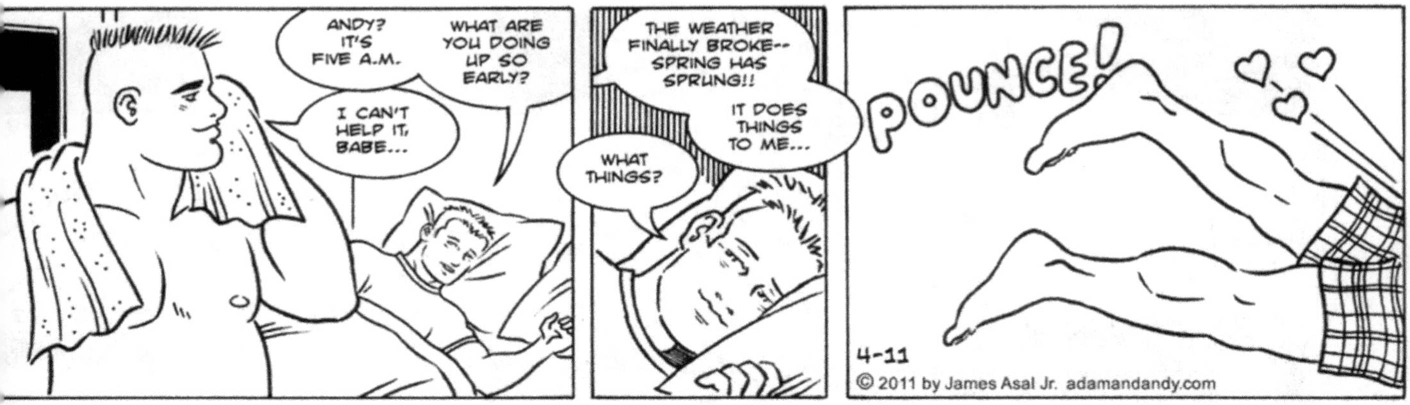
ANDY? IT'S FIVE A.M.
WHAT ARE YOU DOING UP SO EARLY?
I CAN'T HELP IT, BABE...
THE WEATHER FINALLY BROKE-- SPRING HAS SPRUNG!!
IT DOES THINGS TO ME...
WHAT THINGS?
POUNCE!
4-11
© 2011 by James Asal Jr. adamandandy.com

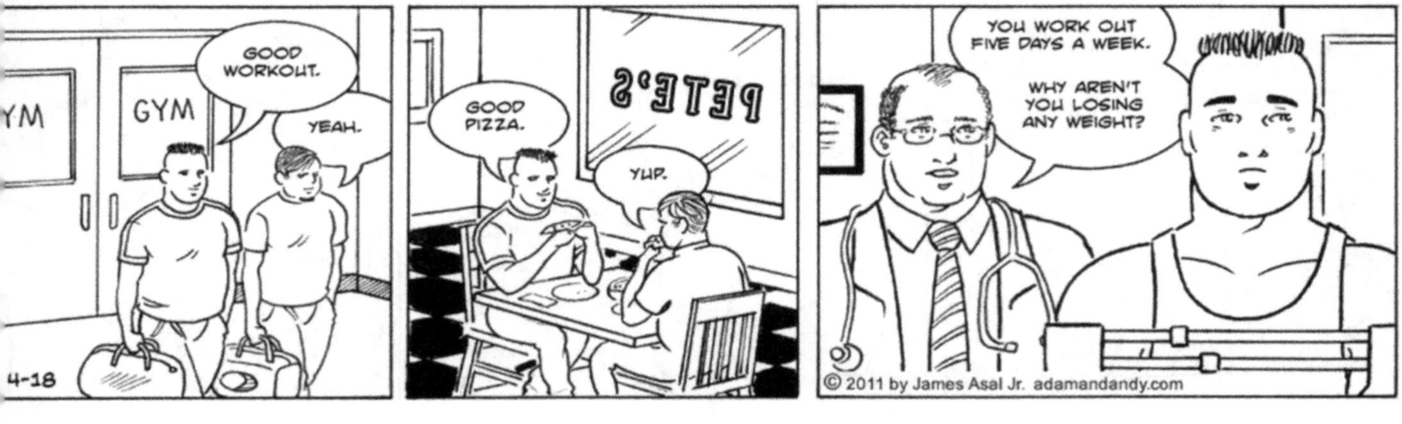
GYM
GOOD WORKOUT.
YEAH.
4-18
PETE'S
GOOD PIZZA.
YUP.
YOU WORK OUT FIVE DAYS A WEEK.
WHY AREN'T YOU LOSING ANY WEIGHT?
© 2011 by James Asal Jr. adamandandy.com

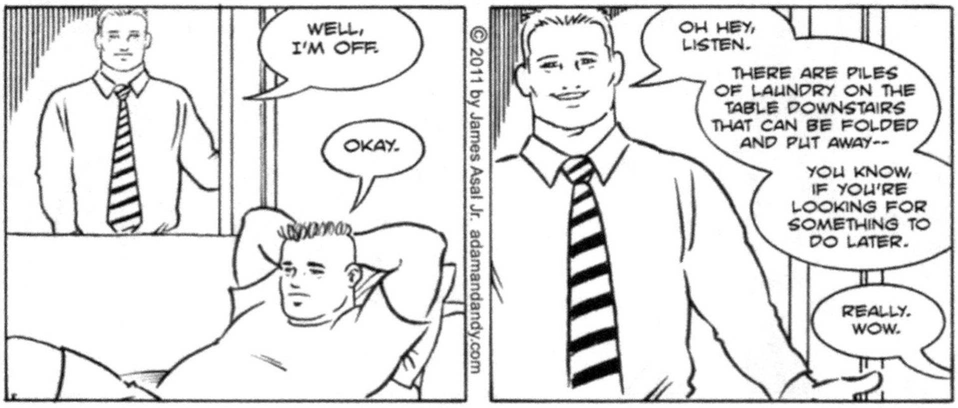
WELL, I'M OFF.
OKAY.
© 2011 by James Asal Jr. adamandandy.com
OH HEY, LISTEN.
THERE ARE PILES OF LAUNDRY ON THE TABLE DOWNSTAIRS THAT CAN BE FOLDED AND PUT AWAY--
YOU KNOW, IF YOU'RE LOOKING FOR SOMETHING TO DO LATER.
REALLY. WOW.
4-25
I WAS JUST THINKING TO MYSELF, "GEE, WHAT AM I GOING TO DO LATER?"

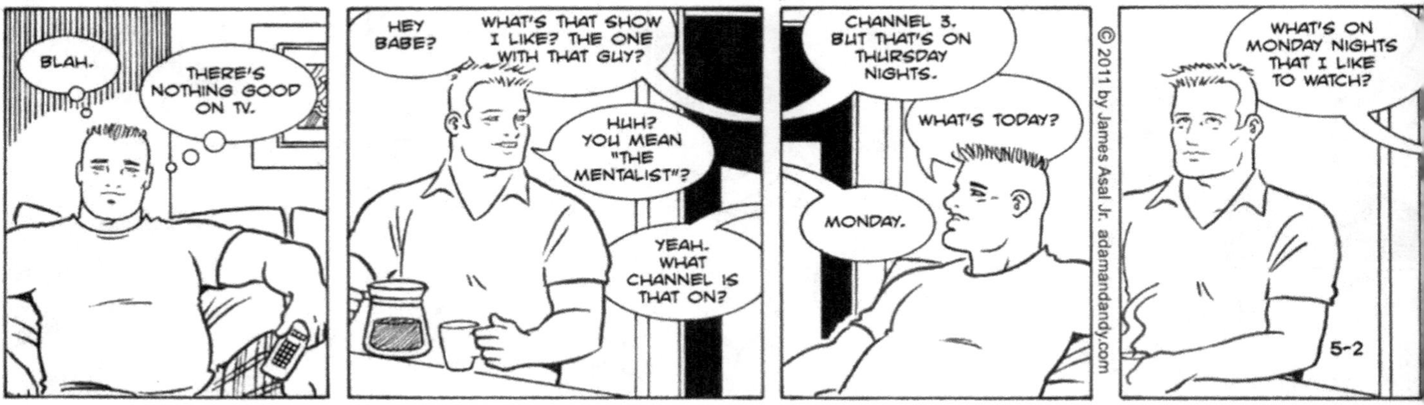
BLAH.
THERE'S NOTHING GOOD ON TV.
HEY BABE?
WHAT'S THAT SHOW I LIKE? THE ONE WITH THAT GUY?
HUH? YOU MEAN "THE MENTALIST"?
YEAH. WHAT CHANNEL IS THAT ON?
CHANNEL 3. BUT THAT'S ON THURSDAY NIGHTS.
WHAT'S TODAY?
MONDAY.
© 2011 by James Asal Jr. adamandandy.com
WHAT'S ON MONDAY NIGHTS THAT I LIKE TO WATCH?
5-2

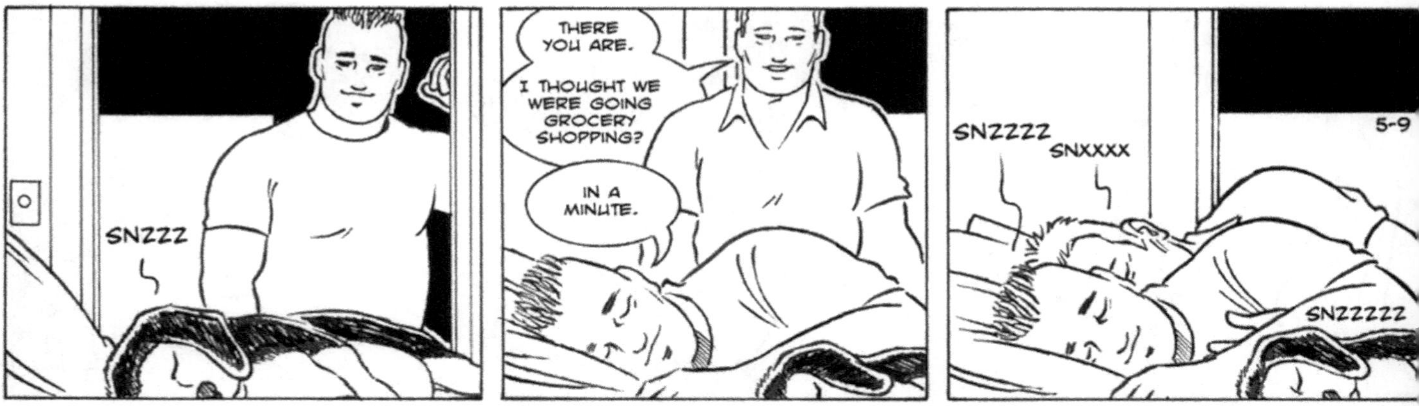
SNZZZ
THERE YOU ARE.
I THOUGHT WE WERE GOING GROCERY SHOPPING?
IN A MINUTE.
5-9
SNZZZZ
SNXXXX
SNZZZZZ

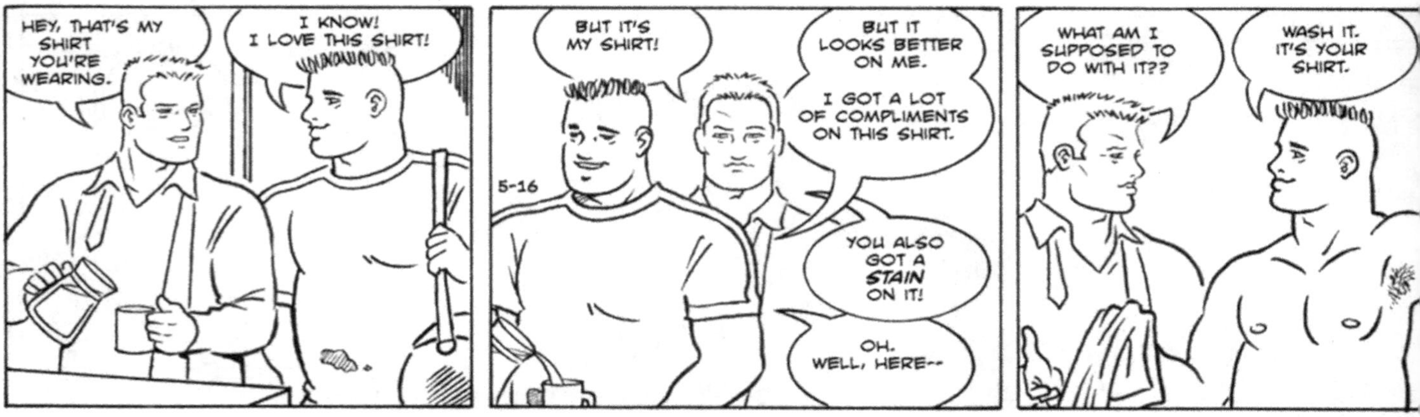
HEY, THAT'S MY SHIRT YOU'RE WEARING.
I KNOW! I LOVE THIS SHIRT!
5-16
BUT IT'S MY SHIRT!
BUT IT LOOKS BETTER ON ME.
I GOT A LOT OF COMPLIMENTS ON THIS SHIRT.
YOU ALSO GOT A STAIN ON IT!
OH. WELL, HERE--
WHAT AM I SUPPOSED TO DO WITH IT??
WASH IT. IT'S YOUR SHIRT.

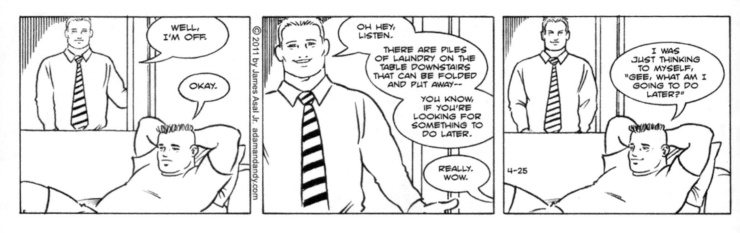

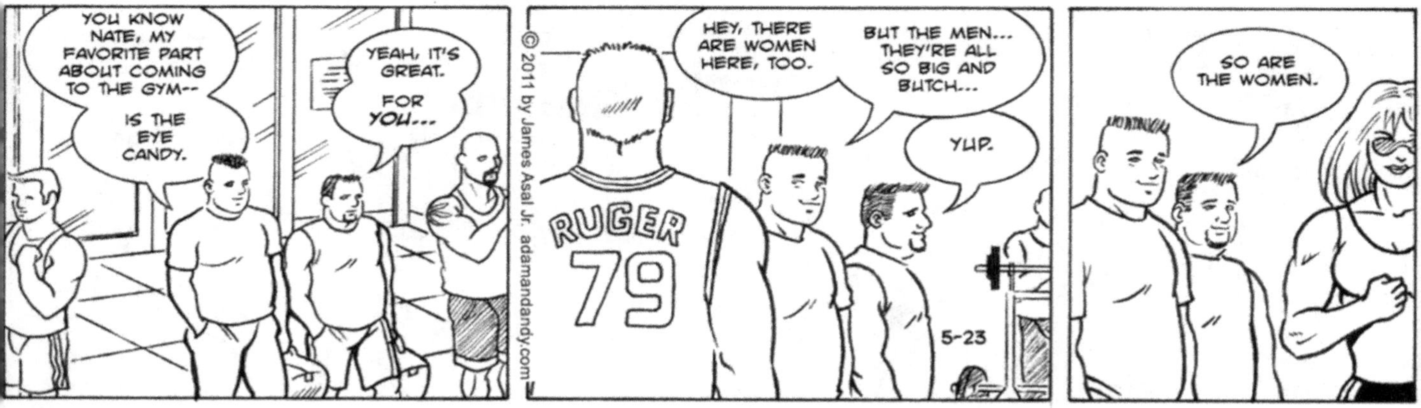
YOU KNOW NATE, MY FAVORITE PART ABOUT COMING TO THE GYM--
IS THE EYE CANDY.
YEAH, IT'S GREAT.
FOR *YOU*...
© 2011 by James Asal Jr. adamandandy.com
HEY, THERE ARE WOMEN HERE, TOO.
BUT THE MEN... THEY'RE ALL SO BIG AND BUTCH...
YUP.
RUGER 79
5-23
SO ARE THE WOMEN.

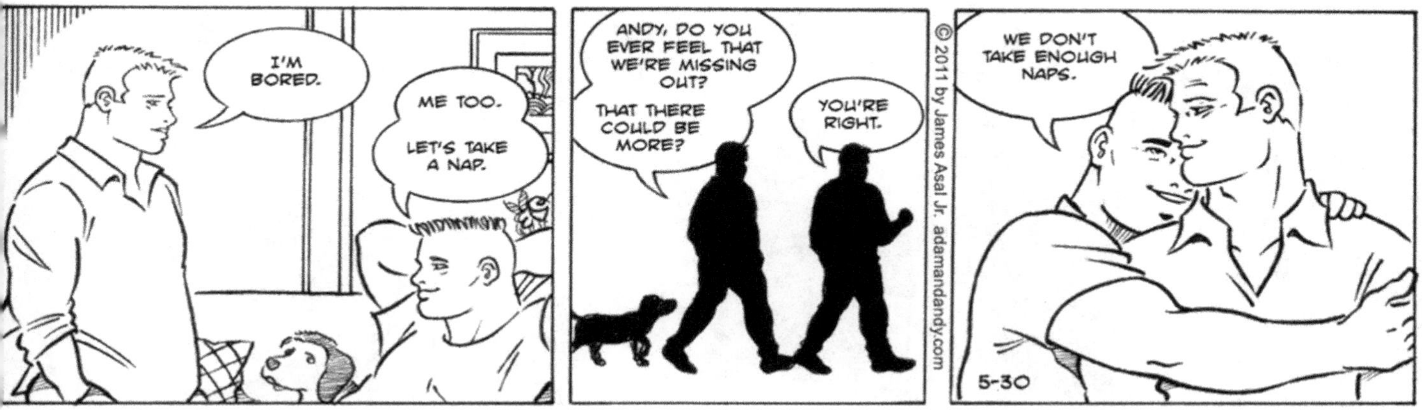
I'M BORED.
ME TOO.
LET'S TAKE A NAP.
ANDY, DO YOU EVER FEEL THAT WE'RE MISSING OUT?
THAT THERE COULD BE MORE?
YOU'RE RIGHT.
© 2011 by James Asal Jr. adamandandy.com
WE DON'T TAKE ENOUGH NAPS.
5-30

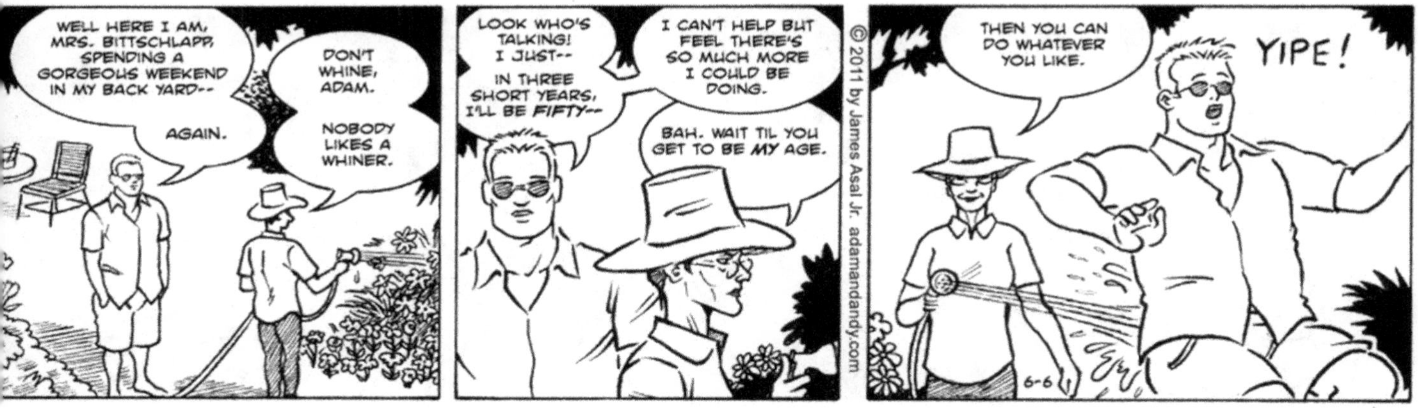
WELL HERE I AM, MRS. BITTSCHLAPP, SPENDING A GORGEOUS WEEKEND IN MY BACK YARD--
AGAIN.
DON'T WHINE, ADAM.
NOBODY LIKES A WHINER.
LOOK WHO'S TALKING! I JUST--
IN THREE SHORT YEARS, I'LL BE *FIFTY*--
I CAN'T HELP BUT FEEL THERE'S SO MUCH MORE I COULD BE DOING.
BAH. WAIT TIL YOU GET TO BE *MY* AGE.
© 2011 by James Asal Jr. adamandandy.com
THEN YOU CAN DO WHATEVER YOU LIKE.
YIPE!
6-6

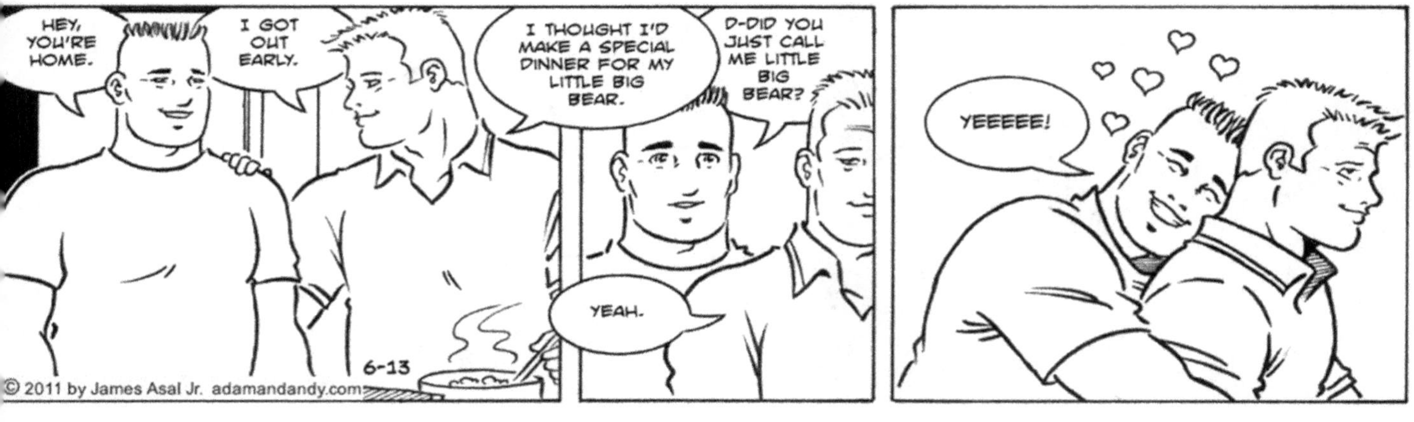
HEY, YOU'RE HOME.
I GOT OUT EARLY.
6-13
© 2011 by James Asal Jr. adamandandy.com
I THOUGHT I'D MAKE A SPECIAL DINNER FOR MY LITTLE BIG BEAR.
D-DID YOU JUST CALL ME LITTLE BIG BEAR?
YEAH.
YEEEEEE!

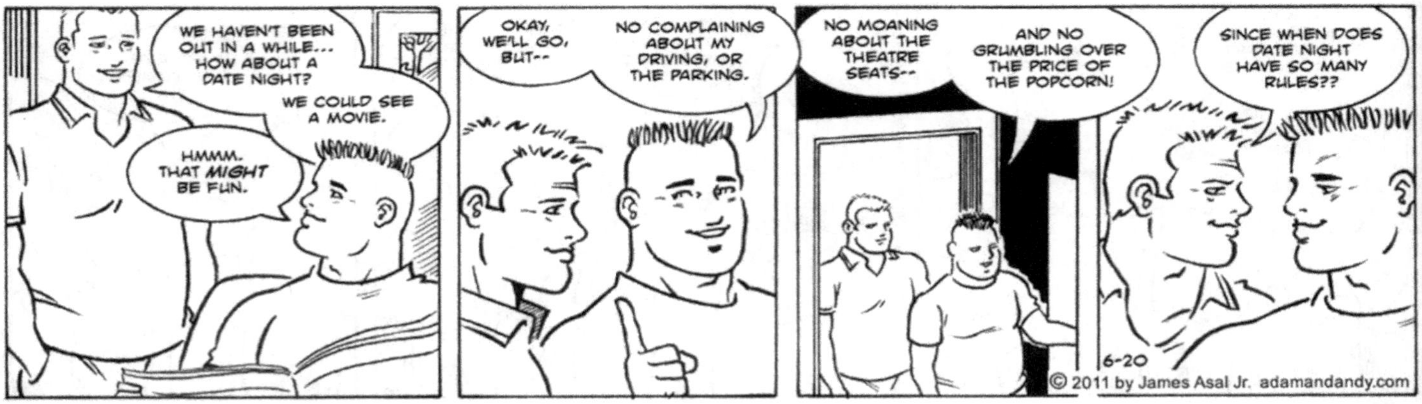
WE HAVEN'T BEEN OUT IN A WHILE... HOW ABOUT A DATE NIGHT?
WE COULD SEE A MOVIE.
HMMM. THAT *MIGHT* BE FUN.
OKAY, WE'LL GO, BUT--
NO COMPLAINING ABOUT MY DRIVING, OR THE PARKING.
NO MOANING ABOUT THE THEATRE SEATS--
AND NO GRUMBLING OVER THE PRICE OF THE POPCORN!
SINCE WHEN DOES DATE NIGHT HAVE SO MANY RULES??
6-20
© 2011 by James Asal Jr. adamandandy.com

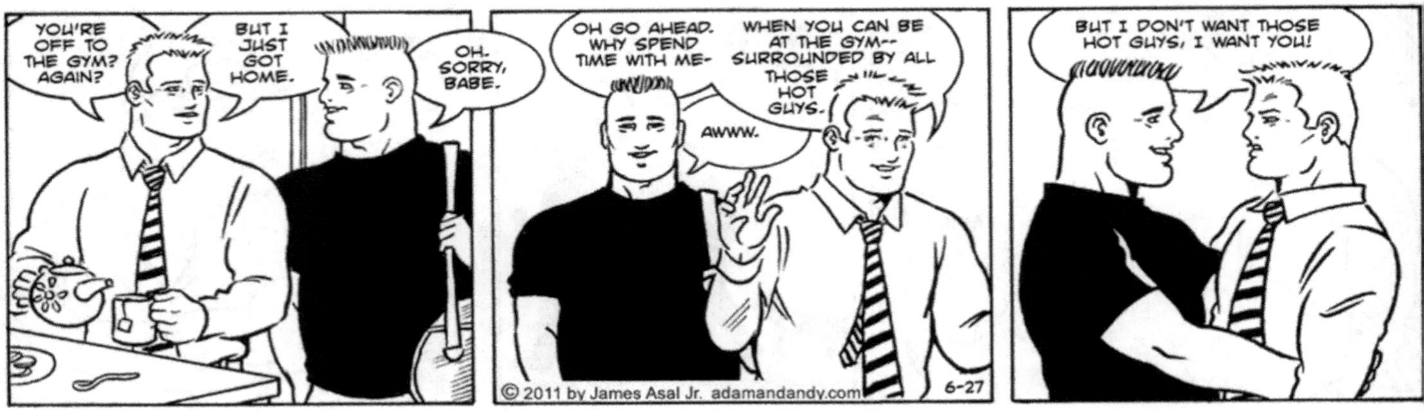
YOU'RE OFF TO THE GYM? AGAIN?
BUT I JUST GOT HOME.
OH. SORRY, BABE.
OH GO AHEAD. WHY SPEND TIME WITH ME-
WHEN YOU CAN BE AT THE GYM-- SURROUNDED BY ALL THOSE HOT GUYS.
AWWW.
BUT I DON'T WANT THOSE HOT GUYS, I WANT YOU!
© 2011 by James Asal Jr. adamandandy.com
6-27

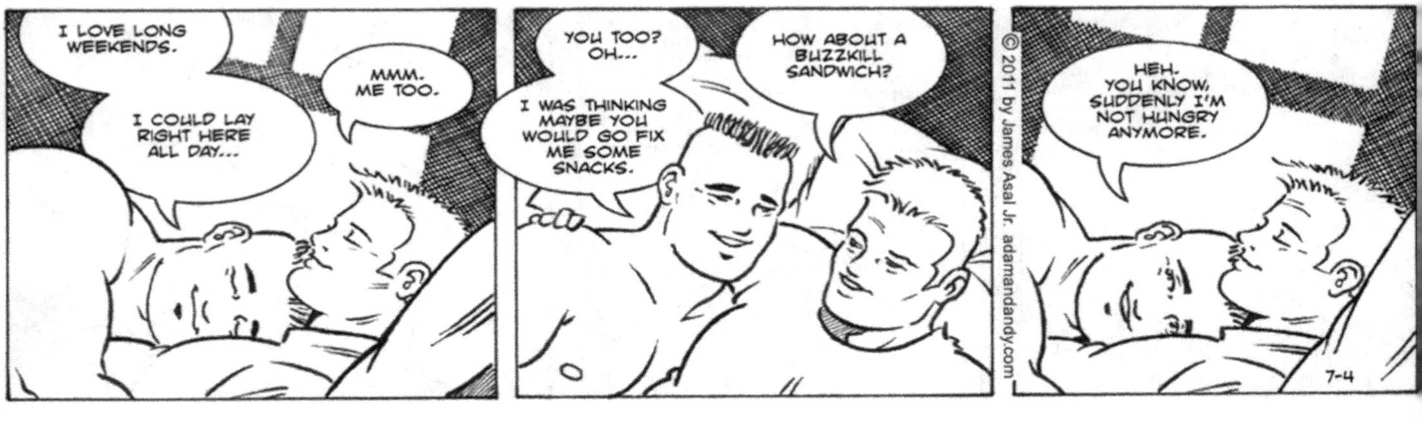
I LOVE LONG WEEKENDS.
MMM. ME TOO.
I COULD LAY RIGHT HERE ALL DAY...
YOU TOO? OH...
HOW ABOUT A BUZZKILL SANDWICH?
I WAS THINKING MAYBE YOU WOULD GO FIX ME SOME SNACKS.
© 2011 by James Asal Jr. adamandandy.com
HEH. YOU KNOW, SUDDENLY I'M NOT HUNGRY ANYMORE.
7-4

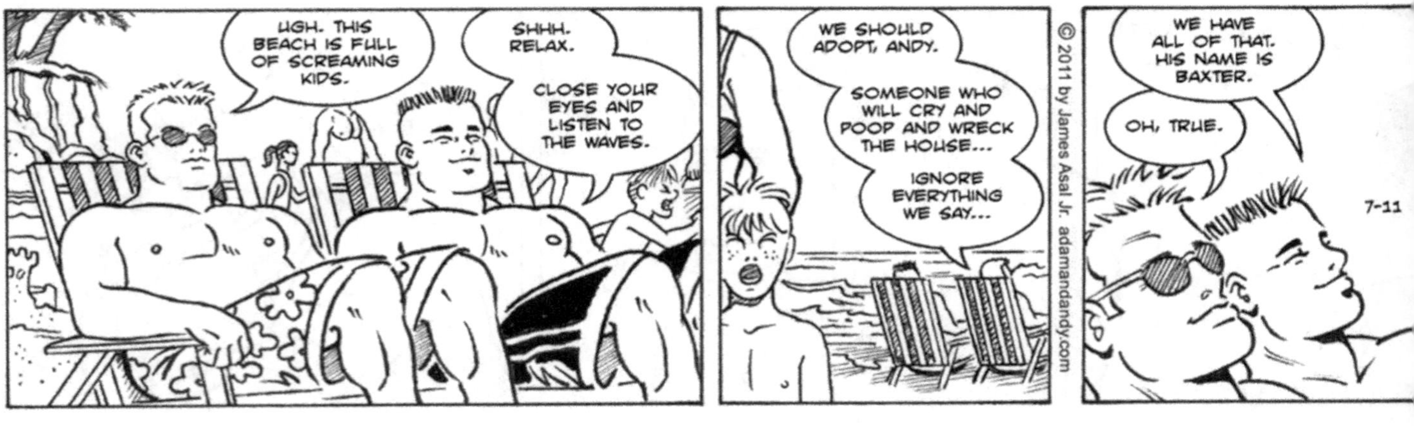
UGH. THIS BEACH IS FULL OF SCREAMING KIDS.
SHHH. RELAX.
CLOSE YOUR EYES AND LISTEN TO THE WAVES.
WE SHOULD ADOPT, ANDY.
SOMEONE WHO WILL CRY AND POOP AND WRECK THE HOUSE...
IGNORE EVERYTHING WE SAY...
© 2011 by James Asal Jr. adamandandy.com
WE HAVE ALL OF THAT. HIS NAME IS BAXTER.
OH, TRUE.
7-11

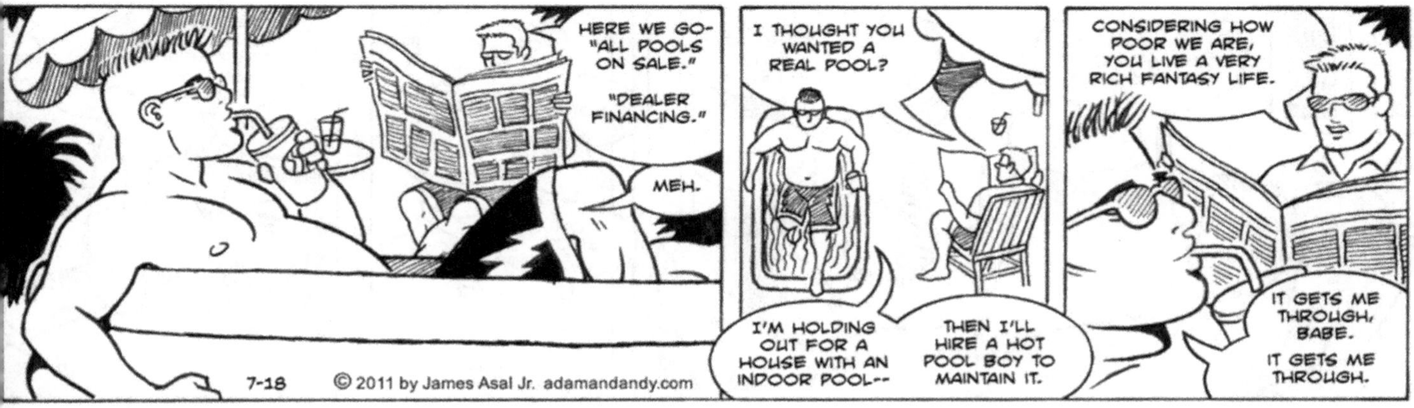
HERE WE GO- "ALL POOLS ON SALE."
"DEALER FINANCING."
MEH.
7-18
© 2011 by James Asal Jr. adamandandy.com
I THOUGHT YOU WANTED A REAL POOL?
I'M HOLDING OUT FOR A HOUSE WITH AN INDOOR POOL--
THEN I'LL HIRE A HOT POOL BOY TO MAINTAIN IT.
CONSIDERING HOW POOR WE ARE, YOU LIVE A VERY RICH FANTASY LIFE.
IT GETS ME THROUGH, BABE.
IT GETS ME THROUGH.

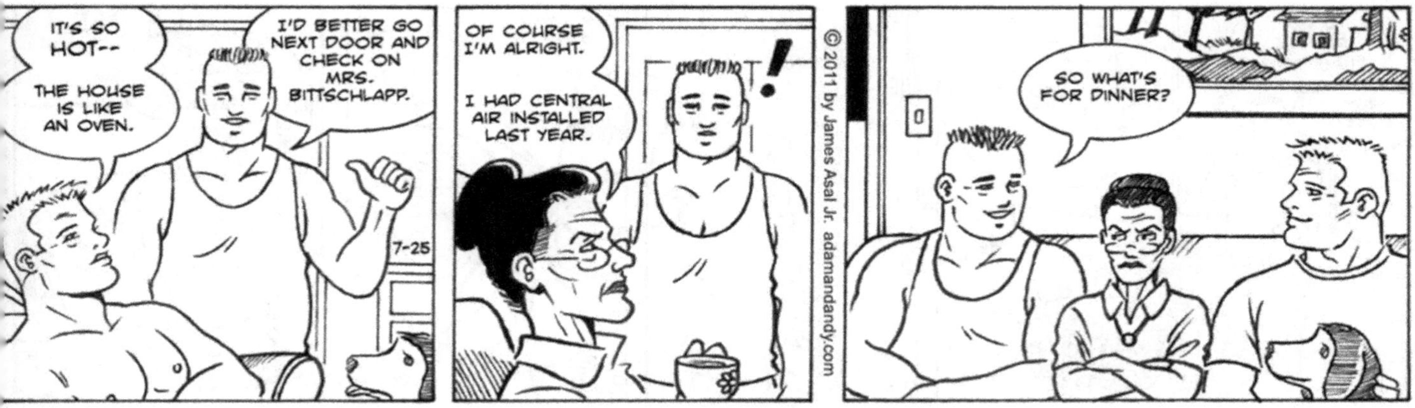
IT'S SO HOT--
THE HOUSE IS LIKE AN OVEN.
I'D BETTER GO NEXT DOOR AND CHECK ON MRS. BITTSCHLAPP.
7-25
OF COURSE I'M ALRIGHT.
I HAD CENTRAL AIR INSTALLED LAST YEAR.
!
© 2011 by James Asal Jr. adamandandy.com
SO WHAT'S FOR DINNER?

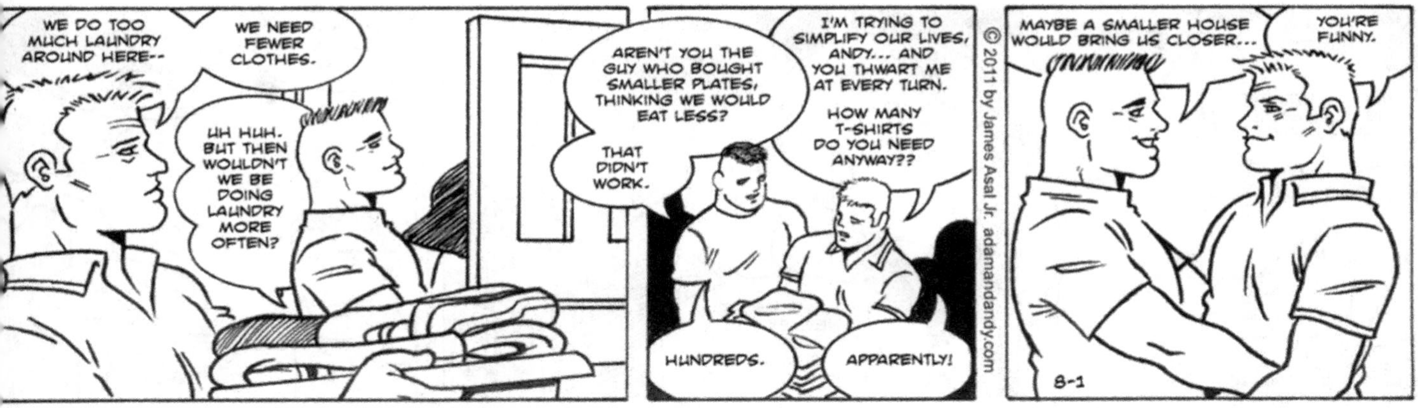
WE DO TOO MUCH LAUNDRY AROUND HERE--
WE NEED FEWER CLOTHES.
UH HUH. BUT THEN WOULDN'T WE BE DOING LAUNDRY MORE OFTEN?
AREN'T YOU THE GUY WHO BOUGHT SMALLER PLATES, THINKING WE WOULD EAT LESS?
THAT DIDN'T WORK.
I'M TRYING TO SIMPLIFY OUR LIVES, ANDY... AND YOU THWART ME AT EVERY TURN.
HOW MANY T-SHIRTS DO YOU NEED ANYWAY??
HUNDREDS.
APPARENTLY!
© 2011 by James Asal Jr. adamandandy.com
MAYBE A SMALLER HOUSE WOULD BRING US CLOSER...
YOU'RE FUNNY.
8-1

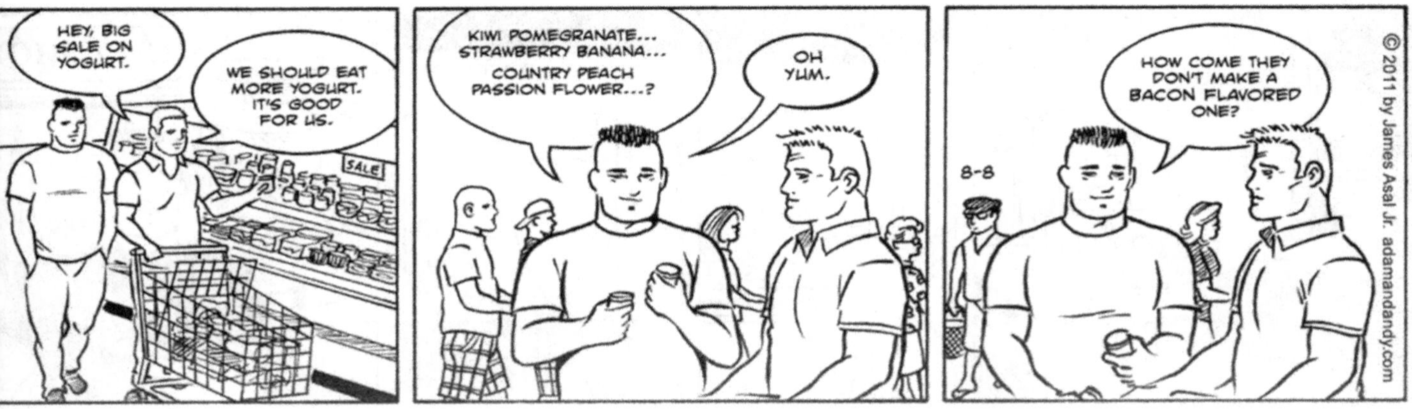
HEY, BIG SALE ON YOGURT.
WE SHOULD EAT MORE YOGURT. IT'S GOOD FOR US.
SALE
KIWI POMEGRANATE... STRAWBERRY BANANA...
COUNTRY PEACH PASSION FLOWER...?
OH YUM.
8-8
HOW COME THEY DON'T MAKE A BACON FLAVORED ONE?
© 2011 by James Asal Jr. adamandandy.com

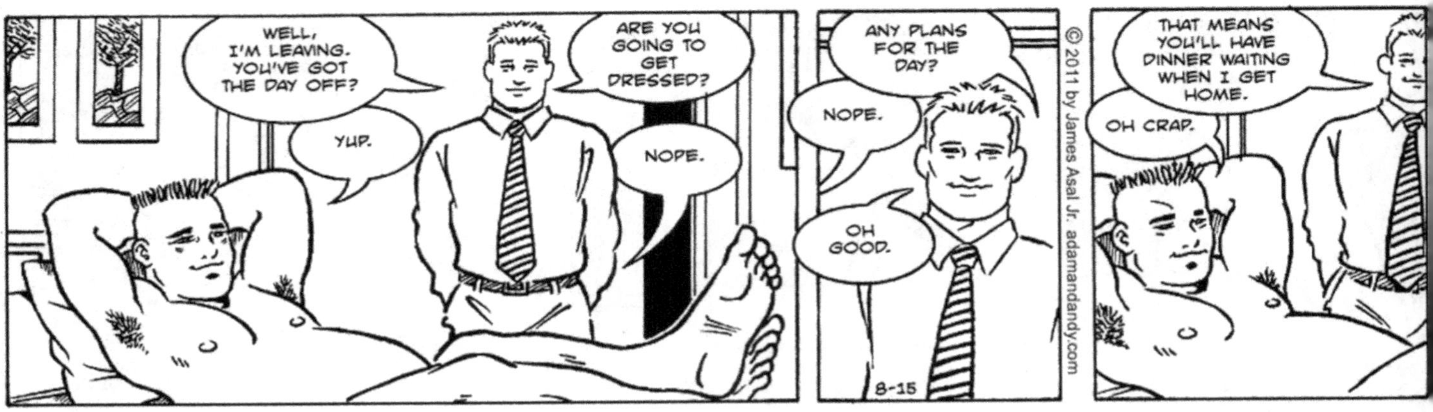
WELL, I'M LEAVING. YOU'VE GOT THE DAY OFF?
YUP.
ARE YOU GOING TO GET DRESSED?
NOPE.
ANY PLANS FOR THE DAY?
NOPE.
OH GOOD.
8-15
© 2011 by James Asal Jr. adamandandy.com
THAT MEANS YOU'LL HAVE DINNER WAITING WHEN I GET HOME.
OH CRAP.

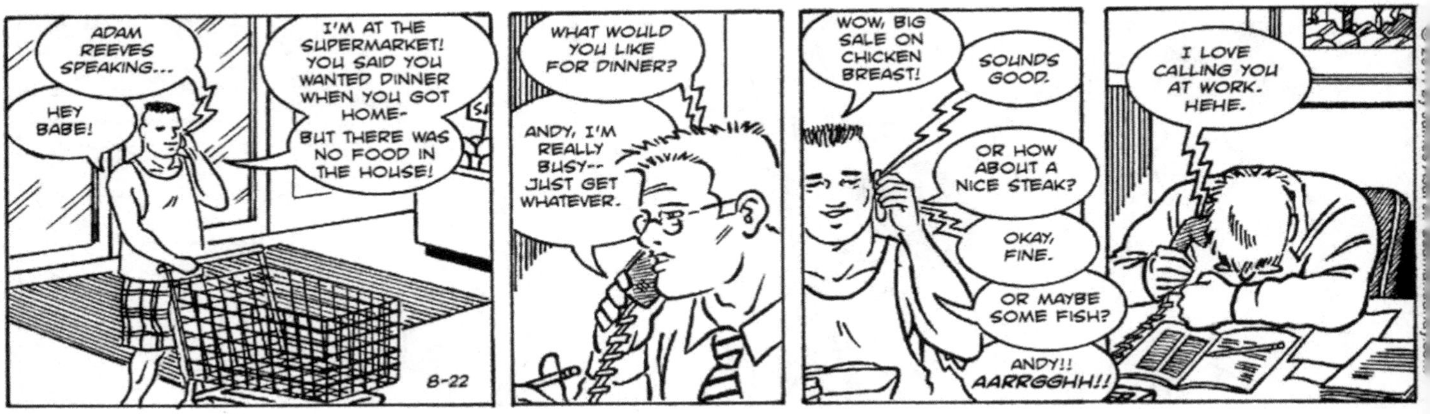
ADAM REEVES SPEAKING...
HEY BABE!
I'M AT THE SUPERMARKET! YOU SAID YOU WANTED DINNER WHEN YOU GOT HOME-
BUT THERE WAS NO FOOD IN THE HOUSE!
8-22
WHAT WOULD YOU LIKE FOR DINNER?
ANDY, I'M REALLY BUSY-- JUST GET WHATEVER.
WOW, BIG SALE ON CHICKEN BREAST!
SOUNDS GOOD.
OR HOW ABOUT A NICE STEAK?
OKAY, FINE.
OR MAYBE SOME FISH?
ANDY!! AARRGGHH!!
I LOVE CALLING YOU AT WORK. HEHE.

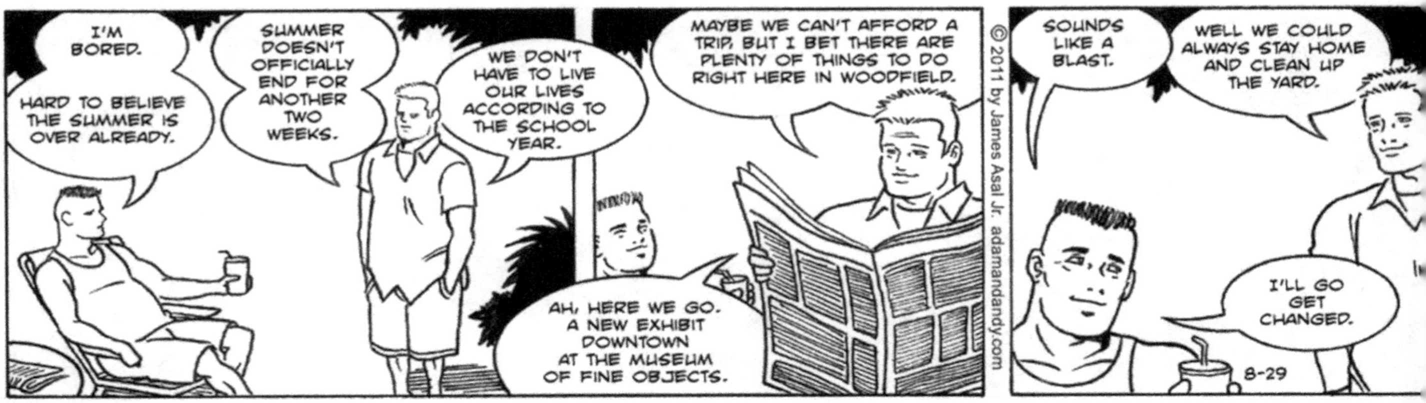
I'M BORED.
HARD TO BELIEVE THE SUMMER IS OVER ALREADY.
SUMMER DOESN'T OFFICIALLY END FOR ANOTHER TWO WEEKS.
WE DON'T HAVE TO LIVE OUR LIVES ACCORDING TO THE SCHOOL YEAR.
MAYBE WE CAN'T AFFORD A TRIP, BUT I BET THERE ARE PLENTY OF THINGS TO DO RIGHT HERE IN WOODFIELD.
AH, HERE WE GO. A NEW EXHIBIT DOWNTOWN AT THE MUSEUM OF FINE OBJECTS.
© 2011 by James Asal Jr. adamandandy.com
SOUNDS LIKE A BLAST.
WELL WE COULD ALWAYS STAY HOME AND CLEAN UP THE YARD.
I'LL GO GET CHANGED.
8-29

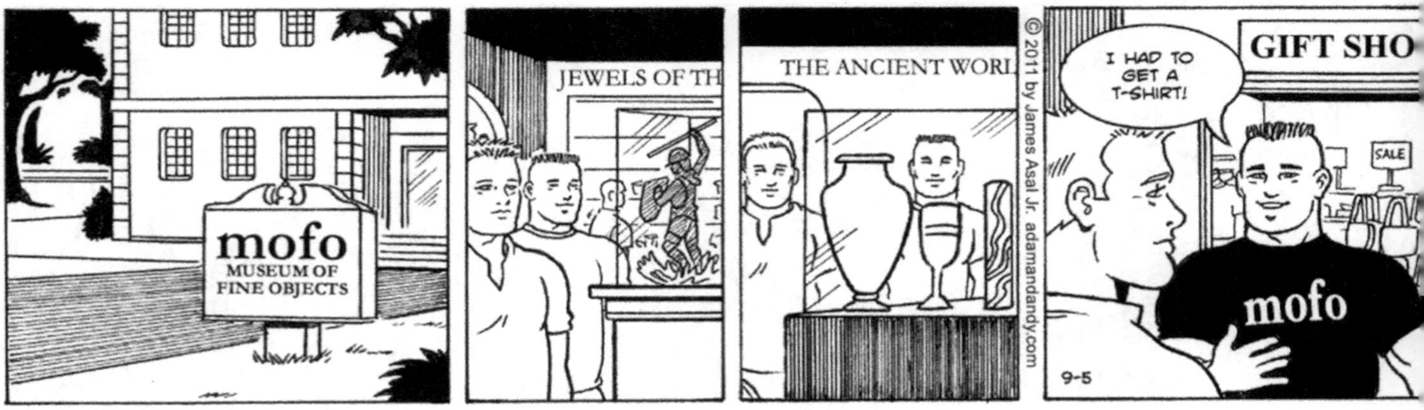
mofo
MUSEUM OF FINE OBJECTS
JEWELS OF TH
THE ANCIENT WORL
© 2011 by James Asal Jr. adamandandy.com
GIFT SHO
I HAD TO GET A T-SHIRT!
SALE
mofo
9-5

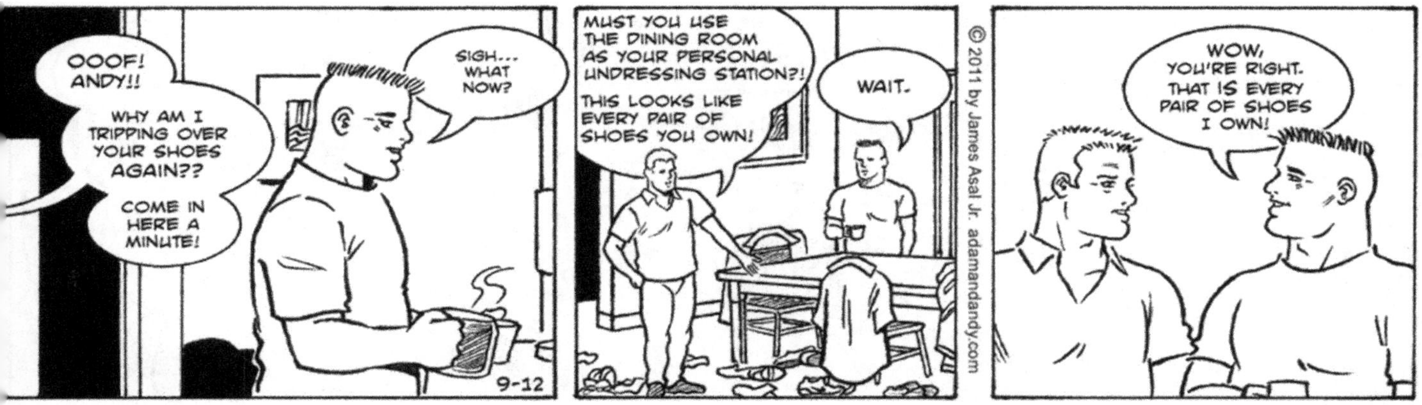
OOOF! ANDY!!
WHY AM I TRIPPING OVER YOUR SHOES AGAIN??
COME IN HERE A MINUTE!
SIGH... WHAT NOW?
9-12
MUST YOU USE THE DINING ROOM AS YOUR PERSONAL UNDRESSING STATION?!
THIS LOOKS LIKE EVERY PAIR OF SHOES YOU OWN!
WAIT.
© 2011 by James Asal Jr. adamandandy.com
WOW, YOU'RE RIGHT. THAT IS EVERY PAIR OF SHOES I OWN!

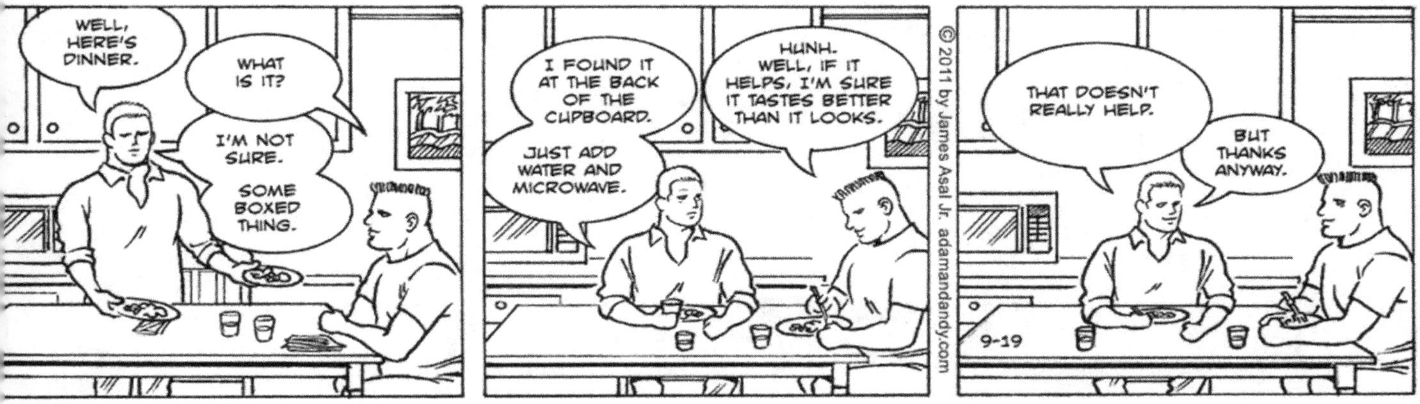
WELL, HERE'S DINNER.
WHAT IS IT?
I'M NOT SURE.
SOME BOXED THING.
I FOUND IT AT THE BACK OF THE CUPBOARD.
JUST ADD WATER AND MICROWAVE.
HUNH. WELL, IF IT HELPS, I'M SURE IT TASTES BETTER THAN IT LOOKS.
© 2011 by James Asal Jr. adamandandy.com
THAT DOESN'T REALLY HELP.
BUT THANKS ANYWAY.
9-19

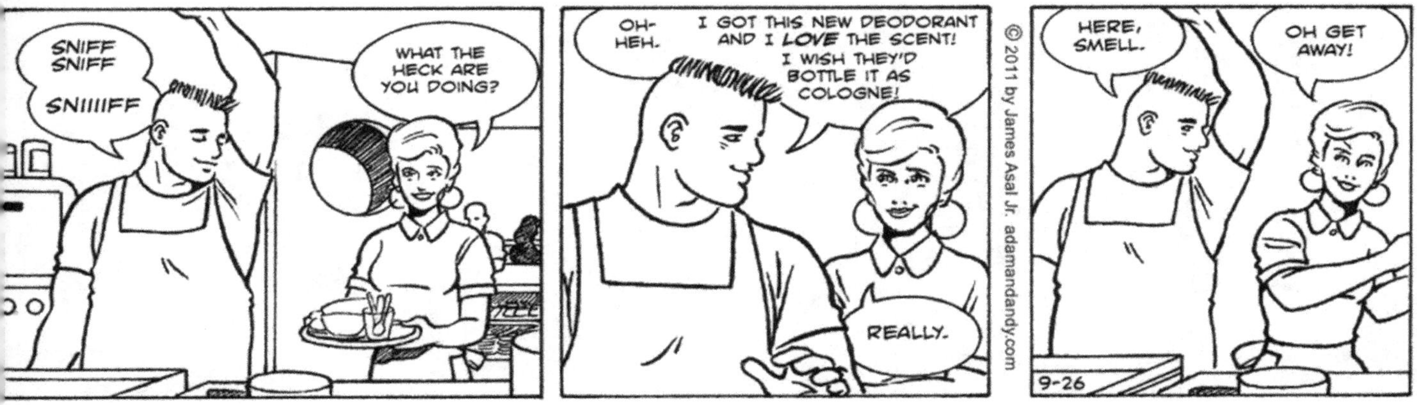
SNIFF SNIFF
SNIIIIFF
WHAT THE HECK ARE YOU DOING?
OH-HEH.
I GOT THIS NEW DEODORANT AND I LOVE THE SCENT! I WISH THEY'D BOTTLE IT AS COLOGNE!
REALLY.
© 2011 by James Asal Jr. adamandandy.com
HERE, SMELL.
OH GET AWAY!
9-26

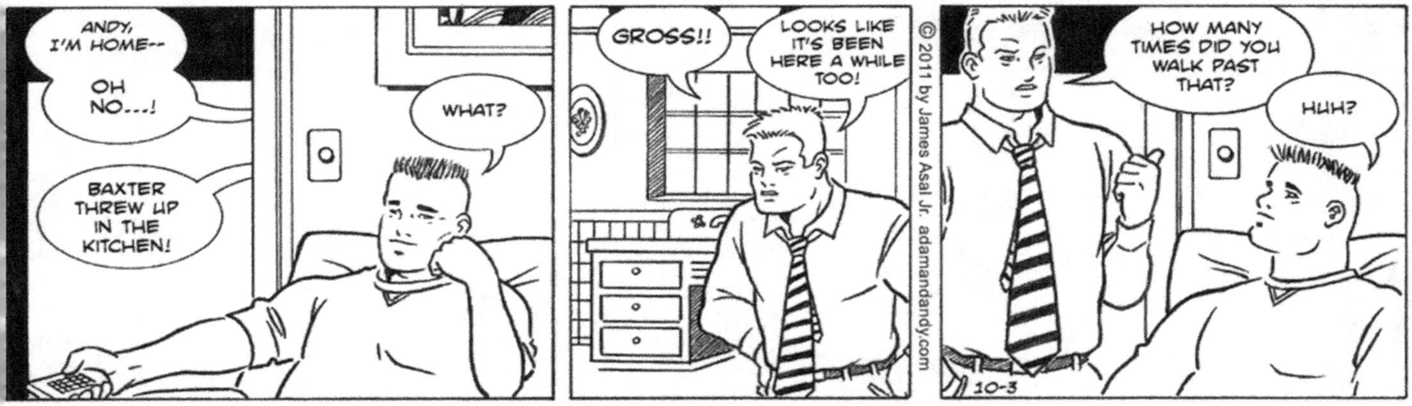
ANDY, I'M HOME--
OH NO...!
BAXTER THREW UP IN THE KITCHEN!
WHAT?
GROSS!!
LOOKS LIKE IT'S BEEN HERE A WHILE TOO!
© 2011 by James Asal Jr. adamandandy.com
HOW MANY TIMES DID YOU WALK PAST THAT?
HUH?
10-3

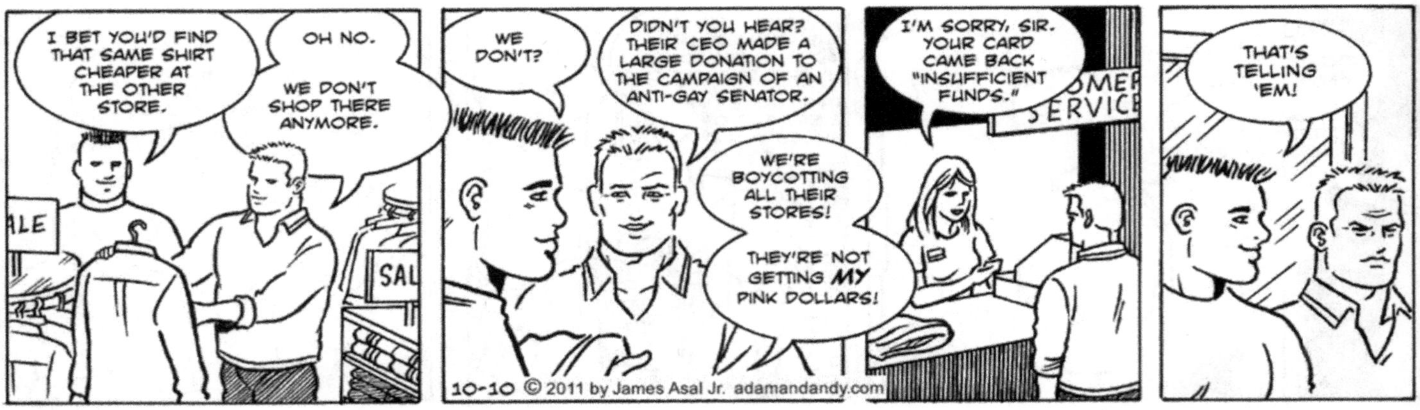

I BET YOU'D FIND THAT SAME SHIRT CHEAPER AT THE OTHER STORE.
OH NO.
WE DON'T SHOP THERE ANYMORE.
ALE
SAL
WE DON'T?
DIDN'T YOU HEAR? THEIR CEO MADE A LARGE DONATION TO THE CAMPAIGN OF AN ANTI-GAY SENATOR.
WE'RE BOYCOTTING ALL THEIR STORES!
THEY'RE NOT GETTING **MY** PINK DOLLARS!
10-10 © 2011 by James Asal Jr. adamandandy.com
I'M SORRY, SIR. YOUR CARD CAME BACK "INSUFFICIENT FUNDS."
SERVICE
THAT'S TELLING 'EM!

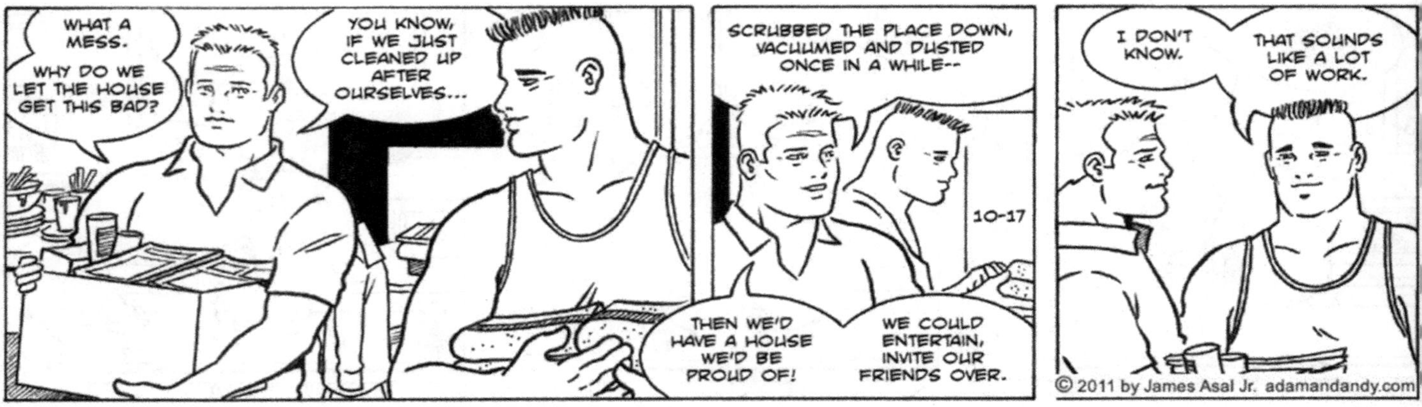

WHAT A MESS.
WHY DO WE LET THE HOUSE GET THIS BAD?
YOU KNOW, IF WE JUST CLEANED UP AFTER OURSELVES...
SCRUBBED THE PLACE DOWN, VACUUMED AND DUSTED ONCE IN A WHILE--
10-17
THEN WE'D HAVE A HOUSE WE'D BE PROUD OF!
WE COULD ENTERTAIN, INVITE OUR FRIENDS OVER.
I DON'T KNOW.
THAT SOUNDS LIKE A LOT OF WORK.
© 2011 by James Asal Jr. adamandandy.com

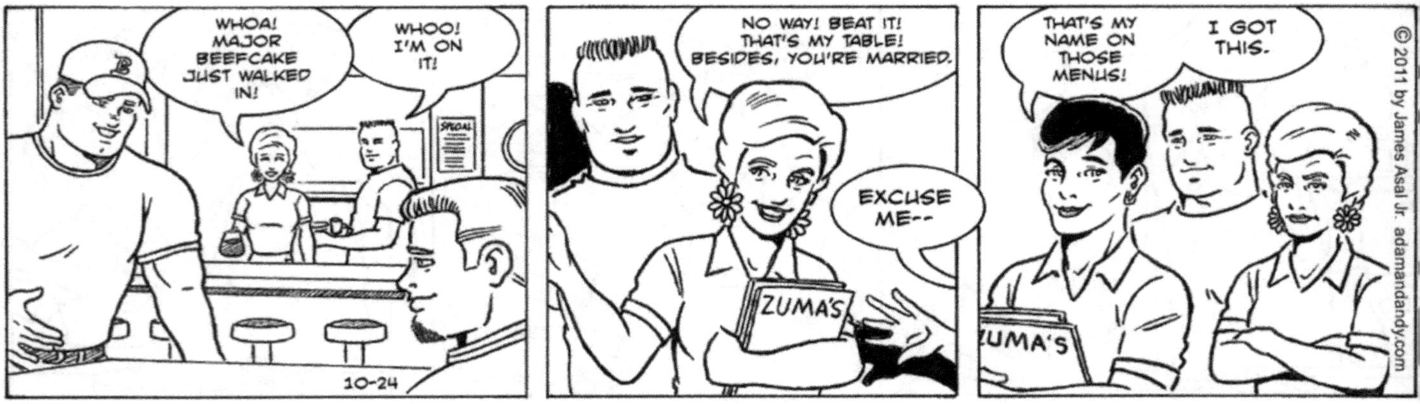

WHOA! MAJOR BEEFCAKE JUST WALKED IN!
WHOO! I'M ON IT!
SPECIAL
10-24
NO WAY! BEAT IT! THAT'S MY TABLE! BESIDES, YOU'RE MARRIED.
EXCUSE ME--
ZUMA'S
THAT'S MY NAME ON THOSE MENUS!
I GOT THIS.
ZUMA'S
© 2011 by James Asal Jr. adamandandy.com

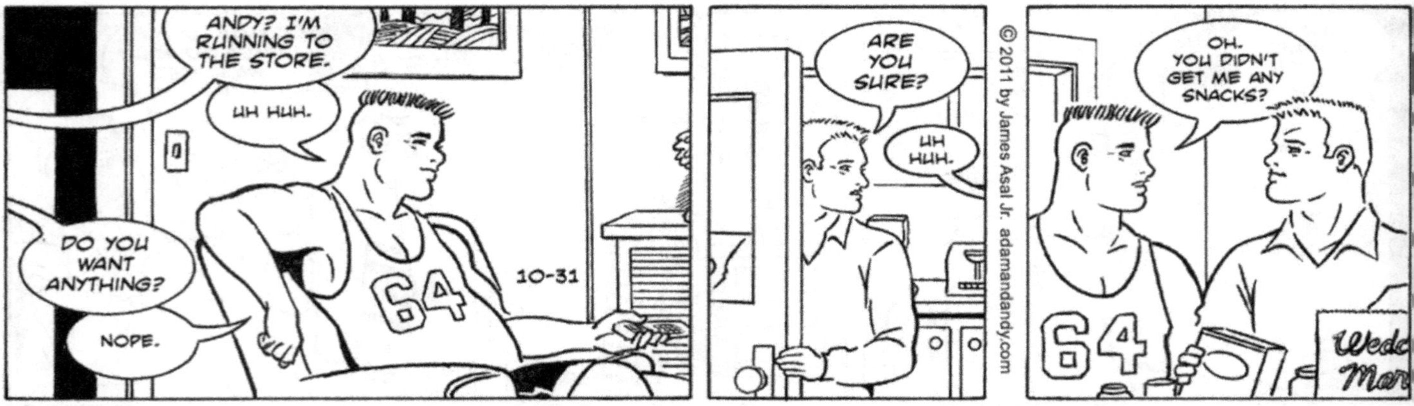

ANDY? I'M RUNNING TO THE STORE.
UH HUH.
DO YOU WANT ANYTHING?
NOPE.
64
10-31
ARE YOU SURE?
UH HUH.
© 2011 by James Asal Jr. adamandandy.com
OH. YOU DIDN'T GET ME ANY SNACKS?
64

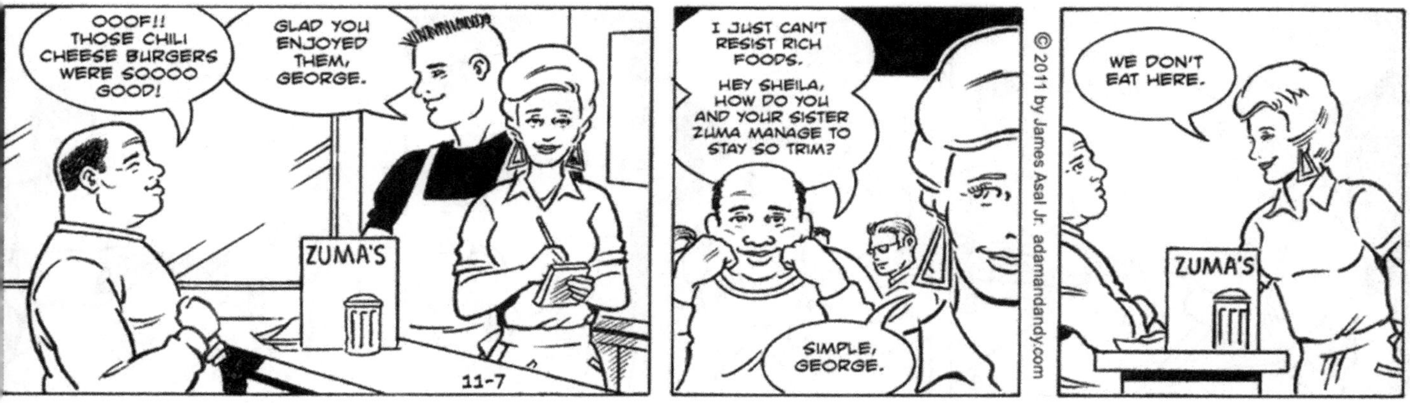
OOOF!! THOSE CHILI CHEESE BURGERS WERE SOOOO GOOD!
GLAD YOU ENJOYED THEM, GEORGE.
ZUMA'S
11-7
I JUST CAN'T RESIST RICH FOODS.
HEY SHEILA, HOW DO YOU AND YOUR SISTER ZUMA MANAGE TO STAY SO TRIM?
SIMPLE, GEORGE.
© 2011 by James Asal Jr. adamandandy.com
WE DON'T EAT HERE.
ZUMA'S

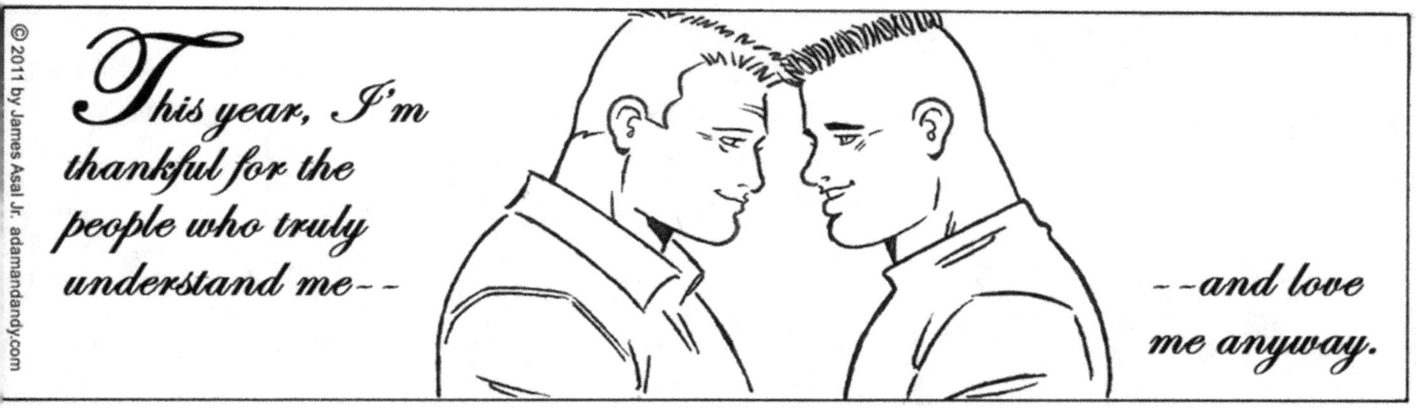
© 2011 by James Asal Jr. adamandandy.com
This year, I'm thankful for the people who truly understand me--
--and love me anyway.

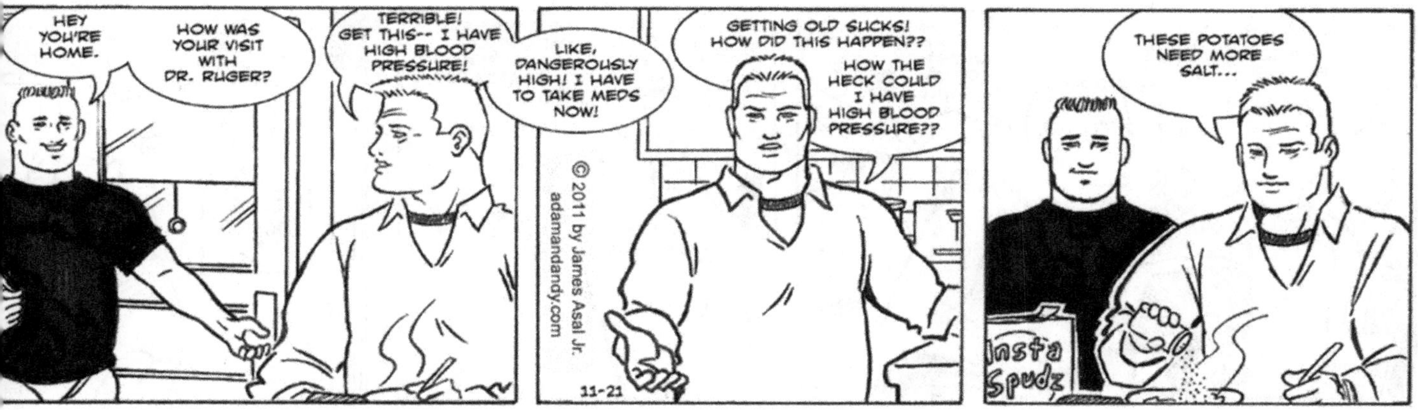
HEY YOU'RE HOME.
HOW WAS YOUR VISIT WITH DR. RUGER?
TERRIBLE! GET THIS-- I HAVE HIGH BLOOD PRESSURE!
LIKE, DANGEROUSLY HIGH! I HAVE TO TAKE MEDS NOW!
© 2011 by James Asal Jr. adamandandy.com
GETTING OLD SUCKS! HOW DID THIS HAPPEN??
HOW THE HECK COULD I HAVE HIGH BLOOD PRESSURE??
11-21
THESE POTATOES NEED MORE SALT...
Insta Spudz

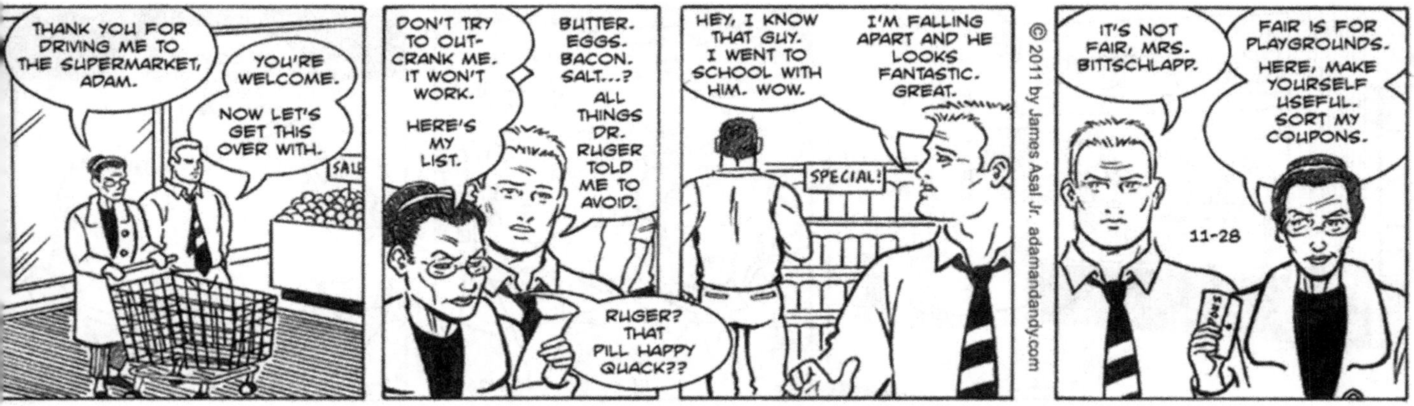
THANK YOU FOR DRIVING ME TO THE SUPERMARKET, ADAM.
YOU'RE WELCOME.
NOW LET'S GET THIS OVER WITH.
SALE
DON'T TRY TO OUT-CRANK ME. IT WON'T WORK.
HERE'S MY LIST.
BUTTER. EGGS. BACON. SALT...?
ALL THINGS DR. RUGER TOLD ME TO AVOID.
RUGER? THAT PILL HAPPY QUACK??
HEY, I KNOW THAT GUY. I WENT TO SCHOOL WITH HIM. WOW.
I'M FALLING APART AND HE LOOKS FANTASTIC. GREAT.
SPECIAL!
© 2011 by James Asal Jr. adamandandy.com
IT'S NOT FAIR, MRS. BITTSCHLAPP.
FAIR IS FOR PLAYGROUNDS. HERE, MAKE YOURSELF USEFUL. SORT MY COUPONS.
11-28

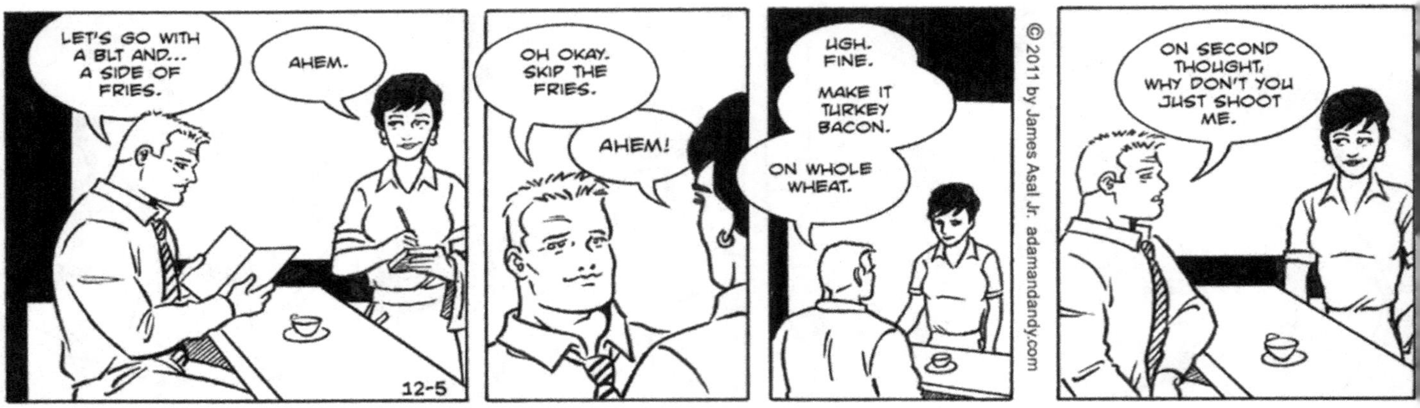
LET'S GO WITH A BLT AND... A SIDE OF FRIES.
AHEM.
12-5
OH OKAY. SKIP THE FRIES.
AHEM!
UGH. FINE.
MAKE IT TURKEY BACON.
ON WHOLE WHEAT.
© 2011 by James Asal Jr. adamandandy.com
ON SECOND THOUGHT, WHY DON'T YOU JUST SHOOT ME.

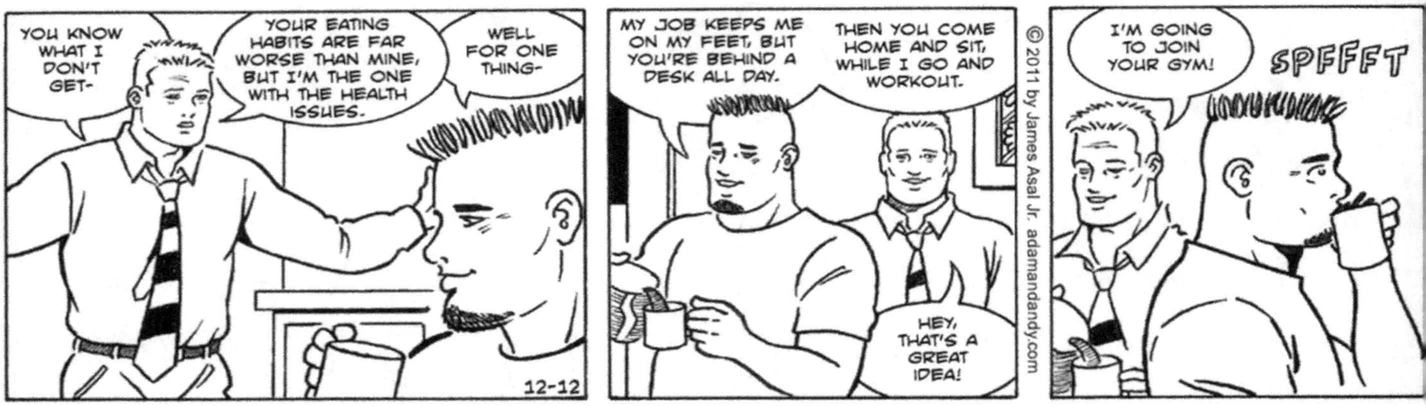
YOU KNOW WHAT I DON'T GET-
YOUR EATING HABITS ARE FAR WORSE THAN MINE, BUT I'M THE ONE WITH THE HEALTH ISSUES.
WELL FOR ONE THING-
12-12
MY JOB KEEPS ME ON MY FEET, BUT YOU'RE BEHIND A DESK ALL DAY.
THEN YOU COME HOME AND SIT, WHILE I GO AND WORKOUT.
HEY, THAT'S A GREAT IDEA!
© 2011 by James Asal Jr. adamandandy.com
I'M GOING TO JOIN YOUR GYM!
SPFFFT

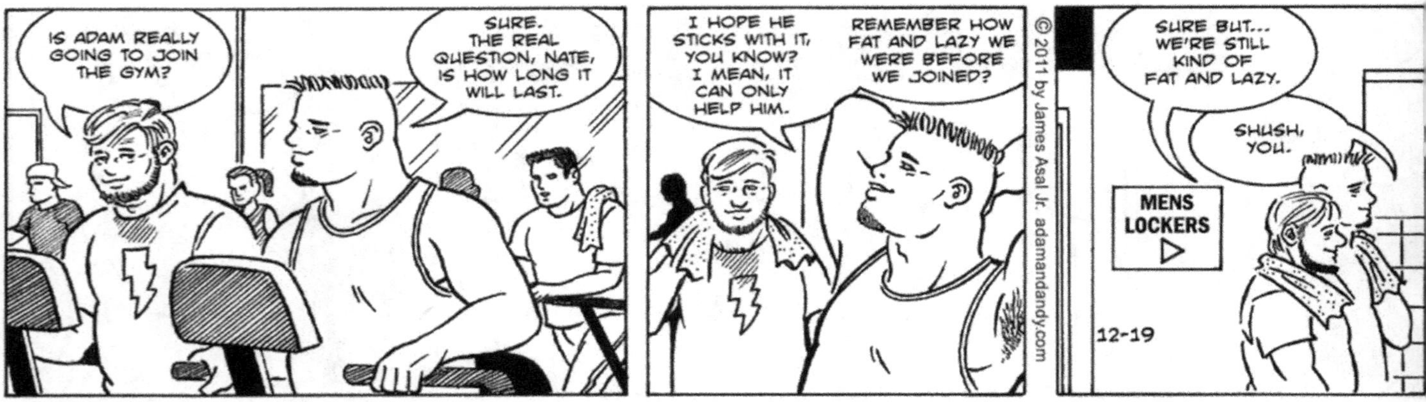
IS ADAM REALLY GOING TO JOIN THE GYM?
SURE. THE REAL QUESTION, NATE, IS HOW LONG IT WILL LAST.
I HOPE HE STICKS WITH IT, YOU KNOW? I MEAN, IT CAN ONLY HELP HIM.
REMEMBER HOW FAT AND LAZY WE WERE BEFORE WE JOINED?
© 2011 by James Asal Jr. adamandandy.com
SURE BUT... WE'RE STILL KIND OF FAT AND LAZY.
SHUSH, YOU.
MENS LOCKERS
12-19

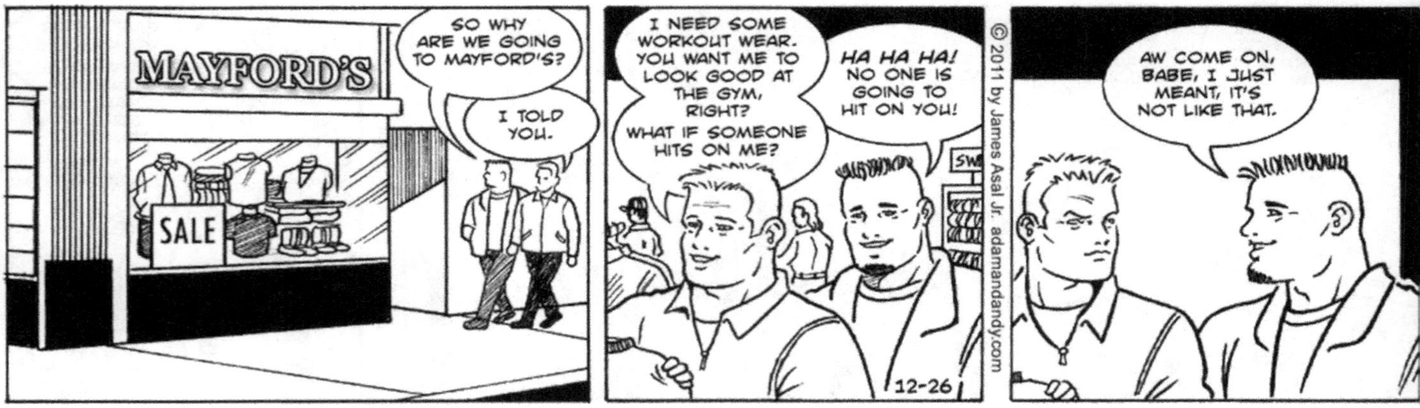
MAYFORD'S
SALE
SO WHY ARE WE GOING TO MAYFORD'S?
I TOLD YOU.
I NEED SOME WORKOUT WEAR. YOU WANT ME TO LOOK GOOD AT THE GYM, RIGHT?
WHAT IF SOMEONE HITS ON ME?
HA HA HA! NO ONE IS GOING TO HIT ON YOU!
12-26
© 2011 by James Asal Jr. adamandandy.com
AW COME ON, BABE, I JUST MEANT, IT'S NOT LIKE THAT.

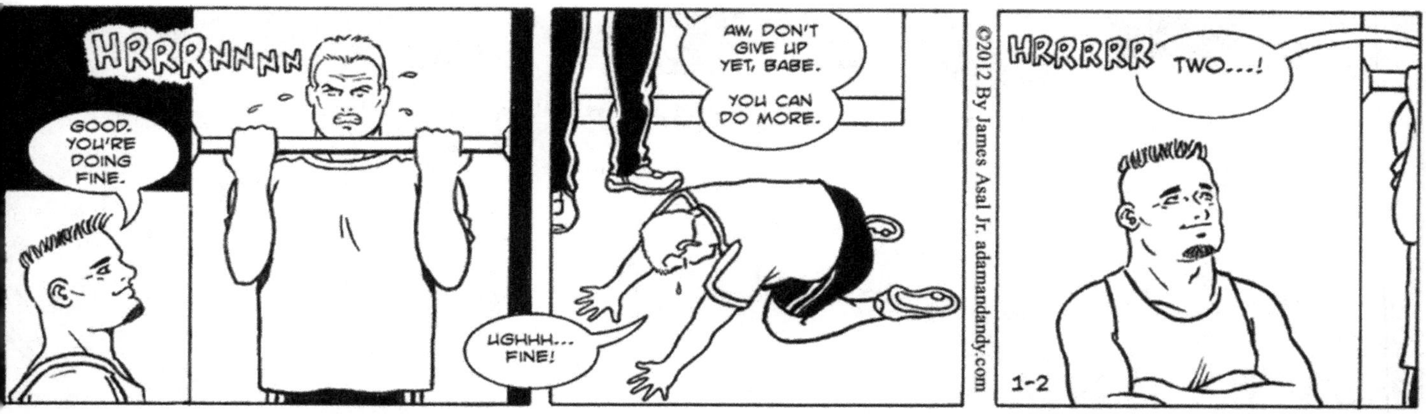
HRRRNNNNN
GOOD. YOU'RE DOING FINE.
AW, DON'T GIVE UP YET, BABE.
YOU CAN DO MORE.
UGHHH... FINE!
©2012 By James Asal Jr. adamandandy.com
HRRRRR
TWO...!
1-2

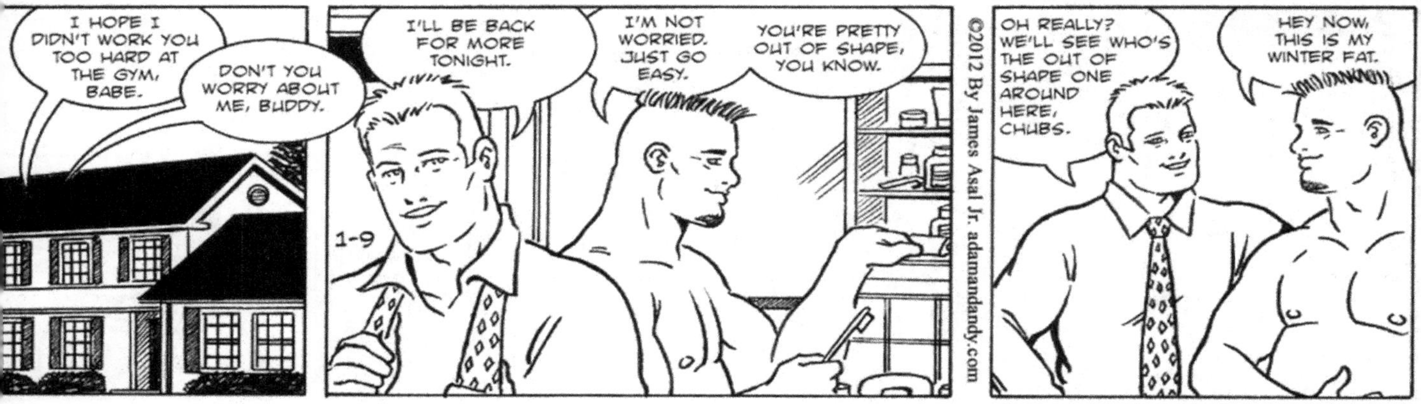
I HOPE I DIDN'T WORK YOU TOO HARD AT THE GYM, BABE.
DON'T YOU WORRY ABOUT ME, BUDDY.
I'LL BE BACK FOR MORE TONIGHT.
I'M NOT WORRIED. JUST GO EASY.
YOU'RE PRETTY OUT OF SHAPE, YOU KNOW.
1-9
©2012 By James Asal Jr. adamandandy.com
OH REALLY? WE'LL SEE WHO'S THE OUT OF SHAPE ONE AROUND HERE, CHUBS.
HEY NOW, THIS IS MY WINTER FAT.

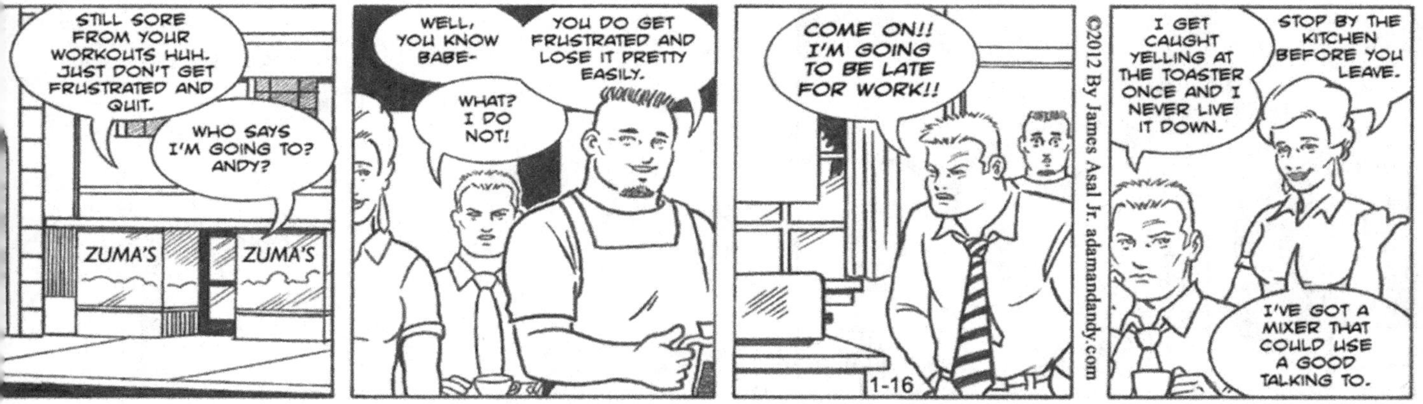
STILL SORE FROM YOUR WORKOUTS HUH. JUST DON'T GET FRUSTRATED AND QUIT.
WHO SAYS I'M GOING TO? ANDY?
ZUMA'S
ZUMA'S
WELL, YOU KNOW BABE-
YOU DO GET FRUSTRATED AND LOSE IT PRETTY EASILY.
WHAT? I DO NOT!
COME ON!! I'M GOING TO BE LATE FOR WORK!!
1-16
©2012 By James Asal Jr. adamandandy.com
I GET CAUGHT YELLING AT THE TOASTER ONCE AND I NEVER LIVE IT DOWN.
STOP BY THE KITCHEN BEFORE YOU LEAVE.
I'VE GOT A MIXER THAT COULD USE A GOOD TALKING TO.

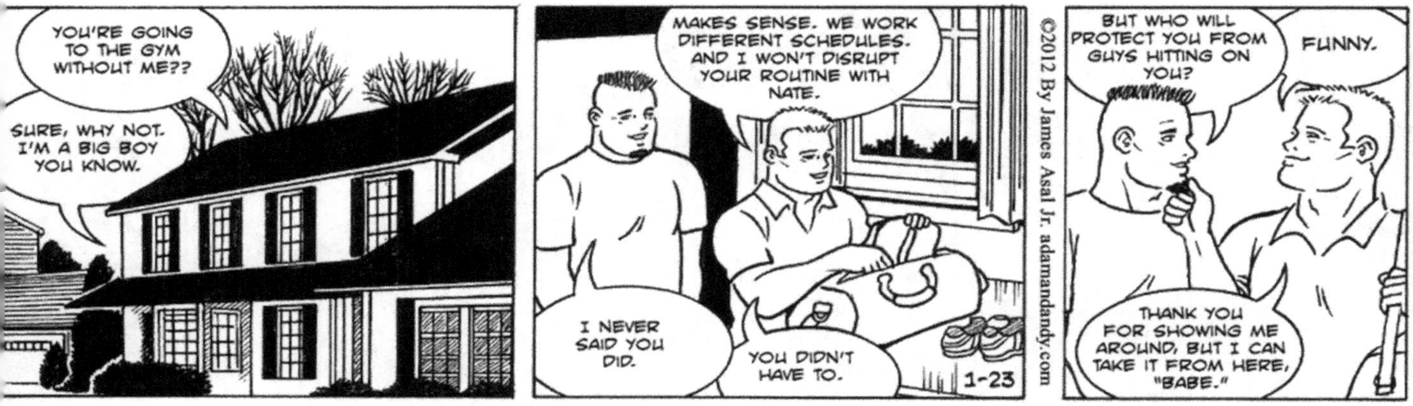
YOU'RE GOING TO THE GYM WITHOUT ME??
SURE, WHY NOT. I'M A BIG BOY YOU KNOW.
MAKES SENSE. WE WORK DIFFERENT SCHEDULES. AND I WON'T DISRUPT YOUR ROUTINE WITH NATE.
I NEVER SAID YOU DID.
YOU DIDN'T HAVE TO.
1-23
©2012 By James Asal Jr. adamandandy.com
BUT WHO WILL PROTECT YOU FROM GUYS HITTING ON YOU?
FUNNY.
THANK YOU FOR SHOWING ME AROUND, BUT I CAN TAKE IT FROM HERE, "BABE."

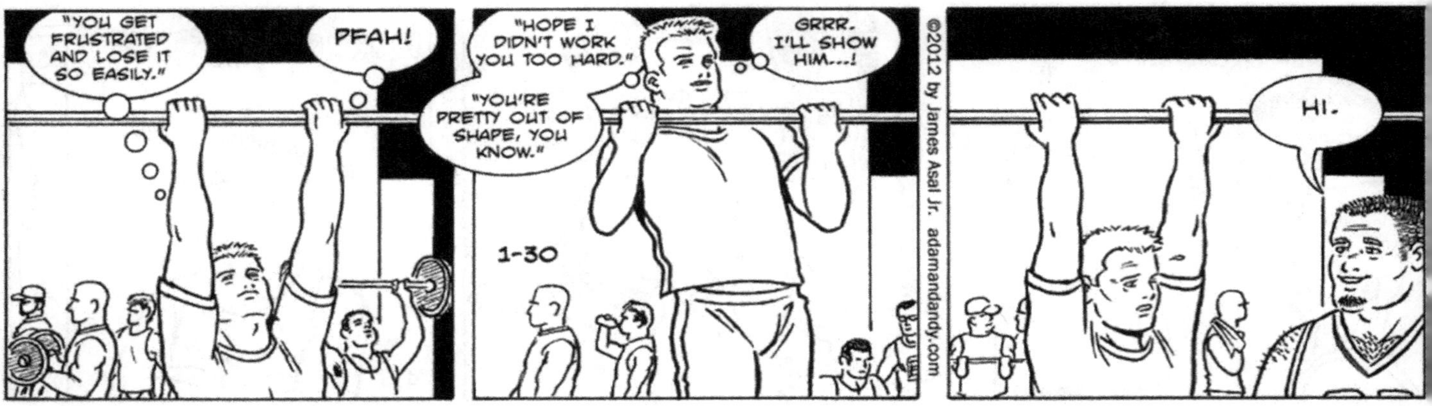
"YOU GET FRUSTRATED AND LOSE IT SO EASILY."
PFAH!
"HOPE I DIDN'T WORK YOU TOO HARD."
"YOU'RE PRETTY OUT OF SHAPE, YOU KNOW."
GRRR. I'LL SHOW HIM...!
1-30
©2012 by James Asal Jr. adamandandy.com
HI.

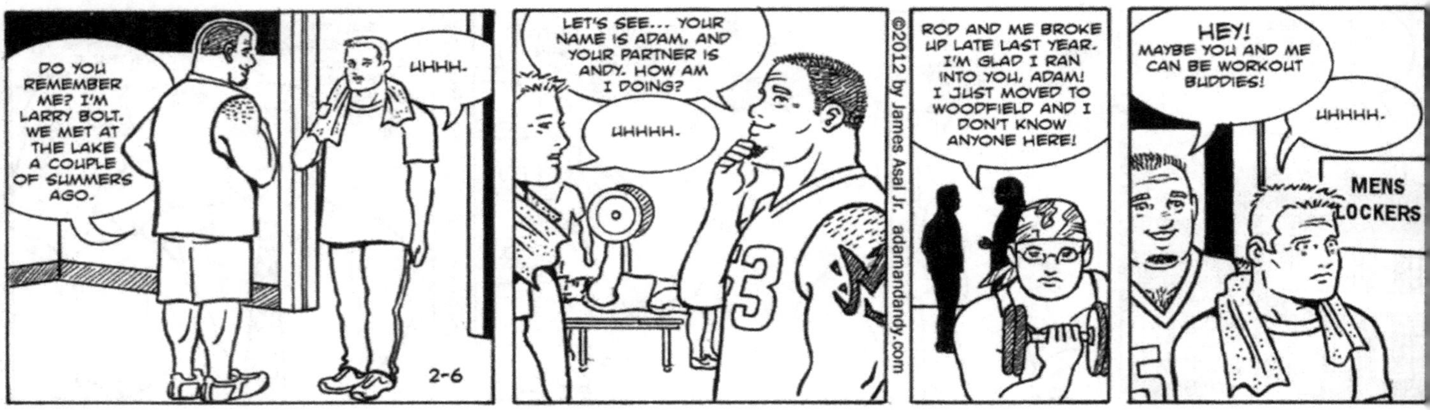
DO YOU REMEMBER ME? I'M LARRY BOLT. WE MET AT THE LAKE A COUPLE OF SUMMERS AGO.
UHHH.
2-6
LET'S SEE... YOUR NAME IS ADAM, AND YOUR PARTNER IS ANDY. HOW AM I DOING?
UHHHH.
©2012 by James Asal Jr. adamandandy.com
ROD AND ME BROKE UP LATE LAST YEAR. I'M GLAD I RAN INTO YOU, ADAM! I JUST MOVED TO WOODFIELD AND I DON'T KNOW ANYONE HERE!
HEY! MAYBE YOU AND ME CAN BE WORKOUT BUDDIES!
UHHHH.
MENS LOCKERS

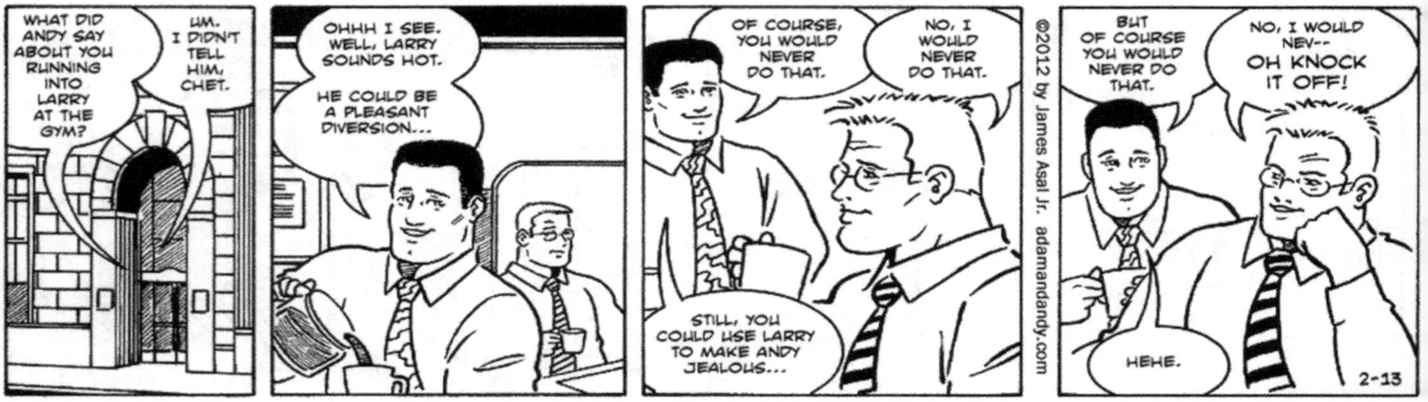
WHAT DID ANDY SAY ABOUT YOU RUNNING INTO LARRY AT THE GYM?
UM. I DIDN'T TELL HIM, CHET.
OHHH I SEE. WELL, LARRY SOUNDS HOT.
HE COULD BE A PLEASANT DIVERSION...
OF COURSE, YOU WOULD NEVER DO THAT.
NO, I WOULD NEVER DO THAT.
STILL, YOU COULD USE LARRY TO MAKE ANDY JEALOUS...
©2012 by James Asal Jr. adamandandy.com
BUT OF COURSE YOU WOULD NEVER DO THAT.
NO, I WOULD NEV-- OH KNOCK IT OFF!
HEHE.
2-13

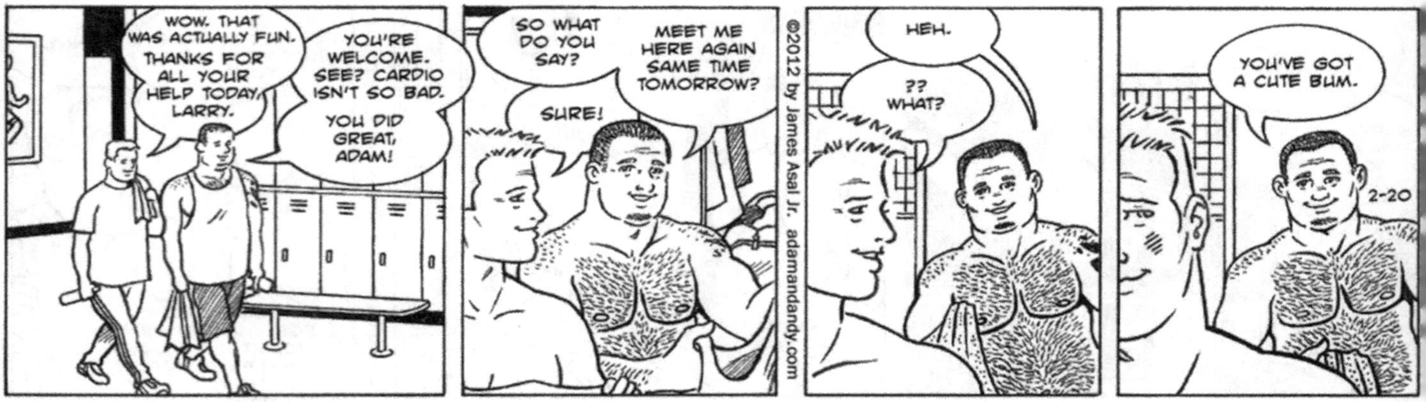
WOW. THAT WAS ACTUALLY FUN. THANKS FOR ALL YOUR HELP TODAY, LARRY.
YOU'RE WELCOME. SEE? CARDIO ISN'T SO BAD.
YOU DID GREAT, ADAM!
SO WHAT DO YOU SAY?
MEET ME HERE AGAIN SAME TIME TOMORROW?
SURE!
©2012 by James Asal Jr. adamandandy.com
HEH.
?? WHAT?
YOU'VE GOT A CUTE BUM.
2-20

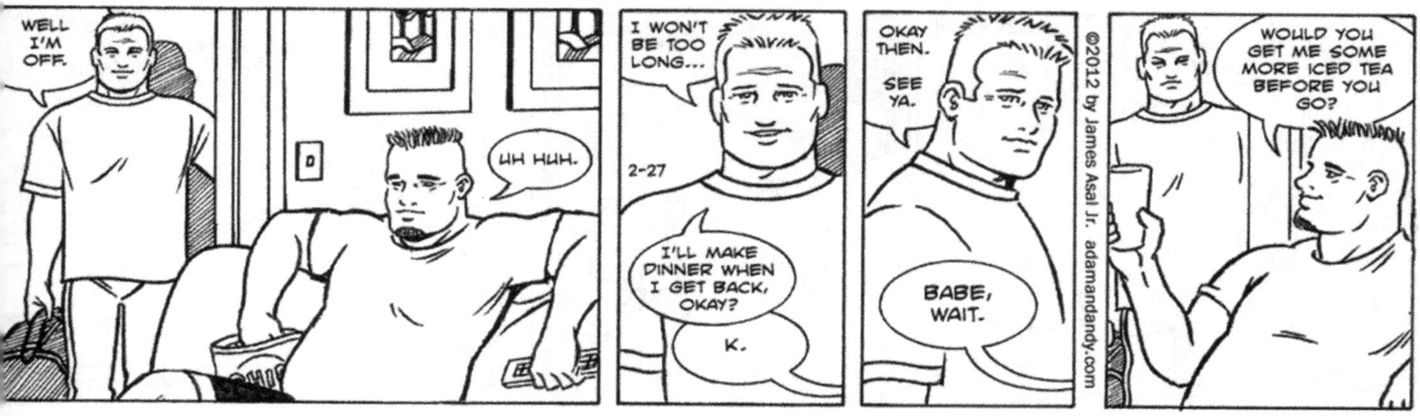
WELL I'M OFF.
UH HUH.
I WON'T BE TOO LONG...
2-27
I'LL MAKE DINNER WHEN I GET BACK, OKAY?
K.
OKAY THEN.
SEE YA.
BABE, WAIT.
©2012 by James Asal Jr. adamandandy.com
WOULD YOU GET ME SOME MORE ICED TEA BEFORE YOU GO?

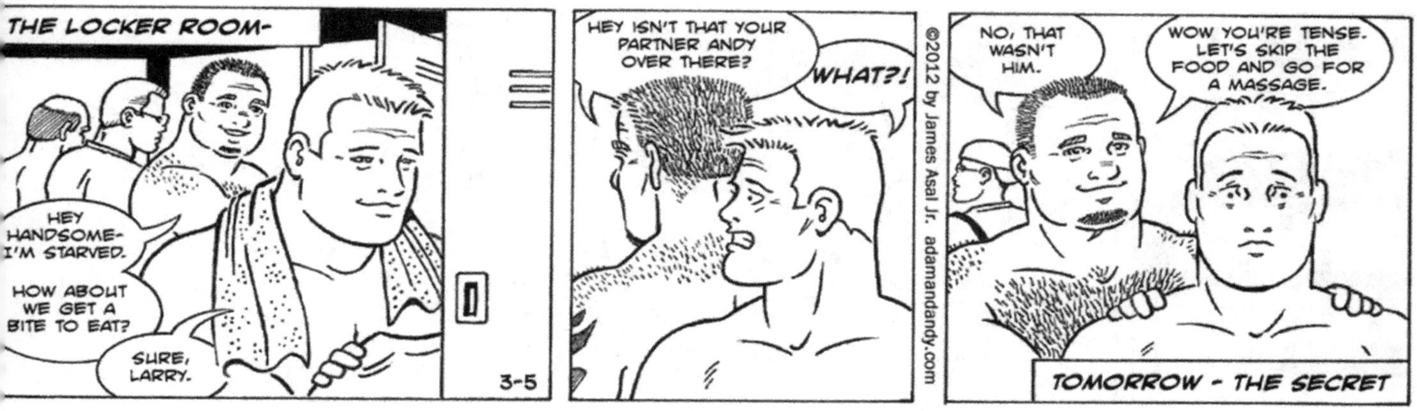
THE LOCKER ROOM-
HEY HANDSOME- I'M STARVED.
HOW ABOUT WE GET A BITE TO EAT?
SURE, LARRY.
3-5
HEY ISN'T THAT YOUR PARTNER ANDY OVER THERE?
WHAT?!
©2012 by James Asal Jr. adamandandy.com
NO, THAT WASN'T HIM.
WOW YOU'RE TENSE. LET'S SKIP THE FOOD AND GO FOR A MASSAGE.
TOMORROW - THE SECRET

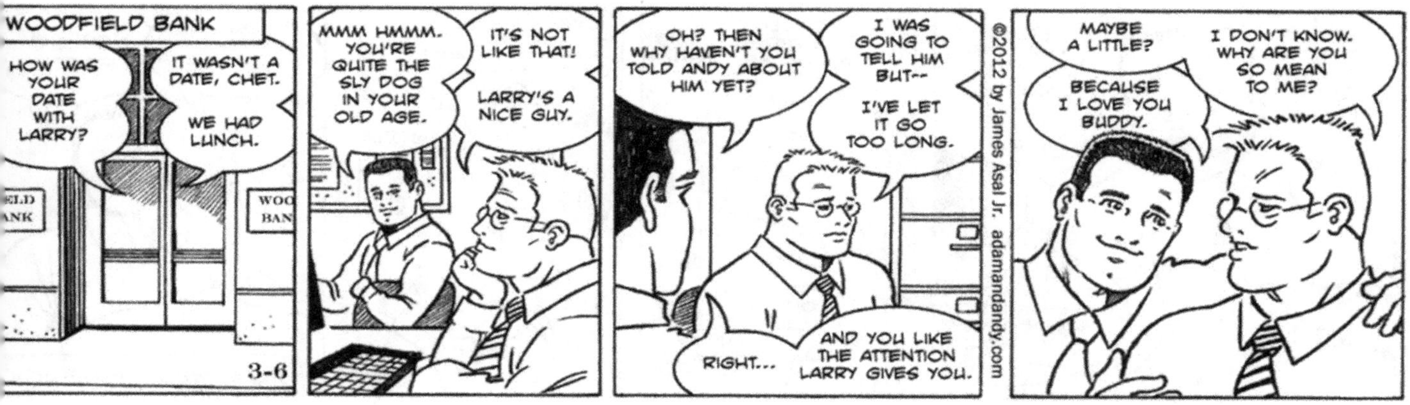
WOODFIELD BANK
HOW WAS YOUR DATE WITH LARRY?
IT WASN'T A DATE, CHET.
WE HAD LUNCH.
3-6
MMM HMMM. YOU'RE QUITE THE SLY DOG IN YOUR OLD AGE.
IT'S NOT LIKE THAT!
LARRY'S A NICE GUY.
OH? THEN WHY HAVEN'T YOU TOLD ANDY ABOUT HIM YET?
I WAS GOING TO TELL HIM BUT--
I'VE LET IT GO TOO LONG.
RIGHT...
AND YOU LIKE THE ATTENTION LARRY GIVES YOU.
©2012 by James Asal Jr. adamandandy.com
MAYBE A LITTLE?
I DON'T KNOW. WHY ARE YOU SO MEAN TO ME?
BECAUSE I LOVE YOU BUDDY.

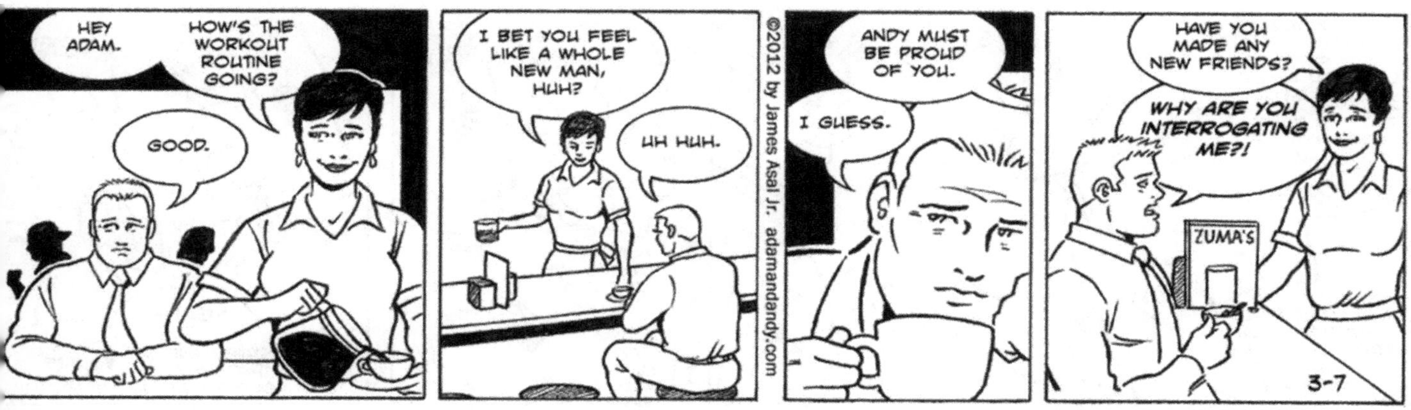
HEY ADAM.
HOW'S THE WORKOUT ROUTINE GOING?
GOOD.
I BET YOU FEEL LIKE A WHOLE NEW MAN, HUH?
UH HUH.
©2012 by James Asal Jr. adamandandy.com
ANDY MUST BE PROUD OF YOU.
I GUESS.
HAVE YOU MADE ANY NEW FRIENDS?
WHY ARE YOU INTERROGATING ME?!
ZUMA'S
3-7

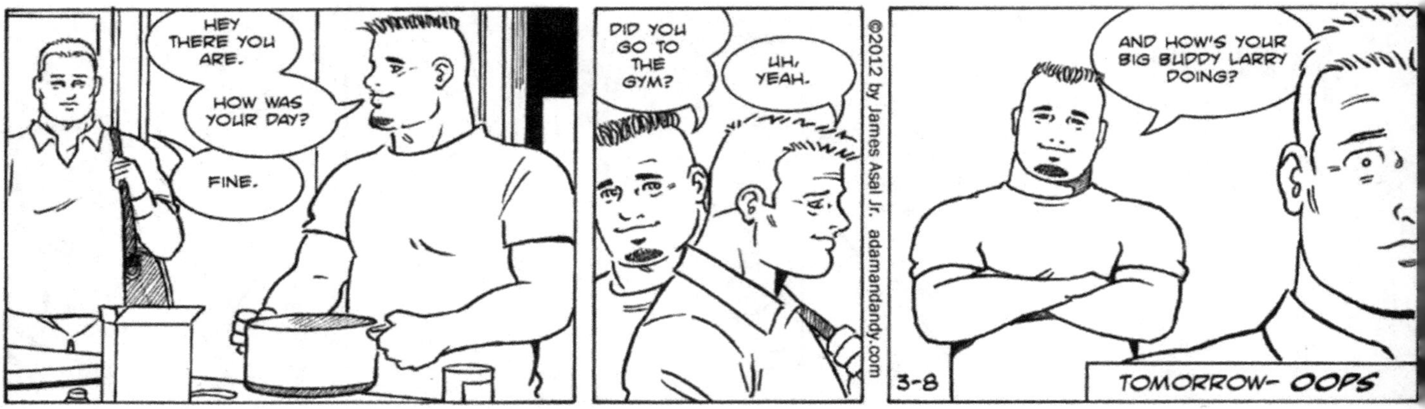
HEY THERE YOU ARE.
HOW WAS YOUR DAY?
FINE.
DID YOU GO TO THE GYM?
UH, YEAH.
©2012 by James Asal Jr. adamandandy.com
AND HOW'S YOUR BIG BUDDY LARRY DOING?
3-8
TOMORROW- OOPS

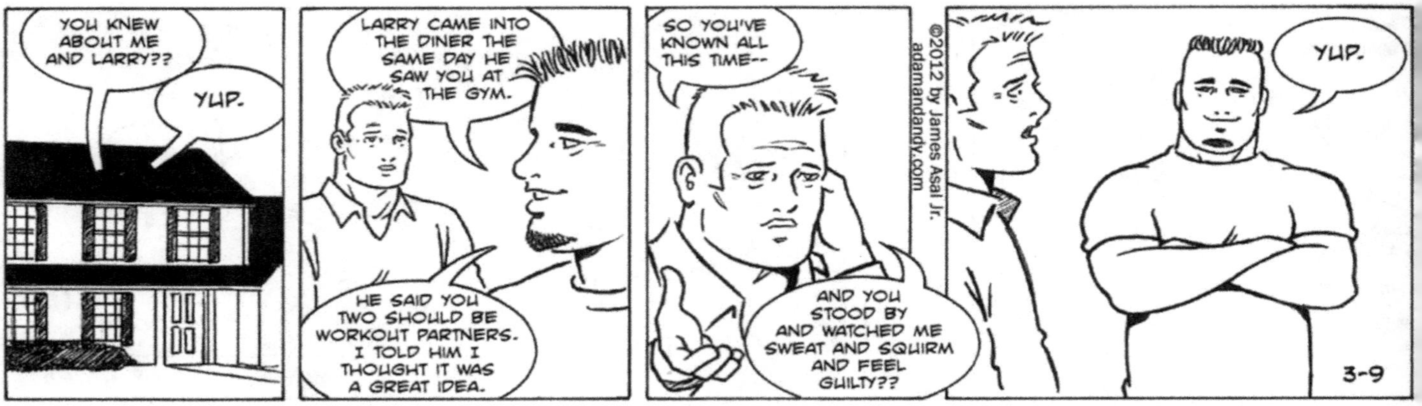
YOU KNEW ABOUT ME AND LARRY??
YUP.
LARRY CAME INTO THE DINER THE SAME DAY HE SAW YOU AT THE GYM.
HE SAID YOU TWO SHOULD BE WORKOUT PARTNERS. I TOLD HIM I THOUGHT IT WAS A GREAT IDEA.
SO YOU'VE KNOWN ALL THIS TIME--
AND YOU STOOD BY AND WATCHED ME SWEAT AND SQUIRM AND FEEL GUILTY??
©2012 by James Asal Jr. adamandandy.com
YUP.
3-9

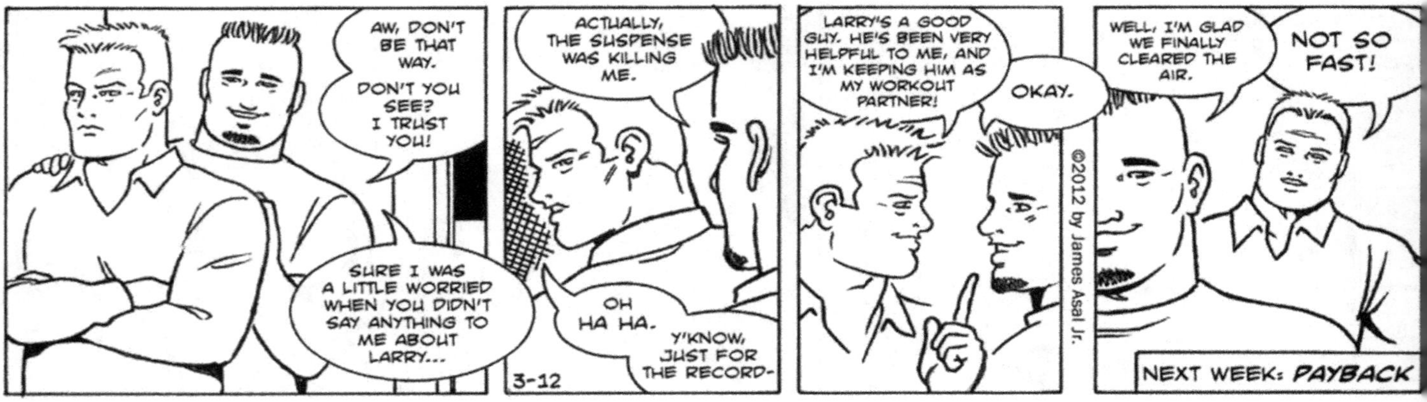
AW, DON'T BE THAT WAY.
DON'T YOU SEE? I TRUST YOU!
SURE I WAS A LITTLE WORRIED WHEN YOU DIDN'T SAY ANYTHING TO ME ABOUT LARRY...
ACTUALLY, THE SUSPENSE WAS KILLING ME.
OH HA HA.
Y'KNOW, JUST FOR THE RECORD-
3-12
LARRY'S A GOOD GUY. HE'S BEEN VERY HELPFUL TO ME, AND I'M KEEPING HIM AS MY WORKOUT PARTNER!
OKAY.
©2012 by James Asal Jr.
WELL, I'M GLAD WE FINALLY CLEARED THE AIR.
NOT SO FAST!
NEXT WEEK: PAYBACK

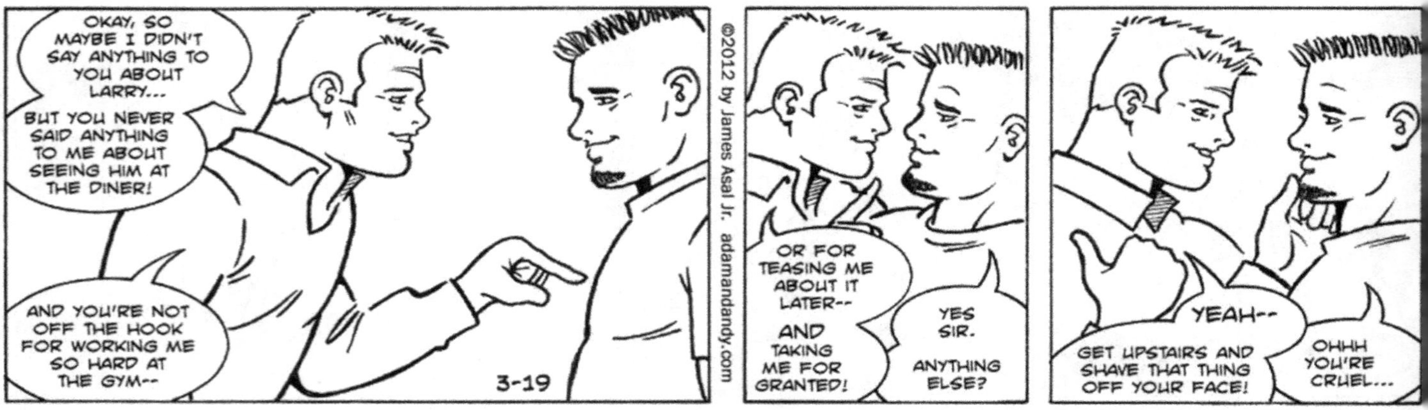
OKAY, SO MAYBE I DIDN'T SAY ANYTHING TO YOU ABOUT LARRY...
BUT YOU NEVER SAID ANYTHING TO ME ABOUT SEEING HIM AT THE DINER!
AND YOU'RE NOT OFF THE HOOK FOR WORKING ME SO HARD AT THE GYM--
3-19
©2012 by James Asal Jr. adamandandy.com
OR FOR TEASING ME ABOUT IT LATER--
AND TAKING ME FOR GRANTED!
YES SIR.
ANYTHING ELSE?
YEAH--
GET UPSTAIRS AND SHAVE THAT THING OFF YOUR FACE!
OHHH YOU'RE CRUEL...

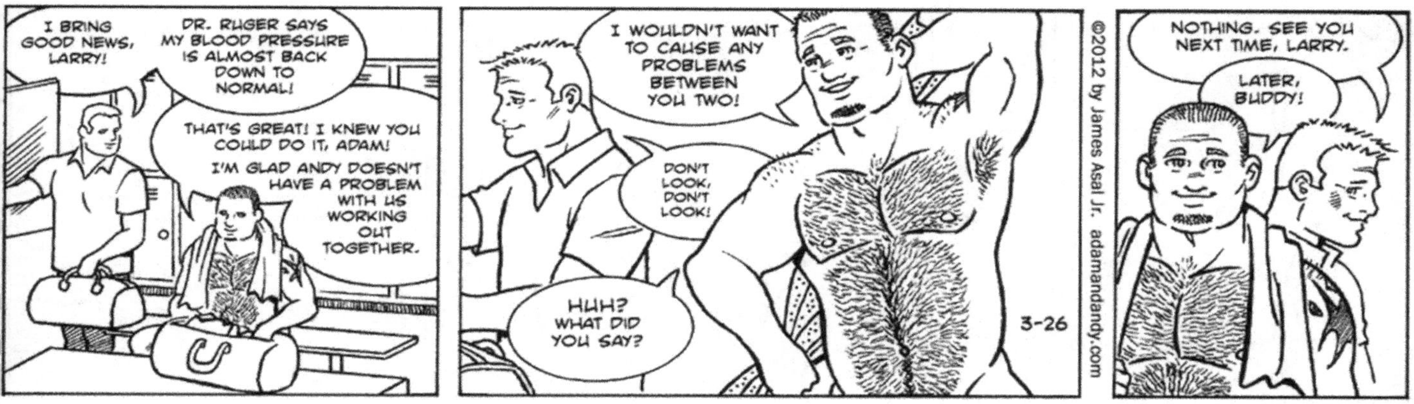
I BRING GOOD NEWS, LARRY!
DR. RUGER SAYS MY BLOOD PRESSURE IS ALMOST BACK DOWN TO NORMAL!
THAT'S GREAT! I KNEW YOU COULD DO IT, ADAM!
I'M GLAD ANDY DOESN'T HAVE A PROBLEM WITH US WORKING OUT TOGETHER.
I WOULDN'T WANT TO CAUSE ANY PROBLEMS BETWEEN YOU TWO!
DON'T LOOK, DON'T LOOK!
HUH? WHAT DID YOU SAY?
3-26
©2012 by James Asal Jr. adamandandy.com
NOTHING. SEE YOU NEXT TIME, LARRY.
LATER, BUDDY!

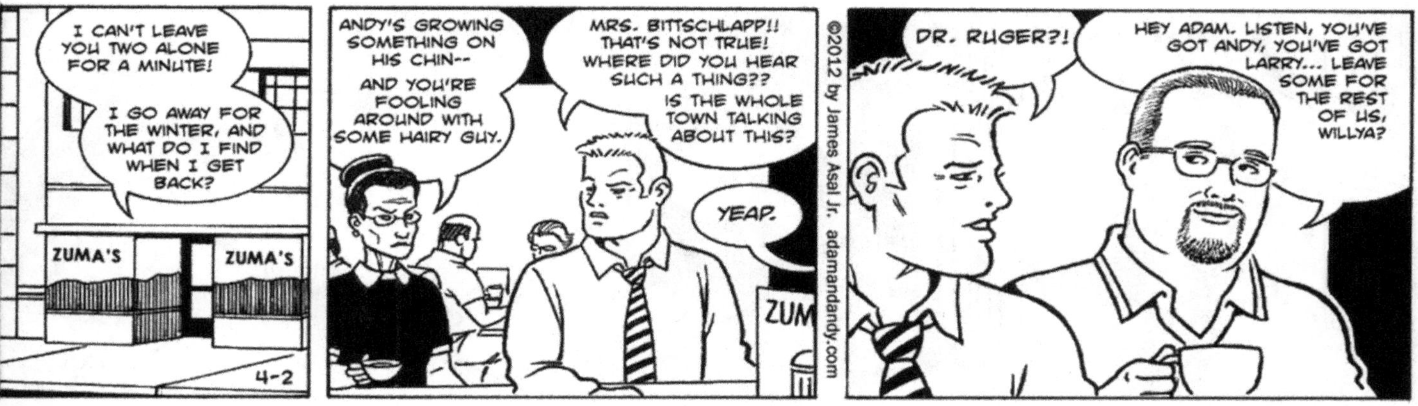
I CAN'T LEAVE YOU TWO ALONE FOR A MINUTE!
I GO AWAY FOR THE WINTER, AND WHAT DO I FIND WHEN I GET BACK?
ZUMA'S
ZUMA'S
4-2
ANDY'S GROWING SOMETHING ON HIS CHIN--
AND YOU'RE FOOLING AROUND WITH SOME HAIRY GUY.
MRS. BITTSCHLAPP!! THAT'S NOT TRUE! WHERE DID YOU HEAR SUCH A THING??
IS THE WHOLE TOWN TALKING ABOUT THIS?
YEAP.
ZUM
©2012 by James Asal Jr. adamandandy.com
DR. RUGER?!
HEY ADAM. LISTEN, YOU'VE GOT ANDY, YOU'VE GOT LARRY... LEAVE SOME FOR THE REST OF US, WILLYA?

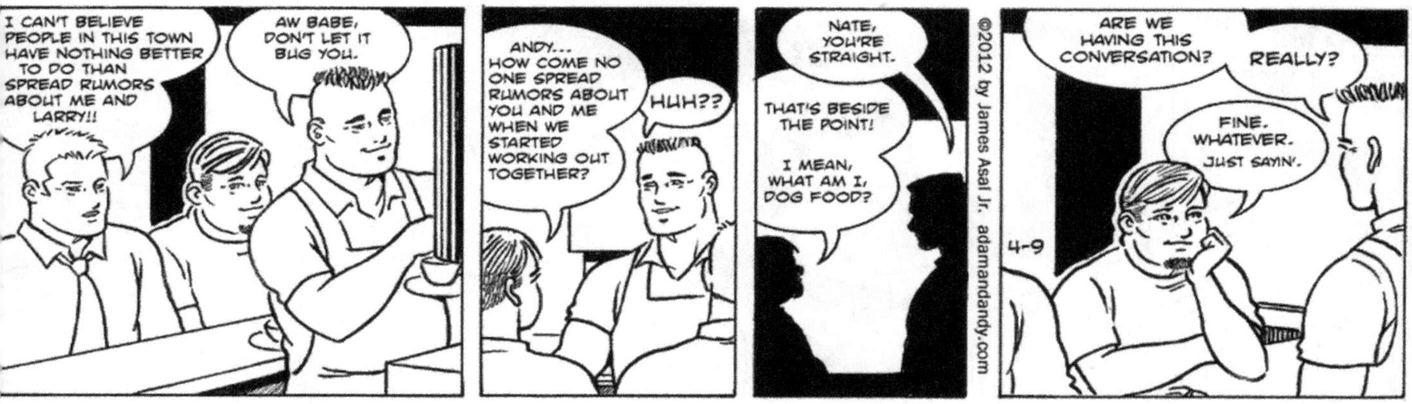
I CAN'T BELIEVE PEOPLE IN THIS TOWN HAVE NOTHING BETTER TO DO THAN SPREAD RUMORS ABOUT ME AND LARRY!!
AW BABE, DON'T LET IT BUG YOU.
ANDY... HOW COME NO ONE SPREAD RUMORS ABOUT YOU AND ME WHEN WE STARTED WORKING OUT TOGETHER?
HUH??
NATE, YOU'RE STRAIGHT.
THAT'S BESIDE THE POINT!
I MEAN, WHAT AM I, DOG FOOD?
4-9
©2012 by James Asal Jr. adamandandy.com
ARE WE HAVING THIS CONVERSATION?
REALLY?
FINE. WHATEVER. JUST SAYIN'.

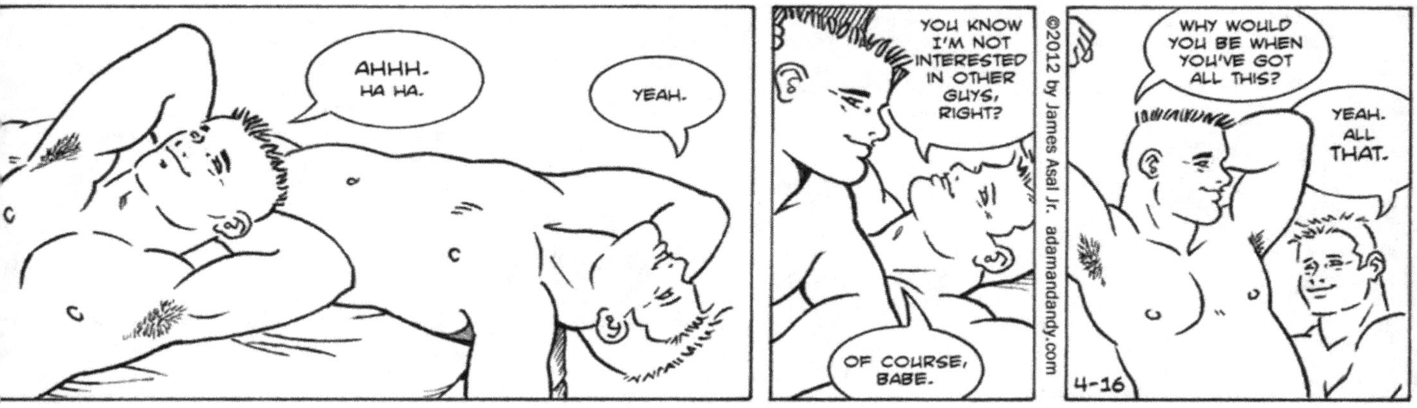
AHHH. HA HA.
YEAH.
YOU KNOW I'M NOT INTERESTED IN OTHER GUYS, RIGHT?
OF COURSE, BABE.
©2012 by James Asal Jr. adamandandy.com
WHY WOULD YOU BE WHEN YOU'VE GOT ALL THIS?
YEAH. ALL THAT.
4-16

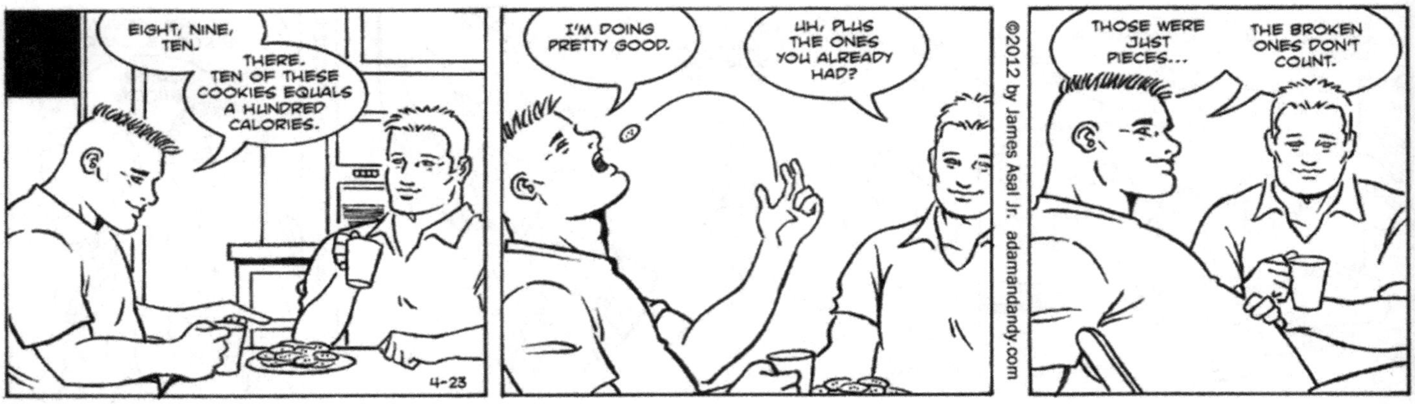
EIGHT, NINE, TEN.
THERE. TEN OF THESE COOKIES EQUALS A HUNDRED CALORIES.
4-23
I'M DOING PRETTY GOOD.
UH, PLUS THE ONES YOU ALREADY HAD?
©2012 by James Asal Jr. adamandandy.com
THOSE WERE JUST PIECES...
THE BROKEN ONES DON'T COUNT.

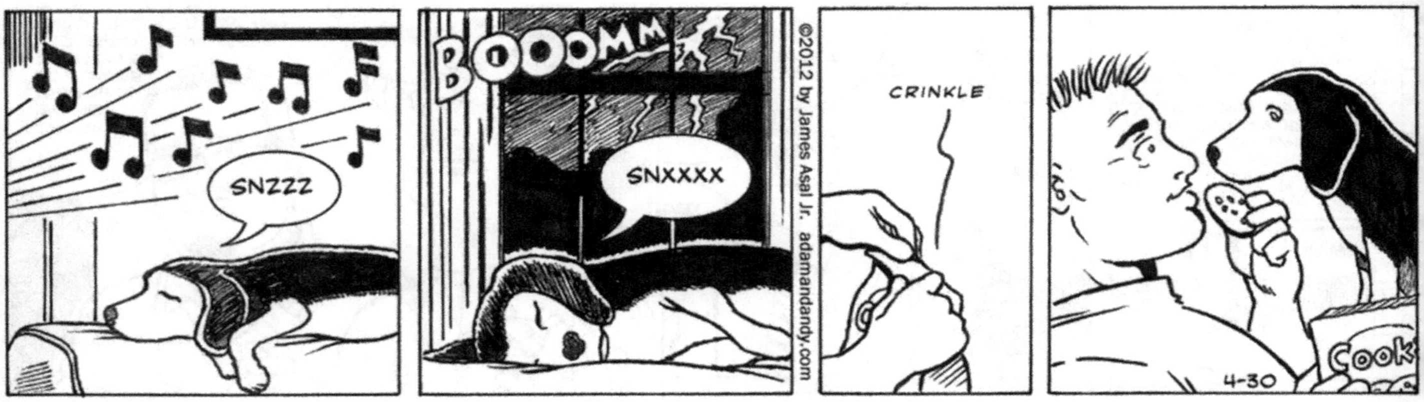
SNZZZ
BOOOMM
SNXXXX
©2012 by James Asal Jr. adamandandy.com
CRINKLE
COOK
4-30

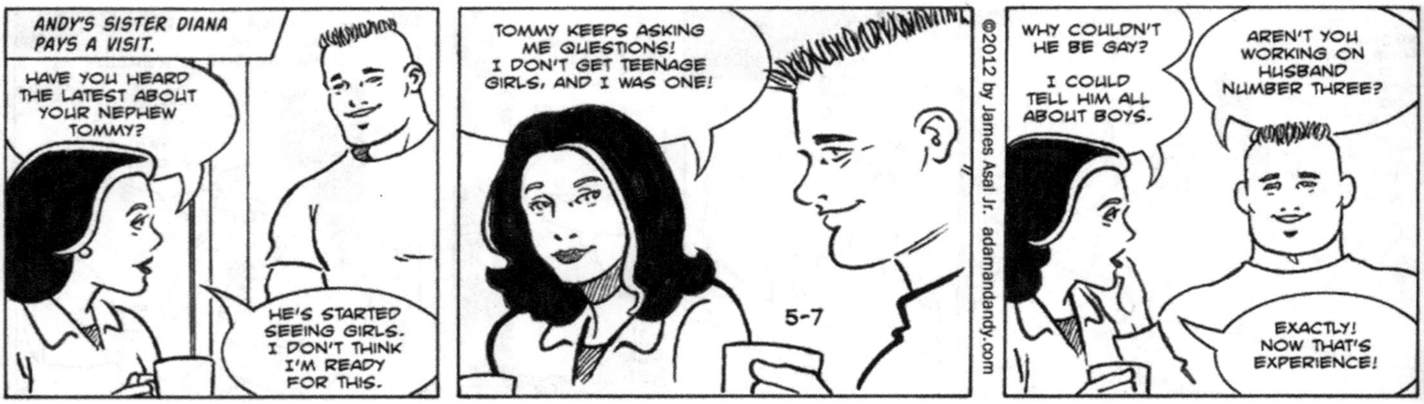
ANDY'S SISTER DIANA PAYS A VISIT.
HAVE YOU HEARD THE LATEST ABOUT YOUR NEPHEW TOMMY?
HE'S STARTED SEEING GIRLS. I DON'T THINK I'M READY FOR THIS.
TOMMY KEEPS ASKING ME QUESTIONS! I DON'T GET TEENAGE GIRLS, AND I WAS ONE!
5-7
©2012 by James Asal Jr. adamandandy.com
WHY COULDN'T HE BE GAY?
I COULD TELL HIM ALL ABOUT BOYS.
AREN'T YOU WORKING ON HUSBAND NUMBER THREE?
EXACTLY! NOW THAT'S EXPERIENCE!

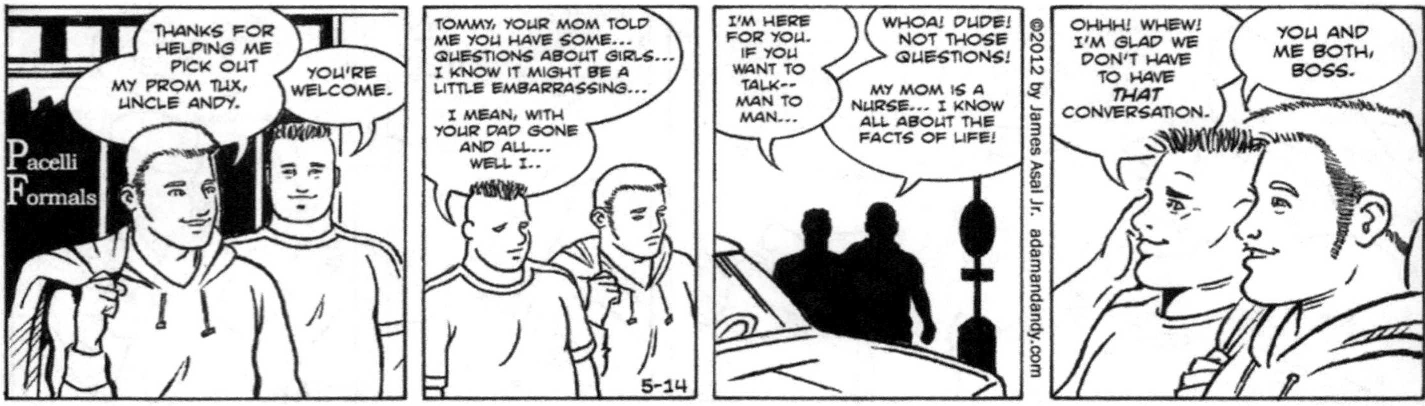
THANKS FOR HELPING ME PICK OUT MY PROM TUX, UNCLE ANDY.
YOU'RE WELCOME.
Pacelli Formals
TOMMY, YOUR MOM TOLD ME YOU HAVE SOME... QUESTIONS ABOUT GIRLS... I KNOW IT MIGHT BE A LITTLE EMBARRASSING...
I MEAN, WITH YOUR DAD GONE AND ALL... WELL I..
5-14
I'M HERE FOR YOU. IF YOU WANT TO TALK-- MAN TO MAN...
WHOA! DUDE! NOT THOSE QUESTIONS!
MY MOM IS A NURSE... I KNOW ALL ABOUT THE FACTS OF LIFE!
©2012 by James Asal Jr. adamandandy.com
OHHH! WHEW! I'M GLAD WE DON'T HAVE TO HAVE *THAT* CONVERSATION.
YOU AND ME BOTH, BOSS.

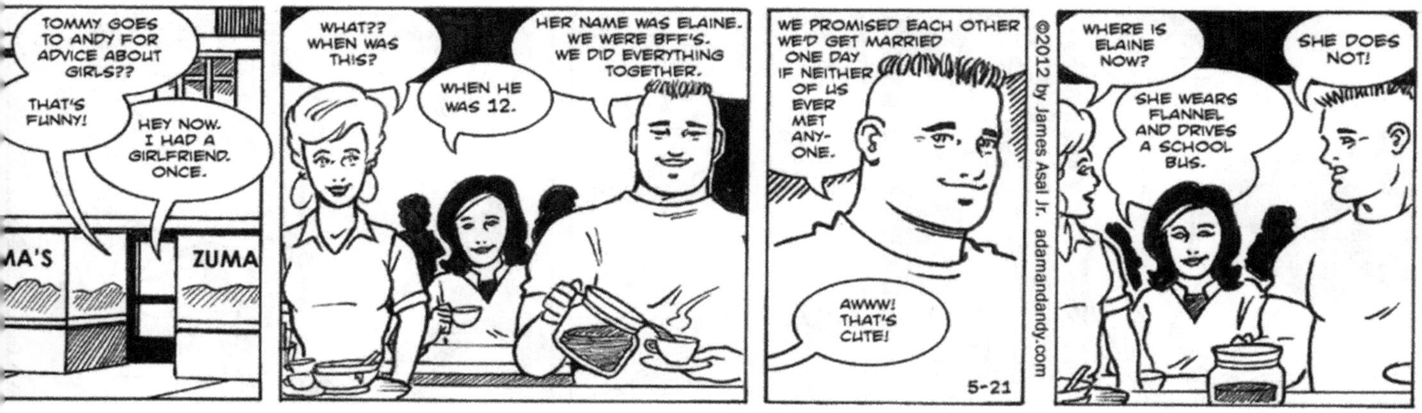
TOMMY GOES TO ANDY FOR ADVICE ABOUT GIRLS??
THAT'S FUNNY!
HEY NOW. I HAD A GIRLFRIEND. ONCE.
MA'S
ZUMA
WHAT?? WHEN WAS THIS?
WHEN HE WAS 12.
HER NAME WAS ELAINE. WE WERE BFF'S. WE DID EVERYTHING TOGETHER.
WE PROMISED EACH OTHER WE'D GET MARRIED ONE DAY IF NEITHER OF US EVER MET ANY-ONE.
AWWW! THAT'S CUTE!
5-21
©2012 by James Asal Jr. adamandandy.com
WHERE IS ELAINE NOW?
SHE WEARS FLANNEL AND DRIVES A SCHOOL BUS.
SHE DOES NOT!

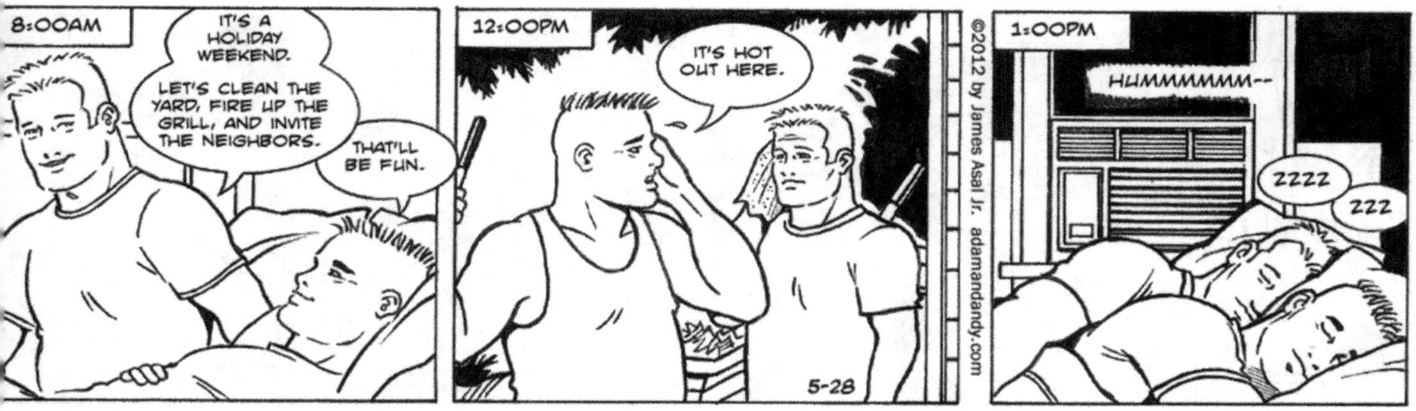
8:00AM
IT'S A HOLIDAY WEEKEND.
LET'S CLEAN THE YARD, FIRE UP THE GRILL, AND INVITE THE NEIGHBORS.
THAT'LL BE FUN.
12:00PM
IT'S HOT OUT HERE.
5-28
©2012 by James Asal Jr. adamandandy.com
1:00PM
HUMMMMMM--
ZZZZ
ZZZ

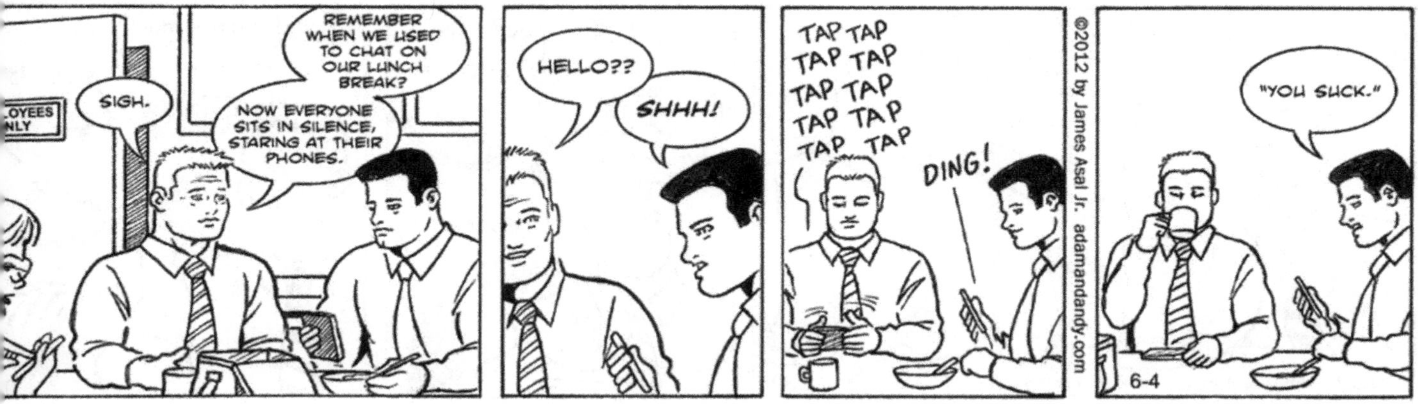
LOYEES NLY
SIGH.
REMEMBER WHEN WE USED TO CHAT ON OUR LUNCH BREAK?
NOW EVERYONE SITS IN SILENCE, STARING AT THEIR PHONES.
HELLO??
SHHH!
TAP TAP TAP TAP TAP TAP TAP TAP TAP TAP
DING!
©2012 by James Asal Jr. adamandandy.com
"YOU SUCK."
6-4

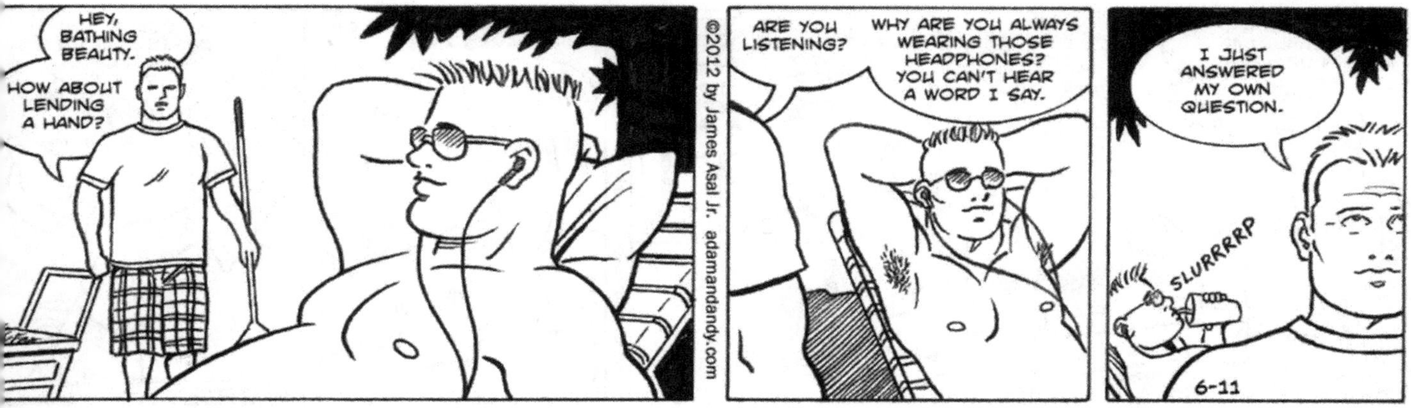
HEY, BATHING BEAUTY.
HOW ABOUT LENDING A HAND?
©2012 by James Asal Jr. adamandandy.com
ARE YOU LISTENING?
WHY ARE YOU ALWAYS WEARING THOSE HEADPHONES? YOU CAN'T HEAR A WORD I SAY.
I JUST ANSWERED MY OWN QUESTION.
SLURRRRP
6-11

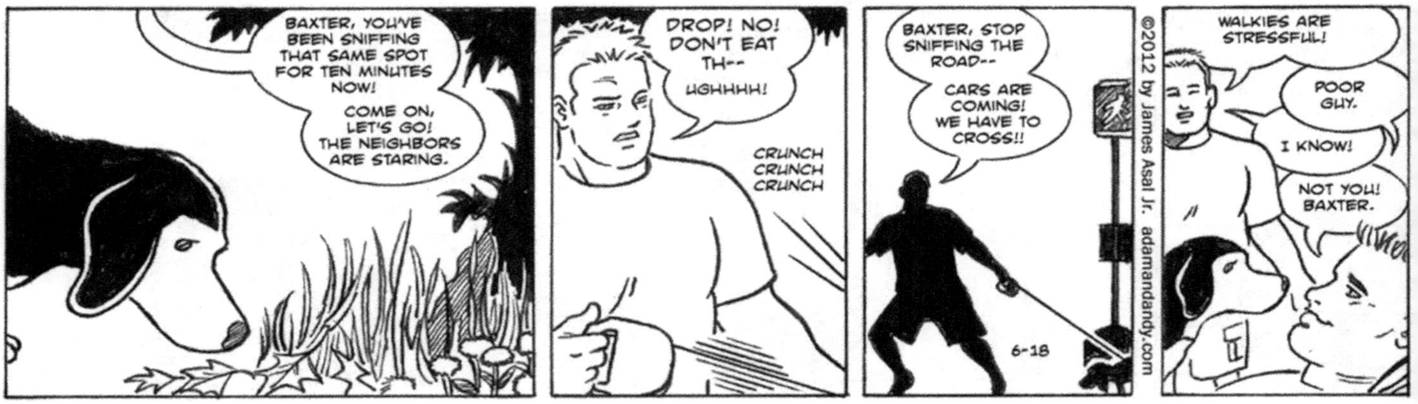
BAXTER, YOU'VE BEEN SNIFFING THAT SAME SPOT FOR TEN MINUTES NOW!
COME ON, LET'S GO! THE NEIGHBORS ARE STARING.
DROP! NO! DON'T EAT TH--
UGHHHH!
CRUNCH CRUNCH CRUNCH
BAXTER, STOP SNIFFING THE ROAD--
CARS ARE COMING! WE HAVE TO CROSS!!
6-18
©2012 by James Asal Jr. adamandandy.com
WALKIES ARE STRESSFUL!
POOR GUY.
I KNOW!
NOT YOU! BAXTER.

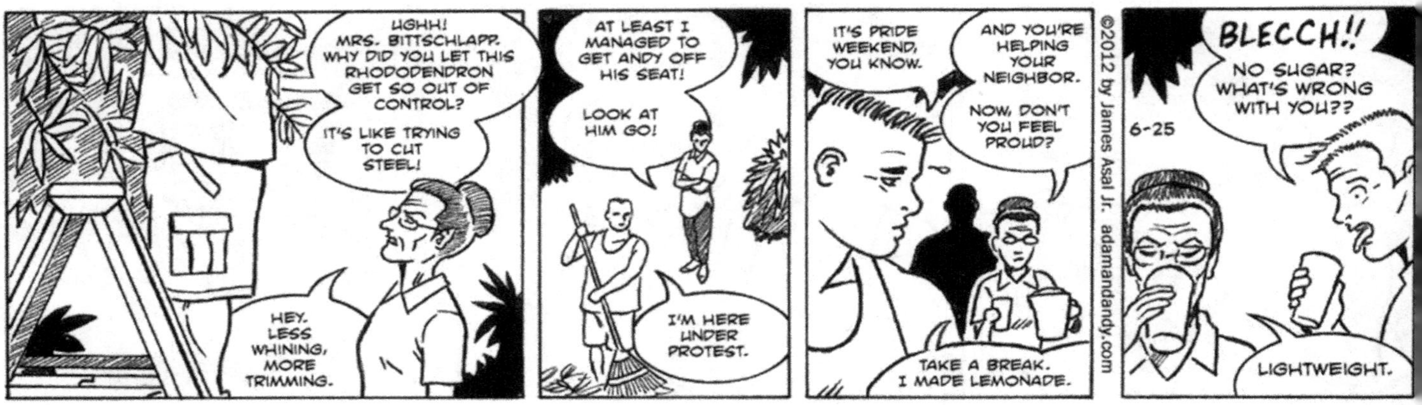
UGHH! MRS. BITTSCHLAPP. WHY DID YOU LET THIS RHODODENDRON GET SO OUT OF CONTROL?
IT'S LIKE TRYING TO CUT STEEL!
HEY. LESS WHINING, MORE TRIMMING.
AT LEAST I MANAGED TO GET ANDY OFF HIS SEAT!
LOOK AT HIM GO!
I'M HERE UNDER PROTEST.
IT'S PRIDE WEEKEND, YOU KNOW.
AND YOU'RE HELPING YOUR NEIGHBOR.
NOW, DON'T YOU FEEL PROUD?
TAKE A BREAK. I MADE LEMONADE.
©2012 by James Asal Jr. adamandandy.com
BLECCH!!
6-25
NO SUGAR? WHAT'S WRONG WITH YOU??
LIGHTWEIGHT.

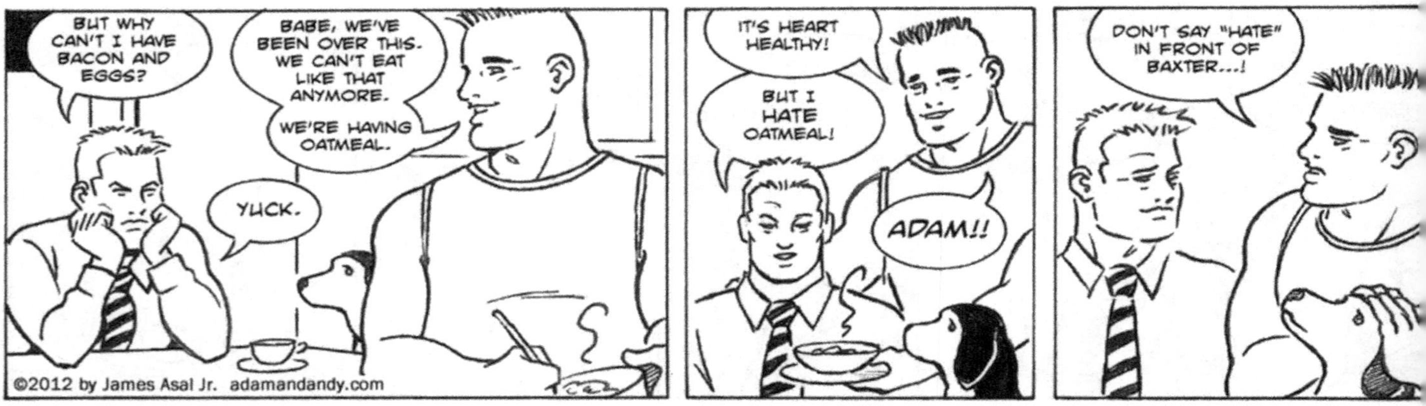
BUT WHY CAN'T I HAVE BACON AND EGGS?
BABE, WE'VE BEEN OVER THIS. WE CAN'T EAT LIKE THAT ANYMORE.
WE'RE HAVING OATMEAL.
YUCK.
©2012 by James Asal Jr. adamandandy.com
IT'S HEART HEALTHY!
BUT I HATE OATMEAL!
ADAM!!
DON'T SAY "HATE" IN FRONT OF BAXTER...!

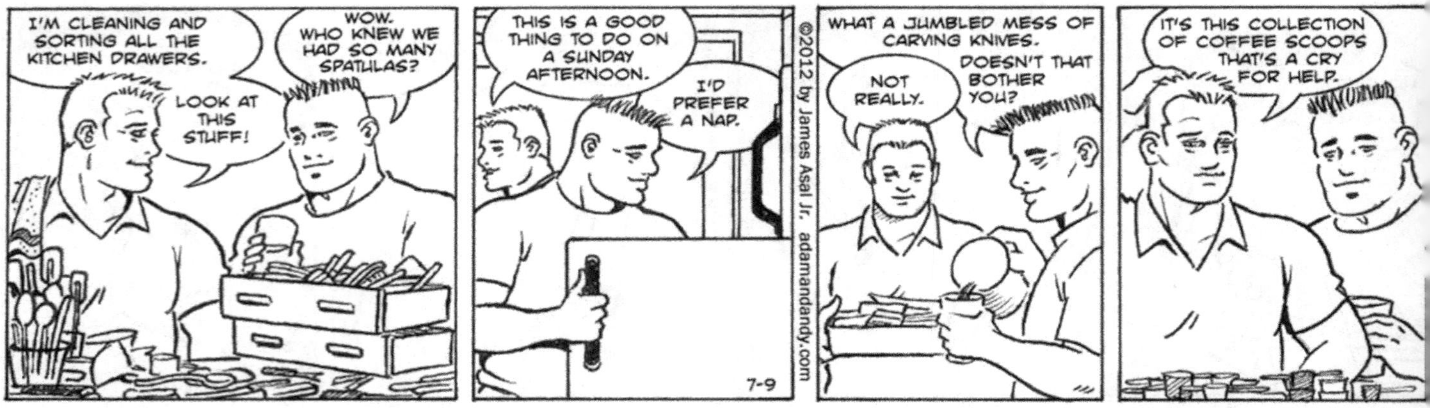
I'M CLEANING AND SORTING ALL THE KITCHEN DRAWERS.
WOW. WHO KNEW WE HAD SO MANY SPATULAS?
LOOK AT THIS STUFF!
THIS IS A GOOD THING TO DO ON A SUNDAY AFTERNOON.
I'D PREFER A NAP.
7-9
©2012 by James Asal Jr. adamandandy.com
WHAT A JUMBLED MESS OF CARVING KNIVES.
NOT REALLY.
DOESN'T THAT BOTHER YOU?
IT'S THIS COLLECTION OF COFFEE SCOOPS THAT'S A CRY FOR HELP.

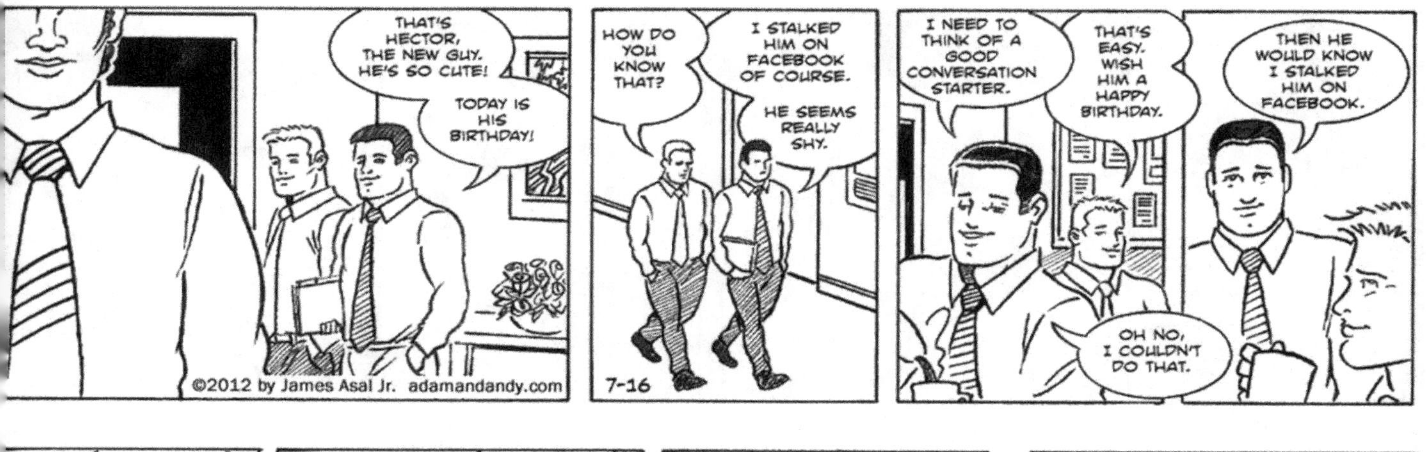
THAT'S HECTOR, THE NEW GUY. HE'S SO CUTE!
TODAY IS HIS BIRTHDAY!
©2012 by James Asal Jr. adamandandy.com
HOW DO YOU KNOW THAT?
I STALKED HIM ON FACEBOOK OF COURSE.
HE SEEMS REALLY SHY.
7-16
I NEED TO THINK OF A GOOD CONVERSATION STARTER.
THAT'S EASY. WISH HIM A HAPPY BIRTHDAY.
OH NO, I COULDN'T DO THAT.
THEN HE WOULD KNOW I STALKED HIM ON FACEBOOK.

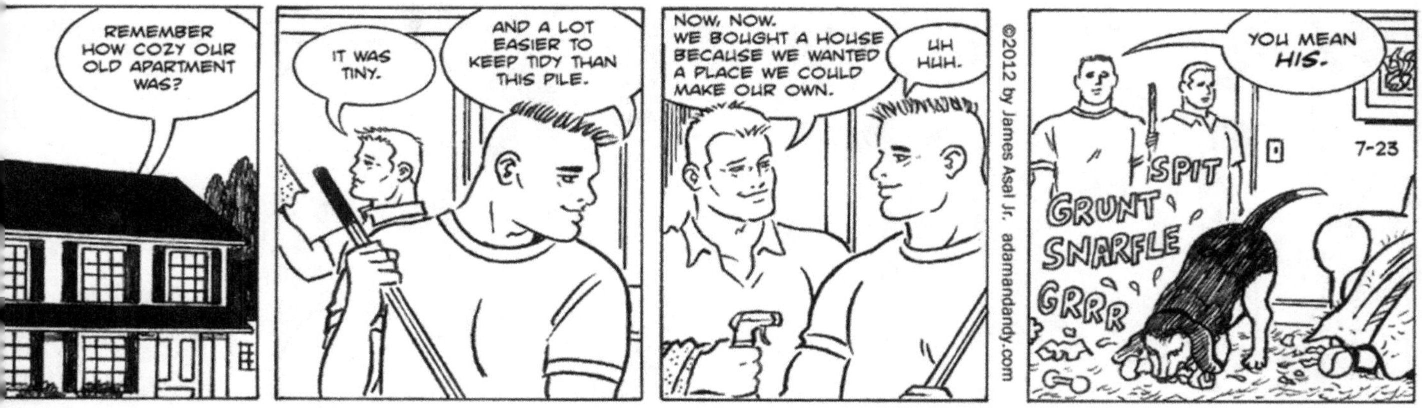
REMEMBER HOW COZY OUR OLD APARTMENT WAS?
IT WAS TINY.
AND A LOT EASIER TO KEEP TIDY THAN THIS PILE.
NOW, NOW. WE BOUGHT A HOUSE BECAUSE WE WANTED A PLACE WE COULD MAKE OUR OWN.
UH HUH.
©2012 by James Asal Jr. adamandandy.com
YOU MEAN *HIS*.
7-23
SPIT
GRUNT
SNARFLE
GRRR

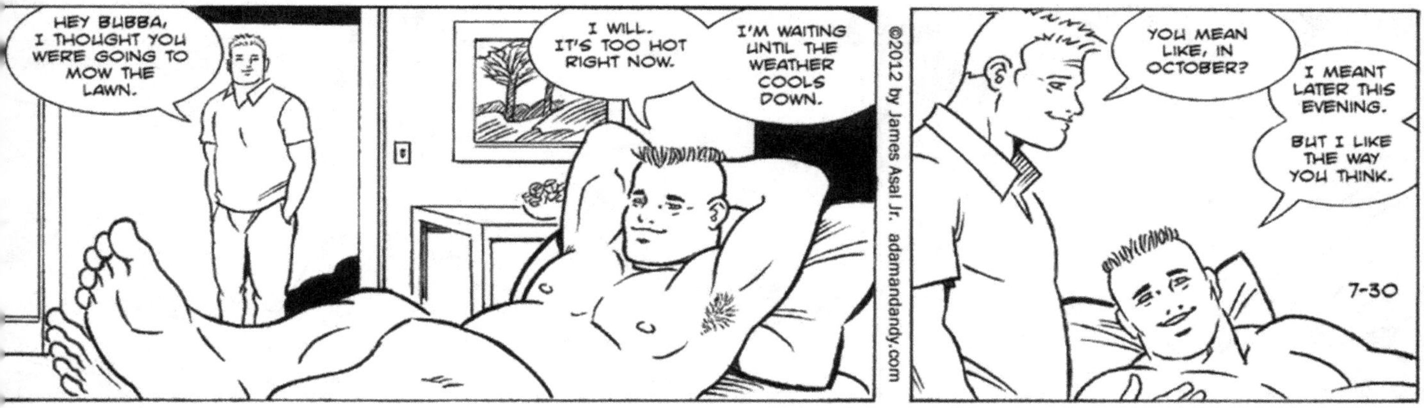
HEY BUBBA, I THOUGHT YOU WERE GOING TO MOW THE LAWN.
I WILL. IT'S TOO HOT RIGHT NOW.
I'M WAITING UNTIL THE WEATHER COOLS DOWN.
©2012 by James Asal Jr. adamandandy.com
YOU MEAN LIKE, IN OCTOBER?
I MEANT LATER THIS EVENING.
BUT I LIKE THE WAY YOU THINK.
7-30

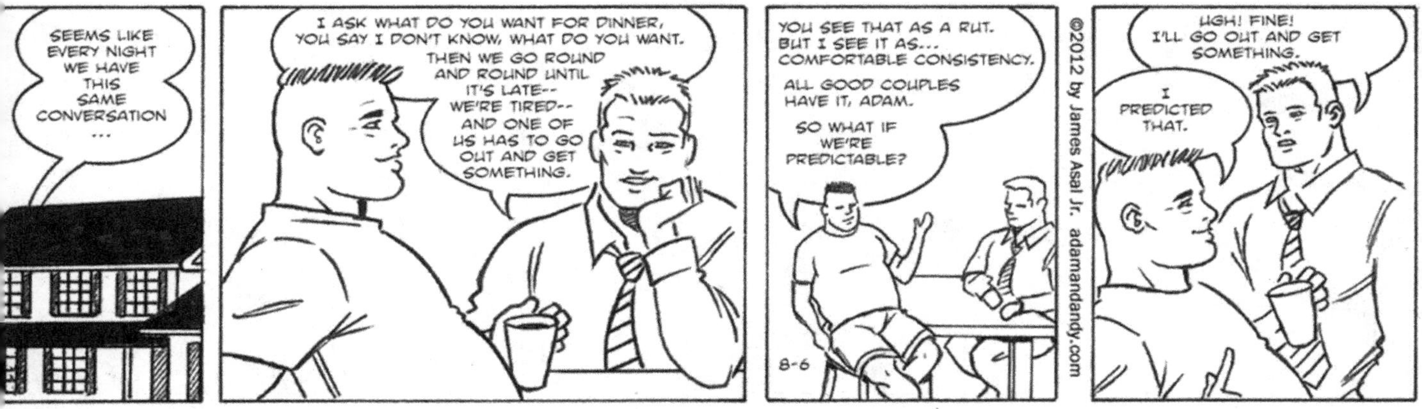
SEEMS LIKE EVERY NIGHT WE HAVE THIS SAME CONVERSATION ...
I ASK WHAT DO YOU WANT FOR DINNER, YOU SAY I DON'T KNOW, WHAT DO YOU WANT.
THEN WE GO ROUND AND ROUND UNTIL IT'S LATE-- WE'RE TIRED-- AND ONE OF US HAS TO GO OUT AND GET SOMETHING.
YOU SEE THAT AS A RUT. BUT I SEE IT AS... COMFORTABLE CONSISTENCY.
ALL GOOD COUPLES HAVE IT, ADAM.
SO WHAT IF WE'RE PREDICTABLE?
8-6
©2012 by James Asal Jr. adamandandy.com
UGH! FINE! I'LL GO OUT AND GET SOMETHING.
I PREDICTED THAT.

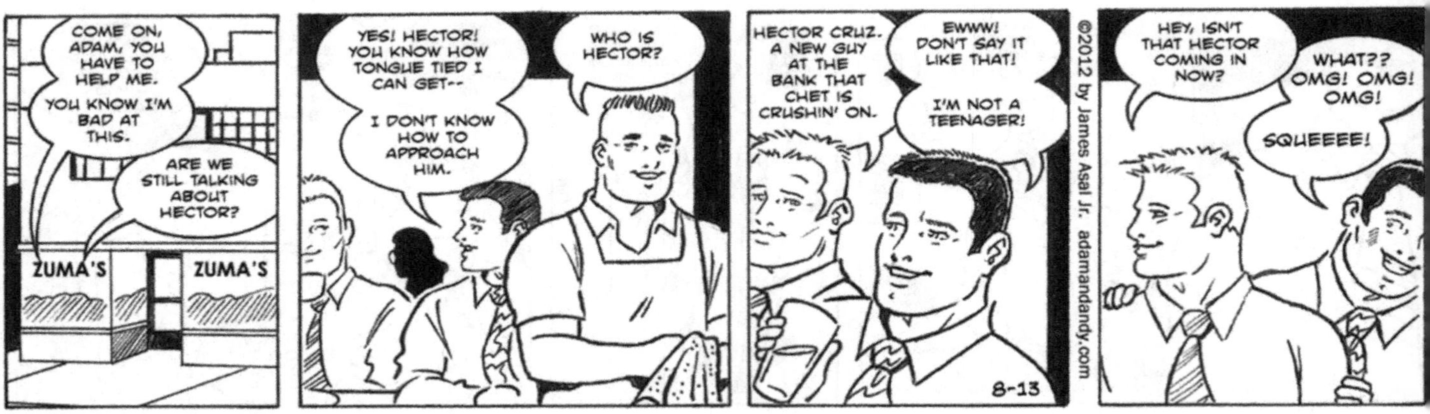
COME ON, ADAM, YOU HAVE TO HELP ME.
YOU KNOW I'M BAD AT THIS.
ARE WE STILL TALKING ABOUT HECTOR?
ZUMA'S
ZUMA'S
YES! HECTOR! YOU KNOW HOW TONGUE TIED I CAN GET--
I DON'T KNOW HOW TO APPROACH HIM.
WHO IS HECTOR?
HECTOR CRUZ. A NEW GUY AT THE BANK THAT CHET IS CRUSHIN' ON.
EWWW! DON'T SAY IT LIKE THAT!
I'M NOT A TEENAGER!
8-13
©2012 by James Asal Jr. adamandandy.com
HEY, ISN'T THAT HECTOR COMING IN NOW?
WHAT?? OMG! OMG! OMG!
SQUEEEE!

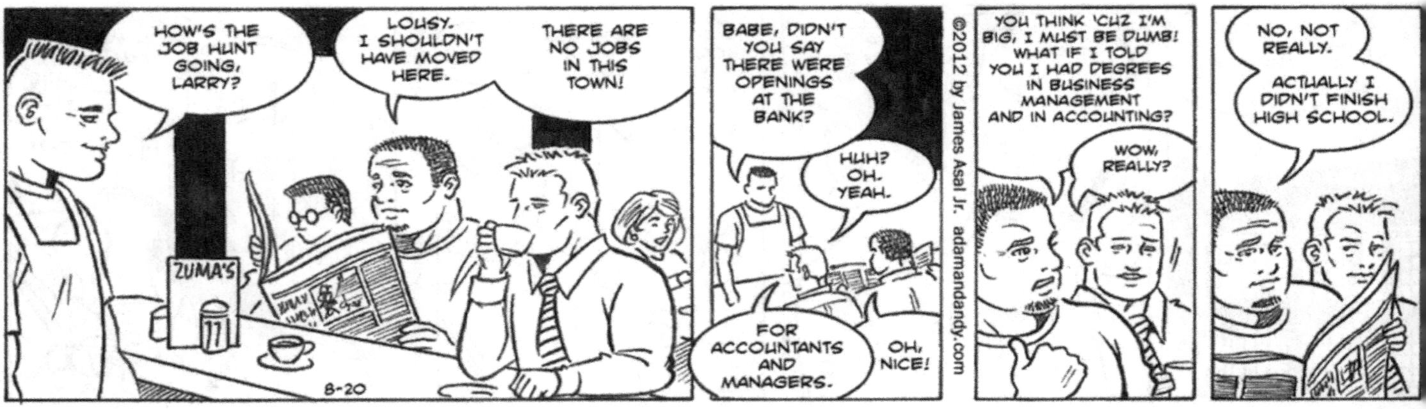
HOW'S THE JOB HUNT GOING, LARRY?
LOUSY. I SHOULDN'T HAVE MOVED HERE.
THERE ARE NO JOBS IN THIS TOWN!
ZUMA'S
8-20
BABE, DIDN'T YOU SAY THERE WERE OPENINGS AT THE BANK?
HUH? OH. YEAH.
FOR ACCOUNTANTS AND MANAGERS.
OH, NICE!
©2012 by James Asal Jr. adamandandy.com
YOU THINK 'CUZ I'M BIG, I MUST BE DUMB! WHAT IF I TOLD YOU I HAD DEGREES IN BUSINESS MANAGEMENT AND IN ACCOUNTING?
WOW, REALLY?
NO, NOT REALLY.
ACTUALLY I DIDN'T FINISH HIGH SCHOOL.

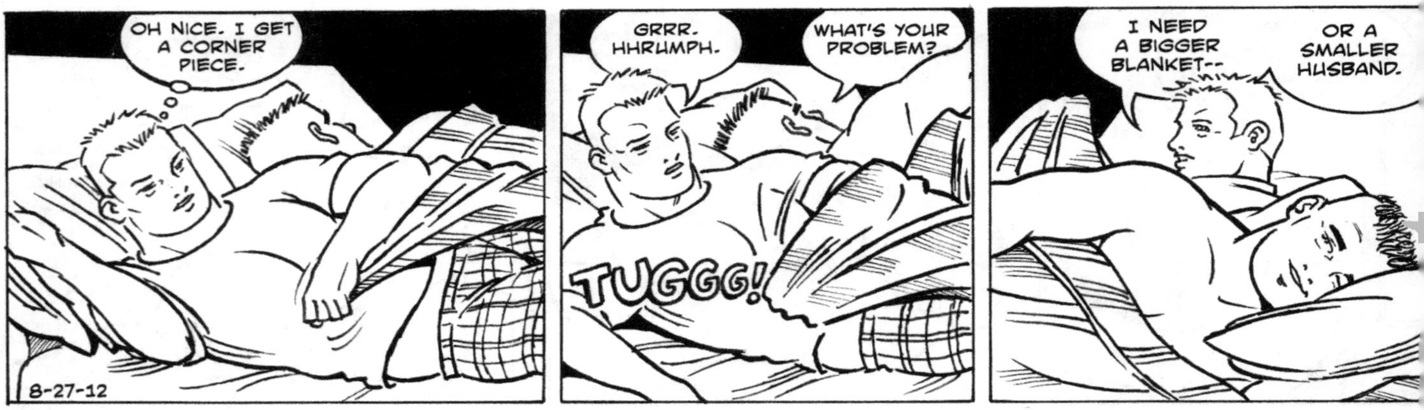
OH NICE. I GET A CORNER PIECE.
8-27-12
GRRR. HHRUMPH.
WHAT'S YOUR PROBLEM?
TUGGG!
I NEED A BIGGER BLANKET--
OR A SMALLER HUSBAND.

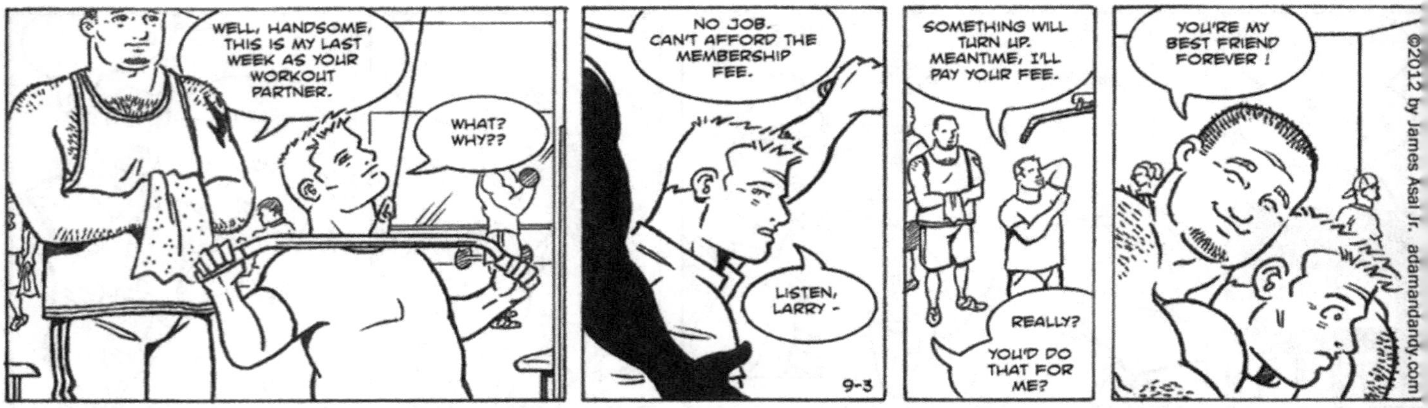
WELL, HANDSOME, THIS IS MY LAST WEEK AS YOUR WORKOUT PARTNER.
WHAT? WHY??
NO JOB. CAN'T AFFORD THE MEMBERSHIP FEE.
LISTEN, LARRY -
9-3
SOMETHING WILL TURN UP. MEANTIME, I'LL PAY YOUR FEE.
REALLY?
YOU'D DO THAT FOR ME?
YOU'RE MY BEST FRIEND FOREVER !
©2012 by James Asal Jr. adamandandy.com

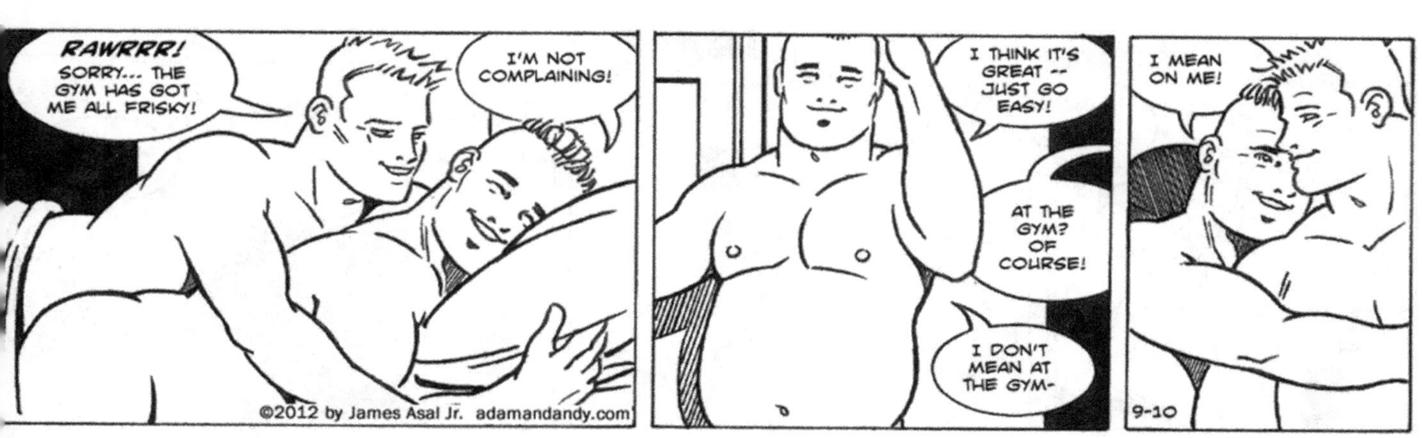
RAWRRR!
SORRY... THE GYM HAS GOT ME ALL FRISKY!
I'M NOT COMPLAINING!
©2012 by James Asal Jr. adamandandy.com
I THINK IT'S GREAT -- JUST GO EASY!
AT THE GYM? OF COURSE!
I DON'T MEAN AT THE GYM-
I MEAN ON ME!
9-10

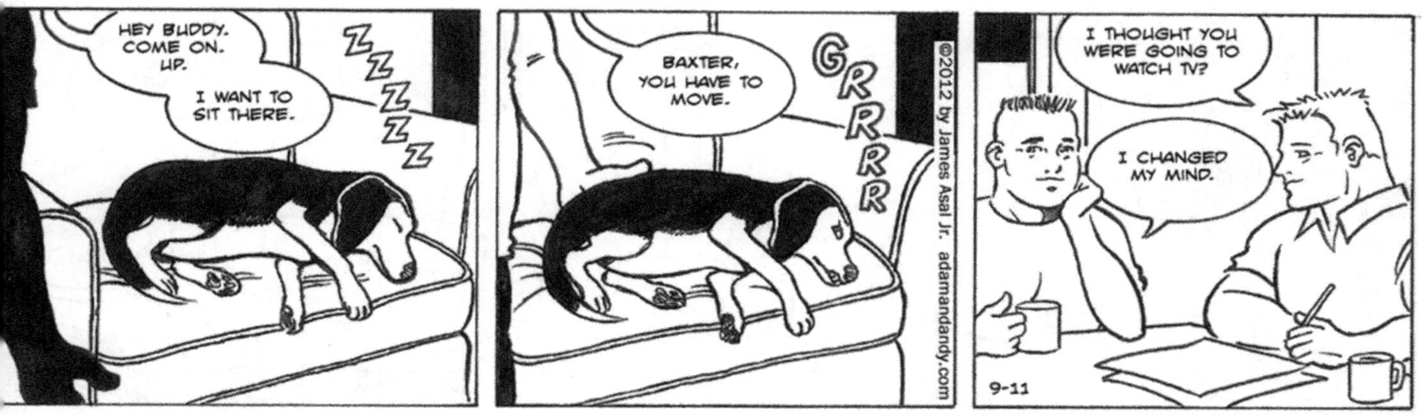
HEY BUDDY. COME ON. UP.
I WANT TO SIT THERE.
ZZZZ
BAXTER, YOU HAVE TO MOVE.
GRRRR
©2012 by James Asal Jr. adamandandy.com
I THOUGHT YOU WERE GOING TO WATCH TV?
I CHANGED MY MIND.
9-11

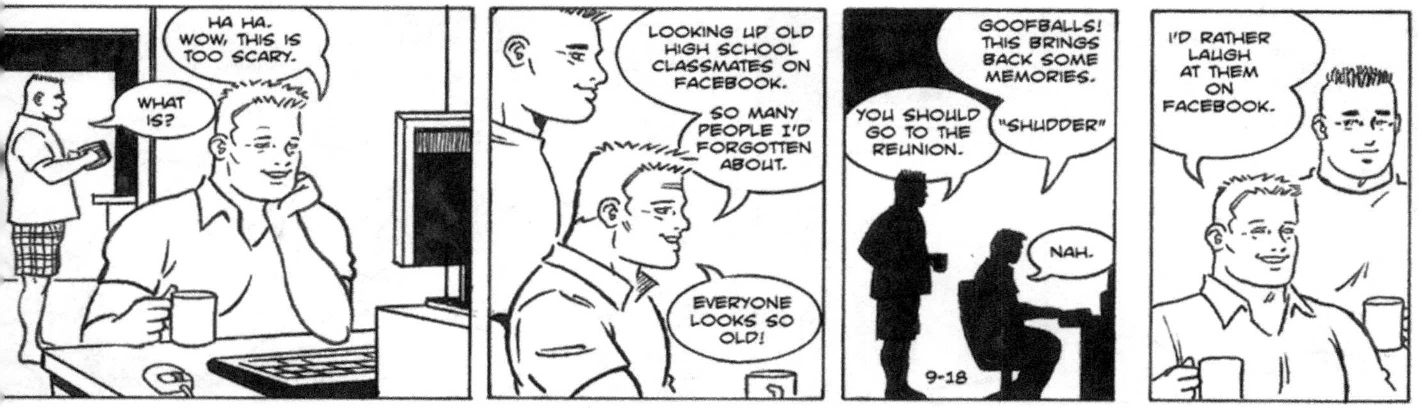
HA HA. WOW, THIS IS TOO SCARY.
WHAT IS?
LOOKING UP OLD HIGH SCHOOL CLASSMATES ON FACEBOOK.
SO MANY PEOPLE I'D FORGOTTEN ABOUT.
EVERYONE LOOKS SO OLD!
GOOFBALLS! THIS BRINGS BACK SOME MEMORIES.
"SHUDDER"
YOU SHOULD GO TO THE REUNION.
NAH.
9-18
I'D RATHER LAUGH AT THEM ON FACEBOOK.

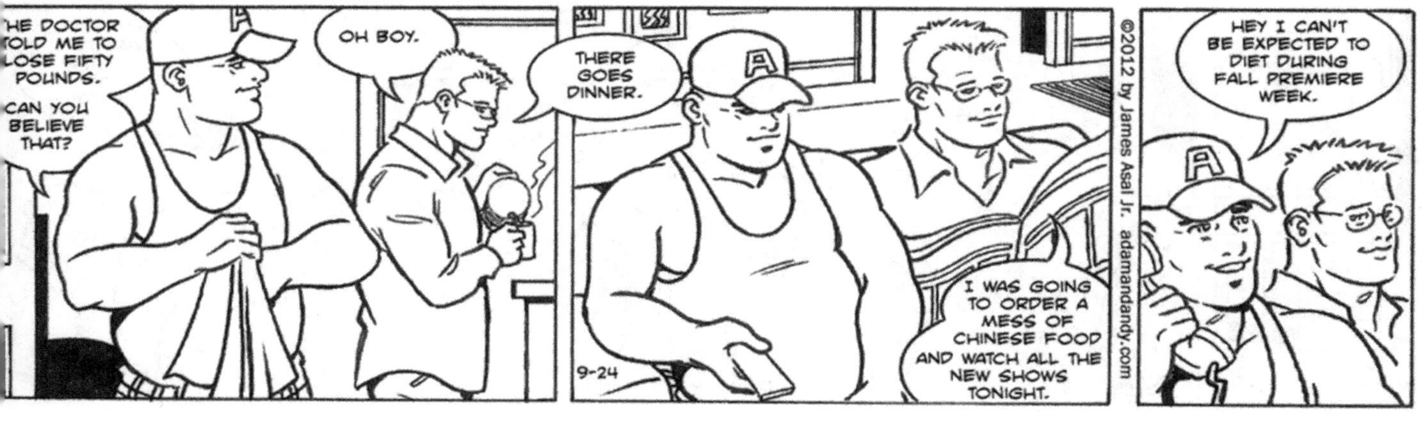
HE DOCTOR OLD ME TO OSE FIFTY POUNDS.
CAN YOU BELIEVE THAT?
OH BOY.
THERE GOES DINNER.
I WAS GOING TO ORDER A MESS OF CHINESE FOOD AND WATCH ALL THE NEW SHOWS TONIGHT.
9-24
©2012 by James Asal Jr. adamandandy.com
HEY I CAN'T BE EXPECTED TO DIET DURING FALL PREMIERE WEEK.

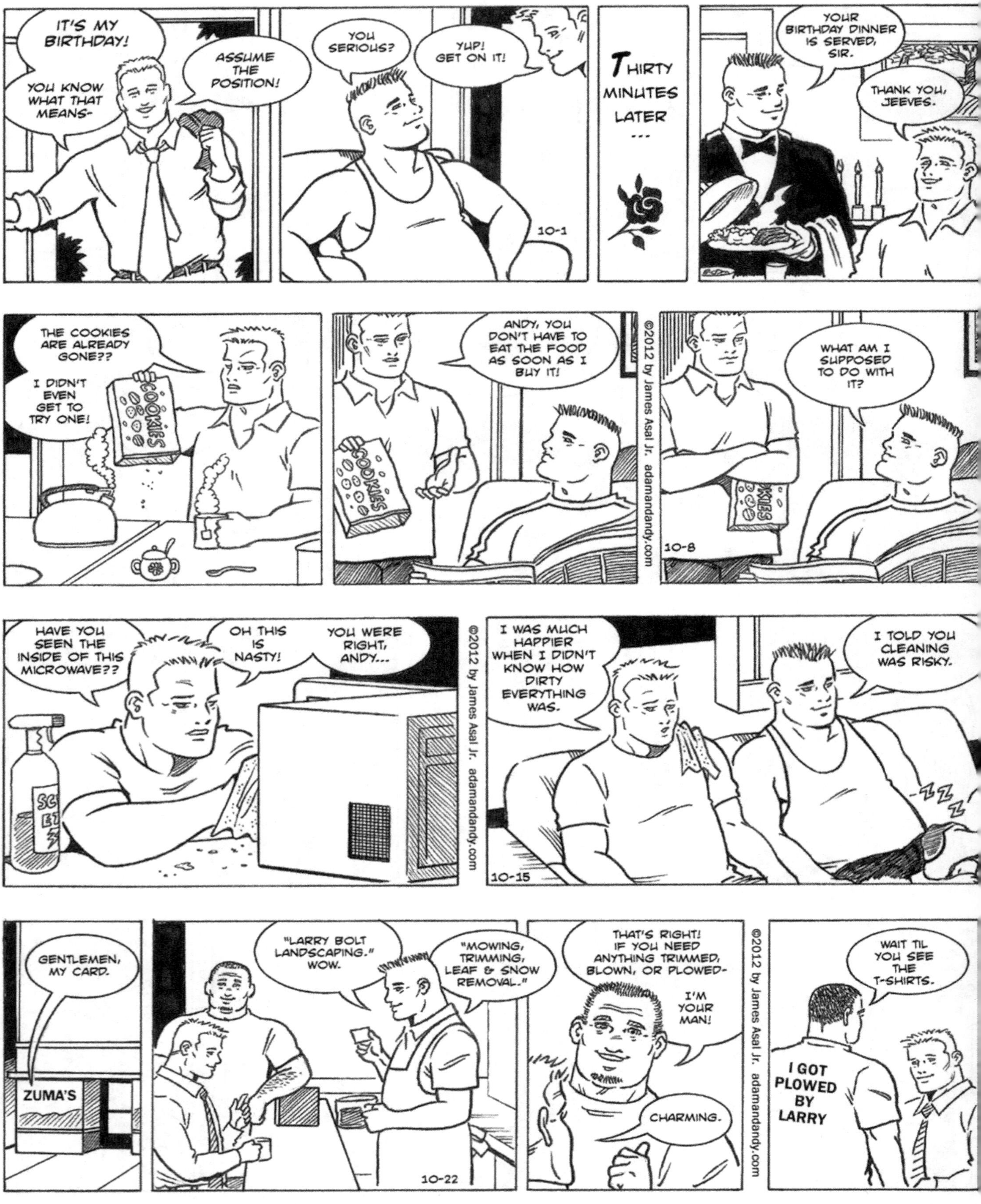
IT'S MY BIRTHDAY!
YOU KNOW WHAT THAT MEANS-
ASSUME THE POSITION!
YOU SERIOUS?
YUP! GET ON IT!
10-1
THIRTY MINUTES LATER ---
YOUR BIRTHDAY DINNER IS SERVED, SIR.
THANK YOU, JEEVES.
THE COOKIES ARE ALREADY GONE??
I DIDN'T EVEN GET TO TRY ONE!
COOKIES
ANDY, YOU DON'T HAVE TO EAT THE FOOD AS SOON AS I BUY IT!
©2012 by James Asal Jr. adamandandy.com
WHAT AM I SUPPOSED TO DO WITH IT?
10-8
HAVE YOU SEEN THE INSIDE OF THIS MICROWAVE??
OH THIS IS NASTY!
YOU WERE RIGHT, ANDY...
©2012 by James Asal Jr. adamandandy.com
I WAS MUCH HAPPIER WHEN I DIDN'T KNOW HOW DIRTY EVERYTHING WAS.
I TOLD YOU CLEANING WAS RISKY.
ZZZ
10-15
GENTLEMEN, MY CARD.
ZUMA'S
"LARRY BOLT LANDSCAPING." WOW.
"MOWING, TRIMMING, LEAF & SNOW REMOVAL."
10-22
THAT'S RIGHT! IF YOU NEED ANYTHING TRIMMED, BLOWN, OR PLOWED-
I'M YOUR MAN!
CHARMING.
©2012 by James Asal Jr. adamandandy.com
WAIT TIL YOU SEE THE T-SHIRTS.
I GOT PLOWED BY LARRY

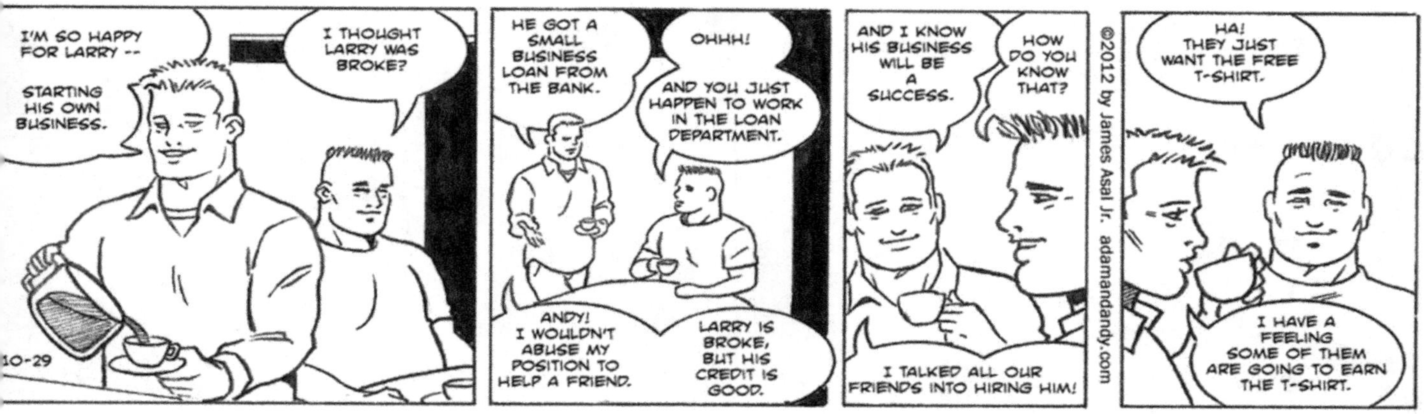
I'M SO HAPPY FOR LARRY --
STARTING HIS OWN BUSINESS.
I THOUGHT LARRY WAS BROKE?
10-29
HE GOT A SMALL BUSINESS LOAN FROM THE BANK.
OHHH!
AND YOU JUST HAPPEN TO WORK IN THE LOAN DEPARTMENT.
ANDY! I WOULDN'T ABUSE MY POSITION TO HELP A FRIEND.
LARRY IS BROKE, BUT HIS CREDIT IS GOOD.
AND I KNOW HIS BUSINESS WILL BE A SUCCESS.
HOW DO YOU KNOW THAT?
I TALKED ALL OUR FRIENDS INTO HIRING HIM!
©2012 by James Asal Jr. adamandandy.com
HA! THEY JUST WANT THE FREE T-SHIRT.
I HAVE A FEELING SOME OF THEM ARE GOING TO EARN THE T-SHIRT.

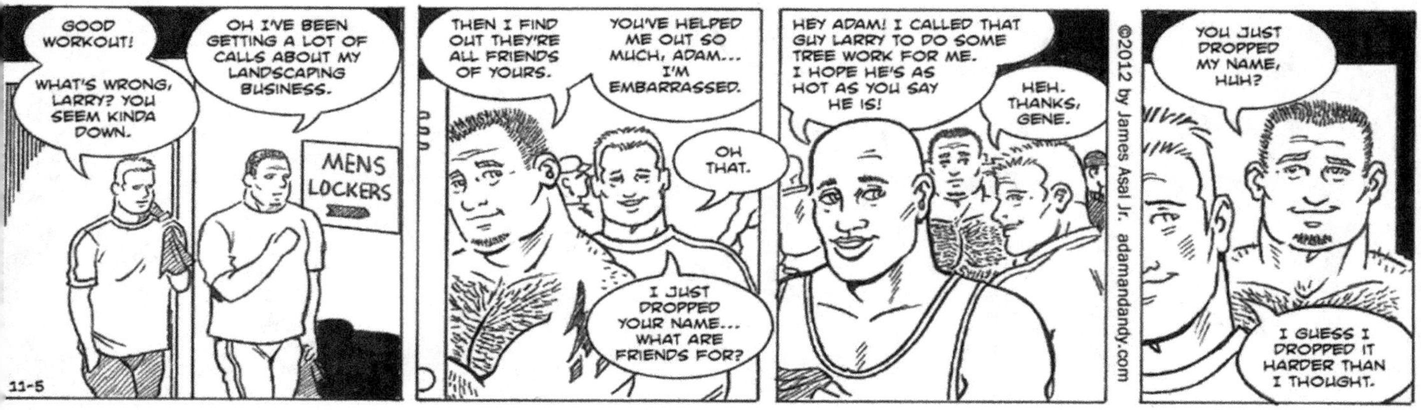
GOOD WORKOUT!
WHAT'S WRONG, LARRY? YOU SEEM KINDA DOWN.
OH I'VE BEEN GETTING A LOT OF CALLS ABOUT MY LANDSCAPING BUSINESS.
MENS LOCKERS
11-5
THEN I FIND OUT THEY'RE ALL FRIENDS OF YOURS.
YOU'VE HELPED ME OUT SO MUCH, ADAM... I'M EMBARRASSED.
OH THAT.
I JUST DROPPED YOUR NAME... WHAT ARE FRIENDS FOR?
HEY ADAM! I CALLED THAT GUY LARRY TO DO SOME TREE WORK FOR ME. I HOPE HE'S AS HOT AS YOU SAY HE IS!
HEH. THANKS, GENE.
©2012 by James Asal Jr. adamandandy.com
YOU JUST DROPPED MY NAME, HUH?
I GUESS I DROPPED IT HARDER THAN I THOUGHT.

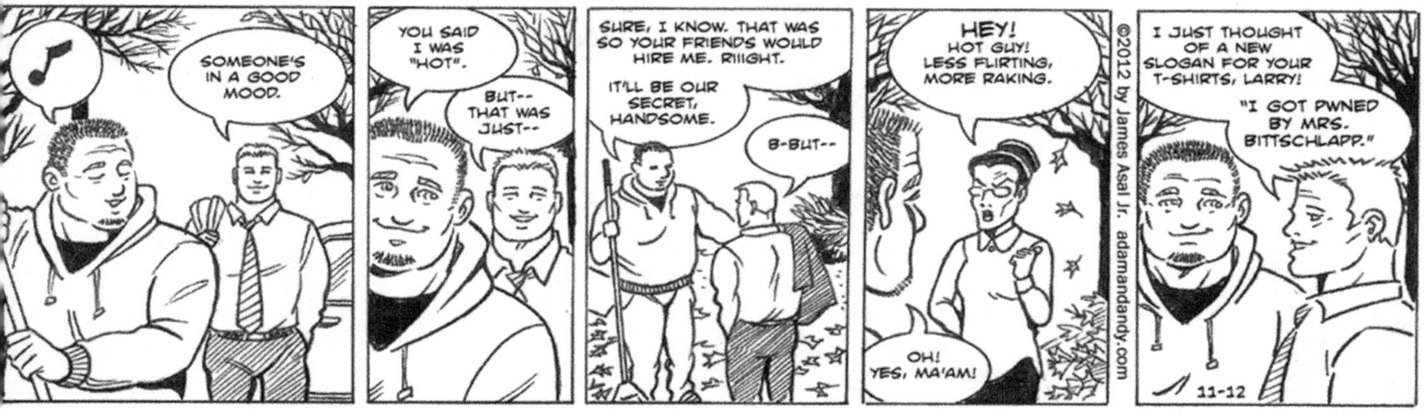
SOMEONE'S IN A GOOD MOOD.
YOU SAID I WAS "HOT".
BUT-- THAT WAS JUST--
SURE, I KNOW. THAT WAS SO YOUR FRIENDS WOULD HIRE ME. RIIIGHT.
IT'LL BE OUR SECRET, HANDSOME.
B-BUT--
HEY! HOT GUY! LESS FLIRTING, MORE RAKING.
OH! YES, MA'AM!
©2012 by James Asal Jr. adamandandy.com
I JUST THOUGHT OF A NEW SLOGAN FOR YOUR T-SHIRTS, LARRY!
"I GOT PWNED BY MRS. BITTSCHLAPP."
11-12

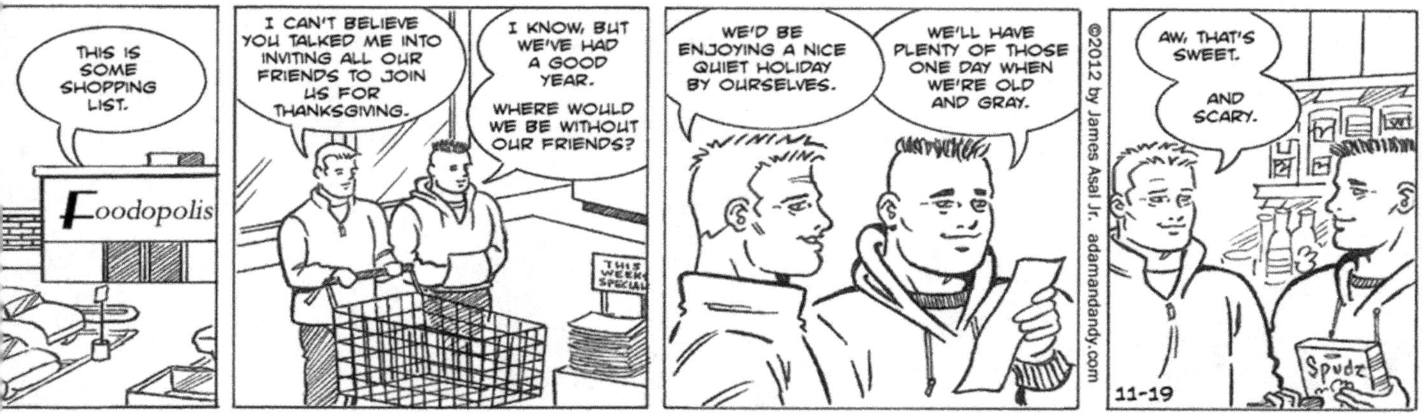
THIS IS SOME SHOPPING LIST.
Foodopolis
I CAN'T BELIEVE YOU TALKED ME INTO INVITING ALL OUR FRIENDS TO JOIN US FOR THANKSGIVING.
I KNOW, BUT WE'VE HAD A GOOD YEAR.
WHERE WOULD WE BE WITHOUT OUR FRIENDS?
WE'D BE ENJOYING A NICE QUIET HOLIDAY BY OURSELVES.
WE'LL HAVE PLENTY OF THOSE ONE DAY WHEN WE'RE OLD AND GRAY.
©2012 by James Asal Jr. adamandandy.com
AW, THAT'S SWEET.
AND SCARY.
Spudz
11-19

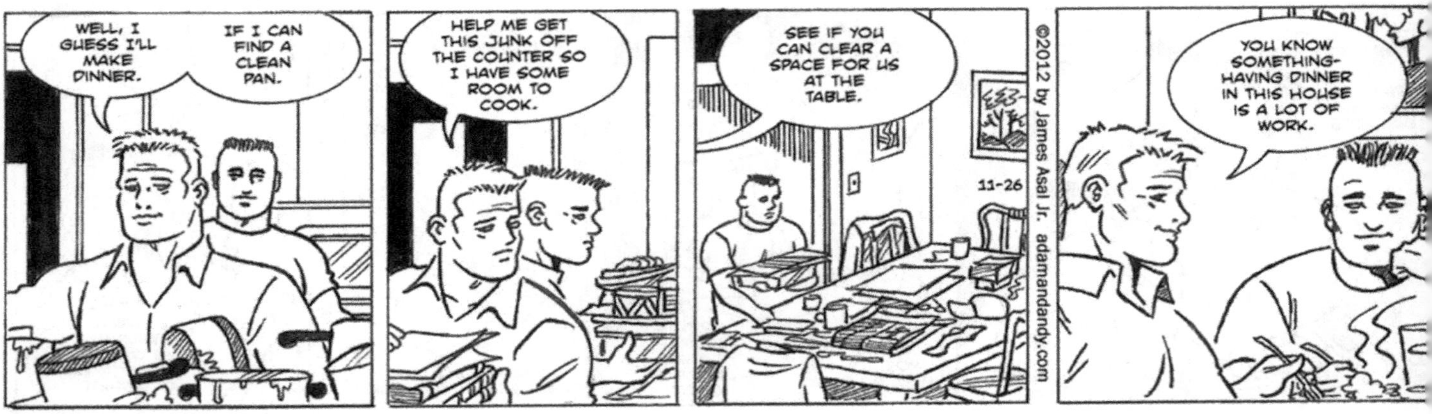
WELL, I GUESS I'LL MAKE DINNER.
IF I CAN FIND A CLEAN PAN.
HELP ME GET THIS JUNK OFF THE COUNTER SO I HAVE SOME ROOM TO COOK.
SEE IF YOU CAN CLEAR A SPACE FOR US AT THE TABLE.
11-26
©2012 by James Asal Jr. adamandandy.com
YOU KNOW SOMETHING- HAVING DINNER IN THIS HOUSE IS A LOT OF WORK.

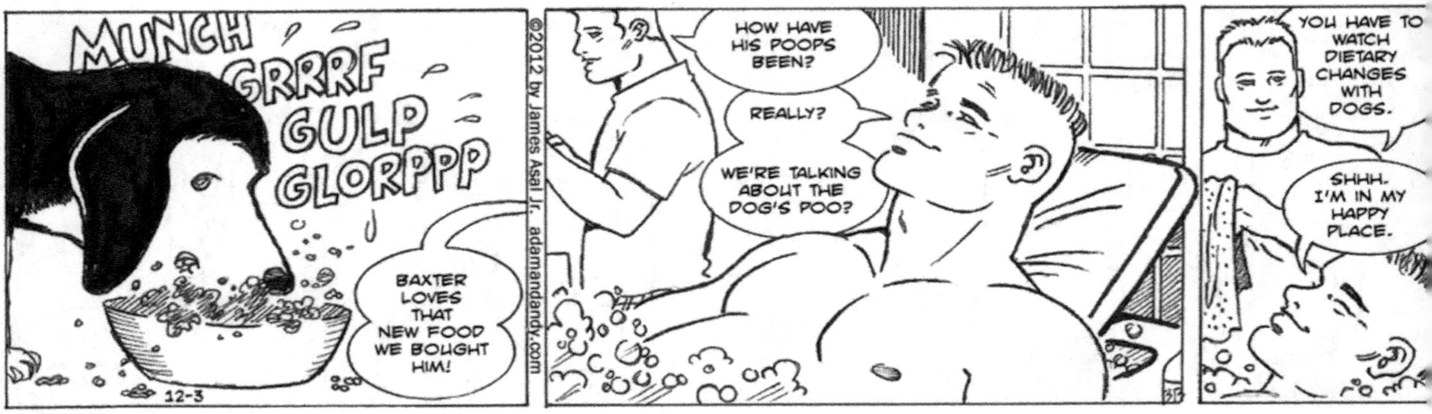
MUNCH
GRRRF
GULP
GLORPPP
BAXTER LOVES THAT NEW FOOD WE BOUGHT HIM!
12-3
©2012 by James Asal Jr. adamandandy.com
HOW HAVE HIS POOPS BEEN?
REALLY?
WE'RE TALKING ABOUT THE DOG'S POO?
YOU HAVE TO WATCH DIETARY CHANGES WITH DOGS.
SHHH. I'M IN MY HAPPY PLACE.

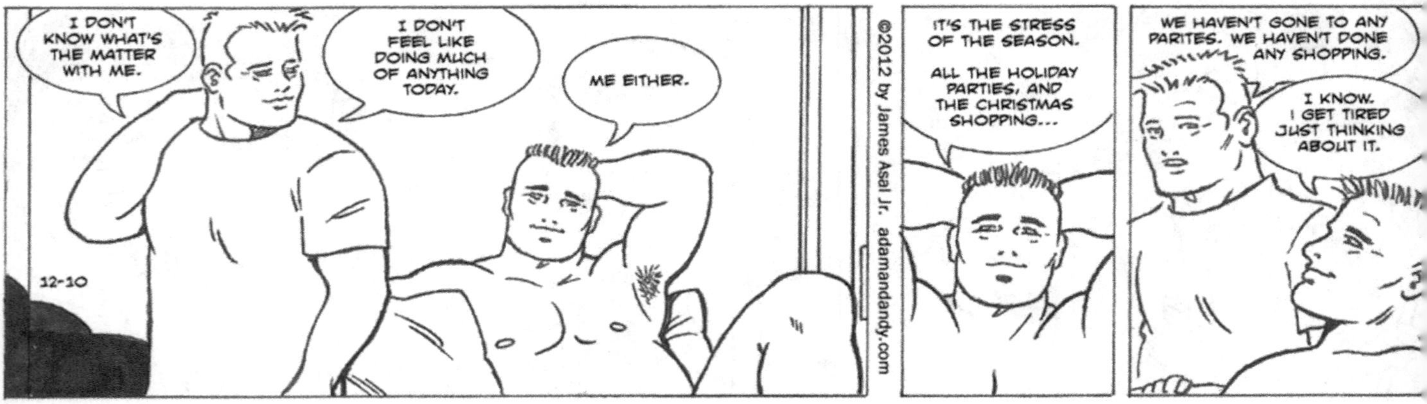
I DON'T KNOW WHAT'S THE MATTER WITH ME.
I DON'T FEEL LIKE DOING MUCH OF ANYTHING TODAY.
ME EITHER.
12-10
©2012 by James Asal Jr. adamandandy.com
IT'S THE STRESS OF THE SEASON.
ALL THE HOLIDAY PARTIES, AND THE CHRISTMAS SHOPPING...
WE HAVEN'T GONE TO ANY PARITES. WE HAVEN'T DONE ANY SHOPPING.
I KNOW. I GET TIRED JUST THINKING ABOUT IT.

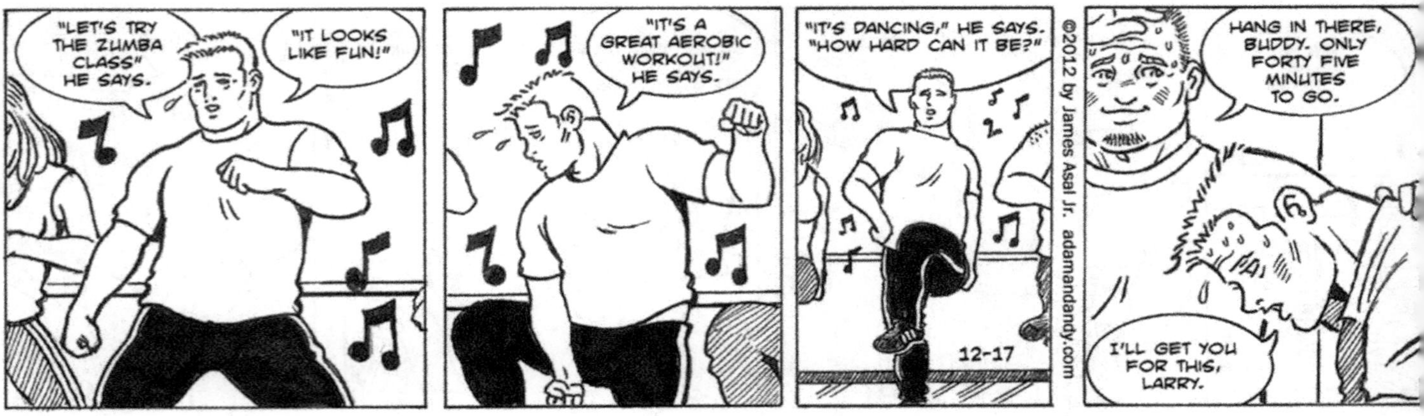
"LET'S TRY THE ZUMBA CLASS" HE SAYS.
"IT LOOKS LIKE FUN!"
"IT'S A GREAT AEROBIC WORKOUT!" HE SAYS.
"IT'S DANCING," HE SAYS. "HOW HARD CAN IT BE?"
12-17
©2012 by James Asal Jr. adamandandy.com
HANG IN THERE, BUDDY. ONLY FORTY FIVE MINUTES TO GO.
I'LL GET YOU FOR THIS, LARRY.

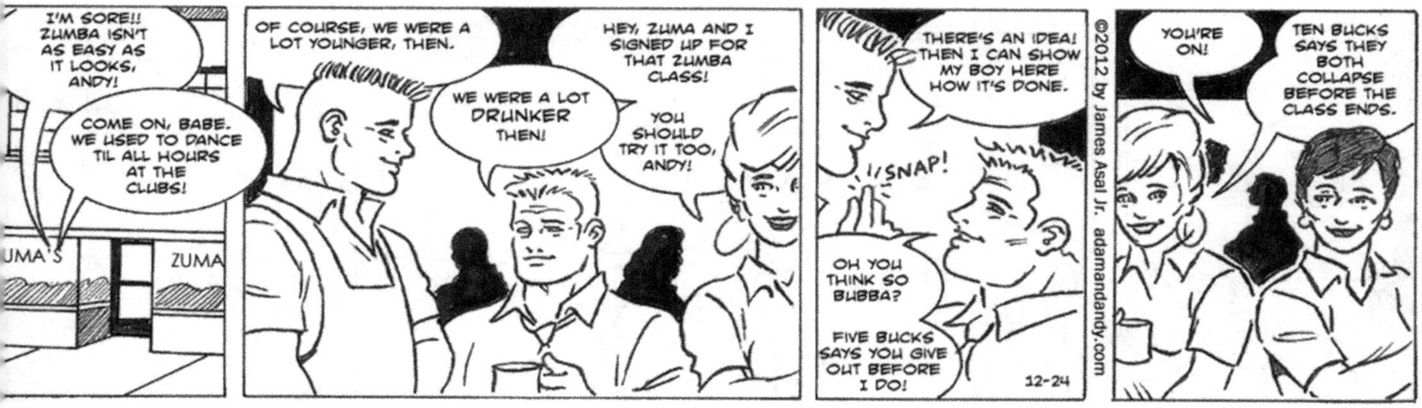
I'M SORE!! ZUMBA ISN'T AS EASY AS IT LOOKS, ANDY!
COME ON, BABE. WE USED TO DANCE TIL ALL HOURS AT THE CLUBS!
UMA'S
ZUMA
OF COURSE, WE WERE A LOT YOUNGER, THEN.
WE WERE A LOT DRUNKER THEN!
HEY, ZUMA AND I SIGNED UP FOR THAT ZUMBA CLASS!
YOU SHOULD TRY IT TOO, ANDY!
THERE'S AN IDEA! THEN I CAN SHOW MY BOY HERE HOW IT'S DONE.
SNAP!
OH YOU THINK SO BUBBA?
FIVE BUCKS SAYS YOU GIVE OUT BEFORE I DO!
12-24
©2012 by James Asal Jr. adamandandy.com
YOU'RE ON!
TEN BUCKS SAYS THEY BOTH COLLAPSE BEFORE THE CLASS ENDS.

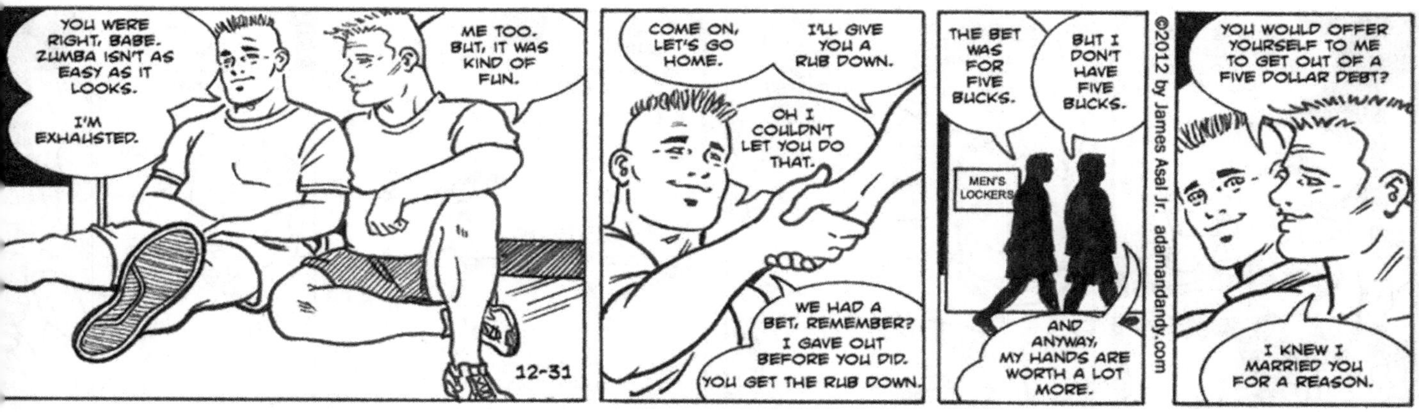
YOU WERE RIGHT, BABE. ZUMBA ISN'T AS EASY AS IT LOOKS.
I'M EXHAUSTED.
ME TOO. BUT, IT WAS KIND OF FUN.
12-31
COME ON, LET'S GO HOME.
I'LL GIVE YOU A RUB DOWN.
OH I COULDN'T LET YOU DO THAT.
WE HAD A BET, REMEMBER? I GAVE OUT BEFORE YOU DID.
YOU GET THE RUB DOWN.
THE BET WAS FOR FIVE BUCKS.
BUT I DON'T HAVE FIVE BUCKS.
MEN'S LOCKERS
AND ANYWAY, MY HANDS ARE WORTH A LOT MORE.
©2012 by James Asal Jr. adamandandy.com
YOU WOULD OFFER YOURSELF TO ME TO GET OUT OF A FIVE DOLLAR DEBT?
I KNEW I MARRIED YOU FOR A REASON.

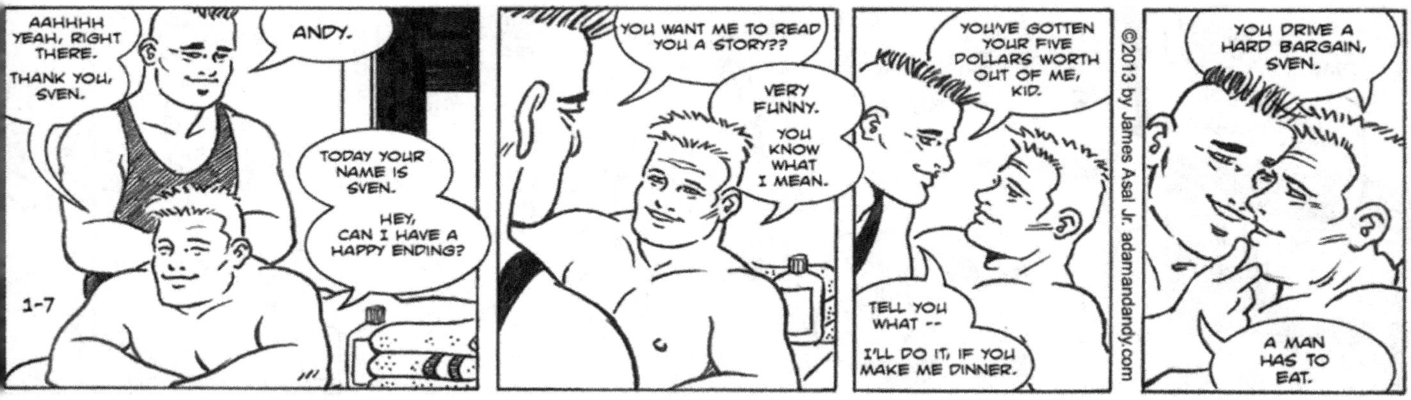
AAHHHH YEAH, RIGHT THERE.
THANK YOU, SVEN.
ANDY.
TODAY YOUR NAME IS SVEN.
HEY, CAN I HAVE A HAPPY ENDING?
1-7
YOU WANT ME TO READ YOU A STORY??
VERY FUNNY.
YOU KNOW WHAT I MEAN.
YOU'VE GOTTEN YOUR FIVE DOLLARS WORTH OUT OF ME, KID.
TELL YOU WHAT --
I'LL DO IT, IF YOU MAKE ME DINNER.
©2013 by James Asal Jr. adamandandy.com
YOU DRIVE A HARD BARGAIN, SVEN.
A MAN HAS TO EAT.

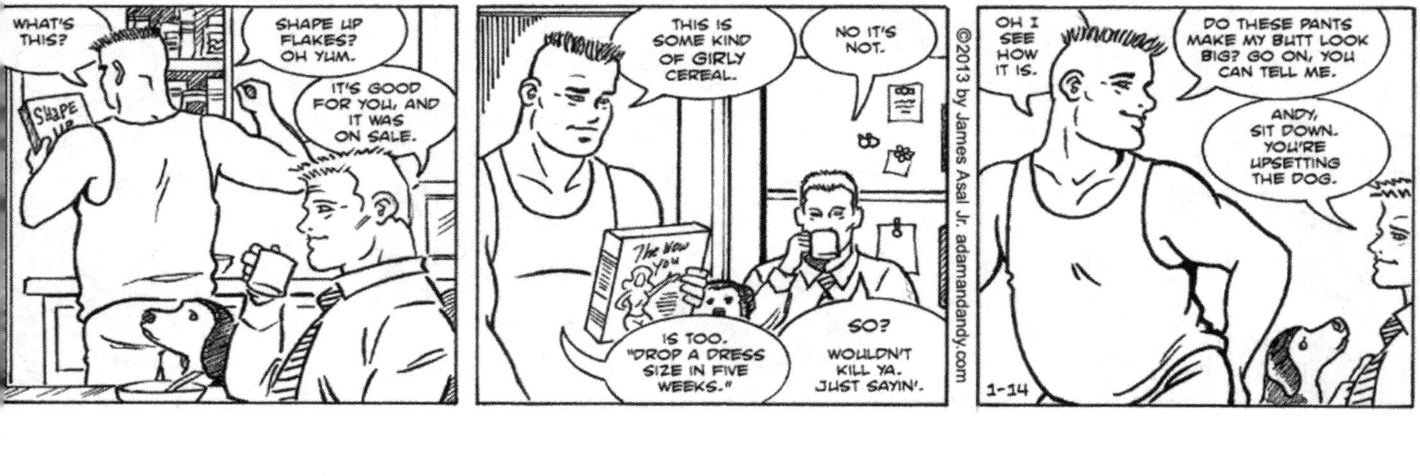
WHAT'S THIS?
SHAPE UP
SHAPE UP FLAKES? OH YUM.
IT'S GOOD FOR YOU, AND IT WAS ON SALE.
THIS IS SOME KIND OF GIRLY CEREAL.
NO IT'S NOT.
IS TOO. "DROP A DRESS SIZE IN FIVE WEEKS."
SO?
WOULDN'T KILL YA. JUST SAYIN'.
©2013 by James Asal Jr. adamandandy.com
OH I SEE HOW IT IS.
DO THESE PANTS MAKE MY BUTT LOOK BIG? GO ON, YOU CAN TELL ME.
ANDY, SIT DOWN. YOU'RE UPSETTING THE DOG.
1-14

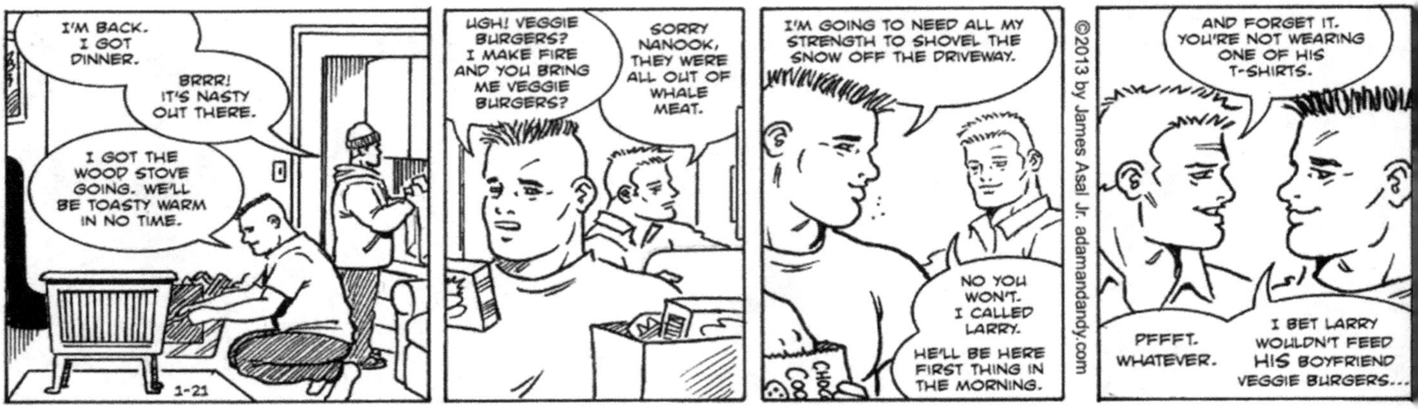
I'M BACK. I GOT DINNER.
BRRR! IT'S NASTY OUT THERE.
I GOT THE WOOD STOVE GOING. WE'LL BE TOASTY WARM IN NO TIME.
1-21
UGH! VEGGIE BURGERS? I MAKE FIRE AND YOU BRING ME VEGGIE BURGERS?
SORRY NANOOK, THEY WERE ALL OUT OF WHALE MEAT.
I'M GOING TO NEED ALL MY STRENGTH TO SHOVEL THE SNOW OFF THE DRIVEWAY.
NO YOU WON'T. I CALLED LARRY.
HE'LL BE HERE FIRST THING IN THE MORNING.
©2013 by James Asal Jr. adamandandy.com
AND FORGET IT. YOU'RE NOT WEARING ONE OF HIS T-SHIRTS.
PFFFT. WHATEVER.
I BET LARRY WOULDN'T FEED HIS BOYFRIEND VEGGIE BURGERS...

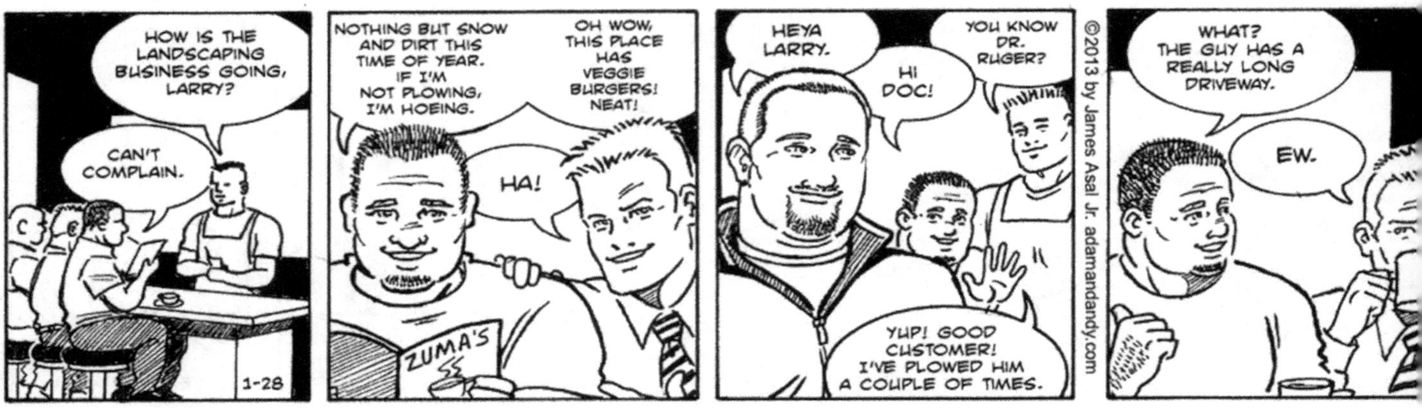
HOW IS THE LANDSCAPING BUSINESS GOING, LARRY?
CAN'T COMPLAIN.
1-28
NOTHING BUT SNOW AND DIRT THIS TIME OF YEAR. IF I'M NOT PLOWING, I'M HOEING.
OH WOW, THIS PLACE HAS VEGGIE BURGERS! NEAT!
HA!
ZUMA'S
HEYA LARRY.
HI DOC!
YOU KNOW DR. RUGER?
YUP! GOOD CUSTOMER! I'VE PLOWED HIM A COUPLE OF TIMES.
©2013 by James Asal Jr. adamandandy.com
WHAT? THE GUY HAS A REALLY LONG DRIVEWAY.
EW.

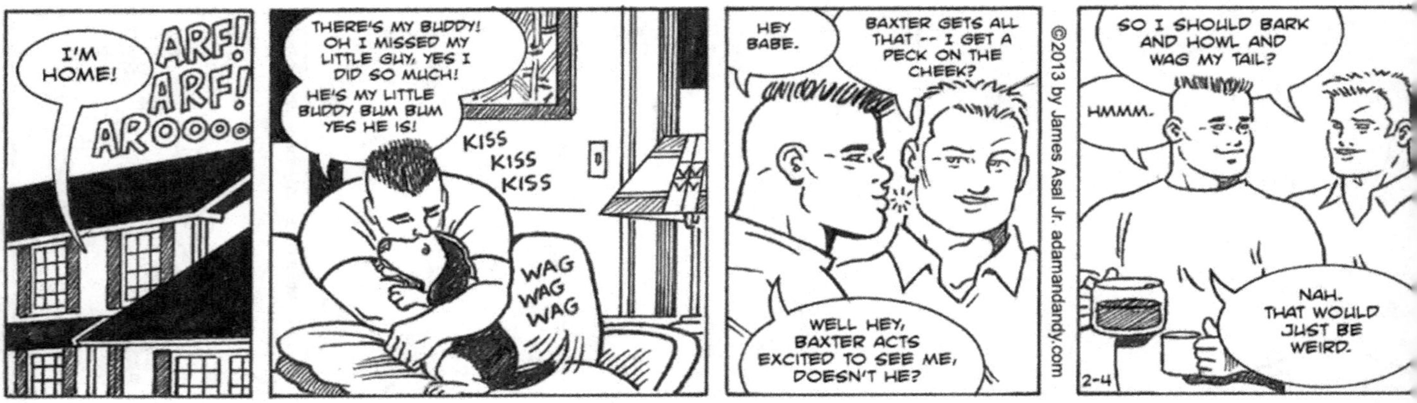
I'M HOME!
ARF! ARF! AROOOO
THERE'S MY BUDDY! OH I MISSED MY LITTLE GUY, YES I DID SO MUCH!
HE'S MY LITTLE BUDDY BUM BUM YES HE IS!
KISS KISS KISS
WAG WAG WAG
HEY BABE.
BAXTER GETS ALL THAT -- I GET A PECK ON THE CHEEK?
WELL HEY, BAXTER ACTS EXCITED TO SEE ME, DOESN'T HE?
©2013 by James Asal Jr. adamandandy.com
SO I SHOULD BARK AND HOWL AND WAG MY TAIL?
HMMM.
NAH. THAT WOULD JUST BE WEIRD.
2-4

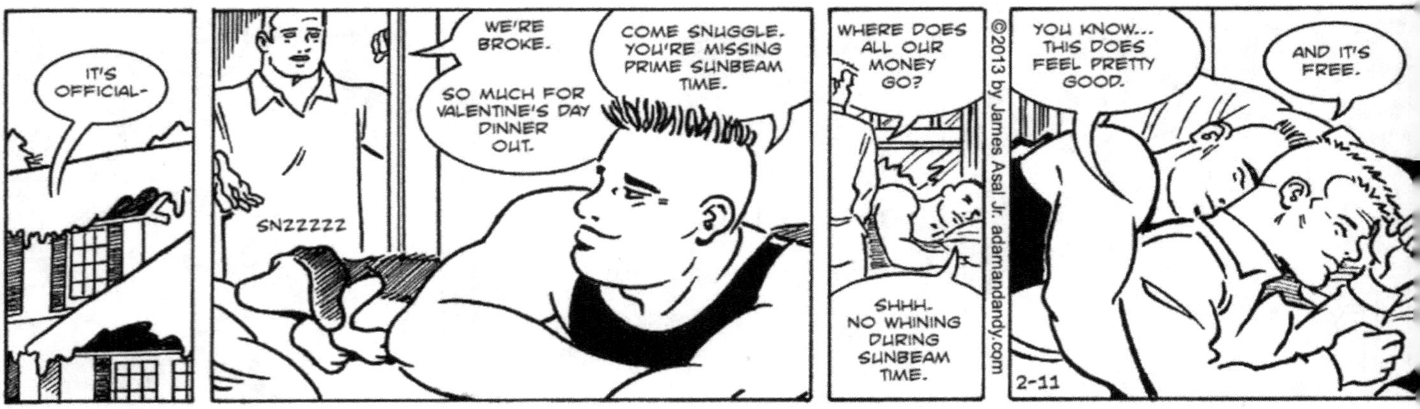
IT'S OFFICIAL-
SNZZZZZ
WE'RE BROKE.
SO MUCH FOR VALENTINE'S DAY DINNER OUT.
COME SNUGGLE. YOU'RE MISSING PRIME SUNBEAM TIME.
WHERE DOES ALL OUR MONEY GO?
SHHH. NO WHINING DURING SUNBEAM TIME.
©2013 by James Asal Jr. adamandandy.com
YOU KNOW... THIS DOES FEEL PRETTY GOOD.
AND IT'S FREE.
2-11

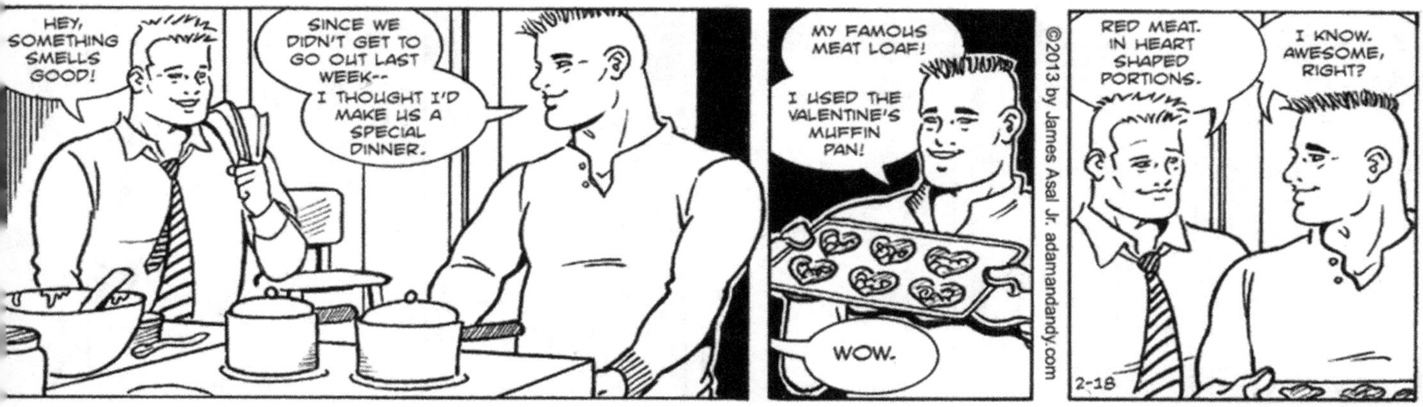
HEY, SOMETHING SMELLS GOOD!
SINCE WE DIDN'T GET TO GO OUT LAST WEEK--
I THOUGHT I'D MAKE US A SPECIAL DINNER.
MY FAMOUS MEAT LOAF!
I USED THE VALENTINE'S MUFFIN PAN!
WOW.
©2013 by James Asal Jr. adamandandy.com
RED MEAT. IN HEART SHAPED PORTIONS.
I KNOW. AWESOME, RIGHT?
2-18

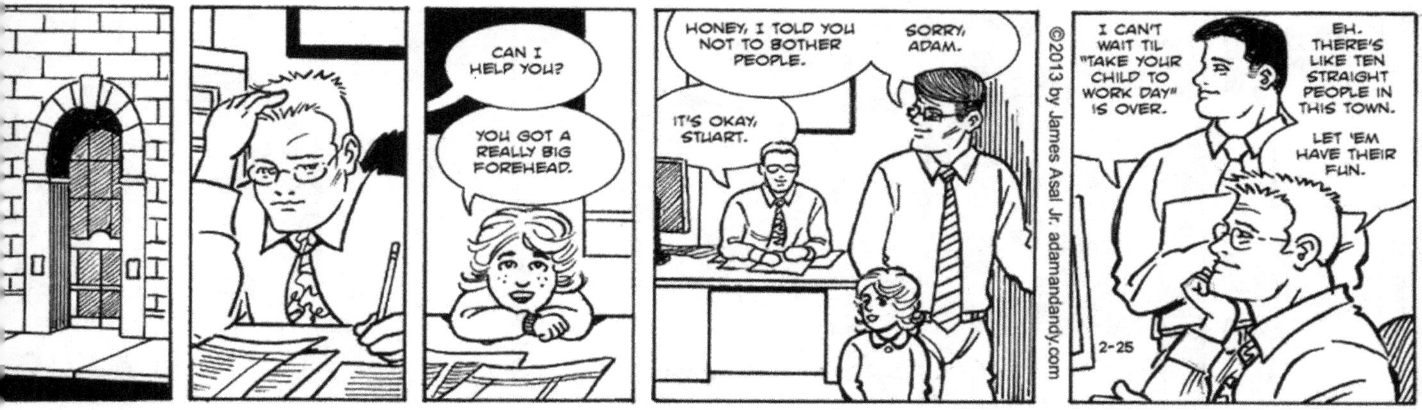
CAN I HELP YOU?
YOU GOT A REALLY BIG FOREHEAD.
HONEY, I TOLD YOU NOT TO BOTHER PEOPLE.
SORRY, ADAM.
IT'S OKAY, STUART.
©2013 by James Asal Jr. adamandandy.com
I CAN'T WAIT TIL "TAKE YOUR CHILD TO WORK DAY" IS OVER.
EH. THERE'S LIKE TEN STRAIGHT PEOPLE IN THIS TOWN.
LET 'EM HAVE THEIR FUN.
2-25

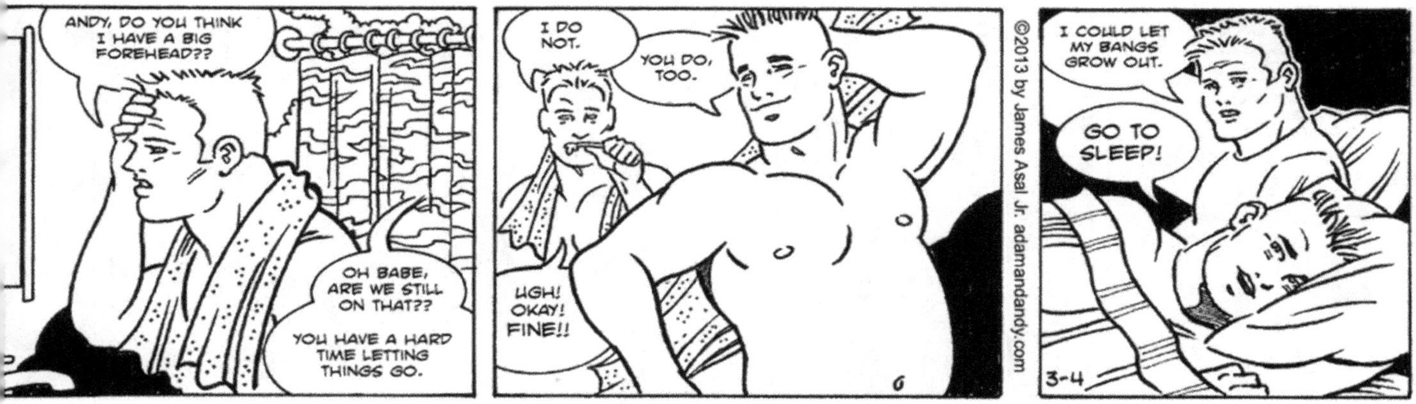
ANDY, DO YOU THINK I HAVE A BIG FOREHEAD??
OH BABE, ARE WE STILL ON THAT??
YOU HAVE A HARD TIME LETTING THINGS GO.
I DO NOT.
YOU DO, TOO.
UGH! OKAY! FINE!!
©2013 by James Asal Jr. adamandandy.com
I COULD LET MY BANGS GROW OUT.
GO TO SLEEP!
3-4

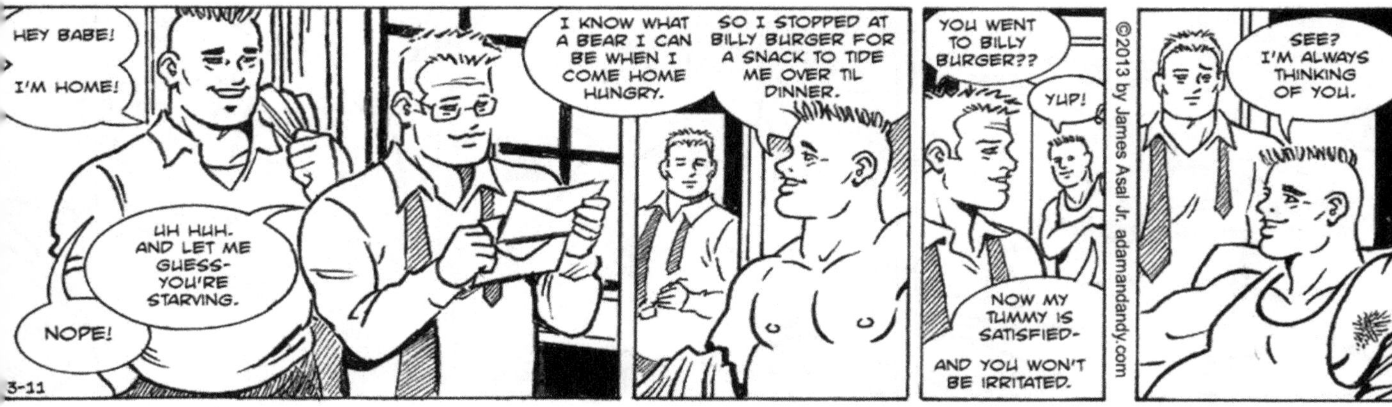
HEY BABE!
I'M HOME!
UH HUH. AND LET ME GUESS- YOU'RE STARVING.
NOPE!
I KNOW WHAT A BEAR I CAN BE WHEN I COME HOME HUNGRY.
SO I STOPPED AT BILLY BURGER FOR A SNACK TO TIDE ME OVER TIL DINNER.
YOU WENT TO BILLY BURGER??
YUP!
NOW MY TUMMY IS SATISFIED-
AND YOU WON'T BE IRRITATED.
©2013 by James Asal Jr. adamandandy.com
SEE? I'M ALWAYS THINKING OF YOU.
3-11

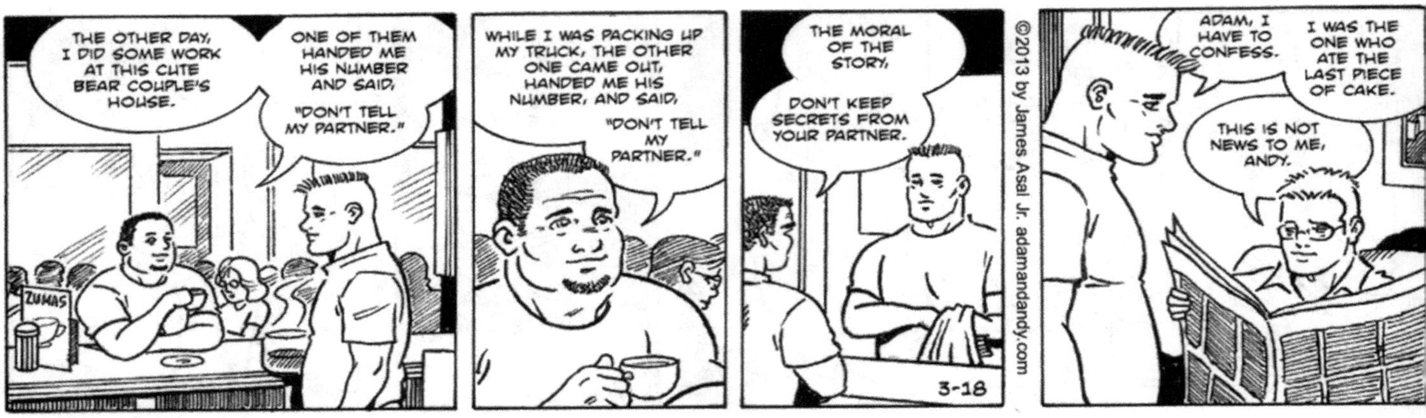
THE OTHER DAY, I DID SOME WORK AT THIS CUTE BEAR COUPLE'S HOUSE.
ONE OF THEM HANDED ME HIS NUMBER AND SAID,
"DON'T TELL MY PARTNER."
ZUMAS
WHILE I WAS PACKING UP MY TRUCK, THE OTHER ONE CAME OUT, HANDED ME HIS NUMBER, AND SAID,
"DON'T TELL MY PARTNER."
THE MORAL OF THE STORY,
DON'T KEEP SECRETS FROM YOUR PARTNER.
3-18
©2013 by James Asal Jr. adamandandy.com
ADAM, I HAVE TO CONFESS.
I WAS THE ONE WHO ATE THE LAST PIECE OF CAKE.
THIS IS NOT NEWS TO ME, ANDY.

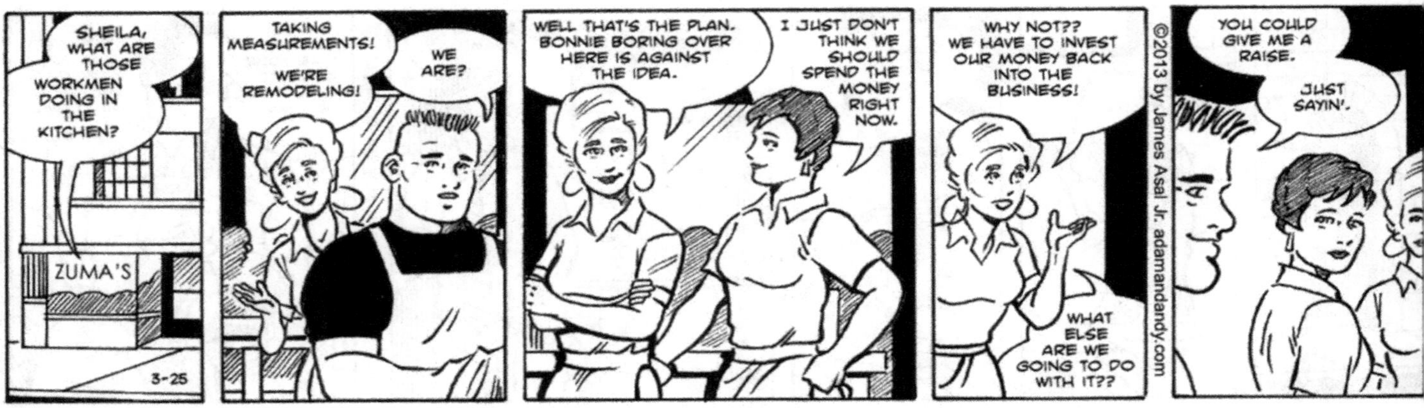
SHEILA, WHAT ARE THOSE WORKMEN DOING IN THE KITCHEN?
ZUMA'S
3-25
TAKING MEASUREMENTS!
WE'RE REMODELING!
WE ARE?
WELL THAT'S THE PLAN. BONNIE BORING OVER HERE IS AGAINST THE IDEA.
I JUST DON'T THINK WE SHOULD SPEND THE MONEY RIGHT NOW.
WHY NOT?? WE HAVE TO INVEST OUR MONEY BACK INTO THE BUSINESS!
WHAT ELSE ARE WE GOING TO DO WITH IT??
©2013 by James Asal Jr. adamandandy.com
YOU COULD GIVE ME A RAISE.
JUST SAYIN'.

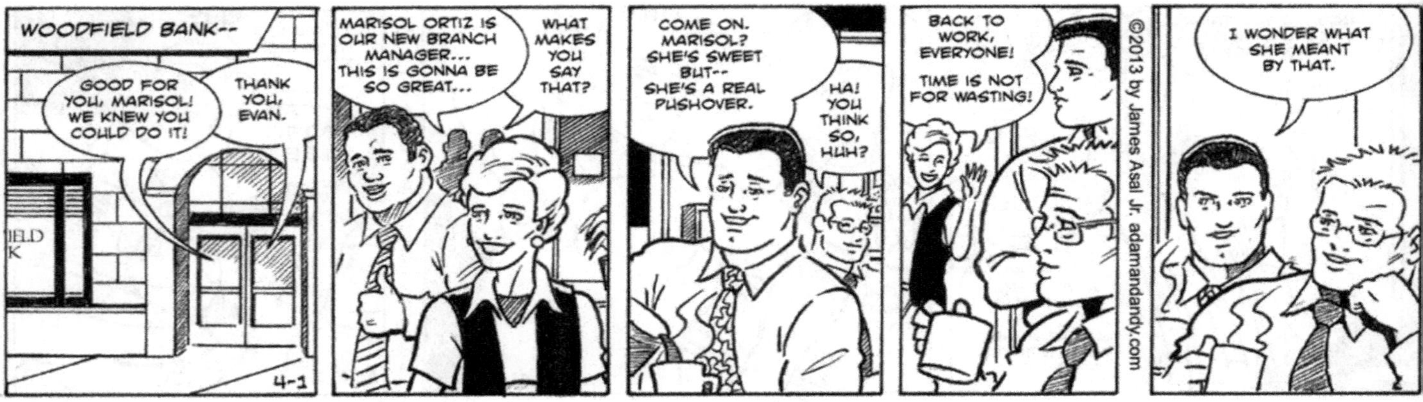
WOODFIELD BANK--
GOOD FOR YOU, MARISOL! WE KNEW YOU COULD DO IT!
THANK YOU, EVAN.
4-1
MARISOL ORTIZ IS OUR NEW BRANCH MANAGER... THIS IS GONNA BE SO GREAT...
WHAT MAKES YOU SAY THAT?
COME ON. MARISOL? SHE'S SWEET BUT-- SHE'S A REAL PUSHOVER.
HA! YOU THINK SO, HUH?
BACK TO WORK, EVERYONE!
TIME IS NOT FOR WASTING!
©2013 by James Asal Jr. adamandandy.com
I WONDER WHAT SHE MEANT BY THAT.

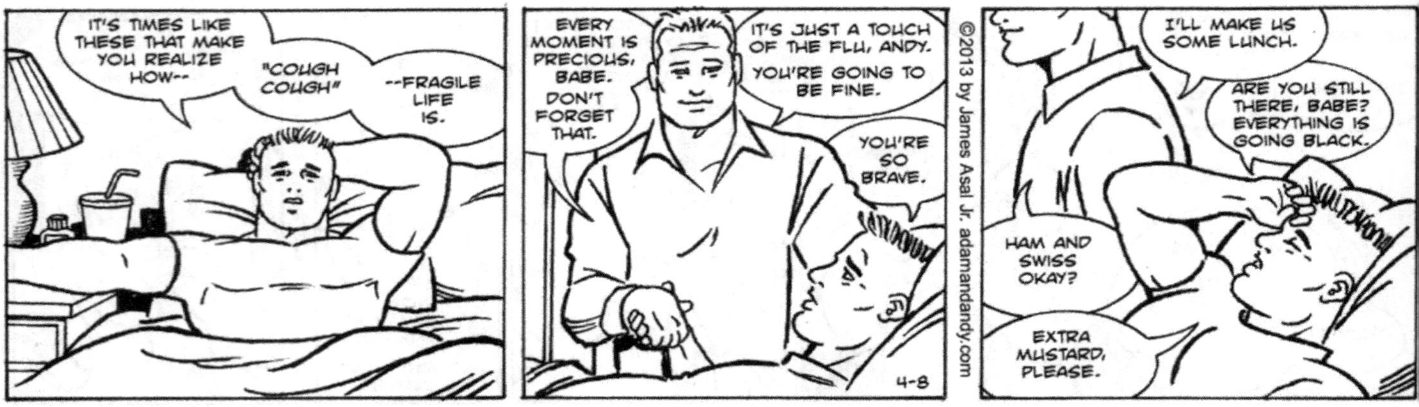
IT'S TIMES LIKE THESE THAT MAKE YOU REALIZE HOW--
"COUGH COUGH"
--FRAGILE LIFE IS.
EVERY MOMENT IS PRECIOUS, BABE.
DON'T FORGET THAT.
IT'S JUST A TOUCH OF THE FLU, ANDY.
YOU'RE GOING TO BE FINE.
YOU'RE SO BRAVE.
4-8
©2013 by James Asal Jr. adamandandy.com
I'LL MAKE US SOME LUNCH.
ARE YOU STILL THERE, BABE? EVERYTHING IS GOING BLACK.
HAM AND SWISS OKAY?
EXTRA MUSTARD, PLEASE.

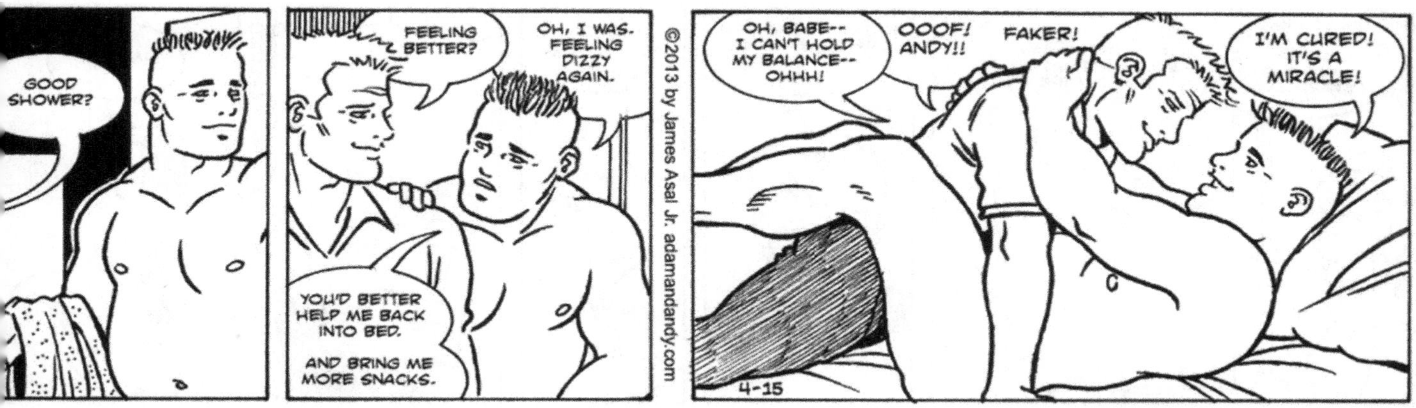
GOOD SHOWER?
FEELING BETTER?
OH, I WAS. FEELING DIZZY AGAIN.
YOU'D BETTER HELP ME BACK INTO BED.
AND BRING ME MORE SNACKS.
©2013 by James Asal Jr. adamandandy.com
OH, BABE-- I CAN'T HOLD MY BALANCE-- OHHH!
OOOF! ANDY!!
FAKER!
I'M CURED! IT'S A MIRACLE!
4-15

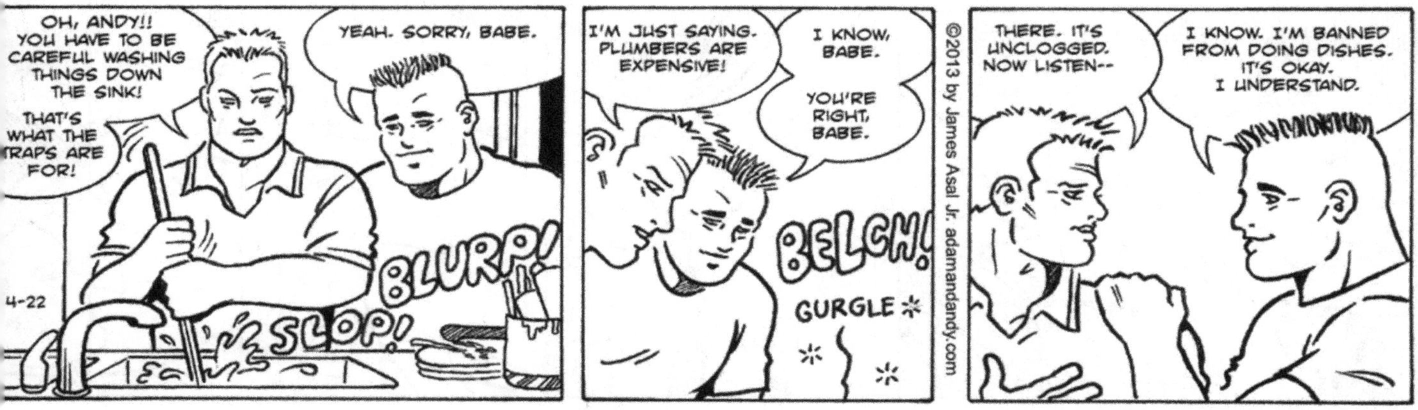
OH, ANDY!! YOU HAVE TO BE CAREFUL WASHING THINGS DOWN THE SINK!
THAT'S WHAT THE TRAPS ARE FOR!
YEAH. SORRY, BABE.
BLURP!
SLOP!
4-22
I'M JUST SAYING. PLUMBERS ARE EXPENSIVE!
I KNOW, BABE.
YOU'RE RIGHT, BABE.
BELCH!
GURGLE
©2013 by James Asal Jr. adamandandy.com
THERE. IT'S UNCLOGGED. NOW LISTEN--
I KNOW. I'M BANNED FROM DOING DISHES. IT'S OKAY. I UNDERSTAND.

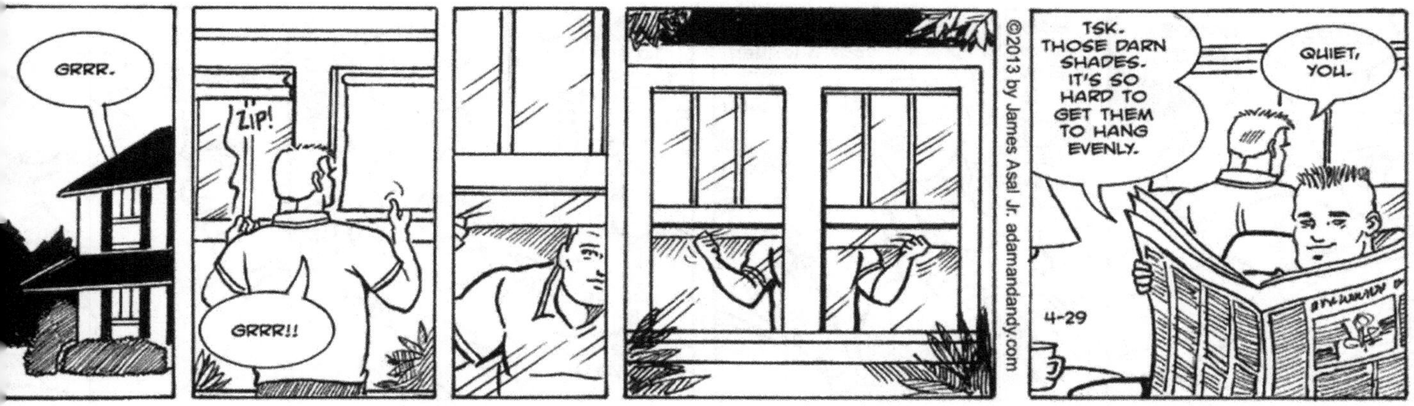
GRRR.
ZIP!
GRRR!!
©2013 by James Asal Jr. adamandandy.com
TSK. THOSE DARN SHADES. IT'S SO HARD TO GET THEM TO HANG EVENLY.
QUIET, YOU.
4-29

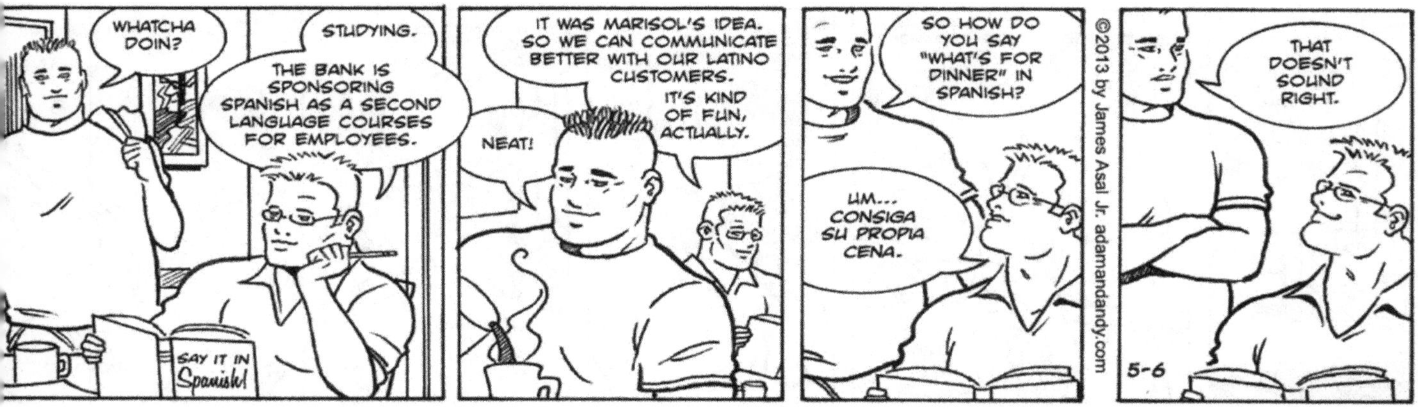
WHATCHA DOIN?
STUDYING.
THE BANK IS SPONSORING SPANISH AS A SECOND LANGUAGE COURSES FOR EMPLOYEES.
SAY IT IN Spanish!
IT WAS MARISOL'S IDEA. SO WE CAN COMMUNICATE BETTER WITH OUR LATINO CUSTOMERS.
IT'S KIND OF FUN, ACTUALLY.
NEAT!
SO HOW DO YOU SAY "WHAT'S FOR DINNER" IN SPANISH?
UM... CONSIGA SU PROPIA CENA.
©2013 by James Asal Jr. adamandandy.com
THAT DOESN'T SOUND RIGHT.
5-6

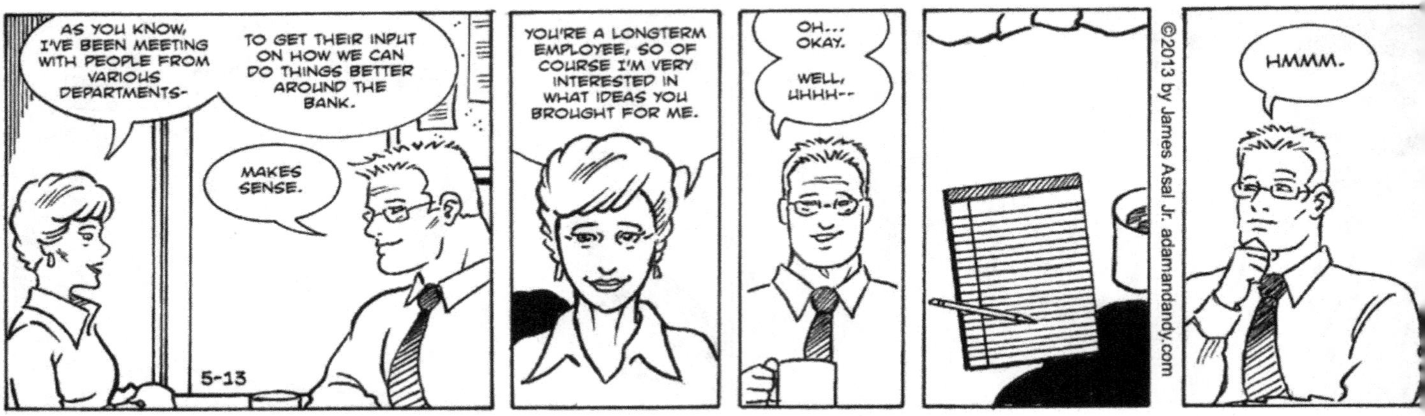
AS YOU KNOW, I'VE BEEN MEETING WITH PEOPLE FROM VARIOUS DEPARTMENTS-
TO GET THEIR INPUT ON HOW WE CAN DO THINGS BETTER AROUND THE BANK.
MAKES SENSE.
5-13
YOU'RE A LONGTERM EMPLOYEE, SO OF COURSE I'M VERY INTERESTED IN WHAT IDEAS YOU BROUGHT FOR ME.
OH... OKAY.
WELL, UHHH--
©2013 by James Asal Jr. adamandandy.com
HMMM.

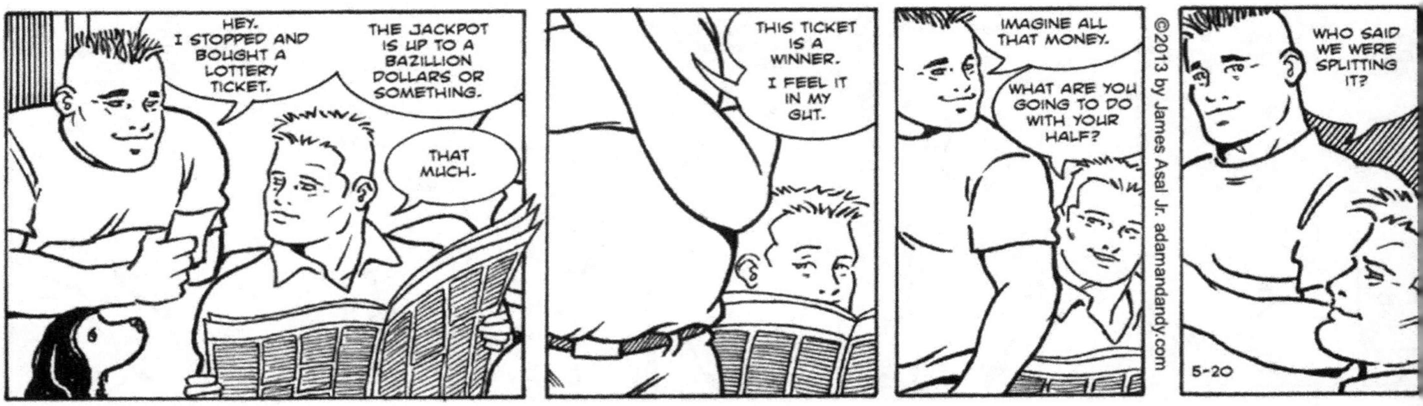
HEY. I STOPPED AND BOUGHT A LOTTERY TICKET.
THE JACKPOT IS UP TO A BAZILLION DOLLARS OR SOMETHING.
THAT MUCH.
THIS TICKET IS A WINNER.
I FEEL IT IN MY GUT.
IMAGINE ALL THAT MONEY.
WHAT ARE YOU GOING TO DO WITH YOUR HALF?
©2013 by James Asal Jr. adamandandy.com
WHO SAID WE WERE SPLITTING IT?
5-20

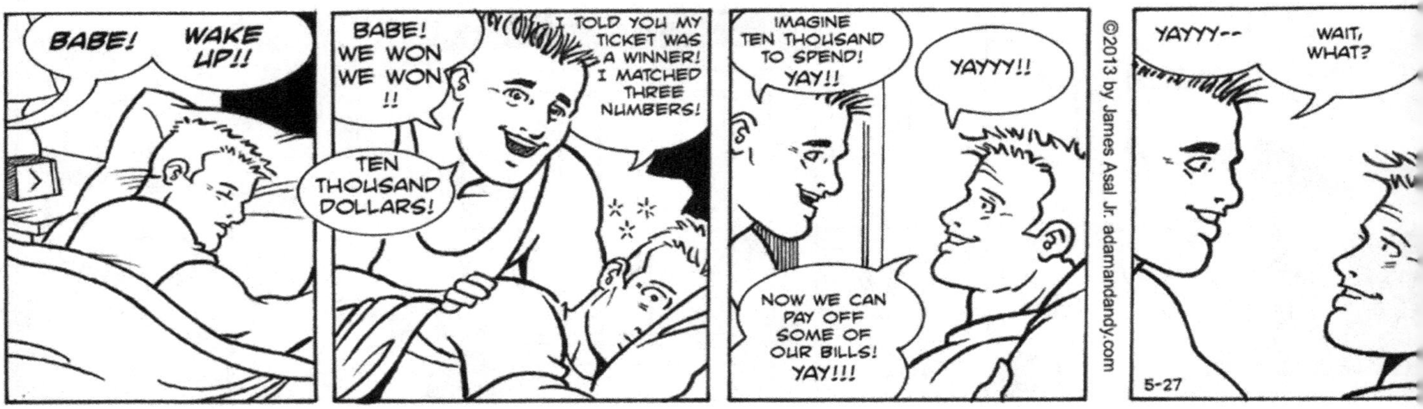
BABE! WAKE UP!!
BABE! WE WON WE WON !!
I TOLD YOU MY TICKET WAS A WINNER! I MATCHED THREE NUMBERS!
TEN THOUSAND DOLLARS!
IMAGINE TEN THOUSAND TO SPEND! YAY!!
YAYYY!!
NOW WE CAN PAY OFF SOME OF OUR BILLS! YAY!!!
©2013 by James Asal Jr. adamandandy.com
YAYYY--
WAIT, WHAT?
5-27

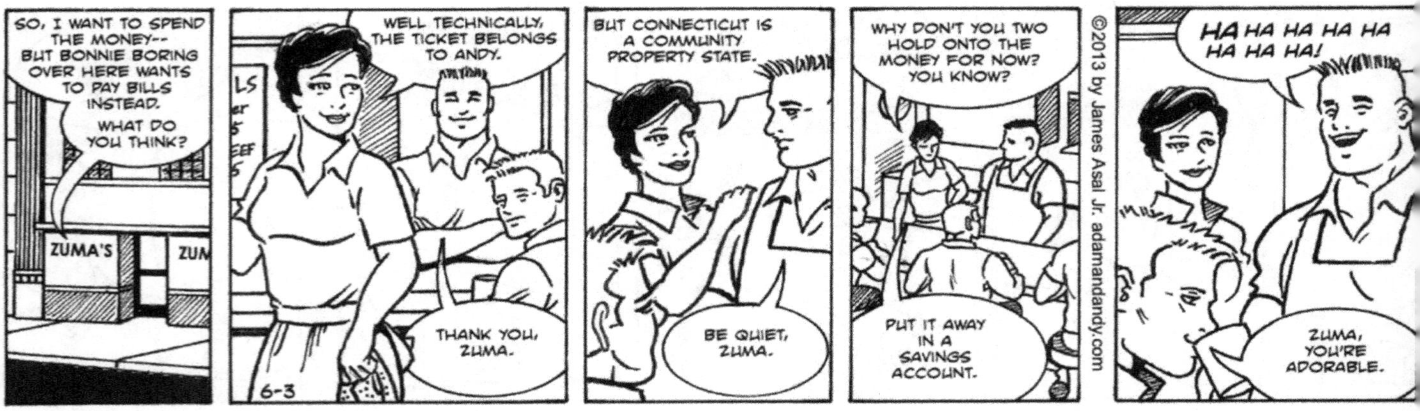
SO, I WANT TO SPEND THE MONEY-- BUT BONNIE BORING OVER HERE WANTS TO PAY BILLS INSTEAD.
WHAT DO YOU THINK?
ZUMA'S
WELL TECHNICALLY, THE TICKET BELONGS TO ANDY.
THANK YOU, ZUMA.
6-3
BUT CONNECTICUT IS A COMMUNITY PROPERTY STATE.
BE QUIET, ZUMA.
WHY DON'T YOU TWO HOLD ONTO THE MONEY FOR NOW? YOU KNOW?
PUT IT AWAY IN A SAVINGS ACCOUNT.
©2013 by James Asal Jr. adamandandy.com
HA HA HA HA HA HA HA HA!
ZUMA, YOU'RE ADORABLE.

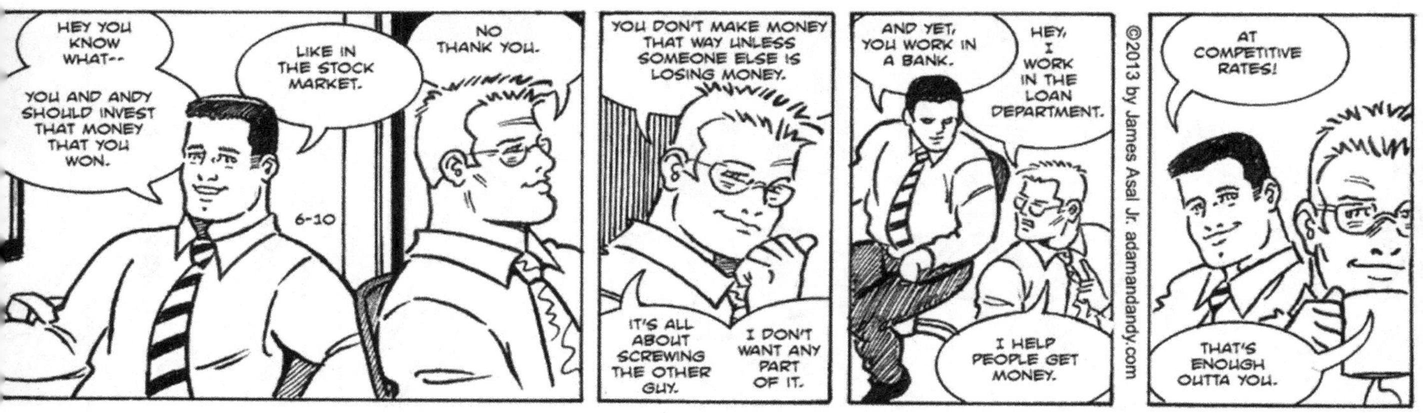
HEY YOU KNOW WHAT--
YOU AND ANDY SHOULD INVEST THAT MONEY THAT YOU WON.
LIKE IN THE STOCK MARKET.
NO THANK YOU.
6-10
YOU DON'T MAKE MONEY THAT WAY UNLESS SOMEONE ELSE IS LOSING MONEY.
IT'S ALL ABOUT SCREWING THE OTHER GUY.
I DON'T WANT ANY PART OF IT.
AND YET, YOU WORK IN A BANK.
HEY, I WORK IN THE LOAN DEPARTMENT.
I HELP PEOPLE GET MONEY.
©2013 by James Asal Jr. adamandandy.com
AT COMPETITIVE RATES!
THAT'S ENOUGH OUTTA YOU.

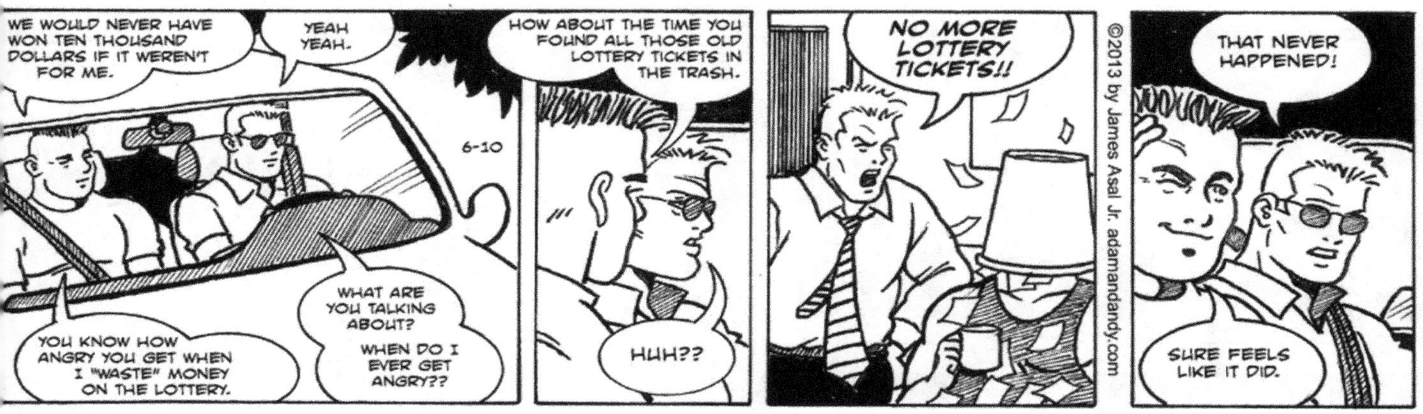
WE WOULD NEVER HAVE WON TEN THOUSAND DOLLARS IF IT WEREN'T FOR ME.
YEAH YEAH.
6-10
YOU KNOW HOW ANGRY YOU GET WHEN I "WASTE" MONEY ON THE LOTTERY.
WHAT ARE YOU TALKING ABOUT?
WHEN DO I EVER GET ANGRY??
HOW ABOUT THE TIME YOU FOUND ALL THOSE OLD LOTTERY TICKETS IN THE TRASH.
HUH??
NO MORE LOTTERY TICKETS!!
©2013 by James Asal Jr. adamandandy.com
THAT NEVER HAPPENED!
SURE FEELS LIKE IT DID.

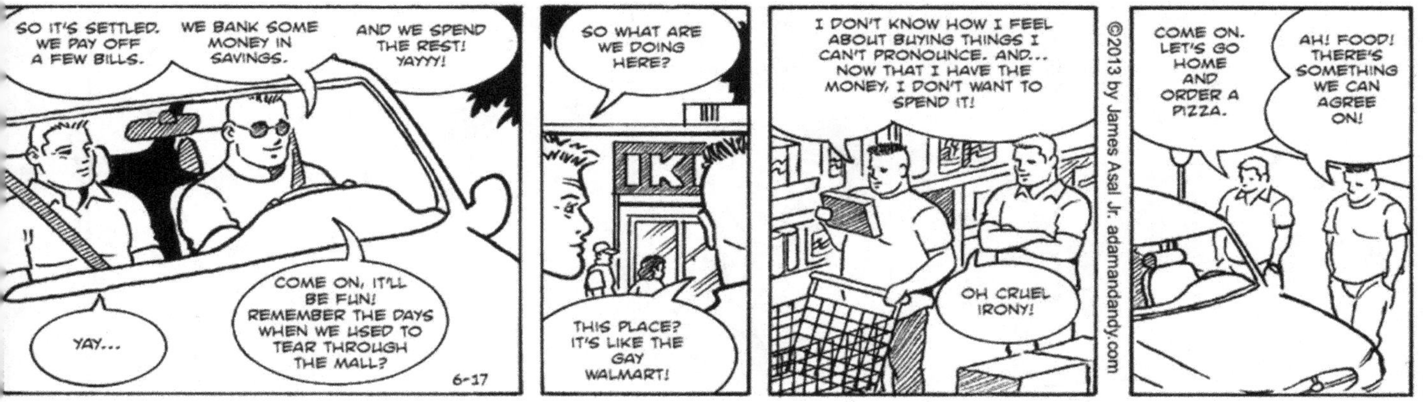
SO IT'S SETTLED. WE PAY OFF A FEW BILLS.
WE BANK SOME MONEY IN SAVINGS.
AND WE SPEND THE REST! YAYYY!
YAY...
COME ON, IT'LL BE FUN! REMEMBER THE DAYS WHEN WE USED TO TEAR THROUGH THE MALL?
6-17
SO WHAT ARE WE DOING HERE?
THIS PLACE? IT'S LIKE THE GAY WALMART!
I DON'T KNOW HOW I FEEL ABOUT BUYING THINGS I CAN'T PRONOUNCE. AND... NOW THAT I HAVE THE MONEY, I DON'T WANT TO SPEND IT!
OH CRUEL IRONY!
©2013 by James Asal Jr. adamandandy.com
COME ON. LET'S GO HOME AND ORDER A PIZZA.
AH! FOOD! THERE'S SOMETHING WE CAN AGREE ON!

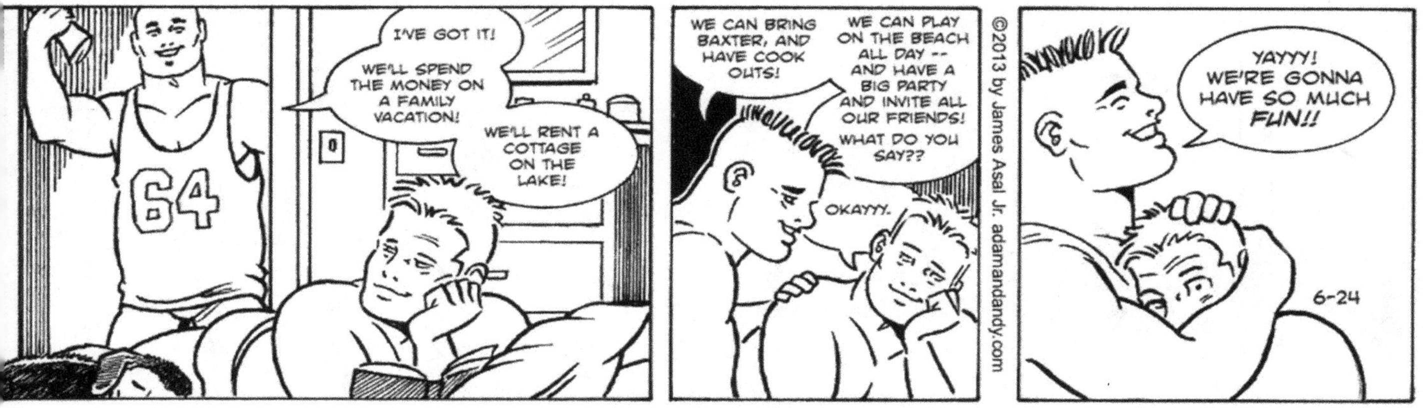
I'VE GOT IT!
WE'LL SPEND THE MONEY ON A FAMILY VACATION!
WE'LL RENT A COTTAGE ON THE LAKE!
64
WE CAN BRING BAXTER, AND HAVE COOK OUTS!
WE CAN PLAY ON THE BEACH ALL DAY -- AND HAVE A BIG PARTY AND INVITE ALL OUR FRIENDS!
WHAT DO YOU SAY??
OKAYYY.
©2013 by James Asal Jr. adamandandy.com
YAYYY! WE'RE GONNA HAVE SO MUCH FUN!!
6-24

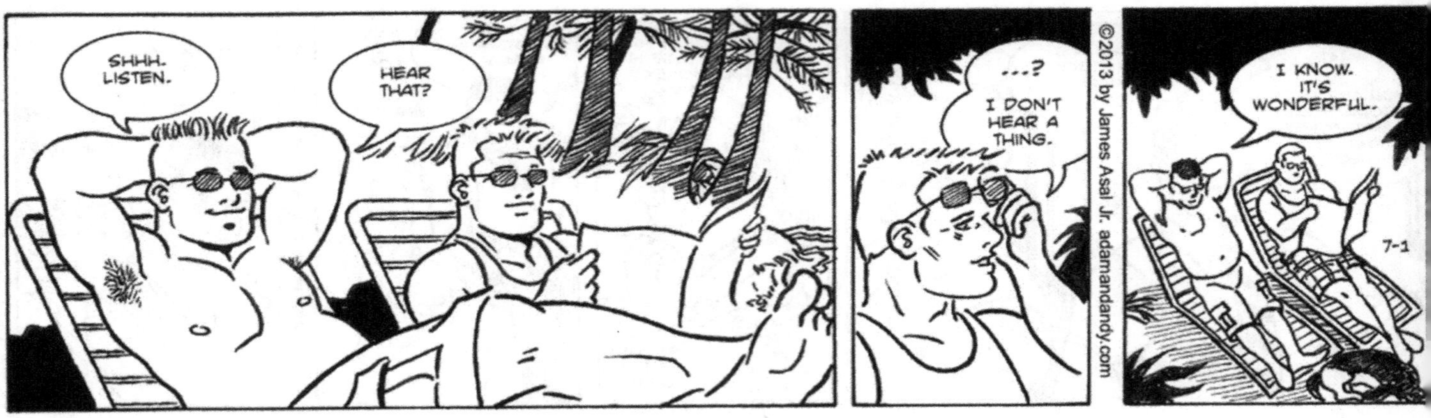
SHHH. LISTEN.
HEAR THAT?
...? I DON'T HEAR A THING.
©2013 by James Asal Jr. adamandandy.com
I KNOW. IT'S WONDERFUL.
7-1

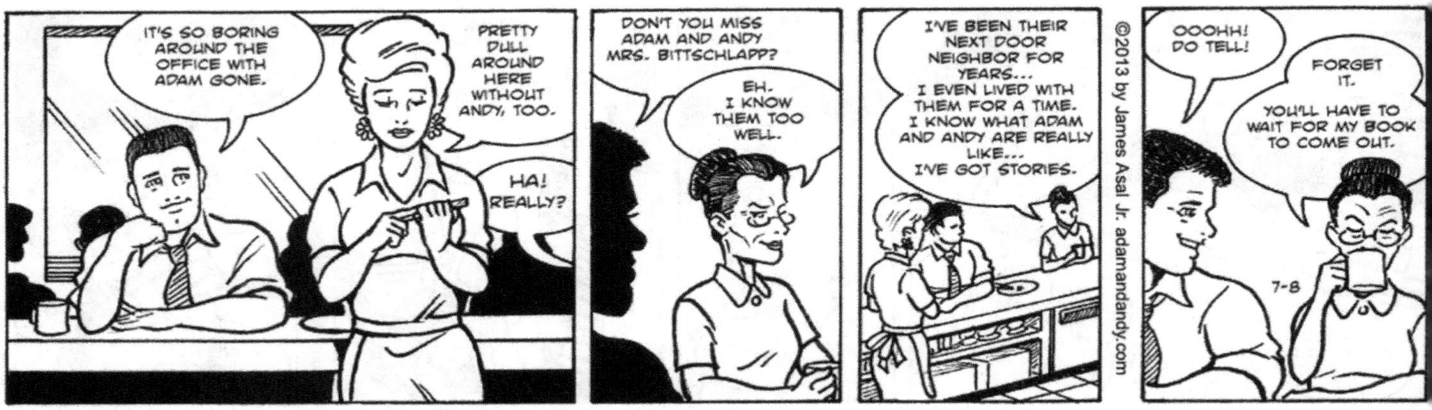
IT'S SO BORING AROUND THE OFFICE WITH ADAM GONE.
PRETTY DULL AROUND HERE WITHOUT ANDY, TOO.
HA! REALLY?
DON'T YOU MISS ADAM AND ANDY MRS. BITTSCHLAPP?
EH. I KNOW THEM TOO WELL.
I'VE BEEN THEIR NEXT DOOR NEIGHBOR FOR YEARS... I EVEN LIVED WITH THEM FOR A TIME. I KNOW WHAT ADAM AND ANDY ARE REALLY LIKE... I'VE GOT STORIES.
©2013 by James Asal Jr. adamandandy.com
OOOHH! DO TELL!
FORGET IT.
YOU'LL HAVE TO WAIT FOR MY BOOK TO COME OUT.
7-8

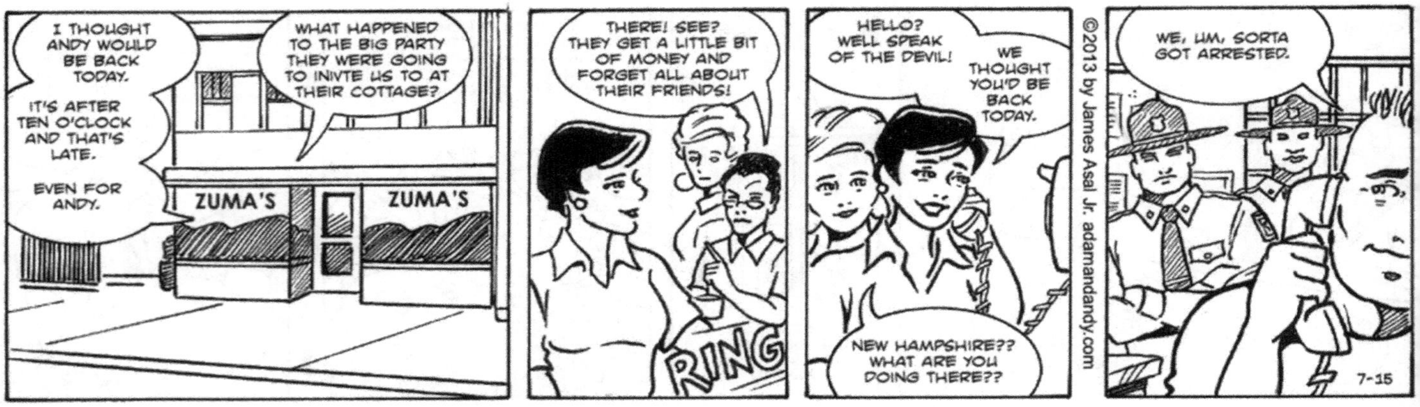
I THOUGHT ANDY WOULD BE BACK TODAY.
IT'S AFTER TEN O'CLOCK AND THAT'S LATE.
EVEN FOR ANDY.
WHAT HAPPENED TO THE BIG PARTY THEY WERE GOING TO INIVTE US TO AT THEIR COTTAGE?
ZUMA'S
ZUMA'S
THERE! SEE? THEY GET A LITTLE BIT OF MONEY AND FORGET ALL ABOUT THEIR FRIENDS!
RING
HELLO? WELL SPEAK OF THE DEVIL!
WE THOUGHT YOU'D BE BACK TODAY.
NEW HAMPSHIRE?? WHAT ARE YOU DOING THERE??
©2013 by James Asal Jr. adamandandy.com
WE, UM, SORTA GOT ARRESTED.
7-15

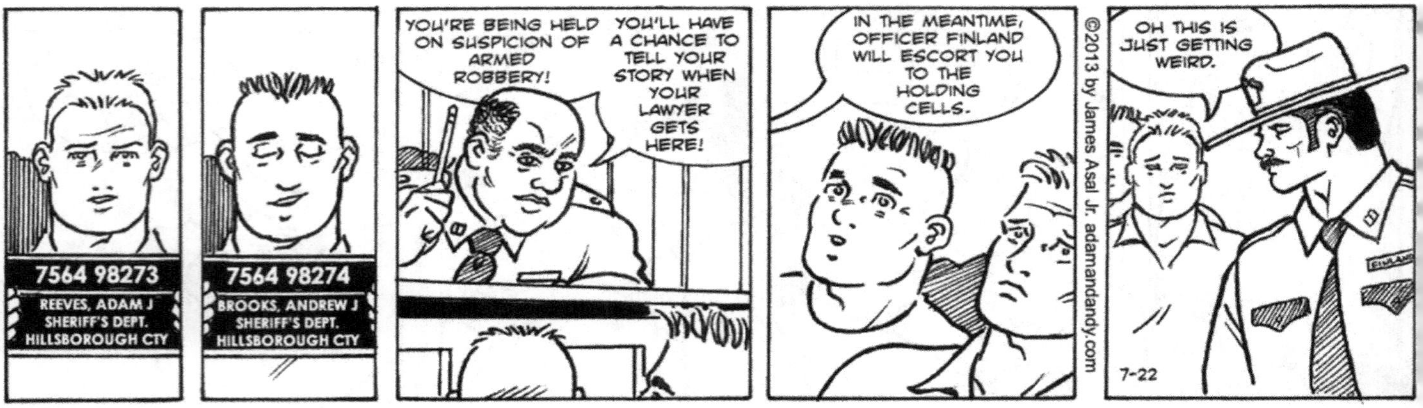
7564 98273
REEVES, ADAM J
SHERIFF'S DEPT.
HILLSBOROUGH CTY
7564 98274
BROOKS, ANDREW J
SHERIFF'S DEPT.
HILLSBOROUGH CTY
YOU'RE BEING HELD ON SUSPICION OF ARMED ROBBERY!
YOU'LL HAVE A CHANCE TO TELL YOUR STORY WHEN YOUR LAWYER GETS HERE!
IN THE MEANTIME, OFFICER FINLAND WILL ESCORT YOU TO THE HOLDING CELLS.
©2013 by James Asal Jr. adamandandy.com
OH THIS IS JUST GETTING WEIRD.
FINLAND
7-22

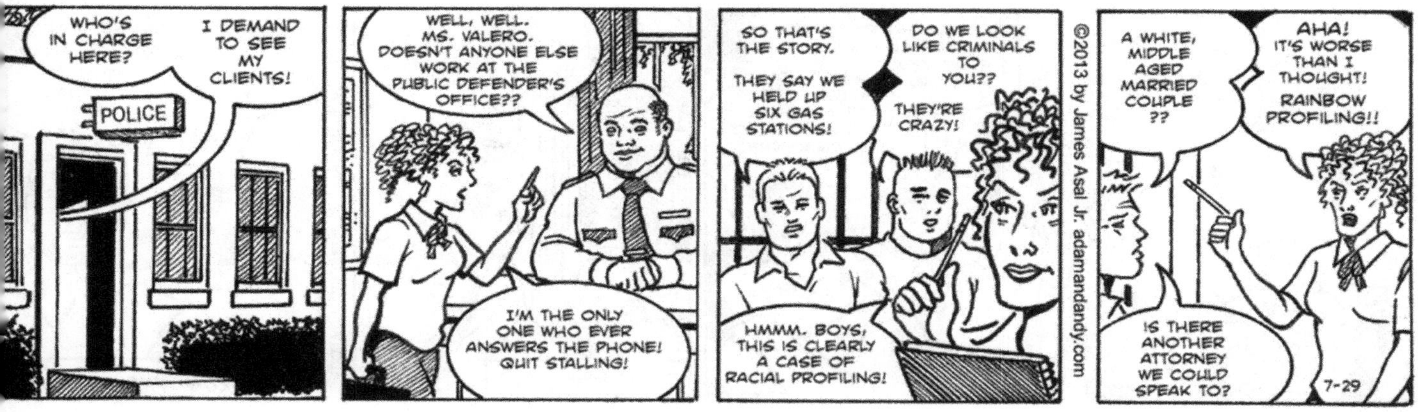
WHO'S IN CHARGE HERE?
I DEMAND TO SEE MY CLIENTS!
POLICE
WELL, WELL. MS. VALERO. DOESN'T ANYONE ELSE WORK AT THE PUBLIC DEFENDER'S OFFICE??
I'M THE ONLY ONE WHO EVER ANSWERS THE PHONE! QUIT STALLING!
SO THAT'S THE STORY.
THEY SAY WE HELD UP SIX GAS STATIONS!
DO WE LOOK LIKE CRIMINALS TO YOU??
THEY'RE CRAZY!
HMMM. BOYS, THIS IS CLEARLY A CASE OF RACIAL PROFILING!
©2013 by James Asal Jr. adamandandy.com
A WHITE, MIDDLE AGED MARRIED COUPLE ??
AHA! IT'S WORSE THAN I THOUGHT!
RAINBOW PROFILING!!
IS THERE ANOTHER ATTORNEY WE COULD SPEAK TO?
7-29

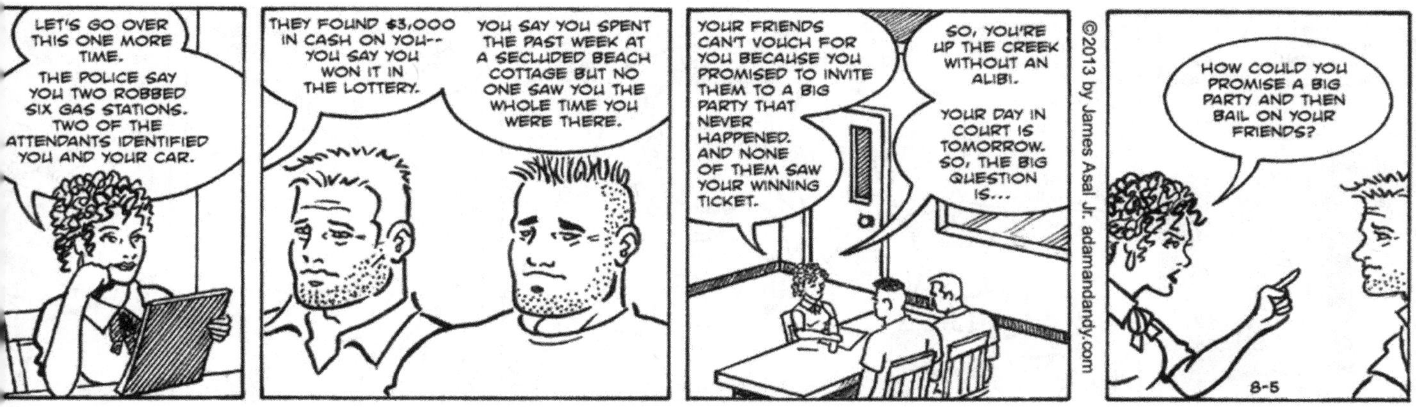
LET'S GO OVER THIS ONE MORE TIME.
THE POLICE SAY YOU TWO ROBBED SIX GAS STATIONS. TWO OF THE ATTENDANTS IDENTIFIED YOU AND YOUR CAR.
THEY FOUND $3,000 IN CASH ON YOU-- YOU SAY YOU WON IT IN THE LOTTERY.
YOU SAY YOU SPENT THE PAST WEEK AT A SECLUDED BEACH COTTAGE BUT NO ONE SAW YOU THE WHOLE TIME YOU WERE THERE.
YOUR FRIENDS CAN'T VOUCH FOR YOU BECAUSE YOU PROMISED TO INVITE THEM TO A BIG PARTY THAT NEVER HAPPENED. AND NONE OF THEM SAW YOUR WINNING TICKET.
SO, YOU'RE UP THE CREEK WITHOUT AN ALIBI.
YOUR DAY IN COURT IS TOMORROW. SO, THE BIG QUESTION IS...
©2013 by James Asal Jr. adamandandy.com
HOW COULD YOU PROMISE A BIG PARTY AND THEN BAIL ON YOUR FRIENDS?
8-5

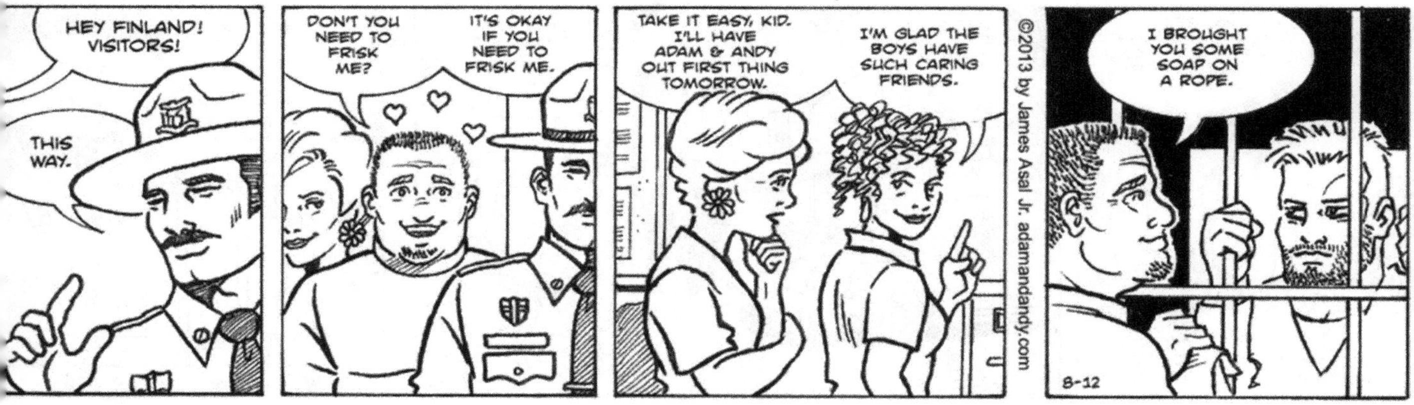
HEY FINLAND! VISITORS!
THIS WAY.
DON'T YOU NEED TO FRISK ME?
IT'S OKAY IF YOU NEED TO FRISK ME.
TAKE IT EASY, KID. I'LL HAVE ADAM & ANDY OUT FIRST THING TOMORROW.
I'M GLAD THE BOYS HAVE SUCH CARING FRIENDS.
©2013 by James Asal Jr. adamandandy.com
I BROUGHT YOU SOME SOAP ON A ROPE.
8-12

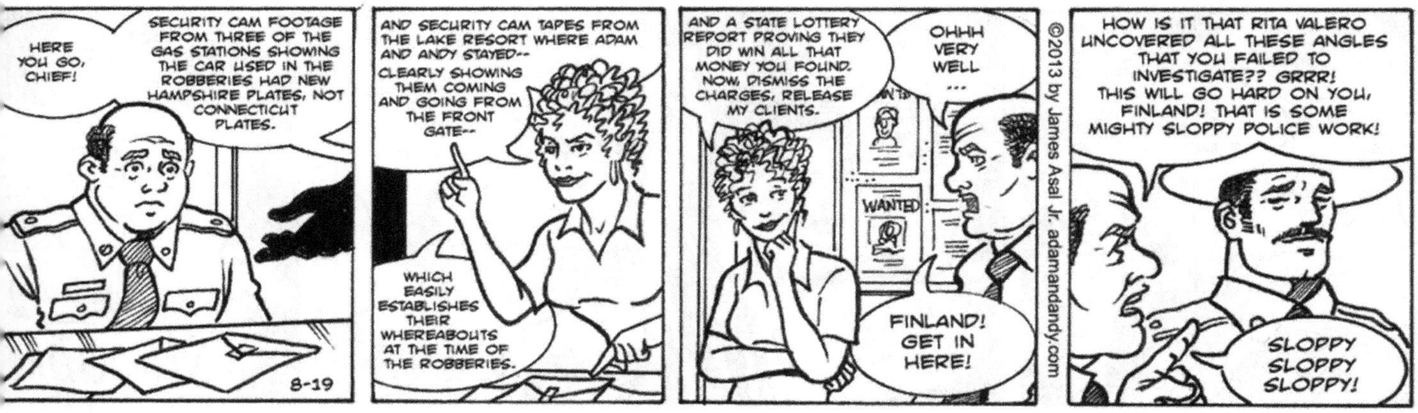
HERE YOU GO, CHIEF!
SECURITY CAM FOOTAGE FROM THREE OF THE GAS STATIONS SHOWING THE CAR USED IN THE ROBBERIES HAD NEW HAMPSHIRE PLATES, NOT CONNECTICUT PLATES.
8-19
AND SECURITY CAM TAPES FROM THE LAKE RESORT WHERE ADAM AND ANDY STAYED--
CLEARLY SHOWING THEM COMING AND GOING FROM THE FRONT GATE--
WHICH EASILY ESTABLISHES THEIR WHEREABOUTS AT THE TIME OF THE ROBBERIES.
AND A STATE LOTTERY REPORT PROVING THEY DID WIN ALL THAT MONEY YOU FOUND. NOW, DISMISS THE CHARGES, RELEASE MY CLIENTS.
OHHH VERY WELL ...
WANTED
FINLAND! GET IN HERE!
©2013 by James Asal Jr. adamandandy.com
HOW IS IT THAT RITA VALERO UNCOVERED ALL THESE ANGLES THAT YOU FAILED TO INVESTIGATE?? GRRR! THIS WILL GO HARD ON YOU, FINLAND! THAT IS SOME MIGHTY SLOPPY POLICE WORK!
SLOPPY SLOPPY SLOPPY!

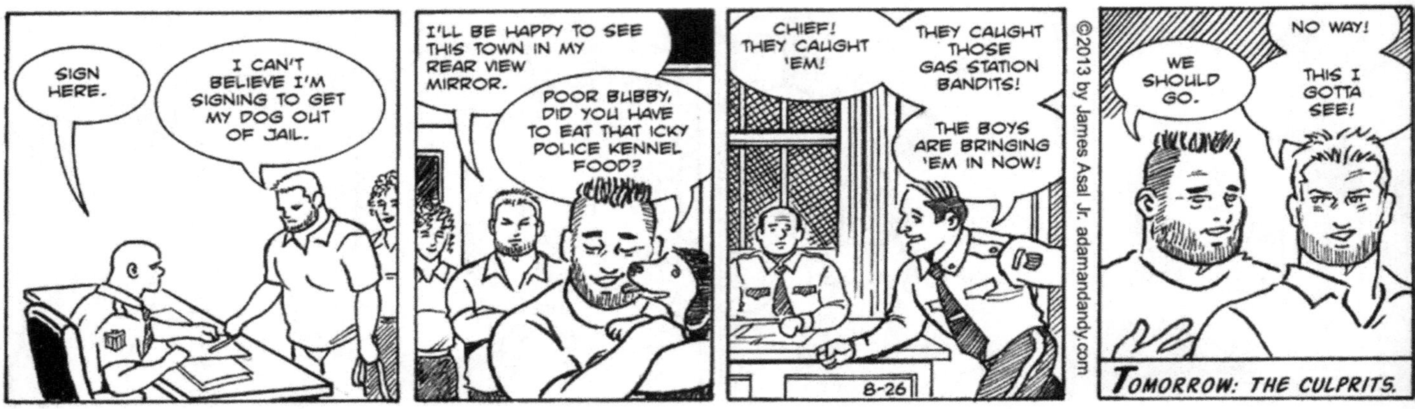
SIGN HERE.
I CAN'T BELIEVE I'M SIGNING TO GET MY DOG OUT OF JAIL.
I'LL BE HAPPY TO SEE THIS TOWN IN MY REAR VIEW MIRROR.
POOR BUBBY, DID YOU HAVE TO EAT THAT ICKY POLICE KENNEL FOOD?
CHIEF! THEY CAUGHT 'EM!
THEY CAUGHT THOSE GAS STATION BANDITS!
THE BOYS ARE BRINGING 'EM IN NOW!
8-26
©2013 by James Asal Jr. adamandandy.com
WE SHOULD GO.
NO WAY!
THIS I GOTTA SEE!
TOMORROW: THE CULPRITS.

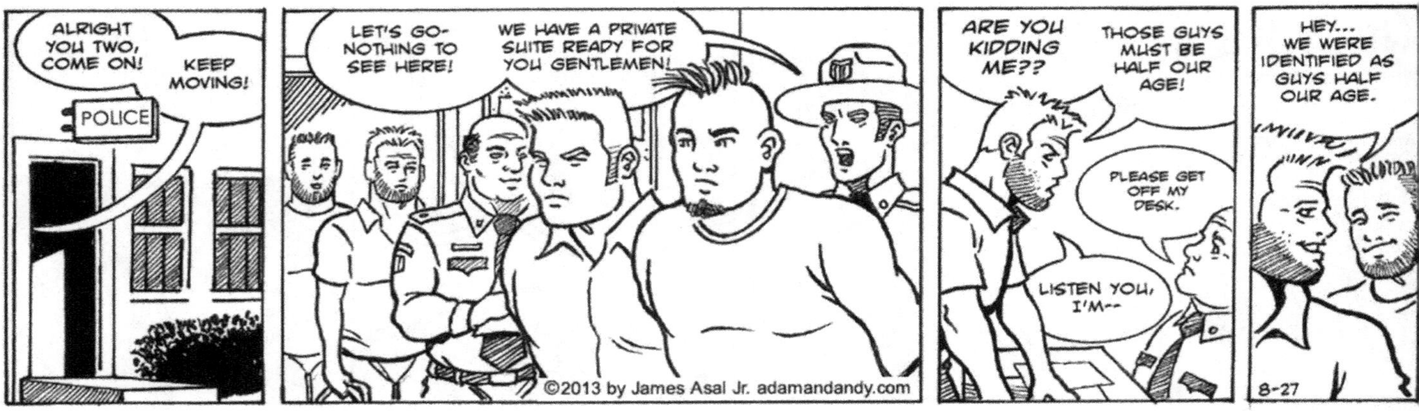
ALRIGHT YOU TWO, COME ON!
KEEP MOVING!
POLICE
LET'S GO- NOTHING TO SEE HERE!
WE HAVE A PRIVATE SUITE READY FOR YOU GENTLEMEN!
©2013 by James Asal Jr. adamandandy.com
ARE YOU KIDDING ME??
THOSE GUYS MUST BE HALF OUR AGE!
PLEASE GET OFF MY DESK.
LISTEN YOU, I'M--
HEY... WE WERE IDENTIFIED AS GUYS HALF OUR AGE.
8-27

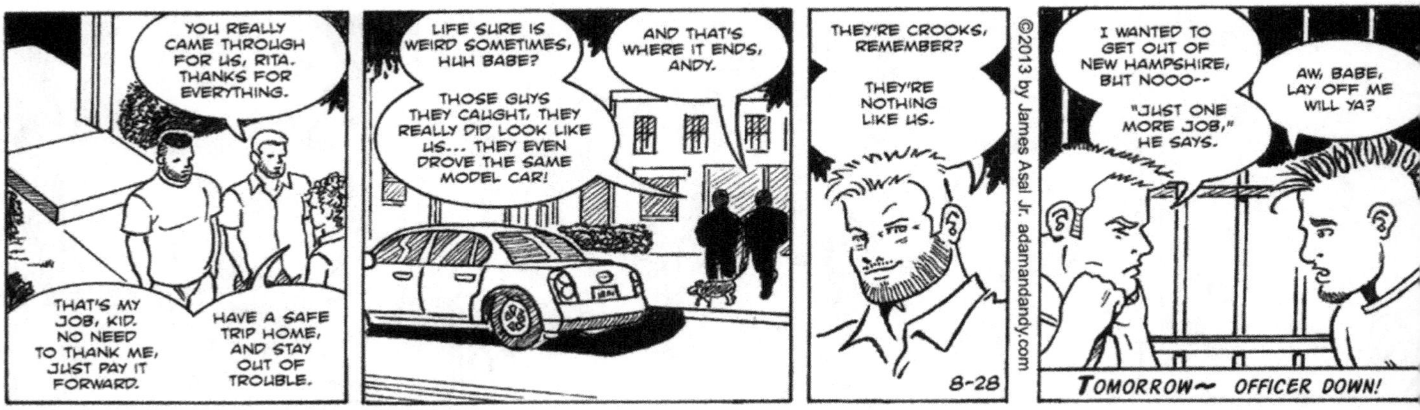
YOU REALLY CAME THROUGH FOR US, RITA. THANKS FOR EVERYTHING.
THAT'S MY JOB, KID. NO NEED TO THANK ME, JUST PAY IT FORWARD.
HAVE A SAFE TRIP HOME, AND STAY OUT OF TROUBLE.
LIFE SURE IS WEIRD SOMETIMES, HUH BABE?
THOSE GUYS THEY CAUGHT, THEY REALLY DID LOOK LIKE US... THEY EVEN DROVE THE SAME MODEL CAR!
AND THAT'S WHERE IT ENDS, ANDY.
THEY'RE CROOKS, REMEMBER?
THEY'RE NOTHING LIKE US.
8-28
©2013 by James Asal Jr. adamandandy.com
I WANTED TO GET OUT OF NEW HAMPSHIRE, BUT NOOO--
"JUST ONE MORE JOB," HE SAYS.
AW, BABE, LAY OFF ME WILL YA?
TOMORROW~ OFFICER DOWN!

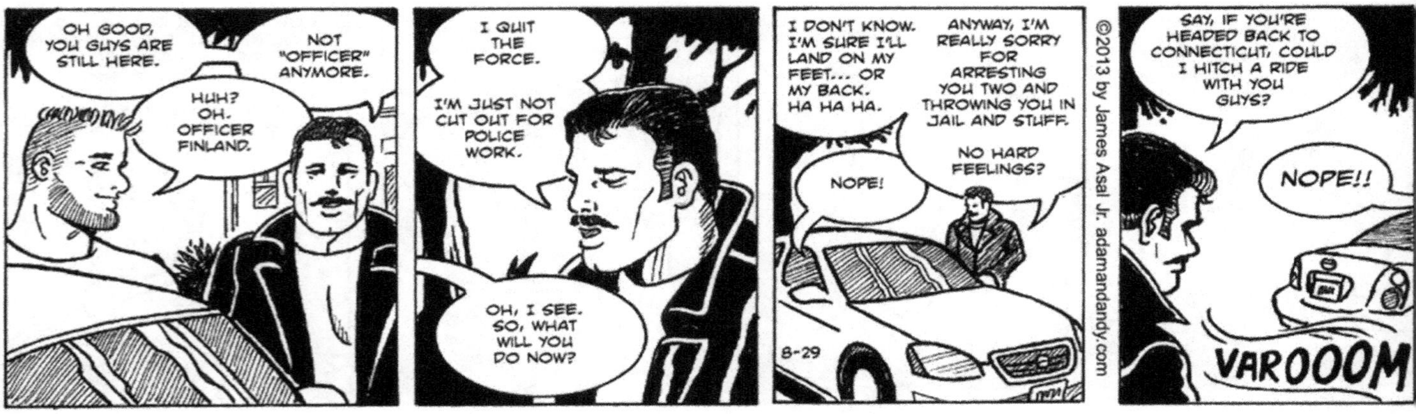
OH GOOD, YOU GUYS ARE STILL HERE.
HUH? OH. OFFICER FINLAND.
NOT "OFFICER" ANYMORE.
I QUIT THE FORCE.
I'M JUST NOT CUT OUT FOR POLICE WORK.
OH, I SEE. SO, WHAT WILL YOU DO NOW?
I DON'T KNOW. I'M SURE I'LL LAND ON MY FEET... OR MY BACK. HA HA HA.
ANYWAY, I'M REALLY SORRY FOR ARRESTING YOU TWO AND THROWING YOU IN JAIL AND STUFF.
NO HARD FEELINGS?
NOPE!
8-29
©2013 by James Asal Jr. adamandandy.com
SAY, IF YOU'RE HEADED BACK TO CONNECTICUT, COULD I HITCH A RIDE WITH YOU GUYS?
NOPE!!
VAROOOM

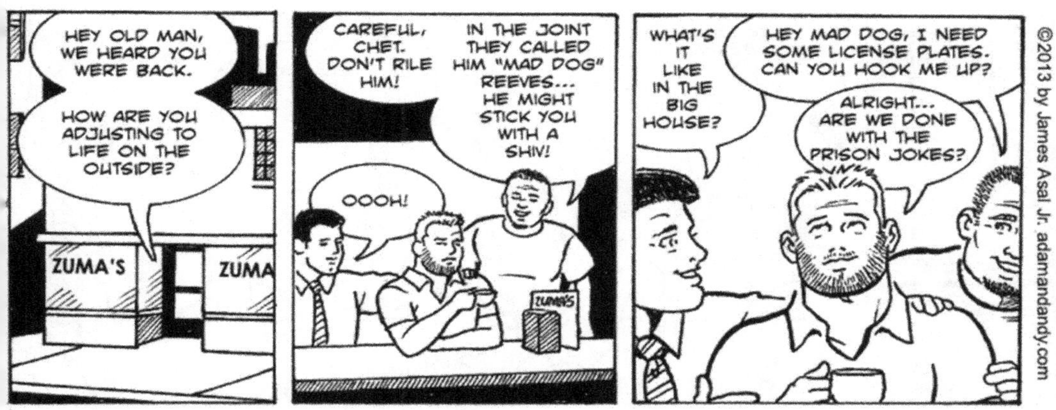
HEY OLD MAN, WE HEARD YOU WERE BACK.
HOW ARE YOU ADJUSTING TO LIFE ON THE OUTSIDE?
ZUMA'S
ZUMA
CAREFUL, CHET. DON'T RILE HIM!
IN THE JOINT THEY CALLED HIM "MAD DOG" REEVES... HE MIGHT STICK YOU WITH A SHIV!
OOOH!
WHAT'S IT LIKE IN THE BIG HOUSE?
HEY MAD DOG, I NEED SOME LICENSE PLATES. CAN YOU HOOK ME UP?
ALRIGHT... ARE WE DONE WITH THE PRISON JOKES?
©2013 by James Asal Jr. adamandandy.com
NOPE!
NOT EVEN CLOSE.
8-30

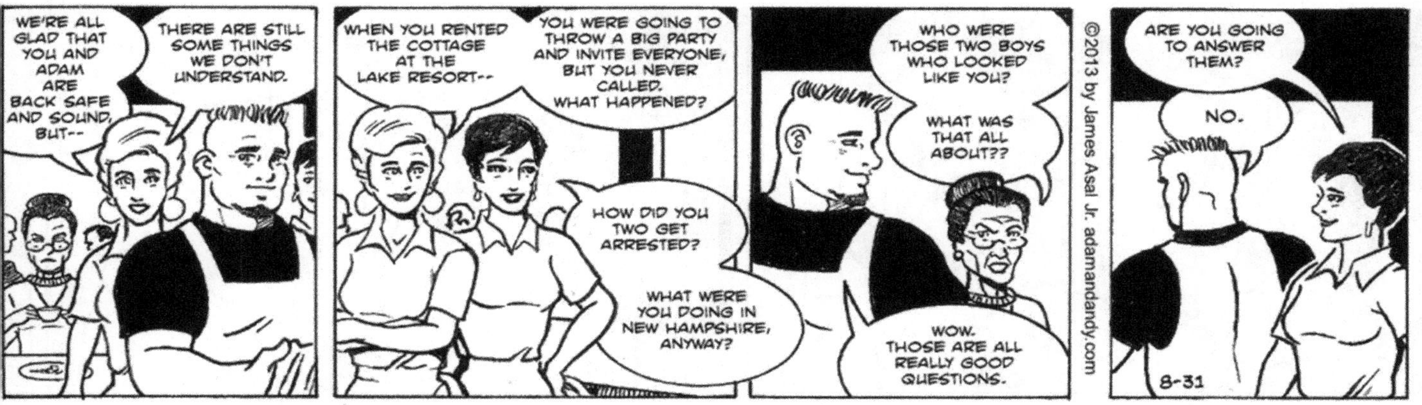
WE'RE ALL GLAD THAT YOU AND ADAM ARE BACK SAFE AND SOUND, BUT--
THERE ARE STILL SOME THINGS WE DON'T UNDERSTAND.
WHEN YOU RENTED THE COTTAGE AT THE LAKE RESORT--
YOU WERE GOING TO THROW A BIG PARTY AND INVITE EVERYONE, BUT YOU NEVER CALLED. WHAT HAPPENED?
HOW DID YOU TWO GET ARRESTED?
WHAT WERE YOU DOING IN NEW HAMPSHIRE, ANYWAY?
WHO WERE THOSE TWO BOYS WHO LOOKED LIKE YOU?
WHAT WAS THAT ALL ABOUT??
WOW. THOSE ARE ALL REALLY GOOD QUESTIONS.
©2013 by James Asal Jr. adamandandy.com
ARE YOU GOING TO ANSWER THEM?
NO.
8-31

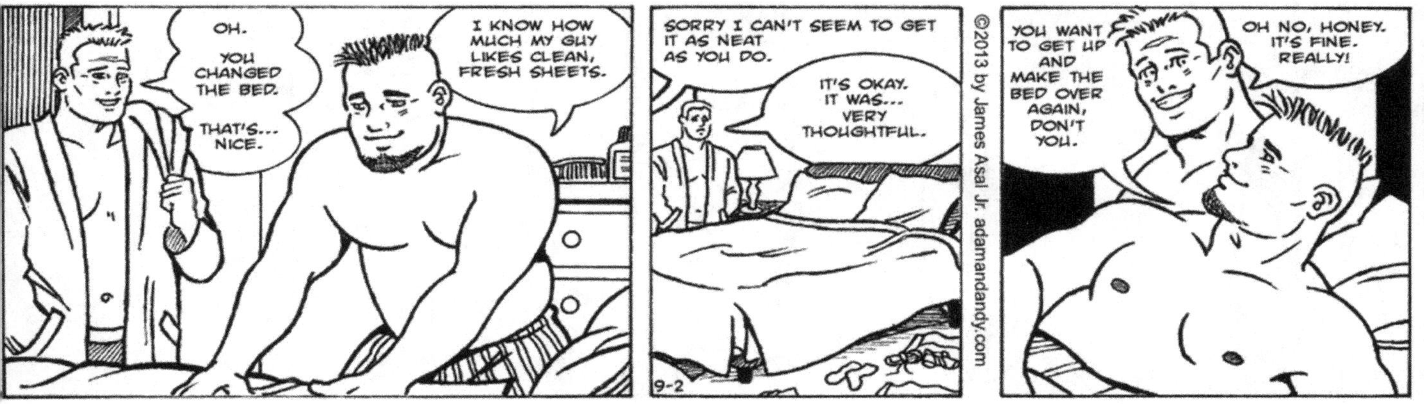
OH. YOU CHANGED THE BED.
THAT'S... NICE.
I KNOW HOW MUCH MY GUY LIKES CLEAN, FRESH SHEETS.
SORRY I CAN'T SEEM TO GET IT AS NEAT AS YOU DO.
IT'S OKAY. IT WAS... VERY THOUGHTFUL.
9-2
©2013 by James Asal Jr. adamandandy.com
YOU WANT TO GET UP AND MAKE THE BED OVER AGAIN, DON'T YOU.
OH NO, HONEY. IT'S FINE. REALLY!

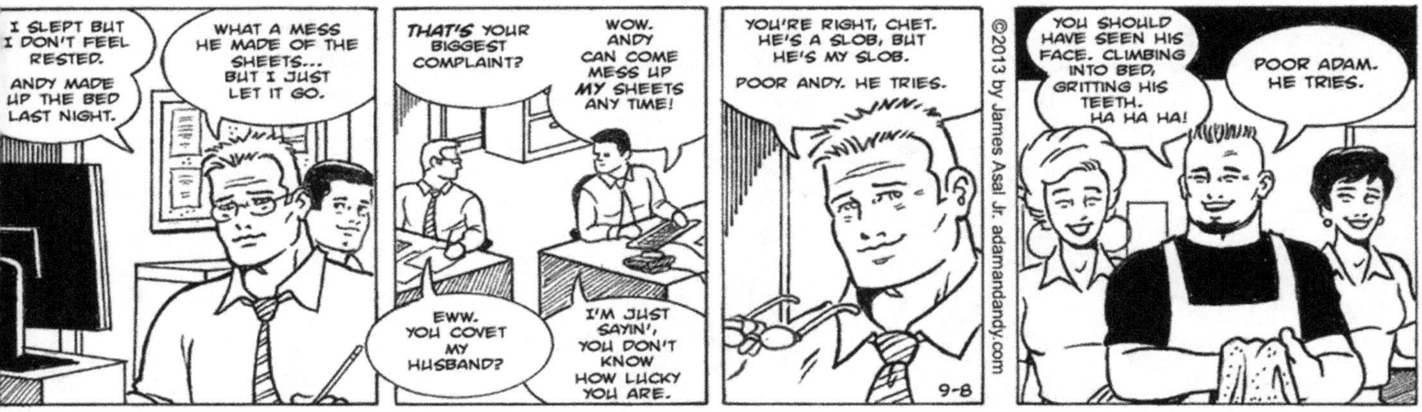
I SLEPT BUT I DON'T FEEL RESTED.
ANDY MADE UP THE BED LAST NIGHT.
WHAT A MESS HE MADE OF THE SHEETS... BUT I JUST LET IT GO.
THAT'S YOUR BIGGEST COMPLAINT?
WOW. ANDY CAN COME MESS UP MY SHEETS ANY TIME!
EWW. YOU COVET MY HUSBAND?
I'M JUST SAYIN', YOU DON'T KNOW HOW LUCKY YOU ARE.
YOU'RE RIGHT, CHET. HE'S A SLOB, BUT HE'S MY SLOB.
POOR ANDY. HE TRIES.
9-8
©2013 by James Asal Jr. adamandandy.com
YOU SHOULD HAVE SEEN HIS FACE. CLIMBING INTO BED, GRITTING HIS TEETH. HA HA HA!
POOR ADAM. HE TRIES.

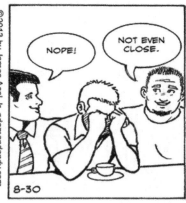

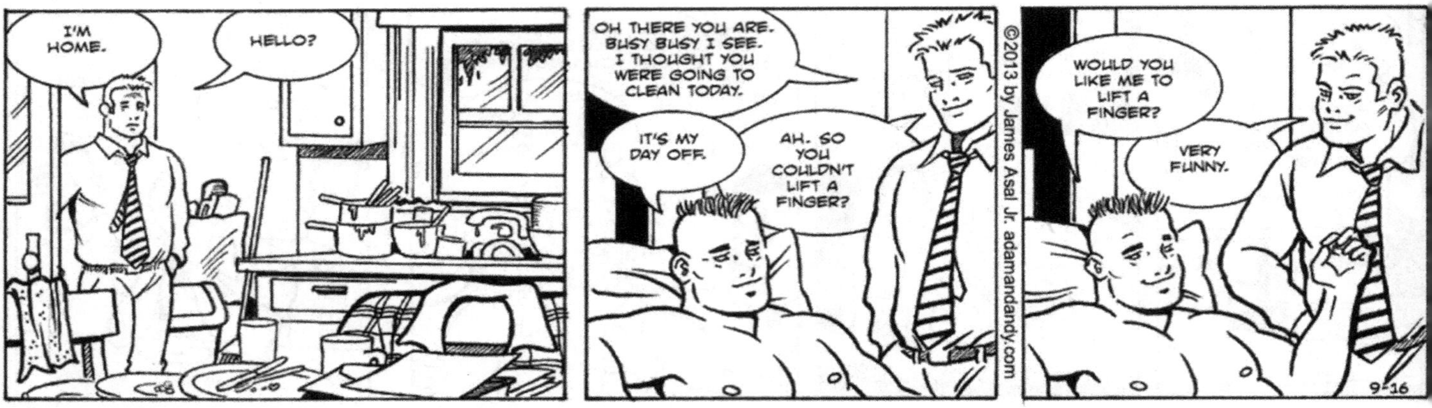
I'M HOME.
HELLO?
OH THERE YOU ARE. BUSY BUSY I SEE. I THOUGHT YOU WERE GOING TO CLEAN TODAY.
IT'S MY DAY OFF.
AH. SO YOU COULDN'T LIFT A FINGER?
©2013 by James Asal Jr. adamandandy.com
WOULD YOU LIKE ME TO LIFT A FINGER?
VERY FUNNY.
9-16

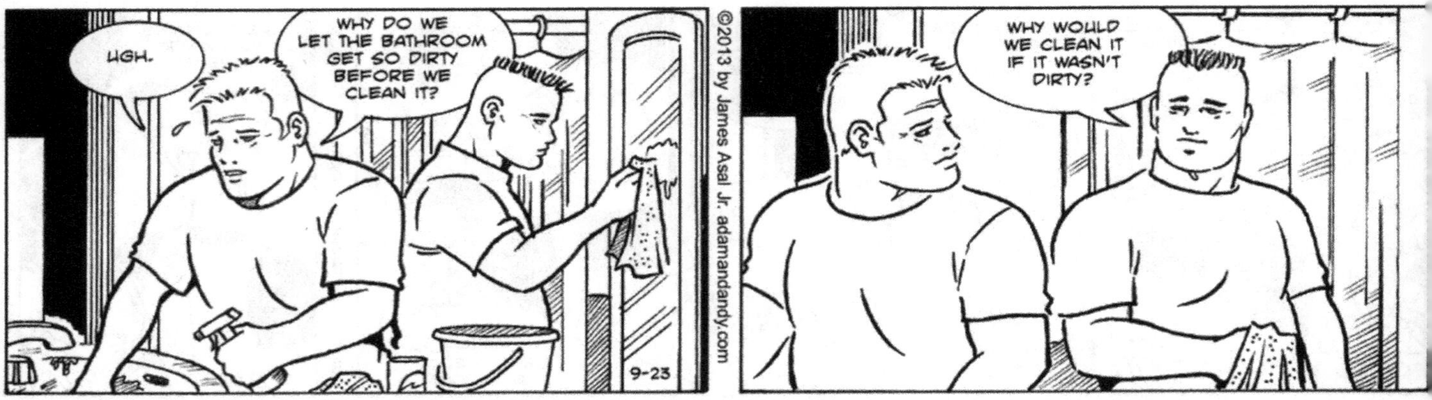
UGH.
WHY DO WE LET THE BATHROOM GET SO DIRTY BEFORE WE CLEAN IT?
9-23
©2013 by James Asal Jr. adamandandy.com
WHY WOULD WE CLEAN IT IF IT WASN'T DIRTY?

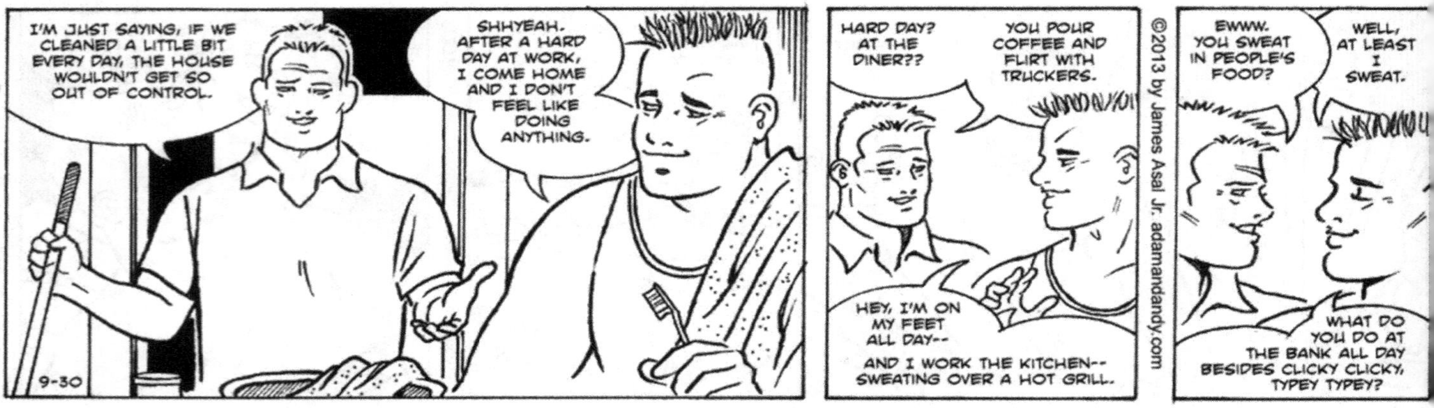
I'M JUST SAYING, IF WE CLEANED A LITTLE BIT EVERY DAY, THE HOUSE WOULDN'T GET SO OUT OF CONTROL.
SHHYEAH. AFTER A HARD DAY AT WORK, I COME HOME AND I DON'T FEEL LIKE DOING ANYTHING.
9-30
HARD DAY? AT THE DINER??
YOU POUR COFFEE AND FLIRT WITH TRUCKERS.
HEY, I'M ON MY FEET ALL DAY--
AND I WORK THE KITCHEN-- SWEATING OVER A HOT GRILL.
©2013 by James Asal Jr. adamandandy.com
EWWW. YOU SWEAT IN PEOPLE'S FOOD?
WELL, AT LEAST I SWEAT.
WHAT DO YOU DO AT THE BANK ALL DAY BESIDES CLICKY CLICKY, TYPEY TYPEY?

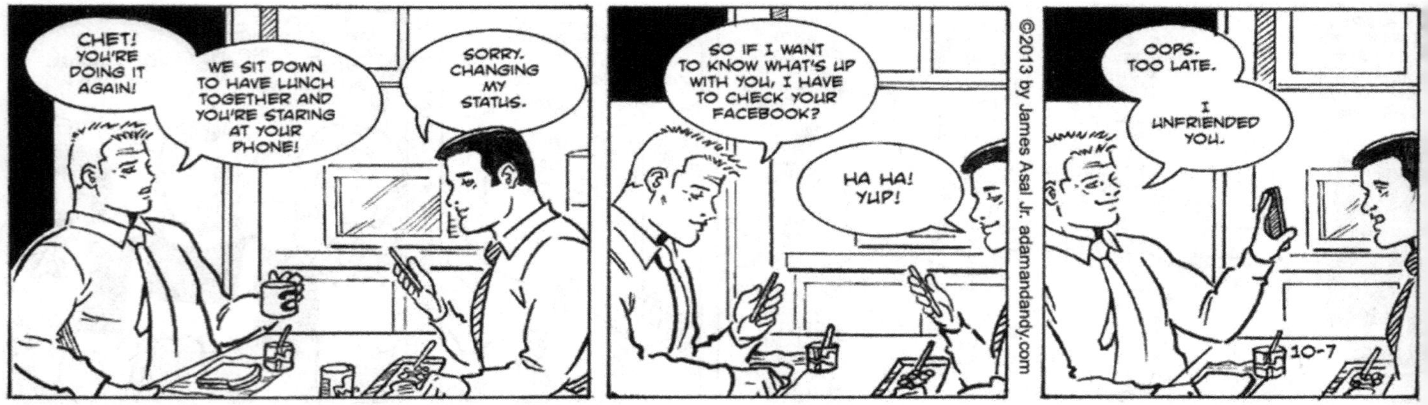
CHET! YOU'RE DOING IT AGAIN!
WE SIT DOWN TO HAVE LUNCH TOGETHER AND YOU'RE STARING AT YOUR PHONE!
SORRY. CHANGING MY STATUS.
SO IF I WANT TO KNOW WHAT'S UP WITH YOU, I HAVE TO CHECK YOUR FACEBOOK?
HA HA! YUP!
©2013 by James Asal Jr. adamandandy.com
OOPS. TOO LATE.
I UNFRIENDED YOU.
10-7

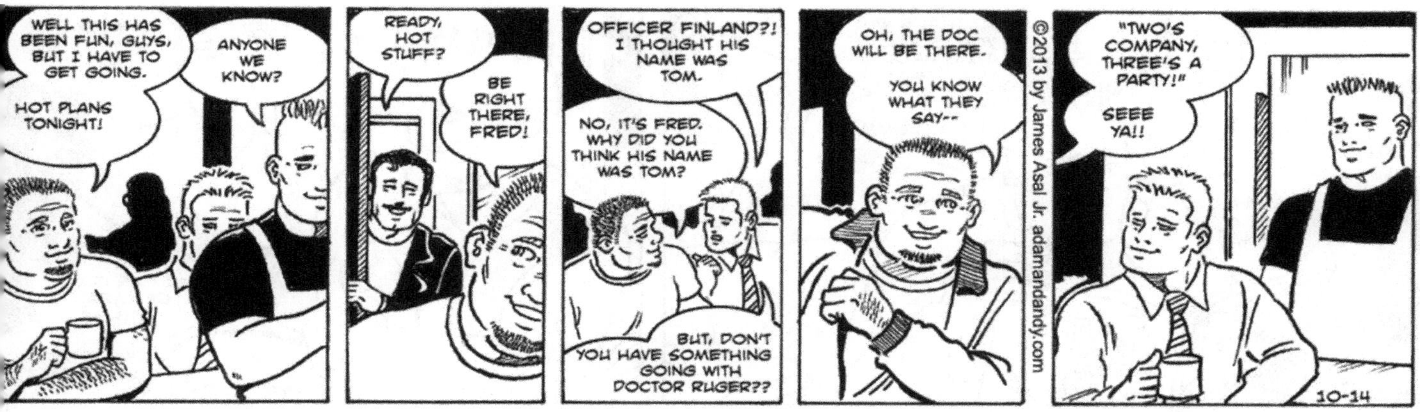
WELL THIS HAS BEEN FUN, GUYS, BUT I HAVE TO GET GOING.
HOT PLANS TONIGHT!
ANYONE WE KNOW?
READY, HOT STUFF?
BE RIGHT THERE, FRED!
OFFICER FINLAND?! I THOUGHT HIS NAME WAS TOM.
NO, IT'S FRED. WHY DID YOU THINK HIS NAME WAS TOM?
BUT, DON'T YOU HAVE SOMETHING GOING WITH DOCTOR RUGER??
OH, THE DOC WILL BE THERE.
YOU KNOW WHAT THEY SAY--
©2013 by James Asal Jr. adamandandy.com
"TWO'S COMPANY, THREE'S A PARTY!"
SEEE YA!!
10-14

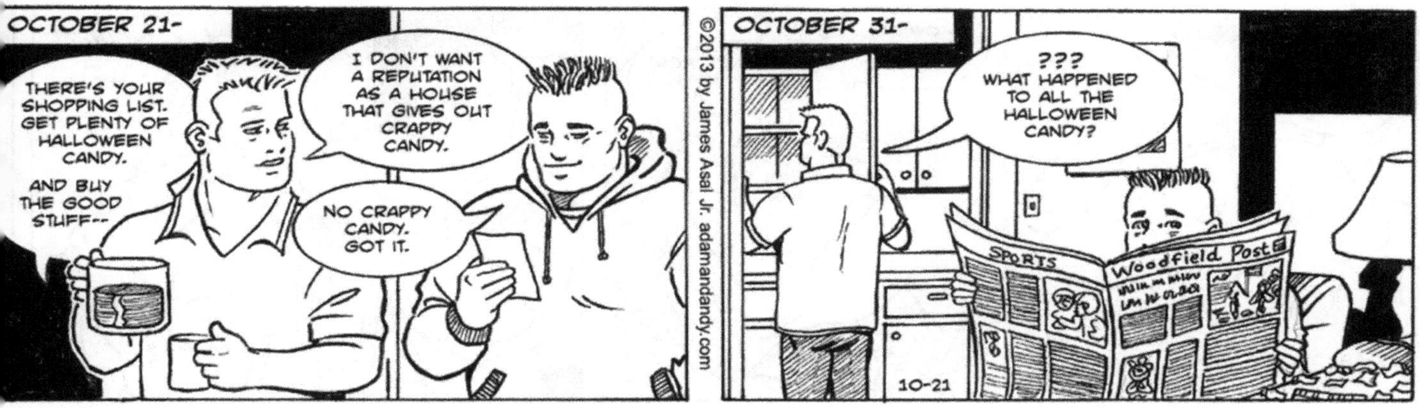
OCTOBER 21-
THERE'S YOUR SHOPPING LIST. GET PLENTY OF HALLOWEEN CANDY.
AND BUY THE GOOD STUFF--
I DON'T WANT A REPUTATION AS A HOUSE THAT GIVES OUT CRAPPY CANDY.
NO CRAPPY CANDY. GOT IT.
©2013 by James Asal Jr. adamandandy.com
OCTOBER 31-
??? WHAT HAPPENED TO ALL THE HALLOWEEN CANDY?
SPORTS
Woodfield Post
10-21

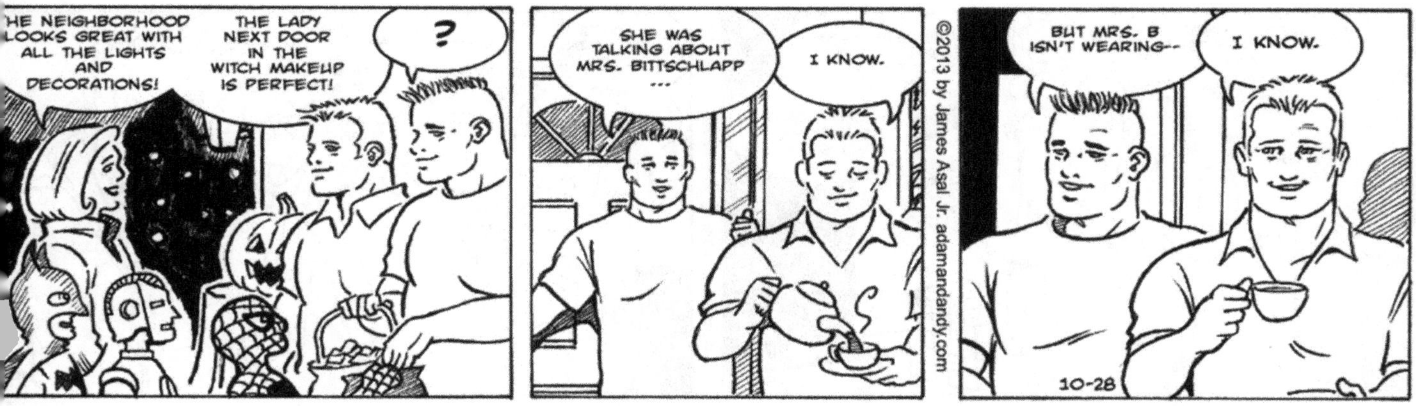
THE NEIGHBORHOOD LOOKS GREAT WITH ALL THE LIGHTS AND DECORATIONS!
THE LADY NEXT DOOR IN THE WITCH MAKEUP IS PERFECT!
?
SHE WAS TALKING ABOUT MRS. BITTSCHLAPP ...
I KNOW.
©2013 by James Asal Jr. adamandandy.com
BUT MRS. B ISN'T WEARING--
I KNOW.
10-28

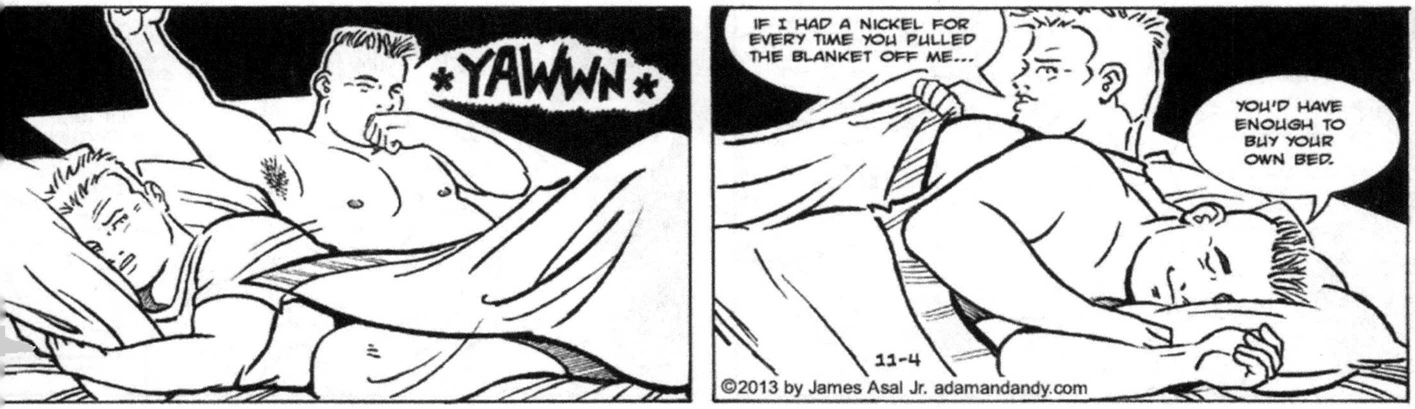
YAWWN
IF I HAD A NICKEL FOR EVERY TIME YOU PULLED THE BLANKET OFF ME...
YOU'D HAVE ENOUGH TO BUY YOUR OWN BED.
11-4
©2013 by James Asal Jr. adamandandy.com

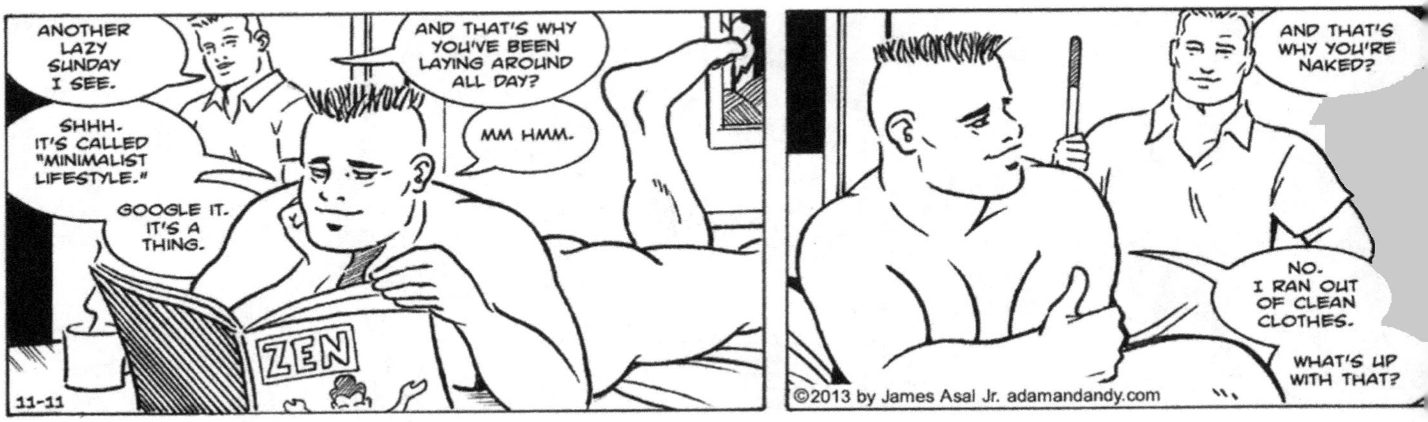
ANOTHER LAZY SUNDAY I SEE.
AND THAT'S WHY YOU'VE BEEN LAYING AROUND ALL DAY?
SHHH. IT'S CALLED "MINIMALIST LIFESTYLE."
MM HMM.
GOOGLE IT. IT'S A THING.
ZEN
11-11
AND THAT'S WHY YOU'RE NAKED?
NO. I RAN OUT OF CLEAN CLOTHES.
WHAT'S UP WITH THAT?
©2013 by James Asal Jr. adamandandy.com

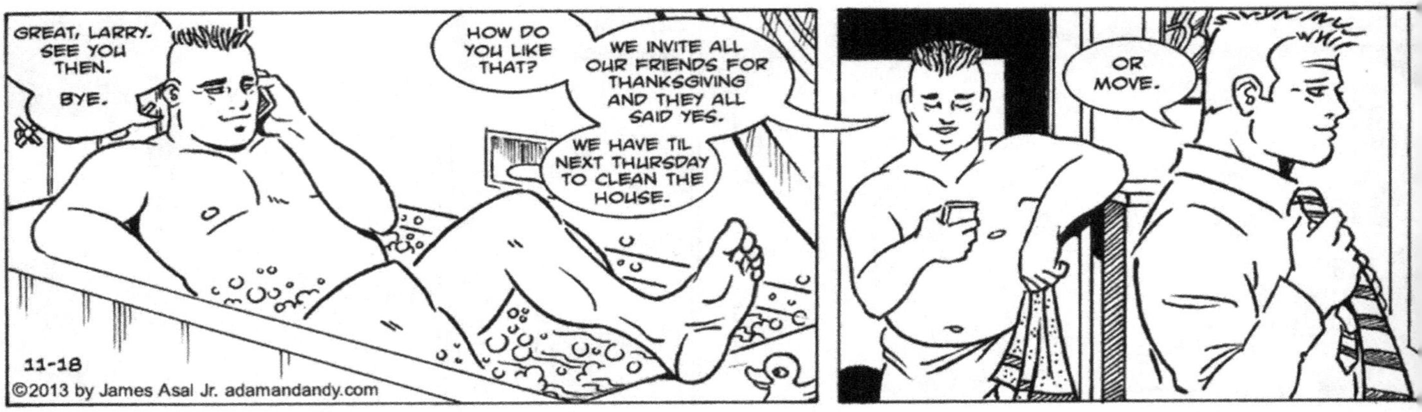
GREAT, LARRY. SEE YOU THEN.
BYE.
HOW DO YOU LIKE THAT?
WE INVITE ALL OUR FRIENDS FOR THANKSGIVING AND THEY ALL SAID YES.
WE HAVE TIL NEXT THURSDAY TO CLEAN THE HOUSE.
11-18
©2013 by James Asal Jr. adamandandy.com
OR MOVE.

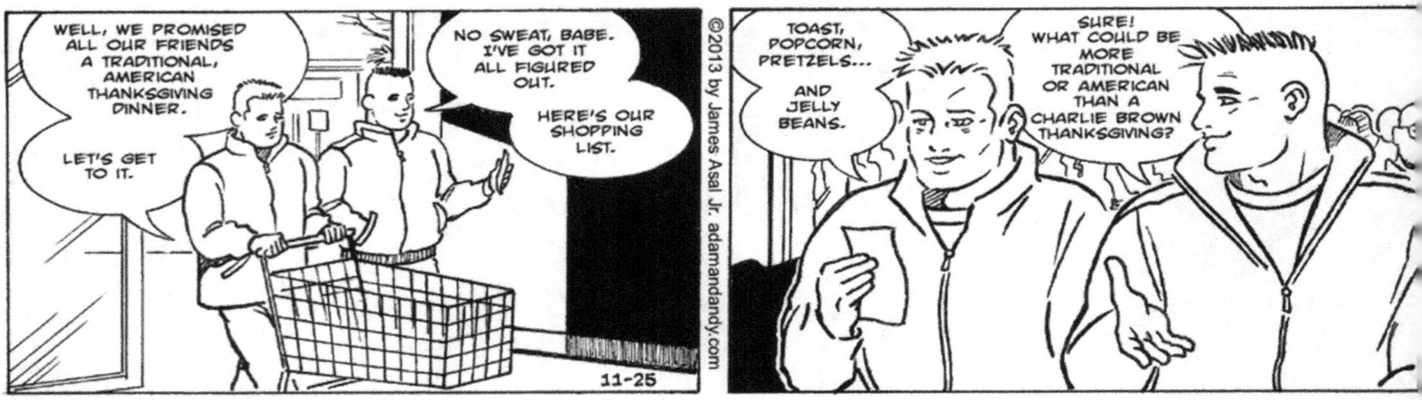
WELL, WE PROMISED ALL OUR FRIENDS A TRADITIONAL, AMERICAN THANKSGIVING DINNER.
LET'S GET TO IT.
NO SWEAT, BABE. I'VE GOT IT ALL FIGURED OUT.
HERE'S OUR SHOPPING LIST.
11-25
©2013 by James Asal Jr. adamandandy.com
TOAST, POPCORN, PRETZELS...
AND JELLY BEANS.
SURE! WHAT COULD BE MORE TRADITIONAL OR AMERICAN THAN A CHARLIE BROWN THANKSGIVING?

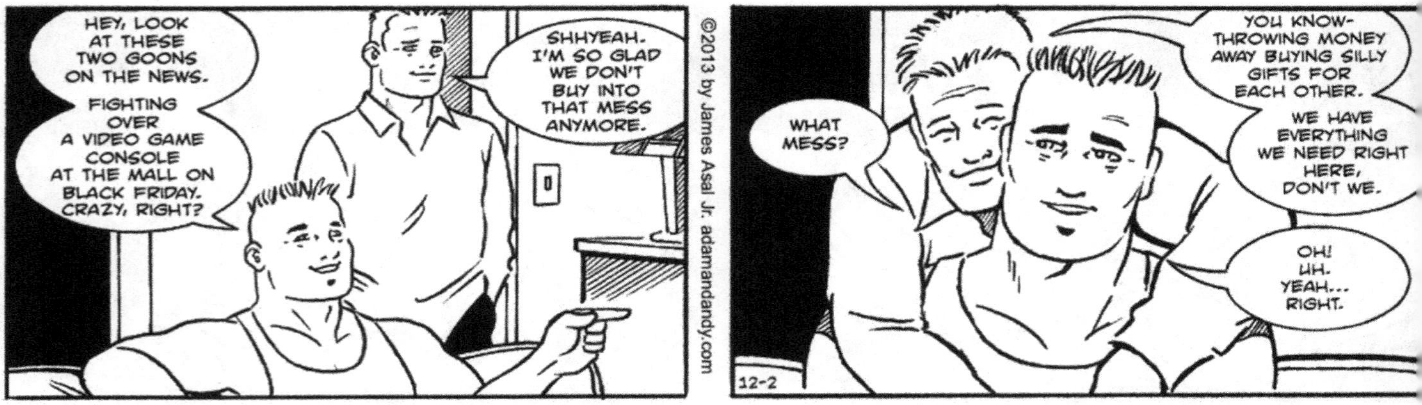
HEY, LOOK AT THESE TWO GOONS ON THE NEWS.
FIGHTING OVER A VIDEO GAME CONSOLE AT THE MALL ON BLACK FRIDAY. CRAZY, RIGHT?
SHHYEAH. I'M SO GLAD WE DON'T BUY INTO THAT MESS ANYMORE.
©2013 by James Asal Jr. adamandandy.com
WHAT MESS?
YOU KNOW- THROWING MONEY AWAY BUYING SILLY GIFTS FOR EACH OTHER.
WE HAVE EVERYTHING WE NEED RIGHT HERE, DON'T WE.
OH! UH. YEAH... RIGHT.
12-2

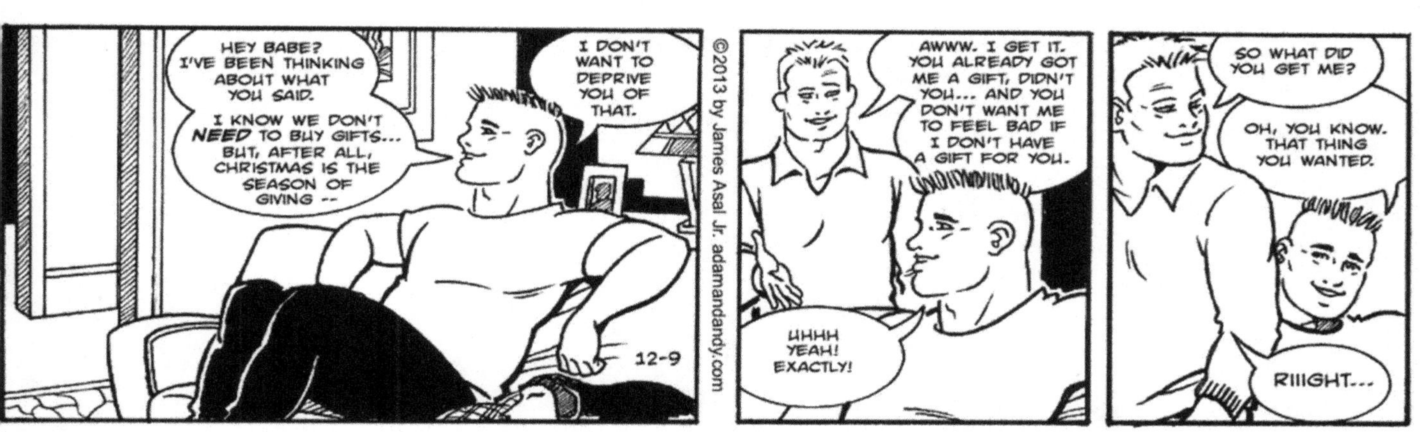
HEY BABE? I'VE BEEN THINKING ABOUT WHAT YOU SAID.
I KNOW WE DON'T NEED TO BUY GIFTS... BUT, AFTER ALL, CHRISTMAS IS THE SEASON OF GIVING --
I DON'T WANT TO DEPRIVE YOU OF THAT.
12-9
©2013 by James Asal Jr. adamandandy.com
AWWW. I GET IT. YOU ALREADY GOT ME A GIFT, DIDN'T YOU... AND YOU DON'T WANT ME TO FEEL BAD IF I DON'T HAVE A GIFT FOR YOU.
UHHH YEAH! EXACTLY!
SO WHAT DID YOU GET ME?
OH, YOU KNOW. THAT THING YOU WANTED.
RIIIGHT...

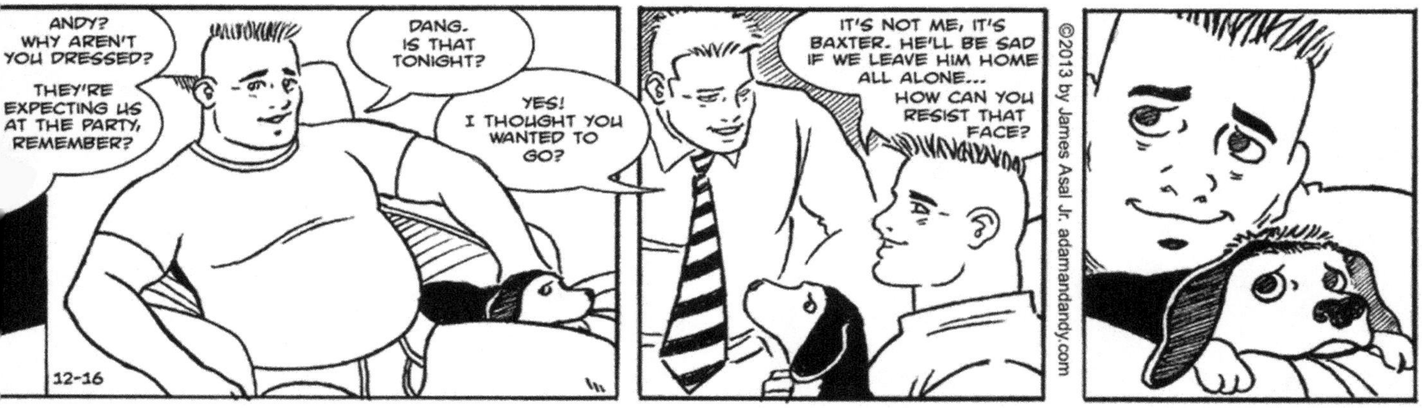
ANDY? WHY AREN'T YOU DRESSED?
THEY'RE EXPECTING US AT THE PARTY, REMEMBER?
DANG. IS THAT TONIGHT?
YES! I THOUGHT YOU WANTED TO GO?
12-16
IT'S NOT ME, IT'S BAXTER. HE'LL BE SAD IF WE LEAVE HIM HOME ALL ALONE...
HOW CAN YOU RESIST THAT FACE?
©2013 by James Asal Jr. adamandandy.com

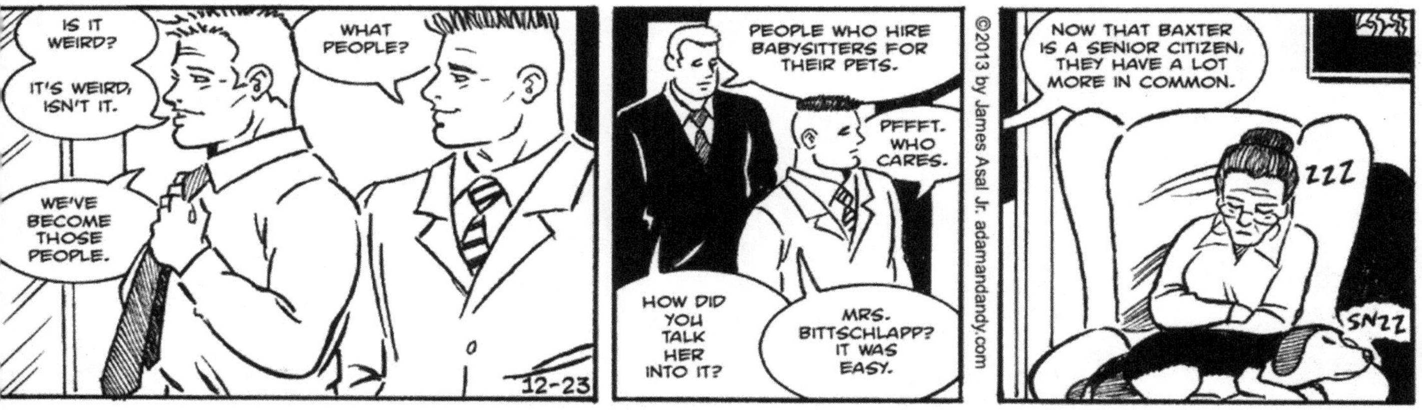
IS IT WEIRD?
IT'S WEIRD, ISN'T IT.
WHAT PEOPLE?
WE'VE BECOME THOSE PEOPLE.
12-23
PEOPLE WHO HIRE BABYSITTERS FOR THEIR PETS.
PFFFT. WHO CARES.
HOW DID YOU TALK HER INTO IT?
MRS. BITTSCHLAPP? IT WAS EASY.
©2013 by James Asal Jr. adamandandy.com
NOW THAT BAXTER IS A SENIOR CITIZEN, THEY HAVE A LOT MORE IN COMMON.
ZZZ
SNZZ

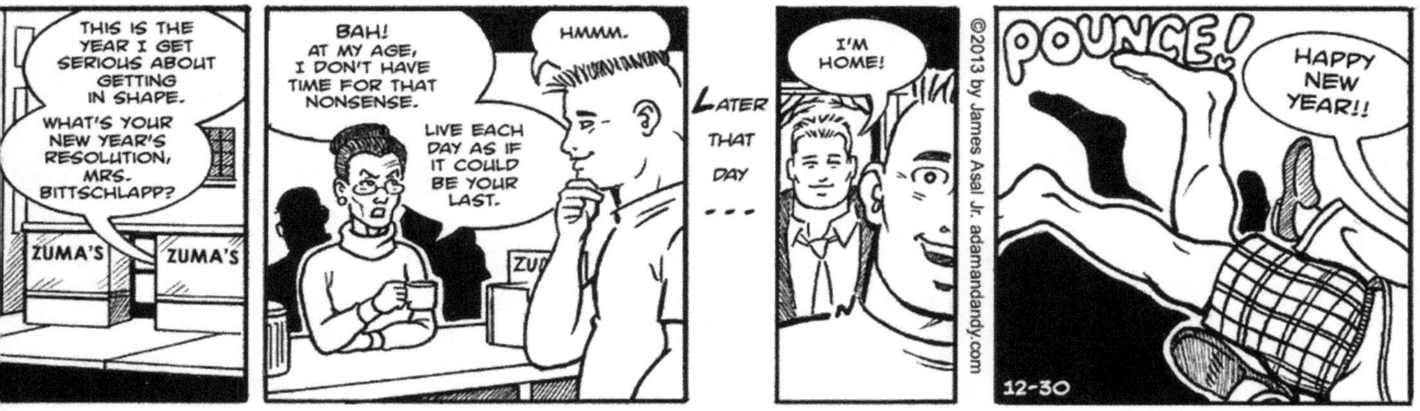
THIS IS THE YEAR I GET SERIOUS ABOUT GETTING IN SHAPE.
WHAT'S YOUR NEW YEAR'S RESOLUTION, MRS. BITTSCHLAPP?
ZUMA'S
ZUMA'S
BAH! AT MY AGE, I DON'T HAVE TIME FOR THAT NONSENSE.
HMMM.
LIVE EACH DAY AS IF IT COULD BE YOUR LAST.
LATER THAT DAY ...
I'M HOME!
©2013 by James Asal Jr. adamandandy.com
POUNCE!
HAPPY NEW YEAR!!
12-30

The adventures continue... adamandandy.com

CPSIA information can be obtained
at www.ICGtesting.com
Printed in the USA
LVHW062000270322
714519LV00008B/402